D1192357

Concise Encyclopedia
of Amish, Brethren, Hutterites,
and Mennonites

CONCISE ENCYCLOPEDIA

of Amish, Brethren, Hutterites, and Mennonites

Donald B. Kraybill

ROLLING MEADOWS LIBRARY
3110 MARTIN LANE
ROLLING MEADOWS, IL 60008

289.7
KRA

THE JOHNS HOPKINS UNIVERSITY PRESS
Baltimore

© 2010 The Johns Hopkins University Press
All rights reserved. Published 2010
Printed in the United States of America on acid-free paper
2 4 6 8 9 7 5 3

The Johns Hopkins University Press
2715 North Charles Street
Baltimore, Maryland 21218-4363
www.press.jhu.edu

Library of Congress Cataloging-in-Publication Data

Concise encyclopedia of Amish, Brethren, Hutterites, and Mennonites / Donald B. Kraybill.
p.   cm.
Includes bibliographical references and index.
ISBN-13: 978-0-8018-9657-6 (hardcover : alk. paper)
ISBN-10: 0-8018-9657-6 (hardcover : alk. paper)
1. Anabaptists—Encyclopedias. I. Title.
BX4931.3.C67 2010
289.7—dc22
2009046015

A catalog record for this book is available from the British Library.

*Special discounts are available for bulk purchases of this book. For more information,
please contact Special Sales at 410-516-6936 or specialsales@press.jhu.edu.*

The Johns Hopkins University Press uses environmentally friendly book materials,
including recycled text paper that is composed of at least 30 percent post-consumer waste,
whenever possible. All of our book papers are acid-free, and our jackets and covers are
printed on paper with recycled content.

Editorial Advisory Council

Jeff Bach, Ph.D., Associate Professor of Religion, Elizabethtown College

Janet M. Breneman, D.Min., Former Professor, Latin American Anabaptist Seminary

Kevin Enns-Rempel, M.A., Archivist, Center for Mennonite Brethren Studies,
Fresno Pacific University

Rachel Waltner Goossen, Ph.D., Professor of History, Washburn University

Amos B. Hoover, Independent Scholar

Rod Janzen, Ph.D., Distinguished Professor, Fresno Pacific University

James Juhnke, Ph.D., Professor Emeritus of History, Bethel College

John A. Lapp, Ph.D., Executive Secretary Emeritus, Mennonite Central Committee

Royden Loewen, Ph.D., Professor of Mennonite Studies, University of Winnipeg

Juan Martínez, Ph.D., Associate Professor of Hispanic Studies, Fuller
Theological Seminary

Steven M. Nolt, Ph.D., Professor of History, Goshen College

John D. Roth, Ph.D., Professor of History, Goshen College

Sara Wenger Shenk, Ed.D., President, Associated Mennonite Biblical Seminary

E. Morris Sider, Ph.D., Professor Emeritus of History, Messiah College

David Rempel Smucker, Ph.D., Independent Scholar

Sam Steiner, M.L.S., Librarian and Archivist (Retired), Conrad Grebel
University College

Diane Zimmerman Umble, Ph.D., Professor of Communication, Millersville University

Contents

Acknowledgments

Many people have contributed their expertise and assisted in gathering information for the *Concise Encyclopedia*. Members of the Editorial Advisory Council deserve special recognition for their advice and suggestions, which have enhanced the accuracy of the text. I especially thank one member, David Rempel Smucker, who played a significant role in helping to conceptualize the project, develop guidelines, and organize the content. Moreover, he researched and wrote an early draft of many of the entries. My Young Center colleague Steve Scott's encyclopedic knowledge of Old Order communities in North America was indispensable in collecting information on those groups. Royden Loewen, Sam Steiner, and Daryl Yoder-Bontrager drafted entries related to their areas of expertise, for which I am grateful.

I owe an enormous debt to my colleague Cynthia Nolt for her exceptional editorial support in all phases of the project and especially for her sharp eye for detail and stylistic consistency. I also thank Kathryn Eisenbise, Megan Memoli, and Lauren Stoltzfus, who performed clerical and research tasks during several stages of the project.

Numerous people generously contributed their time by providing information, suggesting revisions, and reviewing drafts of entries. Some key persons who deserve special recognition include Conrad Kanagy, Eleanor Miller, Linda Shelly, and an anonymous reviewer for the Johns Hopkins University Press. In addition, dozens of staff people representing denominations and agencies as well as leaders and members of various groups graciously gave their time and provided information. Graphic designer Linda Eberly produced the illustrations.

Two books, *Anabaptist World USA* (Kraybill and Hostetter, 2001) and *One Quilt, Many Pieces* (M. Reimer, 2008), provided helpful background resources on numerous church groups. Church Member Profile 2006, a survey of members (in the United States) of the Brethren in Christ, the Church of the Brethren, and Mennonite Church USA, was a key source of attitudinal data. I thank the editors of *Brethren Encyclopedia,* Global Anabaptist Mennonite Encyclopedia Online, and *Mennonite Encyclopedia* for access to and use of their scholarly resources for this project. I am especially grateful for the resources provided by the Young Center for Anabaptist and Pietist Studies at Elizabethtown College and its director, Jeff Bach, for abundant support of my work on the encyclopedia over several years.

Overview

Purpose

This encyclopedia provides a succinct overview of the history, religious beliefs, and cultural practices of four North American religious families: Amish, Brethren, Hutterites, and Mennonites. These families include more than 200 different groups that trace their roots, inspiration, and/or affiliations back to the Anabaptist Movement in Europe during the 16th-century Protestant Reformation. The nearly 350 short entries in this volume offer students, journalists, scholars, and general readers a synopsis of key topics and snapshots of Anabaptist groups in the 21st century. Ample references provide additional resources for more in-depth research.

Scope

The volume focuses on 21st-century Anabaptist communities in North America (Canada, the Caribbean, Central America, Mexico, and the United States), where Anabaptist-related groups are found in 17 of the 23 countries. The United States is home to all four of the Anabaptist families, and Canada is home to three of them (Amish, Hutterites, and Mennonites). Brethren and Mennonites, but no Amish or Hutterites, live in the Caribbean region. Mennonite groups are the primary Anabaptist presence in the Central American countries and Mexico. Although the entries cover a wide range of information, they emphasize culture and 20th-century social history more than theology or European Anabaptist history. This work is not comprehensive or exhaustive. Scholars seeking in-depth treatments of the topics will find electronic resources (web sites) at the end of some entries, as well as printed resources in the References section.

Entries

There is an entry on each of the four Anabaptist families—Amish, Brethren, Hutterites, and Mennonites—as well as entries on a wide range of topics related to religious views and social practices. In addition, each organized church group with 5,000 or more baptized members has an entry, as does each country in North America. Because many Anabaptist groups, especially those in Canada and the United States, have European origins, each of the following countries has an entry: Austria, France, Germany, the Netherlands, Poland, Russia, and Switzerland.

In general, entries focus on topics rather than people. Several leaders of historical significance in the formative years of the major families (Amish, Brethren, Hutterites, Mennonites) have entries. Other people discussed in the text have their birth and death dates noted in parentheses. The Index of Names includes the names of all people mentioned in the encyclopedia.

Table 1   Anabaptist-Related Groups, Congregations, and Baptized Members by Country/Region in North America

	Groups	Congregations	Members[a]
Canada	47	1,313	144,000
Caribbean			
Bahamas	1	1	25
Cuba	3	79	3,350
Dominican Republic	8	138	7,775
Grenada	1	3	50
Haiti	7	68	3,975
Jamaica	3	16	725
Puerto Rico	3	23	900
Trinidad and Tobago	1	6	275
Total	27	334	17,075
Central America			
Belize	10	47	4,400
Costa Rica	4	40	1,825
El Salvador	3	24	650
Guatemala	7	156	7,400
Honduras	5	212	15,050
Nicaragua	5	270	10,925
Panama	1	13	550
Total	35	762	40,800
Mexico	19	169	29,775
United States	77	6,133	578,195
Grand total	**205**	**8,711**	**809,845**

[a] Estimated number of baptized members. If children, unbaptized youth, and nonmember participants are counted, the total population of some groups may be two to three times larger than the baptized membership.

Table 2   Baptized Members by Anabaptist Family and Country/Region in North America

	Amish	Brethren	Hutterites	Mennonites	Total
Canada	2,450	—	14,050	127,500	144,000
Caribbean	—	2,125	—	14,950	17,075
Central America	—	—	—	40,800	40,800
Mexico	—	—	—	29,775	29,775
United States	101,600	175,395	5,075	296,125	578,195
Total	**104,050**	**177,520**	**19,125**	**509,150**	**809,845**

Note: Estimated number of baptized members. If children, unbaptized youth, and nonmember participants are counted, the total population of some groups may be two to three times larger than the baptized membership. Membership estimates for individual countries in the Caribbean and Central America regions appear in table 1 and in the Table of Groups.

The entries are arranged alphabetically. Cross-references to other relevant entries appear in small capital letters in the text and in the "See also" section that follows some entries. The citations that follow each entry indicate the sources of the information in the entry and/or resources for additional information.

Abbreviations

BE	*Brethren Encyclopedia*
ME	*Mennonite Encyclopedia*
GAMEO	Global Anabaptist Mennonite Encyclopedia Online
CMP 2006	Church Member Profile 2006

Classification of Groups

Estimates of the number of congregations and baptized members are based on 2008 and 2009 directories produced by groups and church agencies, and on the reports of informants. Information about church groups appears in three places:

1. Each organized church group with 5,000 or more members in North America has an entry in the main section of the volume.
2. Each group with 300 or more members and/or three or more congregations in North America has an entry in the Directory of Groups, which follows the main section.
3. Each known group, regardless of size, is listed in the Table of Groups.

The Directory of Groups and the Table of Groups are organized by region and country and, within country, by Anabaptist family (Amish, Brethren, Hutterite, Mennonite).

Membership estimates refer to baptized members. If children, unbaptized youth, and nonmember participants are counted, the total population of a group, in some cases, may be two or three times greater than the number of baptized members. This is especially true for traditional groups, whose members typically have large families. Among declining churches with an elderly membership, the actual number of participants may be fewer than the estimated membership.

A group is included in the volume if it meets one or more of the following criteria: (1) use of "Amish," "Brethren," "Hutterite," or "Mennonite" in its name, (2) self-

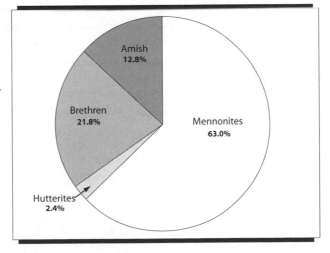

FIGURE 1 Proportional Size of Baptized Membership of Anabaptist Groups in North America

identification as "Anabaptist" in its description of beliefs, (3) inclusion in a directory of Anabaptist churches, (4) association with a network or fellowship of Anabaptist-related churches.

Key Terms

Anabaptist. The four families covered in this encyclopedia—Amish, Brethren, Hutterites, and Mennonites—trace their religious lineage to the Anabaptists of 16th-century Europe. The Anabaptist Movement emerged in 1525 in the wake of the Protestant Reformation of 1517. The early Anabaptists pressed for religious reforms to move more quickly and to break more sharply with established Catholic patterns than did the mainstream reformers. The Anabaptists established voluntary churches, free of state control, consisting of members who made voluntary adult decisions to join the body. Anabaptist leaders raised questions about the Mass, scorned the use of images, criticized the morality of state church officials, refused to baptize babies, and argued that only adults who had made a voluntary decision to follow Jesus should be baptized.

The young reformers were nicknamed "Anabaptists," meaning "rebaptizers," because they had already been baptized as infants in the Catholic Church. Rebaptism was a capital offense in 16th-century Europe because it threatened the longtime marriage of civil and religious authority. Consequently, many Anabaptists were tortured, burned at the stake, or imprisoned because of their "heretical" faith.

Over time the term "Anabaptist" expanded to include three meanings: (1) the dissidents who were baptized twice in the 1500s, (2) the theological heritage that evolved from that radical movement, and (3) contemporary churches and their members that embrace the principles of the 16th-century reform movement.

Amish. The Amish formed in 1693, nearly 170 years after the Anabaptist Movement began. Their name derives from Jakob Ammann (1644–ca. 1730), a convert to the Swiss Anabaptist church who became a prominent leader. Following a schism in 1693, the Swiss–south German stream of Anabaptism formed two branches (Amish and Mennonite), both nourished by a common heritage. The Amish have some 40 subgroups with different cultural customs. They live in rural areas in the Canadian province of Ontario and in 27 states in the United States, mostly east of the Mississippi River. Nearly two-thirds of the Amish live in Ohio, Pennsylvania, and Indiana. They number about 104,000 adults. If children are counted, the total population rises to 233,000. Amish people do not live in the Caribbean, Central America, or Mexico.

Brethren. Alexander Mack Sr. was the leader of the first Brethren, known as German Baptist Brethren or as Dunkers or Dunkards because they baptized (dunked) adults by immersion. The German Baptist Brethren formed near Schwarzenau in central Germany in 1708. They are not an organic offshoot of 16th-century Anabaptism; however, their beliefs and practices were shaped by both Anabaptism and 17th-century Radical Pietism. The North American Brethren world consists of about a dozen groups that trace their origins back to Schwarzenau. There are no Brethren groups in Canada, but there are some congregations in the Dominican Republic, Haiti, and Puerto Rico founded by Brethren missionaries.

Hutterites. Among Anabaptist groups, the Hutterites carry the distinctive mark of rejecting private property and living in rural colonies of about 100 people (adults and children). The Hutterites formed in Moravia (in present-day Czech Republic) in 1528 in the early years of the Anabaptist Movement. Their name derives from an early

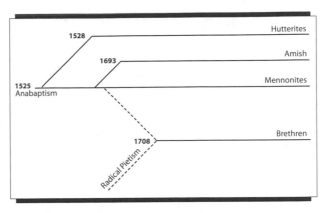

FIGURE 2 Historical Formation of Amish, Brethren, Hutterites, and Mennonites

leader, Jakob Hutter, who was burned alive as a heretic in 1536. The Hutterites have enjoyed remarkable growth since they emigrated from Russia to the United States in the 1870s. About three-fourths of their 480 colonies are in the Canadian provinces of Alberta, Manitoba, and Saskatchewan. In the United States the Hutterites live primarily in South Dakota and Montana. They have four subgroups, each of which has slightly different cultural and religious practices.

Mennonites. Mennonites are the largest and most complex group in the Anabaptist world. They are named for an early Anabaptist leader, Menno Simons, a Catholic priest in the Netherlands who converted to Anabaptism in 1536. Historical, religious, and cultural factors have produced more than 150 different Mennonite groups in North America. Some Mennonites have a Swiss–south German lineage, while others trace their roots to Austria, France, the Netherlands, and northern Germany. In the last half of the 20th century, sizable numbers of Asians, Hispanics, Native Americans / Aboriginals, and African-Americans have expanded what was previously a Eurocentric Mennonite mosaic. Since the mid-20th century, missionaries have planted Mennonite-related churches in several countries in the Caribbean, Central America, and Mexico, as well as in other countries around the world. Mennonites worship in many different languages and are found in rural and metropolitan areas from Costa Rica to Canada.

Assimilated and Traditional Groups. North American Anabaptist groups exhibit a wide diversity of beliefs and practices. Some churches have religious and social practices that distinguish their members from surrounding society. Members of other groups have few distinctive symbols or practices that set them apart from the larger world. The terms "traditional" and "assimilated" are used in many entries to designate a continuum of groups. As shown in figure 3, two fundamental factors mark this spectrum: (1) the locus of *moral authority* and (2) how sharply the community *separates* itself from the larger society. In tradition-centered groups, moral authority rests primarily with the church-community rather than with the individual, and such groups are more likely to reject many of the prevailing practices of the larger society. Assimilated groups, on the other hand, grant individuals more personal moral author-

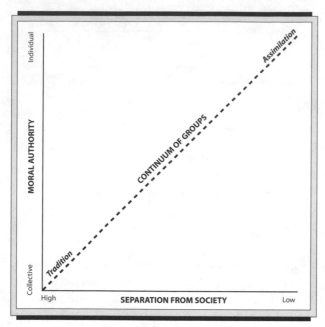

FIGURE 3 Tradition–Assimilation Continuum of Groups

ity on religious matters. Such groups also mingle more freely with the outside world and seek to engage the larger social order.

The tradition–assimilation continuum reflects the degree to which a group rejects or accepts the values, features, and structures of modern society that emerged in North America in the late 19th and 20th centuries. The most visible marker along the continuum is dress. Church-prescribed clothing is a key indicator of how much control a church exercises over individual members and its degree of separation from mainstream culture. Members of traditional groups typically wear some form of church-prescribed dress during worship and when they appear in public settings. Members of assimilated groups blend into the larger society without note because their clothing is not distinctive.

The tradition–assimilation continuum also marks differences related to religious ritual, church organization, leadership, gender roles, education, political involvement, engagement with the larger society, and acceptable technology, to name a few. Groups leaning toward the assimilation end of the range are more likely to accept values and behaviors that are typical of modern culture—flexible religious rituals, gender equality in churches, political involvement, higher education, and widespread use of modern technology.

The distinction between assimilated and traditional groups has many shades of overlap. All groups, including assimilated ones, have traditions; however, assimilated groups tend to borrow and adapt more of their customs from the surrounding society. Moreover, all groups exercise some degree of social control over their members and mark some boundaries with the dominant society. Traditional groups are not isolated from the larger culture. Their members engage in economic activity and participate in many activities in the outside world, but traditional communities tend to have symbols and restrictions that articulate their unique identity in the midst of the larger society. There are many shades of distinction and variation within the broad categories of tradition and assimilation. A specific group, for instance, may embody a mixture of both traditional and assimilational features.

These broad concepts summarize complex social realities and highlight similar traits among dozens of groups within the North American Anabaptist world. This analytical framework applies more readily to churches of European backgrounds than to those of other origins—Asian American, African American, Native American, Hispanic American, and so on. The entries on Traditional Groups and Assimilated Groups provide more clarification of these terms.

Concise Encyclopedia
of Amish, Brethren, Hutterites, and Mennonites

Aboriginal Anabaptists *See* Native American Anabaptists

Abortion

Among TRADITIONAL GROUPS, abortion is considered a serious moral sin. Children are highly desired and welcomed as gifts from God to be cherished and nurtured in the ways of the church. Controversies about the legalization of abortion in the larger culture are seen as a sign of moral decay. Traditional ANABAPTISTS rarely engage in public policy debates or political efforts to shape legislation or influence public officials on moral issues, including the legalization of abortion. One exception occurred in the 2004 U.S. presidential election when some AMISH and OLD ORDER MENNONITES, especially in Pennsylvania and Ohio, voted at a higher than normal rate because abortion was a major issue in the election campaign.

ASSIMILATED GROUPS, more influenced by individualism, changing gender roles, and the media than their traditional counterparts, are also more involved in public discourse about abortion. The 1973 decision by the U.S. Supreme Court and the 1988 decision by Canada's Supreme Court legalizing abortion stirred discussion in some assimilated churches. Several MENNONITE church bodies produced official statements on abortion in 1975, 1980, and 2003, and the CHURCH OF THE BRETHREN issued a statement on abortion at its annual conference in 1984.

The official church statements oppose abortion because it involves the taking of life and is inconsistent with the Anabaptist view that all human life is a gift from God to be valued and protected. The church has the duty, according to these statements, to protect the defenseless regardless of the views of the larger society. The affirmation and preservation of the sanctity of life pertains to all areas, from the unborn child to the enemy in time of war and the criminal on death row. The statements also recognize that the issue of abortion sometimes pits deeply held values against each other—saving the life of the mother and saving the life of the child, for example—which must be discerned within the family and the faith community. This dilemma and other mitigating factors surrounding each situation make a total rejection of all abortions untenable for some assimilated Anabaptists. Church leaders often urge members to develop and support alternatives to abortion in the public communities where they reside.

A survey (CMP 2006) found that a strong majority of the members in three assimilated denominations in the United States embraced a pro-life attitude toward abortion: 62% of Church of the Brethren, 90% of BRETHREN IN CHRIST, and 78% of MENNONITE CHURCH USA members. A minority of members in assimilated groups think that family members and their confidants should have the option to make wise, private decisions rather than categorically rejecting abortion. This pro-choice view was held by 22% of Church of the Brethren, 4% of Brethren in Christ, and 14% of Mennonite Church USA members.

1984 Statement on Abortion by Church of the Brethren (http://www.cobannualconference.org/ac_statements/84Abortion.htm), 2003 Statement on Abortion by Mennonite Church USA (http://www.mennoniteusa.org/Home/About/Statementsandresolutions/Abortion/tabid/114/Default.aspx), CMP 2006, GAMEO ("Abortion"), Kotva (2005)

Abuse, Domestic

As in other communities, some individuals in ANABAPTIST communities experience verbal, physical, and sexual abuse, including incest. Because few, if any, systematic studies have documented the level of abuse, statistical comparisons with other groups or the larger society are not available. Over 80% of MENNONITE CHURCH USA, CHURCH OF THE BRETHREN, and BRETHREN IN CHRIST members in the United States reported in a survey (CMP 2006) that they had never experienced any form of sexual abuse. However, personal stories, anecdotal evidence, and reports from counselors suggest that various forms of domestic abuse are present in Anabaptist communities.

Although church leaders do not condone

abuse, several cultural factors in some of the more TRADITIONAL GROUPS may lend it informal cover. Members of groups that emphasize separation from the world and whose children do not attend public schools may not have access to outside professional services or know how to report abuse. Moreover, they may be afraid to report it. Traditional churches are patriarchal, and male leaders may be unsympathetic to reports of abuse or may minimize its trauma when it is reported by women.

The most conservative and separatist groups prefer to handle infractions within their church community rather than report them to outside civil authorities. The perpetrators of abuse may be censured by the church, but because male leaders do not report the abuse to public officials, the abusers often do not receive professional help. Mild forms of church DISCIPLINE and the lack of professional therapeutic treatment may enable habitual offenders to continue abusive patterns. Abuse is generally more likely to be reported and addressed in ASSIMILATED GROUPS.

See also Sexuality

Block (1990), CMP 2006, Garrett (2001), Labi (2005), E. G. Yoder (1992)

A Cappella Singing   *See* Singing

Acculturation   *See* Assimilated Groups

Adolescence

Adolescence in ASSIMILATED GROUPS may stretch over 10 or more years, as it does in mainstream society, because higher education, travel, or service activities delay marriage and permanent employment. Because they are exposed to mass media and contemporary culture, many young people in assimilated families struggle with tensions between the religious values of their FAMILY and church and the pervasive influence of secular values. Some youth attend ANABAPTIST-related elementary and secondary schools and colleges, where they are exposed to the values of their religious heritage. Many parents look to experts in the fields of psychol-

ogy and counseling to assist them in setting appropriate boundaries and guidelines for their adolescent children. Although certain youth may use alcohol and drugs, this is typically not a serious problem of adolescents in assimilated MENNONITE and BRETHREN groups.

In the more TRADITIONAL GROUPS, the adolescent period is much shorter because youth typically marry and begin permanent employment by age 21. In traditional groups such as the AMISH and OLD ORDER MENNONITES, youth between age 16 and marriage (which usually occurs between the ages of 19 and 22) have a period of freedom, called *RUMSPRINGA* in the Pennsylvania German dialect or "running around" in English. During this time they are between the authority of their parents and the church because they are not yet baptized and thus not official members of the church. On weekends the young people engage in activities with their peers. Many socialize by picnicking, hiking, playing volleyball, and ice skating. More rebellious teens hold dances, use alcohol and drugs, and attend movies, and some Amish youth drive cars. The amount of rowdy behavior varies considerably among communities. An estimated 85% of young people in traditional groups settle down, become baptized, marry, and conform to the regulations of their church.

HUTTERITES recognize a change in status for young persons at age 15. At this time youth begin working at adult tasks under supervision and eat in the adult area of the colony's communal dining room. Some work temporarily at other Hutterite colonies. Between age 15 and baptism, mild and casual deviation from strict colony rules is allowed. Youth have opportunities to get to know members of the opposite sex when members of different colonies mingle for work and social activities. Baptism and then marriage, both of which occur between the ages of 18 and 25, mark the end of the adolescent period among the Hutterites.

Glick and Glick (1988), J. Hostetler (1997), Kraybill (2001), Kraybill and Bowman (2001), S. Shenk (2005), Stevick (2007)

Adult Baptism   *See* Baptism

Africa

The baptized membership of MENNONITE-related churches in Africa is approximately 450,000. These churches witnessed a dramatic 228% increase in membership in the last two decades of the 20th century. The largest African church groups, which are in Ethiopia, Congo, Tanzania, and Kenya, grew out of Mennonite MISSION efforts that began in some countries in the 1890s. Beginning around the same time, BRETHREN IN CHRIST missionaries helped create churches in Zimbabwe and Zambia. Since the 1950s, MENNONITE CENTRAL COMMITTEE has sent millions of dollars worth of material aid and hundreds of volunteers to Africa for development projects, especially in agriculture and education. Recognizing the dramatic increase in the proportion of African ANABAPTISTS in worldwide total membership, the MENNONITE WORLD CONFERENCE held its assembly in Bulawayo, Zimbabwe, in 2003. The Meserete Kristos Church in Ethiopia is the largest national Mennonite body in the world, with more than 130,000 members. The Congo, home to three different Mennonite groups, has the largest number of Mennonites in Africa.

In Nigeria in 1922, the CHURCH OF THE BRETHREN began its first mission work in Africa, which centered on evangelism, church planting, health care, and education. Beginning in 1955, native Nigerians began to take over the leadership of their church. The membership of the Church of the Brethren in Nigeria, known as Ekklesiyar Yan'uwa a Nigeria (EYN), grew rapidly in the last quarter of the 20th century. By 2010, its 200,000 members surpassed the entire North American membership of the Church of the Brethren. The Fellowship of GRACE BRETHREN CHURCHES has some 2,400 related congregations in several African countries.

Significant ethnic and linguistic diversity characterizes Anabaptist churches in Africa. Sub-Saharan Christianity often blends the traditional African practice of ancestor veneration with Christian doctrine. In such a context, JESUS CHRIST is effectively known as the Supreme Ancestor, the source of healing, hope, and salvation.

Except for periods in the 20th century when North American missionaries prohibited dancing and vigorous SINGING in WORSHIP, African Anabaptists often worshiped in an enthusiastic CHARISMATIC style. Some missionaries opposed the use of musical instruments in worship, but eventually their use became widespread. African Anabaptists hold a variety of viewpoints concerning worship, biblical interpretation, PEACEMAKING, and the ORDINATION OF WOMEN for ministry.

The challenges arising from different ethnic groups moving into the cities, as well as the changes induced by the political independence movements of the late 1950s and early 1960s, have led to a strong ecumenical outlook in many African Anabaptist churches. The interaction between Muslims and Christians in northern Africa is another significant challenge for the churches, a development fraught with the danger of interreligious conflict. African Anabaptists' understanding of biblical PACIFISM and of Jesus Christ as a peacemaker serves as an important resource in resolving this conflict.

BE II ("Nigeria"), Bertsche (1998), D. Durnbaugh (1997a), Faw (1974), GAMEO ("Africa"), Lapp and Snyder (2006a), ME V ("Africa"), Mennonite World Conference News Service (2005), D. Miller et al. (2007), http://www.anabaptistwiki.org, http://www.mwc-cmm.org

African-American Anabaptists

TRADITIONAL GROUPS have very few African-American members. However, African-Americans are members of some assimilated Mennonite and Brethren congregations.

Several CHURCH OF THE BRETHREN congregations accepted African-American members in the early 1800s, but it was not until 1872 that the denomination officially ruled that membership and the HOLY KISS were not to be denied due to skin color. Although African-Americans continued to join BRETHREN congregations and some were ordained ministers, only a few predominantly African-American congregations thrived in the first half of the 20th century. In the early 21st century, the Church of the Brethren has about six primarily African-American congregations with a total membership of about 700. In 1988 William Hayes (1928–1993) became the first African-American moderator of Church of the Brethren Annual Conference. In 2007 Belita Mitchell (1946–), the first African-American woman ordained in the Church of the Brethren, served as moderator.

The earliest attempt to establish an African-American MENNONITE congregation was undertaken in 1886 in Elk Park, North Carolina, by the Krimmer Mennonite Brethren (now part of the MENNONITE BRETHREN CHURCH). Some African-Americans joined rural and small-town Mennonite congregations in Pennsylvania during the early 1900s, but more intense interaction developed during the Civil Rights era of the 1950s and 1960s, especially in Chicago and New York City. These efforts were augmented by an influx of young Caucasian Anabaptist men from rural areas doing ALTERNATIVE SERVICE in urban areas in the 1950s and 1960s.

In 1945 James H. Lark (1888–1978) was ordained as a minister at Bethel Mennonite Church in Chicago and in 1954 as the first African-American Mennonite BISHOP. Lark and his wife, Rowena Winters Lark (1892–1970), helped establish two other congregations. From 1945 to 1958, Mennonite Biblical Seminary was located in south Chicago, and a biracial Mennonite congregation developed there. The nonviolent theology and strategy advocated by Martin Luther King Jr. (1929–1968) resonated with some Mennonite leaders desiring to bring biblical PACIFISM to bear on the challenges of race relations in an urban setting. Two rural Pennsylvania Mennonite conferences, Lancaster and Franconia, and the BRETHREN IN CHRIST launched mission efforts in the 1950s in Hispanic and African-American sections of New York City. By 2007 the New York City Council of Mennonite Churches had 16 congregations from various racial and ethnic backgrounds, plus a rural summer camp.

About 60 congregations in MENNONITE CHURCH USA are predominately African-American. Those who attend these congregations represent about 5.7% of the denomination's total membership. African-American congregations tend to be located in urban areas. The largest congregation in Mennonite Church USA is Calvary Community Church in Hampton, Virginia, a predominantly African-American congregation of 2,000 members, which operates two schools: Calvary Christian Academy (preschool through grade 5) and Calvary Bible College.

The African American Mennonite Association (AAMA), a program of Mennonite Church USA, provides its congregations with pastoral and lay leadership skills, advocates for greater African-American representation in denominational leadership, and encourages fellowship and networking of AAMA congregations. In conjunction with the Mennonite Education Agency and Eastern Mennonite University, AAMA operates the Lark Leadership Scholarship Program, which gives financial assistance to leaders of AAMA congregations who are enrolled in college courses to enhance their ministry skills. AAMA congregations vary in size and characteristics.

See also Africa; Anabaptism; Racism; Social Justice

Bechler (1986), BE II ("Minorities, Ethnic and Racial"), BE IV ("Hayes, William [Bill] A."), Kanagy (2007), MacMaster (2006), *Mennonite Church USA* (2009), Shearer (2008, 2010), Stauffer, Sensenig, and Good (1993), P. Toews (1996), http://www.aamamcusa.org

Agriculture

During the late 1500s, intense PERSECUTION forced ANABAPTISTS in Switzerland to flee into rural and isolated areas. Around the same time, Anabaptists in the Netherlands began to spread from urban centers to rural settings. There, Dutch Mennonites became skilled at diverting water and draining low areas for cultivation. MENNONITES in Poland (later Prussia) continued this practice through the 1600s and 1700s.

Mennonites and AMISH in Germany and France developed agricultural innovations that increased the health and productivity of crops and animals. These innovations included growing and feeding clover (whose higher protein content makes it more nutritious than grass and also makes the soil more productive) to cattle and stall-feeding animals on fodder, grains, and root crops (which produces a quicker and more efficient conversion from forage to meat). They began fertilizing uncultivated pastures and using gypsum as a crop fertilizer. They also took advantage of cattle-breeding advances, and they began distilling their grain crops into more economically profitable alcoholic beverages.

Agriculture was the primary economic activity of the Anabaptist groups that immigrated to North America in the 1700s and 1800s. Their high level of agricultural skill, when applied to the fertile soils of North America, produced thriving farming cultures. When Mennonites immigrated to Kansas in the 1870s, for example, they brought with them the highly successful winter wheat known as Turkey Red, which they had developed in the Russian Ukraine. The cultural values associated with family farming, such as frugality, hard work, cooperation, and responsibility, were a major force in shaping the values and worldviews of most North American Anabaptist groups, and they continue to shape the views of traditional Anabaptists living in rural areas.

In the late 1800s and early 1900s, different approaches to agricultural TECHNOLOGY developed within and among the Anabaptist groups. ASSIMILATED GROUPS and the HUTTERITE colonies embraced advanced agricultural technology and modern agronomy. Some TRADITIONAL GROUPS, especially the Amish, rejected tractor farming, an approach that made them visibly separate from their assimilated Anabaptist and non-Anabaptist neighbors. The Old Order Amish do not use tractors for power in the field, but many Amish groups use horses to pull modern harvesting machinery. Gideon L. Fisher (1913–1996), an Amish farmer, writer, and historian in Lancaster County, Pennsylvania, wrote in detail about changes in Amish FARM TECHNOLOGY and rural life during the 1900s.

In the early and mid-1900s, members of assimilated groups began to enter nonagricultural vocations. The shift to nonfarm OCCUPATIONS increased rapidly after World War II. By the late 20th century, members of assimilated groups worked in a wide range of occupations—from trades and factory jobs to professions that required HIGHER EDUCATION.

In a survey conducted in the early 21st century, about 10% of the members of assimilated Anabaptist groups in the United States reported living on a farm, but only half of them earned a living from farming. Types of farming ranged from small produce farms to large corporate-style farms with hundreds of acres of grain or large cattle, swine, or chicken operations. Among traditional groups, fewer than half of the families earn their living from farming. Those who continue to farm typically operate small family-oriented operations. Even in many Amish communities, the majority of men work in nonfarm occupations such as carpentry, construction, and Amish-owned businesses. Despite the shift toward nonagricultural employment, most members of traditional churches continue to live in rural areas.

See also Land

CMP 2006, Correll (1991), Fisher (1978), Jérôme (2005), R. Loewen (2006), Séguy (1973)

Alcohol

European MENNONITES and AMISH produced alcoholic beverages as part of their successful agricultural innovations in Germany and France in the 1600s and 1700s. Moderate use of alcohol was accepted, but drunkenness was rebuked by the church. ANABAPTIST immigrants to North America continued the heritage of alcohol production, and some founded large distilleries and breweries, including the Overholt family in Pennsylvania and the Leisy family in Iowa and Ohio.

By the end of the 1800s in North America, some ASSIMILATED GROUPS accepted the tenets of the temperance movement, and some even permitted involvement in political movements to advocate for temperance legislation. TRADITIONAL GROUPS resisted the temperance movement, however, because it entailed political involvement.

Disagreements over the use of wine in COMMUNION services were entangled in some church schisms. Many Old Order groups use wine for communion, but the majority of assimilated churches use grape juice. Old Order groups generally abstain from alcohol except for its use in communion.

Anabaptist groups exhibit a wide range of behavior—from total abstinence to acceptance of moderate alcohol use. In a survey of assimilated congregations in the United States (CMP 2006), 17% of both CHURCH OF THE BRETHREN and MENNONITE CHURCH USA members and 11% of BRETHREN IN CHRIST members reported drinking alcoholic beverages several times a month. About 1% reported using alcohol daily.

CMP 2006, Correll (1991), D. Durnbaugh (1997a), GAMEO ("Alcohol"), J. Hostetler (1993), Leisy (1976), ME I ("Alcohol")

Alternative Service

As CONSCIENTIOUS OBJECTORS to war (a decision informed by their conviction of biblical PACIFISM), many ANABAPTISTS seek exemptions from universal conscription to military service. In Upper Canada, MENNONITES, QUAKERS, and Tunkers (BRETHREN IN CHRIST) obtained exemption from military service by an act of the legislature in 1793. During the CIVIL WAR in the United States, both the North and the South instituted military drafts of able-bodied adult males. Some Anabaptist church members were able to secure exemptions from this draft by paying a commutation fee or hiring a draft substitute.

During WORLD WAR I, there were no programs of alternative service outside the military for conscientious objectors. In the United States, pacifist draftees were at the mercy of local military commanders, but in Canada, Anabaptists were more readily exempted from military service.

As international tensions increased during the interwar period, Anabaptist groups worked to become more organized in their objection to military service. In 1935, BRETHREN, Mennonites, and Quakers met in North Newton, Kansas, for a conference on peace. The term HISTORIC PEACE CHURCHES was developed at this conference in order to distinguish between the groups' biblically based peaceful NONRESISTANCE and the political pacifism movement that was gaining popularity during this time.

When the United States instituted a program of military conscription in 1940, peace church leaders worked to create an alternative to military service for their members who were conscientious objectors. Beginning with WORLD WAR II, young men of draft age, especially those from Anabaptist groups and the Quakers, could serve in a government-sanctioned program called Civilian Public Service (CPS) in the United States and Alternative Service work in Canada. The young men lived together in large camps and worked on projects such as soil conservation, road construction, firefighting, agricultural experiments, and public health. Others worked in mental hospitals and on various medical and scientific projects. For six years (1941–1947), nearly 12,000 men in the United States and about 7,500 men in Canada participated in some form of alternative service. The historic peace churches paid the U.S. government nearly $7 million to finance the CPS program.

The churches also contributed leadership for the program. M. R. Zigler (1891–1985) of the Church of the Brethren and Mennonites Henry A. Fast (1894–1990) and Orie O. Miller (1892–1977) were important leaders of the Civilian Public Service program. In Canada, Jacob H. Janzen (1878–1950), Benjamin B. Janz (1877–1964), and J. B. Martin (1897–1974) provided leadership.

During the Korean War and the VIETNAM WAR, the U.S. government approved different programs of alternative service for conscientious objectors. These men were required to perform civilian service for the U.S. government, for nonprofit organizations, or in the areas of health care, social welfare, or education. Although the programs were approved by the national government, they were operated by church agencies. A program known as Pax (Latin for peace) was operated by MENNONITE CENTRAL COMMITTEE from the beginning of the Korean War (1951) to the end of the Vietnam War (1976). Nearly 1,200 conscientious objectors who were drafted by Selective Service in the United States served in some 40 countries outside North America. Their service included reconstruction in Europe after World War II, the care and resettlement of refugees, various social services, and agricultural development.

BE I ("Alternative Service," "Civilian Public Service," "Korean War"), Bush (1998b), D. Durnbaugh (1991, 1997a), F. Epp (1974), GAMEO ("Alternative Service [U.S.], "Alternative Service Work Camps," "Civilian Public Service," "Conscientious Objection," "Conscription"), M. Gingerich (1949), Goossen (1997), M. Heisey (2003), W. Janzen (1990), Keim (1990), Keim and Stoltzfus (1988), A. Klassen (1997), Lehman and Nolt (2007), ME I ("Conscientious Objector"), ME V ("Conscription"), C. Redekop (2001), Regehr (1996), T. Schlabach (2009), Speicher and Durnbaugh (2003), http://www.alternativeservice.ca

Altkolonier Mennonitengemeinde   See Old
Colony Mennonite Church, Canada; Old Colony Mennonite Church, Mexico

American Revolution (1775–1783)
ANABAPTIST groups in the American colonies tried to remain neutral as conflict heightened in the 1770s between colonists who demanded fewer political and economic constraints from Great Britain and colonists who were satisfied with British rule.

Anabaptists were willing to pay regular TAXES as well as the fines they were assessed for their refusal to participate in military training. However, they would not hire substitutes to join the military in their place, which was a legal option at the time. Eventually large fines and heavy taxes were demanded from those unwilling to join militias. Some Anabaptists were reluctant to pay these fines and taxes because the money was used for military purposes. The issue triggered a church schism in the Franconia Mennonite Conference of Pennsylvania.

Because Anabaptists generally refused to take OATHS, many would not renounce their allegiance to the British monarch and pledge loyalty to the new revolutionary GOVERNMENT. Therefore, they were denied the right to vote in Pennsylvania between 1777 and 1790.

Most Anabaptists tried to remain neutral and stay out of the conflict. Wealthy and politically vocal BRETHREN publisher and printer Christopher Sauer III (1754–1799) of Germantown (near Philadelphia) was an exception. He openly supported the loyalist British cause, although his father, CHRISTOPHER SAUER II (1721–1784), attempted to remain neutral. Their property was seized, and Christopher Sauer II was imprisoned while his son had to flee to Canada.

Anabaptists often had their goods and properties confiscated for wartime use by armies and by the revolutionary government in lieu of taxes. Even though they were not forced to violate their CONSCIENTIOUS OBJECTION to military service, they suffered minor PERSECUTION from local patriots through physical and verbal abuse. The experience of the war reinforced the Anabaptists' belief in biblical PACIFISM, increased their wariness of involvement with the government, and heightened their sense of NONCONFORMITY to the wider society.

After the United States had been established, a small number of MENNONITES, River Brethren, and German Baptist Brethren immigrated to Upper Canada (now Ontario) in 1786. Although a few applied for the privileges (including free land) given to United Empire Loyalists who had fought for the British, none were successful. Only these earliest immigrants appear to have been motivated by a desire to live under the British crown (as a result of harassment in their former Pennsylvania communities) and to have access to inexpensive land.

BE II ("Revolutionary War, America"), D. Durnbaugh (1997a), F. Epp (1974), E. Good (1988), MacMaster (1985), MacMaster, Horst, and Ulle (1979)

Amish
With roots in the 16th-century Anabaptist Movement, the Amish separated from other

ANABAPTISTS in 1693 in SWITZERLAND and present-day Alsace. They are named for JAKOB AMMANN (1644–ca. 1730), their leader at the time of the 1693 schism. A variety of religious and cultural differences led to the division. Key issues were the degree of separation from the world and the practice of SHUNNING. The Amish migrated to North America in several waves in the 18th and 19th centuries. The last Amish congregation in Europe disbanded in 1937.

In the 1860s and 1870s, many Amish moved away from their older traditions and eventually joined Mennonite groups. However, the majority of Amish groups held to the old ORDNUNG ("regulations"). These groups are now considered Old Order. The various branches of Old Order Amish account for about 95% of the Amish membership. The rest are New Order Amish. The Amish population doubles about every 18 years because of sizable FAMILIES and a retention rate that is 85% or higher in many communities. The total Amish population of adults and children in the United States and Canada is approximately 233,000.

The groups included under the Amish canopy in the 21st century are those that claim the Amish name, use horse-and-buggy transportation, and speak Pennsylvania German or a Swiss German DIALECT. Groups that drive automobiles but use the Amish name, such as the BEACHY AMISH MENNONITE CHURCH and other Amish Mennonite groups, are included with the MENNONITE family of groups because they are more similar to, and associate more with, conservative Mennonites than with the Amish from whom they originated.

The Amish live in nearly 30 states and the Canadian province of Ontario. They have 1,727 local congregations, each comprised of 25 to 35 families. There are more than 40 different affiliations (networks of congregations), which have produced much cultural diversity in areas such as FARM TECHNOLOGY, CLOTHING, occupations, and relationships with the outside world. Although the Amish reside in rural areas, fewer than half are farmers. Many earn their living by working in small businesses that produce furniture, metal products, farm machinery, and crafts. In some communities, men work in non-Amish factories. The Amish place many restrictions on TECHNOLOGY, but they do not reject it; they accept some new technology, modify other forms to fit their cultural values, and also create new tools to serve the special needs of their communities.

Despite numerous differences, most Amish communities have several practices in common. They hold religious services in their homes every other Sunday, select leaders from within their local congregation who serve without advanced training or salary, speak a Pennsylvania German or Swiss German dialect in addition to English, complete their formal education at the end of eighth grade (typically in a one- or two-room Amish-operated school), use horse-and-buggy transportation for local travel, forbid the ownership of electronic media (RADIO, TELEVISION, and

FIGURE 4 Distribution of Amish Congregations in North America
Source: Raber's Almanac (2009), settlement directories, and informants.
Note: Congregations in the following states are not shown: Colorado—3; Maine—3; Montana—5.

Table 3 Largest Amish Settlements in North America		
Settlement area	*State*	*Congregations*
Holmes/Wayne County	Ohio	221
Lancaster/Chester County	Pennsylvania	175
Elkhart/LaGrange	Indiana	132
Geauga/Trumbull County	Ohio	86
Adams/Jay County	Indiana	47
Nappanee	Indiana	37
Arthur	Illinois	27
Daviess County	Indiana	24
Mifflin County	Pennsylvania	20

Note: Amish churches have been established in 420 settlements in 27 states and Ontario.

COMPUTERS), refrain from using ELECTRICITY from public utilities, and wear distinctive clothing prescribed by their particular church community. Men wear BEARDS but not mustaches, and women wear HEAD COVERINGS in public.

With their emphasis on collective culture values—subordination to the church community, self-denial, humility, and obedience to those in authority—the Amish stand apart from the individualism of American culture. They practice MUTUAL AID, helping fellow church members in time of need through work "frolics," barn raisings, benefit auctions, and special offerings. The Amish pay taxes like other citizens but have been exempt from Social Security since 1965 (if self-employed) and in some states do not pay workers compensation insurance. In Canada, a similar arrangement with the government, finalized in 1974, allowed the Amish (and OLD ORDER MENNONITES) to have special Social Insurance numbers that identified them but did not require them to participate in the program. The Amish object to GOVERNMENT handouts and commercial INSURANCE because they believe that church members have a religious duty to care for one another.

A distinctive Amish affiliation known as the New Order Amish formed in Holmes County, Ohio, in the 1960s and 1970s when their leaders emphasized

more personal religious experience, stricter guidelines for youth activities, and fewer restrictions on technology. The New Order Movement eventually developed at least three loosely connected subgroups. Each affiliation has different practices. One key distinction among the subgroups is the use of public utility ELECTRICITY. The New Order Amish have 60 church districts in 13 states, with Ohio claiming about half of them. New Orders constitute less than 5% of the Amish population.

The New Order Amish use horse-and-buggy transportation for local travel and speak the Pennsylvania German dialect, but they are more likely than the Old Order Amish to support church-related relief and mission organizations, encourage a personal faith experience, accept greater individual expression of religious experience, provide formal religious education for youth, hold Sunday school classes, and endorse youth Bible studies. In general they

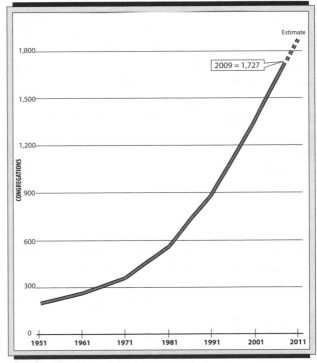

FIGURE 5 Growth of Amish Congregations in North America, 1951–2011
Source: Raber's Almanac (2009), settlement directories, and informants.

embrace a more rationalized and less traditional understanding of faith than the Old Order Amish. New Orders, in general, more readily use technology such as public grid electricity and telephones in their homes and businesses than their Old Order counterparts.

The leading scholar of Amish life in the last half of the 20th century was John A. Hostetler (1918–2001). The first scholar to thoroughly interpret Amish life to the wider society, he wrote the short *Amish Life* (1952) and the longer *Amish Society* (1963).

See also Gelassenheit; Old Order Movement; Traditional Groups

GAMEO ("Amish," "Old Order Amish," "Amish Mennonites"), O. Gingerich (1972), B. Hostetler (1992), J. Hostetler (1993), Hurst and McConnell (2010), Johnson-Weiner (2010), Kraybill (2001, 2003c), Kraybill, Johnson-Weiner, and Nolt (forthcoming), Kraybill and Nolt (2004), Kraybill, Nolt, and Weaver-Zercher (2010), Kraybill and Olshan (1994), D. Martin (2003), Nolt (2003, 2008), Nolt and Meyers (2007), Regehr (1996), Roth (2002b), Waldrep (2008), http://www.etown.edu/amishstudies/

Ammann, Jakob (1644–ca. 1730)

Jakob Ammann was born in SWITZERLAND in the mid-1600s and later immigrated to Alsace because of religious persecution. Many of the details of his life are unknown, but he eventually became the leader of a group of ANABAPTISTS that later became known as AMISH (based on his surname).

Ammann advocated a stricter and more disciplined form of church life than many of the Anabaptist leaders at the time, and he helped to precipitate the division among the Swiss Brethren (MENNONITES). Ammann believed that COMMUNION should be observed twice a year rather than once a year, as was the custom at that time, and that the service include FOOTWASHING. He also insisted that the church community practice a strict SHUNNING of excommunicated members. Other Swiss Brethren ministers maintained that a milder form of shunning—exclusion from communion—was sufficient punishment.

Another area of dispute was whether non-Anabaptist sympathizers would attain salvation because of the aid and protection they offered to persecuted Anabaptists. Some Swiss Mennonite leaders believed that sympathizers would be saved because of their good deeds, but Ammann insisted that they would not. Some of Ammann's ideas reflect the influence of the DORDRECHT CONFESSION OF FAITH written by Mennonites in the Netherlands in 1632.

These issues, along with a variety of other differences of opinion (such as whether fashionable CLOTHING or the trimming of BEARDS should be allowed), eventually led Ammann to excommunicate several of the Swiss ministers. Through this action the Mennonites of Switzerland, Alsace, and southern Germany eventually divided into two factions, and the Amish became a separate Anabaptist group.

See also Amish

Baecher (2000), J. Hostetler (1993), Hüppi (2000), GAMEO ("Ammann, Jakob"), Nolt (2003), Roth (2002b)

Amor Viviente   *See* Living Love

Amusements   *See* Leisure

Anabaptism (Anabaptist)

The Anabaptist Movement began in 1525 in EUROPE as a branch of the RADICAL REFORMATION. It represented an attempt to restore the belief and practice of the New Testament church.

Opponents, both Protestant and Roman Catholic, used the label Anabaptist ("rebaptized") for the radical reformers because they baptized adults who had already been baptized as infants. Anabaptists disliked the term because they did not consider their own infant BAPTISM to be scriptural or valid and therefore did not consider themselves to be *re*baptizers. Even though rebaptizing adults was punishable by death, Anabaptists argued that baptism was only appropriate for adults who could make a voluntary confession of faith and decision to follow Christ. The Anabaptists objected to infant

Table 4   Resources on Amish Groups

Books

The Amish and the Media, Umble and Weaver-Zercher, 2008

The Amish and the State, Kraybill, 2003a

Amish Grace: How Forgiveness Transcended Tragedy, Kraybill, Nolt, and Weaver-Zercher, 2007

The Amish in America, Kraybill, Johnson-Weiner, and Nolt, forthcoming

An Amish Paradox: Diversity and Change in the World's Largest Amish Community, Hurst and McConnell, 2010

The Amish Way: Patient Faith in a Perilous World, Kraybill, Nolt, and Weaver-Zercher, 2010

Growing up Amish, Stevick, 2007

A History of the Amish, Nolt, 2003

New York Amish: Life in the Plain Communities of the Empire State, Johnson-Weiner, 2010

Plain Diversity: Amish Cultures and Identities, Nolt and Meyers, 2007

The Riddle of Amish Culture, Kraybill, 2001

Train up a Child: Old Order Amish and Mennonite Schools, Johnson-Weiner, 2007

Information Centers

Amish and Mennonite Heritage Center, Berlin, OH (http://www.behalt.com; 330-893-3192)

Illinois Amish Interpretive Center, Arcola, IL (http://www.amishcenter.com; 888-45AMISH)

Lancaster Mennonite Information Center, Lancaster, PA (http://www.mennoniteinfoctr.com; 717-299-0954)

Menno-Hof, Shipshewana, IN (http://www.mennohof.org; 260-768-4117)

Libraries and Archives

Heritage Historical Library, Route 4, 52445 Glencolin Line, Aylmer, ON, N5H 2R3

Lancaster Mennonite Historical Society, Lancaster, PA (http://www.lmhs.org; 717-393-9745)

Mennonite Historical Society, Goshen, IN (http://mennohistsoc.mennonite.net; 574-295-3726)

Muddy Creek Farm Library, Ephrata, PA (717-354-7635)

Northern Indiana Amish Library, 4425W 100S, LaGrange, IN 46761 (260-463-2401)

Ohio Amish Library Inc., Millersburg, OH (330-893-4011)

Pequea Bruderschaft Library, PO Box 25, Gordonville, PA 17529

Web Sites

Amish Studies (http://www.etown.edu/amishstudies)

Amish Youth Vision Project (http://ayvp.org)

Clinic for Special Children (http://www.clinicforspecialchildren.org)

Global Anabaptist Mennonite Encyclopedia Online (http://www.gameo.org)

Blog

Amish America (http://amishamerica.com)

Videos

The Amish: Back Roads to Heaven (DVD, 2007, Buller Films LLC)

The Amish: A People of Preservation (DVD, 1996, Heritage Productions)

baptism partly because it was not voluntary, but also because an infant could not confess faith, the main focus of Protestantism.

These 16th-century radical reformers were some of the earliest advocates of the separation of CHURCH AND STATE. They contended that religious issues such as baptism should be de-termined by the AUTHORITY of the church, not the state.

MENNONITES, AMISH, and HUTTERITES are the closest historical descendants of 16th-cen-tury Anabaptism. The BRETHREN originated in the early 1700s in GERMANY and combined Ana-baptist themes with those of Radical PIETISM.

Twentieth-century Mennonite leader Harold S. Bender (1897–1962) provided one of the most influential interpretations of Anabaptist theology in 1944 when he described an Anabaptist vision. According to Bender, there are three key convictions of Anabaptism: (1) DISCIPLESHIP—that the entire way of life of an individual believer be transformed to follow the teachings and examples of JESUS CHRIST; (2) church—that membership be voluntary and based on true conversion; and (3) love and NONRESISTANCE—that these two principles be applied to all human relationships. Most Anabaptist groups emphasize the authority of the BIBLE, especially the teachings of Jesus in the New Testament, and affirm the guidance of the HOLY SPIRIT for the individual believer and the church.

Although the word "Anabaptist" literally means someone who has been baptized twice, it is typically used in a much broader sense. The words "Anabaptism" and "Anabaptists" designate four things: the radical reformers of the 16th century who advocated for adult baptism and a church free from state-imposed authority, the theological beliefs and heritage that have evolved from the 16th-century movement, the religious groups (and their members) that descended from these radical reformers, and other groups (and their members) that have accepted Anabaptist beliefs and perspectives.

See also Anabaptism, Theology of; Believers Church

Bender (1944), BE I ("Anabaptism"), C. Dyck (1993), GAMEO ("Anabaptism"), Klaassen (1973), Kraybill (2003c), ME V ("Anabaptism"), Roth and Stayer (2007), C. Snyder (1995, 1999)

Anabaptism, History of

Most contemporary historians believe that the Anabaptist Movement began independently in three areas of EUROPE (SWITZERLAND, southern GERMANY / AUSTRIA, and the NETHERLANDS / northern Germany) during the Reformation of the early 1500s. The radical reformers were not satisfied by the changes in church life made by Protestant leaders Martin Luther

(1483–1546), Ulrich Zwingli (1484–1531), John Calvin (1509–1564), and their followers.

Swiss ANABAPTISM began under the leadership of Ulrich Zwingli, a reformer in Zurich in the 1520s. However, Anabaptist leaders such as CONRAD GREBEL (ca. 1498–1526) and Felix Manz (1498–1527) rejected Zwingli's idea that GOVERNMENT authorities should control reforms in the church. Instead, these radical reformers believed that the BIBLE and the spirit of Christ were the only authorities for matters of faith. In 1525 the first adult believers BAPTISM occurred and the new (Swiss Brethren) movement separated from Zwingli. In 1527 Manz was drowned for his "heretical" views, and widespread PERSECUTION of Anabaptists soon followed.

In southern Germany and Austria, the Anabaptist Movement began in Württemberg, Bavaria, and Tyrol. Whereas the Swiss Anabaptists stressed daily ethical behavior, the movement in southern Germany emphasized the mystical elements of faith. Anabaptists from various German-speaking areas (especially Tyrol) gathered in Moravia under the leadership of JAKOB HUTTER (d. 1536). His followers became known as HUTTERITES by the early 1530s. Their practice of COMMUNAL LIVING and rejection of private property, which was modeled after the early church as described in the Acts of the Apostles, distinguished them from other Anabaptists.

Melchior Hoffman (1495–1543), a persuasive itinerant preacher in the Netherlands and northern Germany, broke from Lutheranism by 1529. He emphasized prophecy and the apocalyptic return of Jesus Christ. Hoffman's thinking influenced Anabaptists in the north German city of Münster who tried to use violence to take over the city and establish the kingdom of God.

After the suppression of the Münster rebellion in 1535, Anabaptists who opposed the use of violence were attracted to MENNO SIMONS (1496–1561), a former Catholic priest, and other leaders who embraced a pacifist ethic. Menno Simons became the principal Anabaptist leader in the Netherlands, and gradually many Anabaptists become known as Mennonists or MEN-NONITES.

The radical ideas of the Anabaptists (such as the separation of CHURCH AND STATE, RELIGIOUS LIBERTY, and government tolerance of multiple religious groups), as well as their illegal practices (such as adult rebaptism), provoked severe persecution and MARTYRDOM. Although governments responded to the movement with harsh punishment and legal restrictions, missionary zeal led to the rapid spread of Anabaptism throughout central Europe.

The activities of women were especially important in the spread of the movement. Women's roles as teachers, evangelists, elders, and prophets were more prominent than in Catholic or other Protestant groups. About one-third of the 930 martyrs listed in MARTYRS MIRROR are women.

During the 1500s and 1600s, many Anabaptist groups found temporary refuge from persecution with sympathetic rulers in Alsace, Moravia, Poland, the Netherlands, and various German principalities.

In 1693, JAKOB AMMANN (1644–ca. 1730) excommunicated some of the Swiss Anabaptist leaders, thereby precipitating a church schism in Switzerland, Alsace, and southern Germany. Ammann and the AMISH who were named after him sharply separated from the Swiss Anabaptists (Mennonites) and advocated a stricter and more disciplined form of church life further separated from society.

The German Baptist Brethren combined the themes of 16th-century Anabaptism with those of Radical PIETISM. The BRETHREN originated in Germany in 1708 under the leadership of ALEXANDER MACK SR. (1679–1735).

Many Anabaptists migrated during the 18th century. Major waves of Mennonites emigrated from POLAND (later Prussia) to RUSSIA and from southern Germany and Switzerland to North America. By about 1880 the Hutterites and Brethren were found only in North America, and Mennonites in CANADA and the UNITED STATES significantly outnumbered those remaining in Europe. Most of the Amish had im-migrated to the United States by 1860; the last Amish congregation in Europe disbanded in 1937.

In the late 1900s, Anabaptist groups grew rapidly in AFRICA and ASIA, especially through missionary efforts in the countries of Congo, Zimbabwe, Tanzania, Ethiopia, Indonesia, and India. By 2000 there were more members of some Anabaptist churches in Africa, Asia, and South America than in North America.

Research on the history of Anabaptist groups advanced considerably in the 20th century. One early historian in North America was C. Henry Smith (1875–1948). His last and largest contribution, *The Story of the Mennonites* (1941, revised 1981), was the first in English to cover the entire history of Mennonites in Europe and North America. Harold S. Bender (1897–1962) and the MENNONITE QUARTERLY REVIEW also published continuous scholarship on Anabaptism.

The periodical MENNONITE LIFE publishes articles on Mennonite topics and an annual RADICAL REFORMATION and Mennonite bibliography. It became an online-only journal in 2000. Herald Press, Pandora Press, and other publishers have printed numerous monographs and source books on Anabaptist history and theology.

Two influential historians of Brethren groups were Martin G. Brumbaugh (1862–1930) and Donald F. Durnbaugh (1927–2005). Durnbaugh's *Fruit of the Vine: A History of the Brethren, 1708-1995* (1997) provided a comprehensive overview of Brethren history. John A. Hostetler (1918–2001) wrote the earliest comprehensive books on the Amish and Hutterites.

See also Anabaptism, Theology of; Believers Church

Estep (1996), GAMEO (articles on countries and individuals, "Anabaptism," "Women"), I. Horst (1986), ME V ("Anabaptism," "Women"), Packull (1977), J. Roth (1999b), Roth and Stayer (2007), Smith (1962), Smith and Krahn (1981), C. Snyder (1995), Springer and Klassen (1977), J. Weaver (2005), Williams (1992), http://www.bethelks.edu/mennonitelife/bibliographies, http://www.pandorapress.com, http://www.herald press.com

Table 5   Resources on Anabaptist History and Theology

Books

   Anabaptist History and Theology: An Introduction, C. Snyder, 1997a

   The Anabaptist Story: An Introduction to 16th-Century Anabaptism, Estep, 1996

   Becoming Anabaptist: The Origin and Significance of 16th-Century Anabaptism, J. Weaver, 2005

   A Companion to Anabaptism and Spiritualism, Roth and Stayer, 2007

   From Anabaptist Seed: The Historical Core of Anabaptist-Related Identity, C. Snyder, 1999

   Profiles of Anabaptist Women: Sixteenth Century Reforming Pioneers, Snyder and Hecht, 1996

   The Radical Reformation, Williams, 1992

Periodicals

   Conrad Grebel Review (http://www.grebel.uwaterloo.ca/academic/cgreview/index.shtml)

   Mennonite Life (http://www.bethelks.edu/mennonitelife)

   Mennonite Quarterly Review (http://www.goshen.edu/mqr)

Research Centers

   Center for Mennonite Brethren Studies, Fresno, CA (http://www.fresno.edu/library/cmbs)

   Institute of Anabaptist Mennonite Studies, Waterloo, ON (http://www.grebel.uwaterloo.ca/academic/iams)

   Institute of Mennonite Studies, Elkhart, IN (http://www.ambs.edu/ims)

   Mennonite Studies University of Winnipeg, MB (http://mennonitestudies.uwinnipeg.ca)

   Young Center for Anabaptist and Pietist Studies, Elizabethtown, PA (http://www.etown.edu/YoungCenter.aspx)

Libraries and Archives

   Mennonite Brethren Library, Fresno, CA (http://www.fresno.edu/library/cmbs)

   Mennonite Heritage Centre Archives, Winnipeg, MB (http://www.mennonitechurch.ca/
      programs/archives)

   Mennonite Historical Library, Goshen, IN (http://www.goshen.edu/mhl/Home)

   Mennonite Library and Archives, Newton, KS (http://www.bethelks.edu/mla/index.php)

   Menno Simons Historical Library at Eastern Mennonite University, Harrisonburg, VA
      (http://www.emu.edu/library/historical-library)

Web Sites

   Anabaptist Network (http://www.anabaptistnetwork.com)

   Cascadia Press (http://www.cascadiapublishinghouse.com)

   Global Anabaptist Mennonite Encyclopedia Online (http://www.gameo.org)

   Herald Press (http://www.heraldpress.com)

   Pandora Press (http://bookshop.pandorapress.com/index.php)

Video

   The Radicals (VHS, 1989, Gateway Films/Vision Video)

Anabaptism, Theology of

The word ANABAPTIST is based on a Greek word meaning rebaptism. This term was given to the adult baptizers of the RADICAL REFORMATION by their opponents because those being baptized as adults had been previously baptized as infants. The Anabaptists disliked the label because they did not view their initial infant BAPTISM as biblically or theologically valid and therefore did not consider their adult baptism to be *re*baptism.

Anabaptism arose in several regions of western EUROPE, and by 1540, Anabaptist theology, though not entirely unified, expressed six basic themes: (1) baptism is appropriate only for adults who have made a voluntary decision to follow the way of JESUS CHRIST; (2) individual and corporate Christian life is under the authority of the BIBLE (especially the New Testament) as interpreted by the HOLY SPIRIT in COMMUNITY; (3) God gives freedom to individuals to choose lives of DISCIPLESHIP, following the way of Jesus; (4) SALVATION begins with inner regeneration, which is then manifested in outward ethical behavior in social relationships; (5) the church community has authority to discern corporate practice for its members; and (6) the way of Jesus rejects the use of violence and force in human relationships. In addition, some 16th-century Anabaptists had a pronounced eschatology, emphasizing the imminent return of Christ.

Until the late 1800s, mainstream historians and theologians dismissed Anabaptism as representing a heretical or destabilizing threat to church and civil life. Gradually a more neutral or positive interpretation of Anabaptism developed. MENNONITE scholar Harold S. Bender (1897–1962) spearheaded a reinterpretation of the theology of Anabaptism. In December 1943 Bender gave the presidential address at the American Society of Church History in New York City. Entitled "The Anabaptist Vision," the address detailed the essence of 16th-century Anabaptism captured in three concepts: (1) DISCIPLESHIP—that the entire way of life of an individual believer be transformed to follow the teachings and examples of Jesus Christ; (2) church—that membership be voluntary and based on true conversion; and (3) love and NONRESISTANCE—that these two principles be applied to all human relationships.

This address and its ideas were widely distributed and discussed among North American Mennonite groups in the mid-20th century as leaders directed Mennonite institutions, discerned their role in the world, and clarified their identity. Subsequently, scholars of the 1970s and 1980s argued against some of Bender's conclusions. They claimed that the early history of 16th-century Anabaptism had numerous points of origin and included many themes that Bender had excluded, such as MYSTICISM and the use of violence.

Some Anabaptist theologians in CENTRAL AMERICA and SOUTH AMERICA find the Anabaptist vision relevant to their context of poverty, structural violence, and alienation from the political elite. Anabaptist theology blends spirituality with social witness in these themes: following Christ in radical obedience, living and worshiping as a redeemed community, practicing a peaceable lifestyle that rejects violence and apathy, and witnessing against social injustice.

See also Believers Church; Church, Theology of; Confessions of Faith

Bender (1944), Flores (1984), GAMEO ("Anabaptism," "The Anabaptist Vision"), Higueros (1995), Keifer (1990), Keim (1998), Klaassen (1973), Koop (2004, 2006), ME I ("Anabaptist"), Roth and Stayer (2007), C. Snyder (1995, 1999, 2001), Stayer, Packull, and Depperman (1975), J. Weaver (2005), J. H. Yoder (2002)

Anabaptist Financial   *See* Anabaptist Foundation

Anabaptist Foundation

The mission of Anabaptist Foundation is to help AMISH and MENNONITES in TRADITIONAL GROUPS channel their material resources to church organizations and use those resources for Christian projects that are consistent with conservative ANABAPTIST beliefs and values. It provides services to donors, churches, and nonprofits, with a variety of tools that maximize donated money. Anabaptist Foundation has enabled its constituents to provide substantial support for many churches and charities. A public foundation, it is governed by a 10-member board drawn from different sectors of the conservative Anabaptist community; the board has a mix of business experience, professional training, pastoral experience, and experience in nonprofit administration. An advisory group of approximately 40 members provides counsel to the board. The board and staff of Anabaptist Foundation also administer its sister organization, Anabaptist Financial, which provides financial advice and counsel for investors and services for borrowers.

See also Brethren in Christ Foundation; Mennonite Foundation; Mennonite Foundation of Canada http://www.afweb.org/foundation

Anabaptist Groups   *See* Assimilated Groups; Traditional Groups

Anabaptist Groups, International

Beginning with their origins in central and northern Europe and immigration to North America and Russia in the 1600s through 1900, ANABAPTIST-related congregations and conferences spread further over the globe in the 1900s. The primary international Anabaptist organization is MENNONITE WORLD CONFERENCE, a global organization of MENNONITE- and BRETHREN IN CHRIST–related churches from 75 countries on six continents that seeks to link the nearly 1.6 million believers in fellowship, worship, service, and witness. *What We Believe Together* (Neufeld, 2008), a book commissioned by Mennonite World Conference, offers a short overview of the commonly held beliefs of worldwide members of Mennonite-related groups.

Recognizing that a Mennonite population shift to the global South was occurring, Mennonite World Conference began to hold assemblies in ASIA and AFRICA in the late 1900s. By 2010, over half of the 1.6 million Mennonites lived in the global South. All continents showed Mennonite membership growth in the first decade of the 21st century, except Europe, which reported a slight decline. The Meserete Kristos Church in Ethiopia, with more than 130,000 members, is the largest national Mennonite church conference in the world.

BRETHREN WORLD ASSEMBLY held its first meeting at Elizabethtown College in Pennsylvania in 1992. Its goal is to foster communication among the North American Brethren groups and those in other nations. Outside North America, BRETHREN groups are most heavily represented in Africa, especially in Nigeria, where the CHURCH OF THE BRETHREN–related denomination Ekklesiyar Yan'uwa a Nigeria has more than 200,000 members. The GRACE BRETHREN report about 2,600 congregations resulting from mission efforts in 25 countries outside North America, 2,200 of which are in the Central African Republic.

The Council of International Anabaptist Ministries, a group of more than 20 Canadian and U.S. Mennonite, Brethren, and Brethren in Christ mission agencies, coordinates their efforts through the Global Mission Fellowship, which has regional bodies throughout the world.

The HUTTERITES and the AMISH live almost entirely in the United States and Canada and have no international organizations.

Lapp and van Straten (2003), A. Neufeld (2008), C. Snyder (1999), http://www.anabaptistwiki.org, http://www.brethren.org, http://www.mwc-cmm.org

Anabaptist Vision   *See* Anabaptism

Anointing with Oil

This rite, practiced by BRETHREN early in their history, continues into the 21st century. The anointing service was eventually accepted by numerous AMISH and MENNONITE groups. Based on James 5:14–15 and Mark 6:13, where the apostles anointed sick persons with oil, the ceremony is performed privately by a minister in the presence of a few family members or close friends, or in a public worship/healing service. The RITUAL affirms the sick person's faith in the healing power of God and willingness to yield his or her life to God's care, and provides assurance of forgiveness. The anointed person does not necessarily expect immediate healing or prepare for death by this act, unlike the last rite of anointing in some other Christian traditions. Members may also request anointing for the healing of emotional stress or anxiety related to events or psychological transitions in their lives.

See also Ordinance

W. Bowman (1942), GAMEO ("Anointing with Oil"), ME I ("Anointing with Oil"), M. Wenger (2005)

Apostles' Creed   *See* Confessions of Faith

Apostolic Christian Church of America

This group began in 1832 in Switzerland under the leadership of Samuel Froehlich (1803–1857), who was influenced by the ANABAPTISTS and their teaching. Many converts to the Apostolic Church came from Swiss MENNONITE backgrounds. The first Apostolic Christian Church in North America was organized in Lewis County, New York, in 1847, where it attracted a number of AMISH. Sometimes nicknamed "the New Amish," the group shares many Anabaptist principles and practices with conservative Mennonite churches, and has some members from Amish and Mennonite backgrounds. The Apostolic Christian Church occasionally supports projects sponsored by MENNONITE CENTRAL COMMITTEE and MENNONITE DISASTER SERVICE. The group has 12,700 members in the United States in 87 congregations scattered across 23 states, with strong concentrations in Illinois, Indiana, Iowa, and Ohio. It also has two congregations in Canada and two in Mexico.

The Apostolic Christian Church (Nazarene), a related but different group whose members are mostly of Slavic background, formed in 1908. Other small related groups include the German Apostolic Christian Church, the Christian Apostolic Church (a division from the former), and the Nazarene Christian Congregations. (The membership of these related churches is not included in the Table of Groups.)

GAMEO ("Apostolic Christian Church of America"), Klopfenstein (1984), ME I ("Apostolic Christian Church"), http://www.apostolicchristian.org

Architecture   *See* Church Building

Art, Fine

One of the assertions of the Zwinglian-Calvinist streams of the Protestant Reformation was that the presence of God is communicated through the written and spoken word rather than through visual images. Many ANABAPTISTS in the 1500s eliminated overt images in worship, because they associated such images with idolatry, luxury, and pride. A deep suspicion of

fine art and artists developed among Anabaptist groups originating in SWITZERLAND; however, MENNONITES in the NETHERLANDS eventually participated in the high culture of the 1600s. Famous Dutch painters who were Mennonite or associated with Mennonites include Rembrandt van Rijn (1606–1669), Karel van Mander (1548–1606), Jacob van Ruisdael (1628–1682), and Govert Flinck (1615–1660). Dutch engraver Jan Luyken (1649–1712) produced brilliant scenes to illustrate MARTYRS MIRROR, one of the monumental Anabaptist texts.

By the mid-1900s, North American ASSIMILATED GROUPS had members who were fine artists, and church-related colleges eventually developed full-fledged art departments. The Association of the Arts in the CHURCH OF THE BRETHREN was initiated in 1971 in order to connect and encourage artists and to help the arts become an important ministry of the church. Mennonite-related artists have created a web site (http://mennoniteartistproject.com) to foster a sense of community within their ranks. TRADITIONAL GROUPS continue to be suspicious of the fine arts, which they consider impractical and encouraging of pride in individualistic expression.

See also Folk Art

BE I ("Art," "Association for the Arts in the Church of the Brethren"), GAMEO ("Art," individual artists), I. Horst (1956), Krahn (1957), ME I ("Art"), http://mennoniteartistproject.com

Art, Folk   *See* Folk Art

Asia

The first ANABAPTIST missionary to Asia was Mennonite Pieter Jansz (1820–1904), sent in 1851 from the NETHERLANDS to what is now Indonesia. He translated the Bible into Javanese, published a dictionary in a local dialect, criticized aspects of Dutch colonialism, and helped found MENNONITE churches. During and after the tension-filled years of WORLD WAR II and national independence from colonialism, Indonesian Mennonites began to organize their church conferences and engage in MISSION work. In the early 21st century there are approximately 89,000 members of Mennonite-related congregations in Indonesia. Their church conferences include the Evangelical Church of Java, composed primarily of Indonesians of Javanese ethnicity, and Muria Christian Church of Indonesia, composed of persons of Chinese ethnicity.

North American Anabaptist groups sent missionaries to India in the late 1800s and early 1900s—the CHURCH OF THE BRETHREN in 1895, the Mennonites in 1899, and the BRETHREN IN CHRIST in 1905—and they initially drew converts from the lower castes. Mennonite missionaries established schools (emphasizing practical vocational education and Bible teaching), hospitals (including one for people with leprosy), and orphanages. Throughout the 1930s and 1940s the Mennonite churches in India moved toward self-supporting, self-propagating, and self-governing organizations. By the early 20th century, Mennonite and Brethren in Christ conferences were spread over much of the country but concentrated in four states: Andhra Pradesh, Chhattisgarh, Bihar, and West Bengal. The 1997 MENNONITE WORLD CONFERENCE was held in Calcutta. Membership in Mennonite-related congregations in India totals about 157,000. Brethren in Christ mission efforts in India have produced 182 congregations with an estimated membership of 10,000.

In 1895 the first Church of the Brethren missionaries went to India and developed medical and educational ventures, including the Vocational Training School and Rural Service Center. By 1930, membership totaled about 4,000. In 1970, when membership reached 16,000, the Church of the Brethren in India joined with five other Christian denominations to form the Church of North India. The BRETHREN CHURCH has some 180 congregations or preaching stations and more than 10,000 members in India.

In the first decade of the 1900s, Mennonites sent missionaries to China, and by 1952 there were about 5,000 Chinese Mennonites. Following the Communist Revolution that established the People's Republic of China in 1949, some Mennonites joined the new government-sanctioned Protestant church conference and others chose to go underground. In the early 21st century there are several small Chinese Mennonite congregations in Hong Kong and Macau. Mennonite Partners in China (formerly China Educational Exchange) began in 1981 and arranges for North American teachers of English in China and also for Chinese teachers in North American colleges.

The Church of the Brethren sent missionaries to Shanxi Province, China, in 1908 for evangelistic work and later expanded into education, agriculture, and medicine. World War II interrupted that development, but after the war the BRETHREN SERVICE COMMISSION sent 50 volunteers to China with a United Nations operation to help rebuild after the wartime destruction. In 1946 some missionaries returned, but by 1951 the Communist government forced all of them to leave. Some indigenous congregations continued with their own resources in this repressive environment.

In the 1950s, Mennonites sent missionaries to Japan, where they practiced evangelism through radio broadcasting, teaching English, creating kindergartens, and personal contact. There are about 3,000 Mennonites and Brethren in Christ in Japan in five church groups.

In Vietnam a small number of Brethren volunteers were involved in PEACEMAKING activities in the early 1970s. MENNONITE CENTRAL COMMITTEE (MCC) involvement began in the country in the 1950s, and a limited presence of Mennonites continued during the VIETNAM WAR and after the South Vietnamese government collapsed April 1975. Mission efforts resulted in the establishment of a few Mennonite congregations immediately after the war, which have grown to 4,000 members. MCC relief and development programs are found throughout Asia.

BE I ("China"), D. Durnbaugh (1997a), GAMEO ("India," "Indonesia," "International Exchanges"), Juhnke (1979), Lapp (1972), ME V ("India," "Indonesia," "International Exchanges"), Ramseyer and Ramseyer

(1988), W. Shenk (1973), L. Yoder (2006), http://www
.anabaptistwiki.org, http://www.brethrenchurch.org,
http://www.mennonitepartnerschina.org, http://www
.mwc-cmm.org

Asian-American Anabaptists

Asian-Americans who are affiliated with ANA-
BAPTIST churches in North America include
those with the following ethnic/national identities: Chinese, Hmong, Indonesian, Japanese,
Korean, and Vietnamese. The two largest groups
are Chinese and Vietnamese. Congregations
whose members are predominately Asian-American are typically found in large urban areas such
as Toronto, Calgary, Los Angeles, Philadelphia,
San Francisco, Vancouver, and Winnipeg. Most
of the congregations are small, with fewer than
100 members. The MENNONITE BRETHREN
have numerous congregations whose members
have predominantly Asian backgrounds. For the
most part, Asian-American congregations are
affiliated with assimilated Anabaptist groups.

Asian-Americans joined the Anabaptist ranks
through several avenues. Some were converts as
a result of mission outreach in North America
during the last half of the 20th century. Others came as refugees and were hosted by local
congregations. Still others became acquainted
with Anabaptist missionaries or service workers
in their home country prior to coming to North
America.

Two MENNONITE organizations support
Asian-American churches. Lao Mennonite
Ministries, based in St. Catharines, Ontario,
promotes fellowship and cooperation among
Laotian congregations for leadership develop-
ment and church planting. It also serves as a
liaison with other Mennonite agencies in the
United States and Canada. Similarly, the North
American Vietnamese Mennonite Fellowship
promotes collaboration and networking among
Vietnamese Mennonite churches. Founded in
1997, this organization is based in Vancouver,
British Columbia.

The CHURCH OF THE BRETHREN began
Sunday school missions among Chinese immigrants in the early 1900s in Chicago, Detroit,

Washington, D.C., and Los Angeles. Many
Chinese involved in these missions were adult
males who returned to China after a few years.
Some Church of the Brethren members helped
to resettle Japanese-American internees during
World War II, and a few of those internees joined
the church.

See also Vietnam War

BE I ("Americans of Japanese Ancestry," "Chinese
Sunday Schools")

Assimilated Groups

ANABAPTIST groups can be viewed along a continuum stretching from tradition to assimilation.
The terms "traditional" and "assimilated" designate the opposite ends of this continuum, which
reflects the degree to which a group rejects or
accepts the values and structures of modern
culture as it emerged in North America in the
late 19th and 20th centuries.

Two fundamental factors mark this spectrum:
(1) the locus of *moral authority*, and (2) how
sharply the community *separates* itself from the
larger society. Contrasted with TRADITIONAL
GROUPS, assimilated groups grant greater freedom to individual choice, mingle more freely
with the outside world, and seek to engage the
larger social order. For traditional groups, the locus of moral authority is the church-community,
whereas assimilated groups grant greater moral
responsibility for religious matters to individual
members. In other words, individualism is a key
difference between the two groups.

Assimilated Anabaptist groups participate in
North American culture and society more than
traditional groups, which emphasize cultural
and societal separation from the larger society.
The degree of engagement with modern society
has varied by group, region, and historical period in North America; however, the inclination
to assimilate increased in the 20th century, with
the growing influence of mass media, commercial advertising, and HIGHER EDUCATION.

Distinctive CLOTHING is a major dividing
line between assimilated and traditional groups:
members of traditional groups typically wear
dress styles prescribed by the church. Members

of assimilated groups, in addition to wearing fashionable clothing, usually support higher education, work in professions, participate in civic organizations, use electronic media such as RADIO, TELEVISION, and COMPUTERS, live in urban and suburban areas, and have relatively small FAMILIES. Although they may not accept mainstream values such as nationalism and militarism, members of assimilated groups are more likely to accept the individualistic values that are central to mainstream modern culture.

There is a spectrum of diversity among assimilated groups in the extent to which they participate in mainstream social life. Some members of assimilated churches do not work in professions, vote, or own televisions, but the majority do participate in these practices. Assimilated congregations are more likely than traditional ones to revise religious rituals, hire seminary-trained MINISTERS, have well-furnished CHURCH BUILDINGS, support church-related INSTITUTIONS, participate in MISSION and/or peace-and-justice efforts, accept divorced and remarried persons as members of their congregations, and permit the ORDINATION OF WOMEN.

Kraybill and Bowman (2001), Kraybill and Hostetter (2001)

Association of Radical Church Networks
Congregations in this network of several church groups continue to emphasize some ANABAPTIST themes but have also been heavily influenced by ideas of apostolic church governance, which emphasize the authority of male leaders in shaping the vision of their churches. Leaders make connections to the historical radical church, including, but not limited to, the early church described in the New Testament book of Acts and 16th-century Anabaptists. Many of the congregations in the network have a CHARISMATIC emphasis and style of worship and strong outreach and church-planting efforts. Leaders promote a full reliance on the active ministry of the HOLY SPIRIT and a lifestyle of radical discipleship that seeks to practice the values of the kingdom of God taught by Jesus.

Some of the key affiliations in the network include Hopewell Network of Churches (15 congregations) in eastern Pennsylvania, Cornerstone Church and Ministries International (8 congregations) in Virginia, Global Community Network (7 congregations) in Pennsylvania, Hopenet Fellowship of Churches (5 congregations) in Pennsylvania, and the Radical Restoration Network of Churches (6 congregations), which is primarily in Indiana. The Association of Radical Church Networks has an estimated 7,000 members.

Anabaptist (Mennonite) Directory (2009), http://www.CornerstoneNet.org, http://www.hopewellnetwork.org, http://www.radicalrestoration.org/ARCnet.html

Atonement   *See* Salvation

Ausbund
The *Ausbund* ("selection") is the primary hymnbook of the AMISH, and the only one used by most Amish congregations in worship services. Considered the oldest Protestant hymnal in continuous use, the *Ausbund* first appeared in the mid-1500s among descendants of Swiss Brethren ANABAPTISTS in EUROPE. The hymnal contains German texts without musical scores. The texts include ballads that recount the history of the MARTYRDOM and PERSECUTION of Anabaptists, as well as other poetic texts, drawn from Lutheran and Reformed HYMNODY, that seek to admonish believers and inspire faith consistent with the Anabaptist theology. Many *Ausbund* texts have been translated into English, and a few are included in contemporary MENNONITE hymnals.

H. Durnbaugh (1999), GAMEO ("Ausbund"), Peters and Riall (2003), *Songs of the Ausbund* (1998), P. M. Yoder (1964)

Aussiedler (Emigrant) Mennonites
Since 1970 nearly 112,000 MENNONITES and evangelicals with Mennonite ancestry have immigrated to GERMANY from RUSSIA. Much of their theology and ecclesiology has been shaped by their history of PERSECUTION in Russia and

the Soviet Union, and most of these immigrants have created their own church organizations instead of joining existing German Mennonite congregations.

Although the group includes various subgroups with diverse practices, most *Aussiedler* Mennonites maintain a strict interpretation of the Bible. Many members wear simple CLOTHING and object to the use of cosmetics and jewelry. Most ministers do not have a theological education, nor are they paid a salary. Their beliefs and lifestyle set them apart from both the German Mennonite congregations and contemporary German culture. A spectrum of assimilation exists among the subgroups, however, as some members drop the plainer clothing and pursue higher education.

During the decade and a half after 1993, some 15,000 of these immigrants moved once again, this time to rural properties in the southern Manitoba communities of Steinbach and Winkler.

GAMEO ("Umsiedler [Aussiedler]"), Heinrich Loewen (2003), ME V ("Umsiedler [Resettlers]")

Austria

ANABAPTISM flourished in Austria and regions of Moravia (no longer part of present-day Austria) during the 1500s. At about the same time, German-speaking Tyrol (now partially in Italy) witnessed an explosion in its Anabaptist population to an estimated 20,000 adherents. Moravia offered religious tolerance and therefore became a haven for many persecuted sects, including Anabaptists, in the 16th and 17th centuries. Some of these Anabaptist refugees embraced the doctrine of communal living and eventually became known as HUTTERITES. (*Hutterisch,* the dialect of many Hutterites in North America, is closely related to Tyrolean German.)

From about 1550 to 1600, the Hutterite population in Moravia (now Czech Republic) grew numerically, with protection by the nobility— only to be later crushed and totally banished by Emperor Ferdinand II (1578–1637). The Catholic Counter-Reformation also crushed Anabaptism in Austria through executions and banishment,

nearly wiping it out by 1600. By the early 1600s, Anabaptist communities in Austria had largely vanished because of persecution and emigration.

Following WORLD WAR II, MENNONITES and BRETHREN carried out several relief and mission projects in Austria, which produced a few new Anabaptist congregations there.

BE I ("Austria"), GAMEO ("Austria"), ME I ("Austria"), Packull (1977, 1995)

Authority

ANABAPTISM arose as a countercultural protest against powerful government-supported church authorities. Hence, some Anabaptist groups continue to feel ambivalence toward power, leadership, and authority (both in the church and in society).

Many ASSIMILATED GROUPS accept the individualism that characterizes the cultures of contemporary liberal democracies. As an assimilated part of the wider culture, they embrace a philosophy that champions individual rights and freedom and personal autonomy at the expense of individual submission to COMMUNITY standards. On the traditional end of the spectrum, the HUTTERITE practice of COMMUNAL LIVING illustrates an extreme form of community authority over individual choice and freedom.

TRADITIONAL GROUPS believe that social authority is centered in the Scriptures and the traditions of the community rather than in the subjective preferences of the individual. In church matters, ordained adult males typically have more authority than other members. In home matters, older persons, both male and female, have authority in their defined spheres of responsibility, which are usually determined by clear GENDER ROLES.

Religious authority in Anabaptist groups is based on four principles: (1) the life, teaching, and redemptive work of JESUS CHRIST; (2) the BIBLE, especially the New Testament; (3) the guidance of the HOLY SPIRIT; and (4) the witness of both the early church and the contemporary church as it discerns God's will and guides believers.

Among most Anabaptist groups, the CON-GREGATION tends to hold the highest ecclesiastical authority. Certain groups also grant a high level of authority to regional networks of congregations.

The Brethren Annual Conference is a variation on this Anabaptist practice. Beginning in the 1700s, BRETHREN met to discuss important issues facing its congregations, and the decisions of the participants at the national conference became the binding authority for the congregations. Although the authority of Annual Conference still has binding power among traditional Brethren groups, its authority has largely dissolved among the more assimilated Brethren groups. Likewise, regional conferences of some of the North American MENNONITE groups of Swiss-German origin held considerable authority over local congregations in the 19th and 20th centuries, but in assimilated groups that authority had largely eroded by the early 21st century.

In the 20th century many assimilated groups began creating church-related institutions such as mission agencies, hospitals, and publishing organizations. These institutions operate on legal patterns of authority that are different from the traditional forms of authority espoused in the leadership patterns of the church. The older patterns of congregational or conference authority persist in traditional groups.

See also Church Authority

BE I ("Authority"), GAMEO ("Authority"), ME V ("Authority"), B. Redekop and C. Redekop (2001), Sawatsky (1997), M. Schrag (1964)

Automobile

North American ANABAPTIST groups reacted in diverse ways to the arrival of the automobile in the early decades of the 20th century. Members of ASSIMILATED GROUPS adopted the car as it became widely accepted in society. HUTTER-ITES accepted the communal ownership and operation of motor vehicles and farm equipment.

Some TRADITIONAL GROUPS, such as the AMISH and certain OLD ORDER MENNONITES, rejected the car because it symbolized pride, individualism, and status and, in its early stages, was associated with URBAN LIFE and culture. These traditional groups feared that the mobility provided by individually owned cars would encourage greater individual freedom, fragment their locally based COMMUNITIES, lead youth away to the city, and compromise personal accountability to the community.

For example, in the 1920s and 1930s, in some Old Order Mennonite groups, the car became a contentious issue and divided some groups into car-driving and horse-driving factions. A few Old Order Mennonite churches accepted the use of the car for its members but placed restrictions on the type of car they could own. One group required its members to paint all the chrome black, leading to the nickname "black bumper MENNONITES." Although this practice was relaxed, some traditional groups still encourage their members to drive black vehicles. A horse and buggy are still used for daily transportation by most Old Order Amish and some Old Order Mennonite groups in the United States and Canada, and by many OLD COLONY MENNO-NITES in Belize, Mexico, and South America.

Some Old Order groups forbid ownership of cars but permit their members to hire vehicles with drivers for BUSINESS purposes and trips out of the local community. Public transportation—buses, trains, and boats—is widely used by the most traditional groups. Some Old Order groups prohibit air travel except in the case of emergencies.

See also Technology

BE I ("Automobile"), GAMEO ("Automobile"), Heidebrecht (2006), A. Hoover (2006), Kraybill (2001), Kraybill and Bowman (2001), Kraybill and Hurd (2006), D. Martin (2003), ME V ("Automobile")

Avoidance   *See* Shunning

b

Bahamas

The only ANABAPTIST group in the Bahamas, the Eastern Pennsylvania Mennonite Church, began a mission there in the early 1980s. The project eventually included a farm and several mechanical shops providing training and employment for local people. The mission consists of one congregation of 25 members. Religious services are held at two sites, one on North Andros Island and the other on South Andros Island.

C. Martin (1994), http://www.mwc-cmm.org

Ban   *See* Shunning

Baptism

For ANABAPTIST groups, baptism is a public ORDINANCE that acknowledges a believer's confession of Christian faith and entry into a local church COMMUNITY. Before and during the Protestant Reformation, most churches baptized infants. In contrast, all Anabaptist groups practiced adult or believers baptism. They believed that only an adult could decide to repent, confess faith, enter into a baptismal covenant with fellow believers in the church, and show signs of a regenerated life. These convictions were confirmed by biblical examples of baptism. Because adults were given a choice (instead of automatically being baptized into the state church as infants), adult baptism radically challenged the longstanding medieval integration of CHURCH AND STATE.

When Anabaptism began in 16th-century German- and Dutch-speaking territories, opponents of Anabaptism used various Baptist labels to identify the movement. In GERMANY they were called *Wiedertäufer* ("baptized again"), in SWITZERLAND, *Täufer* ("baptists"), and in the NETHERLANDS, *Doopsgezinde* ("baptism-minded"). Anabaptists' refusal to bear arms and use force on behalf of civil authorities as well as their practice of baptizing adults advocated a then-heretical separation of church and state.

Anabaptist groups developed different modes of baptism: sprinkling, pouring, and immersion. Contention sometimes surrounded the mode.

BRETHREN groups required a total immersion in water three times successively (trine immersion), using the names of the Trinity upon each immersion. MENNONITE BRETHREN CHURCHES also required total immersion. All AMISH, HUTTERITES, and most MENNONITES baptized by pouring or sprinkling. Each group provided biblical justification for their particular mode of baptism. In the 21st century some assimilated churches allow the baptismal candidate to select the mode.

For TRADITIONAL GROUPS, joining the church through baptism is a momentous step. With their act of baptism, new members signal their willingness to obey the specific rules of conduct set by their church. Serious violations of their baptismal vows may incur DISCIPLINE and/or EXCOMMUNICATION and, in some groups, SHUNNING.

Although Anabaptist groups have generally insisted upon adult baptism, the age at which baptism occurs varies widely because the rite is requested by the individual. It typically takes place between ages 12 and 25, but in some instances it occurs as early as age 8; those who confess their faith in Christ are baptized at any age. Some ASSIMILATED GROUPS permit early baptism, while others question whether young teens and preteens have the spiritual maturity to fully understand the baptismal covenant. Most Anabaptist groups hold several instructional meetings, sometimes called catechism, for those who request baptism. Some assimilated Anabaptist congregations only require a reaffirmation of faith and do not require adult baptism of committed believers who were baptized as infants in other churches.

See also Believers Church; Church, Theology of
Armour (1966), BE I ("Baptism"), D. Brown (1983),
C. Dyck (1993), GAMEO ("Baptism," "Immersion"),
J. Hostetler (1993), Jeschke (1983), ME I ("Baptism"),
M. Miller (1990), Roth (2005a)

Beachy Amish Mennonite Church

The Beachy Amish emerged in the 1920s in Somerset and Lancaster counties (Pennsylvania) under the leadership of Bishop Moses Beachy

(1874–1946). Many of the group's members come from Old Order Amish backgrounds. Unlike the Old Order, the Beachy Amish use automobiles and public electricity and worship in meeting-houses. They typically do not permit television and radio. Members use English in their church services and wear plain dress, and men wear abbreviated BEARDS. Many Beachy Amish Mennonite congregations support evangelistic and outreach initiatives. Although of AMISH origin, the Beachy Amish interact and participate much more with conservative MENNONITE groups than with Old Order Amish.

The Beachy Amish have about 7,350 members in the United States, in 97 congregations in 20 states with heavy concentrations in Ohio, Pennsylvania, Indiana, Kentucky, and Virginia. In Canada they have eight congregations with about 225 members. In Central America they are involved with some 30 congregations in Belize, Costa Rica, El Salvador, and Nicaragua.

Since 1990, three groups have branched from the Beachy Amish and formed their own affiliations: Ambassadors Amish Mennonites (the most conservative group, with four congregations and about 250 members); Maranatha Amish Mennonite Church; and Berea Amish Mennonite Fellowship.

GAMEO ("Beachy Amish Mennonite Fellowship"), ME V ("Beachy Amish Mennonite Fellowship"), Nolt (2003), Scott (1996), E. S. Yoder (1987), http://www .beachyam.org

Beard
In the early 1800s, following the French Revolution, Napoleon's soldiers often wore mustaches with no beards. Hence, descendants of Swiss-origin ANABAPTIST pacifists often associated hair on the upper lip with the military. In the mid-1700s most BRETHREN and MENNONITE men wore beards, but mustaches were eventually disallowed or discouraged by many Anabaptist groups.

In the 21st century, beards, mustaches, and shaven faces are a matter of personal choice among men in ASSIMILATED GROUPS. With the exception of CHURCH OF GOD IN CHRIST,

MENNONITES, men in traditional Mennonite groups generally do not wear beards. AMISH and HUTTERITE adult men are required by church rules to wear an untrimmed beard, but mustaches are forbidden because of their association with the military. OLD GERMAN BAPTIST BRETHREN and some other traditional Brethren groups require ministers to wear beards and encourage laymen to wear them as well.

See also Clothing; Nonconformity

BE I ("Beard"), D. Durnbaugh (1997a), GAMEO ("Beard"), ME I ("Beard")

Becker, Peter (1678–1758)
As the first BRETHREN minister in North America, Becker helped to organize new Brethren congregations in Pennsylvania. He emigrated from Krefeld, GERMANY, in 1719, was chosen as a minister in 1723, and presided over the first Brethren baptism and LOVE FEAST in North America. Known as a deeply caring counselor, Becker worked harmoniously with Brethren founder ALEXANDER MACK SR. (1679–1735) in Pennsylvania until Mack's death. Initially Becker lived in Germantown (near Philadelphia) and later moved north to the Skippack area. Both in Krefeld and in Pennsylvania, he and his fellow Brethren lived adjacent to MENNONITE communities, with whom they shared many ANABAPTIST beliefs and practices.

See also Pietism

BE I ("Becker, Peter"), D. Durnbaugh (1997a)

Beissel, Conrad   *See* Ephrata Cloister

Believers Church
This theological term reflects a view of the church as a gathered body of believers who have made voluntary confessions of faith and decisions as adults to follow Jesus Christ and to commit themselves to participate in a church that is free from GOVERNMENT control or supervision. The concept can be traced back to the RADICAL REFORMATION and the Free Church Movement in 16th-century EUROPE. It encompasses ANABAPTIST groups and other denominations such as Baptists, QUAKERS,

Churches of God, Churches of Christ, and some Pentecostal groups, as well as many of the rapidly growing Christian churches throughout AFRICA and ASIA.

For the 16th-century Anabaptists, the doctrine of the church separated them most sharply from the rest of Christendom, both Catholic and Protestant. They rejected completely the medieval concept of a Christian social order in which church, society, and civil government blended together. The Anabaptists were some of the first to envision a free church, composed only of disciples who had committed their lives to the way of Jesus, which was separate from the state and separated from the world by cultural values. They viewed this believers church as a brotherhood with leaders, but without a hierarchy. All the members held responsibility for the total life of the church, for mutual aid, and for mutual discipline and order. Their TWO-KINGDOM THEOLOGY drew a clear line between the church and the general social order.

A 1967 ecumenical conference in Louisville, Kentucky, spread the term "believers church" and spawned a series of additional meetings. Following the conference, BRETHREN scholar Donald F. Durnbaugh (1927–2005) wrote *The Believers' Church: The History and Character of Radical Protestantism,* a widely distributed book that explores the history and character of believers churches and is often used to study their tradition. Since 1986 the Believers Church Bible Commentary Series project, a cooperative venture of MENNONITE and Brethren churches, has published 22 major interpretive volumes on books of the Bible and projects covering the entire Bible.

See also Anabaptism, Theology of; Baptism; Religious Liberty

BE I ("Believers' Church"), D. Durnbaugh (1968), GAMEO ("Believers Church"), Koop and Shertz (2000), ME V ("Believers' Church"), J. H. Yoder (1991)

Belize

The 10 ANABAPTIST-related groups in Belize have about 4,400 members. The Belizean Anabaptist story began in 1958, when two groups

of conservative Dutch-Russian MENNONITES with Canadian origins (OLD COLONY MENNONITES and Kleine Gemeinde) moved from MEXICO to British Honduras, which became the independent country of Belize in 1981. These Mennonites had settled in Mexico in the 1920s and 1940s to avoid assimilation in CANADA. During the 1950s some of them feared that Mexico's social welfare system would undermine the religious values of their colonies, so several hundred emigrated from Mexico to Belize. The Old Colony Mennonites established two agricultural colonies in Belize: Shipyard and Blue Creek. (A colony is a block of hundreds of acres of adjacent land.) The Kleine Gemeinde founded a colony known as Spanish Lookout. Both groups were traditional in religious doctrine and practice as well as in their use of TECHNOLOGY.

During the 1970s and 1980s an unstable economy and endemic violence in Belize encouraged some members of the Old Colony and Kleine Gemeinde churches to return to Canada, especially to southern parts of Ontario, Alberta, and Manitoba, but also to British Columbia and Nova Scotia.

Blue Creek gradually underwent a transformation when evangelical-minded Mennonites from Canada moved in during the 1960s and the traditional horse-and-buggy culture disappeared. Shipyard is still a horse-and-buggy community of the Old Colony Mennonites.

The Hoover Mennonites, with two communities (Springfield and Upper Barton Creek), have members from Swiss, Russian, Belizean, and indigenous backgrounds. The members of a similar community at Lower Barton have mostly Russian (Old Colony) backgrounds. These ultraconservative Mennonites reject all engines and any form of ELECTRICITY. Members of these groups wear plain CLOTHING, and the men grow BEARDS. Not including children, the three communities claim 175 members as well as many seekers attracted to their extremely conservative horse-and-buggy lifestyle.

The tradition-minded Mennonites in Belize have prospered in their agricultural productivity, and they dominate the fruit, poultry, and dairy sectors of the country's economy. In the early years of the 21st century the Old Colony Mennonites have about 2,050 baptized members, and the Kleine Gemeinde have about 800 baptized members.

The Belize Evangelical Mennonite Church began in 1973. This church grew out of SERVICE and MISSION activities of MENNONITE CENTRAL COMMITTEE and Eastern Mennonite Missions in the 1960s. These agencies worked with the Low German–speaking Mennonites and eventually with other Belizeans. Incorporated in 1981, the Belize Evangelical Mennonite Church has 10 congregations and 425 members. While the official language of Belize is English, the church holds worship services in English, Spanish, and Garifuna, or a combination of these languages.

The EVANGELICAL MENNONITE MISSION CONFERENCE, based in Manitoba, began to establish congregations in Belize in the 1960s. Their EVANGELICAL approach contrasted sharply with the traditional views of the Old Colony Mennonites and the Kleine Gemeinde. The Evangelical Mennonite Mission Conference established congregations near the Blue Creek (1966), Spanish Lookout (1995), and Shipyard (2002) colonies in an attempt to evangelize colony members, a move that led to several internal divisions among the colonies. The Evangelical Mennonite Mission Conference has three congregations and about 475 members.

Five conservative, plain-dressing TRADITIONAL GROUPS based in the United States have a total of 25 small congregations and mission outreach sites in Belize with a total of about 400 members. Immediately following the destruction wrought by Hurricane Hattie in 1961, Amish Mennonite Aid, the relief agency of the BEACHY AMISH MENNONITE CHURCH, began reconstruction work in Belize. The first Beachy Amish church in the country was organized in 1962. The Beachy Amish have six congregations with some 175 members. Twelve churches (150 members) in Belize belonging to the Caribbean Light and Truth organization trace their roots to mission work begun in the

1970s by the Salem Mennonite Church of Keota, Iowa. Three other conservative Mennonite churches, two affiliated with the Bethel Mennonite Fellowship and one with the Western Conservative Mennonite Fellowship, have a combined membership of about 100. The Church of God in Christ, Mennonite group has two congregations and five mission sites in Belize, with an estimated 50 members.

GAMEO ("Belize"), R. Loewen (2008), ME V ("Belize"), Mennonite World Conference (2005), http://www.emmc.ca, http://www.mwc-cmm.org

Benevolence

Benevolence involves acting in kind ways toward other people and/or giving them financial gifts. North American ANABAPTISTS have a significant record of both SERVICE and financial benevolence. Benevolence can be sorted into three types: to others inside the Anabaptist community, to non-Anabaptists in the same country, and to non-Anabaptists outside the benefactor's country. Numerous factors—biblical teaching, human compassion for those who suffer, obligations within a church community, and forces in the larger social context—may motivate Anabaptists to be benevolent.

A few examples illustrate the significant history of organized benevolence programs beyond spontaneous aid within local congregations. Dutch Mennonites in the 1600s and 1700s established a tradition of benevolence when they invested considerable energy and financial resources (advice, funds, and lobby efforts) to aid Anabaptists of Swiss origin who were experiencing severe persecution and forced migration because of their religious convictions. The memories of this assistance established a foundation for future generations of Anabaptists to assist immigrants and refugees both within and outside the Anabaptist family.

A major burst of benevolent activity among MENNONITE groups occurred in the context of WORLD WAR I (1914–1918). For some Mennonites this benevolence toward refugees became the moral equivalent of the wartime sacrifices made by other Americans. As CONSCIEN-

TIOUS OBJECTORS with a German heritage, many Mennonites faced severe resentment in the United States. In response to this wartime persecution and to gain respect as citizens, they donated several million dollars to Mennonite organizations, Protestant relief bodies, and civic organizations such as the Red Cross to help those suffering from the devastation in Europe. In addition to money and other relief supplies, Mennonites helped to send some 800 cows to Germany to help farmers rebuild their herds.

The wartime devastation in Europe and the suffering of Mennonites in Russia led to the formation in 1920 of a new inter-Mennonite relief agency, MENNONITE CENTRAL COMMITTEE (MCC). In time it became a major North American body for relief and service activities around the world in the 20th century. In addition to providing aid to refugees and a wide variety of social services and agricultural development, MCC frequently assisted and coordinated Anabaptist emigrants leaving war-torn European countries to find new homes in North and South America.

The conditions surrounding WORLD WAR II prompted another outpouring of organized service activities and financial giving from BRETHREN and Mennonite communities. In the United States, many men and women served in Civilian Public Service as an alternative to military service. The BRETHREN SERVICE COMMISSION sent volunteers to reconstruction projects in Europe after the war. The commission also recruited some 5,000 volunteers known as "seagoing cowboys," who tended cattle on ships as they were being transported to Europe. Heifer International, begun by Brethren leader Dan West (1893–1971) in 1939, organized operations and solicited farmers to send cattle from Brethren and Mennonite farms in the United States to farmers in Europe.

Following World War II, various ALTERNATIVE SERVICE programs in lieu of military service (including Pax), as well as other voluntary service programs, enabled Anabaptists in North America to serve others at home as well as in other countries. In the last half of the 20th century, MENNONITE DISASTER SERVICE and BRETHREN DISASTER MINISTRIES were founded to send Anabaptist volunteers to help those ravaged by floods, hurricanes, and tornados. In the last quarter of the 20th century, through contributions and the proceeds of charity benefit auctions known as relief sales, Mennonite Central Committee has raised millions of dollars to support its relief and service work around the world. Traditional Mennonite and AMISH groups have made significant financial contributions to support the work of CHRISTIAN AID MINISTRIES, which provides some $150 million worth of relief supplies and services annually to people in nearly 90 countries. These groups also actively support annual relief sales in various regions of the United States that send supplies and financial aid to Haiti.

See also Mutual Aid

Juhnke (1986), J. Kreider (2001), Lowry (2007), Nolt (2005)

Bezaleel Education Center

This educational center of the NATIONAL EVANGELICAL GUATEMALAN MENNONITE CHURCH, begun in 1999, is a bilingual Spanish and K'ekchi' boarding school that offers vocational training and other educational programs. The goal of Bezaleel (named for a craftsman mentioned in Exodus 31:1–5) is to provide a transformational, holistic, bilingual education for K'ekchi' youth that gives dignity to their history and culture, and empowers them to become future leaders in their communities and churches. The school offers secondary education and vocational classes for residential students.

See also K'ekchi' Mennonite Foundation
http://bezaleel.mennonite.net/

Bible

ANABAPTIST groups accept the Bible as the Word of God and as central to Christian faith and practice. Similar to Protestant Reformers such as Martin Luther (1483–1546) and John Calvin (1509–1564), Anabaptists turned to the Bible, more than to church tradition, for the norms of faith and practice.

Anabaptists generally believe that the Bible should be interpreted through a process that involves the discernment of the church and the guidance of the HOLY SPIRIT. Disagreements over biblical interpretation about faith practices in daily life have spawned numerous church schisms among Anabaptist groups. Yet in spite of these disagreements, Anabaptist groups generally emphasize four themes: (1) The New Testament—especially the sections on the life, teachings, death, and resurrection of JESUS CHRIST in the four Gospels—is the interpretive key to the entire Bible. This Christocentric understanding asserts that God's progressive revelation culminates in Jesus of Nazareth. The New Testament, especially the life and teachings of Jesus and the SERMON ON THE MOUNT (Beatitudes), provides spiritual and ethical guidance for faithful Christian living. (2) Interpreting and applying the Word of God to daily living is most fully accomplished in COMMUNITY rather than as an isolated individual. (3) Understanding the Bible as the Word of God should produce obedient DISCIPLESHIP to the way of Jesus. (4) The Holy Spirit embodies God's presence and guides believers as they seek to understand God's will through biblical study.

Anabaptist scholars have generally avoided using the term "inerrancy"—the view that the Bible is without error—when interpreting the Scripture. Biblical interpretation in Anabaptist groups, however, has been influenced by widespread movements such as scholarly biblical criticism, EVANGELICALISM, PIETISM, FUNDAMENTALISM, modernism, and postmodernism. Pietism was an especially important influence on Brethren-related groups at their inception in 18th-century GERMANY. TRADITIONAL GROUPS, which emphasize separation from the larger culture, have somewhat avoided such movements because they have less exposure to higher education and mass media.

The HUTTERITE practice of radically rejecting private property is based on their interpretation of Acts 2:43–47. By practicing COMMUNAL LIVING for all their members, the Hutterites are attempting to restore the New Testament church's practice of community of goods.

In North America in the late 1800s and early 1900s, more than 50 church-operated educational ventures called Bible institutes or Bible schools were founded. Many of these did not endure, but a few developed into colleges or expanded Bible schools. The Believers Church Bible Commentary Series project, a cooperative venture of BRETHREN and MENNONITE churches, has published 23 interpretive volumes on books of the Bible since 1986 and anticipates covering the entire Bible in future volumes.

See also Schools, Bible; Theology

M. Augsburger (1967b), BE I ("Bible"), GAMEO ("Bible," "Bible Colleges and Institutes," "Biblical Interpretation"), Gardner (1983), Kissinger (1983), ME I ("Bible"), ME V ("Bible Colleges and Institutes," "Biblical Interpretation"), C. Snyder (2001), Snyder and Peters (2002), Swartley (1984), P. B. Yoder (1982)

Bible School   *See* Education; Schools, Bible

Birth Control
Most TRADITIONAL GROUPS discourage the use of artificial methods of birth control because they believe that limiting conception is contrary to the will of God. As a result, many OLD ORDER MENNONITE, AMISH, and HUTTERITE families have six or more children. Some traditional families do use birth control, however. Natural methods of birth control are preferred, but some families use artificial means or medical procedures if recommended by a physician.

ASSIMILATED GROUPS generally believe that medically approved forms of birth control are consistent with responsible Christian behavior and leave such decisions to the discretion of each family.

See also Demography

GAMEO ("Birth Control"), J. Hostetler (1993), ME V ("Birth Control")

Birth Rate   *See* Demography

Bishop

The role of bishop is one of three ordained church offices among AMISH and other TRADITIONAL GROUPS of Swiss origin. The other two offices are MINISTER (or preacher) and DEACON. Instead of "bishop," MENNONITES of Dutch and north German origins tend to use the term *Ältester* or "elder" for a similar office. In the Pennsylvania German DIALECT spoken by some Swiss-origin groups, the office was called *völliger Diener* (head servant), not *Bischof*, although it is often translated as "bishop" in English.

Among the Amish, a bishop holds the highest authority in a congregation; among traditional Mennonites, his authority stretches over a cluster of congregations. Bishops administer BAPTISM, COMMUNION, ORDINATIONS, WEDDINGS, and EXCOMMUNICATION. From about 1850 to 1950, some bishops in the Mennonite Church had great authority. Bishop Daniel Kauffman (1865–1944), an effective speaker, writer, and organizer, at one time served on 22 church committees. As editor of two church publications, *Gospel Witness* (1905–1908) and *Gospel Herald* (1908–1943), he exercised great influence in defining the church's stand on many issues.

The OLD GERMAN BAPTIST BRETHREN have three levels of elders, who are elected by the congregation. The most senior, or presiding elder, is comparable to a bishop in traditional Mennonite churches. Assimilated BRETHREN have only two ministerial offices: licensed ministers and fully ordained ministers. The office of bishop does not exist in HUTTERITE communities either. Instead, each colony is governed by a council of five to seven men, including the head preacher (sometimes called elder), who represents the colony to the outside world. For Mennonites of Dutch, Prussian, and Russian origins, the office of elder somewhat corresponds to that of bishop.

Although most assimilated groups no longer use the term "bishop," it is still used by the Brethren in Christ and by a few regional Mennonite conferences. Since the 1960s, assimilated Mennonites have ascribed more authority to lay leaders in congregations and less to the office of bishop. The terms "overseer" or "conference minister" are used by certain assimilated Mennonite groups for leaders who are responsible for overseeing the pastors and church life of several congregations. In these groups both the title and the role of bishop have changed from their traditional meanings in the last half of the 20th century.

See also Church Authority

BE I ("Degrees of Ministry"), GAMEO ("Bishop," "Elder [Ältester]"), L. Gross (1986), J. Hostetler (1993, 1997), ME I ("Bishop"), ME V ("Bishop [Swiss-Pennsylvania]")

Brethren

Brethren groups trace their roots to the German Baptist Brethren who emerged near the village of Schwarzenau, GERMANY, in 1708 under the leadership of ALEXANDER MACK SR. (1679–1735). The group arose out of the Pietist Movement that began in the late 17th century in Germany. Strictly speaking, the German Baptist Brethren were not an organic offshoot of any 16th-century ANABAPTIST group. Nevertheless, the Schwarzenau Brethren blended themes from PIETISM (love and personal devotion) and ANABAPTISM (adult BAPTISM, the separation of CHURCH AND STATE, NONRESISTANCE, and church DISCIPLINE).

Unlike many of the Anabaptist groups that baptized by pouring, the German Baptist Brethren practiced immersion baptism and therefore were sometimes known as Dunkers or Dunkards. Reflecting the Pietist emphasis on love, Brethren groups celebrated a LOVE FEAST that included COMMUNION, FOOTWASHING, and a simple liturgical meal. This periodic practice was a highlight of their church life.

The Brethren migrated to North America shortly after their formation in EUROPE. By 1728, 20 years after their first baptisms in the Eder River in Germany, most of them had settled in Pennsylvania and then eventually established settlements west and south of Pennsylvania, often in close proximity to MENNONITE communities.

Numerous groups trace their roots to the Brethren of Schwarzenau. A three-way division in 1880 resulted in three major groups: the OLD GERMAN BAPTIST BRETHREN, the BRETHREN CHURCH, and the German Baptist Brethren (who changed their name to the CHURCH OF THE BRETHREN in 1908). The Church of the Brethren is the largest Brethren group, with about 124,000 members. The Dunkard Brethren and the Fellowship of GRACE BRETHREN CHURCHES emerged as separate groups in the 20th century. A 1989–1991 division in the latter group resulted in the Conservative Grace Brethren Churches International. These six Brethren groups cooperate in publication efforts, such as *BRETHREN ENCYCLOPEDIA*, and participate in BRETHREN WORLD ASSEMBLY.

Henry R. Holsinger (1833–1905) was a key 19th-century Brethren leader. As a pastor and publisher, Holsinger became the leader of the progressive Brethren. He advocated major changes in German Baptist Brethren practice: a salaried ministry, simple but not uniform CLOTHING regulations, MISSION activity, secondary and HIGHER EDUCATION, SUNDAY SCHOOLS, and evangelistic meetings. In 1882 he was disfellowshiped by the Brethren, and in 1883 his supporters organized a new denomination called the Brethren Church. In 1901 Holsinger wrote *The History of the Tunkers and the Brethren Church.*

Apart from the Dunkard Brethren and the Old German Baptist Brethren, there are very few groups of Brethren that wear plain dress. The Brethren fuse the legacies of Pietism and Anabaptism and consider themselves to be noncreedal churches that view the New Testament as their authoritative guide for living. Traditionally among these churches, the spirit of truth takes precedence over formal doctrine, and the compassion of Jesus supersedes denominational dogma.

In North America, virtually all of the descendant groups of the German Baptist Brethren are in the United States. There are no Brethren-related groups in Canada that trace their roots directly to Schwarzenau. Some Brethren-related congregations are found in Puerto Rico, the Dominican Republic, and Haiti.

BE I ("Brethren, 1708–1883," "Holsinger, Henry Ritz"), C. Bowman (1995), D. Brown (1996, 2005), Clouse (1979), D. Durnbaugh (1997a), Longenecker (2006), Stoffer (1989)

Brethren Church

The Brethren Church formed in 1883 when it branched off from the German Baptist Brethren, who originated in 1708 in Schwarzenau, GERMANY. Known as the "progressive" wing at the time of the three-way division, the Brethren Church is headquartered in Ashland, Ohio. Sometimes called the Ashland Brethren, the group's 119 congregations are located in 18 states. Ashland University and Ashland Seminary were founded by members of the Brethren Church. The denomination participates in BRETHREN ENCYCLOPEDIA, INC. projects and other inter-BRETHREN activities. About 78% of the 10,400 members live in Ohio, Indiana, and Pennsylvania. Church-planting efforts are under way in Mexico and Canada, as well as in some countries outside of North America.

BE I ("Brethren Church"), Stoffer (1989), http://www.brethrenchurch.org

Brethren Colleges Abroad (BCA)

This organization was founded in

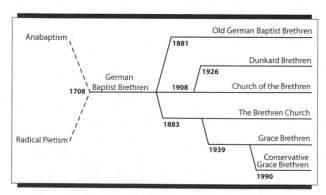

FIGURE 6 Historical Formation of Brethren Groups

Table 6   Resources on Brethren Groups

Books

Another Way of Believing, D. Brown, 2005
Brethren Encyclopedia, 1983, 1984, 2005 (http://www.brethrenencyclopedia.org)
Brethren Society, C. Bowman, 1995
A Cup of Cold Water, J. Kreider, 2001
Fruit of the Vine, D. Durnbaugh, 1997a
The Love Feast, Ramirez, 2000
Portrait of a People, C. Bowman, 2008

Periodicals

The Brethren Evangelist (http://www.brethrenchurch.org/web/brethren/library/the-brethren-evangelist)
Brethren Life and Thought (http://www.bethanyseminary.edu/node/43)
FGBC World (http://www.fgbcworld.com)
Messenger (http://www.emconf.ca/Messenger/index.htm)
The Vindicator (6952 N. Montgomery County Line Road, Englewood, OH 45322)

Information Centers

Crossroads Valley Brethren-Mennonite Heritage Center, Harrisonburg, VA (http://www.vbmhc.org; 540-438-1275)
Brethren Heritage Center, Brookville, OH (http://www.brethrenheritagecenter.org; 937-833-5222)

Libraries and Information Resources

Ashland Theological Seminary Library, Ashland, OH (http://seminary.ashland.edu/academics/academics-library.html)
Brethren Encyclopedia (http://www.brethrenencyclopedia.org)
Brethren Historical Library and Archives, Elgin, IL (http://www.cob-net.org/fobg/library.htm)
Bridgewater College Special Collections, Bridgewater, VA (http://www.bridgewater.edu/StudentServices/Alexander
   MackMemorialLibrary/SpecialCollections)
Juniata College Archives and Special Collections, Huntingdon, PA (http://www.juniata.edu/services/library)
Young Center for Anabaptist and Pietist Studies, Elizabethtown, PA (http://www.etown.edu/YoungCenter.aspx)

Web Sites

Brethren Church (http://www.brethrenchurch.org)
Church of the Brethren (http://www.brethren.org)
Church of the Brethren Network (http://www.cob-net.org)
Dunkertown Workshop (http://www.dunkertownworkshop.com/home.html)
Fellowship of Grace Brethren Churches (http://www.fgbc.org)

1962 by the Committee on Higher Education in the CHURCH OF THE BRETHREN in order to encourage students at BRETHREN colleges to study in EUROPE. The program emphasizes foreign language study as well as intercultural learning in many subjects. Students are integrated into classes at universities in the host countries. BCA expanded through cooperation with non-Brethren colleges and now serves hundreds of students each year at 20 sites on five continents.

BE I ("Brethren Colleges Abroad"), Keating (1982), http://www.bcanet.org

Brethren Disaster Ministries

In 1973 the CHURCH OF THE BRETHREN created this organization to recruit short-term volunteers to help clean up and rebuild after natural disasters. Volunteers from local congregations travel to disaster sites across the country after hurricanes, floods, and tornados. In addition to cleanup and rebuilding efforts, some volunteers provide emergency childcare in the aftermath of disasters. The main office is at the BRETHREN SERVICE CENTER in New Windsor, Maryland, where supplies such as blankets and medicines are stored.

See also Brethren; Mennonite Disaster Service; Voluntary Service

BE I ("Disaster Relief"), http://www.brethren.org/site/PageServer?pagename=serve_brethren_disaster_ministries

Brethren Encyclopedia

This four-volume (2,918-page) work published in 1983, 1984, and 2005 is the most comprehensive source of information on BRETHREN-related topics. Under the editorship of Donald F. Durnbaugh (1927–2005), this cooperative publishing effort was guided by representatives of the five major Brethren groups (with a sixth group added in 1999). Volumes 1 and 2 contain over 6,000 entries contributed by more than 1,000 people. In addition to a large bibliography, the third volume contains extensive maps, statistics, and lists of congregations, ministers and elders, institutions, and missionaries. Volume 4 contains new entries, updated lists of ordained ministers and elders, and a new bibliography on Brethren topics. Brethren Encyclopedia, Inc., overseen by a board of directors, publishes books, videos, and other resources related to Brethren history.

Brethren Encyclopedia (1983, 1984, 2005), http://www.brethrenencyclopedia.org

Brethren Encyclopedia, Inc.

The dream of producing a Brethren encyclopedia grew out of the leadership of M. R. Zigler (1891–1985) and Brethren historians and writers. Representatives of the five largest Brethren groups (CHURCH OF THE BRETHREN, BRETHREN CHURCH, Fellowship of GRACE BRETHREN CHURCHES, OLD GERMAN BAPTIST BRETHREN, and Dunkard Brethren Church) met in 1973 to lay the foundation for the project. Donald F. Durnbaugh (1927–2005) was appointed editor-in-chief along with a board of editors representing each of the five Brethren groups. Volumes 1 and 2 of BRETHREN ENCYCLOPEDIA were published in 1984, Volume 3 in 1985, and Volume 4 in 2005.

In 1984 the board of directors (with representatives of the five groups) of Brethren Encyclo-pedia, Inc., wishing to continue historical work in the interests of all the Brethren groups, approved plans to publish scholarly monographs and dissertations. (In 1999 a representative of the newly formed Conservative Grace Brethren Churches International joined the board of directors.)

In addition to their publishing efforts, Brethren Encyclopedia, Inc. has supported numerous study conferences and raised funds for the Alexander Mack Museum in Schwarzenau, Germany. The organization continues to publish scholarly and historical studies that contribute to an understanding of Brethren history and the various Brethren groups.

BE IV ("Brethren Encyclopedia, Inc.), http://www.brethrenencyclopedia.org

Brethren Foundation   *See* Church of the Brethren Benefit Trust

Brethren in Christ

JACOB ENGEL (1753–1833) is considered the founder of the Brethren in Christ denomination (known earlier as the River Brethren), which formed in the late 1770s in western Lancaster County, Pennsylvania, near the Susquehanna River. Engel was born in SWITZERLAND in 1753 and came to Lancaster County in 1754 as the child of an immigrant Swiss MENNONITE mother. Sometime before 1780 he experienced a heartfelt CONVERSION typical of the adherents of REVIVALISM, an experiential religious movement that Pennsylvania Mennonite leaders discouraged.

Engel and his followers were influenced by numerous German Baptist Brethren practices, including BAPTISM by immersion and the LOVE FEAST. Engel contended that trine immersion was the only scriptural mode for baptism. Since he had earlier been baptized by Mennonites, probably by pouring, Engel and a few others baptized each other and began a new church known as the River Brethren. Their name derived from the fact that they were known as the Brethren who lived near the Susquehanna River (in western Lancaster County). The new denomination integrated PIETIST and ANABAPTIST themes.

As early as 1788, some River Brethren moved to Ontario, where they became known as Tunkers (from the German word *tunken*, meaning "to dip") because they baptized by immersion. They likely formed the first Anabaptist congregation in CANADA. The bulk of the members remained in Pennsylvania. In the mid-19th century the group experienced some transitions when two TRADITIONAL GROUPS, the United Zion Church and the Old Order River Brethren, separated from the Brethren in Christ in 1855 and 1856 respectively. About a decade later, the main body of River Brethren adopted the name Brethren in Christ.

Christian N. Hostetter Jr. (1899–1980) was a prominent leader in the mid-20th century, providing leadership for the group's mission, evangelism, and educational ventures. He served as president of Messiah College in Grantham, Pennsylvania, from 1934 to 1960 and as chair of MENNONITE CENTRAL COMMITTEE from 1953 to 1967. Although they have been shaped by Anabaptist, Pietist, and Wesleyan theological streams, the Brethren in Christ relate more closely to Mennonite groups than to the BRETHREN groups that emerged from Schwarzenau, Germany, in 1708. The Brethren in Christ participate in the worldwide work of Mennonite Central Committee and MENNONITE WORLD CONFERENCE.

The Brethren in Christ have 270 congregations and about 23,000 members in the United States and 48 congregations and about 3,600 members in Canada, mostly in Ontario. In the United States, congregations are located in 20 states, with Pennsylvania, Florida, Ohio, and California dominating. Several large Cuban-background congregations are located in Miami, Florida. Brethren in Christ missionaries initiated churches in Cuba in 1954, and the Brethren in Christ Missionary Society remained in the country after Fidel Castro (1926–) assumed power in 1959. In the early 21st century, the Cuban church has about 3,275 members in 75 congregations. There are several small congregations in the Dominican Republic. About 4,350 members in Honduras and Nicaragua belong to some 150

congregations established by Brethren in Christ missionaries, and in Mexico there are 250 members in 8 congregations. The denomination also has congregations in Colombia and Venezuela.

See also Brethren in Christ History and Life
BE I ("Brethren in Christ"), Brensinger (2000), GAMEO ("Brethren in Christ," "Engel, Jacob [1753–1833]," "Hostetter, Christian N. Jr. [1899–1980]"), M. Heisey (2003), ME V ("Engel, Jacob," "Hostetter, Christian N. Jr."), Ruth (2001), E. M. Sider (1982, 1988), Wittlinger (1978), http://www.bic-church.org

Brethren in Christ Foundation
This charitable agency, created in 1972 by the BRETHREN IN CHRIST, manages funds in the form of gifts and loans for church-related projects. In 1990 its offices moved from Upland, California, to Grantham, Pennsylvania. The agency was originally called the Jacob Engle Foundation (for the founder of the Brethren in Christ), but in 2000 its name was changed to Brethren in Christ Foundation.

See also Anabaptist Foundation; Engel, Jacob; Mennonite Foundation; Mennonite Foundation of Canada
GAMEO ("Engel, Jacob [1753–1833]," "Brethren in Christ Foundation"), ME V ("Engel, Jacob," "Jacob Engle Foundation"), http://www.bicfoundation.org

Brethren in Christ History and Life
Begun in 1978, this journal is published three times a year by the Brethren in Christ Historical Society. The periodical carries major articles on the past and present life of the BRETHREN IN CHRIST and related groups. Articles cover a wide range of subjects: prominent people, institutions, doctrines, missions, current issues, music, and reviews of books and visual media. An index covering the years 1978 to 2008 was published in 2009.
http://www.bicweb.org/ministries/histsoc/pub_act.htm

Brethren Life and Thought
Begun in 1955, this quarterly journal is published by Bethany Theological Seminary and the Brethren Journal Association in the interests of

the CHURCH OF THE BRETHREN. The periodical contains articles, essays, and book reviews pertaining to the history, theology, and culture of the Church of the Brethren and related movements. Many of its articles provide theological reflections on various aspects of contemporary Brethren church life. Occasionally issues are devoted to special topics, such as BRETHREN poets and poetry (Summer 2008 issue). In 1964 the journal published an extensive annotated bibliography of Brethren writings, edited by Donald F. Durnbaugh (1927–2005) and Lawrence W. Shultz (1892–1982); the bibliography was updated in 1966 and 1970.

BE I (*"Brethren Life and Thought"*), http://dev.bethanyseminary.edu/node/43

Brethren Mutual Aid Agency (BMAA)
Founded in 1885 to provide MUTUAL AID for the members of the German Baptist Brethren (now CHURCH OF THE BRETHREN), this organization provides insurance services for Church of the Brethren homeowners, businesses, automobile owners, retreat centers, and church facilities.

See also Brethren
http://MAABrethren.com

Brethren Revival Fellowship
This network of CHURCH OF THE BRETHREN congregations holds membership in the parent body and operates inside the denominational structure. It formed in 1959 to advocate for more traditional BRETHREN standards of doctrine and practice. The Fellowship holds workshops and conferences, organizes work camps and voluntary service units, and publishes a newsletter. It also founded and operates Brethren Bible Institute, an annual weeklong series of Bible classes.

http://www.brfwitness.org

Brethren Service *See* Brethren Service Commission; Voluntary Service

Brethren Service Center
Located in New Windsor, Maryland, and operated by the CHURCH OF THE BRETHREN, this center provides a base for extensive VOLUN-
TARY SERVICE training as well as a location for the collection of relief materials for distribution to victims of poverty, war, and disaster in North America and around the world. Almost from its beginning in 1944, the center has attracted various ecumenical relief organizations. Church World Service, Lutheran World Relief, CHRISTIAN RURAL OVERSEAS PROGRAM (CROP), and other groups use it as a collection and distribution center.

The center has served as a headquarters for HEIFER INTERNATIONAL, founded by BRETHREN leader Dan West (1893–1971), as well as for ON EARTH PEACE ASSEMBLY, initiated by Brethren leader M. R. Zigler (1891–1985). The center has also served as a coordination point for various refugee resettlement programs and SERVICE organizations.

BE I ("Brethren Service Center, New Windsor, MD"), J. Kreider (2001)

Brethren Service Commission
Established in 1939 under the leadership of M. R. Zigler (1891–1985), this CHURCH OF THE BRETHREN organization helped administer the Civilian Public Service program of ALTERNATIVE SERVICE during WORLD WAR II. After the war the commission developed extensive VOLUNTARY SERVICE, relief, and rehabilitation programs in North America and abroad. BRETHREN groups donated massive amounts of material and significant personnel for postwar reconstruction in EUROPE. These wartime service activities evolved into the Brethren Volunteer Service (BVS) program in 1948. The BRETHREN SERVICE CENTER in New Windsor, Maryland, hosted the Brethren Service Commission programs and continues to serve as the initial training location for many BVS units. The Brethren Service Commission concluded its work in 1969, and its functions were transferred to other Church of the Brethren agencies.

BE I ("Brethren Service Commission"), D. Durnbaugh (1975, 1997a), J. Kreider (2001)

Brethren Volunteer Service *See* Voluntary Service

Brethren World Assembly

The first Brethren World Assembly was held in 1992 at Elizabethtown College in Pennsylvania. M. R. Zigler (1891–1985) laid the groundwork for a world assembly in the 20 years before the first gathering as he traveled around the United States urging leaders and members of various BRETHREN groups to meet together "just to shake hands." Leaders of the five largest Brethren bodies in the United States—BRETHREN CHURCH, CHURCH OF THE BRETHREN, Dunkard Brethren, Fellowship of GRACE BRETHREN CHURCHES, and OLD GERMAN BAPTIST BRETHREN—initiated the first assembly and have continued to direct subsequent meetings. The first assembly's theme was "Christ Is Lord: Affirming Our Faith Heritage," and it commemorated the 250th anniversary of the first Brethren annual meeting, which was held in 1792.

Subsequent gatherings have convened in 1998 at Bridgewater College in Virginia and in 2003 at Grace College in Indiana. A fourth gathering was held in Schwarzenau, GERMANY, in 2008, the 300th anniversary year of the Brethren movement. The assemblies usually include lectures on Brethren-related topics, tours, and worship services. BRETHREN ENCYCLOPEDIA, INC. has published proceedings from the World Assembly gatherings.

See also Anabaptist Groups, International; Mennonite World Conference

Brethren World Assembly (1994, 1999, 2004)

Bruderhof

Also called the Society of Brothers and Church Communities International, this group of communal Christians originated in 1920 in GERMANY under the leadership of Eberhard Arnold (1883–1935). Arnold attempted to place radical DISCIPLESHIP, COMMUNITY, PACIFISM, and the SERMON ON THE MOUNT at the center of Bruderhof life. He visited North American HUTTERITE colonies in 1930 and found many similarities between his convictions and their faith and practice. All three branches of Hutterites accepted the Bruderhof into fellowship, but they had only intermittent contact from 1930 to 1950.

The Bruderhof opened a refugee community in Liechtenstein in 1934, and then temporarily relocated to England when they were expelled from Germany by the Nazis in 1937. In 1941 they moved to Paraguay and in the 1950s began to establish communities in the United States. (The Paraguay settlement closed in 1961.) In the United States the Bruderhof came into closer contact with the Hutterite groups. Fellowship with the Hutterites was broken from 1955 to 1974, reestablished from 1974 to 1990, and then continued with the Schmiedeleut group alone until 1995, when that relationship dissolved. Cultural and historical differences made it difficult for the two communities to continue to affiliate.

Unlike Hutterite colonies, Bruderhof communities are comprised of people from a wide variety of ethnic and social backgrounds. They reject private property, have common dining areas, and live in modest apartments in a village-like arrangement where they have strong community bonds. Unlike the Hutterites, Bruderhof communities are not involved in farming.

Entrepreneurial efforts of the Bruderhof have included publications and the manufacture of children's toys and equipment for playgrounds and special education. In 1987 the Bruderhof published the first English translation of *The Chronicle of the Hutterian Brethren,* a significant historical account written in German in the 1500s and 1600s. There are 10 Bruderhof communities in New York, Pennsylvania, New Jersey, England, Germany, and Australia. Although the group had important connections to the Hutterites, it does not identify itself as ANABAPTIST or maintain association with any Anabaptist groups. Its communities and members are not included in the Table of Groups.

See also Communal Living

Baum (1998), C. Dyck (1993), GAMEO ("Arnold, Eberhard [1883–1935]," "Hutterian Brethren [Hutterische Brüder]"), Rod Janzen (1999, 2005), ME I ("Arnold, Eberhard"), ME V ("Hutterian Brethren"), J. H. Yoder (1984a), Zablocki (1971), http://www.churchcommunities.org

Business

AGRICULTURE was the primary OCCUPATION
of many members of ANABAPTIST groups when
they settled in North America. A small number
were involved in various types of business in
colonial times, but farming predominated until
the middle of the 20th century. As BRETHREN
and MENNONITES began to assimilate into the
larger society during that time, many became
business owners and ENTREPRENEURS. The
traits of frugality, integrity, hard work, and problem solving, which were valued as part of their
farming culture, proved to be valuable resources
for business as well. There are hundreds of
examples of Mennonite and Brethren entrepreneurs who have built successful businesses in
the manufacturing and service sectors.

HUTTERITE colonies, which often own
several thousand acres and have large farming
operations, function as large corporations. In
addition, some of the colonies have branched
into manufacturing and other types of business
in order to supplement their income from agriculture.

One of the largest and most rapid shifts
from agriculture to business occurred among
the Old Order Amish in the 1980s and 1990s. In
many AMISH communities more than half of the
households receive their income from nonfarm
employment. Some operate small family-based
cottage industries that provide supplemental
income; others own non-home-based businesses engaged in manufacturing, construction, construction-related trades, or retail sales.
Although many of these businesses have been
very successful, they are all generally small, with
a dozen or fewer employees. Furniture-making
has become a prime occupation in many Amish
communities. Some Amish people are also employed in businesses owned by non-Amish. The
shift into business is transforming the lifestyle
and culture of Amish communities even though
they remain primarily rural.

For all Anabaptist groups, involvement in
business raises many questions for members
and leaders regarding profit, accumulation of
WEALTH, LITIGATION, and LABOR UNIONS.
The Marketplace, a magazine published since
1971 by MENNONITE ECONOMIC DEVELOP-
MENT ASSOCIATES (MEDA), encourages
business owners to integrate their theological
commitments into their business decisions. The
professional conferences sponsored by MEDA,
as well as its international economic development projects, encourage Mennonite businesspeople to apply their faith to the world of business and to use their expertise to serve those in
economically depressed areas.

GAMEO ("Business"), Kraybill and Nolt (2004),
C. Kreider (1980), Redekop, Ainlay and Siemens (1995),
Redekop, Krahn, and Steiner (1994), C. Redekop and
B. Redekop (1996)

Camps and Retreat Centers

Because most North American ANABAP-
TISTS lived in rural settings in the 1800s, they
had little interest in recreational camping. The
first Anabaptist-related camps—summer camps
for youth and young adults—were begun by
ASSIMILATED GROUPS in the 1920s. During
the 1940s and 1950s the number of camps grew
rapidly and served people of all ages. The rise of
camp programs coincided with the move of many
Anabaptists away from farming and rural settings
to more urban or suburban environments.

Camp ministries served many needs: the nur-
ture and education of youth within the church,
a setting in which to evangelize urban youth,
family vacations, leisure activities, leadership
training for youth, nature education, and Bible
education. Beginning in the 1970s, many camps
transformed themselves into year-round facilities and provided additional services. Besides
the usual summer camping opportunities, many
camps now offer weekend retreats, theme-based
retreats, camps for youth in trouble with the
law, and adventure camps with activities such
as canoeing and spelunking.

There are more than 50 Anabaptist-related
camps and retreats centers in the United States
and Canada. Many of these are affiliated with
the Mennonite Camping Association, which
was founded in 1960. There are nearly 30 camps
across the country that are affiliated with the
CHURCH OF THE BRETHREN. The BRETHREN
IN CHRIST have seven camps in Canada and
the United States. TRADITIONAL GROUPS
generally do not own and operate church camps
but sometimes rent camp facilities owned by
other church groups for special conferences or
retreats.

BE I ("Camping Movement"), Eby and Eby (2006),
GAMEO ("Camps and Retreat Centers"), Jess Kauffman (1984), ME V ("Camps and Retreat Centers"),
Ziegler (1979), http://www.cob-net.org/oma.htm,
http://www.mennonitecamping.org

Canada

The earliest ANABAPTIST settlers in Canada
were MENNONITE and BRETHREN IN CHRIST
families who emigrated from Bucks County,
Pennsylvania, to the Niagara Peninsula
in 1786. These settlers left the United States
because they suffered PERSECUTION due to
their British sympathy during the AMERICAN
REVOLUTION. However, they were never formally recognized as United Empire Loyalists
because, as pacifists in the colonies, they did
not join the militia—one of the requirements.
The first Brethren in Christ (Tunker) congregation likely formed soon after 1788. The first
Mennonite congregation was organized in what
is now Vineland, Ontario, in 1801. A few BRETH-
REN families also migrated to Ontario after the
American Revolution.

Throughout the 19th century, waves of Mennonites and Brethren in Christ from Pennsylvania, AMISH from Alsace and Bavaria, and Mennonites from Russia and West Prussia migrated
to Upper Canada (now Ontario) and Manitoba.
They established informal and formal block
settlements whereby their land was adjoining,
which created a kind of colony. These block settlements, less familiar in the United States, were
later replicated in Central and South America
by Mennonites of Dutch-Russian origin. Not all
Mennonite immigrants to Canada settled on des-
ignated Mennonite tracts of land, but they did so
in sufficient numbers to ensure a strong measure
of cultural, if not always religious, stability.

In the first decade of the 1800s, Pennsylvania investors purchased over 100,000 acres in
what became Waterloo County, Ontario, for
resale to extended families and fellow Mennonites. In the 1820s the government of Upper
Canada set aside almost 30,000 acres adjacent
to the Mennonite block for about 1,000 Amish
immigrants from Bavaria and Alsace who arrived between 1824 and 1850. In the 1870s the
Canadian government established two land reserves in Manitoba for about 7,000 Mennonites
emigrating from Russia. This area consisted of
25 townships that covered more than 500,000
acres. These immigrants were later referred to
as KANADIER by other Mennonites. Two more
Mennonite reserves were established in Saskatchewan between 1895 and 1904, when Mani-

toba Mennonites pressed westward and another 2,000 immigrants arrived from Russia, Prussia, and the United States.

Later migrations included about 1,000 HUT-TERITES from the United States during WORLD WAR I. This move resulted in an order-in-council barring further migration of Anabaptist groups, a law rescinded in the early 1920s by newly elected Prime Minister W. L. Mackenzie King (1874–1950), who knew Mennonites from growing up in Berlin (Kitchener), Ontario. Also in the 1920s, about 20,000 Mennonites known as RUSSLÄNDER fled the Soviet Union for Canada. After WORLD WAR II another 7,700 refugees came to Canada.

Economic opportunity and cheaper land were the primary motivations for the 19th-century migrations. The Mennonite immigrants from Russia also feared loss of military exemption privileges and community autonomy. The migrations in the 1900s were driven by war displacement, ethnic and religious persecution, and concern about maintaining the culture and language of the church community.

In the 1920s about 8,000 conservative Mennonites (from TRADITIONAL GROUPS) emigrated from Canada. About 6,000 of them, mostly Old Colonists, moved to MEXICO, and the others, mostly Chortitzer Mennonites, settled in Paraguay. Over time many of their descendants returned to Canada.

Prior to World War II, Canadian Anabaptists remained overwhelmingly agricultural and rural. The greatest exceptions were the Russländer, who began to find work in urban areas such as Winnipeg, Kitchener-Waterloo, Saskatoon, and Vancouver. Because German-speaking Mennonites from both Russia and Latin America continued to immigrate to Canada throughout the 1900s, the German language and culture persisted into the 21st century, even among some assimilated congregations. The most traditional groups, such as the OLD ORDER MENNONITES, Old Order Amish, and OLD COLONY MENNO-NITES, speak German DIALECTS in daily life and worship.

Three streams of traditional Mennonite groups can be found in Canada. The Old Colony churches, part of the 1870s Kanadier migration, have Russian roots. A second stream of plain-dressing Mennonites has Swiss–south German roots. Their ancestors first came to Pennsylvania in the early 1700s and then, in the late 18th and early 19th centuries, moved to Upper Canada. Some members of this branch supported the OLD ORDER MOVEMENT in the last quarter of the 19th century and today are known as Old Order Mennonites. The third stream of traditional Mennonites is composed of churches that separated from assimilated groups in the second half of the 20th century because they wanted to retain more conservative and separatist practices.

Although Canadian Mennonites did not have as much internal conflict concerning FUN-DAMENTALISM as Mennonites in the United States did, they experienced a steady stream of church schisms among their communities beginning in the 1830s.

A higher percentage of Canadian Mennonites belong to ASSIMILATED GROUPS, are more urbanized, and in some ways are more integrated into the larger society than their counterparts in the United States. They are more likely to live in cities and to permit the use of alcohol. Members show greater flexibility on CHURCH AND STATE issues by operating social and educational agencies that receive government assistance. Their level of POLITICAL PARTICIPA-TION, such as running for provincial or national office, is also higher.

Frank H. Epp (1929–1986), an influential Canadian Mennonite historian and church leader who was an advisor to the federal government in the areas of immigration and multiculturalism, served as the executive director of the World Federalists of Canada, and was an active member of the United Nations Association of Canada. He ran in federal parliamentary elections as a Liberal in 1979 and 1980. Brad Wall (1965–), a MENNONITE BRETHREN, was elected premier of Saskatchewan in 2007. In 2009, 7 members (out of 308) of Canada's House of Commons identified themselves as Mennonite.

Table 7   Anabaptist-Related Churches in Canada with 5,000 or More Baptized Members

Group	Membership	Web site
Mennonite Brethren Church	37,000	http://www.usmb.org
Mennonite Church Canada	33,000	http://www.mennonitechurch.ca
Hutterites	14,050	—
Old Colony Mennonites	9,000	—
Evangelical Mennonite Conference	7,000	http://www.emconf.ca
Church of God in Christ, Mennonite	5,000	http://churchofgodinchristmennonite.net

Note: Estimated number of baptized members. If children, unbaptized youth, and nonmember participants are counted, the total population of some groups may be two to three times larger than the baptized membership.

In urban Canadian areas today, Mennonite and Brethren in Christ congregations worship in English, German, French, Spanish, Lao, Mandarin, and at least 12 other languages. In part this ethnic diversity resulted from mission work and sponsorship of refugee families from Southeast ASIA and Central America in the late 1900s. Although MENNONITE CENTRAL COMMITTEE is headquartered in the United States, Canadian Mennonites have been heavily involved in its international relief and development efforts from the agency's beginning in 1920. In 1963, Mennonite Central Committee Canada was created to oversee domestic service programs in Canada.

The baptized membership of Anabaptist groups in Canada is approximately 127,500 Mennonites, 14,050 Hutterites, 3,600 Brethren in Christ, and 2,450 Amish. Four urban centers—Winnipeg, Vancouver, Abbotsford, and Kitchener-Waterloo—contain over 25% of the Mennonites in Canada. The largest denominational groups are the Canadian Conference of Mennonite Brethren Churches and MENNONITE CHURCH CANADA, with 37,000 and 33,000 members respectively. The Brethren groups that originated in Schwarzenau, Germany, in 1708 do not have churches in Canada.

Ens (2004), F. Epp (1974, 1982), M. Epp (2008), GAMEO ("Epp, Frank H.," "Canada"), Regehr (1996, 2000), M. Reimer (2008), E. M. Sider (1988)

Canadian Foodgrains Bank

In 1976, Mennonite Central Committee Canada began collecting surplus grain for distribution overseas, largely through the impetus of a MEN-

NONITE entrepreneur. In 1983 this program, under the leadership of C. Wilbert Loewen (1922–), expanded into an ecumenical movement involving non-Mennonite church groups. Now owned by 15 Canadian church denominations, the foodgrains bank collects donations of cash, grain, and other agricultural commodities for distribution to the world's hungry people. From 1999 to 2003, the annual average value of grain and cash was $6.31 million Canadian. In 2007–2008 the total was $8.4 million Canadian.

See also Agriculture; Canada; Mennonite Central Committee (MCC)

Kroeker (2005: 105), http://www.foodgrainsbank.ca

Capital Punishment

Because the ANABAPTIST ethic of NONRESISTANCE precludes killing people, many assimilated and traditional Anabaptists do not support government executions. On the other hand, some Anabaptists in both TRADITIONAL GROUPS and ASSIMILATED GROUPS cite Romans 13 to support the death penalty as a legitimate use of power by the state to suppress evil and maintain order. Differing interpretations of the Bible have fueled the debate over capital punishment among Anabaptist groups. Some argue that the Old Testament clearly sanctions the taking of life in punishment for murder (Gen. 9:6). Others claim that the ethic of Jesus prohibits all taking of human life, especially because Jesus refused to advocate the death penalty for the woman caught in adultery (John 8:1–11). Those opposed to the death penalty believe that it inflicts the ultimate violation of

RELIGIOUS LIBERTY and ends the redemptive possibilities for persons charged with capital offenses. In general, traditional groups do not lobby the government regarding issues such as capital punishment.

BE I ("Capital Punishment"), GAMEO ("Capital Punishment"), Hanks (1997), Lind (2004), ME V ("Capital Punishment"), J. H. Yoder (1961)

Caribbean Nations and Territories

ANABAPTIST-related groups are present in PUERTO RICO and in 7 of the 12 countries of the Caribbean region (BAHAMAS, CUBA, DOMINICAN REPUBLIC, GRENADA, HAITI, JAMAICA, and TRINIDAD AND TOBAGO). No HUTTERITE or AMISH mission groups or congregations are in the region. The BEACHY AMISH MENNONITE CHURCH, with historic Amish roots in the United States, is active in several Caribbean countries, but it is more aligned with conservative MENNONITE groups than with Amish ones. Although the CHURCH OF THE BRETHREN has been active in Puerto Rico, the Dominican Republic, and Haiti, Mennonite-related groups dominate the Anabaptist influence in the Ca-

ribbean region. The first expatriate mission and service personnel came to the Dominican Republic and Puerto Rico in the 1940s, to Cuba and Jamaica in the 1950s, to Haiti and Trinidad and Tobago in the 1960s, and to the Bahamas in the 1980s.

In addition to numerous mission endeavors and indigenous churches, two major Mennonite service agencies are also active in the Caribbean area. CHRISTIAN AID MINISTRIES, supported by many TRADITIONAL GROUPS in the United States, has operations in Haiti for the distribution of food, clothing, medicine, seeds, and Christian literature. MENNONITE CENTRAL COMMITTEE supports about a dozen expatriate personnel, primarily in Haiti, as well as Haitian national staff who are involved in educational and development programs related to agriculture, health, and peacebuilding activities.

http://www.mwc-cmm.org

CASAS   *See* Central America Study and Service

Casting of Lots   *See* Ordination

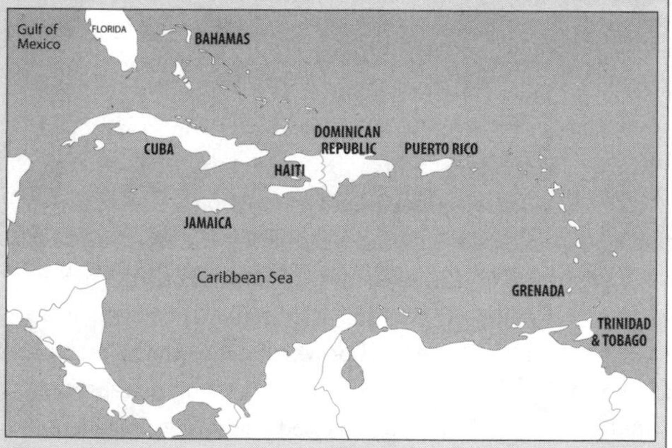

Catechism   *See* Baptism

Central America

ANABAPTIST-related groups are active in all seven countries of Central America: BELIZE, COSTA RICA, EL SALVADOR, GUATEMALA, HONDURAS, NICARAGUA, and PANAMA. One Latin American scholar (Martínez 1999) has noted six diverse types of Anabaptist-related churches in the Central American region: (1) urban professional congregations whose members, active in professions and university life, use advanced technology; (2) urban congregations in lower-middle-class or poor neighborhoods whose leaders are self-educated and bi-vocational; (3) rural peasant congregations whose members have very little education and may live in a subsistence economy; (4) indigenous congregations (mostly

Country	Congregations	Members
Bahamas	1	25
Cuba	79	3,350
Dominican Republic	138	7,775
Grenada	3	50
Haiti	68	3,975
Jamaica	16	725
Puerto Rico	23	900
Trinidad and Tobago	6	275

FIGURE 7 Anabaptist-Related Congregations and Baptized Membership in the Caribbean Region

in Guatemala) who worship in their native language and whose culture is often oppressed by the dominant society; (5) Afro-Caribbean congregations mainly on the Caribbean coast who may have lost their native language and whose historic culture is also under assault; and (6) conservative German-speaking MENNONITE colonists who emigrated from Canada in the 1920s. In addition, hundreds of missionaries and service workers from Anabaptist groups in Canada and the United States are an active part of the Anabaptist presence in Central America. This enormous diversity makes it risky to make sweeping generalizations about the Anabaptist profile of the Central American region.

No AMISH, HUTTERITE, or BRETHREN groups have congregations in Central American countries. The BEACHY AMISH MENNONITE CHURCH, with historic Amish roots in the United States, is active in several countries, but this group is more aligned with conservative Mennonite groups than with Amish churches. Mennonite groups dominate the Anabaptist influence in the region.

Two different types of TRADITIONAL GROUPS are found in MEXICO and Central America: (1) Low German–speaking Mennonites of Canadian and Russian background who in 1922 established colonies in Mexico in order to preserve their traditional culture, and (2) those of Swiss–south German ancestry from the United States who came after 1950 to do SERVICE and MISSION work.

The first Mennonites to establish a presence in Central America were missionaries from the United States who were based in Colombia. They started an educational and literacy program in Panama in the 1940s. In the 14-year period from 1950 to 1964, Anabaptist missionaries and/or settlers with Canadian and U.S. origins established an Anabaptist presence in the other six Central American countries—Honduras in

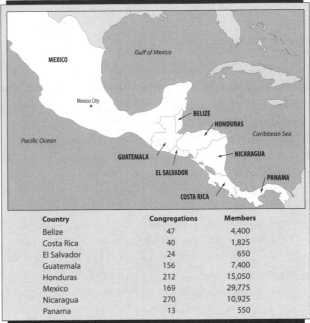

Country	Congregations	Members
Belize	47	4,400
Costa Rica	40	1,825
El Salvador	24	650
Guatemala	156	7,400
Honduras	212	15,050
Mexico	169	29,775
Nicaragua	270	10,925
Panama	13	550

FIGURE 8 Anabaptist-Related Congregations and Baptized Membership in Central America and Mexico

1950, British Honduras (now Belize) in 1958, followed by Costa Rica, El Salvador, Guatemala, and Nicaragua, all in the early 1960s. Apart from Belize, where OLD COLONY MENNONITES from Mexico (emigrants from Canada in the 1920s) established colonies to preserve their culture, the expatriate Mennonites entering Central America in the last half of the 20th century came to provide social services, do agricultural development, evangelize, and start indigenous churches.

In the first decade of the 21st century, expatriate missionaries are affiliated with both assimilated and traditional Mennonite groups in the United States and Canada. In fact, by 2008, 12 different traditional Mennonite groups had established over 100 congregations and mission outposts in all the Central American countries except Panama.

In addition to the mission personnel who focus primarily on evangelization, two major Mennonite service agencies are also active in the region. CHRISTIAN AID MINISTRIES, supported by many traditional Amish and Mennonite groups in the United States, has operations in Nicaragua for the distribution of food, clothing, medicine, seeds, and Christian literature. MENNONITE CENTRAL COMMITTEE (MCC) supports some three dozen expatriate personnel in several countries, mostly in Guatemala, Honduras, and Nicaragua. MCC also supports national staff who are involved in a variety of educational and development programs related to AGRICULTURE, health, and peacebuilding.

Although Brethren groups have not established congregations, Brethren Volunteer Service has placed volunteers with various service agencies in Guatemala, Honduras, Nicaragua, and El Salvador since the late 20th century.

The CENTRAL AMERICAN ANABAPTIST MENNONITE CONSULTATION, known as CAMCA (Consulta Anabautista Menonita Centroamericana), is a biannual gathering of delegates from Mennonite member conferences and organizations in Central America. This regional group, which has been meeting since 1973, provides a venue for fellowship, worship, and collaboration. The LATIN AMERICAN ANABAPTIST SEMINARY (SEMILLA) is located in Guatemala.

GAMEO ("Central America"), R. Loewen (2004, 2008), Martínez (1999, 2000, 2005), ME V ("Central America," "Old Colony Mennonites"), Mennonite World Conference (2005), http://www.anabaptistwiki.org, http://www.mwc-cmm.org

Central American Anabaptist Mennonite Consultation (CAMCA)

Known as CAMCA (Consulta Anabautista Menonita Centroamericana), this gathering of delegates from MENNONITE member conferences and organizations in the CENTRAL AMERICAN region provides a venue for fellowship, worship, and collaboration. It has been meeting annually since 1973. Statements produced by the gathering in Belize (1978) and Nicaragua (1982) provided helpful guidance for ANABAPTIST churches facing social, spiritual, and political challenges to peace in the region. Meeting in its 34th assembly in 2007 in Guatemala City, CAMCA decided to meet every other year, alternating with the LATIN AMERICAN

ANABAPTIST SEMINARY's biennial Hans Denck lecture series. Other groups of Anabaptists in the Central American region—the Central American Anabaptist Women Theologians, for example—often meet in conjunction with the CAMCA gatherings.

GAMEO ("Consulta Anabautista Menonita de Centroamericana"), Mennonite World Conference News Service (2008)

Central America Study and Service (CASAS)

CASAS offers Spanish-language study and cultural orientation to Guatemalan society, politics, economics, and religious groups for individuals and student groups from ANABAPTIST-related and non-Anabaptist-related colleges and universities in North America. Students are usually housed with families in marginal communities to introduce them to Guatemalan culture firsthand. The program includes visits to human rights organizations and development agencies, lectures on Guatemalan issues, and trips to archaeological sites and tourist areas. It also includes an optional short-term service component.

http://semilla.org.gt/casas%20en.html

Charismatic

The term refers to an emphasis on the HOLY SPIRIT'S influence on believers who practice the spiritual gifts described in the New Testament. These gifts may include prophecy, speaking in tongues, healings, and miracles. This emphasis on spiritual gifts has been institutionalized in Pentecostal groups.

Many 16th-century ANABAPTISTS emphasized the role of the Holy Spirit without a special accent on spiritual gifts such as speaking in tongues. While TRADITIONAL GROUPS do not welcome charismatic expressions in WORSHIP, some assimilated groups began to embrace this lively and emotional movement in the 1950s. Although initially met with strong resistance, charismatic modes of WORSHIP and THEOLOGY gained acceptance within some MENNONITE and BRETHREN groups through the establishment of Mennonite Renewal Services in 1970—a network of individuals and congregations that promoted charismatic views and expressions. In 1974 the Holy Spirit Renewal Group, which focused on charismatic healing, was founded within the CHURCH OF THE BRETHREN. These efforts eventually merged into Believers Church Renewal Ministries and then later into Empowered Ministries, which ended in 1995.

About half of the members of three assimilated denominations in the United States— BRETHREN IN CHRIST (48%); CHURCH OF THE BRETHREN (53%); MENNONITE CHURCH USA (44%)—report that they have personally experienced some of the gifts of the Spirit (CMP 2006). Various Anabaptist congregations accept mildly charismatic styles of worship, such as raising hands in worship. Although they are not highly charismatic, some assimilated congregations use contemporary praise songs and spontaneous expressions in worship.

Brethren, Mennonite, and Brethren in Christ congregations with a predominant Hispanic identity often participate in charismatic forms of worship. Initially, Latin American Anabaptist groups rejected charismatic forms of church life, but by the 1980s most of the indigenous Spanish-speaking congregations in Central American countries had adopted various modes of charismatic worship.

See also Pietism

BE I ("Charismatic Movement"), CMP 2006, Davis (1979), GAMEO ("Charismatic Movement"), J. H. Kauffman (1996), Martínez (2000, 2006), ME V ("Charismatic Movement"), Rutt (1997)

Children

ANABAPTIST theology rejects both the practice of infant BAPTISM and the belief that children inherit original sin at birth. Various 16th-century Anabaptist leaders considered the age of accountability to be as young as 7 to as old as 30, depending on the leader. Twenty-first-century Anabaptist churches generally teach that children younger than the age of accountability (about 12 years and older) are innocent with respect to SALVATION or damnation. Anabaptists believe that upon reaching the age of ac-

countability, individuals are responsible and accountable for the eternal consequences of their faith-related decisions. (See Mark 10:13–16.) Parents diligently instruct children in the faith but advocate a voluntary decision to accept Christ as Savior and Lord and join the church at the age of moral maturity. However, during the 1800s, as REVIVALISM influenced ASSIMILATED GROUPS, the age of baptism drifted downward from early adulthood to early ADOLESCENCE.

Children are valued in Anabaptist communities, and parents take seriously their responsibility to teach them Christian beliefs and values. The average number of children per family varies considerably. Families in TRADITIONAL GROUPS may have 8 to 10 children, whereas families in assimilated groups may have only 2 or 3.

In traditional groups the education of children is controlled by the community and emphasizes submission to social and religious norms through self-control. The themes of obedience, self-denial, respect for elders, frugality, and hard work are important values in childhood socialization. HUTTERITE children, for example, learn the values of communal living by spending more time in the community kindergarten than with their own parents. Most children in traditional Anabaptist communities attend private schools operated by their own religious groups.

Parents in assimilated groups send their children to either public schools or private religious schools. There are numerous MENNONITE-operated elementary and secondary schools in the United States and Canada. Most of these schools also enroll students from other religious groups.

See also Anabaptism, Theology of; Schools, Elementary; Schools, Secondary

GAMEO ("Dock, Christopher [d. 1771]," "Children"), Graber Miller (2001), J. Hostetler (1997), Jeschke (1983), ME II ("Dock, Christopher"), ME V ("Children"), Schwartz (1973), http://www.mennoniteschools.org

Christian Aid Ministries (CAM)

Created in 1981 in response to need in Romania, this charitable organization supported by AMISH and MENNONITES in TRADITIONAL

GROUPS in the United States and Canada responds to physical and spiritual needs around the world. Its purpose, according to its annual report, is to "encourage God's people and bring the gospel to a lost and dying world."

Administrative centers are located in Ohio, Pennsylvania, and Ontario. International centers are located in Romania, Moldova, Ukraine, Haiti, Nicaragua, and Liberia. In addition to many volunteers, CAM has over 300 employees. In a typical year the organization gathers more than $186 million for programs in about 30 foreign countries. This includes nearly $25 million in cash and $160 million worth of donated products (86% of revenue). Much of the material aid (such as food, seeds, medicine, and clothing) is shipped to people suffering from poverty, famine, war, and natural disasters. Orphanages and medical clinics serve as distribution points for some of the aid.

CAM also distributes Christian literature (353,600 pieces a year), such as Bibles and devotional writings in foreign languages, and the staff presents Bible education programs. CAM provides material support for church planting, but existing North American churches provide the leadership support for this program. The rapid growth of Christian Aid Ministries reflects the significant demographic increase in Amish and Mennonites in traditional groups since 1960, as well as their growing willingness to support some para-church institutions.

Christian Aid Ministries 2008 Annual Report, http://www.anabaptists.org/places/cam/index.html

Christian Education   *See* Education

Christian Peacemaker Teams (CPT)

Christian Peacemaker Teams began in the mid-1980s. Initiated by MENNONITES, BRETHREN, and QUAKERS, the group is supported by a variety of faith traditions. CPT's ministry of biblically based and spiritually centered PEACEMAKING emphasizes creative public witness events, nonviolent direct action, and the protection of human rights.

CPT's goal is to devote the same discipline and self-sacrifice to nonviolent peacemaking that armies devote to war. Enlisting people of faith in organized, nonviolent alternatives to war, CPT places violence-reduction teams in crisis situations and militarized areas around the world at the invitation of local peace and human rights workers. These teams, ready to risk injury and death, make bold unarmed interventions in attempts to transform lethal conflict through the nonviolent power of God's truth and love.

CPT provides organizational support to persons committed to faith-based nonviolent alternatives where lethal conflict is an immediate reality or is supported by public policy. CPT promotes CONSCIENTIOUS OBJECTION to war, the development of nonviolent institutions, skills and training for intervening in conflict situations, and violence-reduction work.

The organization has some 40 full-time peacemakers and nearly 200 part-time volunteers, from many different backgrounds and age groups.

T. Brown (2005, 2008), Kern (2009), http://www.cpt.org

Christian Rural Overseas Program (CROP)

After WORLD WAR II this ecumenical program organized the shipment of donated foodstuffs from North America to overseas countries, primarily to populations devastated by the war. It began in 1947 among BRETHREN, MENNONITE, Catholic, and Evangelical and Reformed Church members. John D. Metzler (1898–1993), a member of the CHURCH OF THE BRETHREN, was the first executive director of CROP. The first office was at Bethany Biblical Seminary, the Church of the Brethren school then in Chicago, and the first staff member came from the BRETHREN SERVICE COMMISSION. Lutheran World Relief and Catholic Relief Services soon joined the effort. In 1952 CROP was placed under the Church World Service rubric of the National Council of Churches. CROP is still administered by Church World Service and raises funds to combat world hunger through direct aid and long-range agricultural development projects.

BE ("Christian Rural Overseas Program [CROP]"),
C. Bowman (1995), D. Durnbaugh (1997b), GAMEO
("Christian Rural Overseas Program [CROP]"), Morse
(1977)

Christology   *See* Jesus Christ, Doctrine of

Chronicle of the Hutterian Brethren, The

This two-volume history of the HUTTERITES
describes their ANABAPTIST origins from the
early 1500s to their emigration from Russia to
the United States in the 1870s. Translated into
English in 1987 and 1998, these two large volumes are based on a series of handwritten manuscripts that were written and copied at various
times and passed down through Hutterite leaders. They are indispensable for understanding
the history and identity of the Hutterites, the
oldest known Christian group in continuous
existence that practices COMMUNAL LIVING.

These volumes contain a wide variety of
forms — narratives, doctrinal statements, letters,
and hymn texts. They describe more than three
centuries of events in territories stretching from
Switzerland to Moravia, Russia, and the United
States, and they include information on important leaders such as JAKOB HUTTER (d. 1536)
and PETER RIEDEMANN (1506–1556). The theological motif of the suffering church guides the
narrative, as stated in the introduction to the
1998 volume: "Indeed, this history is written in
the blood of suffering, MARTYRDOM, and PER-
SECUTION, and in the tears of despair, human
frailty, and struggle."

GAMEO ("Hutterite Chronicles"), Hutterian Brethren (1987, 1998), ME I ("Chronicles, Hutterite")

Church   *See* Believers Church

Church and State

As a theory of GOVERNMENT, the idea of the
separation of church and state developed slowly
in EUROPE with contributions from ANABAP-
TISTS in the 1500s and 1600s. With the exceptions of Balthasar Hubmaier (1481–1528) and the
Anabaptist Kingdom at Münster, most Anabaptists believed that civil authorities should not

exercise authority over the church or over spiritual matters of individual conscience. Through
their opposition to governmental control of
religion and their willingness to suffer MARTYR-
DOM for this belief, the 16th-century Anabaptists eloquently advocated for the separation
of church and state. Sometimes called the Free
Church Movement, Anabaptists argued that the
church should be free from government control.
Although adult BAPTISM was the public sign of
the Anabaptist Movement, the deeper underlying issue was the separation of powers — the
radical idea that government should not have
authority over religious matters such as baptism. PILGRAM MARPECK (ca. 1490s–1556), a
hydraulic engineer and Anabaptist leader, ex-
emplifies a rare posture of cooperation between
Anabaptists and civic authorities in the 16th
century.

Even in political systems where separation of
church and state is the official policy, informal
traditions of civic or civil religion may develop
public rituals and symbols that imbue governments with religious meaning. Distinguishing
between a government's legitimate demands and
those that violate Anabaptist NONRESISTANT
beliefs (especially during times of war) sometimes produces tensions within North American
Anabaptist churches.

In British North America in the 1600s, especially in the colonies of Rhode Island and
Pennsylvania, the separation of church and
state found a welcome stage for development.
MENNONITE, BRETHREN, and AMISH groups
eagerly sought RELIGIOUS LIBERTY in Pennsylvania and participated in the QUAKER-led social
and political experiment from its early years.

Anabaptist views of the separation of church
and state vary widely by group and country.
Leaders of TRADITIONAL GROUPS that have
a TWO-KINGDOM THEOLOGY seek a sharp
separation of church and state. Such groups discourage members from accepting government
subsidies, participating in government pension
or Social Security systems, and participating in
politics and voting. Members of ASSIMILATED
GROUPS are more likely to vote, hold political

office, participate in government programs, and influence government policies through various means including lobbying.

See also Nationalism

BE I ("Church-State Relations"), Estep (1988), GAMEO ("Church State Relations," "Government, Theory and Theology of"), ME IV ("State, Anabaptist-Mennonite Attitude Toward"), ME V ("Church-State Relations," "Government, Theory and Theology of"), S. Peters (2003), T. Schlabach (2009), http://mcc.org/canada/ottawa, http://mcc.org/un, http://mcc.org/us/washington

Church Authority

Although 16th-century ANABAPTISTS rejected the traditional sacramental understanding that Christ was actually present in the celebration of the Mass, they did argue that the true church on earth was imbued with the presence of Christ through the HOLY SPIRIT. This belief created a very high view of church AUTHORITY, which emphasized a visible church defined by how it practiced the Christian faith. When adult members of a local CONGREGATION gathered together to discern the Scriptures and the will of God, they understood that they were empowered to make decisions for the membership that would be binding in heaven and on earth. Members were held accountable to the decisions that the gathered church ratified under the direction of its lay leaders.

The strong Anabaptist emphasis on practice rather than doctrine, along with an acceptance of the strong authority of the church, led to the development of specific rules and regulations for membership often known as ORDNUNG. Matthew 18:15–17 provided a biblical threefold process for rebuking and correcting a member who violated the authority of the church. Wayward members who did not submit to the authority of the church or confess their infractions before the gathered body faced sanctions through some form of DISCIPLINE by the community, possibly even EXCOMMUNICATION. This theological understanding of authority assumed that adult church membership required a submission

of personal preferences to the discernment of the church.

Most of the TRADITIONAL GROUPS continue to emphasize the submission of the individual to the collective authority of the church and will excommunicate members who refuse to comply with the teachings and practice of the church. The scope of church authority covers areas of social practice, dress, use of force, and TECHNOLOGY. By contrast, many of the ASSIMILATED GROUPS, influenced by the cultural value of individualism, do not have explicit rules for membership and place a higher priority on grace, tolerance, and participation in the life of the church than on adherence to specific guidelines. Although the church remains an important, persuasive influence in these groups, individual preference based on personal experience has become the typical source of authority on many matters.

BE I ("Authority"), GAMEO ("Authority"), Koop and Schertz (2000), ME V ("Authority"), B. Redekop and C. Redekop (2001), Sawatsky (1987, 1997), C. Snyder (1997a)

Church Building

The initial PERSECUTION of ANABAPTISTS in Europe and the subsequent legal and social restrictions under which they lived often resulted in obscure or hidden worship spaces and buildings. Anabaptists gathered in fields, forests, and boats as well as in houses and barns. As legal restrictions were lifted in Europe, they began to meet in church buildings called meetinghouses with several distinctive patterns inside the rectangular structure: (1) the congregation sat in a face-to-face arrangement, along the longer sides of the building; (2) the ministers (usually several) sat behind a table or a pulpit along one of the long sides facing the congregation; (3) the exterior decoration was simple and functional, with clear windows allowing sunlight to reach the interior; (4) the seating was organized by gender and age; and (5) the interior decoration was plain, without ornamentation. A few exceptions to this pattern emerged in urban areas such as Amsterdam where some church buildings had a high pulpit and some ornamentation.

In North America in the 1700s most AMISH, BRETHREN, and MENNONITE congregations met for worship services in homes, mills, or barns rather than in separate church buildings. In the 19th century many North American Mennonite and Brethren groups began to build meetinghouses, which usually followed the simple meetinghouse styles from Europe.

In the 20th century many assimilated Anabaptist congregations adopted architectural features from other religious groups. These features included steeples, exterior ornamentation, stained glass windows, raised pulpits, choir areas, projection screens, offices, libraries, Christian education classrooms, fellowship halls, and sometimes multipurpose gymnasiums. Although some sanctuaries have their seating arranged in a partial circle of chairs facing the pulpit area, many have traditional pew seating facing the pulpit area in front. A few assimilated Anabaptist congregations do not have a church building; instead, they own or rent functional spaces for worship and fellowship, or meet in homes.

TRADITIONAL GROUPS continue to use plain, simple meetinghouse architecture without a steeple, stained glass windows, or ornamentation. The Old Order Amish still worship in houses, shops, and barns because they believe that a separate building for worship is unnecessary. The HUTTERITES use simple, plain meeting rooms that are often part of larger buildings in their colonies.

GAMEO ("Architecture," "Meetinghouses"), L. Miller (1977), Roth (1999a)

Church of God in Christ, Mennonite

Also known as the Holdeman Mennonites, this group formed in Ohio in 1859 under the leadership of John Holdeman (1832–1900). The church gradually spread to other midwestern states and to Ontario and western Canada by the early 1880s. Members of AMISH and various other MENNONITE groups eventually joined the Holdemans.

In the 21st century, members of the Church of God in Christ, Mennonite maintain a sharp separation from the outside world by their distinctive dress, rejection of worldly entertainment, and shunning of ex-members. Men wear abbreviated BEARDS, and women wear black scarves or bonnets. Although similar in some ways to other conservative Mennonite groups, the Holdeman church teaches that they are the one true church of Christ. Their doctrine of the one true church, based on Matthew 16:18 and other Scriptures, emphasizes the succession of true doctrine, practice, and teachers through the centuries, and the authority of the church under Christ. This group, unlike some traditional ones, accepts revivalism and conversions marked by an abrupt and emotional acceptance of Christian faith.

The Holdemans have 130 congregations with approximately 14,500 members in 33 states in the United States, with a large concentration in Kansas. In Canada they have nearly 5,000 members and over 50 congregations in eight provinces, with large concentrations in Alberta and Manitoba. The group also has 22 small mission congregations in the Caribbean, 7 in Central America, and 31 in Mexico. Outside of North America the Holdeman Mennonites have congregations and mission ventures in 24 countries. Their total worldwide membership stands at about 22,000.

Bible Doctrine (1998), GAMEO ("Church of God in Christ, Mennonite"), C. Hiebert (1973), ME V ("Church of God in Christ, Mennonite"), http://churchofgod inchristmennonite.net

Church of the Brethren

The Church of the Brethren, the largest of the BRETHREN bodies, traces its roots to the German Baptist Brethren who formed in Schwarzenau, GERMANY, in 1708. The German Baptist Brethren were influenced by both Radical PIETISM and ANABAPTISM. At its bicentennial in 1908 the body changed its name to the Church of the Brethren. The Brethren are one of the three HISTORIC PEACE CHURCHES, along with the QUAKERS and the MENNONITES. In addition to active PEACEMAKING, the Brethren participate in ecumenical conversations with the National Council of Churches in the United States and with the World Council of Churches. Six colleges and Bethany Theological Seminary are affiliated with the Church of the Brethren. *Messenger* is the official publication of the denomination, whose Mission and Ministry Board programs and administrative offices are located in Elgin, Illinois. BRETHREN DISASTER MINISTRIES and the BRETHREN SERVICE CENTER provide leadership to the denomination's service ministries. Scholars from the denomination have played key roles in the historical projects sponsored by BRETHREN ENCYCLOPEDIA, INC. The Church of the Brethren meets yearly in Annual Conference, which is comprised of delegates from all congregations. Annual Conference is the highest decision-making body for the Brethren.

The denomination's 1,000 congregations are located in 39 states, mostly east of the Mississippi River. About 70% of its 124,000 members live in Pennsylvania, Virginia, Ohio, and Indiana. The Church of the Brethren has six predominately AFRICAN-AMERICAN congregations (about 700 members) and four Haitian congregations (about 450 members) in the United States. There are also 16 HISPANIC-AMERICAN congregations (some 700 members) as well as 7 congregations in Puerto Rico (about 375 members.) The church has started numerous congregations in the Dominican Republic and Haiti, but it does not have affiliated congregations in Canada, Central America, or Mexico.

See also Brethren Life and Thought; Higher Education
BE I ("Church of the Brethren"), C. Bowman (1995, 2008), D. Brown (2005), D. Durnbaugh (1958, 1997a), Stoffer (1989), http://www.brethren.org, http://www.cob-net.org

Church of the Brethren Benefit Trust

Founded in 1943 as a pension board, this agency of the CHURCH OF THE BRETHREN includes the Brethren Foundation. It provides a variety of financial services, including pension management for churches, asset management, deferred gift management, educational resources, and health insurance. By the beginning of the 21st century, the agency had more than 4,000 members, and the Brethren Foundation distributed about $1.3 million per year in gifts through its planned giving program. In 2004, Brethren Benefit Trust became the administrator of the Church of the Brethren Credit Union, which had more than 1,200 members.

See also Brethren; Credit Unions; Mutual Aid
http://www.brethrenbenefittrust.com

Church, Polity of

ANABAPTIST groups exhibit a wide variety of patterns for governing and ordering the life of the church. CHURCH AUTHORITY tends to originate from the CONGREGATION and then flow to regional or national bodies beyond the congregations. ASSIMILATED GROUPS tend to grant more AUTHORITY to the members of congregations, whereas TRADITIONAL GROUPS invest more authority in ordained leaders who act on behalf of a congregation or a cluster of congregations. Among the AMISH, decisions are ratified by the vote of a local congregation, whereas among OLD ORDER MENNONITES, polity issues are determined by a regional or national conference of ordained leaders.

Among BRETHREN groups, major decisions are made by Annual Conference. This yearly meeting of church members from the entire denomination began around the middle of the 18th century. Members and ordained leaders met to discuss issues and make decisions for the church based on their understanding of gospel principles. Until the late 1800s these decisions were made by consensus. The OLD GERMAN BAPTIST BRETHREN continue this practice, but other Brethren groups now make decisions by majority vote. The decisions of Annual Conference applied to all congregations, but in the 20th century the Conference's authority over local congregations began to wane. In the 21st century the authority of Annual Conference varies considerably among Brethren groups.

Among Amish and traditional MENNONITE groups of Swiss origin, the amount of authority granted to BISHOPS varies. The bishop is ordained for life (as is the MINISTER and the DEACON) and is the highest spiritual authority for a group of congregations (for Mennonites) or for a single congregation (for Amish). He administers COMMUNION and other ORDINANCES such as BAPTISMS, ORDINATIONS, WEDDINGS, and EXCOMMUNICATIONS. Despite his influence, the bishop usually makes recommendations to a group of ministers or members of a congregation, rather than outright decisions. For example, among the Amish only a vote of all baptized members can excommunicate another member.

Among HUTTERITES, each colony has a council—usually a group of five to seven men elected by church members—who makes all important decisions for the colony. The head preacher, the second preacher, and the steward (business manager) serve on this council. The head preacher delivers sermons and conducts all important church services such as baptisms, marriages, and FUNERALS. Unlike the Amish, Hutterite women have no formal vote in council decisions, and their GENDER ROLES are tightly defined. Each individual colony is linked into the central leadership councils of one of the four large Hutterite conferences.

The specific polity of assimilated churches varies by denomination. Various levels of decision-making and authority reside in local congregations and in regional and national bodies. Although greater authority has shifted toward the local congregation since the last quarter of the 20th century, the authority to credential and ordain leaders generally is held by a church body beyond the local congregation.

BE I ("Authority"), BE II ("Polity"), GAMEO ("Authority," "Polity"), J. Hostetler (1993, 1997), ME V ("Authority"), Sawatsky (1987, 1997), M. Schrag (1964), E. Thomas (1996)

Church Rules and Regulations   *See* Church
Authority; *Ordnung*

Church, Theology of
According to ANABAPTIST theology, the church is the body of Jesus Christ (Rom. 12:5), which means that the spirit of Christ is present in the lives of believers—those spiritually regenerated, adult-baptized, mutually accountable disciples who make up the church. As a gathered fellowship patterned after the New Testament church, they seek to discern and obey Christ's will.

The five basic marks of the church are adult BAPTISM, COMMUNION, MUTUAL AID, mutual accountability, and witness to the larger world. In its life together and its compassion for the world, the body of believers seeks to demonstrate the righteousness, justice, love, and peace of Jesus Christ. Anabaptists believe that the church, not the government, has the AUTHORITY, under the lordship of Christ, to define the practices and ethical standards for believers, both individually and corporately.

Many of the 16th-century Anabaptists also said that suffering was a mark of the church. BRETHREN up through the 19th century viewed unity as the primary sign of a church. Anabaptists believe that the church needs to be a visible body separated from the worldly society. Citing Scriptures such as Romans 12:2 and Ephesians 5:27, members believe that the church should not be conformed to the values of the secular society.

TRADITIONAL GROUPS believe that members who disobey the regulations of the church should be disciplined in order to maintain the integrity of the church body. This may involve EXCOMMUNICATION and, for the Old Order Amish, the ban or SHUNNING. Traditional churches expect a high degree of visible unity of belief and practice, which sometimes produces schisms as groups seek to determine practical guidelines for their faith. ASSIMILATED GROUPS tend to grant greater freedom to individual conscience, which leads to a higher degree of theological and social DIVERSITY among their members.

See also Anabaptism, Theology of; Believers Church; Church Authority; Church, Polity of

BE I ("Church, Doctrine of"), C. Bowman (1995), GAMEO ("Church, Doctrine of"), Koop and Schertz (2000), ME V ("Church, Doctrine of"), Roth (2005a, 2009), C. Snyder (1995)

Cinema

When movies emerged in the early 1900s, most ANABAPTIST groups prohibited attendance and sanctioned members who violated this restriction. In their view, movies glorified crime, dishonesty, violence, and sexual promiscuity. Twenty-first-century TRADITIONAL GROUPS still censure attendance at movies.

As some MENNONITES and BRETHREN began to assimilate into the wider culture, they developed a cautious but positive attitude toward watching movies. Among most ASSIMILATED GROUPS, decisions about theater attendance and viewing movies at home are now largely left to the discretion of individual members. Some assimilated churches use various forms of media in order to communicate the gospel to a wider audience. For example, Third Way Media produces films and DVDs with a religious message for churches and the general public. Church periodicals often include movie reviews in order to help readers distinguish helpful movies from harmful ones. In rare instances members own public theaters. Others work as filmmakers and producers of church-related and secular media.

In 1984, *And When They Shall Ask* used both documentary footage and dramatic vignettes to describe Mennonite life in RUSSIA from about 1880 to 1930. This period included times of great prosperity as well as WORLD WAR I, the Communist Revolution, civil war, famine, and repression of the church. *The Radicals,* produced in 1989 by a Mennonite film company, told the story of Anabaptist beginnings in Switzerland in 1525–1530. Both films were widely shown in Mennonite communities throughout North America.

In 1984–1985, Paramount Studios filmed *Witness* in Lancaster County, Pennsylvania. In the movie an urban police officer (Harrison Ford) seeks protection from retribution by living temporarily among the AMISH. The plot involves a romance between the officer and a widowed Amish woman (Kelly McGillis). The film was distributed internationally and sparked renewed interest in Amish life and culture. Some Mennonites lauded it as providing an accurate and sensitive representation of Amish life in that genre.

Others led vociferous protests against the film's producers and promoters for exploiting the Amish lifestyle for financial gain. A 2007 drama, *Stellet Licht* (Silent Light), was authentically set in an OLD COLONY MENNONITE community in northern Mexico.

See also Leisure

And When They Shall Ask (1984), BE II ("Motion Pictures"), GAMEO ("Motion Pictures"), M. Good (1985), Hostetler and Kraybill (1988), ME V ("Motion Pictures"), *The Radicals* (1989), *Stellet Licht* (2007), J. Thiesen (1984), Umble and Weaver-Zercher (2008), Weaver-Zercher (2001), *Witness* (1985)

Civilian Public Service   *See* Alternative Service

Civil Religion   *See* Nationalism

Civil Rights Movement   *See* Racism; Social Justice

Civil War, U.S.

During the Civil War (1861–1865) the PACIFIST convictions of ANABAPTISTS were severely tested, especially when the Union and the Confederacy first instituted compulsory conscription. Most eligible Anabaptist men received exemptions by paying an additional TAX (commutation fee) or securing a substitute (paying someone else to enlist in the military in their place), even though some Anabaptists thought this practice was hypocritical. Due to the Confederacy's urgent need for soldiers and supplies, exemption fees were higher in the South. A few men immigrated to Canada, and some did join the armies despite their denominations' official stance of NONRESISTANCE.

MENNONITES and BRETHREN in Virginia felt the brunt of the Civil War as the Shenandoah Valley became the site of battles and plundering armies. Families had crops and food stolen, buildings burned, and fields ruined. Some men secured military substitutes; others fled to northern states to escape serving in the Confederate Army. Although most Virginia Mennonites and Brethren had more sympathy for the Union, a few joined the Confederate Army. John Kline

(1797–1864), moderator of the Brethren Annual Meeting in 1864 and a well-known Brethren preacher, was murdered in 1864 in Virginia, likely because of his vocal public advocacy for peace and his opposition to slavery.

BE I ("Civil War"), BE II ("Kline, John"), GAMEO ("American Civil War [1861–1865]"), Juhnke and Hunter (2004), Lehman and Nolt (2007), T. Schlabach (1988), Wright (1931)

Clergy   *See* Bishop; Deacon; Elder; Minister; Ordination

Clothing

Prior to the 20th century, most ANABAPTIST groups emphasized the principles of modesty and simplicity of dress rather than uniformity. With the rise of mass-produced clothing and fashion advertising in the late 19th century, some Anabaptist groups began to require uniformity of church-prescribed clothing for their members. The shift to uniformity was a reaction to factory-made clothing, rising income, and greater access to costly ornaments such as silk ribbon and fancy buttons. This shift predated mass advertising, but fashion had an impact on MENNONITES and BRETHREN even without it.

In the 20th century the more ASSIMILATED GROUPS gradually relaxed their expectations for distinctive dress, and members increasingly purchased clothing from commercial retailers. Although assimilated groups do not require specific styles of clothing, many of their members purchase clothing that reflects the values of simplicity, modesty, and frugality.

Distinctive dress is one of the key differences between assimilated and TRADITIONAL GROUPS. Clothing in American culture is frequently used to display individual taste and style. Among traditional groups, church-prescribed patterns of dress symbolize a rejection of individualism and the willingness of members to submit to the standards of the church. Moreover, the embrace of plain and modest clothing signals a rejection of the fads and fashions of mainstream consumer culture.

The distinctive clothing worn by the mem-

bers of traditional groups strengthens in-group solidarity and sharpens their social boundaries with the larger society. Moreover, dress practices frequently carry important symbolic signals to distinguish members of Anabaptist subgroups from one another. The dozens of different traditional groups exhibit a multitude of unique patterns of dress.

In general, the guidelines for dress are more exact and specific for women than for men, including some kind of HEAD COVERING for women. In some traditional groups, clothing is made at home using store-bought cloth. In others, a seamstress in the community or an ethnic retailer is the major producer of the group's clothing, and in still others, some clothing is purchased from mainstream stores. Often, multiple sources are used.

Conservative and distinctive clothing among traditional groups reflects several deeply held religious convictions: NONCONFORMITY to the values of the world, and obedience to the scriptural standards of humility, simplicity, and modesty taught in the New Testament. Frequently cited Bible verses include Romans 12:2, I Timothy 2:9–10, and I Peter 3:3–4.

Jewelry and cosmetics are forbidden by many of the more conservative groups. This includes wristwatches for some AMISH groups and wedding rings for most traditional groups.

See also Gender Roles

Arthur (1997), D. Durnbaugh (1997a), GAMEO ("Dress"), M. Gingerich (1970), Graybill (2002), Kraybill and Bowman (2001), Rupel (1994), Scott (1986)

College   *See* Higher Education

Communal Living

The HUTTERITES are the only ANABAPTIST group that has practiced communal living from its beginning. Finding some protection from intense PERSECUTION for their Anabaptist beliefs in Moravia, the Hutterites began living communally there in 1528. Private property, except for a few small personal items, is not allowed in Hutterite colonies. All the material needs of the individual from infancy to death are supplied by the colony, which in return expects diligent labor. The longest enduring communal society in European and North American history apart from monastic religious orders, the Hutterites base their practice on the early church as described in Acts 2:44. Their communal life continues to flourish in nearly 500 colonies in rural areas of the United States and Canada.

The AMISH, BRETHREN, and MENNONITES emphasize MUTUAL AID within their church groups but do not practice economic communalism, as the Hutterites do. Celibate members of the Ephrata Cloister (derived from the Brethren) had a somewhat communal economy in the 18th century. In the 20th century, small groups of Mennonites and Brethren, in an attempt to practice Christian equality and mutual support, formed small communal groups, with varying levels of success. Two examples are Reba Place Fellowship in Evanston, Illinois, and Plow Creek Community in Tiskilwa, Illinois. The BRUDER-HOF, a group similar to the Hutterites, practices communal living in several of their communities.

Bach (2003), BE II ("Reba Place Fellowship"), GAMEO ("Community of Goods"), J. Hostetler (1997), Rod Janzen (2005), Janzen and Stanton (2010), Kraybill and Bowman (2001)

Communion

This central ORDINANCE of Christian WORSHIP is based on Jesus' sharing of bread and wine with his disciples in the Last Supper as recorded in the BIBLE (see Mark 14:12–25 and I Cor. 10:16). Rejecting Catholic views of transubstantiation, most ANABAPTISTS understand the rite of communion to be a symbolic remembrance of and thanksgiving for Jesus' suffering on the cross. Anabaptists believe that the communion elements signify not only the death of Jesus but also a renewed commitment to the church, his spiritual body. Communion helps to unite believers and to reenergize their commitment to live a Christlike life.

Anabaptists have emphasized the communal and collective meaning of this sacred RITUAL, rather than viewing communion as an individualistic transaction between God and a believer.

Because many Anabaptists view communion as part of the reconciling work of Christ in the church, some groups hold a special preparation service before the communion service. This service encourages each member to seek peace with God and to reconcile any conflicts with fellow church members. In some TRADITIONAL GROUPS the preparation service includes giving verbal assent to the beliefs and practices of the congregation's DISCIPLINE. In some conservative groups, the communion service is a celebration of unity and peace in the congregation. The AMISH and OLD ORDER MENNONITES, for example, postpone the communion service if conflict in the congregation cannot be reconciled.

The traditional BRETHREN communion involves a LOVE FEAST, which includes FOOTWASHING, a simple agape (love) meal, and the sharing of unleavened bread and wine or grape juice. The Amish and some MENNONITE groups also practice footwashing with the communion service. The HUTTERITES, who do not practice footwashing, hold communion once per year, on the day after Easter. Old Order Amish and Old Order Mennonites celebrate communion twice per year and have a long preparation service prior to communion.

Among ASSIMILATED GROUPS, communion practices vary widely. Communion may be a short service added to the regular WORSHIP service without any emphasis on church unity and covenant renewal, or it may include these elements in a special service apart from the regular one. Communion is celebrated several times a year in some Mennonite congregations, in various formats, and also in retreat settings and other gatherings outside regular church settings. Many assimilated Brethren congregations have a "bread and cup" communion service within their regular worship service twice per year, in addition to a love feast. In general, assimilated groups have more individualized communion services than traditional churches.

BE I ("Communion"), BE II ("Love Feast"), GAMEO ("Communion"), J. Hostetler (1993, 1997), E. Kreider (1997), ME I ("Communion"), ME V ("Communion"), Ramirez (2000), Rempel (1993), Roth (2009)

Community

In the ANABAPTIST world, "community" is a prominent word with layers of meaning. The religious persecution in EUROPE that forced some Anabaptists into rural enclaves fostered an enduring sense of community. Historically, "community" connoted a rural neighborhood with face-to-face interaction. This is still the case among HUTTERITES, who live in 100-person colonies segregated from the surrounding society. Automobile-rejecting AMISH and MENNONITES also emphasize the importance of a community grounded in daily interaction within a local neighborhood, maintained by walking, horse-and-buggy travel, and small congregations with explicit geographical boundaries. For TRADITIONAL GROUPS, church, extended family, and neighborhood often blend into the tight social fabric of daily life.

The forces of modernization in the 20th century unraveled the ties of many communities. HIGHER EDUCATION, mobility, occupational specialization, the Internet, MISSION and social SERVICE activities, as well as individualism, weakened the social bonds and intimate character of geographically based communities. In the world of ASSIMILATED GROUPS, expressions of community evolved into new forms. As church-related organizations emerged in the 20th century, some members found a renewed sense of community by creating, supporting, and working in church-related INSTITUTIONS, mission agencies, schools, hospitals, PUBLISHING, service organizations, and RETIREMENT COMMUNITIES. Church-related professional organizations and gatherings of Anabaptists such as mental health providers, historians, and peace activists also provided a sense of community beyond the local congregation for some members. For assimilated Anabaptists, the Internet has offered new forms of virtual community with like-minded believers who may be separated by distance. Some congregations have made explicit attempts to create small Bible study groups, education classes, support groups, and fellowship activities to foster the bonds of community.

Anabaptist theology assumes that Christian faith is practiced in the context of community. Faith, in other words, has social expressions. Biblical teaching about caring for fellow members in times of need, because they are members of the "body of Christ," also heightens the significance and centrality of community in the Anabaptist mind.

The word "community" carries religious meanings, not merely social ones, in the Anabaptist world. In a religious tradition that emphasizes the importance of the wisdom and authority of the collective body—the body of Christ—over the individual, community is important. Some Anabaptist historians, citing Jesus' promise that where two or three are gathered he is in their midst, have suggested that the gathered church—the community—is the only sacrament in the Anabaptist tradition.

See also Anabaptism, Theology of; Mutual Aid
GAMEO ("Community"), Kraybill and Bowman (2001), C. Snyder (1997b), P. Toews (1996)

Community of Goods   *See* Bruderhof;
Communal Living; Hutterites

Computer

ASSIMILATED GROUPS have accepted the computer and the Internet for personal, business, and church use. In a survey (CMP 2006), about three-fourths of CHURCH OF THE BRETHREN, BRETHREN IN CHRIST, and MENNONITE CHURCH USA members reported having one or more computers in their homes. Many church organizations and congregations have web sites, and some members' vocations involve the design, programming, sale, or service of computers.

Some TRADITIONAL GROUPS restrict or ban the use of computers. They limit their members' access to media material that they deem spiritually harmful. Some of these groups allow the use of word-processing software on computers but prohibit Internet access. Others permit the use of computers with Internet access in businesses, but not in members' homes. Some AMISH groups prohibit computers but permit battery-operated word processors and allow business owners to outsource web site creation and maintenance for business purposes. HUT-TERITES permit community-owned computers for business purposes, but not for home use.

Many ANABAPTIST-related publications have online editions. Thousands of entries on Mennonite topics can be found entirely online at www.gameo.org.

See also Technology

CMP 2006, Kraybill and Hostetter (2001), Kraybill and Hurd (2006), D. Martin (2003)

Conference of Mennonites in Canada (CMC)

The Conference of Mennonites in Canada (CMC) began in 1902–1903 with the union of congregations from the Rosenorter Mennonites of Saskatchewan and the Bergthaler Mennonites of Manitoba. CMC eventually included new congregations composed of families who came from the United States along with immigrants who came from the Soviet Union in the 1920s, then after World War II, and finally in the 1960s and 1970s. The conference, which was affiliated with the GENERAL CONFERENCE MENNONITE CHURCH, was involved in various MISSION, publication, SERVICE, and EDUCATION projects including Canadian Mennonite Bible College.

The Conference of Mennonites in Canada became inter-MENNONITE in 1988 when the Conference of United Mennonite Churches of Ontario (a provincial conference related to CMC) joined two MENNONITE CHURCH district conferences in Ontario to form the Mennonite Conference of Eastern Canada (MCEC). The Mennonite Church congregations became associate members of CMC at that time, and in 1995 all but one became full members. By 1998, CMC had 222 congregations with over 35,000 members.

In 2002, the Conference of Mennonites in Canada, together with the Mennonite Church and the General Conference Mennonite Church, completed a long process of integration and transformed into two national bodies — MENNO-NITE CHURCH USA and MENNONITE CHURCH CANADA — thus ending CMC.

See also Canada

GAMEO ("Conference of Mennonites in Canada")

Confession   *See* Communion; Discipline; Excommunication

Confessions of Faith

Given their size relative to other Protestant denominations, MENNONITE groups have written many theological statements of belief. Most of these statements affirm the basic Christian convictions found in the Apostles' Creed, but ANABAPTISTS generally do not recite creedal statements of faith in their worship services. They view confessions of faith as less important than biblical texts, not universally valid for all time, and not to be used by governments to force adherence. Most important, Anabaptists tend to emphasize faithful practice (DISCIPLE-SHIP) over correct belief (doctrine).

Whereas some creeds focus only on the death, suffering, and resurrection of JESUS CHRIST, Anabaptists accent his life and teachings, especially the SERMON ON THE MOUNT, along with his redemptive death and resurrection. They tend to use confessions of faith in pragmatic ways — as a witness to those outside their groups, as an instructional tool for young people, and as a source of unity among diverse Mennonite groups.

The largest North American Mennonite denomination, MENNONITE CHURCH USA, subscribes to a 1995 statement of belief, *Confession of Faith in a Mennonite Perspective*. A 2004 Mennonite Brethren Confession of Faith is widely used by Mennonite Brethren churches. AMISH and OLD ORDER MENNONITE groups look to the DORDRECHT CONFESSION, written in 1632 in the Netherlands, for guidance. They use its 18 articles of faith in their catechism classes before baptism. Through discussion and traditional practice, Old Order groups develop regulations that are transmitted orally to new members. These regulations or ORDNUNG, which are revised as needed, focus on the practical expression of their religious beliefs in daily life as it relates to technology, dress, and interaction with the outside society.

The BRETHREN, in contrast to the Mennonites and Amish, frequently declare that they are noncreedal. Brethren often say that they have "no creed but the New Testament." A Brethren's Card, in use in the early 20th century, provided a handy summary of beliefs for lay members. A few confessions of faith were written by individual Brethren in the 18th and 19th centuries. Annual Conference minutes provided doctrinal clarification of Brethren beliefs and applications throughout the 19th and 20th centuries. Traditional Brethren groups continue to emphasize the authority of their Annual Conference to define their faith and practice so that they can consistently and uniformly uphold their application of biblical principles. Assimilated Brethren groups grant considerable individual freedom for interpretations of faith and belief.

The HUTTERITES have no specific list of doctrines, but many of their basic emphases can be gleaned from the THEOLOGY of PETER RIE-DEMANN (1506–1556), a 16th-century European leader whose writings continue to guide and inspire Hutterian leaders.

BE I ("Confession of Faith"), BE II ("Noncreedalism"), D. Brown (2005), *Confession of Faith* (1995), D. Durnbaugh (1997a), GAMEO ("Confessions, Doctrinal"), Koop (2004, 2006), Howard Loewen (1985), ME V ("Confessions, Doctrinal"), http://www.usmb.org

Conflict

Because of their PACIFIST commitments, ANA-BAPTIST groups may appear to be harmonious and tranquil. Like other societies, however, these groups are not immune to conflict. Although they reject violence and seek to live in harmony among themselves and with others, Anabaptist groups have experienced schism. North American AMISH, BRETHREN, HUTTER-ITE, and MENNONITE churches have all witnessed multiple divisions in the 19th and 20th centuries.

Indeed, the very character of the Anabaptist faith may encourage conflict because of its emphasis on ethical practice rather than doctrine. Seeking to apply the teachings of Jesus to daily life sometimes leads to squabbles over applications of faith values to lifestyle, CLOTHING,

TECHNOLOGY, and vocation. DISCIPLESHIP focuses on social ETHICS and the integrity of daily life, which can cultivate a literalism that may lead to divisions. Furthermore, the historical Anabaptist emphasis on a visible church, with clear lines of membership and boundaries with the outside culture, has also spawned divisions. The Anabaptist focus on the SERMON ON THE MOUNT and the view that the church already embodies the kingdom of God on earth has led, in some cases, to a perfectionism that can also fuel the fires of conflict.

In addition to these theological influences, social, cultural, economic, ethnic, and racial factors have played a role in conflicts in Anabaptist communities. Moreover, dogmatic leaders, family quarrels, personality clashes, and power plays by leaders and subgroups have brought about breaches in Anabaptist groups.

The significant division among Swiss-origin Anabaptists in the 1690s in FRANCE and SWIT-ZERLAND that separated the Amish and the Mennonites resulted from different views of excommunication and of relations with the outside world, as well as regional and cultural differences. Among Brethren groups, 21 schisms occurred between 1700 and 1883, creating numerous small groups, many of which did not endure. A three-way schism in 1880–1883 resulted in three major groups of Brethren.

A higher incidence of schism exists among traditional Mennonites and Brethren than among assimilated ones. Their strong emphasis on dress and restrictions on technology and participation in popular culture spawn frequent disagreements that can lead to schisms.

ASSIMILATED GROUPS are more diverse theologically, if not socially. Thus, when assimilated churches splinter, it is more likely because of theological differences than controversies over practice, as is typically the case among more tradition-minded groups.

Assimilated Anabaptist churches also occasionally merge. One such union occurred in 2002 when the MENNONITE CHURCH, the GENERAL CONFERENCE MENNONITE CHURCH, and the CONFERENCE OF MENNONITES

IN CANADA realigned to form MENNONITE CHURCH USA, the largest group of Mennonites in the UNITED STATES, and MENNONITE CHURCH CANADA, the second largest group of Mennonites in CANADA.

Conflict can have positive consequences. Divisions sometimes spur spiritual renewal, revitalization, stronger in-group solidarity, and clarity of identity. Despite the pain they cause, schisms reflect the fact that people care deeply enough about their convictions to make difficult decisions that may lead to separation.

BE II ("Schism"), GAMEO ("Schisms"), Kniss (1997), Kraybill and Hostetter (2001), ME V ("Schisms"), Roth (1998, 2002b), D. Smucker (1993)

Congregation

BRETHREN and MENNONITE groups have a modified congregational form of CHURCH AU-THORITY that is less hierarchical than episcopal or synodal forms. Many decisions, such as order of WORSHIP, selection of MINISTERS, and DISCIPLINE, rest with the local congregation. The ORDINATION of leaders and the supervision of pastors and other leaders are facilitated by regional districts or conferences. In general, however, much AUTHORITY rests with the congregation.

The HUTTERITES, who live in colonies, concede more spiritual and church authority to their head ministers than do most Anabaptist groups. The AMISH grant much authority to the BISHOP, although the ORDNUNG, EXCOM-MUNICATION, and other matters are decided by a vote of the entire congregation. Many TRADITIONAL GROUPS choose their leaders by casting lots, a means of ordination with biblical roots that combines nominations by the congregation with a belief in divine selection.

See also Church, Polity of

BE II ("Polity"), D. Durnbaugh (1997a), GAMEO ("Congregationalism," "Polity"), Juhnke (1983), ME V ("Congregationalism," "Polity")

Conrad Grebel Review

This interdisciplinary journal (published three times a year) began in 1983 at Conrad Grebel College, Waterloo, Ontario. The periodical encourages reflection from ANABAPTIST perspectives on a broad range of contemporary issues, such as spirituality, ethics, theology, and culture. It has more contemporary theological content than *MENNONITE QUARTERLY REVIEW* or *JOURNAL OF MENNONITE STUDIES*, which focus more on historical studies. In addition to articles and book reviews, *Conrad Grebel Review* fosters dialogue by including lengthy responses to articles and authors' responses to their critics.

GAMEO ("Conrad Grebel University College"), http://www.grebel.uwaterloo.ca/academic/cgreview/

Conscientious Objectors

This term, which originated in North America during WORLD WAR I, describes those whose conscience and/or religious convictions forbid them to perform military service. NONRESIS-TANCE to evil, one of the central themes of ANABAPTISM, precluded participation in the military. The meaning and interpretation of nonresistance has varied in Anabaptist groups over the centuries. When Anabaptists faced military conscription in western Europe, some of them migrated to Russia, Canada, and the United States, rather than face compulsory military service; some of those who remained joined the armed forces.

Anabaptist groups typically sought pacifist ways of serving their countries during times of universal conscription. Beginning in 1793 in Canada, MENNONITES, QUAKERS, and BRETH-REN IN CHRIST successfully petitioned for exemption from military service. Later, in the United States, Anabaptists first appealed for exemptions from universal military service during the CIVIL WAR.

During World War I, Canada recognized Mennonite and Brethren in Christ conscientious objectors and provided exemptions for them based on the Militia Act of 1793 and formal agreements reached with Mennonite immigrants from Russia in the 1870s. In the United States, noncombatant military service was offered during World War I, but many Anabaptist groups forbade joining the military and wearing a uniform, even in noncombatant roles. Imprisonments, torture, and harassment ensued, resulting in the death of two young HUTTERITE men.

In the United States during WORLD WAR II, the government provided the options of non-combatant military service and ALTERNATIVE SERVICE in church-administered programs, which was known as Civilian Public Service. Canada also offered a program for conscientious objectors: alternative service work camps administered by the government. Groups of conscientious objectors in both countries typically lived and worked together performing various services—conservation, construction, agricultural, medical—in the national interest.

In the United States during the Korean War, the alternative service program, called I-W Service for the draft classification, placed individuals in service assignments approved by local draft boards. Many of these assignments were in medical and psychiatric hospitals.

During the VIETNAM WAR, a few Mennonite and BRETHREN men objected to any cooperation with the government in matters of conscription and practiced civil disobedience by burning their draft cards, refusing to register with selective service, or migrating to Canada. Objections to participating in war have motivated Anabaptists in different countries and time periods to face imprisonment or to migrate in order to honor their deeply held convictions.

A survey (CMP 2006) of assimilated groups in the United States found that 27% of Brethren in Christ, 37% of CHURCH OF THE BRETHREN, and 70% of MENNONITE CHURCH USA members would serve as conscientious objectors in alternative service if drafted for the armed forces.

See also Peacemaking; Voluntary Service

BE I ("Conscientious Objector"), C. Bowman (2008), Bush (1998b), CMP 2006, F. Epp (1974), GAMEO ("Alternative Service [U.S.]," "Alternative Service Work Camps [Canada]," "Conscientious Objection"), M. Heisey (2003), W. Janzen (1990), Keim and Stoltzfus (1988), Klippenstein (1979), Klippenstein and Dick (2002), ME I ("Conscientious Objector"),

Mock (2003), J. Oyer (1992), http://www.alternative service.ca

Conscription   *See* Alternative Service

Conservative Anabaptist Groups   *See* Traditional Groups

Conservative Mennonite Conference
Organized in 1910 in Pigeon, Michigan, this group was first known as the Conservative Amish Mennonite Conference but dropped the "Amish" part of its name in 1954. Virtually all of the early members came from AMISH backgrounds. The Conservative Mennonite Conference is an autonomous body with fraternal relations with numerous MENNONITE bodies and organizations. The group emphasizes the authority of the Scriptures and NONCONFORMITY to the world. Plain dress is worn by some members living in rural areas but by few members of urban congregations. The group's denominational headquarters and school, Rosedale Bible College, are located in Irwin, Ohio. In the United States the group has over 11,000 members attending 106 congregations. They are scattered in 24 states, with the largest concentration in Ohio. Mission efforts in Central America have resulted in 4,600 members in 117 congregations in Nicaragua and 1,400 members in 26 congregations in Costa Rica. In Haiti, the Gospel Light Chapel (700 members) is affiliated with the Conservative Mennonite Conference.

Anabaptist (Mennonite) Directory (2009), GAMEO ("Conservative Mennonite Conference"), ME V ("Conservative Mennonite Conference"), I. Miller (1985), Scott (1996), N. Yoder (2011), http://www.cmcrosedale .org

Conversion
In the Christian context, conversion means turning from unbelief or agnosticism to a committed faith in Jesus Christ (Matt. 4:17–19). Repentance for sin and immoral behavior is the first stage in the conversion process. ANABAPTISTS insist that genuine repentance results in righteousness, ethical regeneration, becoming a

disciple of Jesus Christ, and a willingness to be baptized into his church. Conversion can also include a personal transformation through God's grace. MENNO SIMONS (1496–1561), a prominent early Dutch Anabaptist leader, emphasized the centrality of this new birth in his writings.

After their beginnings in Europe, some second- and third-generation Anabaptist communities became somewhat self-contained, culturally distinct, and nonconformist. As their ethnic identity solidified, younger generations grew up within the culture of the church. For these young people, conversion did not always produce a dramatic change in life. As a response to these challenges, some Anabaptist groups, especially BRETHREN, MENNONITE BRETHREN, and BRETHREN IN CHRIST churches, accepted revivalism, as well as PIETIST and CHARISMATIC expressions of faith, which stressed a personal, subjective experience of repentance and conversion.

Many TRADITIONAL GROUPS emphasize the seriousness of conversion (signaled by adult BAPTISM) as a personal promise to follow Jesus Christ and to obey the behavioral norms of their particular church group. ASSIMILATED GROUPS display a wide variety of understandings about the age, style, and theological meaning of conversion. Some 96% or more of CHURCH OF THE BRETHREN, Brethren in Christ, and MENNONITE CHURCH USA members in the United States reported that at one time in their lives they had "accepted Christ as Savior and Lord" (CMP 2006).

BE I ("Conversion, Doctrine of"), CMP 2006, GAMEO ("Conversion"), Jeschke (1983), Kraybill and Bowman (2001), ME V ("Conversion"), E. M. Sider (2002)

Converts   *See* Evangelism; Mission

Cookbooks
Based on their successful agricultural and rural life, ANABAPTIST groups developed a reputation for a simple, hearty, and bountiful cuisine. By the 1900s that reputation merged with the desire of some Anabaptists to preserve the recipes of their ancestors. Soon after the CHURCH OF

THE BRETHREN established a publishing house in 1897, it published *Inglenook Cookbook* (1901), which was reprinted many times and remained available into the 1980s. An updated version, *Granddaughter's Inglenook Cookbook,* appeared in the 1940s.

Another example from the Pennsylvania German tradition is *Mennonite Community Cookbook: Favorite Family Recipes* (1950). It remains in print because it describes the most common and highly cherished foods eaten in the 1900s by Swiss-origin North American MENNONITES. Good Books, in Intercourse, Pennsylvania, has compiled many cookbooks, some from the Swiss-origin Pennsylvania German tradition. OLD ORDER MENNONITES and AMISH, from the same tradition, have also published numerous cookbooks since 1990.

Cookbooks from the Russian Mennonite tradition include *Melting Pot of Mennonite Cookery, 1874–1974* (1974) and the two-volume *Mennonite Foods and Folkways from South Russia* (1990 and 1991). The latter provides an extensive description of the history, folklore, Low German DIALECT, recipes, and traditions of Russian Mennonites. *Celebration of Hospitality: A Brethren in Christ World Cookbook* is the best-known cookbook in that denomination. Published in 1998, it includes recipes from all the regions of the world where Brethren in Christ members live.

MENNONITE CENTRAL COMMITTEE (MCC), an international relief and development organization, published a very popular cookbook, *More-with-Less Cookbook: Suggestions by Mennonites on How to Eat Better and Consume Less of the World's Limited Food Resources,* in 1976. Using ingredients readily accessible in North America, it provides simple recipes with an underlying theology of respect for God's creation and stewardship of the earth's resources. A later MCC cookbook, *Extending the Table: A World Community Cookbook* (1991), includes recipes from many nations and cultures. In a later melding of theology and recipes, MCC published *Simply in Season* in 2005, a cookbook that describes how the choice of foods impacts local and global neighbors.

Books on Amish-style cooking abound. "The Amish Cook," a nationally syndicated newspaper column that appears in more than 100 newspapers around the country, was written by Elizabeth Coblentz (1936–2002), an Old Order Amish woman from Missouri. For 11 years she wrote about the events of her life and her activities in the kitchen, ending each column with a recipe. Her daughter Lovina Eicher (1971–) has continued to write the column. Eicher and her editor, Kevin Williams (1973–), published two cookbooks: *The Amish Cook at Home* in 2008 and *The Amish Cook's Baking Book* in 2009.

Congregations, small groups, and church-related institutions have also published cookbooks as fundraising projects. Cookbooks highlight the role of food in community life and social interaction. Amish worship services end with a shared meal. In many Anabaptist groups various aspects of congregational life, including weddings and funerals, integrate eating together as part of the ritual. Growing and preserving food are key roles for women in TRADITIONAL GROUPS.

See also Folklife

Bailey-Dick (2005), BE I ("Cookbooks," "Cooking"), Eicher and Williams (2008), P. Good (2000), *Granddaughter's Inglenook Cookbook* (1942), *Inglenook Cook Book* (1901), E. Kaufman (1974), Lind and Hockman-Wert (2005), D. Longacre (1976), Preheim (2005), J. Schlabach and Burnett (1991), Showalter (1950), E. Sider (1998), Voth (1990–1991), http://www.oasis newsfeatures.com

Costa Rica

The Convention of Mennonite Churches of Costa Rica (Asociación Convención de Iglesias Menonitas de Costa Rica) formed in 1974 through the efforts of missionaries from Rosedale (Ohio) Mennonite Missions. The MISSION staff arrived in the 1960s and for over a decade was engaged in community development projects and translating the Bible into an indigenous language. Throughout the 1960s and 1970s, more than 90 North American volunteers worked in social SERVICE assignments with the Convention of Mennonite Churches. The group

has 26 congregations in urban and rural areas, with about 1,475 members.

A second, more conservative MENNONITE group in Costa Rica, the Beachy Amish Mennonite Fellowship, emerged in 1968. The group began by developing colonies where members lived close together on large blocks of land, similar to the colony pattern of Mennonite groups in BELIZE and MEXICO. The BEACHY AMISH MENNONITES have 11 congregations in Costa Rica, with about 275 members. Many of the members, including some of the ministers, are native Costa Ricans.

The Mennonite Christian Fellowship (a conservative offshoot of the Beachy Amish) has one congregation in the country, with 25 members. In addition, an Amish Mennonite group from Tennessee has two mission outreach centers in Costa Rica.

GAMEO ("Beachy Amish Mennonite Fellowship," "Convención Evangélica Menonita de Costa Rica"), ME V ("Convención Evangélica Menonita de Costa Rica"), Mennonite World Conference (2005), http://www.mwc-cmm.org

Counterculture

Numerous ANABAPTIST groups could properly be dubbed countercultural. This does not mean that they are against culture—an impossibility for any group, because all societies embody a particular culture. Anabaptist counterculture groups reject some cultural values and practices of the dominant society because they seek to practice the values taught by Jesus and the church.

Several historical and theological influences have produced this countercultural stance. The religious PERSECUTION of Anabaptists in EUROPE fostered a suspicion and critique of the larger society. An emphasis among some Anabaptist groups on NONCONFORMITY to the world and separation from it has also underscored a countercultural mindset and encouraged distinctive practices related to dress and the use of technology. The teachings of Jesus and other biblical admonitions to not love the world or the things in the world also undergird these nonconformist beliefs (see, for example, Matt. 3–6, Rom. 12:2, James 4:4, John 17:14, Luke 16:15, I John 2:15–16).

Members of many Anabaptist groups view Christian teachings related to humility, honesty, modesty, simplicity, forgiveness, and nonviolence as counter to some mainstream cultural values, which champion excessive consumption, fashions, promiscuity, violence, and assertive individualism.

In a U.S. survey (CMP 2006), over half of MENNONITE CHURCH USA members agreed that the church should clearly stand apart from popular culture, and almost half of this group said that Christians should participate in popular culture but not let it shape them. About half of CHURCH OF THE BRETHREN members who participated in the survey thought that Christians should engage popular culture in order to make it better.

TRADITIONAL GROUPS appear countercultural because of their rejection of modern fashions; however, members of ASSIMILATED GROUPS also manifest countercultural traits to the extent that they reject violence, nationalism, and conspicuous consumption in the larger society.

See also *Gelassenheit*; Sect

CMP 2006, D. Friesen (2000), Kraybill (2003b), T. Neufeld (1989)

Court of Law   *See* Jury Duty; Litigation; Oath, Swearing of

Courtship

Patterns of courtship vary considerably across different ANABAPTIST groups. Among the HUTTERITES, courtship occurs informally when youth from different colonies meet at work projects. Dating couples, however, rarely spend time together in private. Although marriages are not arranged, parents have veto power over mate selection. The bride typically moves to the colony of the groom.

The Old Order Amish allow more freedom. Couples are permitted to spend time together privately during their courtship. Single males

and females often meet at Sunday night youth singings, and a couple will often travel by horse and buggy back to the girl's home. For most Anabaptists in TRADITIONAL GROUPS, marriage is endogamous, because the church allows only members of the same religious group to marry.

Youth in ASSIMILATED GROUPS generally follow prevailing dating customs, which often involve participation in unsupervised groups and private time for couples. Courtship behavior is influenced by individual preferences, romantic attraction, and parental guidance, but usually not church regulations. Marriage between persons from different assimilated Anabaptist groups and other Christian churches is generally accepted, although parents may express concern if their child dates someone from a different or nonreligious background or from a different cultural or racial background.

See also Adolescence; Diversity, Social; Family

GAMEO ("Courtship Customs"), ME V ("Courtship Customs"), Stevick (2007)

Credit Unions

These member-owned and not-for-profit cooperatives offer financial services similar to banks. Credit unions are composed of members with some common bond, and they usually share any profits among the members rather than among the directors.

Early ANABAPTIST credit union activity began in RUSSIA. MENNONITES in 19th-century Russia were granted significant civil powers to control the economy of their colonies. Hence, they had experience in being responsible for financial matters such as taxation and public works. In addition, the *Waisenamt* (Orphans' Office), a MUTUAL AID organization that administered estates for orphans, became a type of Mennonite bank with a wide impact. By 1900, some economic cooperatives had also developed as credit institutions where loans could be obtained.

The idea of credit unions accompanied Russian Mennonites, especially the RUSSLÄNDER, to Canada and then to the United States. One of the first large Mennonite credit unions was Crosstown Credit Union, created in 1944 in Winnipeg, Manitoba. In the early 21st century, large Mennonite-related credit unions include Steinbach Credit Union in southern Manitoba (over 60,000 members and ca. $2 billion in assets in 2007) and Mennonite Savings and Credit Union in Ontario (over 16,000 members and over $600 million in assets in 2007). Mennonite Financial Federal Credit Union, created in 1955 by Mennonite Publishing House employees in Scottdale, Pennsylvania, has some 8,000 members in various states. MENNONITE ECONOMIC DEVELOPMENT ASSOCIATES has encouraged the creation of credit unions in countries outside North America.

The Church of the Brethren Credit Union was organized in 1938 by employees of the Brethren Publishing House. In 2004 its charter was expanded to include the families of all CHURCH OF THE BRETHREN members and employees of BRETHREN institutions. It has about 1,200 members. The CHURCH OF THE BRETHREN BENEFIT TRUST administers the credit union.

See also Business; Economics

BE I ("Credit Unions"), J. Friesen (1989), GAMEO ("Credit Unions," "Waisenamt"), ME IV ("Waisenamt"), ME V ("Credit Unions"), http://www.cobcu.org, http://www.mennonitefinancial.com, http://www.mscu.com

Creed   See Confessions of Faith

CROP   See Christian Rural Overseas Programs

Cuba

The efforts of several missionaries from the United States resulted in churches in Cuba in the 1950s. Most missionaries left the country after Fidel Castro (1926–) assumed power in 1959. Only one church, the Brethren in Christ Missionary Society (Sociedad Misionera Cubano Hermanos en Cristo), was legally registered in 1959. In the early 21st century the BRETHREN IN CHRIST have about 3,275 members and an additional 5,000 participants that meet in 75 congregations and outreach sites in Cuba. A second ANABAPTIST church, the Mennonite Church in Cuba (Iglesia Menonita en Cuba), emerged in 2008 as a result of contact with Canadian MENNONITES over two decades. Strongly committed to an Anabaptist vision, the group has three congregations and about 50 members. Conservative Mennonites established mission churches in Cuba in the 1990s. Two small missions are under the auspices of the Southern California Bible Fellowship. A congregation with about 25 members was planted by the Mennonite Christian Fellowship in 1999, with Costa Rican oversight.

GAMEO ("Cuba"), ME V ("Cuba"), Mennonite World Conference (2005), http://www.mwc-cmm.org

Cult   See Sect

Cultural Diversity   See Diversity, Social

Culture   See Assimilated Groups; Traditional Groups

Dancing

Many ANABAPTIST churches discouraged social dancing during the 17th through 20th centuries. Objections to dancing were that it encouraged sexual relations, was related to other worldly amusements including smoking and alcohol use, and violated the religious principle of nonconformity to the world. Most TRADITIONAL GROUPS continue to hold these objections in the 21st century; however, square dancing is practiced in some OLD ORDER MENNONITE and AMISH groups.

Among ASSIMILATED GROUPS, the taboo on dancing declined, especially in the last half of the 20th century, although it occasionally was a controversial issue for some church-related colleges. A 1972 survey of assimilated MENNONITES found that 43% thought that social dancing was always wrong. Thirty-four years later, 18% of MENNONITE CHURCH USA members thought that dancing is always or usually wrong (CMP 2006). Similarly, about 15% of CHURCH OF THE BRETHREN and BRETHREN IN CHRIST members agreed that dancing is always or usually wrong. In the 21st century, liturgical dance is practiced in the worship services of some assimilated groups.

CMP 2006, GAMEO ("Dance"), Kauffman and Harder (1975), ME V ("Dancing")

Dariusleut Hutterites

The earliest HUTTERITE churches emerged about 1528 in the context of the Anabaptist Movement during the Protestant Reformation in Europe. Their distinctive trademark is their rejection of private property and insistence on COMMUNAL LIVING and sharing. Facing severe persecution, the Hutterites migrated to several countries in Europe, and the Dariusleut formed in Russia in about 1860. Their name derives from their first leader, preacher Darius Walter (1835–1903). More moderate than the Lehrerleut, the Dariusleut have the most internal cultural diversity of the four Hutterite groups, in areas such as technology and home furnishings. This group has about 6,320 members (16,000 adults and children) living in 158 colonies in North America; 22 colonies are in the United States, mostly in Montana, and 136 colonies are in Canada, over 100 of them in Alberta.

See also Anabaptism; Lehrerleut Hutterites; Schmiedeleut Hutterites, Gibb Group; Schmiedeleut Hutterites, Kleinsasser Group

J. Hostetler (1997), Rod Janzen (2005), Janzen and Stanton (2010), Kraybill and Bowman (2001), Packull (1995)

Dating   *See* Courtship

Deacon

Along with BISHOP (or ELDER) and MINISTER (or preacher), deacon is one of the traditional spiritual leadership roles in ANABAPTIST groups. The biblical meaning of the word "deacon," which is mentioned in Acts 6:3 and Romans 16:1, pertains to service. The responsibilities of the deacon vary among different Anabaptist groups and different historical periods. In general, the deacon assists the minister(s) in administering the ORDINANCES and caring for the material needs of the congregation.

In the 19th and early 20th centuries in many MENNONITE congregations, the deacon handled financial matters, administered the mutual aid fund, assisted the bishop or minister(s) in administering BAPTISM and COMMUNION, assisted in visiting sick or erring members, read the BIBLE and offered prayer(s) in WORSHIP, and if necessary led worship in the absence of a minister or bishop. Among General Conference Mennonites of Russian origin, a deacon board served as trustees of the congregation and often hired the minister. The traditional deacon role continues in many conservative congregations, but its function has changed or been renamed "financial secretary" or a similar title among assimilated Mennonite groups.

Among the BRETHREN, deacons made a yearly visit to the homes of members in preparation for the LOVE FEAST. The visit provided an opportunity for members to discuss their spiritual lives and air their concerns, and for deacons to remind members of the churches' expectations for attire and other lifestyle issues. The OLD GERMAN BAPTIST BRETHREN and Dunkard Brethren still place high emphasis on the annual deacon visit, but it is no longer practiced among ASSIMILATED GROUPS. In the 21st century, Brethren deacons in many congregations not only prepare and serve the love feast; they also assist with pastoral care for infirm, sick, and lonely members. The Association of Brethren Caregivers of the CHURCH OF THE BRETHREN provides training and resources for deacons, including a *Deacons Manual.*

Some ASSIMILATED GROUPS have eliminated the office of deacon. The HUTTERITES do not ordain deacons, but they do have a steward who is in charge of all colony finances.

BE I ("Deacon"), GAMEO ("Deacon," "Ordination"), ME I ("Deacon"), ME V ("Ordination")

Deaconess   *See* Gender Roles

Death   *See* Funeral Customs

Demography
The number of CHILDREN in the nuclear families of TRADITIONAL GROUPS averages 5 to 6, but in some OLD ORDER MENNONITE and AMISH families it is 10 or more. Over half the population in traditional groups is under 18 years of age, which means that much more of the groups' energy is focused on child-rearing and educational efforts than on services for the ELDERLY. Many of the HUTTERITE, Old Order Mennonite, and Amish groups double in size about every 20 years. With a few exceptions, the growth in traditional communities comes from their large nuclear families and their ability to retain their youth. Many have retention rates of 85% or higher. The practice of endogamy (marriage within the group) in traditional groups also fuels their growth.

The demographic profile of ASSIMILATED GROUPS is quite different, largely because their members began using artificial methods of birth control as they became available in the mid-20th century. In a survey (CMP 2006), nearly 60% of married women in CHURCH OF

THE BRETHREN, BRETHREN IN CHRIST, and MENNONITE CHURCH USA churches in the United States reported having two or three children. With a low rate of conversion of outsiders and a modal number of two or three children per family, the size of the extended FAMILY shrinks and reduces the proportion of the population under 18 years of age. Small nuclear families means that greater attention is given to elder care because the proportion of aged is significant. The growth of assimilated groups largely depends on their ability to evangelize and recruit members from outside the group. Assimilated groups have difficulty retaining their youth because of mobility, HIGHER EDUCATION, exogamy, and loss to other religious groups.

CMP 2006, GAMEO ("Demography"), Janzen and Stanton (2010), Kraybill and Bowman (2001)

Denomination
Sociologists typically distinguish among three types of religious organizations: cult, SECT, and denomination. These three types vary by their inclusiveness, separation from society, and bureaucratic complexity. Social analysts have noted a tendency for cults and sects to evolve toward denominations. Compared with sects, denominations are more *inclusive* (having relatively few membership requirements, which make it easy for outsiders to join), more *accepting* of the values of the larger society, and more *bureaucratic* in their structure.

Most assimilated ANABAPTIST churches can be characterized as denominations. Some members in these churches joined as adults from other religious backgrounds. Because they do not wear distinctive dress, the members of assimilated churches are not visibly different from members of the larger society, as are those in the more TRADITIONAL GROUPS. Assimilated churches have numerous institutions, formal organizations, and a more complex bureaucratic structure than traditional churches.

Many of the denominational institutions and agencies were founded between 1875 and 1975. Anabaptists who built denominational structures fervently believed they were doing it to advance the gospel through missions, education, hospitals, and publications. Although they were building modern forms of social organizations, they were motivated by Bible-based intentions and fervent religious convictions.

Many of the traditional groups fit the definition of an established sect, but not a cult. These groups, with few large bureaucratic-style organizations, tend to operate more informally, like an extended family, than assimilated churches.

Yinger (1970)

Devotional Literature

ANABAPTIST groups have written and published a considerable amount of literature to strengthen the faith of the individual and the religious life of the church. Some developed themes common to and accepted by most Christians, and others focused on topics emphasized by Anabaptists. Hymnbooks are the oldest and most widespread type of devotional literature; these texts were also read by individuals for inspiration outside of WORSHIP services. Other early types of devotional literature include catechisms, dialogues, CONFESSIONS OF FAITH, letters, allegorical meditations, and prayers.

Most European MENNONITE and AMISH traditions include the writings of MENNO SIMONS (1496–1561), the 16th-century leader of Dutch Mennonites, in their devotional traditions. Key devotional sources for Anabaptists and their spiritual descendants include the massive collection of martyrs' stories in MARTYRS MIRROR (1660 in Dutch and 1837 in English), the hymnal entitled AUSBUND (1564 in German), and *Prayer Book for Earnest Christians* (1708 in German and 1997 in English). Additional devotional books published prior to 1800 include *Golden Apples in Silver Bowls* (1702, 1745; in German only until 1997), *Paradies Gärtlein* (1612), and *The Wandering Soul* (1635 in Dutch).

In 1660, probably in Elbing near Danzig, Mennonites published a catechism that was widely reprinted for more than a century. Mennonite bishop Georg Hansen (d. 1703) wrote a confession of faith in 1671, which was reprinted in Russia and North America in the 1800s. In 1702 in

Altona, Germany, Gerhardt Roosen (1612–1711) wrote *Christliches Gemüthsgespräch*, a catechism in a question-and-answer format. German and English editions are kept in print by OLD ORDER MENNONITES in Ontario and Pennsylvania, respectively.

In the 1700s, BRETHREN groups in Europe read widely available PIETIST literature, especially Johann Arndt's *True Christianity*, but soon began to publish their own hymnals. In 1720 in Germany they published GEISTREICHES GESANGBUCH, and in 1744 in Pennsylvania, DAS KLEINE DAVIDISCHE PSALTERSPIEL DER KINDER ZIONS. The Ephrata Community (EPHRATA CLOISTER) created a large body of unique devotional literature and hymn texts. When progressive BRETHREN and Mennonites began to publish periodicals in the mid-1800s in North America, they printed a wide range of devotional literature to promote their SPIRITUAL LIFE, often borrowing some from other religious groups.

The *(Great)* CHRONICLE OF THE HUTTERIAN BRETHREN, a massive volume, serves as a prime devotional work for HUTTERITES. It covers the earliest Swiss Anabaptist history from the 1520s to about 1665, and includes history, statements of faith, exhortations, martyrs' accounts, sermons, letters, and regulations for communal life. The *(Small) Chronicle of the Hutterian Brethren* summarizes some of the earlier work and adds material from the period 1665 to 1802. These two books were first translated into English in North America in 1987 and 1998.

Contemporary assimilated Anabaptists read many types of devotional literature, even as they maintain their own publishing efforts. The Believers Church Bible Commentary Series and the Christian education curriculum as well as the prayer and devotional books of some Mennonite and Brethren groups have helped bolster denominational identity. On the other hand, Anabaptist use of paraphrased versions of the BIBLE, the lectionary cycle, and church-growth materials from para-church organizations have also exposed members to other ecumenical devotional sources.

BE I ("Devotional Literature"), Boers et al. (2005),

Braght (1998), Friedmann (1949), GAMEO ("Devotional Literature"), L. Gross (1997), Hutterian Brethren (1987, 1998), ME II ("Devotional Literature"), ME V ("Devotional Literature")

Dialects

As a regional expression of LANGUAGE, a dialect has some unique pronunciations, vocabulary, and grammar at variance with a more formal written language. Because of their specific European origins, ANABAPTIST groups in North America spoke dialects related to German and Dutch. As they encountered persecution and immigrated to language areas outside their homelands, their dialects helped to reinforce distinctive theological and cultural identities, especially in FOLKLIFE practices.

When many German-speaking Anabaptist groups in North America assimilated into the larger culture, they lost their native dialect. Some of the more TRADITIONAL GROUPS continue to use a dialect in everyday communication and/or church services, however, which helps to maintain their cultural identities, especially as communities set apart from the wider society.

Two major German-based dialects are spoken in some traditional groups in North America in the 21st century. Pennsylvania German, also known as Pennsylvania Dutch *(Deitsch)*, is spoken among AMISH and some traditional Swiss-origin MENNONITES. Pennsylvania German emerged from elements of Swiss, Swabian, Alsatian, and Palatinate dialects in the 18th century in Pennsylvania. The total number of Pennsylvania German speakers (children and adults) is about 256,000. (This estimate is a conservative one that only includes people affiliated with a group that uses German or Pennsylvania German or both in church services. It excludes speakers whose churches now use English in their services but who may still speak some Pennsylvania German at home.)

An Amish-Mennonite Conference Line, established in 2006, enables members of Amish and conservative Mennonite groups to hear news from their communities, discuss historical topics, and listen to special speakers via telephone. As many as 8,000 calls are made a day on a Pennsylvania German line and an English line. The Pennsylvania German line is open 24 hours per day (except between 10:00 p.m. Saturday and 1:00 p.m. Sunday) for informal conversations. These conversations help to reinforce and perpetuate the use of the dialect.

Low German *(Plautdietsch)* is spoken by traditional and some assimilated Dutch-Russian-origin Mennonites in Belize, Canada, Mexico, and the United States who have produced a significant body of literature in the dialect. Some segments of the following Mennonite groups speak the dialect: Old Colony, Reinländer, Sommerfelder, Kleine Gemeinde, Bergthaler, and Chortitzer. The approximate numbers of Low German speakers (adults and children) in all of these groups by country are 6,500 in Belize, 40,500 in Canada, 58,000 in Mexico, and 5,000 in the United States.

HUTTERITES speak *Hutterisch*, a dialect derived from the province of Carinthia, Austria.

Buffington (1942), Burridge and Enninger (1992), R. Epp (1993), GAMEO ("Dialect Literature and Speech, Low German," "Dialect Literature and Speech, Pennsylvania German"), J. Hostetler (1997), Huffines (1988), Louden (2006), ME V ("Dialect Literature and Speech, Low German," "Dialect Literature and Speech, Pennsylvania German"), Scheer (1980)

Direction

Direction is a semiannual journal, begun in 1972, that addresses theological issues, church-related theory and practice, sociological issues, and discipleship matters. Neither a purely academic journal nor a denominational magazine, *Direction* highlights the interdependence of Christian reflection and mission. With articles in print and online, it is supported by six MENNONITE BRETHREN higher educational institutions and the U.S. and Canadian Mennonite Brethren Conferences.

http://www.directionjournal.org

Dirk Philips (1504–1568)

This ANABAPTIST leader may be second only
to MENNO SIMONS (1496–1561) in terms of his
influence on the first decades of the Anabaptist Movement in the NETHERLANDS. Little is
known of Dirk Philips' early life. He was born
in Leeuwarden, the illegitimate son of a Dutch
priest. He eventually became a Franciscan
monk, but by 1534 he had been baptized as an
adult into the Anabaptist fellowship. Soon after
his BAPTISM he was ordained an ELDER, and
he baptized several people. Dirk Philips lived
in the Netherlands and later in East Friesland,
Holstein, and Prussia. In a major church division
in 1567 among the Dutch Anabaptists, he sided
with the Flemish over the Frisians.

Dirk Philips was the leading theologian
among the Dutch and north German MENNO-
NITES in the mid-16th century. He preached
the doctrines of NONRESISTANCE and the
Trinity. He advocated the strict application of
the ban, with SHUNNING of those who were
excommunicated. He also wrote on topics such
as baptism, conversion, the visible church, and
marriage. His writings are clearer and more systematic than those of Menno Simons. Leaders
of TRADITIONAL GROUPS have had the most
enduring interest in Dirk Philips' teachings, especially his writings on excommunication and
shunning.

Before his death, Dirk Philips compiled all of
his writings and published them in a single volume. This volume, *Enchiridion oft Hantboecxken
van de Christelijcke Leere . . .* , has since been
published in French, German, and English, in
addition to the original Dutch.

GAMEO ("Dirk Philips," "Enchiridion Oft Hantboecxken"), ME II ("Dirk Philips," "Enchiridion Oft
Hantboecxken . . . "), Dirk (1992)

Disabilities

ANABAPTISTS have long emphasized the
themes of love, COMMUNITY, SOCIAL JUSTICE,
and SERVICE to others—themes that pertain directly to serving and understanding people with
disabilities. Although Russian MENNONITE immigrants organized a program for people with
mental retardation and mental illness in Ontario
in 1932, the bulk of church-related services for
the disabled emerged after 1950. Much of the
growth of agencies and services concerned
with mental illness and developmental disabilities in the Mennonite world was propelled by
hundreds of young adults who had performed
ALTERNATIVE SERVICE in public mental hospitals as CONSCIENTIOUS OBJECTORS during
WORLD WAR II and later. They were appalled by
the deplorable and inhumane conditions they
found, and some of them resolved to address
these issues when they returned to their home
communities. As programs began in the 1950s
and 1960s, they typically combined services for
both the mentally ill and the developmentally
disabled.

In 1957, Mennonites in Ohio established
Adriel School, a residential and educational center for mentally retarded and emotionally troubled slow learners. By 1987 some 40 agencies
related to several different Mennonite bodies
were providing residential, vocational, advocacy,
and other support services to both Mennonite
and non-Mennonite people with developmental
disabilities. As the number of local service providers grew, several interchurch agencies and
networks emerged to provide resources and coordination. In 1973, Mennonite Health Services,
an agency of MENNONITE CENTRAL COMMIT-
TEE, established a developmental disabilities
services unit that offered services, resources,
consultation, and coordination to local providers, including retreats for families. In Canada,
the Manitoba Mental Health and Disabilities
Program was formed under the umbrella of Mennonite Central Committee in 1980.

By the first decade of the 21st century, the
interchurch agency Mennonite Health Services
offered coordination and resources for local providers of services for the disabled. In 2003 the
Anabaptist Disability Network emerged to provide encouragement and resources to congregations, families, and persons with disabilities.
One of their projects involves support for people
with Asperger Syndrome who relate to Anabaptist churches.

Some OLD ORDER MENNONITE and AMISH groups have developed support services and resources for families with disabled children in their communities. These include short-term residential facilities for mentally disabled persons and various types of vocational workshops, as well as special schools and classes for students with disabilities.

See also Hospitals, Mental; Mental Health

GAMEO ("Disabilities," "Wiebe, Henry Peter[(1898–1980]"), P. Leichty (2006), ME V ("Disabilities"), http://www.adnetonline.org, http://manitoba.mcc.org/programs/mhdp, http://www.mhsonline.org

Discipleship

ANABAPTIST groups of all types view discipleship as a central feature of their faith. Because they emphasize the daily practice of faith over doctrinal belief, Anabaptists commit themselves to being disciples of JESUS CHRIST in everyday life. "No one may truly know Christ except one who follows him in life," said 16th-century Anabaptist Hans Denck (1495–1527). Indeed, four out of five CHURCH OF THE BRETHREN, BRETHREN IN CHRIST, and MENNONITE CHURCH USA members reported that following Jesus in daily life is very important to their personal faith (CMP 2006).

Because they aim to be his disciples, Anabaptists emphasize the importance of the life and teachings of Jesus, especially the SERMON ON THE MOUNT, in their theological framework. Theological discussions tend to focus either on the believer's imitation of Jesus in his nonresistant love or the believer's participation in Jesus' way in the world.

The writings of Harold S. Bender (1897–1962), especially his essay on the Anabaptist vision, highlight discipleship as a cornerstone of Anabaptist theology. Other Mennonite writers also articulate the meaning of discipleship in their writings (D. Augsburger 2006, J. H. Yoder 1972/1994). ALEXANDER MACK SR. (1679–1735), founder of the Church of the Brethren, penned a hymn, "Count the Cost," which underscored discipleship's importance in Brethren faith and life.

See also Anabaptism, Theology of; Ethics

D. Augsburger (2006), Bender (1944, 1962), CMP 2006, Eberly (1991), GAMEO ("The Anabaptist Vision [Text, 1944]," "Denk, Hans [ca. 1500–1527]," "Discipleship"), Kraybill (2003b), ME II ("Denk, Hans"), ME V ("Discipleship"), C. Snyder (2004), J. H. Yoder (1972/1994)

Discipline

The accountability of members to the collective discernment of the local congregation is central to the historic ANABAPTIST view of the nature of the church. In the heritage of adult believers BAPTISM, the baptism vow was not only a confession of faith in Jesus Christ but also a pledge to participate in the body of Christ (the local congregation) and to be accountable to it for any moral failures. This process of accountability, often referred to as church discipline, is based on four verses in the Gospel of Matthew (18:15–18).

In this passage, Jesus speaks about the authority of the church to "bind and loose"—to make decisions about membership that are ratified in heaven. The process outlined in the four verses involves three steps. If an offense occurs between two members, they should first seek to resolve their differences privately. If that fails, the offended member should take one or two witnesses along and approach the offender a second time. If the visit with witnesses does not heal the breach, the issue should be taken to the church. EXCOMMUNICATION is appropriate if the offender refuses to heed the counsel and wisdom of the church.

This process of church discipline underscores both the seriousness of the baptismal vow and the authority of the church to hold members accountable for ethical failure or behavior that threatens the well-being of the church community and its witness. Different Anabaptist groups have sought to implement this biblical process in different ways, with various levels of success.

Among TRADITIONAL GROUPS, members who do not respect the counsel of the church are excommunicated. In addition, some churches shun ex-members with rituals of shame intended to encourage them to confess their wrongdoing and return to the church. This practice of discipline runs counter to the high value placed on individualism in the dominant society. Thus, many ASSIMILATED GROUPS emphasize biblical teachings of acceptance, grace, and forgiveness, and use personal counseling for ethical lapses, rather than a collective process of accountability.

See also Believers Church; Shunning

BE I ("Discipline"), GAMEO ("Discipline, Church"), Jeschke (1988), Koop (2004), Koop and Schertz (2000), Ulrich and Fairchild (2002)

Diversity, Social

The public mythology that ANABAPTISTS in North America are a homogeneous people shaped by the same cultural cookie-cutter belies the facts. From the rural regions of Guatemala to Vancouver, British Columbia, diversity abounds in the Anabaptist world. Variations in lifestyle, social class, race, cultural origin, LANGUAGE, OCCUPATION, WEALTH, politics, TECHNOLOGY, and religious belief are plentiful. Diversity varies by region, country, and church affiliation. Anabaptists living in or near major metropolitan areas exhibit the most diversity.

TRADITIONAL GROUPS of BRETHREN, MENNONITES, AMISH, and HUTTERITES who live in rural areas practice a different lifestyle and worship in a different manner from members of ASSIMILATED GROUPS who live in urban areas. Thousands of Mennonites hold professional jobs in the Winnipeg, Manitoba, area—home to some 50 Mennonite churches, and the largest urban concentration of Anabaptists in the world. Anabaptists in cities such as Mexico City, Miami, and Los Angeles add even more ethnic diversity to the cultural mosaic. In Philadelphia, Anabaptists worship in a dozen different languages including Chinese, Vietnamese, and Spanish. Vancouver offers yet another example of a multiethnic Anabaptist urban community that worships in multiple languages. Anabaptist groups span a wide social spectrum. Some members refrain from any political activity while others serve as elected officials in county,

state, and provincial offices. Differences abound on views of biblical interpretation, the HOLY SPIRIT, miracles, EVOLUTION, ABORTION, HOMOSEXUALITY, and women in leadership, to name but a few.

Some Anabaptists read by kerosene lamps, while others surf the Internet. Some live without credit cards, while others work as stockbrokers. Hundreds study in one-room schools, while others teach at Harvard University. Some are recent immigrants from Asia, while others claim nine generations of German lineage. Some are gay and some are straight. Some are black and some are white. Some travel by horse and buggy on back country roads, and others drive high-performance cars on superhighways. Some use hand tools to till the soil in Central America; others work in high-rise urban offices. Many are forbidden by their churches to access the Internet, yet others design computer software and own high-tech companies. Some live on the edge of poverty, and others are wealthy entrepreneurs who operate large corporations. Some churches eschew art, while some Anabaptists make their living as artists and writers. Social diversity abounds in all of these ways among North American Anabaptists. The diverse social contexts raise new theological questions and lead to an ever-growing religious diversity.

Kraybill and Hostetter (2001)

Divorce

The legal dissolution of the marriage bond has been strongly discouraged and/or made subject to church DISCIPLINE at times among most ANABAPTIST groups. This censure is based on Jesus' words (Matt. 5:32, 19:9 and Mark 10:7–9) and on the destabilizing effect divorce has on the family.

TRADITIONAL GROUPS permit only marital separation. Indeed, divorce is cause for EXCOMMUNICATION in many of these churches. Some ASSIMILATED GROUPS allow divorce in cases of adultery or abandonment but forbid remarriage while the ex-spouse is living. Many other assimilated Anabaptist churches, influenced by individualism, mobility, urbanization, and modern culture, experience divorce among their members. Such groups have developed various redemptive and counseling programs to address marital conflict and prevent divorce whenever possible. In the last half of the 20th century, many assimilated groups accepted divorce and remarriage of church members, although some congregations continued to oppose the remarriage of divorced persons. A survey (CMP 2006) found that fewer than 10% of MENNONITE CHURCH USA members and 18% of CHURCH OF THE BRETHREN and BRETHREN IN CHRIST members in the United States had been divorced or separated—a much lower rate than among the general public.

BE I ("Divorce"), Bontrager (1978), CMP 2006, GAMEO ("Divorce and Remarriage"), Kauffman and Driedger (1991), ME I ("Divorce"), ME V ("Divorce and Remarriage"), Ziegler (1976)

Doctrine *See* Confessions of Faith; Theology

Dominican Republic

At least seven ANABAPTIST related groups are present in the Dominican Republic. The Conference of the Dominican Evangelical Mennonites was begun by the FELLOWSHIP OF EVANGELICAL CHURCHES (formerly EVANGELICAL MENNONITE CONFERENCE) in the mid-1940s. It has some 2,450 members in 60 congregations. Two churches were planted by missionaries from the Eastern Mennonite Missions: the Dominican Evangelical Mennonite Council, which has about 275 members in 6 congregations, and a related body, the Divine Light National Assembly of Mennonites, which has some 2,500 members in 23 congregations. Koinonia Fellowship of Churches, another MENNONITE-related group, has about 400 adherents.

Two traditional, U.S.-based Mennonite churches have about a dozen congregations and mission outreach sites. The NATIONWIDE FELLOWSHIP CHURCHES began mission work in the Dominican Republic in 1981 and has five churches with about 100 members. The CHURCH OF GOD IN CHRIST, MENNONITE group has established three congregations and

five mission outreach sites. Their membership is about 50. Blue Ridge International for Christ, a mission organization supported by the BEACHY AMISH MENNONITE CHURCH in the United States, also conducts mission work in the Dominican Republic.

The Bethel Brethren in Christ Church (Iglesia Bethel Hermanos en Cristo) established by BRETHREN IN CHRIST missionaries in 1997, has about 300 members plus 500 participants in 15 congregations and numerous worship centers.

CHURCH OF THE BRETHREN members from Puerto Rico began mission efforts in the Dominican Republic following Hurricane David in 1979. BRETHREN congregations and agencies from the United States soon assisted the growing churches. Thirty years later the Church of the Brethren had some 1,700 members and 20 congregations and mission outposts in the Dominican Republic. A micro-loan community development project involves about 500 people related to many of the congregations. The church also supports health education and a medical clinic.

Some of the Anabaptist churches in the Dominican Republic have joined with the Anabaptist churches in Puerto Rico to form the Caribbean Anabaptist Seminary, in order to offer Anabaptist theological training for pastors and church leaders.

BE IV ("Dominican Republic"), Mennonite World Conference (2005)

Dordrecht Confession of Faith

Written in 1632 in the Netherlands by MENNONITE leaders, the 18 articles that make up this statement of faith cover a wide range of Christian theological issues and practices. Articles with special significance for ANABAPTIST theology include those on believers BAPTISM, FOOTWASHING, SHUNNING of excommunicated members, non-swearing of OATHS, NONRESISTANCE (biblical PACIFISM), and church DISCIPLINE. This statement of faith was eventually endorsed by ministers in Alsace in 1660 and influenced the formation of the AMISH in 1693. Adopted by the Franconia and Lancaster Mennonite conferences in Pennsylvania in 1725, the

Dordrecht Confession is widely used today as a guide to faith and practice by most traditional Mennonites of Swiss–south German origin and by virtually all Amish groups. Most assimilated Mennonite groups eventually replaced the Dordrecht Confession with their own confessions or statements of faith.

See also Anabaptism, Theology of; Confessions of Faith; Schleitheim Articles

GAMEO ("Dordrecht Confession of Faith [Mennonite, 1632]"), I. Horst (1982, 1988), Koop (2004, 2006), ME II ("Dordrecht")

Draft   See Alternative Service

Dress   See Clothing

Dunkard Brethren   See Brethren

Dutch Anabaptists   See Netherlands

Dutch Language

The Dutch LANGUAGE of the NETHERLANDS, a key region of the Anabaptist Movement in the 1500s, was used in many ANABAPTIST religious publications such as hymnals, DEVOTIONAL LITERATURE, and CONFESSIONS OF FAITH. North American MENNONITES and AMISH utilized the Dutch writings of MENNO SIMONS (1496–1561) and the DORDRECHT CONFESSION OF FAITH, especially after they were translated into German and, later, into English.

Many Mennonites living in the northern province of Friesland (in the Netherlands) adopted the dialect of Low German (Plattdeutsch or Plautdietsch) as their daily tongue when they immigrated to POLAND (later Prussia). However, they continued to use Dutch for their written and formal religious language until the 1700s, when they changed to High German. In the late 1700s some of these people with Dutch roots immigrated to RUSSIA and, later, in the 1870s, 1920s, and 1950s, to North and South America.

Knowledge of the Dutch language became important for scholars studying original sources as research on Anabaptist groups grew in the 1800s and 1900s. Pennsylvania German, frequently known as Pennsylvania Dutch, is sometimes mistaken for a Dutch dialect.

R. Epp (1993), GAMEO ("Netherlands"), ME III ("Netherlands"), Menno (1956), J. Thiessen (1989)

Eastern Pennsylvania Mennonite Church

This group of churches began in 1969 in eastern Pennsylvania when 5 conservative bishops and some 40 other ordained leaders withdrew from the Lancaster Mennonite Conference over issues related to dress, television, and other cultural changes. The Eastern Pennsylvania Mennonite Church developed a more conservative discipline and continues to uphold traditional MENNONITE standards of doctrine, dress, and practice. With some 4,500 members in the United States, this group has 56 congregations in 13 states, the majority of them in Pennsylvania. The group also has four affiliated congregations in Canada with about 200 members, one congregation in the Bahamas, and about 200 members in five congregations in Guatemala.

GAMEO ("Eastern Pennsylvania Mennonite Church"), ME V ("Eastern Pennsylvania Mennonite Church"), Ruth (2001), Scott (1996)

Ecology   *See* Environment

Economics

Apart from the HUTTERITES, who practice COMMUNAL LIVING based on Christian economic principles, North American ANABAPTISTS accept private property and participate in the broader capitalist economic system. Members buy and sell products in public markets, charge interest, make investments in stock markets, and operate for-profit corporations. Although members participate in the wider economic system, church leaders admonish them to do so while adhering to Christian principles of honesty and integrity. Historic Anabaptist values discourage greed, the use of fraudulent business practices, the exercise of force for economic gain, and other activities that undermine the ethics of the kingdom of God and the witness of the church.

Leaders in most Anabaptist churches encourage members to embrace Christian principles of stewardship, MUTUAL AID, and SERVICE to others. Biblical teaching suggests that Christians are stewards of God-given gifts—skills, talents, wealth—that should be used in ways that honor God and benefit the larger world. Moreover, the Scripture also teaches that church members are duty-bound to give time, money, and material goods to help those in their church with special needs. Members are also encouraged to use their means to serve others beyond their church. Numerous social service and relief agencies have been founded by church groups for this purpose. Materialism and the conspicuous consumption that erodes spiritual values, promotes vanity, and wastes resources are strongly eschewed by most Anabaptist churches.

Despite teachings on stewardship and mutual aid, the economic disparities across the North American Anabaptist world run deep. Not only do they exist within congregations, but they also vary by region and country. National economies have a significant impact on the living standards of church members and amplify economic differences within the church.

Many Anabaptists who have had success in the BUSINESS world have used their resources to support church agencies that serve both those within the church and those outside it.

See also Anabaptist Foundation; Benevolence; Brethren in Christ Foundation; Church of the Brethren Benefit Trust; Credit Unions; Entrepreneurs; Mennonite Economic Development Associates; Mennonite Foundation; Mennonite Foundation of Canada

Burkhardt (2006), P. J. Klassen (1964), C. Redekop (1989), Redekop, Krahn, and Steiner (1994)

Ecumenism

Cooperation with outside church bodies varies greatly among ANABAPTIST groups. Anabaptists emerged as a persecuted religious protest movement at the time of the Protestant Reformation and later lived as a marginal German-speaking cultural minority in North America and RUSSIA. Therefore, many Anabaptists, especially those in TRADITIONAL GROUPS, have shown marked caution toward or outright rejection of ecumenical movements. The ecumenical activity of ASSIMILATED GROUPS varies by denomination and region.

The CHURCH OF THE BRETHREN has been the most ecumenical of all the Anabaptist groups. It first participated in formal ecumenical activity in 1941 when it joined the Federal Council of Churches and the World Council of Churches (WCC). M. R. Zigler (1891–1985) served as the BRETHREN representative to the National Council of Churches and the World Council of Churches. In the late 1940s Zigler and BRETHREN SERVICE COMMISSION provided the initial impetus for the ecumenical CHRISTIAN RURAL OVERSEAS PROGRAM (CROP), a conduit for food relief. Zigler also became involved in the creation of various ecumenical relief organizations such as Church World Service (CWS) and Cooperative for American Remittances to Europe (CARE). Brethren Dan West (1893–1971) established Heifer Project, which eventually became HEIFER INTERNATIONAL. In the 1960s the Church of the Brethren participated (with observer status) in discussions of the Consultation on Church Union, an ecumenical movement among some traditional Protestant denominations. However, in 1966 the church declined to become a full participant. Brethren representatives continue to be active in the World Council of Churches and the National Council of Churches in the 21st century.

Assimilated MENNONITES generally participate in local ecumenical bodies and send individual representatives (some with observer status) to meetings of national ecumenical groups such as the World Council of Churches, the National Council of Churches, and the National Association of Evangelicals. MENNONITE CHURCH CANADA has been an affiliate or member of both the Evangelical Fellowship of Canada and the Canadian Council of Churches since 2004. European Mennonite churches have been members of the World Council of Churches since 1948, and several of their members have served on its Central Committee. Mennonites and especially Church of the

Brethren leaders played an important role in the "Decade to Overcome Violence 2001–2010" initiative of the WCC.

Between 1986 and 2003, Church of the Brethren and Mennonite representatives participated in a series of consultations on the RADICAL REFORMATION. These gatherings brought together members from a variety of Radical Reformation groups, with dialogue partners from Protestant, Roman Catholic, and Orthodox traditions. MENNONITE CHURCH USA and the Church of the Brethren are also members of Christian Churches Together, an ecumenical group that offers an alternative to the National Council of Churches and the National Association of Evangelicals.

The amount of inter-Anabaptist ecumenical activity also varies by group and region of the country. Many Mennonite groups cooperate in historical activities, relief auctions, and support for two major inter-Mennonite organizations, MENNONITE WORLD CONFERENCE and MENNONITE CENTRAL COMMITTEE, both of which include the BRETHREN IN CHRIST denomination. The MENNONITE ENCYCLOPEDIA of the 1950s was a cooperative effort of various Mennonite groups. BRETHREN ENCYCLOPEDIA and BRETHREN WORLD ASSEMBLY have been important cooperative ventures among the six major Brethren groups.

Traditional groups rarely, if ever, participate in ecumenical activities with non-Anabaptist churches. Some of the more traditional churches also strongly discourage their members from attending WORSHIP services in other churches. Because considerable authority resides within local congregations, the AMISH and OLD ORDER MENNONITES do not join overarching church organizations of fellow Anabaptists or other Christians, but they do support some church-related service organizations for international relief and development, such as Mennonite Central Committee and CHRISTIAN AID MINISTRIES. Although HUTTERITE colonies are organized into district conferences, they rarely cooperate in a formal way with non-Hutterite religious groups.

BE I ("Consultation on Church Union," "Ecumenism"), D. Durnbaugh (1989), Enns (2007), GAMEO ("Ecumenism"), ME V ("Ecumenism"), J. H. Yoder (1958), Ziegler (1966)

Education

ANABAPTISTS of Swiss origin initially distanced themselves from formal education for several reasons. Some of the 16th-century Anabaptist leaders were university trained and highly educated. Nevertheless, they were critical of clergy, both Protestant and Catholic, who had formal theological education but lived lives of hypocrisy and disobedience to Scripture. When Anabaptists were persecuted and tried as heretics, the interrogators were typically educated and learned men, which added to the disdain for education. PERSECUTION by GOVERNMENTS forced many Anabaptists into rural areas, where they became farmers who saw no practical utility in formal education. Their lack of interest in formal schooling was also based on their emphasis on DISCIPLESHIP over doctrine, their NONCONFORMITY to the broader culture, and their understanding of the scriptural admonition that "the wisdom of this world is foolishness with God" (I Cor. 3:19).

The Anabaptist theology of the priesthood of all believers meant that lay people were responsible for reading the Bible and understanding it sufficiently to respond to it and to share it. In this context, congregations selected self-educated ministers from their own ranks who were not formally or specifically educated for the ministry.

Formal HIGHER EDUCATION was often discouraged or even prohibited by many Anabaptist groups, except in the Netherlands. As Dutch Anabaptists became more assimilated, they sought higher education, and they established the first MENNONITE seminary in Europe in 1735. In the late 1800s, Mennonites in Russia sent some young people to study at Russian and European universities, and they also created secondary schools in Mennonite colonies.

In North America some Anabaptist groups began to create church-related educational INSTITUTIONS in the late 1800s. They founded BRETHREN and Mennonite secondary schools and colleges to prepare young people for a wide variety of vocations while still maintaining their Anabaptist identity. About a dozen small Anabaptist-related colleges, universities, and seminaries operate in the 21st century. Some of them are closely related to the church, but others have only a weak association with a denominational body and serve mostly non-Anabaptist students. Church-related colleges, universities, and graduate schools contribute Anabaptist perspectives on a wide variety of academic disciplines and have made significant contributions to the life of the church.

TRADITIONAL GROUPS generally operate their own elementary and secondary schools, but do not encourage or even permit higher education. OLD ORDER MENNONITES and the AMISH, as well as many HUTTERITE colonies, terminate formal education at the eighth grade. A 1972 U.S. Supreme Court decision, *Wisconsin v. Yoder,* granted the Amish and other Old Order groups permission to end formal schooling at age 14. In the late 1960s, informal understandings with the Ontario government permitted the operation of parochial schools with Old Order teachers in that Canadian province. Some traditional groups operate Bible schools or short-term institutes to provide biblical and religious instruction for members and leaders.

See also Anabaptism, Theology of; Schools, Bible; Schools, Elementary; Schools, Secondary; Theological Education

C. Bowman (1995), GAMEO ("Christian Education"), D. Martin (2003), ME V ("Christian Education," "Education"), Weaver-Zercher (2002)

Elder

This term, *Ältester* in German, has been applied to the highest office of ordained ministry among some ANABAPTIST groups. It is especially used by TRADITIONAL GROUPS that emigrated from RUSSIA (some traditional MENNONITES and the HUTTERITES), while groups with Swiss–south German origins (AMISH) use the English term BISHOP for this office.

The elder may perform all the functions of ministry, and among some traditional groups certain ORDINANCES, such as communion, can only be conducted by the elder. Among the OLD GERMAN BAPTIST BRETHREN, the presiding elder, often the oldest of several elders, coordinates the LOVE FEASTS, baptisms, and installation of ministers.

In general, traditional groups have retained this office. In many ASSIMILATED GROUPS the role of elder or bishop declined with the rise of seminary-trained, salaried pastors or was transformed into an overseer and/or leader of a cluster of pastors.

BE I ("Elder"), GAMEO ("Elder [Ältester]"), Krahn (1956), ME II ("Elder"), Paton Yoder (1991)

Elderly

In TRADITIONAL GROUPS such as the AMISH and the HUTTERITES, older persons are granted special respect and authority. They are typically cared for in the homes of their children or other relatives rather than in RETIREMENT COMMUNITIES. Rather than retiring at a set age, most traditional ANABAPTISTS, often self-employed, decrease their work load gradually. In many traditional groups a couple will begin active retirement by passing a farm or business to one of their children when they reach age 50. The semiretired couple may create a new BUSINESS and/or help their adult children on a farm or business.

Anabaptists in ASSIMILATED GROUPS have generally followed mainstream retirement trends. In the 20th century, MENNONITE and BRETHREN groups created a number of INSTITUTIONS for the elderly, including nursing homes and retirement centers. Many of these facilities have a large percentage of residents who come from non-Anabaptist groups.

BE II ("Retirement Homes"), GAMEO ("Aged, Care for," "Homes, Retirement and Nursing"), J. Hostetler (1993), ME V ("Aged, Care for," "Homes, Retirement and Nursing"), Stone (1987)

Electricity

Most ANABAPTIST groups permit full access to electricity. However, the AMISH and some very conservative MENNONITE groups restrict and regulate their members' use of electricity from the public grid. Groups that restrict access do so because their religious convictions dictate that the church should be separate from the world and not conform to the values of the larger society. In their view, easy access to electricity from the public grid would encourage modern conveniences and connections to mass media, such as television and COMPUTERS, which would open their communities to negative influences from the outside culture.

The electricity-restricting groups usually permit the use of 12-volt electricity from batteries but do not permit tapping 110-volt current from public utilities. Many small battery-powered devices, such as hand tools, flashlights, clocks, and lights on buggies are allowed. Some groups permit the use of inverters to convert 12-volt from batteries into 110-volt to power small electronic devices such as copiers, word processors, scales, and cash registers. Other groups permit the use of on-site generators powered by small diesel engines to generate electricity. Solar panels are increasingly used to generate electricity. Propane gas, naphtha gas, kerosene, gasoline, wind, and wood provide alternative energy power for lighting and heating in lieu of electricity from the public grid. Many Amish groups permit the use of pneumatic (air) and hydraulic (oil) devices to operate the state-of-the-art machinery in their manufacturing and woodworking shops.

See also Technology

BE I ("Electricity"), Kraybill (2001), Scott and Pellman (1990)

Elementary Schools   *See* Schools, Elementary

El Salvador

In 1968, relations between El Salvador and Honduras became strained when Hondurans began to object to the many illegal Salvadoran immigrants in their country. Tensions flared dramatically in June 1969 when the soccer teams from both countries met in a three-game elimination match leading up to the World Cup. Interactions between the fans became vicious, and violence broke out against Salvadorans throughout Honduras. Tens of thousands of Salvadorans fled Honduras, and an unknown number were killed. On July 14, 1969, El Salvador invaded Honduras, which initiated the so-called Soccer War.

Some of the Salvadorans who fled had become members of MENNONITE churches in Honduras, and they eventually formed a national Mennonite conference, the Evangelical Mennonite Church of El Salvador, which has 425 members in 11 congregations.

A second ANABAPTIST group, the Evangelical Mennonite Church, was begun by the BEACHY AMISH MENNONITES. Several Beachy Amish service and development workers started an agricultural aid project in El Salvador in 1962 under Amish Mennonite Aid sponsorship. A church eventually emerged as a result of a social service project that included an orphanage, and evangelization efforts have produced 10 congregations with about 200 members. In addition, the CHURCH OF GOD IN CHRIST, MENNONITE denomination has three congregations (about 25 members) and several mission outposts, as well as a gospel tract distribution center in the country. The CHURCH OF THE BRETHREN has had occasional Brethren Volunteer Service workers in El Salvador since the 1980s.

In 1981, MENNONITE CENTRAL COMMITTEE (MCC) began assisting victims of El Salvador's civil war. Throughout the war, MCC personnel worked in various areas affected by the conflict and aided local churches. After the 1992 ceasefire, MCC staff created a peacebuilding program to heal communities scarred by the violence. Following two devastating earthquakes in 2001, MCC contributed nearly $1 million to rebuild homes for some 3,000 people. MCC funds the construction of concrete-block houses, the construction of rainwater storage tanks, and sustainable-agriculture training in several rural communities. The organization also supports HIV/AIDS prevention education and counseling, mental health education and care, and conflict resolution training for El Salvadoran organizations and government officials.

GAMEO ("El Salvador"), ME V ("El Salvador"), Mennonite World Conference (2005), http://www .mwc-cmm.org

Emigration   *See* Migration

Engel, Jacob (1753–1833)

Engel, who came to North America as an immigrant child of a Swiss MENNONITE mother, is considered the founder of the River Brethren (later known as the BRETHREN IN CHRIST) of eastern Pennsylvania in the late 1770s. Engel, eventually the first bishop of the group, was one of eight who signed a confession of faith that showed influences of the revivalist and PIETIST movements prominent in Pennsylvania at the time. Although six of the leaders had ethnic Mennonite names, the movement also borrowed the following practices from their BRETHREN neighbors, the German Baptist Brethren (later CHURCH OF THE BRETHREN): the LOVE FEAST, trine (threefold) immersion, the BEARD, the election of ministers rather than the casting of lots, and an annual visit to each member's home by deacons. Engel's group performed trine immersion baptisms in streams, but their name (River Brethren) derived from the fact that they were known as the Brethren who lived near the Susquehanna River (in western Lancaster County). By 1788, members of the group had settled in Canada where they became known as Tunkers, a derivative of the German word *tunken* (to dip), which referred to their mode of baptism. Several groups in the 21st century—the Brethren in Christ, the United Zion Church, the Old Order River Brethren—trace their religious lineage to the Engel group that formed in the 1770s.

GAMEO ("Engel, Jacob [1753–1833]"), ME V ("Engel, Jacob"), Ruth (2001), Wittlinger (1978)

English Language

When German-speaking ANABAPTIST groups immigrated to British North America in the late 1600s, they found themselves immersed in an English-speaking society. These German-speaking immigrants gradually became proficient in English, but their ability varied widely by region, time period, and individual. Many of the German-speaking Anabaptists lived in German speaking-communities and regions and did not shift to English until the last half of the 19th century.

Successive waves of German-speaking Anabaptist immigrants arrived in Canada and the United States in the 1800s and 1900s. Three significant periods of MENNONITE emigration from POLAND/Prussia and RUSSIA occurred in the 1870s, the 1920s, and the 1940s and 1950s. These new immigrants reinvigorated church activities and daily life with German culture, but despite this cultural influx, many of the immigrant Mennonites had shifted to English by the early 21st century.

The transition to English often stirred controversy and division among Anabaptist groups because the identity of some churches was wedded to GERMAN LANGUAGE and culture. LANGUAGE differences heightened generational tensions. Biblical, devotional, and hymnological resources in German became irrelevant for younger generations. Some schisms occurred due to conflicts over the growing use of English. The language transition was one of several factors that prompted the emergence of the OLD ORDER MOVEMENT between 1870 and 1910 because the Old Orders favored the German language.

Most ASSIMILATED GROUPS in the United States and Canada speak only English in their daily lives, but some TRADITIONAL GROUPS in these two countries still speak a German or Swiss DIALECT in their everyday discourse. Many OLD COLONY MENNONITES and similar Low-German-speaking groups in Belize and Mexico speak Spanish when conversing with outsiders. The AMISH, HUTTERITES, and some traditional Mennonites use German-related dialects for worship services, while other conservative Mennonites use English. The groups that speak a German dialect also learn English in order to communicate with outsiders for business and other activities. The Low German dialect (*Plautdietsch*) survives among some Mennonite groups with Dutch-Russian roots in Canada, Belize, Mexico, and the United States.

Scholarship on Anabaptist groups has most typically been written in German, DUTCH, French, and English. These are also the primary languages used at MENNONITE WORLD CONFERENCE gatherings. More recently Spanish has become an important language for Mennonites as the number of Spanish-speaking congregations continues to grow in both North and SOUTH AMERICA. Asian immigrants who have joined Anabaptist churches in Canada and the United States speak a variety of languages in their homes and churches, in addition to English.

GAMEO ("English Language"), Ediger (2001), ME II ("English"), Scheer (1980)

Entertainment   *See* Leisure

Entrepreneurs

Entrepreneurs in ANABAPTIST communities whose businesses operate in a capitalist economy often face tensions between their faith commitments and the demands for success in the marketplace. The Anabaptist theological tradition grounded in the teachings of Jesus carries critiques of materialism, WEALTH, greed, cutthroat competition, and LITIGATION. In contrast, the tradition values simplicity, humility, stewardship, honesty, MUTUAL AID within the church community, and service to others beyond the church. These religious values often conflict with the ethics, tactics, and strategies necessary to advance in the corporate world. Many successful Anabaptist entrepreneurs have found creative ways to negotiate the tensions between their faith and the complexities of the capitalist market economy. Other Anabaptist businesspeople have drifted away from the church or joined non-Anabaptist churches that are more comfortable with mainstream values and the corporate business ethos.

Anabaptist entrepreneurs range from small BUSINESS owners to CEOs of large corporations. In Old Order communities, thousands of entrepreneurs have been remarkably successful operating small businesses despite church restrictions on their use of technology. One U.S. study found the rate of AMISH business failures to be under 10%, compared with a small business failure rate of over 65% nationwide. Members of other TRADITIONAL GROUPS also have found success in the business world.

Among ASSIMILATED GROUPS, entrepreneurs typically do not face technological restrictions from their churches, but they may face challenges trying to operate a corporation or professional agency in ways that are consistent with their Christian ethical commitments. Many successful entrepreneurs have contributed generously of their wealth and resources to support church-related institutions as well as their local congregations.

Several factors may explain the success of Anabaptist entrepreneurs. Many see themselves as stewards of God's resources with a responsibility to use the resources in ways that serve others. Some business owners, one or two generations from the farm, retain a rigorous work ethic that facilitates the profitability of their enterprises. Simplicity and frugality rather than extravagance are values that can also increase profitability. Honesty, integrity, SERVICE, and product quality that reflect Christian values are also valued in the marketplace. Strong involvement from extended families and members of the church community also contribute to the success of entrepreneurs.

See also Economics; Mennonite Economic Development Associates

Kraybill and Nolt (2004), C. Kreider (1980), Redekop, Ainlay, and Siemens (1995), C. Redekop and B. Redekop (1996)

Environment

Some of the earliest ANABAPTISTS in Europe lived in cities, but PERSECUTION in the 16th century pushed many of them into rural areas. As farmers, they developed a strong attachment to the land and its care. Immigrants to the New World who continued the agrarian tradition felt a special affinity with the created order. A new environmental consciousness that encompassed the larger created order emerged in the last quarter of the 20th century. Reflecting this new ecological concern, several Anabaptist groups issued statements on the responsibility of church members to care for the earth.

In 1971, Annual Conference of the CHURCH OF THE BRETHREN issued a statement on ecology, followed by resolutions in 1973 from the denomination's General Board on strip mining and the energy crisis. Annual Conference again spoke in 1991 in a statement entitled "Creation: Called to Care," which urged church members to be stewards and partners in God's continuing creation. The statement noted that Christian ecology and stewardship involve doing God's will in caring for the earth with respect while striving to preserve and restore its integrity, stability, and beauty.

The MENNONITE CHURCH issued a statement, "Stewardship of the Earth," in 1989. This was followed in 1994 by one from MENNONITE CENTRAL COMMITTEE, "Stewards of God's Creation." In addition, the 1995 Mennonite Confession of Faith notes that the biblical view of peace embraces personal peace with God, peace in human relations, peace among nations, and peace with God's creation.

To support their environmental efforts, many Anabaptist advocates of environmental care cite biblical teachings: God's creation is good (Gen. 1), God owns the earth (Ps. 24:1–2), nature itself praises and glorifies God (Pss. 19 and 96), among others. Additional Scriptures suggest that people of faith, as God's stewards, should care for the natural creation (Gen. 1:26–28, Exod. 20:8–11, Lev. 25 and 26, Luke 4:16–22). The emphasis on simplicity by many Anabaptist groups has encouraged their members to avoid highly consumptive lifestyles that excessively deplete nonrenewable resources. *Creation and the Environment: An Anabaptist Perspective on a Sustain-*

able World offers an assortment of scholarly essays on Anabaptist understandings of creation, ecology, and sustainability. Several cookbooks—*More-with-Less Cookbook, Simply in Season, Simply in Season Children's Cookbook*—offer recipes and suggestions that support sustainability and environmental care.

Although the official church statements declare Anabaptist views on the importance of Christian stewardship of all creation, the actual practice of members varies considerably—in areas such as recycling, energy-efficient housing, solar energy, and energy-efficient vehicles. Some people support the Mennonite Creation Care Network (MCCN), a binational Christian organization affiliated with MENNONITE CHURCH USA and MENNONITE CHURCH CANADA. The movement encourages people to claim the theological teachings on caring for creation, discover the ties that link all created beings together, and act faithfully to restore the earth. Similarly, the New Community Project encourages BRETHREN to live more sustainably and more fairly with all people.

About 85% of Mennonite Church USA, Church of the Brethren, and BRETHREN IN CHRIST members in the United States reported in a survey (CMP 2006) that living a simple lifestyle is important to them, and some 75% said that they regularly recycle used materials.

Beach and Kauffman (2006), CMP 2006, Lind and Hockman-Wert (2005), R. Loewen (2005), Longacre (1976), C. Redekop (2000), http://www.cobannual conference.org/ac_statements/91Creation.htm, http://www.mcusa-archives.org/library/resolutions/ stewardshipoftheearth.html, http://www.mennocre ationcare.org, http://www.newcommunityproject.org

Ephrata Cloister

After a bitter division from the German Baptist Brethren in 1728, Conrad Beissel (1691–1768), a charismatic leader, founded an independent Protestant monastic community in Pennsylvania that became known as Ephrata Cloister.

Beissel, born in Eberbach, GERMANY, was orphaned at a young age. He was influenced by Radical PIETISM and eventually immigrated to Pennsylvania in 1720 for religious freedom. He had intended to join a community of solitary hermits, but when he arrived in Pennsylvania he found that the community had disintegrated. Instead, Beissel became apprenticed to BRETHREN leader PETER BECKER (1687–1758), and in 1724 he was baptized and became the leader of the Conestoga (Pennsylvania) congregation.

In 1728 Beissel split with the Brethren. He formed the communal experiment at Ephrata in 1732. Members came from Brethren, MENNONITE, and other religious backgrounds. The community of men and women was based on the mystical theology of Jacob Boehme (1575–1624), with an emphasis on celibacy, self-denial, Saturday worship, and extensive printing. By 1750 the community had 300 members, divided into three groups: celibate women ("sisters"), celibate men ("brothers"), and families ("householders") who lived in farmhouses scattered near the celibate residences. In 1748–1749, with the support of Pennsylvania Mennonites, celibate members translated and printed a German edition of the 1,290-page MARTYRS MIRROR—the largest book printed in colonial North America.

Some Cloister rituals followed classic Brethren practices: LOVE FEAST, FOOTWASHING, and BAPTISM by trine immersion. Beissel wrote many unique hymns and essays. The community was the first group in Pennsylvania to create fraktur, a decorative calligraphy. The community ended in 1934, and the Ephrata site, with its remaining buildings of distinctive architecture, eventually became a Pennsylvania state museum.

Bach (2003), BE I ("Beissel, Johann Conrad," "Ephrata Community"), GAMEO ("Martyrs' Mirror"), ME III ("Martyrs Mirror"), http://www.ephratacloister.org

Ethics

Discerning how to live according to God's will has been a central concern of ANABAPTIST groups from their beginnings. The desire to faithfully practice obedient DISCIPLESHIP as described in the New Testament, especially in the teachings of Jesus in the SERMON ON THE MOUNT (Matt. 5–7), has influenced Anabaptist thinking about personal and social ethics. Churches encourage individuals to be obedient disciples of Jesus, sharing God's love in the church and the world.

In various modes and in different time periods, churches have developed ORDINANCES and guidelines for proper ethical behavior. In TRADITIONAL GROUPS, members who violate the behavioral standards without remorse may face DISCIPLINE and EXCOMMUNICATION, depending on the circumstance.

Anabaptist groups have been criticized for emphasizing behavior rather than articulating their spirituality. However, these groups affirm the New Testament's assertion that faith without works is dead (James 2:20). Anabaptist theologians contend that confessing Jesus as Lord should produce ethical "fruits" (values and behavior) of righteousness in daily life. Guy F. Hershberger's (1896–1989) writings on various topics related to Christian social ethics were influential in shaping MENNONITE thinking in the United States in the mid-20th century. John Howard Yoder (1927–1997) played a key role in communicating Anabaptist ethical perspectives to ecumenical audiences.

Traditional groups continue to emphasize cultural forms of dress and other separatist ethical behavior, while many ASSIMILATED GROUPS have fewer distinctive ethical standards for their congregations and members.

See also Theology

M. Augsburger (1990), BE I ("Ethics"), Kraybill (2003b), Rogers (1988), T. Schlabach (2009), J. Weaver (1997), J. H. Yoder (1984b)

Ethnicity

Members of ethnic groups view themselves as having a common ancestry related to religion, culture, LANGUAGE, country of origin, skin color, or any combination of these factors. Those outside an ethnic group perceive and treat members of the group based on their affiliation with the group. Ethnic groups typically share cultural customs related to DIALECT, dress, food, holidays, and many other facets related to their unique IDENTITY.

Within the ANABAPTIST world, there is a variety of ethnic group identity wedded to language, cultural background, skin color, and country of origin. Many subgroups have an ethnic affinity with their country of origin. Examples include members with Chinese, Korean, Japanese, African, Dutch, and Swiss cultural origins. In North America dozens of regional and national identities shape the psychological and social identities of Anabaptist subgroups.

Some church groups are strongly formed by a particular ethno-religious tradition. The membership of the NATIONAL EVANGELICAL GUATEMALAN MENNONITE CHURCH, for example, is mostly comprised of people from a K'ekchi' ethnic background. Many of the TRADITIONAL GROUPS in the United States reflect Swiss-German or Dutch-Russian cultural influences. Some MENNONITES in ASSIMILATED GROUPS in the United States and Canada also have many members with either Swiss-German or Dutch-Russian ethnic ties.

Anabaptists in North America speak more than a dozen different languages. Nevertheless, a U.S. survey (CMP 2006) found that the majority of CHURCH OF THE BRETHREN, BRETHREN IN CHRIST, and MENNONITE CHURCH USA members self-identified as white-Caucasian.

The multitude and complexity of ethnic subgroups influence the beliefs and behaviors of members and shape the politics of cooperative ventures within church bodies, especially those primarily composed of one ethnic group. Church-related associations based on ethnic, cultural, and racial identities provide avenues of ethnic-based fellowship, as well as political vehicles to voice concerns about RACISM and ethnic discrimination to official church bodies.

CMP 2006, Juhnke (1988), Kanagy (2007), Kraybill (1988), Redekop and Steiner (1988)

Eucharist   *See* Communion

Europe

ANABAPTISM originated in SWITZERLAND, the NETHERLANDS, and GERMANY during the early 1500s. In 1708 in Schwarzenau, Germany, a handful of illegal adult BAPTISMS took place in the Eder River, signaling the beginning of numerous BRETHREN groups. Most of the first Anabaptist groups spoke DIALECTS related to GERMAN and DUTCH. Though Swiss Anabaptists and Dutch Anabaptists held many similar theological beliefs, such as baptism only for adults and no direct political leadership in society, the Swiss emphasized the separation of the church from society, and the Dutch, by contrast, were more willing to engage the larger society. PERSECUTION in the 1500s resulted in MIGRATION within Europe. Especially after the Thirty Years War (1618–1648), persecution in certain European locations caused some regional rulers to invite Anabaptists to immigrate to their territories in order to rebuild and stimulate the economy.

Until 1900, persecution, migration (for reasons other than persecution), and MISSION efforts spread Anabaptism outside Europe, especially to Canada, Russia, and the United States. Although the pacifist MENNONITES tended to live at the periphery of power in the major political and intellectual centers, the impact of nationalism, Enlightenment thought, PIETISM, and wars influenced Anabaptist church life and beliefs. For example, in the 1800s, Dutch Mennonites shed many of their distinctive theological and cultural traits. However, a renewal movement in the early 1900s among a small group of Dutch Mennonites encouraged Bible study, biblical pacifism, and abstinence from alcohol.

Mennonites in European Russia experienced rapid growth in the 19th century and quick disintegration in the 20th under the brutal impact of Soviet communism.

In Germany during the 1800s, Mennonites gradually escaped their status as a legally restricted minority; they were accepted by their neighbors and accorded equal political status. In many congregations the belief in biblical pacifism and nonparticipation in the military disappeared. By the 1930s most German Mennonites supported or acquiesced to National Socialism, although some harbored suspicion toward Hitler's policies. At the end of WORLD WAR II all Mennonite congregations in POLAND/Prussia were dissolved during the invasion of the Soviet army, though some Mennonites managed to flee west to existing Mennonite congregations, also often devastated by the war.

In the repressive atmosphere of the Soviet Union, some Russians of Mennonite German descent joined Baptist churches after 1944. From 1951 to 2004, Germany accepted about 2.3 million Soviet citizens of German descent as immigrants, and it is estimated that about 12% (ca. 275,000) had connections to Mennonite or Baptist churches that Mennonites had joined in Russia. With natural growth and new converts, the number with Russian-Mennonite ties in modern Germany is about 340,000, though some are not members of Mennonite churches. Fewer than 1,000 members known as Mennonites remain in the former Soviet Union.

WORLD WAR I and World War II caused great suffering and some distrust among European Mennonites. Complex and pressing needs for material relief after World War II brought North American relief workers from MENNONITE CENTRAL COMMITTEE and missionaries from various North American Mennonite denominations to Europe. They helped European Mennonites to recover economically and spiritually, and the Europeans were energized by a renewed Anabaptist vision and the creation of a Bible school at Bienenberg near Basel, Switzerland, supported by French, Swiss, and German Mennonites. Eventually the European Mennonites developed their own mission strategies, in cooperation with the European Mennonite Evangelization Committee.

In the early 21st century, Mennonites in Switzerland, Germany, FRANCE, and the Netherlands have a small presence in a secularized culture in which Christianity has been increasingly demoted to the sphere of the individual. The proportion of Europeans in the Anabaptist world has dropped greatly. AMISH, Brethren, and HUTTERITES no longer live in Europe. Since 1950, Mennonite and Brethren churches have been growing rapidly in AFRICA, SOUTH AMERICA, and ASIA, while the number of Men-

nonites in Europe has declined. European Mennonite churches report a baptized membership
of about 64,500, a small percentage (4%) of the
worldwide figure of about 1.6 million Mennonites and BRETHREN IN CHRIST. Some Anabaptist European mission organizations have
planted congregations in European countries
outside the four countries with an Anabaptist
presence since the 16th century. The activities
of the European Mennonite Regional Conference have revitalized the Anabaptist peace
witness in its personal and social dimensions in
various countries.

See also Anabaptism, History of

C. Dyck (1993), GAMEO ("Europe"), Lapp and
Snyder (2006b), Lichdi and Kreider (1990), ME II ("Europe"), J. B. Toews (1982), http://www.mwc-cmm.org

Evangelicalism

As a 20th-century movement, evangelicalism
comprises a diverse set of Christian beliefs and
practices that has influenced many ASSIMI-
LATED GROUPS in the ANABAPTIST world. It
typically includes an emphasis on biblical authority; EVANGELISM, inviting non-Christians
to accept Jesus Christ as their personal Savior;
and REVIVALISM, revitalizing those within
the church by encouraging them to renew and
strengthen their faith and practice. Congregational revival meetings welcome both members
and outsiders, thus blending revivalism and
evangelism.

Evangelicalism shares some characteristics
with Anabaptism, PIETISM, and FUNDAMEN-
TALISM, but it also has different connotations in
substance and in its association with different
time periods and geographical areas. All four
theological perspectives emphasize a personal
and living faith in Jesus Christ, the inspiration
and authority of the Bible, right ethical behavior, and witnessing to nonbelievers with the
intention of conversion.

Anabaptism refers to the religious movement that began with the Reformation of the
early 1500s in Europe as an attempt to restore
the New Testament church. Pietism, with Protestant origins, emerged in Europe in the 1600s.

Fundamentalism refers to the reaction of some
conservative North American Christians, between 1875 to 1925, to the challenges of Darwinian evolution, historical criticism of the Bible,
and psychological explanations of religious
experience. Contemporary evangelicalism took
shape in North America during and after World
War II. Although it shared some basic theological continuity with fundamentalism, it was less
suspicious of wider culture, less individualistic
in ethics, less futuristic in eschatology, and
less exclusive in relating to other Christian
groups.

TRADITIONAL GROUPS do not identify with
evangelicalism. They see the church as a visibly
separated community and hesitate to embrace
missionary calls to aggressively convert and incorporate nonbelievers in their churches. Traditional groups also forbid or discourage political
participation and ecumenical efforts, and they
are uncomfortable with the patriotic and nationalistic themes often embraced by American
evangelicalism.

Assimilated groups display a wide range of
attitudes and behavior toward evangelicalism.
The MENNONITE BRETHREN, BRETHREN IN
CHRIST, and the BRETHREN CHURCH, as well
as many congregations within the CHURCH OF
THE BRETHREN, are aligned with contemporary
evangelical practices, attitudes, and national
organizations such as the National Association
or Evangelicals and Evangelical Fellowship of
Canada. Other congregations and some leaders
in these denominations oppose a close align-
ment with evangelicalism for fear it will erode
some classic Anabaptist values such as PEACE-
MAKING, DISCIPLESHIP, and the rejection of
nationalism.

To the degree that both traditional and assimilated groups emphasize biblical PACIFISM,
they encounter resistance from evangelicalism,
which often supports patriotic nationalism and
military participation. To the degree that assimilated groups emphasize the believer's religious
status as dependent on the church community
and expect the church to model the present
and coming kingdom of God, they encounter

resistance from evangelicalism, which generally stresses only the individual believer's relationship with God and often relegates the ethics of God's kingdom to a future age.

When evangelicals explore the theological implications of caring for God's creation, the Christian's attitude toward ameliorating the plight of the poor, and questions of SOCIAL JUSTICE, some assimilated Anabaptists identify with and participate more readily in evangelicalism. Indicative of such activity is the leadership of some Anabaptists in the Council for Christian Colleges and Universities and in Evangelicals for Social Action.

See also Ecumenism

C. Bowman (1995), GAMEO ("Evangelicalism"), Kraus (1979), Lehman (2002), ME V ("Evangelicalism")

Evangelical Mennonite Conference

With Russian roots and formerly known as the Kleine Gemeinde ("small church"), this church emerged from a renewal movement among Low German–speaking MENNONITES in southern RUSSIA in 1812. Concerns about educational control and objection to military service prompted the church to migrate to North America in 1874–1875. The group selected the name Evangelical Mennonite Church in 1952 and then adopted the name Evangelical Mennonite Conference in 1959. Based in Steinbach, Manitoba, the conference spans five Canadian provinces and is organized into nine regions. Steinbach Bible College educates many of the group's ministers, missionaries, and laity. The cultural makeup of the conference is growing diverse, although its Low German roots remain visible. About one-third of the congregations have leaders from other cultural backgrounds. Committed to nonviolence and mission efforts, the group embraces both an evangelical and an ANABAPTIST identity. It supports several educational programs and cooperates with numerous inter-Mennonite agencies. Some 7,000 members worship in about 60 congregations, with the majority in Manitoba. The conference has about 150 outreach workers in 25 countries. It has daughter churches organized as national autonomous conferences in Mexico, with 850 members in 16 congregations, and in Nicaragua, with 2,300 members in 32 congregations.

See also Kanadier Mennonites

GAMEO ("Evangelical Mennonite Conference [Kleine Gemeinde]"), http://www.emconf.ca/

Evangelical Mennonite Mission Conference

Ancestors of this group were part of a migration from Russia to Manitoba in the 1870s. Based in Winnipeg, the group began in 1937 as a revivalist, evangelical division from the more traditional Sommerfeld Mennonite Church. It adopted the name Evangelical Mennonite Mission Conference in 1959. The majority (16) of its 27 congregations (4,300 members) are located in Manitoba. Some congregations still use German in their church services. The group has been active in mission work among OLD COLONY MENNONITES in Belize and Mexico and among those who returned to Canada from Mexico. It has four congregations in the United States with about 400 members and three in Belize with some 480 members.

GAMEO ("Evangelical Mennonite Mission Conference [EMMC]"), Heppner (1987), http://www.emmc .ca/

Evangelism

By its very nature and in order to survive, the BELIEVERS CHURCH must encourage adults to voluntarily commit themselves to JESUS CHRIST as their Lord and Savior. As a voluntary church chosen freely by adult members, ANABAPTISTS in the early 1500s grew through evangelism, even in the face of PERSECUTION. However, some Swiss Anabaptist groups became isolated countercultures, dependent solely on internal growth when MARTYRDOM and sustained repression by civil and religious authorities stifled evangelism in the mid-1600s. Similarly, in order to immigrate into specific territories in RUSSIA in the 1800s, some Anabaptist groups had to agree not to evangelize indigenous peoples.

In sharp contrast, the German Baptist

Brethren, who were evangelistic in Europe, dramatically increased their membership through evangelism after they reorganized in Pennsylvania in 1723. Their vigorous evangelistic preaching tours triggered a 20-fold increase in their membership (from fewer than 100 members to more than 2,200) in about 40 years in colonial America.

In the late 1800s, assimilated European and North American MENNONITES and BRETHREN accepted REVIVALISM in their local CONGREGATIONS and began foreign MISSIONS. In the 1900s this mission outreach increased the international spread of Mennonites and Brethren, especially in AFRICA and ASIA.

By the mid-1900s some Mennonites and Brethren were engaged in full-scale evangelistic campaigns. Contemporary evangelistic efforts use a variety of methods to explain the Christian gospel and to establish new churches as well as to welcome new members into existing churches. The amount of support and interest in evangelism varies considerably among assimilated Anabaptist denominations and congregations. In a recent survey in the United States (CMP 2006), over 60% of MENNONITE CHURCH USA members and 78% of BRETHREN IN CHRIST members completely agreed that Christians should do all they can to convert nonbelievers to Christ. Over 43% of CHURCH OF THE BRETHREN members agreed that evangelizing nonbelievers is very important in their personal faith commitments, and 46% thought that the church should place more emphasis on evangelism. Most of the ASSIMILATED GROUPS have organized mission agencies to coordinate evangelism efforts in North America and around the world. However, most members of assimilated churches believe that these mission agencies should combine evangelism and social service.

Many TRADITIONAL GROUPS emphasize NONCONFORMITY more than evangelism in their witness to and understanding of the Christian faith. They believe that the quality of their life in community should be a countercultural witness to the rest of the world. Some of these groups believe that evangelism emphasizes individualistic, subjective, and emotional expressions of faith that they consider dangerous to the stability and preservation of their community. Although they accept new members from the outside, their cultural, linguistic, and religious traditions make it challenging for outsiders to join.

M. Augsburger (1983), BE I ("Evangelism"), CMP 2006, D. Durnbaugh (1997a), GAMEO ("Evangelism"), ME II ("Evangelism"), ME V ("Evangelism"), H. Schmidt (1986)

Everence

This MUTUAL AID organization, formerly known as Mennonite Mutual Aid and then MMA, was founded in 1945 in northern Indiana as a way for MENNONITES to share financial burdens and support the stewardship of material resources. It started by offering loans to church service volunteers. Since then this tax-exempt charitable corporation has grown rapidly and added numerous related services, which provide health INSURANCE, automobile insurance, casualty and property insurance, life insurance, long-term care insurance, investment management, estate management, annuities, loans for church buildings, pension plans, charitable programs, and educational resources on stewardship. Originally developed within the MENNONITE CHURCH, Everence now serves church members, congregations, businesses, and related institutions from 25 ANABAPTIST-related denominations in the United States as well as a broader audience of people who want to integrate faith and finance.

Everence has over $1.6 billion in assets and disburses some $40 million to church-related programs annually through the MENNONITE FOUNDATION. These figures reflect the growing wealth of Anabaptist groups in the early 21st century.

In contrast to most secular insurance and investment companies, Everence gives outright grants for various needs to its constituents and congregations; these grants total about $3 million per year. Everence uses underwriting guidelines that are more inclusive and flexible than those of comparable secular insurance companies, as well as investment guidelines that reflect careful stewardship and social responsibility.

GAMEO ("Mennonite Mutual Aid"), ME V ("Mennonite Mutual Aid"), T. Schlabach (2009), Swartley and Kraybill (1998), http://www.mma-online.org

Evolution

The views of Darwinian evolution held by ANABAPTISTS reflect their theological worldviews. Anabaptists with a more conservative view of the Bible reject all understandings of evolution and subscribe to a literal six-day creation as reported in Genesis. Those with a less literal view of Scripture and a scientific view of the world emphasize God's role in creation and hold various views of how evolution may have occurred and of God's role in the process.

TRADITIONAL GROUPS reject evolution and see belief in it as an example of the moral decay and secular values typical of the larger unregenerate society. Some Old Order groups do not teach science in their private schools, explaining that they do not want their children exposed to evolution (thus equating it with science).

The influence of FUNDAMENTALISM in the 1920s and 1930s shaped heated discussions about faith and evolution, particularly on the campuses of colleges operated by or affiliated with Anabaptist churches. Some of these colleges have taught a theistic view of evolution since the early 20th century. In the last half of the century the science faculty of most of the Anabaptist-affiliated colleges taught some type of theistic evolution that emphasized both God's role in creation and God's hand in evolution.

Education levels are typically associated with views of evolution among the members of many Anabaptist groups. In general, the higher the level of education, the greater the acceptance of theistic evolution.

A survey (CMP 2006) of CHURCH OF THE BRETHREN, BRETHREN IN CHRIST, and MENNONITE CHURCH USA members in the United States found that two-thirds or more believe that God created human beings in their present form at creation. By contrast, the view that God created life and then guided the emergence of humans over millions of years was supported by 21% of BRETHREN, 11% of Brethren in Christ, and 22% of MENNONITE survey respondents.

BE I ("Evolution"), CMP 2006, GAMEO ("Evolution"), ME V ("Evolution")

Excommunication

This historic ANABAPTIST practice of excluding a member from church fellowship is based on Jesus' instructions for dealing with sin (Matt. 5:29–30, 18:15–20) as well as the advice of the Apostle Paul (Gal. 5:19–21, Titus 3:10, I Cor. 5:1–5, 6:9–10). Early Anabaptists taught that church DISCIPLINE sometimes required excluding a disobedient member from the church community. The process of discipline outlined in Matthew's Gospel (18:15–20) may lead to excommunication if the offender is unwilling to repent. This biblical passage and process is the central text in understanding church discipline in Anabaptist churches.

According to Anabaptist theology, the church is a visible community of committed adult members—a BELIEVERS CHURCH—that spiritually represents the body of Christ. Therefore, in order to maintain the purity of Christ's body and the integrity of baptismal vows, members who violate the teachings of the Scriptures and the church should be confronted about their sin, and asked to confess their errors and amend their ways if they want to continue as members. Members who refuse to repent and change their behavior may face excommunication. The goal of excommunication, according to biblical teaching, is to inspire repentance and to restore a sinner into full membership.

Excommunication is termination of membership. Some Anabaptist churches believed that ex-members should thereafter be excluded or shunned from some aspects of church life and social interaction according to the teaching of the Apostle Paul. MENNO SIMONS (1496–1561), the influential Anabaptist leader in the Netherlands from whom MENNONITES take their name, advocated excommunication and SHUN-NING. A debate over shunning was a key point of contention in the church division in the 1690s in Switzerland and Alsace that led to the formation of the AMISH.

In the 21st century, Amish, HUTTERITES, and traditional BRETHREN and Mennonites continue to practice excommunication. An ex-member can be restored to membership in the church upon confession of sin. Some Anabaptist groups require a vote of the whole congregation to initiate excommunication as well as to accept the repentant member back into the community, while others give this power to ordained leaders. Groups that practice excommunication typically make extensive efforts to reconcile wayward members before resorting to excommunication.

The use of excommunication typically declines as groups become more assimilated. As they come to accept individualistic interpretations of faith and modern values such as tolerance and pluralism, assimilated churches become reluctant to challenge the behavior of their members. Excommunication is rarely, if ever, practiced by ASSIMILATED GROUPS in the 21st century. Informal discussions or asking an offender to participate in an accountability group may be used, however, as milder forms of church discipline that attempt to rehabilitate wayward members.

BE I ("Avoidance," "Ban," "Disfellowshiping"), GAMEO ("Ban [1953]," "Excommunication"), J. Hostetler (1993, 1997), Kraybill, Nolt, and Weaver-Zercher (2007), ME I ("Ban"), ME II ("Excommunication")

Family

ANABAPTIST teaching emphasizes the importance of the family for nurturing religious values in CHILDREN and raising them to join the church as young adults. Although churches provide various types of educational programs, parents are the ones who carry God-given responsibilities to teach and train their children in Christian values.

The role and size of the nuclear family typically changes as communities become more urbanized. Anabaptist groups reflect the general worldwide pattern that becomes typical as industrialization shrinks not only the size of families but also the economic contribution of children to the family economy.

Families in TRADITIONAL GROUPS are much larger than families in ASSIMILATED GROUPS, and children play a bigger role in the economic welfare of the family. Marriage and having children are highly esteemed values in traditional communities. Men and women typically marry by age 21. The number of single adults is relatively low, and DIVORCE is taboo. Artificial methods of BIRTH CONTROL are discouraged in many traditional groups. Families with 5 to 10 children are common in these groups, which typically live in rural areas where children play an important role in providing labor for the family economy. Children acquire a strong work ethic, frugal values, and practical vocational skills. Some traditional churches frown on women with young children working outside the home. It is impossible to overestimate the influence of the extended family in traditional groups. An individual typically may have 60 to 80 first cousins. Aunts, uncles, and cousins often influence key family decisions and provide assistance when needed. The ELDERLY are typically cared for by their adult children or other relatives, rather than living in RETIREMENT COMMUNITIES.

The family structure of assimilated groups differs dramatically from that of traditional groups; it reflects the familial patterns of North American society in general. Families in assimilated churches are smaller (two or three children) on average, which shrinks the size and influence of the extended family. Because of higher education and professional occupations, nuclear families are more mobile and less connected to grandparents and other members of the extended family. The age of marriage is later—sometimes 25 or older—and more people choose to remain single than is typical in traditional groups. In two-parent families, both parents are more likely to hold jobs outside the family. Divorce and remarriage are acceptable in some assimilated groups. Many of the elderly live in retirement communities, rather than being cared for by their adult children.

See also Demography

Graber Miller (2001), Kauffman and Driedger (1991), Roth (2001), Ziegler (1956)

Family History   *See* Genealogy

Farming   *See* Agriculture

Farm Technology

Variations in farm TECHNOLOGY among ANABAPTISTS largely emerged in the first half of the 20th century with the availability of tractors and mechanized farm equipment. Variations have been driven by religious convictions, but some regional and national differences, related to unique crops and specialized AGRICULTURE, have also produced variations.

Most farmers in ASSIMILATED GROUPS use the same type of farm technology as their non-Anabaptist neighbors. Farmers in some TRADITIONAL GROUPS, especially in Old Order communities, have rejected some forms of modern farm technology or adapted it to fit the rules of their particular church. They associate the technology with modernization and what they see as its potentially harmful effect on families and social relations in small separatist communities.

Many, but not all, AMISH groups use horses or mules for field work, but some do permit tractors or other types of power units at the barn for high-power needs. Some OLD ORDER MENNONITES and Amish place steel wheels on their tractors to inhibit their use as vehicles on public roads. Church leaders fear that rubber tires on tractors would, over time, lead to the use of cars. For the same reason, some Old Order groups prohibit the ownership of self-propelled harvesting equipment or require steel wheels on it. Many Amish farmers adapt commercially manufactured harvesting equipment designed to be powered by tractors by mounting gas engines on the implements and towing them across their fields using horses or mules. Dozens of adaptations of this nature enable Amish farmers to combine horse power with mechanized equipment.

Some traditional groups prohibit the use of computer-controlled equipment in barns or in other aspects of their farming operations. Certain church groups place limits on the size of farming operations to promote small family farming rather then corporate-style agriculture.

The HUTTERITES use state-of-the-art farm equipment that is often very large, because a colony typically farms several thousand acres on prairies. Unique among Anabaptist farming communities, Hutterite colonies own the farm equipment; it is controlled by the community rather than by an individual farmer, as in other groups.

The restrictions on farm technology among some traditional groups rest on several concerns. Acceptance of modern farm technology could (1) erode the viability of small family-owned operations, (2) encourage young people to work away from home in factories, (3) destroy cooperation within the community, which is needed for labor-intensive tasks such as planting and harvesting, (4) lead to mechanization in other areas of life such as household appliances or automobiles, and (5) encourage members to engage in large corporate-style agriculture, which would increase social inequities in the community and increase interaction with and dependence on the larger society.

Kraybill (2001), Kraybill and Bowman (2001), R. Loewen (2006)

Feetwashing   *See* Footwashing

Fellowship of Evangelical Churches
Formed in 1865 by people with AMISH background, this group was known for many years as the Egly Amish because its leader was Henry Egly (1824–1890). In 1908 the group changed its name to the Defenseless Mennonite Church, and in 1948, to the Evangelical Mennonite Church. In 2003 the group became the Fellowship of Evangelical Churches. Strongly shaped by modern evangelicalism, many of its congregations have a weak MENNONITE identity. Nevertheless, the group commits itself to adhering to ANABAPTIST principles and to participating with other Anabaptist groups in responding to global social needs. The denomination views its evangelical commitments as rooted in historical Anabaptist teachings. Headquartered in Fort Wayne, Indiana, the group has 43 congregations in nine states, with about one-third of them in Illinois. The baptized membership numbers about 6,950.

http://fecministries.org

Feminism   *See* Gender Roles

Fiction   *See* Literature

First Nation Anabaptists   *See* Native American Anabaptists

Flag   *See* Nationalism

Folk Art
Material items designed for decorative and aesthetic appeal are typically considered folk art. Some, such as QUILTS, combine both artistic features and utilitarian features usually associated with crafts. Many ANABAPTIST immigrants to North America brought distinctive folk art traditions that have persisted over several generations. Anabaptist groups have produced many beautiful objects in various art forms using techniques and designs learned through imitation and example. Many of the folk arts in Anabaptist communities have artistic characteristics similar to those of regional or ethnic groups outside Anabaptist circles. There are no

common folk arts that are shared across all Anabaptist communities. Distinctive artistic expressions are shaped by ethnic tradition, country of origin, regional setting, and religious affiliation. The folk art varies, for example, among Anabaptists of Dutch-Russian, Swiss–south German, Native American, Mexican, and Caribbean cultural heritage.

Examples of folk art include ceramics, quilts, decorated furniture, wood carvings, needlework, painting on glass, painting on objects (such as milk cans), scenic watercolor painting, wheat weaving, and fraktur.

Fraktur lettering of hand-decorated texts, often in striking colors, was used by Anabaptist artists as well as other Pennsylvania Germans to create family records, BIBLE verses, religious POETRY, bookplates, school exercises, and other commemorative certificates. Colonial MEN-NONITE schoolteacher Christopher Dock (ca. 1698–1771) taught fraktur to his students and spawned an interest in this folk art, which they produced for several generations. Barbara Ebersol (1846–1922) was a noted AMISH folk artist from Pennsylvania. She created colored bookplates and family registers for Amish friends and relatives with simple drawings of flowers, hearts, and stars along with stylized fraktur lettering. Collectors began to notice her folk art in the 1970s and 1980s, and paid high prices for some small, simple pieces.

One popular art form in many Anabaptist homes in the first half of the 20th century involved various types of painting on glass. Such paintings hung on walls in the home and included mottos with colorful lettering of Bible verses, proverbs, family records of births, marriage, and deaths, and listings of children.

The quilts of various design made by women in Anabaptist communities, especially Amish women, have become highly prized works of art since the 1970s and are frequently made for retail sale.

Scholars and collectors have taken a keen interest in various types of folk art produced by Anabaptist FOLKLIFE traditions. Some of the more traditional groups have retained their folk art styles and expressions into the 21st century. At the same time, artists in ASSIMILATED GROUPS are developing new forms of art related to ceramics, textiles, and other materials.

Abrahams (1980), Beck (1989, 1997), BE I ("Art"), Bird (1977, 2002), Earnest and Earnest (2003), GAMEO ("Folk Arts," "Fraktur"), Hershey (2003), Hess (2002), Janzen and Janzen (1991), Luthy (1995), ME V ("Folk Arts"), L. Stoltzfus (1995)

Folklife

"Folklife" is a broad term that covers many of the traditions and customary practices of a people in daily life, including their rituals, crafts, customs, food, furnishings, architecture, and other forms of material culture that are distinctive to a particular people. FOLK ART (artistic expression), FOLKLORE (oral expression), and MATERIAL CULTURE (artifacts) are subfields under the larger rubric of folklife. In a broad sense the customs and traditions that bind a community together and shape its identity reflect the life ways of its people. There are few, if any, common strands of folklife that are shared across all ANABAPTIST communities. The particular practices of each community are shaped by its setting (urban, suburban, or rural), ethnic tradition, country of origin, regional context, and religious affiliation. The line between social and religious customs blurs in many aspects of Anabaptist life, especially in areas such as SINGING, WEDDINGS, and FUNERALS.

Examples of folklife in various Anabaptist communities include customs related to CLOTHING, food, medical remedies, religious rituals, births, weddings, BAPTISM, ORDINATION, LOVE FEAST, FOOTWASHING, funerals, quilting parties, social gatherings, games, furnishings, architecture, and so on.

Dress styles, often regulated by the church in TRADITIONAL GROUPS, provide a public identity for the group. Customs related to styles and colors of dress for men and women are typically longstanding traditions in the more conservative communities.

Food traditions are recorded in hundreds of COOKBOOKS, some published by local congregations and others by commercial presses for national distribution. Potluck meals are important to promote fellowship and community in many congregations.

Public auctions to sell household items and farm equipment or to benefit charitable causes often have a festive atmosphere and include people from outside the local Anabaptist community. Dozens of relief auctions supporting the worldwide efforts of MENNONITE CENTRAL COMMITTEE to assist refugees and victims of famine and war are organized by local MENNONITE and AMISH communities each year. There are also similar BRETHREN-based auctions for disaster relief. These auctions take on a festival flavor that features good food, fellowship, and games in the context of raising money for international benevolence. Long-established traditions in some communities involve groups of volunteers serving outside the community on short-term projects through MENNONITE DISASTER SERVICE and BRETHREN DISASTER MINISTRIES.

Although the content of song is an element of folklore, the practice of singing is an important aspect of the folklife in both traditional groups and ASSIMILATED GROUPS. A cappella singing without instruments both in church and social gatherings is an important means of building community and solidarity in some churches.

Some customs that have been lost in contemporary society have persisted in the more rural and isolated Anabaptist communities. For example, some Mennonites and Amish in 17th-century EUROPE had a reputation for unusual medicinal remedies for humans and animals, which some of the Amish and OLD ORDER MENNONITES continue to use.

Beck (2004, 2005), Bronner (2006), GAMEO ("Folk Arts," "Quilts"), Hess (2002), McCauley and McCauley (1988), ME V ("Folk Arts"), Ramirez (2000), Scott (1988)

Folklore

This term typically denotes oral expressions—songs, ballads, sayings, jokes, proverbs, stories, and legends—that reflect and shape the tradi-

tions and identity of a specific society. Folk tales may highlight the virtues or flaws of an ethnic tradition or place a group in a positive or negative light in comparison with other groups. In many communities, songs and proverbs provide ways of transmitting and reinforcing key values and wisdom. The DIALECTS spoken by ANABAPTIST groups and the stories transmitted in dialect form are also part of their folklore.

Several books that offer a humorous look at MENNONITES in the United States and their practices contribute to the folklore of Mennonite-related groups. A collection of Mennonite folklore (Beck 2004) includes chapters on "Inter-Mennonite Ethnic Slurs," "Origin Tales and Beliefs," "Trickster Tales," and a widespread urban legend about an encounter of two Mennonite women with Major League Baseball player Reggie Jackson (1946–) on a New York elevator. In a volume of BRETHREN tales, Ramirez (2008) recounts the legends about famous people who supposedly become Brethren or were connected to them in some way as well as Brethren who became famous. Examples include the likes of Abraham Lincoln (1809–1865), Annie Oakley (1860–1926), Daniel Boone (1734–1820), James Earl Jones (1931–), and many more.

SINGING, both religious and nonreligious, is an important form of oral expression in Anabaptist communities. From the slow tunes of the AUSBUND, sung in unison by the AMISH, to the popular praise songs written and recorded by aspiring young Anabaptist artists, musical styles and content express the heartfelt desires and cultural forms of Anabaptist peoples. Music written and sung by Anabaptist groups and choirs has been recorded and sold in many forms. "Sound in the Lands" festivals featuring Mennonite music took place at Conrad Grebel University College in 2004 and 2009. Many church groups have produced hymnbooks, some of which include songs written by members.

The ballads written and sung by Andy (1942–) and Terry Murray (1943–) have brought listeners a deeper understanding of Brethren values, a broader knowledge of Brethren "heroes," and a wider appreciation of Brethren heritage through their CDs and performances at many gatherings across the United States.

Several songs written by Anabaptists have attained legendary status in some groups. These include, for example, "I Owe the Lord a Morning Song," written (text and tune) by Pennsylvania Mennonite preacher Amos Herr (1816–1897) in the 1880s, and "Move in Our Midst," written by Brethren leader Kenneth I. Morse (1913–1999) in 1942; the latter is sometimes called the national anthem of the Church of the Brethren. "Praise God from Whom All Blessings Flow," a song with the same designation in some Mennonite groups, was not written by an Anabaptist. Sometimes simply called "606" for its page number in *The Mennonite Hymnal* published in 1969, it has beautiful harmonic qualities when sung without musical accompaniment.

Beck (2004, 2005), Fike (1979), GAMEO ("Folklore"), Gates (1987), Haas and Nolt (1993), Kehrberg (2007), D. Klassen (1989), Lesher (1985), Ramirez (2004, 2008), Roth (2006), Sharp (2001), http://www.dunkertownworkshop.com/products.html

Food   *See* Cookbooks

Footwashing

Many, but not all, ANABAPTIST groups practice this ORDINANCE, in which members wash one another's feet as a symbol of Jesus' ministry (based on John 13:2–17). The ritual washing of feet as part of LOVE FEAST, COMMUNION, or WORSHIP demonstrates the willingness to serve others in humility. In addition to embodying the virtues of SERVICE and humility, some interpreters such as MENNO SIMONS (1496–1561) and DIRK PHILIPS (1504–1558) also view it as a metaphor for cleansing from sin.

For MENNONITES, the rite is usually practiced in sex-segregated pairs—two members take turns washing each other's feet in a small basin of water and then drying them with a towel. After washing, the pair typically embrace and offer each other words of blessing or, in the case of traditional groups, a HOLY KISS. In some churches six or eight members sit in a circle or around a table and, proceeding around

the circle, wash the feet of the person next to them. The ritual is performed in different ways depending on the occasion and the tradition of the church.

For BRETHREN, footwashing is traditionally practiced while seated at tables, segregated by sex, prior to the love (agape) meal at the love feast. One member kneels and washes and dries the feet of the member seated next to him or her. After exchanging a blessing and perhaps the holy kiss, the second member then washes the feet of the next member and so on until all have taken their turn. The OLD GERMAN BAPTIST BRETHREN practice the double mode of footwashing. In this mode, two members share in administering the ritual to one or two members next to them. One of the pair washes, the other dries. Then both greet the person whose feet they have washed with the holy kiss and a blessing.

The AMISH and many Mennonite groups practice footwashing as a part of the communion service. Brethren groups generally practice footwashing as the first part of the love feast. HUTTERITES do not observe footwashing as a special ceremony but believe they practice it symbolically in daily life as they serve each other in community. Footwashing is sometimes also practiced at special events or conferences to symbolize servant leadership. Visual images of the basin and the towel are often used as symbols in Anabaptist publications to reflect the themes of servanthood and humility.

In general, the practice of footwashing has somewhat declined among assimilated Anabaptists since the mid-20th century. Some 70% of MENNONITE CHURCH USA and BRETHREN IN CHRIST members in the United States viewed footwashing as "a symbol of humility and service," according to a survey (CMP 2006). Likewise, two-thirds of CHURCH OF THE BRETHREN members saw the ritual as "spiritually moving and very meaningful."

See also *Gelassenheit*

BE I ("Feetwashing"), CMP 2006, GAMEO ("Feetwashing"), ME II ("Footwashing"), Ramirez (2000), Roth (2009)

Force, Use of *See* Nonresistance; Peacemaking

Fraktur *See* Folk Art

France

From about 1526 to 1550, the city of Strasbourg (now part of France) provided a haven for persecuted ANABAPTISTS. However, the congregations located there gradually disappeared as the government began issuing harsh mandates against Anabaptists and anyone who offered them assistance.

Beginning in 1648, Anabaptists from Canton Bern, SWITZERLAND, were invited by some noble families of northeastern France to settle in Ste. Marie-aux-Mines in Haut-Rhin (Upper Alsace region) and rebuild there. The Thirty Years War had destroyed much of the landholdings of these families, and they welcomed the Anabaptists because they could cultivate their fields.

These Anabaptist immigrants to Alsace remained separate from their new culture. Their farms were often in isolated locations, and the immigrants retained their Swiss-German DIALECT. The PERSECUTION they had experienced in Switzerland made them wary of becoming too involved in French culture. In contrast, the Anabaptists who remained in Switzerland became more assimilated. They participated somewhat in local politics, and some accepted military service. The religious and cultural tensions between the groups in Alsace and Switzerland eventually led to a schism in 1693, when many of the Anabaptists in Alsace followed JAKOB AMMANN (1644–ca. 1730) and became known as the AMISH.

In the 1600s and 1700s, MENNONITES and Amish in France made important innovations in AGRICULTURE that increased the health and productivity of their crops and animals. They also developed a new cattle breed called Montbéliard. During the 1800s an agricultural almanac that was started by a Mennonite gained widespread popularity for its information about these innovations.

During the French Revolution (1789–1799), Anabaptists were granted citizenship by the government and legal permission to buy land, but they also became subject to military service. Some efforts at partial exemption from military service were successful, but no general exemption was granted. In order to escape military conscription, over 1,000 Amish and Mennonites migrated to the United States between 1830 and 1860.

In the late 1800s, French Mennonites struggled with spiritual and cultural tensions within their churches. For example, the older leaders wanted to use only German in church, but the young people were educated in French. Spiritual renewal began in Mennonite churches in France around 1900 with the acceptance of REVIVALISM, ministerial training, publications, MISSION activity, and attention to Mennonite history.

At the beginning of the 21st century, the baptized membership of Mennonites in France numbers about 2,100. There are no longer any Amish living in France.

GAMEO ("France," "Strasbourg [Alsace, France]"), Jérôme (2005), ME II ("France"), ME IV ("Strasbourg"), Séguy (1984), http://www.mwc-cmm.org

Free Church *See* Radical Reformation; Believers Church

Freedom of Religion *See* Religious Liberty

Friends, Religious Society of *See* Quakers

Fundamentalism

This movement began as a reaction to modernism among North American evangelical Protestants in the early 1900s. It defined certain "fundamentals" as essential to genuine, biblical Christianity. These fundamentals included biblical inerrancy, the virgin birth, the bodily resurrection of Jesus Christ, premillennial dispensationalism, and the historical accuracy of the biblical account of creation. American fundamentalism opposed the critical study of biblical texts, the theory of human evolution, and the Social Gospel Movement. Fundamentalism not only had to do with religious doctrine, it also was a cultural movement that vigorously protested many social changes identified with modernism.

Among ANABAPTISTS, most TRADITIONAL GROUPS were not influenced by this movement because of their separatist stance. Some MENNONITE and BRETHREN leaders in AS-SIMILATED GROUPS borrowed theological concepts and vocabulary from fundamentalism in order to bolster their opposition to modernity, despite the fact that many historical Anabaptist beliefs and practices, such as DISCIPLESHIP, nonresistant PACIFISM, NONCONFORMITY, and noncreedalism, directly conflicted with many of the tenets of fundamentalism.

The impact of fundamentalism caused bitter CONFLICTS within some Mennonite and Brethren groups, especially at their colleges. Goshen College (Indiana), for example, closed for the 1923–1924 school year because of conflicts related to fundamentalist controversies. The Fellowship of GRACE BRETHREN CHURCHES, which embraces some fundamentalist beliefs, separated from the BRETHREN CHURCH in 1939 in response to controversies provoked by the movement. Some conference divisions and congregational withdrawals from various Anabaptist denominations in the 1950s and 1960s also stemmed from disagreements about fundamentalism. Fundamentalism continues to influence and create tensions among many contemporary Mennonite and Brethren groups, especially in the areas of biblical interpretation and other religious doctrines.

BE I ("Fellowship of Grace Brethren Churches," "Fundamentalism"), D. Durnbaugh (2002), GAMEO (Fundamentalism"), Juhnke (1989), A. Martin (2007), ME V ("Fundamentalism"), P. Toews (1983, 1996), N. Yoder (1999)

Funeral Customs

The burial customs of TRADITIONAL GROUPS are virtually identical for each person in their church because they are dictated by traditions that emphasize simplicity, humility, and frugal-ity. The expenses of an AMISH or HUTTERITE funeral are very modest, reflecting only the cost of a plain wooden coffin and the embalming and burial fees, if any. In some of the cemeteries of traditional groups, simple gravestones are placed in family order; in others, they are placed in rows in chronological order of death without regard to family groupings. In some churches the gravestones for adults are of equal size, and none have ornamentation.

The onset of public laws pertaining to burial and the commercialization of funerals during the 1900s altered funeral customs among MEN-NONITES and BRETHREN in ASSIMILATED GROUPS. Funeral customs and costs, influenced by individual choice, vary greatly. Some funerals are elaborate, while others reflect the values of simplicity and modesty. Memorial services and cremations are preferred by some individuals. The traditional practice of holding a public viewing of the deceased is left to the discretion of the family. The practice of having someone stay with the deceased body throughout the night in a home (known as a wake), practiced by some groups in the 19th and early 20th centuries, has largely but not entirely died out, even among traditional groups. The OLD GERMAN BAPTIST BRETHREN and some Amish groups have a unique burial custom of wrapping the deceased in a white cloth, dress, suit, or bathrobe, in imitation of the shroud in which Christ was buried.

Regardless of other variations, most funerals in both assimilated and traditional ANABAPTIST groups include visitation with the family and a meal for family and friends. These two rituals reflect the significance of community in the Anabaptist tradition.

BE I ("Funerals"), GAMEO ("Funerals"), J. Hostetler (1993, 1997), ME V ("Funerals"), M. Schmidt (1980), Scott (1988)

Furniture   *See* Material Culture

GAMEO *See* Global Anabaptist Mennonite Encyclopedia Online

Games *See* Leisure

Geistreiches Gesangbuch

Two different hymnals are named *Geistreiches Gesangbuch* (Spiritual Hymnal).

A hymnal with this name was published by the BRETHREN in Europe in 1720. Their first hymnal, it contained "Count Well the Cost," a baptismal hymn by ALEXANDER MACK SR. (1679–1735), and about 100 hymns written by a Brethren man while he was imprisoned with five other Brethren in Jülich for being baptized.

A completely different hymnal with the same name was published in 1767 in Königsberg, East Prussia. This early and foundational German MENNONITE hymnal was used primarily by Mennonites in Prussia and northern GERMANY, whose descendants migrated to Russia and later to North America and South America. Over half of the texts in the first edition were borrowed from PIETIST hymns in Lutheran or Reformed hymnals. The remaining texts were either translations of hymns from Dutch Mennonite hymnals or original German hymns composed by German Mennonites. This hymnal had many editions and is still used by traditional Mennonites—OLD COLONY MENNONITE groups—in Belize, Canada, Mexico, and South America, especially.

See also *Ausbund;* Hymnody; Singing; Traditional Groups; *Unpartheyisches Gesangbuch*

GAMEO ("Geistreiches Gesangbuch," "Hymnology of the Mennonites of West and East Prussia, Danzig, and Russia"), Letkemann (2001), ME II ("Hymnology of the Mennonites of West and East Prussia, Danzig, and Russia")

Gelassenheit

The German word *Gelassenheit* has multiple translations: yieldedness; surrender; submission; resignation; abandonment. Reflecting the views of some late-medieval spiritual writers, 16th-century ANABAPTISTS called for a deep and unconditional spiritual surrender to God. For those burned at the martyrs' stake, *Gelassenheit* meant a literal abandonment of one's body into the hands of God. Over the centuries the mystical meanings have been translated into cultural forms of plain and simple living in many traditional Anabaptist communities. *Gelassenheit* is less prevalent in ASSIMILATED GROUPS; they accept more expressions of individualism.

Although the word itself is not spoken in daily discourse within TRADITIONAL GROUPS, scholars have used it as a conceptual tool to describe the cultural ethos of these communities, especially Old Order groups. Among the HUTTERITES, *Gelassenheit* means a willingness to surrender one's life so completely to God that members willingly give up private property and yield their economic interests to the COMMUNITY. *Gelassenheit* is a deep and broad disposition that undergirds the entire worldview of AMISH, OLD ORDER MENNONITE, OLD COLONY MENNONITE, and Hutterite groups. It stands in sharp contrast to the individualism of American culture, which nurtures an assertive self that demands individual freedom and choice. Those who embody the virtues of *Gelassenheit* surrender themselves to God, yield to the authority of the church, and defer to those in authority over them. They exhibit a meek and mild personality that is willing to suffer rather than defend itself.

Gelassenheit is a crucial bridge between the individual and the church community. Members who embody this virtue are willing to deny self-interest for the welfare of the community. Leaders of traditional groups also frequently extol a related virtue, humility, and contrast it with the vice of pride (bold individualism). As a deep cultural disposition in traditional groups, *Gelassenheit* expresses itself in both values and behaviors, in attitudes and practices—not only in individual behavior, but in the architecture of church buildings, the rituals of the community, dress practices, and other aspects of life.

See also Martyrdom; Nonresistance; Old Order Movement

Cronk (1977), Kraybill (2001), D. Martin (2003), C. Snyder (2004)

Gender Roles

In the 1500s, ANABAPTIST women held roles as teachers, evangelists, elders, and prophets more frequently than women in Catholic and Protestant groups. About one-third of the 930 martyrs listed in MARTYRS MIRROR are women. However, after the 1500s most Anabaptist churches began to restrict the church leadership roles of women. As Anabaptist groups were forced into more rural and agricultural settings, motherhood and homemaking eventually constituted the sphere of women's work.

In the 1800s, controversies began to arise among more ASSIMILATED GROUPS regarding the participation of women in the life of the church. Although all Anabaptist groups prohibited the ORDINATION OF WOMEN at this time, some women took active leadership roles in Christian education and missionary activities. Foreign MISSION assignments typically had fewer restrictions on women's roles, which allowed them to serve as evangelists, teachers, nurses, and doctors.

During the 1900s, a variety of women's organizations emerged in the congregations of assimilated groups. For example, sewing circles became popular in many congregations; women prepared clothing, textiles, and other goods for overseas relief and mission projects.

The deaconess movement among MENNONITES from 1908 to 1958 is another important example of women's unordained leadership in the church. Without making formal vows, a small number of young women agreed to remain single, live communally, and devote lifetime service to the church-related ministry of caring for the sick. They administered and staffed hospitals in Kansas, Minnesota, Nebraska, Idaho, and Oregon. By the 1930s the professionalization of nursing as well as other societal trends brought about the demise of the movement, but the hospitals staffed by the deaconesses usually continued under different auspices.

Throughout the 1900s, women in assimilated groups began to enter both secular and church-related PROFESSIONS outside the home. This change, coupled with the feminist movement that began in the 1960s and new interpretations of biblical teaching on gender, influenced women in some assimilated groups to seek fuller participation in church leadership and more equal AUTHORITY with men in the FAMILY structure. Some men also supported this shift in gender roles.

In the 1970s, authors began writing and publishing biographies of Anabaptist women, and by the 1990s, scholars were studying Anabaptist and PIETIST history specifically from the perspective of gender. Eventually scholarship and teaching by women about women's issues found acceptance among assimilated Anabaptist groups.

In 1973 the Committee on Women's Concerns was formed within MENNONITE CENTRAL COMMITTEE. From 1973 to 2004 it produced *Women's Concerns Report,* which covered issues such as spirituality, abuse, gender relations, ordination of women, family dynamics, artistic creativity, immigration, race relations, sexuality, infertility, children, theology, and aging. A similar group known as the Womaen's Caucus was formed in the CHURCH OF THE BRETHREN in 1973.

Among Anabaptist groups, church-related organizations for men first arose in 1920 in the Church of the Brethren. With the goal of enabling more men to participate in the life of the church, Men's Work provided counsel for men who decided to join the military, advocated for men's Bible study classes, and encouraged men to become active in their local congregations (as ushers and maintenance workers) as well as in civic and community affairs. Mennonite Men, a ministry of MENNONITE CHURCH USA and MENNONITE CHURCH CANADA, provides opportunities for fellowship and spiritual growth in local congregations, and assists with leadership training, disaster relief, and youth activities. It also provides grants to young congregations for the purchase of their first church building.

The concept of headship is taught and promoted by most TRADITIONAL GROUPS in the

21st century. This understanding of the husband's dominant leadership role in the religious affairs of the family is based on I Corinthians 11:3–12, where the Apostle Paul spells out a divine order of headship authority: God, Christ, man, woman. These groups continue to restrict the roles that women may hold in the church, and few, if any, of these churches ordain women for any aspect of official ministry or public church leadership. OLD ORDER MENNONITES encourage ministers' wives to assist in some church matters such as privately counseling other women and receiving new members with a kiss at baptism. Women in many groups are allowed to vote in church business meetings, and exert considerable influence through their husbands and informal channels in these patriarchal communities.

BE II ("Womaen's Caucus," "Women"), Brubaker (1985), Carter (1985), M. Epp (1987, 2000, 2008), GAMEO ("Men's Work," "Mennonite Men [General Conference Mennonite]," "Women"), Goossen (1994), Johnson-Weiner (2001), Juhnke (1989), ME V ("Men's Work," "Mennonite Men," "Women"), Rich (1983), Schmidt, Umble, and Reschly (2002), Siegrist (1996), Snyder and Hecht (1996), Ziegler (1977), http://www.mennonitemen.org, http://www.mennonitewomenusa.org, http://www.womaenscaucus.org

Genealogy

Both their emphasis on NONCONFORMITY and their historical experiences of PERSECUTION led many ANABAPTIST groups to emphasize the study of FAMILY history. Persecution scattered Anabaptists into different countries, and stable marriage patterns provided some security in the midst of complex MIGRATION and legal restrictions. Their theology of being a close community encouraged endogamy (marriage within the group), and their emphasis on being separate from the world also accentuated family relationships.

Certain Anabaptist surnames are often associated with particular geographical areas, time periods, and subgroups. This information provides helpful resources for genealogical re-

search. Aided by computerized databases and software, the study of family history among North American Anabaptist groups has experienced explosive growth since 1975 in the form of conferences, books, researchers, and the expansion of local and regional historical societies. As more Anabaptists in ASSIMILATED GROUPS have married people from different racial and cultural backgrounds, their interest in genealogical research has grown. This interest has also been fostered by travel, computerization, and additional leisure time.

Major genealogical databases have been established by the Swiss Anabaptist Genealogical Association and the California Mennonite Historical Society (Genealogical Registry and Database of Mennonite Ancestry, known as GRANDMA), which emphasize Prussian/Russian MENNONITE family lines. Over one million names are included between the two databases.

Because of their comprehensive family records, relative stability, and INTERMARRIAGE, TRADITIONAL GROUPS provide an excellent resource for GENETIC STUDIES for geneticists and others studying the transmission of inherited diseases.

GAMEO ("Genealogy"), Gingerich and Kreider (1986), ME V ("Genealogy"), http://calmenno.org/index.htm, http://www.mennonitegenealogy.com/canada, http://www.mennonites.ca, http://www.omii.org

General Conference Mennonite Church

The General Conference Mennonite Church formed in 1860 in West Point, Iowa, when representatives from various MENNONITE bodies, seeking common fellowship, organized a new conference. As the conference grew, its membership included older immigrants of German stock as well as many new immigrant congregations of Dutch-Russian background. Historically, the General Conference Mennonite Church membership was divided between the United States and Canada.

The General Conference Mennonite Church emphasized congregational authority more than the MENNONITE CHURCH, which gave greater authority to regional conferences. Thus, on many issues (dress, voting, civic engagement) in the mid-20th century, the General Conference was considered more liberal and less sectarian than the Mennonite Church.

In 2002 the General Conference Mennonite Church in the United States merged with the Mennonite Church to form MENNONITE CHURCH USA. Prior to the merger, the General Conference in the United States had 179 congregations and about 27,500 members. A similar merger occurred in Canada in 2002, when MENNONITE CHURCH CANADA was formed, thus ending the General Conference Mennonite Church in both the United States and Canada.

GAMEO ("General Conference Mennonite Church [GCMC]"), Kraybill and Hostetter (2001)

Genetic Studies

OLD ORDER MENNONITE, AMISH, and HUT-TERITE groups have attracted many genetic researchers studying inherited diseases and their interaction with social and cultural factors. Living in somewhat geographically isolated TRA-DITIONAL GROUPS, many ANABAPTISTS have shown high levels of INTERMARRIAGE for many generations, and most keep accurate GENEA-LOGICAL records. They also tend to have more uniform environmental influences and more uniform behavior than the general population of Anabaptists in ASSIMILATED GROUPS. Traditional groups may have a higher incidence of some genetically based diseases than the general population, but a similar or lower incidence of other diseases. For these reasons traditional groups provide an excellent source of data for studying genetic diseases and their interaction with cultural influences.

Since 1962, Johns Hopkins School of Medicine in Baltimore, Maryland, has conducted extensive studies of genetic diseases among the Amish, and to a lesser degree among the Hutterites. Since 1989, the Clinic for Special Children in Strasburg, Pennsylvania, which treats primarily Amish and Old Order Mennonite children with genetically based metabolic diseases, has conducted research on the genetic roots of

these diseases. The Amish Research Clinic, established in 1995 in affiliation with the University of Maryland, has numerous medical-genetic research projects in Amish communities that are funded by the National Science Foundation and other agencies. Some of the topics investigated in Old Order populations include bipolar disorder, diabetes, obesity, deafness, and heart disease.

Cross and Crosby (2008), J. Hostetler (1993, 1997), McKusick (1978), Miller, Brubaker, and Peterson (2005), http://www.clinicforspecialchildren.org, http://www.umm.edu/news/releases/amish_res_clinic.htm

German Baptist Brethren   *See* Brethren; Mack, Alexander, Sr.; Old German Baptist Brethren

German Language

German was the original LANGUAGE of most ANABAPTISTS in the 1500s. During that time the Dutch spoken by Anabaptists in the NETH-ERLANDS was similar to a German DIALECT of northern GERMANY. Numerous German-related dialects are still spoken by many European and some North American MENNONITES.

AMISH, BRETHREN, HUTTERITE, and Mennonite groups have all spoken various German dialects throughout their history. Swiss German continues to be spoken by the Mennonites who remained in SWITZERLAND, and the Alsatian German dialect, similar to what became Pennsylvania German, is still spoken by the Swiss-origin Anabaptists living in the French-speaking region of Alsatian FRANCE. The Hutterites speak *Hutterisch*, a dialect derived from the province of Carinthia, Austria.

Mennonites who emigrated from the Netherlands to northern Germany and POLAND/Prussia in the 1500s spoke the north German dialect known as Low German or *Plautdietsch*. To varying degrees they retained their native tongue during their later settlement in Russia, South America, and North America. Approximately 110,000 adults and children in several Mennonite groups in BELIZE, CANADA, MEXICO, and the United States continue to speak the Low German dialect in the 21st century.

The Palatinate German dialect originating in southwestern Germany served as the basis for Pennsylvania German, which developed among German-speaking immigrants (including Mennonites, Amish, and other religious groups) in Pennsylvania in the 1700s. A few Amish groups that immigrated to the United States directly from Switzerland in the 19th century speak Swiss German instead of Pennsylvania German.

As most German-speaking Anabaptist groups in North America assimilated into the larger culture, they shed their native tongue for English. Only the most traditional groups have retained some form of German for everyday communication and/or church services. The Amish and horse-and-buggy-driving Mennonites continue to use Pennsylvania German in daily conversation among themselves and in their church services. Although they learn English in school, Pennsylvania German serves as a crucial cultural mark of separatist identity and group solidarity for these Old Order groups, regardless of where they live. The same is true for those groups who speak Low German or other dialects.

Burridge and Enninger (1992), R. Epp (1993), GAMEO ("German Language"), Huffines (1988), Louden (2006), ME V ("German Language")

Germany

Although the modern German nation did not take shape until the late 1800s, many semi-autonomous German-speaking principalities existed for centuries prior to that within the loosely structured Holy Roman Empire. Along with the NETHERLANDS and German-speaking SWITZERLAND, these German principalities witnessed the emergence and spread of ANABAPTISM in the 1500s. The cities of Augsburg and Strasbourg in southern Germany were centers of Anabaptist activity, but the movement also had adherents in other areas.

Anabaptists faced intense PERSECUTION and severe legal restrictions because of their unique religious beliefs and practices. Even after Protestants and Roman Catholics, exhausted by religious wars, agreed to provide limited RELIGIOUS LIBERTY for each other within specific territories, both still wanted to expel Anabaptists. In German areas such as Roman Catholic Bavaria and Austria, rulers successfully exterminated Anabaptism by the early 1600s. By the mid-1600s most of the Anabaptists in southern and central Germany had been converted, exiled, or executed.

Generally, persecuted Anabaptists migrated to whichever principalities would tolerate them. During this time the HUTTERITES in Germany fled east to Moravia. The Palatinate, at different times, tolerated Anabaptists. The German Baptist Brethren originated in Wittgenstein in the town of Schwarzenau in 1708, but by the mid-1700s the entire BRETHREN movement had left Germany for North America. In the 1700s and 1800s, many Anabaptists from southern Germany immigrated to eastern North America, searching for freedom to practice their religious beliefs—especially their nonresistant PACIFISM—and for fertile land on which to establish agricultural communities.

The principalities in northern Germany also persecuted Anabaptists, but they were more tolerant than those in the south. The cities of Hamburg and Emden on the north coast were important centers of Anabaptism in the 1500s. A few MENNONITE families there became wealthy as merchant whalers and shipbuilders. Further south, the city of Krefeld offered considerable tolerance of Mennonites, and by the mid-1700s they had helped to make it an important center for textile (especially linen) manufacturing.

German PIETISM had considerable influence on Mennonites and Brethren in Germany, especially in the north. Pietistic influences shaped their HYMNODY, CHURCH BUILDINGS, and DEVOTIONAL LITERATURE.

Since 1970, contemporary Mennonite church life in Germany has been shaped by the arrival of nearly 112,000 Russian Mennonite immigrants, known as AUSSIEDLER. Not all of the *Aussiedler* remained in Germany or joined Mennonite congregations. At the beginning of the 21st century, the baptized membership of Mennonites in Germany, including the *Aussiedler* who affiliated with the established German congregations, numbers about 46,000. No Brethren or AMISH remain in Germany.

See also German Language

BE I ("Germany"), C. Dyck (1993), GAMEO ("Germany"), Guth (1995), Lapp and Snyder (2006b), Heinrich Loewen (2003), ME II ("Germany"), http://www.mennoniten.de, http://www.mwc-cmm.org

Global Anabaptist Mennonite Encyclopedia Online (GAMEO)

This online encyclopedia, known as GAMEO, was initiated in 1996 when the Mennonite Historical Society of Canada began posting a database of Canadian congregations. The project gradually added additional partners, grew to include other MENNONITE-related topics, and expanded significantly when entries from the five-volume MENNONITE ENCYCLOPEDIA were added to the database. GAMEO offers over 14,000 entries in a searchable database about Mennonite groups and topics worldwide.

http://www.gameo.org

Global Anabaptists   *See* Anabaptist Groups, International

Global Mennonite History Project

One of the most remarkable developments of modern church history has been the growth of the Christian movement in the global South. During the 1990s the majority of Christian adherents in the world shifted from EUROPE and North America to AFRICA, ASIA, and SOUTH AMERICA. MENNONITES and BRETHREN were no exception. This global transition prompted some ANABAPTIST churches to revise and update their histories to document the new demographic reality.

The Global Mennonite History Project, launched at the 1997 Mennonite World Conference in Calcutta, India, is an attempt to write the history of the worldwide Mennonite and BRETHREN IN CHRIST churches. This five-volume project, sponsored by MENNONITE WORLD CONFERENCE, involved researchers and writers from each of the most populous continents. The history of Africa was published in 2003 (1st ed.; 3rd ed. 2006) and the history of Europe in 2006. The histories of Latin America, Asia, and North America are under way.

Lapp and Snyder (2006a, 2006b), www.anabaptistwiki.org

God, Doctrine of

The doctrine of God is central to Christian THEOLOGY. ANABAPTIST understandings of God are based primarily on the BIBLE, especially on God's revelation through JESUS CHRIST—his life, teachings, death, and resurrection. The classical doctrine of the Trinity—God as Father, Son, and Holy Spirit—has been generally accepted by Anabaptist groups but not highly developed. Rather than basing their views on philosophical ideas, Anabaptists' views of God arose from their understandings of biblical texts as interpreted by the lay leaders of the church.

Two 16th-century Anabaptists who wrote about the Trinity were PILGRAM MARPECK (ca. 1490s–1556) and PETER RIEDEMANN (1506–1556). Anabaptists, however, wrote little formal systematic theology until the late 20th century. Instead, they expressed their views of God in various CONFESSIONS OF FAITH. Some contemporary MENNONITE and BRETHREN theologians debate whether Anabaptist theology has its own unique foundations, or whether it stands on the classical confessions of faith of the early Christian tradition and then develops or adds special Anabaptist emphases.

In the last quarter of the 20th century, Anabaptist scholars devoted attention to developing more systematic understandings of God. The writings of Gordon D. Kaufman (1925–), professor emeritus of Harvard Divinity School and former president of the American Academy of Religion, as well as other theologians have been influential in shaping Anabaptist academic understandings of God.

BE II ("Trinity, Doctrine of"), Finger (1985, 1989, 2004), GAMEO ("God [Trinity], Doctrine of"), G. Kaufman (1968, 1993), Klaassen and Klassen (2008), Koop (2006), McClendon (1994, 2000, 2002), ME V ("God [Trinity], Doctrine of"), Packull (2007), A. Reimer (2001, 2003), J. H. Yoder (1972/1994, 2002)

Government

Both their history and their theology lead many ANABAPTIST groups to be wary of government. During the origins of the Anabaptist Movement in the 1500s, many Anabaptists were victims of hostile governments, which persecuted, exiled, and even executed them.

According to historic Anabaptist theology, there are two kingdoms in the world. The lower kingdom, which includes the state, is based on strife and conflict. In contrast, the church is part of a higher kingdom, which is anchored in the radical pacifist ethic of Jesus Christ. This so-called TWO-KINGDOM THEOLOGY assumes two different ethical standards for the church and the state.

Even though governments were seen as part of the lower kingdom, early Anabaptists believed that God had ordained a specific role for the state: to maintain order by restraining evil and promoting justice. They urged followers to pray for government officials and to obey government laws when they did not conflict with Christian ETHICS (see Rom. 13:1–7). They generally, but not always, forbade members to hold government offices because the action of campaigning and executing the duties of government involved the use of, or the threat of, force. Early Anabaptist views of government are found in the SCHLEITHEIM ARTICLES (1527).

As some Anabaptist groups found themselves in more tolerant and democratic societies, especially in the 1600s in the NETHERLANDS and later in the representative democracies of North America, they began to develop a more positive view of government. This change is reflected in the DORDRECHT CONFESSION of 1632. In 18th- and 19th-century monarchical Russia and 20th-century Paraguay, MENNONITES were encouraged to create their own colonies and local governmental structures to meet the social and economic needs of their communities.

In contemporary North America, Anabaptists in TRADITIONAL GROUPS retain the two-kingdom approach to government. They refuse to accept government subsidies and strongly discourage POLITICAL PARTICIPATION.

Anabaptists in ASSIMILATED GROUPS exhibit a wide range of political attitudes and behavior. Some—both those of liberal and those of conservative persuasions—become very active in politics. Others shy away from political participation. Some merge their Christian convictions with particular political and social ideologies, such as socialism, capitalism, and NATIONALISM. Others seek to develop an engaged social and political critique of the state that is based on biblical principles and that calls on the government to uphold the highest expression of its own values: justice, order, and equal opportunities and responsibilities for all citizens. In a survey (CMP 2006), a majority of assimilated MENNONITE CHURCH USA, BRETHREN IN CHRIST, and CHURCH OF THE BRETHREN members in the United States said that Christians should try to influence governments to do what is right.

Political participation, such as voting, is widespread among assimilated Anabaptists, but holding political office beyond the local level, while acceptable, is not common.

See also Church and State

BE I ("Church-State Relations"), CMP 2006, GAMEO ("Church-State Relations," "Government, Theory and Theology of"), W. Janzen (1990), Klaassen (1981), ME IV ("State, Anabaptist-Mennonite Attitude Toward"), ME V ("Church-State Relations," "Government, Theory and Theology of"), J. H. Yoder (1972/1994)

Grace Brethren Churches, Fellowship of

This group traces its roots back to the BRETHREN movement that originated in Schwarzenau, Germany, in 1708. The Fellowship of Grace Brethren Churches emerged in 1939 from a division within the Ashland (Ohio)-based BRETHREN CHURCH over theological issues related to FUNDAMENTALISM. A related group, the Conservative Grace Brethren Churches International, branched off from the main body in 1989–1991.

The Fellowship emphasizes the verbal inspiration of all the books of the Old and New Testaments—that is, the belief that the Bible is without error as originally given of God. The denomination accepts more militaristic and patriotic views than is typical of most Brethren-related groups. Grace College and Grace Theological Seminary are key educational institutions for the Fellowship. In the United States the Fellowship has about 30,400 members and over 260 congregations in 29 states, with the largest clusters in Pennsylvania, Ohio, and California. The group has begun mission efforts to establish churches in Canada and in several states of Mexico. Grace Brethren International Missions has an active presence in many countries outside North America, involving some 2,600 congregations of various sizes.

BE I ("Grace Brethren Churches"), http://www .fgbc.org

Grebel, Conrad (ca. 1498–1526)

Conrad Grebel is usually considered the leading founder of Swiss–south German ANABAPTISM and an early leader of the Swiss Brethren. His aristocratic family was prominent in Zurich because of its involvement in business and politics. Grebel studied at some of the best universities of the time: Basel, Vienna, and Paris. Eventually he became a student of Ulrich Zwingli, the prominent Reformed pastor in Zurich, with whom he later parted ways over the issue of adult BAPTISM. Grebel likely performed the first adult baptism of the RADICAL REFORMATION in January 1525. He died at 28 years of age (likely from the plague or another illness) after only three years as public spokesperson for the emerging Anabaptist Movement. Except for 69 letters that he wrote between 1517 and 1525, few of his writings have been preserved.

GAMEO ("Grebel, Conrad [ca. 1498–1526]"), ME II ("Grebel, Conrad"), ME V ("Grebel, Conrad")

Grenada

Olive Branch Mennonite Missions, affiliated with the Keystone Mennonite Fellowship based in eastern Pennsylvania, has three mission churches in Grenada with a membership of about 50. The CHURCH OF GOD IN CHRIST,

MENNONITE group also has a mission outreach on the island but few, if any, members.

Mennonite Church Directory (2009)

Growth   *See* Demography

Guatemala

There are at least seven church bodies with ANABAPTIST connections in Guatemala. Five different plain-dressing MENNONITE groups in the United States are affiliated with 30 small congregations or mission outreach sites with some 700 members. The earliest Mennonite involvement in Guatemala began in 1964 when members of the Conservative Mennonite Fellowship established a MISSION project at Chimaltenango. Their efforts eventually produced congregations that affiliated with other church groups in the United States when the Conservative Mennonite Fellowship disbanded in the 1990s. At the beginning of the 21st century, five congregations with a total of about 175 members relate to the NATIONWIDE FELLOWSHIP CHURCHES in the United States. Another congregation, also an heir to the 1964 mission efforts, affiliates with the Bethel Mennonite Fellowship and has about 25 members.

In 1970 the EASTERN PENNSYLVANIA MENNONITE CHURCH began mission efforts in Guatemala and now has five congregations with about 200 members. Mennonite Air Missions began in 1972 as an outgrowth of the Conservative Mennonite Fellowship mission efforts. Using airplanes to reach isolated areas in the roadless interior of the country, the Air Missions group established numerous churches and now claims 17 congregations with about 275 members. Two mission congregations established by the CHURCH OF GOD IN CHRIST, MENNONITE group have about 25 members.

The two largest bodies of Mennonite-related churches in Guatemala formed after missionaries from Eastern Mennonite Missions and the Franklin-Washington Mennonite Conference (both based in Pennsylvania) arrived in Guatemala in 1968. The first church, the Evangelical

Mennonite Church of Guatemala, emerged in Guatemala City. It has about 1,700 members in 11 congregations throughout the capital city area. The second one, whose members come mostly from indigenous K'ekchi' backgrounds, is the NATIONAL EVANGELICAL GUATEMALAN MENNONITE CHURCH. This church has 115 congregations and 5,000 baptized members.

The first K'ekchi' baptisms occurred in September 1972, and the church grew rapidly in the 1980s and 1990s. The congregations are located in the K'ekchi'-speaking area of northeastern Guatemala, mostly in the department of Alta Verapaz. Linguists associated with Wycliffe Bible Translators translated the Bible into the K'ekchi' language and helped to mentor some of the missionaries in the 1970s.

The K'EKCHI' MENNONITE FOUNDATION is the social justice arm of the K'ekchi' church. It began as a social service agency to build connections between the church and the community. It now administers a government health program that attends to a population of 80,000, and operates BEZALEEL EDUCATION CENTER.

The National Evangelical Guatemalan Mennonite Church relates to MENNONITE WORLD CONFERENCE and is a part of the inter-Mennonite CENTRAL AMERICAN ANABAPTIST MENNONITE CONSULTATION (CAMCA). The church also relates to the LATIN AMERICAN ANABAPTIST SEMINARY, which is based in Guatemala City and provides biblical and theological education for 10 Anabaptist/Mennonite groups in Central America and Mexico.

MENNONITE CENTRAL COMMITTEE (MCC) first began work in Guatemala in 1976 with reconstruction following a major earthquake. There are about 10 expatriate workers in the country engaged in numerous projects, including assisting the K'ekchi' (through the K'ekchi' Mennonite Church) and Ixil indigenous communities with educational and agricultural projects. MCC supports HIV/AIDS prevention programs and conflict resolution workshops in Guatemala through a partner organization, Redpaz (REGIONAL NETWORK OF JUSTICE AND PEACE), and supports Bezaleel Education Center through its Global Family sponsorship program.

GAMEO ("Central America," "Guatemala"), ME V ("Central America"), Mennonite World Conference (2005), http://www.lindale.org/sent/trottertg/index .asp, http://www.mwc-cmm.org

Haiti

An ANABAPTIST presence first began
in Haiti in the 1958 with service workers from
MENNONITE CENTRAL COMMITTEE (MCC)
conducting medical and health-related projects.
MCC promotes human rights, provides food and
basic supplies, and sponsors reforestation and
environmental education. Since it began reforestation work in 1983, MCC has helped to plant
more than six million seedlings. In 2007, for
example, a team of eight MCC workers helped
community tree nurseries distribute more than
400,000 seedlings to farmers.

The CHURCH OF GOD IN CHRIST, MEN-
NONITE group conducted disaster relief work in
Haiti after it was devastated by Hurricane Flora
in 1963. Missionaries followed in 1968, and the
group grew to 17 congregations and about 600
members. The Gospel Light Chapel churches
grew from a mission begun in 1978 and supported by the Palm Grove Mennonite Church
of Sarasota, Florida, which is affiliated with the
CONSERVATIVE MENNONITE CONFERENCE.
The 14 congregations affiliated with the Chapel
have some 700 members.

The Mennonite Sonlight Mission began
as an indigenous Haitian church in 1980. It is
supported by several Conservative Mennonite
groups, primarily from Ohio and Pennsylvania.
The Mission has five congregations and 200
members. The Washington-Franklin Mennonite
Conference, based in Maryland and Pennsylvania, which began mission activities in Haiti in
1993, has about 25 members in one congregation. The largest Anabaptist-related church is
Assembly of Grace, with 25 congregations and
2,375 members. It formed in 1990 through the
efforts of Haitian pastors to plant indigenous
churches. The group is affiliated with Mennonite World Conference.

At the initiative of a Haitian congregation in
Miami, the CHURCH OF THE BRETHREN began
mission and service programs in Haiti early in
the 21st century. There are five congregations
and other outreach sites with more than 50
members. Following several devastating hurricanes in 2008, BRETHREN DISASTER MINIS-

TRIES began a major effort to build homes
and engage in other hurricane recovery
projects.

CHRISTIAN AID MINISTRIES (CAM) maintains a material aid base and a clinic in Haiti.
A 25-member congregation, established by the
organization in 1997, is affiliated with the Salem
Amish Mennonite Church of Ohio.

Some 20 different Anabaptist-related service and relief organizations are active in Haiti.
Most receive their funding and direction from
church-related organizations in the United
States. Many of the relief endeavors are supported by AMISH and conservative MENNO-
NITES through Haiti Benefit Auctions in various
regions of the United States. In addition to MCC
and CAM, some of the other prominent agencies
supported by Anabaptists in the United States
include Blue Ridge International for Christ,
Christian Witness Mission, Haiti Relief Mission, International Faith Missions, International
Fellowship Haven, Life Ministries, Mennonite
Gospel Missions, Palm Grove Mission, Son Light
Missions Ministries, and Water for Life.

Following the disastrous earthquake in January 2010, many North American Anabaptist
church groups and agencies contributed funds,
supplies, and volunteers to the immediate relief
efforts and the long-term rebuilding activities in
the country.

GAMEO ("Haiti"), Mennonite World Conference
(2005), S. Miller (1998), http://www.mwc-cmm.org

Head Covering

ANABAPTIST women have worn some form of
head covering since the 16th century. Until the
19th century, it was usually a variation on the
traditional headgear worn by women where
the Anabaptists lived. In North America the
distinctive European characteristics disappeared, and different Anabaptist groups created their own standardized head coverings.
Nineteenth-century Anabaptist women typically
wore these head coverings in church services,
when they appeared in public, and sometimes
at home. The covering styles and the patterns
of use varied considerably. Some reflected the

regional or national patterns of women in Protestant churches. The head-covering practice was based on the Apostle Paul's admonition in I Corinthians (11:3–12) that women, but not men, should cover their heads during prayer and worship as a sign of respect for a divine order of authority. This teaching is known as the headship principle, with four steps of divine order: God, Christ, men, women.

As mass-produced CLOTHING and headgear appeared in the late 19th century in North American society, some Anabaptist churches created more specific styles of women's head coverings. Wearing plain, simple veilings was viewed as an act of obedience to scriptural teaching and a symbolic rejection of the fancy fashions of the wider society. Moreover, in patriarchal churches the woman's veiling symbolized the subjection of women to men, who typically dominated church leadership. When wearing church-prescribed head coverings in public, women in some TRADITIONAL GROUPS carried the public burden of ethnicity more than men, whose clothing was less distinctive.

During the 20th century, the wearing of head coverings declined in more ASSIMILATED GROUPS, which gradually interpreted the Pauline teaching as referring to a cultural practice in the early church without relevance for women in the modern world. Some churches in the mid-20th century had long and contentious discussions about wearing head coverings because proponents saw its decline as a serious erosion of obedience to scriptural teaching.

In the most conservative churches, a woman's refusal to wear a church-prescribed veiling is cause for excommunication. In the 21st century, virtually all traditional churches require women to wear a head covering for church services as well as when they appear in public. The patterns and styles of church-prescribed head coverings very considerably from group to group, which makes a group's particular style a key element of its religious identity.

See also Gender Roles; Nonconformity

GAMEO ("Grebel, Conrad"), M. Gingerich (1970), Kraybill (1978), Scott (1986)

Health Practices   *See* Medicine

Heifer International

This nonprofit relief organization, formerly named Heifer Project, works to end hunger and poverty in many countries through the donation of animals. It was sponsored, directed, and supported by the CHURCH OF THE BRETHREN when it began at the outset of WORLD WAR II, but it soon became an ecumenical project.

The program was conceived by Dan West (1893–1971), a BRETHREN farmer from northern Indiana. When he served as a relief worker in Spain during the Spanish Civil War, he saw that the relief supplies donated to war victims were insufficient to sustain them. West approached his farming neighbors when he returned home and proposed that they donate and ship dairy cattle overseas so that families devastated by the war could restock their farms. The cattle would provide fresh milk for the families, and in turn, each family would be expected to pass along their cow's first calf to another family in need. In this way, they would be passing on the gift.

In June 1942 the project was approved as an official program of the BRETHREN SERVICE COMMISSION. After World War II, thousands of heifers were donated to families in countries across EUROPE, and many young Brethren men accompanied these shipments as "seagoing cowboys." In 1948 an interdenominational group took responsibility for the program and in 1953 incorporated Heifer Project as an independent nonprofit. The organization has been headquartered near Little Rock, Arkansas, since 1979 and was later renamed Heifer International.

Since its inception, Heifer International has donated many kinds of animals (from water buffalo to llamas to bees) to people in developing countries all over the world. The organization also offers training in animal care and reproduction as well as in new agricultural technology and sustainable farming practices. In the 60 years since its creation, Heifer International has aided over one million families in 110 countries.

See also Agriculture; Voluntary Service

BE I ("Heifer Project International"), D. Durnbaugh (1997a), G. Yoder (1978), http://www.heifer.org

Higher Education

Although some 16th-century ANABAPTIST leaders were trained in universities, prior to the late 1800s formal EDUCATION beyond the basic level was not encouraged or permitted by many Anabaptist groups, except in the NETHERLANDS, GERMANY, and RUSSIA. Many Anabaptist groups distanced themselves from educational institutions other than the church because the members wanted to be nonconformed to the broader culture and because they were persecuted by governments. These Anabaptists valued the practical skills used in agricultural vocations and theological self-education over formal schooling.

As Anabaptists assimilated in the 1800s in the Netherlands, the UNITED STATES, CANADA, and Russia, they created institutions of higher learning in order to train ministers and missionaries and to prepare members for nonagricultural vocations. The Dutch MENNONITES started a small seminary in 1735, which was enlarged in 1811 with the support of all Dutch Mennonite groups. In North America in the late 1800s, BRETHREN and Mennonites created educational institutes and Bible schools, some of which later developed into colleges and universities.

In addition to numerous Bible schools and institutes, assimilated Mennonite groups have nine liberal arts colleges and universities and four graduate-level seminaries located near Mennonite population centers in North America. According to a recent survey in the United States (CMP 2006), almost 60% of MENNONITE CHURCH USA members have some college education, with nearly 40% holding at least a four-year college degree. About 30% of CHURCH OF THE BRETHREN and BRETHREN IN CHRIST members are college graduates. The various Brethren groups have eight colleges and three seminaries in the United States.

As church-related colleges and universities developed more sophisticated and varied programs, students, faculty, and administration from non-Anabaptist backgrounds began to attend and staff them. This created opportunities for spreading Anabaptist perspectives, but it also encouraged the secularization of some of these institutions. Across the various church-related colleges, the percentage of students with Anabaptist backgrounds ranges from more than 50% to less than 5%.

The majority of Anabaptist youth and adults who attend college graduate from a state-sponsored or private institution not affiliated with an Anabaptist denomination. Among assimilated Anabaptists in the United States whose schooling included some higher education, those who attended a college related to their denomination for at least one year included 52% of Mennonite Church USA, 23% of Church of the Brethren, and 21% of Brethren in Christ members (CMP 2006).

Most TRADITIONAL GROUPS do not allow higher education, believing that it will lead youth away from the church and erode the church's identity and social boundaries. They also believe that higher education is simply not necessary to prepare young people for vocations in agriculture, business, construction, and trades.

See also Schools, Bible

BE I ("Higher Education"), Bittinger (1980), CMP 2006, D. Durnbaugh (1997b), GAMEO ("Colleges and Universities, Mennonite"), Kauffman and Driedger (1991), ME I ("Colleges")

Hispanic-American Anabaptists

This entry focuses on Hispanic-American ANABAPTISTS living in the United States and Canada rather than on Spanish-speaking Anabaptists living in the Caribbean Territories, Central America, and Mexico.

MENNONITE BRETHREN and MENNONITE CHURCH workers began mission outreach efforts in the 1930s among multigenerational families in south Texas who had maintained their Spanish culture and language for several genera-

Table 8　Anabaptist-Related Colleges and Universities

Brethren-related

Ashland University	Ashland, OH	http://www.ashland.edu
Bridgewater College	Bridgewater, VA	http://www.bridgewater.edu
Elizabethtown College	Elizabethtown, PA	http://www.etown.edu
Grace College	Winona Lake, IN	http://www.grace.edu
Juniata College	Huntingdon, PA	http://www.juniata.edu
La Verne University	La Verne, CA	http://www.laverne.edu
Manchester College	North Manchester, IN	http://www.manchester.edu
McPherson College	McPherson, KS	http://www.mcpherson.edu

Mennonite-related

Bethel College	North Newton, KS	http://www.bethelks.edu
Bluffton University	Bluffton, Ohio	http://www.bluffton.edu
Canadian Mennonite University	Winnipeg, MB	http://www.cmu.ca
Columbia Bible College	Abbotsford, BC	http://www.columbiabc.edu
Conrad Grebel University College	Waterloo, ON	http://grebel.uwaterloo.ca
Eastern Mennonite University	Harrisonburg, VA	http://www.emu.edu
Fresno Pacific University	Fresno, CA	http://www.fresno.edu
Goshen College	Goshen, IN	http://www.goshen.edu
Hesston College	Hesston, KS	http://www.hesston.edu
Messiah College	Grantham, PA	http://www.messiah.edu
Rosedale Bible College	Irwin, OH	http://www.rosedale.edu
Tabor College	Hillsboro, KS	http://www.tabor.edu

tions. During the same time period, other mission efforts began among Hispanic immigrants in Chicago.

In the 1970s, Hispanic congregations organized a fellowship (National Council of Hispanic Mennonite Churches) to strengthen their congregations and their mission outreach to fellow Spanish-speakers. Although relatively small in numbers, Spanish-speaking MENNONITES in North America increased at a rapid rate—about 30% annually in the 1970s and 1980s. Iglesia Menonita Hispana, an organization of Mennonite Hispanics that formed in 2000, represents about 20 different Spanish-speaking nationalities.

Three major clusters include Mexican-Americans, especially in large border states such as Texas and California; first-generation immigrants eager to maintain their native language and resist assimilation into North American culture; and descendants of first-generation immigrants who speak English and are more culturally assimilated. Anabaptists of Hispanic origin in North America are predominantly from Cuban, Mexican, and Puerto Rican backgrounds.

Congregations are concentrated in California, Florida, and Texas and in urban centers of the eastern and southern UNITED STATES. Mennonite Hispanic congregations are affiliated with MENNONITE CHURCH USA, MENNONITE CHURCH CANADA, and Mennonite Brethren denominations in Canada and the United States. Mennonite Church USA has about 80 Spanish-identity congregations with a membership of nearly 4,500. The Mennonite Brethren have over 50 Latino congregations.

There are some three dozen Hispanic congregations in Florida and several in California that relate to the BRETHREN IN CHRIST. Many of the church members in the Miami area are immigrants from Cuba.

The CHURCH OF THE BRETHREN, the BRETHREN CHURCH, and the GRACE BRETHREN have Spanish-speaking congregations in numerous states.

BE IV ("Hispanic Ministries"), Falcon (1986), Flores (2001), GAMEO ("Hispanic Mennonites"), Hinojosa (2009), Kanagy (2007), Martínez (2005), ME V ("Hispanic Mennonites"), http://www.bic-church.org/about/find.asp#

Historic Peace Churches

By the late 1930s, the BRETHREN, QUAKERS, and MENNONITES were known as the historic peace churches. This designation, suggested by Henry Peter Krehbiel (1862–1940), emerged from a joint peace conference in Kansas in 1935. The leaders of the three groups affirmed their religious pacifist stance while distinguishing themselves from the political PACIFISM movement that was becoming popular at that time.

The three groups have cooperated at various times throughout the 20th and 21st centuries, especially when trying to protect their status as CONSCIENTIOUS OBJECTORS during times of war. One notable example of their collaboration was the development of the Civilian Public Service program, which provided opportunities for ALTERNATIVE SERVICE in the UNITED STATES during WORLD WAR II.

Through their cooperation and advocacy for a PEACEMAKING theology, the three denominations have encouraged ecumenical peace conversations and initiatives in the World Council of Churches (WCC). For example, CHURCH OF THE BRETHREN and Mennonite leaders actively developed the WCC program "Decade to Overcome Violence 2001–2010."

BE I ("Historic Peace Churches"), D. Durnbaugh (1978), GAMEO ("Historic Peace Churches"), Keim and Stoltzfus (1988), ME V ("Historic Peace Churches"), Speicher and Durnbaugh (2003)

Holdeman Mennonites   *See* Church of God in Christ, Mennonite

Holidays, Religious

European ANABAPTISTS rejected the religious holidays that were based on Roman Catholic saints, but they did observe many of the basic Protestant and Catholic holy days, such as Good Friday, Easter, Pentecost, and Christmas, with special WORSHIP services, fasting, and celebrations. Some MENNONITE and BRETHREN groups in North America, both traditional and assimilated, were influenced by the Puritan rejection of certain religious seasons such as Advent, Epiphany, and Lent. Thus, many groups observe Christmas, Ascension Day, Good Friday, Easter, and Pentecost, but not Epiphany or Lent.

The North American Anabaptist groups that have retained more of their European roots have the most extensive church calendar. For example, the HUTTERITES celebrate days such as Annunciation Day and the Day of Jesus' Circumcision. Some AMISH groups observe the day after Christmas and Easter Monday as special times for social visiting and family gatherings. Many AMISH in the Midwest observe Epiphany (which they call Old Christmas) as a holiday and avoid making much of December 25, which they consider an overly commercialized day. In general, most Anabaptist groups tend to avoid the excessive commercialization and secularization of religious holidays.

In the last quarter of the 20th century, some ASSIMILATED GROUPS began to incorporate aspects of the broader Christian calendar into their worship by including the seasons of Advent and Lent. Some of these groups also rely on the lectionary cycle of biblical texts used in many Protestant and Catholic churches and have created Anabaptist-oriented lectionary aids.

Most Anabaptist groups hold their primary worship services on Sunday. Apart from attending worship services, other Sunday activities vary widely among Anabaptist groups. Many members of assimilated groups engage in recreation and leisure activities, and some do not object to employment on Sunday. Most of the TRADITIONAL GROUPS do not allow members to buy and sell or engage in any work or commercial activities on Sunday, other than caring for animals.

See also Holidays, Secular

GAMEO ("Christian Calendar"), J. Hostetler (1997),

ME II ("Holidays and Anniversaries"), ME V ("Christian Calendar"), L. Schmidt (1995)

Holidays, Secular

The types of secular holidays vary greatly by country because they are shaped by national themes and ethnic traditions. The involvement of ANABAPTIST groups in national holidays also varies, making it risky to make sweeping generalizations.

Members of ASSIMILATED GROUPS typically observe secular holidays by participating in family, friendship, or civic activities. TRADITIONAL GROUPS, in keeping with their separatist stance, are more likely to ignore holidays such as Halloween in the United States or its equivalent in other countries, and holidays that emphasize nationalistic military themes. The celebrations of national independence and war-related holidays (Memorial Day and Remembrance Day) have caused tensions in churches in the UNITED STATES and CANADA. Most Anabaptist groups have traditionally opposed participating in parades or other patriotic celebrations. They view militaristic NATIONALISM as compromising their peace witness as well as the separation of CHURCH AND STATE.

See also Holidays, Religious

BE I ("Independence Day"), GAMEO ("Christian Calendar"), J. Hostetler (1997), ME II ("Holidays and Anniversaries"), ME V ("Christian Calendar"), L. Schmidt (1995)

Holy Kiss

Following the instructions of the Apostle Paul and Middle Eastern custom, Christians in the early church (Acts 20:37) greeted one another with a kiss in both WORSHIP settings and informal gatherings. Many TRADITIONAL GROUPS, except the HUTTERITES, continue to use this mode of greeting (male to male and female to female) as a salutation and as a sign of spiritual fellowship during the ORDINANCES of BAPTISM, FOOTWASHING, and COMMUNION. The practice has largely disappeared within ASSIMILATED GROUPS.

In some groups it is primarily the ordained leaders who practice the holy kiss, while in other groups, lay members also participate in the RITUAL. The kiss symbolically confirms the genuine affection that believers feel for one another, and it serves as a boundary marker identifying who is part of the church community. Members of some traditional groups use the kiss as a sign of intergroup fellowship with members of other groups with similar beliefs and practices.

BE II ("Kiss, Holy"), GAMEO ("Kiss, Holy"), Kraybill (2001), E. Kreider (1987), ME III ("Kiss")

Holy Spirit

ANABAPTIST groups believe that the Holy Spirit, the third person of the Trinity, regenerates, guides, activates, and purifies the believer, as is then expressed in the believer's CONFESSION OF FAITH. Some early Anabaptists advocated the direct inspiration of the Spirit apart from the BIBLE, but most believed that any inner revelation by the Spirit required confirmation and congruence with the "outer" Word of God, the Scripture. A believer's inspiration by the Holy Spirit required affirmation by the church and consistency with the Holy Spirit's fruits as described in the Bible (Gal. 5:22–26).

With their PIETIST roots, the BRETHREN groups, especially those that accepted REVIVALISM, have often highlighted the experience of the Holy Spirit more than other Anabaptist groups. In the 1970s, members of some ASSIMILATED GROUPS responded to the wider CHARISMATIC movement by organizing conferences and ongoing committees centered on Holy Spirit renewal. In 1974 the Holy Spirit Renewal Group, which focused on charismatic healing, was founded within the CHURCH OF THE BRETHREN.

Anabaptist churches in Mexico and Central American countries and those with strong Hispanic influences in Canada and the United States tend to emphasize the gifts of the Holy Spirit more than churches with European cultural roots. Some of the newer immigrant congregations in Canada and the United States place a strong emphasis on the Holy Spirit in their WORSHIP services. Likewise, some assimilated groups that focus on evangelism and church growth have a more Pentecostal style of worship.

BE I ("Holy Spirit"), D. Brown (1978), Brunk (1972), GAMEO ("Holy Spirit"), Martínez (2006), ME II ("Holy Spirit"), ME V ("Holy Spirit"), C. Snyder (2004)

Home Schooling   *See* Schools, Elementary

Homosexuality

While not specifically mentioning homosexuality, official ANABAPTIST denominational statements written in the 1980s affirm that any sexual relations outside of a marriage covenant between a man and a woman are contrary to the will of God. TRADITIONAL GROUPS do not condone homosexuality or accept practicing homosexuals in their churches.

Until the mid-20th century the subject of sexuality, especially homosexuality, received little formal attention among Anabaptist groups. Members of ASSIMILATED GROUPS began to discuss it in the 1970s. The Brethren-Mennonite Council for Lesbian and Gay Concerns (later renamed the Brethren Mennonite Council for Lesbian, Gay, Bisexual, and Transgender Interests) was created in 1976 to provide support for homosexuals and their families and to advocate acceptance of homosexuals in the church. The organization was never officially accepted in MENNONITE and BRETHREN denominations, but it has provided significant resources and support for individuals, FAMILIES, and CONGREGATIONS interested in issues of SEXUALITY.

The topic of homosexuality stirs intense controversy among assimilated Mennonites and Brethren, as it does in the broader culture. Many assimilated Brethren and Mennonite congregations do not accept practicing homosexuals as church members, but some do, and others are known as "open and affirming" congregations that welcome everyone, regardless of sexual orientation.

A survey (CMP 2006) of assimilated Anabaptists in the United States found that almost 64% of MENNONITE CHURCH USA members, 55% of CHURCH OF THE BRETHREN members, and 79% of BRETHREN IN CHRIST members thought that their congregation should not accept homosexuals as members. In some denominations and regions, contentious differences over homosexuality have led to divisions within congregations and regional bodies.

BE II ("Sexuality, Human"), Bucher (1994), CMP 2006, GAMEO ("Sexuality"), Kraus (2001), ME V ("Sexuality"), Swartley (2003), http://www.bmclgbt.org

Honduras

Five ANABAPTIST groups in Honduras have some 15,000 members attending over 200 CONGREGATIONS. Most of the churches tend toward the CHARISMATIC style of WORSHIP that is common in the evangelical churches of Central America.

The oldest church, the Honduran Evangelical Mennonite Church, has about 4,750 members in 136 congregations. It was started by missionaries from Eastern Mennonite Missions who arrived on the northeastern coast of Honduras in 1950. This missionary effort began in the small coastal town of Trujillo and grew along the coast in Garifuna communities and then inland into the large banana-growing areas, and finally to La Ceiba and other urban centers. In the early 1970s about 40 Mennonite CONSCIENTIOUS OBJECTORS from the United States performed ALTERNATIVE SERVICE by working Peace Corps–style in agricultural development in rural villages. The Honduran Evangelical Mennonite Church emerged out of these mission and service efforts. The metropolitan area around San Pedro Sula has seen the greatest growth of the church in the 21st century.

The Honduran Evangelical Mennonite Church seeks to minister to both the spiritual and physical needs of people. When civil wars broke out in neighboring countries in the 1980s, refugees fled to Honduras where MENNONITES worked with the United Nations to help build emergency housing. This ministry eventually grew into a major development agency, the Mennonite Social Action Commission. The Peace and Justice Committee of the Honduran Evangelical Mennonite Church provided national leadership for a successful effort to abolish obligatory military service in 1995.

A second denomination, LIVING LOVE (Amor Viviente), formed in 1973 as the result of a Mennonite missionary couple's work with youth and alcoholics. Establishing small cell groups of new members, the church grew rapidly. The charismatic-style movement began in Tegucigalpa, the capital city, and attracted urban nominal Catholics. It is the largest Anabaptist denomination in Honduras, with 8,650 members in 32 congregations. Ten years after it began, Living Love sent its first missionaries to the UNITED STATES, where it has several affiliated churches.

The Evangelical Brethren in Christ Church formed in the arid areas of southern Honduras when BRETHREN IN CHRIST missionaries from Nicaragua arrived there in 1989. The congregations are mostly located in rural areas of southern Honduras, although a large congregation meets in Tegucigalpa. About 1,450 members attend 37 Brethren in Christ congregations.

Old Order AMISH from Ontario and Indiana started a settlement at Guaimaca in 1968. The group eventually divided, and those who favored farming with horses returned to Canada and the United States. Those who stayed in Honduras eventually became part of the Mennonite Christian Fellowship, a group that has five congregations and about 150 members. The Pilgrim Mennonite Conference in the United States established a mission in Honduras in 2005, which has two congregations and 50 members.

MENNONITE CENTRAL COMMITTEE (MCC) began working in Honduras in 1981, helping Salvadoran refugees coming across the border. Following the devastation of Hurricane Mitch in 1998, MCC provide $5.9 million in funds and volunteers to rebuild some 500 homes. MCC, with about a dozen expatriate staff, supports several Anabaptist organizations in educational projects, HIV/AIDS prevention, agricultural development, and the rehabilitation of gang members. MCC also sponsors educational efforts to prevent domestic violence and agricultural development work through Mennonite Christian Service, a Honduran Evangelical Mennonite Church organization, and the Committee of Social Development, a committee of the Evangelical Brethren in Christ.

GAMEO ("Honduras"), ME IV ("Honduras"), ME V ("Honduras"), Mennonite World Conference (2005), P. Schrag (2004), http://www.bic-church.org/wm/who-we-are/honduras.asp, http://www.mwc-cmm.org,

Horse-Drawn Transportation   *See* Amish; Old Colony Mennonite Church, Mexico; Old Order Mennonites, Groffdale Conference; Old Order Movement

Hospitals, Medical

MENNONITES in North America and RUSSIA began founding hospitals around 1900. Over the next 45 years, assimilated Mennonites established some 20 hospitals in or near Mennonite communities. In the prairie states and provinces, these Mennonite hospitals relied heavily on the service of single women called deaconesses. From 1960 to 1990, many Mennonite hospitals were merged, closed, or transferred to nonprofit corporations because of rising medical costs and the competitive nature of corporate-style health care, especially in the United States.

The Mennonite Medical Association is an organization of about 600 doctors, dentists, and medical/dental students who are members of Mennonite and BRETHREN IN CHRIST churches. It provides a network for consultation, encouragement, and service for these ANABAPTIST health care professionals.

ASSIMILATED GROUPS have often included various forms of health care in their domestic and foreign MISSIONS. In numerous instances mission efforts resulted in the establishment of hospitals. The BRETHREN built more hospital institutions in foreign mission settings (such as India, China, Nigeria, and French Equatorial Africa) than in North America. One exception was the Bethany Brethren Hospital in Chicago (founded in 1921). The hospital later merged with the Evangelical Hospital Association and the Lutheran General Hospital Association, but the CHURCH OF THE BRETHREN is still represented by members on the hospital's governing council.

TRADITIONAL GROUPS have not created medical hospitals, although some RETIREMENT COMMUNITIES operated by members of these groups provide nursing care, and some of these groups operate clinics as part of their mission programs.

See also Hospitals, Mental; Mennonite Health Services Alliance

BE I ("Bethany Brethren Hospital," "Hospitals"), BE IV ("Bethany Hospital"), GAMEO ("Hospitals, Clinics and Dispensaries"), ME II ("Hospitals"), G. Snyder (1995), Ziegler (1959), http://www.mennmed.org

Hospitals, Mental

The first ANABAPTIST mental hospital, Bethania, was founded by MENNONITES in 1910 in RUSSIA, but by 1927 the destruction of WORLD WAR I had forced the hospital to close. Significant Anabaptist interest in MENTAL HEALTH organizations began during WORLD WAR II. During the war about 1,500 Anabaptist men and 300 Anabaptist women worked along with other conscientious objectors in public mental health facilities as part of Civilian Public Service, an ALTERNATIVE SERVICE program. Witnessing the harsh conditions imposed on the mentally ill encouraged Mennonites to form a number of mental health facilities in the decades after the war: Brook Lane in Hagerstown, Maryland (1947); Kings View in Reedley, California (1951); Philhaven near Lebanon, Pennsylvania (1952); Prairie View in Newton, Kansas (1954); Penn Foundation in Sellersville, Pennsylvania (1955); Oaklawn in Elkhart, Indiana (1963); Kern View in Bakersfield, California (1966); Eden in Winkler, Manitoba (1967). These initiatives contributed to the emerging national conversations about improving care for the mentally disabled. Mennonite Mental Health Services, founded in 1952 as a part of MENNONITE CENTRAL COMMITTEE, managed these mental health centers until they became more independent. The facili-

ties are licensed by professional and governmental organizations to serve persons of all religions and races, but they still retain ties to Anabaptist churches.

See also Hospitals, Medical; Mennonite Health Services Alliance

BE II ("Mental Hospital Service"), Al Dueck (1989), GAMEO ("Mental Health Facilities and Services, North America"), ME III ("Mental Hospitals, Mennonite"), ME V ("Mental Health Facilities and Services, North America"), V. Neufeld (1983), J. Oyer (1982), Sareyan (1994), Taylor (2009), http://www.brooklane.org, http://www.edenhealth.mb.ca, http://www.kingsview.org, http://www.oaklawn.org, http://www.pennfoundation.org, http://www.philhaven.org, http://www.pvi.org

Humility   *See Gelassenheit*

Humor   *See Folklore*

Hutter, Jakob (d. 1536)

This leader of the HUTTERITES was a native of the Austrian Tyrol. Around 1533, he gave leadership to persecuted ANABAPTISTS in Moravia, where they had found temporary refuge. Several clusters of people committed to COMMUNAL LIVING had formed there in 1528. Hutter reinforced communal ownership of possessions and united competing factions into one cohesive group, which was later named for him. He led the Moravian Hutterites until his imprisonment, torture, and MARTYRDOM on February 25, 1536, in Innsbruck, AUSTRIA.

GAMEO ("Hutter, Jakob [d. 1536]"), J. Hostetler (1997), ME II ("Hutter, Jakob"), Packull (1995)

Hutterites

Faced with bitter persecution for their religious faith, some ANABAPTISTS in Europe fled to safe havens in Moravia, in present-day Czech Republic, where the Hutterites formed in 1528. They rejected private property and began sharing material goods in the spirit of the apostolic church as described in the New Testament book of Acts. In 1536, JAKOB HUTTER (d. 1536), an early leader for whom the group was eventually

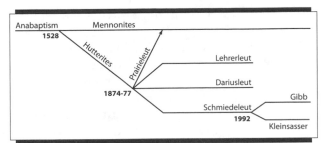

FIGURE 9 Historical Formation of Hutterite Groups

named, was captured and burned at the stake as a heretic. The foremost apologist for Hutterite belief was PETER RIEDEMANN (1506–1556).

The early years of Hutterite history were filled with frequent migration and PERSECU-TION. According to *The Chronicle of the Hutterian Brethren,* more than 1,000 Hutterites gave their lives for the sake of their faith. Vicious propaganda spread lies about them in the 16th and 17th centuries, and many faced cruel means of torture: burning, branding, amputation, drowning, and starvation in dungeons. Against incredible odds, the Hutterites survived. Several times during the 18th century their communal living pattern ended but later was restored. In 1770 they moved to Russia and, a century later, to the United States.

The Hutterites have enjoyed remarkable growth since they arrived in the United States in the 1870s. Three immigrant colonies multiplied to some 480 colonies, with an average of 100 people in each. Persecuted for being conscientious objectors during WORLD WAR I, many Hutterites moved to Canada. About three-fourths of the colonies are in the Canadian provinces of Alberta, Manitoba, and Saskatchewan. Hutterites in the United States reside primarily in South Dakota and Montana. They number about 19,100 members (or 49,000 when counting children as well as adults). They have four subgroups: Dariusleut, Lehrerleut, and two branches of Schmiedeleut.

Hutterites live in large agricultural colonies segregated from the larger so-ciety. Colony buildings, clustered like a small village on 5,000 to 10,000 acres of land, are often hidden from major highways. Huge tractors pull modern equipment across vast stretches of prairie. A growing number of colonies operate flourishing businesses as well.

The colony lives as an extended family—eating meals together in a common dining hall and sharing laundry facilities. Each family has an apartment with a coffee area, living room, bathroom, and bedrooms. Long barrack-like houses with several apartments typically encircle the dining hall and church building. The average family has five or six children. Youth are usually baptized between 21 and 25 years of age.

Hutterites speak an Austrian DIALECT called *Hutterisch.* They also learn to read High German, which is used in sermons and other religious writings. Young people learn English in colony schools operated by public school districts.

Hutterite beliefs emphasize the importance of COMMUNAL LIVING—sharing material goods, surrendering self-will for communal harmony, and separating from an evil world. Communal property, the hallmark of Hutterite culture, distinguishes them from other Anabaptist groups. Private property, in Hutterite eyes, symbolizes selfishness, greed, and vanity, and causes many other forms of evil. Sharing material goods is seen as the highest form of Christian love. Hutterites seek to follow the example

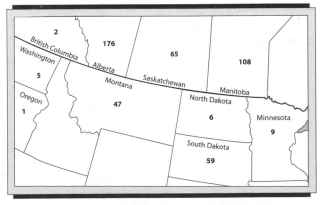

FIGURE 10 Distribution of Hutterite Colonies in North America
Source: Janzen and Stanton (2010).

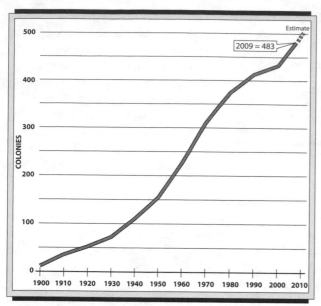

500 ┈┈┈┈┈┈┈┈┈┈┈┈┈┈┈┈┈ Estimate

2009 = 483

400

COLONIES

300

200

100

0

1900 1910 1920 1930 1940 1950 1960 1970 1980 1990 2000 2010

FIGURE 11 Growth of Hutterite Colonies in North America, 1900–2010
Source: Janzen and Stanton (2010).

of the early church described in Acts (2:44–45), where Christians held their economic property in common and shared with each other without claiming property rights.

Apart from a few personal belongings— clothes, knickknacks, dishes, books, furniture— individual Hutterites have no private property. Land, farm machinery, vehicles, and household furniture are owned by the colony. Everyone works without pay. At baptism, members relinquish any claim to colony property. Those who abandon colony life may take only a few clothes and family items.

The Hutterite "experiment" has endured nearly 500 years, making Hutterites the oldest communal group in North America. But communalism is not just an interesting experiment in their eyes; it is a sincere attempt to practice Christian teachings that point to eternal life.

See also Bruderhof

J. Friesen (1999), L. Gross (1980), P. Gross (1965), Harrison (1997), J. Hostetler (1997), Hutterian Brethren (1987, 1998), Rod Janzen (2005), Janzen and Stanton (2010), Kraybill and Bowman (2001), Packull (1995, 2007), Scheer (1980), Schlachta (2009)

Hutterisch   *See* Dialects

Hymnal: A Worship Book

This hymnbook was published in 1992 by three ASSIMILATED GROUPS: the CHURCH OF THE BRETHREN, the MENNONITE CHURCH, and the GENERAL CONFERENCE MENNO- NITE CHURCH. These groups also published *Accompaniment Handbook* (1992), *Companion* (1996), and a series of supplements including *Sing the Jour- ney* (2005) and *Sing the Story* (2007). The *Handbook* provides instrumental (primarily keyboard) accompaniment scores, essays on musical topics, and specific suggestions on congregational SINGING for many of the hymns. The *Companion* includes historical back- ground on each hymn and biographical sketches of the composers and authors, and the supplements contain some familiar and many new hymns that were not in- cluded in the hymnal.

Hymnal: A Worship Book draws on the com- mon core of ecumenical HYMNODY among North American Protestants, but it also includes hymns by MENNONITE and BRETHREN com- posers and authors, hymns that emphasize specifically Anabaptist themes such as FOOT- WASHING and DISCIPLESHIP, and German chorales. The hymnal includes American folk hymns and hymns from outside North America too, but very few contemporary praise choruses typical of CHARISMATIC styles of WORSHIP. Some gender-specific words have been altered to reflect contemporary inclusive language, but the words of older, well-known hymns that use male terminology for God are rarely altered.

Hymnal (1992), Moyer (1994), D. Smucker (1994)

Hymnody

ANABAPTIST groups possess complex tradi- tions of hymnody that were influenced by their Anabaptist and PIETIST origins in EUROPE and by many other churches. The first edition of the AUSBUND, the oldest Christian hymnal in

Table 9	Resources on Hutterite Groups

Books

From the Tyrol to North America: The Hutterite Story through the Centuries, Schlachta, 2009

The Golden Years of the Hutterites: Witness and Thought of the Communal Moravian Anabaptists during the Walpot Era, 1565–1578, L. Gross, 1980

Hutterite Beginnings: Communitarian Experiments during the Reformation, Packull, 1995

The Hutterites in North America, Janzen and Stanton, 2010

Hutterite Society, J. Hostetler, 1997

On the Backroad to Heaven: Old Order Hutterites, Mennonites, Amish, and Brethren, Kraybill and Bowman, 2001

Information Centers and Libraries

Archives of the Mennonite Church, Goshen, IN (http://www.mcusa-archives.org)

Heritage Hall Museum and Archives, Freeman, SD (http://www.freemanmuseum.org)

Mennonite Library and Archives, Newton, KS (http://www.bethelks.edu/mla/index.php)

Young Center for Anabaptist and Pietist Studies, Elizabethtown, PA (http://www.etown.edu/YoungCenter.aspx)

Video

The Hutterites: To Care and Not to Care (DVD/VHS, 1984, Gateway Films/Vision Video)

continuous use, was published in GERMANY in 1564. This collection of martyr ballads and hymn texts written in German remains the only hymnal used for Sunday WORSHIP among the Old Order AMISH, and it serves as a source of hymn texts in translation for some other Anabaptist groups.

MENNONITES in the NETHERLANDS published many hymnals in Dutch, which were also used by the Mennonites living in POLAND/Prussia until the mid-1700s, when the Prussian Mennonites began to speak German. They published their first German hymnal, GEISTREICHES GESANGBUCH, in 1767 in Königsberg, East Prussia.

For centuries, HUTTERITE song leaders used only handwritten hymn texts. Those manuscripts served as the basis for *DIE LIEDER DER HUTTERISCHEN BRÜDER*, their first published hymnal, which was printed in 1914 in South Dakota.

Mennonites of Swiss–south German origin and many BRETHREN groups emphasized SINGING hymns in unison in a cappella style (without instrumental accompaniment). The first hymnals compiled by Mennonites in North America were *Zions Harfe* (1803) and *UNPARTHEYISCHES GESANGBUCH* (1804), both of which were printed in southeastern Pennsylvania.

In the mid-1800s, assimilated Mennonites and Brethren began using English in their worship services and four-part singing of hymns. As a result, their unison singing and their German-language hymn traditions almost disappeared, although some TRADITIONAL GROUPS continue to sing and worship in German.

Many ASSIMILATED GROUPS continue to sing a cappella occasionally, but they also use a wide variety of musical instruments in worship, including pipe organs, guitars, and drums. *HYMNAL: A WORSHIP BOOK*, which was published in 1992 as a joint effort of the largest assimilated Mennonite and Brethren groups in North America, has an *Accompaniment Handbook* (1992), which provides scores for instrumental accompaniment of many of the hymns.

Mennonite and Brethren groups outside Canada and the United States usually sing hymn texts and tunes shaped by their national and ethnic traditions.

See also Devotional Literature

BE I ("Hymnals," "Hymns"), H. Durnbaugh (1986), Faus (1988), GAMEO ("Hymnology," "Singing"), Kropf and Nafziger (2001), H. Martens (2002), ME II ("Hymnology"), ME V ("Hymnology," "Singing"), Slough and King (2007), P. M. Yoder (1964)

Identity

The identity of a group, both for in-group members and for outsiders, is shaped by unique beliefs and practices. Identities change slowly over time as distinctive customs and values change. The most enduring and widely known identity of most ANABAPTIST groups relates to their PACIFISM and CONSCIENTIOUS OBJECTION to military service. The MENNONITES and BRETHREN along with the QUAKERS have been known as HISTORIC PEACE CHURCHES since 1935. The RITUALS or ORDINANCES of Anabaptist groups have traditionally shaped their identities as well.

Among TRADITIONAL GROUPS, distinctive practices related to dress and the use of TECHNOLOGY shape each group's identity. Some OLD ORDER MENNONITE groups drive horse and buggy, whereas others drive automobiles. The head scarf/kerchief worn by HUTTERITE women distinguishes different groups. For some AMISH groups, the color of their buggy tops—brown, yellow, white, black, grey—is one symbol of the group's identity. In general, the identities of traditional groups are rooted in specific daily practices while those of ASSIMILATED GROUPS are molded more by abstract values and beliefs.

Social change in assimilated groups transforms their identities as long-held customs or beliefs erode. Pacifism has been a central component of the identity of many assimilated groups. One scholar (Peachey) in 1968 argued that the MENNONITE CHURCH was undergoing an "identity crisis" related to rapidly changing lifestyles, dress, and use of media such as television. Many of these shifts were prompted by a trend away from an agrarian way of life, greater mobility, and increasing higher education. Thirty years later, other scholars described another "identity crisis," related to a different set of issues: declining church membership, loss of historic beliefs, growing ethnic diversity, and the growing influence of popular-brand Christianity in the United States. Changing social conditions raise new questions about identity. Group identities that are tied to abstract values and beliefs are more fluid and able to change more discretely than those anchored in external practices.

See also Ethnicity

C. Bowman (2008), Groff (1975), Juhnke (1988), Kanagy (2007), Kraybill (1988), Peachey (1968), Redekop and Steiner (1988), Scott (1986), Ziegler (1975)

Iglesia Nacional Evangélica Menonita Guatemalteca   *See* National Evangelical Guatemalan Mennonite Church

Immigration   *See* Migration

Infant Baptism   *See* Baptism

Institutions

In the late 19th century, ASSIMILATED GROUPS began building church-related organizations to address needs of and provide services for regional and national associations of churches. The pace of institution building accelerated in the 20th century and reflected the institution-building patterns in the larger society—demonstrating how ANABAPTIST churches were assimilating the practices and values of the larger society. By the mid-20th century, Anabaptist institutions included CREDIT UNIONS, educational agencies, historical societies and libraries, HOSPITALS, MENTAL HEALTH institutions, MISSION agencies, MUTUAL AID programs, PUBLISHING ORGANIZATIONS, schools and colleges, service agencies, INSURANCE providers, seminaries, RETIREMENT COMMUNITIES, and recreational CAMPS.

Despite theological differences, most assimilated and a few traditional Anabaptist church groups cooperate in national and international church-related organizations such as MENNONITE WORLD CONFERENCE, BRETHREN WORLD ASSEMBLY, and MENNONITE CENTRAL COMMITTEE (MCC).

John H. Oberholtzer (1809–1895), one of the founders of the GENERAL CONFERENCE MENNONITE CHURCH, helped to develop MISSIONS, THEOLOGICAL EDUCATION, and publications. He introduced a written constitution, a catechism, and SUNDAY SCHOOLS in the group he helped to form in 1847.

MENNONITE Orie O. Miller (1892–1977) was an architect of institutional building and management whose influence shaped numerous institutions in the mid-20th century. Miller was the first executive director of MCC, serving from 1935 to 1958. He served as a key leader in creating and sustaining some of the many programs that developed out of MCC: Civilian Public Service, MENNONITE ECONOMIC DEVELOPMENT ASSOCIATES, Mennonite Mental Health Services, National Service Board for Religious Objectors, Mennonite Camp Association, Menno Travel Service, Mennonite Mutual Aid (now EVERENCE), and MENNONITE FOUNDATION.

BRETHREN leader Michael Robert "M. R." Zigler (1891–1985) was a contemporary of Orie Miller. Zigler played an influential role in creating and shaping Brethren institutions in the 20th century including BRETHREN SERVICE COMMISSION, BRETHREN ENCYCLOPEDIA, INC., and ON EARTH PEACE ASSEMBLY. He represented Brethren interests in many ecumenical conversations worldwide.

This plethora of ethnic-religious organizations has shaped and reinforced the identity of specific denominations by providing significant service to their members as well as a robust Christian witness to the larger world. Anabaptists who erected denominational structures strongly believed they were doing it to advance the gospel through missions, education, hospitals, and publications. Although they were building modern forms of social organizations, they were motivated by Bible-based intentions and fervent religious convictions.

TRADITIONAL GROUPS have fewer formal organizations than assimilated groups. Groups such as the AMISH and HUTTERITES have some informal committees and networks stretching across congregational and colony boundaries, but they do not have highly bureaucratized institutions like the assimilated churches. Some conservative church groups have developed publishing, service, and mission organizations. (Examples include CHRISTIAN AID MINISTRIES, PATHWAY PUBLISHERS, Christian Light Publications, and ANABAPTIST FOUNDATION.) In general, the growth of institutions reflects the degree of assimilation into the larger world; nevertheless, many Anabaptist organizations have retained a distinctive ethnic identity that shapes their corporate values and practices.

See also Higher Education; Schools, Bible; Schools, Elementary; Schools, Secondary

C. Bowman (1995), D. Durnbaugh (1989, 1997a), C. Redekop (1989), Ruth (1984)

Insurance

Throughout their history, ANABAPTIST groups have generally relied on informal, spontaneous MUTUAL AID to assist fellow members who faced financial and property losses. Beginning in the 1600s, MENNONITES in Prussia and RUSSIA operated church-based insurance funds for property loss.

When commercial life insurance became available in North America in the 1800s, Anabaptist groups forbade their members to utilize it because they believed it encouraged individualism and self-sufficiency, lessened dependence on God and the church COMMUNITY, and placed a monetary value on human life created in the image of God. However, beginning in the 1860s some Mennonites and BRETHREN created insurance companies for material loss from fire and storm. With the rise of the automobile and accompanying governmental regulations in the early 1900s, the need for liability insurance became pressing; some Mennonite-related companies eventually arose to meet this need.

Mennonite Mutual Aid (now called EVERANCE) was created in 1945 and eventually provided life, health, and, later, auto liability insurance. Today it covers many Anabaptist groups, provides various insurance products, including health insurance, and offers many financial services. CHURCH OF THE BRETHREN BENEFIT TRUST, established in 1943, offers similar financial and insurance services to members of that denomination.

The rapidly rising cost of medical treatment has strained the health insurance resources of both TRADITIONAL GROUPS and ASSIMILATED GROUPS. Most members of assimilated groups purchase private health, auto, home, disability, long-term care, and life insurance from commercial insurance companies or through their employers. Others purchase it from Anabaptist-related insurance agencies. Because CANADA instituted provincially administered health insurance programs with extensive governmental regulation, Anabaptists groups there do not have their own health insurance plans. Most, but not all, members of traditional groups in Canada participate in the public health programs.

Many traditional groups have their own mutual aid programs that cover health costs and hospitalization as well as property damage and losses from fire and storm damage. These simple, informal programs have virtually no administrative costs and are available only to church members. Some traditional groups also have voluntary liability aid plans in the event that LITIGATION is brought against them because of a member's negligence or the malfunctioning of products or services.

The HUTTERITES need no insurance plans because they practice COMMUNAL LIVING. All individual needs are covered by the colony. In the case of large disasters or special needs, colonies assist one another.

BE I ("Insurance"), GAMEO ("Insurance"), Kraybill (2001), P. Lederach (2002), ME III ("Insurance"), ME V ("Insurance"), T. Schlabach (2009), Swartley and Kraybill (1998)

Intermarriage

Until the 1900s, most ANABAPTIST groups discouraged or prohibited marriage between their members and persons outside their group (unless the outsider joined the group). Some groups permitted marriage to outsiders who were Christian, if church leaders approved. Their practice of endogamy (marrying within the group) was based not only on cultural custom but also on an understanding that the church was composed of members who agreed to particular ethical standards of behavior and beliefs. Their experience of PERSECUTION made many Anabaptists wary of people outside their COMMUNITY, which also contributed to the practice of endogamy.

TRADITIONAL GROUPS have a high level of endogamy. A member of a traditional Anabaptist group will typically leave the group voluntarily if he or she plans to marry an outsider. The HUTTERITES have almost no marriage with outsiders (exogamy), and rates for other traditional groups are very low because many of them excommunicate members who marry outside their group. One exception is the OLD GERMAN BAPTIST BRETHREN; they permit members to marry nonmembers.

In ASSIMILATED GROUPS, marriage to outsiders is widely accepted. Exogamy is higher among urban Anabaptists and those exposed to greater social DIVERSITY. In general, greater assimilation means more frequent intermarriage. Exogamy involves both loss and gain of members for assimilated groups.

See also Family

Driedger, Vogt, and Reimer (1983), GAMEO ("Intermarriage"), Kauffman and Harder (1975), ME III ("Mixed Marriage"), ME V ("Intermarriage")

International *See* Anabaptist Groups, International

Internet *See* Computer

Iraq War

The U.S.-led invasion of Iraq in March 2003 troubled many members of ANABAPTIST churches in North America. In 2002, when U.S. government officials began to talk publically about invading Iraq, numerous MENNONITE and BRETHREN groups engaged in discussions and public witness against war and searched for nonviolent alternatives.

Several peace gatherings for leaders and lay members were held in January 2002, and on Palm Sunday of that year about 4,000 Mennonites sent faxes to the White House to protest a possible invasion. Various forms of protest and witness throughout 2002 included prayer vigils and the printing and distribution of "Pray for Peace" pins, peace flags, t-shirts, and bumper stickers. Over 17,000 Mennonites signed a letter to President George W. Bush (1946–) protesting an invasion. CHRISTIAN PEACEMAKER TEAMS entered Iraq in November 2002, the same month that members of many Mennonite congregations were encouraged to fast for peace and to sign a peace pledge. In January 2003 some 10,000 people (Mennonites and others), in a "peace blitz," promised to take 10 actions to avert war.

The activists were disheartened when the U.S.-led invasion of Iraq began in March 2003. Members of TRADITIONAL GROUPS were largely silent about the war; even though they are CONSCIENTIOUS OBJECTORS, they think it is inappropriate for Christians to try to influence or protest GOVERNMENT policies or actions. Several ASSIMILATED GROUPS eventually issued statements on the war. In 2004, Annual Conference of the CHURCH OF THE BRETHREN called its members to prayer and repentance and to witness constantly against all war and violence. Two years later the General Board of the same denomination endorsed a resolution urging the U.S. and other governments to remove their troops from Iraq. In 2005 the delegate assembly of MENNONITE CHURCH USA reiterated its commitment to peace and to searching for alternatives to war and called for an end to the U.S. military presence in Iraq.

Despite numerous statements and peace activities from denominational leaders and grassroots organizers, not all members of assimilated groups opposed the war. In some congregations different views of the war stirred controversy, and some young people voluntarily enlisted for military service. In a survey (CMP 2006), some members of assimilated groups in the United States expressed support for the U.S. invasion of Iraq; 24% of MENNONITE CHURCH USA respondents, 47% of CHURCH OF THE BRETHREN respondents, and 61% of BRETHREN IN CHRIST respondents agreed that the United States did the right thing by going to war in Iraq.

See also Nationalism; Peacemaking

T. Brown (2008), CMP 2006, http://www.coban nualconference.org/ac_statements/2004Iraq.html, http://www.cobannualconference.org/ac_statements/2006IraqWarResolution.pdf, http://www.mennonite usa.org/Default.aspx?tabid=110, http://peace.menno link.org/articles/mennoiraq02.html

Jamaica

The Jamaica Mennonite Church began when missionaries from the Virginia Mennonite Board of Missions began a MISSION outreach in 1955. The Jamaican church has about 675 members in 13 congregations scattered across the country. In addition to caring for the spiritual needs of its members, the church founded and operates Maranatha School for the Deaf. The church maintains ties with the Virginia Mennonite Conference and the MENNONITE churches of Trinidad and Tobago.

Several small conservative BRETHREN groups supported Christ's Ambassadors, a mission effort in Jamaica for many years. In 2007 this mission (one congregation with 25 members) became affiliated with Biblical Mennonite Alliance. The CHURCH OF GOD IN CHRIST, MENNONITE group has two congregations in Jamaica with about 25 members. From 1970 to 2008, MENNONITE CENTRAL COMMITTEE (MCC) workers in Jamaica actively advocated for people with mental illnesses through various counseling services. MCC staff also worked with education and mentoring programs for children and youth in organizations that work for human rights. The MCC program closed in 2008.

GAMEO ("Jamaica"), ME V ("Jamaica"), Mennonite World Conference (2005)

Jesus Christ, Doctrine of

ANABAPTIST theology centers on the life, teachings, death, and resurrection of Jesus Christ. It views all of these as expressions of God's love for creation. These aspects also form the foundation for Anabaptist faith and practice. Anabaptists emphasize the believer's joyful obedience to Christ and faith in Christ as Redeemer and Lord. This obedience is expressed through Christian DISCIPLESHIP and is patterned on the life and teachings of Jesus as revealed in the BIBLE.

Anabaptist theology views Jesus as the first martyr in a long line of believers who were willing to suffer death in order to be faithful to the will of God. This theology relies on the New Testament, especially the SERMON ON THE MOUNT, in which Jesus describes the virtues for faithful, pacifist, humble disciples.

Anabaptists understand the church to be the "body of Christ" (Eph. 4:15), which is knit together though love and loyalty to Jesus Christ. The church is the visible community of Jesus' disciples, so the doctrine of Jesus Christ is closely related to the doctrine of the church. By the mid-1900s, Anabaptist theologians began to develop the dimensions of this Christ-centered ecclesiology. One of the most influential books in this regard, both within and outside Anabaptist circles, was *The Politics of Jesus* (1972 and 1994) by MENNONITE John Howard Yoder (1927–1997). Yoder based Christian social ETHICS on Jesus' call for the church as an alternative, called-out, covenantal community. James McClendon (1924–2000), a CHURCH OF THE BRETHREN member, wrote extensively on Christology in a three-volume series on Anabaptist theology.

Some Anabaptist theologians in the late 20th century placed more emphasis on the HOLY SPIRIT. They argued that this CHARISMATIC element was necessary to prevent Christian faith and experience from shrinking to merely ethical practices. Theological currents from the broader church context, such as FUNDAMENTALISM, ECUMENISM, EVANGELICALISM, and REVIVALISM, have also influenced the image of Jesus Christ held by ASSIMILATED GROUPS. Because of their separatist stance and limited use of mass media, TRADITIONAL GROUPS have been more immune to non-Anabaptist theological influences.

See also Anabaptism, Theology of

BE I ("Christology"), GAMEO ("Christology"), Kraus (1987), McClendon (1994, 2000, 2002), ME V ("Christology"), C. Snyder (2004), J. Weaver (1983), J. H. Yoder (1972/1994)

Journal of Mennonite Studies

This interdisciplinary annual PERIODICAL began in 1983 at the University of Winnipeg in Manitoba. The articles, book reviews, and occasional fiction offer literary, historical, social historical, and cultural perspectives on MENNO-NITE topics. While most of the articles pertain to the history and culture of Mennonites from RUSSIA and CANADA, some include the experience of Mennonites in the NETHERLANDS, northern GERMANY, POLAND/Prussia, the UNITED STATES, and Latin America. The journal covers a wide range of ANABAPTIST themes.

    http://mennonitestudies.uwinnipeg.ca/jms/

Jury Duty

Many ANABAPTIST groups traditionally empha-sized the separation of CHURCH AND STATE and nonparticipation in political offices. There-fore, they prohibited jury service, because jury members must assent to the use of coercion, force, and possibly even CAPITAL PUNISH-MENT against a defendant. Some groups also cite Jesus' teaching, "Judge not that you be not judged" (Matt. 7:1), as a reason for not sitting on juries.

Beginning in the late 1800s, ASSIMILATED GROUPS increasingly participated in a wider range of economic, social, and political arenas, including jury service. Some assimilated Anabap-tists who oppose capital punishment refuse jury service in capital cases but serve on other cases.

Many TRADITIONAL GROUPS have retained the prohibition against jury duty in general and especially when capital cases are involved. The legal systems of CANADA and the UNITED STATES usually grant exemptions from specific jury service for those with religious objections.

See also Litigation

BE I ("Jury Service"), D. Martin (2003), Ruth-Heffelbower (1991), T. Schlabach (1988)

Justice   *See* Social Justice

Kanadier Mennonites

In 1871 the Tsarist government in RUSSIA eliminated many of the special privileges that GERMAN-speaking MENNONITES had enjoyed for 80 years, and announced plans to reexamine the exemption from military service. Although they were promised various types of ALTERNATIVE SERVICE options, the more traditional Mennonites, approximately one-third of those in Russia, decided to emigrate.

Beginning in 1874 and continuing for about 10 years, some 7,000 Russian Mennonites moved to CANADA and about 10,000 to the UNITED STATES. Canada promised the immigrants exemptions from military service and public education and allowed them to settle in compact agricultural reserves in the prairie provinces. Mennonites of Swiss origin in both Canada and the United States provided MUTUAL AID to some of the new immigrants.

Starting in 1923 and continuing for about seven years, another large group of about 20,000 Russian Mennonites immigrated to North America, primarily to Canada. To distinguish between the two waves of immigration, the group that came earlier (1874) became known as Kanadier and the group that came later (1923) were called RUSSLÄNDER.

The Kanadier Mennonites constituted three distinct groups. The largest one (about 3,200 people) became known as the OLD COLONY (or Reinländer) MENNONITE CHURCH. It originated from Chortitza (Khortitsa) Colony, the first or "oldest" Mennonite colony in Russia, which was founded in 1789, and its offspring, Fuerstenland Colony. The second group was the Bergthal Mennonite Church, named after its colony of origin in Russia, which was founded in 1836. Third, the Kleine Gemeinde (literally, "small church") was a small reform group of some 900 people that had begun in 1812 in Molotschna Colony and relocated to Borosenko Colony in the 1860s. During the 1870s immigration to North America, the Kleine Gemeinde divided into two subgroups, one in Manitoba and one in Nebraska.

These groups all spoke a West Prussian Low German DIALECT (*Plautdietsch*) and in Manitoba settled on exclusively Mennonite blocks of contiguous acres called the East and West Reserves, one on either side of the Red River. Here they replicated their Old World farm village system, and most of them constructed conjoined house-barns. They also recreated INSTITUTIONS from their Russian homeland: schools, fire insurance agencies, mutual aid societies, and farm village councils.

Of the three groups, the Old Colony Mennonite Church (or Reinländer) was the most conservative. Most of its members settled on the open prairie land of the West Reserve, in the vicinity of present-day Winkler, Manitoba.

During the 1920s about two-thirds of the Old Colony community relocated to MEXICO after governments in Manitoba and Saskatchewan passed laws requiring English-language instruction for children. Many of those who remained in Canada moved to more isolated communities in the northern parkland regions of Alberta, Saskatchewan, and British Columbia. In the second half of the 20th century many Old Colony Mennonites living in Mexico moved to Bolivia. Others returned to Canada and established new congregations in Leamington and Aylmer (Ontario) and Tabor (southern Alberta).

The Bergthal Mennonite Church was the second major conservative church group that arrived in Manitoba from Imperial Russia in the 1870s. About 20 years later the group splintered into three distinct groups.

A small progressive group retained the name Bergthal Mennonite Church. (This body founded the Conference of Mennonites of Canada in 1902, which evolved into MENNONITE CHURCH CANADA). The conservative majorities formed two churches: Chortitzer Mennonite Church (East Reserve) and Sommerfeld Mennonite Church (West Reserve), named for the villages of their bishops. The Chortitzer and Sommerfeld churches resisted fashionable clothing, town life, and public schools. Many Sommerfelder Mennonites moved to present-day Saskatchewan in the 1890s and reverted to the name Bergthaler or Saskatchewan Bergthaler.

In the 1920s and 1940s, many Chortitzer, accompanied by some Sommerfelder and Saskatchewan Bergthaler Mennonites, moved to Paraguay to maintain their private schools and conservative ways. Those who remained in Canada continued to live in German-speaking, Plain communities, often in new settlements in the northern parkland regions of Alberta, Saskatchewan, and British Columbia. In 1936 some members of the Sommerfeld church in Manitoba formed the mission-minded EVANGELICAL MENNONITE MISSION CONFERENCE (also known as Rudnerweide).

In 1958, other, more conservative Sommerfelders formed the Reinländ Mennonite Church, which eventually grew into a network of churches in southern Manitoba, northwestern Ontario, Texas, and Bolivia. By the end of the 20th century these groups in Canada had become more open: the Sommerfelders showed strong support for MENNONITE CENTRAL COMMITTEE, while the Chortitzers supported Bible college education and also allowed fashionable clothes and musical instruments. Each group also established a congregation in Winnipeg.

The third conservative group to arrive in Manitoba in the 1870s was the Kleine Gemeinde. It emphasized strict NONRESISTANCE, nonparticipation in municipal GOVERNMENT, and simplicity in architecture and dress. It was, however, more open to educational reform, including teacher training, and it even registered its schools with the provincial government to qualify for public grants. In a schism in the early 1880s, about half of the Kleine Gemeinde, including its bishop, Peter Toews (1839–1914), and most of its ministers, joined the CHURCH OF GOD IN CHRIST, MENNONITE group, founded by John Holdeman (1832–1900) of Ohio and known popularly as the Holdeman Mennonites.

The two groups had many similarities, including openness to some educational reform, nonparticipation in local government, and avoidance of fashionable clothes, musical instruments, higher education, and photography. The Holdeman Mennonites, however, used English

in some services, allowed women to vote, were more open to the automobile, embraced revival meetings, and emphasized the doctrine of one true church of God.

After World War I the Holdeman Mennonites became more conservative, while the Kleine Gemeinde began to accept missions and town life, thus alienating a conservative wing, which moved to Mexico in 1948. In 1952 the Kleine Gemeinde changed its name to EVANGELICAL MENNONITE CONFERENCE (EMC), signaling support for missions and the English language. It also embraced town life, higher education, and support for such broader organizations as Mennonite Central Committee. Both the EMC and the Holdeman Mennonites were active in "colonization" programs, establishing new rural settlements and mission outreach programs in non-Mennonite communities.

Conservative Kleine Gemeinde congregations were reestablished in Manitoba's interlake district, southern Ontario, and Nova Scotia in the 1970s and 1980s, when members began returning from Mexico. Some of these members also established conservative Kleine Gemeinde congregations in the United States. During the same time the Holdeman Mennonites established small congregations across Canada.

GAMEO ("Old Colony Mennonite Church"), R. Loewen (2004, 2008), ME V ("Old Colony Mennonites")

K'ekchi' Mennonite Foundation

The K'ekchi' Mennonite Foundation is the social justice arm of the K'ekchi' Mennonite Church of GUATEMALA. The church began in 1972 and legalized the Foundation in 1998 to administer and strengthen three programs: education, health, and development. The Foundation began as a social service agency to build connections between the church and the community. The health program, funded by the government, serves a population of 80,000. The educational program includes literacy work, an adult secondary degree completion program, and BEZALEEL EDUCATION CENTER—a bilingual Spanish and K'ekchi' boarding school that offers vocational and other educational programs. The development program includes agricultural projects supported by HEIFER INTERNATIONAL and a resettlement community, Bethel, which helps K'ekchi' families acquire legitimate land titles.

http://bezaleel.mennonite.net/

Kiss *See* Holy Kiss

Kleine Davidische Psalterspiel der Kinder Zions, Das *(The Small Davidic Psaltery of the Children of Zion)*

This 1744 hymnal, published by Christopher Sauer I (1695–1758) in Pennsylvania, was the first hymnal published by the BRETHREN in North America. It included 56 hymns from the first Brethren hymnal, GEISTREICHES GESANG-BUCH (1720), published in GERMANY. Most of the hymn texts were written by Brethren or PIETIST poets; no musical notes were included. Reprinted until 1830, it was the longest-lived Brethren hymnal, and it defined the core of Brethren HYMNODY in the German language.

BE I (*"Geistreiches Gesang-Buch"*), BE II (*"Kleine Davidische Psalterspiel der Kinder Zions, Das"*), H. Durnbaugh (1986)

Labor Unions

Before World War I, most ANABAPTISTS in North America lived in rural areas or small towns. Therefore, few of them worked in industries where labor unions were common. Later, when some Anabaptists became employed in industry, they tended to avoid labor unions because their pacifist ethic of NONRESISTANCE rejected the use or threat of force and coercion typical of labor strikes. Their rejection of membership in SECRET SOCIETIES also predisposed them against participation in labor unions.

TRADITIONAL GROUPS that are largely rural still prohibit membership in unions, while members of ASSIMILATED GROUPS display a variety of responses.

BRETHREN member Martin G. Brumbaugh (1862–1930) was governor of Pennsylvania from 1915 to 1919. He reformed labor law, especially regarding children. However, he also called out the Pennsylvania National Guard against striking steel workers in Pittsburgh. One Brethren leader, Kermit Eby (1903–1962), had a career in labor union administration. Some Anabaptist owners of large businesses have attempted to prevent unions from forming within their companies. Sometimes members of the same CONGREGATION find themselves on opposite sides in a strike situation. Some church leaders attempt to bring a biblical perspective to such conflicts by rejecting coercion, violence, militancy, and threats by either labor unions or management. Other church leaders are more open to nonviolent coercive actions because they see them as resources for SOCIAL JUSTICE.

BE I (Brumbaugh, Martin Grove"), BE II ("Labor Unions"), GAMEO ("Labor Unions"), G. Hershberger (1939, 1958), ME V ("Labor Unions"), Sappington (1985), T. Schlabach (2009)

Land

Although ANABAPTISM first arose in the cities of central EUROPE, PERSECUTION often drove the movement to rural areas. Here Anabaptists developed agricultural survival skills, often in isolated areas and on rather infertile land. The primary economic activity of the Anabaptist groups who immigrated to North America in the 1700s and 1800s was AGRICULTURE. Their agricultural skill and emphasis on hard work produced thriving farming communities in their major settlements in the UNITED STATES and CANADA. Their rural identity and their theology of NONRESISTANCE merged in the phrase *Die Stillen im Lande* ("the quiet in the land"), which was sometimes used to describe Anabaptists and PIETISTS.

Many Anabaptists felt a spiritual connection to God through tilling the soil and harvesting the crops it produced. They echoed the words of the Psalmist—"The earth is the Lord's" (Psalm 24:1)—and saw themselves as stewards of God's creation. In the late 20th and early 21st centuries, numerous writers articulated theological concerns for land conservation.

MENNONITE colonies in 19th-century RUSSIA set up their own structures of civic administration, including land distribution. Complex laws were developed to distribute small tracts of land to all families and to create new colonies throughout Russia. In the United States in the mid-1800s, land companies in the western states worked closely with railroad companies to encourage BRETHREN individuals to buy tracts of land and establish agricultural settlements near the railroads.

HUTTERITE colonies own large tracts of thousands of acres in the prairie states and provinces. A single colony may own 10,000 acres or more. When land is purchased for a new Hutterite colony, it causes a major impact on the local economy.

From 1900 to 1950, members of ASSIMILATED GROUPS gradually left their plows for nonfarm jobs. As the percentage of farmers in the larger society plummeted, the TRADITIONAL GROUPS retained their agricultural OCCUPATIONS. For the younger generation in traditional agricultural communities, finding farmland at reasonable prices is a high priority and prompts some families to move to other areas. Since 1975 many AMISH have continued to live in rural areas but have found work in self-employed trades, Amish-owned shops, construction, or factories owned by non-Amish. Although many Amish still value farming, some settlements have a large percentage of households that no longer own land or farm on a full-time basis.

BE II ("Land Companies"), GAMEO ("Land Distribution [Canada and Latin America]," "Land Distribution [Russia]," "Landless [Landlose]"), J. Hostetler (1997), Kraybill and Nolt (2004), R. Loewen (2005), ME III ("Landless"), ME V ("Land Distribution"), C. Redekop (2000), Ruth (2001)

Language

As ANABAPTISTS migrate and adapt to new cultures, many learn to speak several languages. For example, OLD COLONY MENNONITES in Mexico and Belize speak both Low German and Spanish. Anabaptists in CANADA and the UNITED STATES who speak a dialect typically speak English as well. Recent immigrants to the United States and Canada who have joined Anabaptist churches speak a variety of languages including Spanish, Korean, Vietnamese, and Chinese. One result of missionary zeal among MENNONITE and BRETHREN groups in the 1800s and 1900s is that many different languages and dialects are spoken by Anabaptists around the world. Worldwide, the congregants in Anabaptist-related churches speak at least 75 different languages.

DUTCH and GERMAN were the primary written languages of the early Anabaptists because the movement originated and expanded in Dutch- and German-speaking European areas. For everyday use these Anabaptists spoke the DIALECT of their particular region. When they immigrated they often took their native language(s) into different linguistic/cultural settings. Many Anabaptists were nonconformed to the larger society, and they often retained their native dialects in these new settings as a way of preserving their religious and cultural heritage.

Some TRADITIONAL GROUPS in North America continue to speak German-related dialects. Approximately 110,000 children and adults in several Mennonite groups in Belize, Canada, Mexico, and the United States speak *Plautdietsch,* a Low German dialect. The AMISH and

some OLD ORDER MENNONITES in Canada and the United States speak Pennsylvania German. Some assimilated MENNONITES who are more recent immigrants to CANADA have also retained their German-related dialects. The use of non-English dialects is a powerful marker of religious and cultural identity. Linguists have fruitfully studied these dialects and their evolution, especially the Pennsylvania German spoken by the Amish and the Low German spoken among the Mennonites of Russian origin.

The BRETHREN groups transitioned from German to English in the mid-1800s, earlier and with less conflict than other Anabaptist groups. The PIETIST roots of the Brethren encouraged them to spread their beliefs among English-speaking people and thus provided the impetus for their language transition.

The acceptance of ENGLISH is a key marker of assimilation into mainstream society. Within Mennonite congregations, generational and theological CONFLICTS arose over transitions to English. The opposition to English in WORSHIP was a major catalyst in forming the OLD ORDER MOVEMENT in the late 1800s. Many of these Old Order groups continue to use German in their worship services.

The communal HUTTERITE groups in North America speak *Hutterisch* in their daily discourse. This German dialect originated in Carinthia (in what is now AUSTRIA). A number of borrowed words have entered their dialect from the various regions in which the Hutterites lived, such as Czech words from Slovakia, Russian words from Ukraine, and English words from North America. The Hutterites use an older form of German in their religious writings, and they also learn to speak English in school.

The 1900s saw a rapid growth of Anabaptism both within and outside of North America. Therefore, many people affiliated with Anabaptist churches in North America and beyond have no cultural or linguistic connection to German, Dutch, or English.

A wide variety of languages are presently spoken by Anabaptists in North America. Spanish, for example, is the primary language of thousands of Anabaptists living in Canada, Central America, Mexico, and the United States. Many Spanish-speaking members residing in Canada and the United States whose families are immigrants also speak English. For others living in Latin America, Spanish is their only language.

BE II ("Language Shift"), Ediger (2001), GAMEO ("Language Problem"), ME III ("Language Problem"), http://www.mwc-cmm.org

Latin American Anabaptist Seminary (SEMILLA)

SEMILLA, which means "seed" in Spanish, is the acronym for the original name of the Latin American Anabaptist Seminary (Seminario Anabautista Latinoamericano), based in Guatemala City. SEMILLA provides biblical and THEOLOGICAL EDUCATION for 10 ANABAPTIST/MENNONITE conferences in CENTRAL AMERICA and MEXICO. It was initiated by Central Americans in the early 1980s to train church leaders who were already involved in ministry. The seminary uses a distance education model so that students can attend short courses in their own country. SEMILLA also publishes books with a focus on Anabaptist theology, anthologies for the regional Bible institutes, and guides for women's studies. Seminary staff, along with Central American grassroots writers, also collaborate with South American Mennonites to produce children's Christian Education curriculum written specifically for a Latin American context from an Anabaptist perspective. The seminary played a role in organizing the first Consultation of Anabaptist Hispanic Theological Institutions, which met in 2007 in Guatemala to share visions for theological education and enhance their collaboration.

Emaus House, a guesthouse that can accommodate more than 50 people, and CASAS, Central America Study and Service, a Spanish-language immersion program, are on the SEMILLA campus in Guatemala City and part of the SEMILLA program.

http://semilla.org.gt/english%20home.html

Latino Anabaptists *See* Hispanic-American Anabaptists

Law *See* Government; Litigation

Lawsuits *See* Litigation

Leadership *See* Authority; Bishop; Church Authority; Deacon; Elder; Minister; Ordination

Lehrerleut Hutterites

The earliest HUTTERITE churches emerged around 1528 in the context of the Anabaptist Movement during the Protestant Reformation in Europe. Their distinctive trademark is their rejection of private property and instance on COMMUNAL LIVING and sharing. Facing severe PERSECUTION, the Hutterites migrated to several countries in Europe. The Lehrerleut emerged as a distinctive group around 1877 after they immigrated to the United States from Russia in the 1870s. Their leader, Jacob Wipf (1835–1896), was a teacher (*Lehrer*), and thus his followers became known as *Lehrerleut* ("teacher's people"). They are the most conservative and homogeneous of the four Hutterite groups.

The Lehrerleut live in rural colonies that typically own several thousand acres of land. The Lehrerleut have about 5,600 members (or 14,000 when counting children as well as adults) in 140 colonies in North America, mostly in the Canadian provinces of Alberta and Saskatchewan. In the United States, they have 35 colonies in Montana.

See also Anabaptism; Dariusleut Hutterites; Schmiedeleut Hutterites, Gibb Group; Schmiedeleut Hutterites, Kleinsasser Group

J. Hostetler (1997), Rod Janzen (2005), Janzen and Stanton (2010), Kraybill and Bowman (2001), Packull (1995)

Leisure

Recreational and leisure activities vary widely among ANABAPTIST groups. Such activities reflect local and national practices as well as church teaching in some communities. In general, members of ASSIMILATED GROUPS participate rather freely in the recreational activities of their surrounding society with few church restrictions or guidelines. Members of these groups participate in spectator sports as well as play on teams in local church or civic leagues. A survey (CMP 2006) of MENNONITE CHURCH USA, CHURCH OF THE BRETHREN, and BRETHREN IN CHRIST members in the United States found that 39%, 35%, and 32% respectively reported that sports were fairly or very important in their lives.

In the first half of the 20th century many assimilated churches had religious restrictions on activities such as DANCING and attendance at plays, motion pictures, and spectator sports. The restrictions reflected the religious principle of NONCONFORMITY to the world, sometimes labeled "separation from the world." Involvement in these activities was viewed as superfluous, too tied to worldly acclaim, fashion, and celebrity culture, and unbecoming for the followers of Jesus seeking to live a simple and plain lifestyle. Moreover, the prominence of agriculture and the physical activity it required in rural communities diminished the appeal of some of these opportunities for physical exercise.

In the 21st century, assimilated churches have few leisure-related restrictions; recreational practices are the choice of individual members. Church-sponsored camping and retreat centers exist in many denominations. Some congregations have gymnasiums as part of their facilities for use by members and for outreach to others.

As an application of their commitment to nonconformity to the world, TRADITIONAL GROUPS continue to place restrictions on recreational activities such as attending movies and plays, amusement parks, carnivals, fairs, casinos, and boardwalk amusements. The word "amusement" has a pejorative meaning for many traditional people; it connotes a self-indulgent waste of time and money. Their recreational activities are often nature-related: hiking, swimming, camping, and skating. Many men go game hunting and sport fishing in local areas or go on guided expeditions away from home. Some

community activities in traditional groups blend work and socializing—quilting bees and barn- or house-building work parties, for example. Many traditional churches prohibit leisure-time technological devices—televisions, video players, DVD players, computers, tape players, and radios.

See also Camps and Retreat Centers; Cinema

BE II ("Recreation"), CMP 2006, GAMEO ("Amusements and Entertainment," "Recreation"), ME ("Amusements and Entertainment")

Lieder der Hutterischen Brüder, Die

This HUTTERITE hymnal was published in 1914 in South Dakota. Before its publication the Hutterites had no printed hymnal. Some leaders had handwritten texts preserved from the Hutterite martyrs of the 1500s and 1600s, and most Hutterites learned these texts and tunes through oral tradition. A Hutterite elder compiled the texts for the hymnal, but it was published without tunes. The melodies come from a wide variety of sources: ANABAPTIST hymns, court songs, medieval *Meistersinger* songs, Lutheran chorales, Reformed Church hymns, and Gregorian chants.

In the last two decades of the 20th century some Hutterites learned four-part singing and began to play musical instruments. Nevertheless, unison a cappella singing remains the standard in their WORSHIP services.

See also Hymnody; Martyrdom

GAMEO ("Lieder der Hutterischen Brüder, Die"), H. Martens (2002), ME III ("Lieder der Hutterischen Brüder, Die")

Literacy   *See* Education

Literature

Members of ANABAPTIST groups read a wide array of literature that varies by type of church group and level of education. The range of reading materials goes from simple religious writings to sophisticated theology, from biographies for children to postmodern fiction.

Although basic literacy was very important to early Anabaptist groups, reading and writing fiction was discouraged because it violated the ethic of truth-telling. One major exception to this prohibition was the literature by and about MENNONITES in the NETHERLANDS. Some Dutch Mennonites made important contributions to the national literary and artistic scene as early as the late 1500s. *The Wandering Soul*, a popular devotional novel, was published in 1635 by Dutch Mennonite Jan Philip Schabaelje (1585–1656).

The distinctive cultural patterns of many Anabaptist groups enticed outsiders to portray them in fiction, but not always accurately or sympathetically. As mainstream culture increasingly diverged from the lifestyle of TRADITIONAL GROUPS in the 1900s, these groups often became subjects of fictional interpretations by outsiders. The AMISH have received the most attention in this regard, as they have been highlighted by the TOURISM and entertainment industries (especially CINEMA) as well as by dozens of Amish-themed novels.

Members of ASSIMILATED GROUPS began to write fiction in the early 1900s in North America. Anabaptists have written novels, dramas, poems, criticism, and scholarly analysis of Anabaptist fiction. Canadian Rudy Wiebe (1934–) is one of numerous Mennonite novelists from the Russian Mennonite tradition. Two of his novels, *The Temptations of Big Bear* (1973) and *A Discovery of Strangers* (1994), won the Governor General's Literary Award for fiction. Five major conferences of Mennonite writers and poets since 1990 have stimulated significant interest and collaboration in writing and POETRY. The Center for Mennonite Writing at Goshen College (Indiana) seeks to encourage writers through a variety of resources and events.

In the late 20th century, some writers from traditional groups began to write light fiction based on stories from Old Order culture for the popular market. Other writers from these groups have published widely through PATHWAY PUBLISHERS, CHRISTIAN AID MINISTRIES, and Christian Light Publications.

BE II ("Literature, Brethren in"), GAMEO ("Literature, Mennonites in—United States and Canada,"

"Literature, North American Mennonite [1950–1985]"), Gundy (1997, 2005), Harry Loewen (1999), ME III ("Literature, Mennonites in"), ME V ("Literature," "Literature, Mennonites in"), Regehr (1996), Roth (2003), Ruth (1978), Weaver-Zercher (2001), http://www.mennonitewriting.org

Litigation

Historically, many ANABAPTIST groups, especially those of Swiss origin, did not allow members to engage in litigation. Following the New Testament teaching (Matt. 18:15–20 and I Cor. 6:1–2), they believed that CONFLICT among church members should be resolved peaceably within the church. Their relationships outside the church were generally guided by the doctrine of loving one's enemies and returning good for evil. These groups did allow participation in court action for settling estates, except when suits were involved.

In North America in the late 1800s and early 1900s, some ASSIMILATED GROUPS relaxed the ban on litigation. Nevertheless, most Anabaptists prefer to use less coercive measures to cope with conflict. Assimilated MENNONITES and BRETHREN have created various programs of mediation, reconciliation, and RESTORATIVE JUSTICE to pursue ways of resolving conflict.

Most TRADITIONAL GROUPS forbid their members to file lawsuits. In some groups, initiating litigation will result in excommunication. This prohibition of lawsuits hampers some members of traditional groups who own sizable business enterprises. Members of groups such as the AMISH sometimes will permit nonmembers to file lawsuits on their behalf. This was the case in *Wisconsin v. Yoder*, a major decision in 1972 by the U.S. Supreme Court that permitted Old Order (Amish and Mennonite) youth to terminate formal schooling at age 14. A controversy between HUTTERITE factions in the 1990s resulted in several years of highly publicized litigation.

BE II ("Law"), Church (2008), Erb (1939), A. Esau (2004), GAMEO ("Lawsuits"), J. Lederach (1999), ME III ("Litigation"), ME V ("Lawsuits"), S. Peters (2003), Sampson and Lederach (2000), Scott (1996)

Living Love

Living Love (Amor Viviente) formed in 1973 in HONDURAS as the result of a MENNONITE missionary couple's work with youth and alcoholics. The CHARISMATIC-style movement began in Tegucigalpa, the capital city. Establishing small cell groups of new members, the church grew rapidly. It is the largest ANABAPTIST denomination in Honduras with about 8,650 members in 32 congregations. Ten years after it began, Living Love sent its first missionaries to the United States. It has missionaries and churches in several countries outside of Honduras.

The visibility of Rene Peñalba (1954–) helped to make Living Love a national movement. Peñalba had been a popular musician and band leader before becoming the successful pastor of the mother church in Tegucigalpa, which had about 5,000 participants in the mid-1990s, and he was widely known among evangelical leaders all over Honduras. He left Living Love in 2000 to form a new group, Christian Churches International. Some of the members of his congregation followed him into the new church, which soon developed a network of congregations in some 20 countries. This network has few, if any, ties to Anabaptist churches.

GAMEO ("Honduras"), ME V ("Honduras")

Lord's Supper   *See* Communion

Lot, Selection by   *See* Ordination

Love Feast

Churches whose theological heritage has been shaped by PIETISM typically incorporate into their COMMUNION services a commemorative meal resembling the Last Supper and other early Christian rituals that combine WORSHIP with a meal. The inclusion of a meal with communion and FOOTWASHING is based on Jesus' last supper, Paul's reference in I Corinthians 11, and a reference to love feasts in Jude 12. The love feast typically includes five elements: footwashing, breaking and eating bread (symbolic of Christ's broken body), drinking wine or grape juice (symbolic of Christ's shed blood on the cross), a modest liturgical fellowship meal, and worship.

The formula for the love feast ritual varies from church to church, and within church groups its patterns have evolved in the course of the 19th and 20th centuries. It is typically celebrated twice a year, in the spring and fall. In addition, some assimilated churches periodically offer their members a "bread and cup" communion during the regular worship service.

For many congregations, celebrating the love feast is the ritual high point of their faith and congregational life. Some TRADITIONAL GROUPS celebrate the love feast in the main room of their meetinghouse by using special benches that can be converted into tables. Other groups observe the love feast in the church basement or fellowship hall. The BRETHREN developed simple kitchens in their meetinghouses in the 19th century for preparing the love feast.

Participation in the love feast is a strong expectation for members in many congregations; however, love feast attendance is sporadic in others. In general, participation is highest in the most traditional congregations. In one survey, 65% of a sample of CHURCH OF THE BRETHREN members reported that they regularly attend the love feast (CMP 2006).

Brethren-related churches that trace their roots to the origins of the German Baptist Brethren in 1708 typically observe the love feast. The BRETHREN IN CHRIST and the Old Order River Brethren, as well as related groups that originated from the River Brethren in 1780, also observe the love feast, although the fellowship meal is not officially part of their liturgical service. Most AMISH, HUTTERITE, and MENNONITE churches do not include a meal in their communion observances, nor do they describe them using the term "love feast."

BE II ("Love Feast"), CMP 2006, Ramirez (2000), E. M. Sider (1988)

Low German   *See* Dialects

Mack, Alexander, Jr. (1712–1803)

This son of the first minister of the German Baptist Brethren groups was the most influential BRETHREN leader of the 18th century. He served as pastor at Germantown (near Philadelphia), and he wrote important works describing Brethren beliefs and practices, a historical account of Brethren beginnings in Pennsylvania, and hymn texts.

BE II ("Mack, Alexander Jr."), D. Durnbaugh (1997a), Eberly (1991), GAMEO ("Church of the Brethren"), ME I ("Brethren, Church of the")

Mack, Alexander, Sr. (1679–1735)

Considered the first minister of the Schwarzenau German Baptist Brethren groups, Mack embraced the Radical Pietist Movement as a young adult. A prosperous miller from a locally prominent family, he began to hold BIBLE study and prayer meetings in his home. These gatherings were prohibited by law. He and his wife fled PERSECUTION in 1706 from his birthplace, Schriesheim in the German Palatinate, to Schwarzenau in Wittgenstein, where a sympathetic count offered a haven for religious dissenters. In 1708, Mack and seven other leaders illegally baptized each other by trine immersion. All of the BRETHREN groups with German background trace their roots to these BAPTISMS.

Mack and his followers zealously practiced MISSION outreach and adult baptisms, which were usually conducted in public. In order to escape persecution and to find better economic opportunities, the German Baptist Brethren eventually immigrated to Pennsylvania. Most of the settlers arrived in two groups—one in 1719 and a larger one in 1729 with Mack. Mack and his sons (his wife and daughters died in EUROPE) settled in Germantown (near Philadelphia). The Brethren remaining in Europe did not continue long as a church, and North America eventually became the primary home of all of the Brethren groups.

BE II ("Mack, Alexander"), D. Durnbaugh (1997a), Eberly (1991), GAMEO ("Church of the Brethren"), ME I ("Brethren, Church of the")

Marpeck, Pilgram (ca. 1490s–1556)

This leader of the south German Anabaptist Movement was born into a wealthy family in Rattenburg, a town in the province of Tyrol, AUSTRIA. He eventually became a city councilor and mining magistrate, but when he converted to ANABAPTISM, he resigned his post and fled. To escape PERSECUTION, Marpeck went to Strasbourg (now in FRANCE) in 1528, where he led a group of Anabaptists. He served as the city lumber supervisor and hydraulic engineer until 1532, when Strasbourg expelled him. From 1532 to 1544 he lived in SWITZERLAND but traveled widely to establish congregations in Tyrol, Moravia, southern GERMANY, and Alsace. From 1544 until his death, he lived in Augsburg, Germany, and worked as the city engineer overseeing the waterworks and lumbering operations.

Marpeck represented the Anabaptist Movement in debates, writings, and church leadership. He criticized the spiritualistic and apocalyptic strains that were developing among fellow Anabaptists, wrote on the theology of the Lord's Supper, and forged a middle way between the restrictive legalism of the Swiss BRETHREN and HUTTERITES and the permissive attitude of the Spiritualists. Marpeck's emphasis on the incarnation was the lynchpin of his entire theological worldview. In his writings he advocated using the New Testament to interpret the Old Testament, and he believed that the whole COMMUNITY of believers is necessary in order to interpret the BIBLE.

GAMEO ("Marpeck, Pilgram"), Klaassen and Klassen (2008), Klassen and Klaassen (1978), ME III ("Pilgram Marpeck"), ME V ("Marpeck, Pilgram")

Marriage   *See* Family

Martyrdom

The willingness to follow Jesus Christ, even if it leads to death, is a central theme of ANABAPTIST theology and a characteristic of Anabaptists' historical experiences in early Reformation EUROPE. Their insistence on adult-only BAPTISM, non-swearing of OATHS, and nonparticipation in the military often resulted in PERSECUTION and martyrdom. MARTYRS MIRROR, first published in the NETHERLANDS in 1660, is a massive compilation of testimonies of Christian martyrs, including testimonies of many 16th-century Anabaptists. An estimated 5,000 Christians were martyred in Europe during the 16th century, including some 2,000 to 2,500 Anabaptists.

Throughout their history Anabaptist groups have lived in tension with GOVERNMENTS. Some of these governments have resorted to persecution and even executions of Anabaptists. For example, thousands of MENNONITES were killed during the Communist Revolution in RUSSIA in 1917, either through outright execution or through hardship and starvation. However, many of these were likely killed because they were Germans, not because they were Mennonites or Christians.

See also Anabaptism, Theology of; Discipleship; Jesus Christ, Doctrine of

Braght (1998), C. Dyck (1985), GAMEO ("Martyrdom, Theology of," "Martyrs"), Gregory (1999), Hallock (1998), Juhnke (1999), Lowry (2003), ME III ("Martyr"), Oyer and Kreider (1990), E. Stauffer (1945), Stayer (2002), A. Toews (1990)

Martyrs Mirror

First published in the NETHERLANDS in 1660, *Martyrs Mirror* (complete title: *The Bloody Theater, or Martyrs Mirror of the Defenseless Christians Who Baptized Only upon Confession of Faith, and Who Suffered and Died for the Testimony of Jesus, Their Saviour, from the Time of Christ to the Year A.D. 1660*) is a compilation of testimonies of Christian martyrs. It was compiled by a MENNONITE ELDER, Thieleman Jansz van Braght (1625–1664), and was first written in DUTCH. The book is divided into two parts: the first, written by van Braght, covers Christian MARTYRDOM from the time of Christ to the year 1500; the second contains accounts of 803 martyrs in the 16th century (many gathered from previous publications). Most of the martyrs in the second part of the book are Anabaptists, and a full third of them are women.

These stories about remaining faithful to

Christ in the face of PERSECUTION, torture, and death were meant to inspire readers with similar convictions. Van Braght hoped that Dutch Mennonites would remember their radical DISCIPLESHIP in the face of their assimilation to the prosperous Dutch culture. In many instances the book was used for devotional purposes. Throughout *Martyrs Mirror,* van Braght emphasizes distinctive ANABAPTIST themes, such as DISCIPLESHIP, NONRESISTANCE, and using the BIBLE as the standard for church life and witness.

Since its original publication, *Martyrs Mirror* has been revised and reprinted many times. The first German translation and the first English translation were both published in Pennsylvania: the German at Ephrata Cloister in 1748–1749, and the English in 1836–1837. This foundational book remains in print in both languages. Although not widely read, it is nevertheless a highly revered symbol of martyrdom in Anabaptist history. A short (100-page) English edition of selected stories, *Mirror of the Martyrs,* was published in 1990.

The 1685 edition contained 104 reproductions of etchings by Jan Luyken (1649–1712), a prominent Dutch Mennonite printmaker. Between 1977 and 1989, North American Mennonites purchased 30 of the original copper plates etched by Luyken. Some of these plates are held in various museums, while 23 are featured in an exhibit entitled "Mirror of the Martyrs" at the Kaufman Museum of Bethel College in North Newton, Kansas. The exhibit traveled to venues throughout Canada and the United States in the 1990s.

Braght (1998), C. Dyck (1985), GAMEO ("Martyrs," "Martyrs' Mirror," "Women"), Juhnke (1990), Lowry (2003), ME III ("Martyr," "Martyrs' Mirror"), ME V ("Women"), Oyer and Kreider (1990), http://www.homecomers.org/mirror

Material Culture

This term describes the totality of a group's artifacts—the material objects of their everyday lives. Scholars have been particularly interested in the material culture of ANABAPTIST groups because their strong ethnic and religious identities have encouraged them to retain certain forms of European material culture even as they moved from place to place. Some of the most-studied artifacts include CHURCH BUILDINGS, farm machinery, furniture, clocks, CLOTHING, ceramics, textiles, QUILTS, and fraktur manuscripts. Books and publications are another category of material culture.

Some Anabaptist people were renowned for their FOLK ART in Europe. The HUTTERITES excelled as craftspeople, especially in ceramics, in Moravia from the mid-1500s to 1621. Their colorfully decorated and skillfully produced Habaner pottery is prized by museums and studied by European scholars. Likewise, MENNONITE clockmakers in GERMANY in the 1700s and in RUSSIA in the 1800s were noted for their fine pieces.

Polish Mennonites and their descendants who immigrated to Russia and North America were known for their distinctive furniture pieces, such as the dowry chest. The chest was given to CHILDREN for the storage of items they would eventually use to set up their own households. The unique form and function of the chest and other types of furniture reveals the cultural practices of Mennonite families. Generally, Mennonite immigrant furniture was large, sturdy, and constructed of ash or pine. The furniture was decorated with inlaid veneer, paint, or stain.

Russian Mennonites brought to North America the European architectural feature of attaching the barn to the house. In North America, Mennonites of Dutch-Russian background established museums of collected artifacts several decades before other groups did.

TRADITIONAL GROUPS, which remain somewhat separated from mainstream culture, retain older forms of material culture. As ASSIMILATED GROUPS conformed to mainstream culture, they began to lose much of their distinctive material culture. Aware of this disappearance, scholars and collectors have begun gathering traditional items of folk art. Books and PERIODICALS such as *Mennonite Life, Pennsyl-*

vania Mennonite Heritage, and *Preservings* have published many articles about traditional forms of Anabaptist material culture.

Abrahams (1980), Bird (2002), Friedmann (1958), GAMEO ("Clocks," "Furniture and Woodworking"), Hess (2002), Reinhild Janzen (1992, 1994), Janzen and Janzen (1991), ME V ("Clocks," "Furniture and Woodworking"), Roth (1999a), http://www.bethelks.edu/kauffman/MennoniteFurniture/Mennonite FurnitureStory.html

Media   *See* Cinema; Publishing; Radio; Television

Medicine

In countries where ANABAPTISTS were persecuted and marginalized, they often needed to furnish their own health practitioners and medicine. In some instances these rural Anabaptists became known among non-Anabaptist Europeans for their advanced knowledge of methods of natural healing. HUTTERITE health practitioners enjoyed good reputations in the 17th century, for example.

When professional occupations became accepted among ASSIMILATED GROUPS in the early 1900s, some members were trained in medicine and served as doctors and nurses in domestic or missionary settings. MENNONITES in RUSSIA created both medical and mental health hospitals in the early part of the 20th century.

During WORLD WAR II some Anabaptists served in medical settings as an alternative to military service. This context provided opportunities for members of Anabaptist groups to perform service in the national interest outside their communities. Several Mennonite and BRETHREN hospitals and INSTITUTIONS for the mentally ill grew out of these ALTERNATIVE SERVICE experiences.

Anabaptist groups do not place restrictions on blood transfusions or organ transplants for religious reasons. However, new and controversial medical technologies pose some ethical questions for Anabaptist health care providers and church leaders. In 2001 the Anabaptist Center for Healthcare Ethics was founded at Associated Mennonite Biblical Seminary in Elkhart, Indiana. The center provides guidance on issues of health care and biotechnology through consultation, printed resources, networking, and advocacy.

Although most TRADITIONAL GROUPS do not allow their members to receive the formal education necessary to become doctors and nurses, members of these groups do go to medical practitioners and hospitals for medical treatment. Many members of traditional groups, however, prefer homeopathic and alternative forms of medicine.

See also Genetic Studies; Hospitals, Medical; Hospitals, Mental; Mennonite Health Services Alliance

BE II ("Medicine"), GAMEO ("Medicine"), ME V ("Medicine"), Rogers (1988), G. Snyder (1995)

Meetinghouse   *See* Church Building

Men   *See* Gender Roles

Mennonite Brethren Churches, Canadian Conference of

With about 37,000 members, this is the largest body of MENNONITES in CANADA. Established in 1860, the Mennonite Brethren trace their roots to a renewal movement in Russian Mennonite communities under way in the late 1850s. The earliest Canadian congregations originated through evangelistic work among Old Colony communities in the 1880s as well as from secondary migrations from the United States in the 1890s and later, and from RUSSIA beginning in the 1920s. The Northern District (which included all Canadian congregations) was established in 1909. The name Canadian Conference was adopted in 1946.

With some 250 congregations in eight provinces, members worship in more than a dozen different languages. The beliefs of this group appear in a 2004 confession of faith. The denomination operates numerous mission and education programs and also cooperates in many areas with the United States Conference of Mennonite Brethren. The Canadian Conference supports MENNONITE CENTRAL COMMITTEE

projects as well as other inter-Mennonite organizations including MENNONITE WORLD CONFERENCE. Mennonite Brethren Mission and Service International is the global mission agency of the Mennonite Brethren churches in Canada and the United States. It works in about a dozen countries including Mexico and Panama.

J. Friesen (2007), GAMEO ("Mennonite Brethren," "Canadian Conference of Mennonite Brethren Churches"), ME V ("Mennonite Brethren of North America"), M. Reimer (2008), Toews and Enns-Rempel (2002), http://www.mbconf.ca, http://www.mbmsi.org

Mennonite Brethren Churches, United States Conference of

The result of a renewal movement, the Mennonite Brethren emerged among Russian MENNONITES in 1860 and migrated to the UNITED STATES in the late 19th century. In 1960 the Krimmer Mennonite Brethren, also of Russian origin, merged with the larger Mennonite Brethren conference. Some 200 Mennonite Brethren congregations are located in 19 states, with more than 60 in California alone. Most of the congregations are located west of the Mississippi River. A 2004 confession of faith summarizes their religious convictions. Maintaining a strong evangelical orientation, they support MENNONITE CENTRAL COMMITTEE projects as well as other inter-Mennonite organizations including MENNONITE WORLD CONFERENCE. Fresno Pacific University, Tabor College, and Mennonite Brethren Biblical Seminary are key educational institutions for the Mennonite Brethren.

As a result of their evangelistic outreach and the entry of some 35 Slavic congregations into their denomination, nearly half of the Mennonite Brethren congregations have strong Asian, Slavic, or Hispanic identities, and about half of their congregations worship in a language other than English. These ethnic congregations account for some 16,000 of the denomination's 35,875 members. The Mennonite Brethren Churches also have a Canadian Conference. Mennonite Brethren Mission and Service International is the global mission agency of the Mennonite Brethren churches in Canada and the United States. It works in about a dozen countries including Mexico and Panama.

GAMEO ("Mennonite Brethren"), ME V ("Mennonite Brethren of North America"), Toews and Enns-Rempel (2002), http://www.usmb.org

Mennonite Central Committee (MCC)

This relief agency was founded in 1920 to coordinate the relief efforts of North American MENNONITES for people in war-torn RUSSIA. Based in Akron, Pennsylvania, it coordinates relief, development, SERVICE, and PEACEMAKING activities for many Mennonite and BRETHREN IN CHRIST groups in the UNITED STATES and CANADA. As its website states, "MCC seeks to demonstrate God's love by working among people suffering from poverty, conflict, oppression, and natural disaster." MCC volunteers work with and participate in churches and church organizations, but starting new churches is not the primary focus. Instead, MCC works in developing countries around the world in areas such as education, health care, relief work, and job creation. The organization was also instrumental in creating programs for refugee resettlement, victim-offender reconciliation, drug rehabilitation, legislative advocacy, and the reconstruction of communities destroyed by natural disasters. About 1,175 people (staff and volunteers) work in MCC programs in 50 countries. Since its inception, over 15,000 people have served with MCC for more than one year. In addition, numerous volunteers process clothing, food, and health supplies for worldwide distribution, work in thrift shops, and help at relief sales.

Orie O. Miller (1892–1977) served as the first executive director of MCC, from 1935 to 1958. He was a key leader in creating and sustaining some of the many programs that MCC developed: Civilian Public Service, MENNONITE ECONOMIC DEVELOPMENT ASSOCIATES, Mennonite Mental Health Services, National Service Board for Religious Objectors, Menno-nite Camp Association, Menno Travel Service, Mennonite Mutual Aid (now EVERENCE), and MENNONITE FOUNDATION.

MCC Canada was created in 1963 with head-quarters in Winnipeg, Manitoba. The Canadian arm of MCC, it is supported by 15 different Mennonite and Brethren in Christ groups. Committed to relief, development, and peace issues, MCC Canada operates projects in all the provinces as well as in other countries. MCC Canada staff members have assisted thousands of OLD COLONY MENNONITES who have returned to Canada from Belize, Mexico, and some South American countries.

In 1946 MCC created Self-Help Crafts, renamed Ten Thousand Villages in 1996. Ten Thousand Villages pays artisans in developing countries a fair price for their crafts and markets them in North America. Ten Thousand Villages is a founding member of the International Fair Trade Association, which seeks to improve the economic situations of people in developing countries by changing the unfair structures of international trade.

In 1976 MCC commissioned the *More-with-Less Cookbook* and in 1991, *Extending the Table: A World Community Cookbook*. These best-selling COOKBOOKS provide resources for simple living and responsible use of the earth's resources.

In a typical year MCC receives approximately $65 million in gifts and grants to support its international work. Approximately $5 million is raised each year through relief sales, about 45 of which are held each year throughout the United States and Canada. Quilts, woodcrafts, food, and other items are sold at these events, with proceeds going to MCC programs.

Although some TRADITIONAL GROUPS in North America participate in Mennonite Central Committee on a small scale, those groups are more active with CHRISTIAN AID MINISTRIES (created in 1981), which also distributes material relief, supplies, and Christian literature to countries throughout the world.

See also Voluntary Service

F. Epp (1983), Erb (1969), GAMEO ("Mennonite Central Committee Canada," "Mennonite Central Committee [International]," "Mennonite Central Committee United States," "Miller, Orie O. [1892–1977]"), Graber Miller (1996), Kraybill (1996), Kreider and Goossen (1988), Marr (2003), ME V ("Mennonite

Central Committee Canada," "Mennonite Central Committee United States," "Miller, Orie O."), J. Oyer (1970, 1996), Prieb (1990), P. Toews (1996), http://www.mcc.org, http://www.mcc.org/canada, http://www.tent housandvillages.com

Mennonite Church

Swiss–south German MENNONITES in the United States were primarily organized into regional conferences until 1898, when a national conference was formed. Some of the regional conferences joined the national body later; others remained independent. For much of the 20th century the national body with regional conferences was known as the (Old) Mennonite Church. On some issues (dress, voting, civic engagement), this body was considered more conservative and separatist in the mid-20th century than the GENERAL CONFERENCE MENNONITE CHURCH. However, it had a more progressive outlook than the OLD ORDER MENNONITES, and it built church-related institutions such as mission agencies, colleges, and publishing agencies. At the turn of the 21st century the Mennonite Church had 20 regional conferences, some 800 congregations in 41 states, and a baptized membership of about 92,000. In 2002 the Mennonite Church merged with the General Conference Mennonite Church to form MENNONITE CHURCH USA.

GAMEO ("Mennonite Church [MC]"), Kraybill and Hostetter (2001)

Mennonite Church Canada

This is the second largest body of MENNONITES in CANADA, with some 33,000 members in over 220 congregations. The denomination formed in 2002 with the restructuring of the MENNONITE CHURCH, the GENERAL CONFERENCE MENNONITE CHURCH, and the CONFERENCE OF MENNONITES IN CANADA. Many members of these groups historically came to Canada as emigrants from Russia, Switzerland, and Germany in different time periods. Mennonite Church Canada has congregations in seven provinces. It is affiliated with several colleges and universities as well as the Associated Mennonite Biblical Seminary in Elkhart, Indiana. Members actively support relief and service projects of MENNONITE CENTRAL COMMITTEE. Mission activities have resulted in some two dozen congregations whose members are of Asian or Hispanic background. The denomination partners with MENNONITE CHURCH USA on a number of educational and publishing endeavors and is a member of MENNONITE WORLD CONFERENCE. Its key beliefs are expressed in the 1995 Confession of Faith in a Mennonite Perspective.

J. Friesen (2007), GAMEO ("Mennonite Church Canada"), M. Reimer (2008), http://www.mennonitechurch.ca

Mennonite Church USA

This is the largest MENNONITE body in the United States. It formed in 2002 through the restructuring of the MENNONITE CHURCH and the GENERAL CONFERENCE MENNONITE CHURCH. Mennonite Church USA has 916 congregations in 44 states with a baptized membership of about 106,000. About 18% of the congregations and 11% of the members are non-Caucasian. Within the non-Caucasian portion of the members, about 50% are African-American, 35% are Latino/Hispanic, 9% are Asian, and 4% are Native American.

The 1995 Confession of Faith in a Mennonite Perspective summarizes the key beliefs of this group. The denomination supports numerous mission programs, publishing efforts, and mutual aid programs, and is affiliated with two seminaries, several colleges, and some secondary schools. Many of its members support international service and relief programs operated by MENNONITE CENTRAL COMMITTEE and activities of MENNONITE WORLD CONFERENCE. Denominational leaders participate in various ecumenical discussions with representatives of other religious bodies.

GAMEO ("Mennonite Church USA"), Kanagy (2007), http://www.mennoniteusa.org, http://www.thirdway.com

Mennonite Disaster Service (MDS)

This relief agency mobilizes volunteers to clean up, repair, and rebuild after natural disasters in North America. Volunteers come from both ASSIMILATED GROUPS and TRADITIONAL GROUPS of MENNONITES, AMISH, and BRETHREN IN CHRIST. The work of MDS is rooted in the ANABAPTIST spirit of MUTUAL AID and the desire to help one's neighbors as described by Jesus in the parable of the Good Samaritan. Most of these VOLUNTARY SERVICE projects focus primarily on non-Anabaptists who are victims of natural disasters.

MDS began informally in 1950 near Hesston, Kansas, among adult Sunday school participants who wanted to assist flood victims. In 1955, MDS became a part of MENNONITE CENTRAL COMMITTEE (MCC) and expanded its scope to include both Canada and the United States. In 1993, MDS was separately incorporated; it maintains a minimum staff in Akron, Pennsylvania, near MCC headquarters.

It is estimated that more than 50,000 volunteers have participated in MDS since its creation. Having more than 60 units of trained volunteers across North America enables the agency to respond quickly to disasters. MDS cooperates with other relief agencies, especially the Red Cross and BRETHREN DISASTER MINISTRIES. Although some Amish and traditional Mennonites participate in MDS, several of these groups have formed their own disaster service programs.

Detweiler (2000), GAMEO ("Disaster Services"), ME V ("Disaster Services"), http://www.mds.mennonite.net

Mennonite Economic Development Associates (MEDA)

The goal of this agency is to alleviate poverty through economic development. North American MENNONITES created MEDA in 1953 in response to requests from Mennonites in Paraguay for assistance in developing BUSINESS ventures. The organization supplied business advice and loans, especially for creating cooperatives and small businesses. These skills and financial resources were later used to assist disadvantaged persons in CENTRAL AMERICA, AFRICA, and ASIA who sought to operate small businesses.

Foreign MEDA programs generally developed in countries where MENNONITE CENTRAL COMMITTEE already had relief and community development programs established. The work of MEDA is an expression of the ANABAPTIST desire to integrate biblical values and business principles and to express faith in business and work settings.

Fretz (1978), GAMEO ("Mennonite Economic Development Associates"), Kroeker (2003), ME V ("Mennonite Economic Development Associates"), http://www.meda.org

Mennonite Encyclopedia

This massive compilation was first published in four volumes between 1955 and 1959. A large part of it was a translation of the earlier *Mennonitisches Lexikon*. A fifth volume was added in 1990. Harold (1897–1962) and Elizabeth Bender (1895–1988), assisted by Melvin Gingerich (1902–1975) and Nelson P. Springer (1915–2004), provided editorial leadership for the first four volumes. Cornelius J. Dyck (1921–) and Dennis D. Martin (1952–) edited volume 5. The encyclopedia was a significant cooperative venture of different MENNONITE groups, and it remains the most authoritative single print source on ANABAPTIST and Mennonite topics. All of the entries in *Mennonite Encyclopedia* are available electronically in GLOBAL ANABAPTIST MENNONITE ENCYCLOPEDIA ONLINE (GAMEO).

GAMEO ("Mennonite Encyclopedia"), M. Gingerich (1964), Keim (1998), ME I–V (1955–1959, 1990), Waltner (1982)

Mennonite Foundation

This foundation was organized as a charitable corporation by Mennonite Mutual Aid (now called EVERENCE) in 1952. It offers estate planning and planned giving services for individuals, CONGREGATIONS, and church INSTITUTIONS. Donors direct the disbursement of the funds. Its publications and regional staff have played an important role in encouraging stewardship of material resources.

See also Anabaptist Foundation; Brethren in Christ Foundation; Mennonite Foundation of Canada; Mennonites

GAMEO ("Mennonite Foundation, United States"), ME V ("Mennonite Foundation, United States"), http://www.mmaonline.org/a.aspx?id=675

Mennonite Foundation of Canada

This national charitable organization was chartered in 1973 as a merger of two regional church foundations. It provides estate planning and planned giving services, such as the administration of endowment funds and charitable bequests. Donors to this charity recommend where and how their gifts are distributed. As a result, many of the funds are invested back into the supporting community through loans to congregations and church-related institutions.

See also Anabaptist Foundation; Brethren in Christ Foundation; Mennonite Foundation; Mennonites

GAMEO ("Mennonite Foundation of Canada"), ME V ("Mennonite Foundation, Canada"), http://www.mennofoundation.ca

Mennonite Health Services Alliance (MHS Alliance)

MHS Alliance is an organization that brings ANABAPTIST-related health and human service providers together for networking, collaboration, consultation, financial stewardship, leadership development, and an annual conference (Mennonite Health Assembly). The alliance traces its roots to the late 1940s, following the service of Mennonite CONSCIENTIOUS OBJECTORS assigned to state mental hospitals during and after World War II. The present form of the organization was set up in 2002 with three mandating denominations: MENNONITE CHURCH USA, MENNONITE BRETHREN CHURCHES, and BRETHREN IN CHRIST.

MHS Alliance members include retirement communities, nursing homes, other senior services, inpatient and/or outpatient mental and behavioral health care services, acute care

hospitals, and agencies serving those with developmental disabilities as well as troubled families, youth, and children. The network of Anabaptist-related health and human service providers embrace common values: care of the spirit, human dignity, justice for the vulnerable, peace and reconciliation, community, mutuality, and service.

The Peace Church Purchasing Group (PCPG) is a collaborative effort among MHS Alliance, the Association of Brethren Caregivers, and Friends Services for the Aging. Participant organizations gain buying power and significant cost savings through access to national purchasing contracts. The Peace Church Risk Retention Group (PCRRG) is a similar joint venture among the same three religious groups. This self-funded and self-governed insurance model offers its approximately 40 members relief from volatile general and professional liability insurance costs through shared risk management.

See also Alternative Service; Hospitals, Medical; Hospitals, Mental; Mental Health

http://www.mhsonline.org/php/about/index.php

Mennonite Life

This journal explores many facets of the MENNONITE experience across several disciplines for a wide readership. In a broad approach to Mennonite studies, the essays in *Mennonite Life* discuss historical as well as social, political, and theological questions. One of the journal's strengths has been its extensive use of visual materials as well as its focus on the arts. Published by Bethel College in North Newton, Kansas, from 1946 to 1999 in paper form, *Mennonite Life* became a free, online-only journal in 2000. Its web site makes past issues readily available.

http://www.bethelks.edu/mennonitelife/

Mennonite Mutual Aid   *See* Everence

Mennonite Quarterly Review

This scholarly journal, begun in 1927 at Goshen College (Indiana), contains material concerning ANABAPTIST history and MENNONITE studies. It is the oldest and most comprehensive Mennonite-related scholarly periodical in North America. Harold S. Bender (1897–1962) was the journal's founder and first editor (1927–1962), and his interests in history, THEOLOGY, and other church-related issues have provided the primary focus for the PERIODICAL. In 2000 a cumulative index of subjects, authors, and reviewed books was published, making the material much more accessible for research. In 2009 about 1,000 copies of each quarterly issue were distributed.

GAMEO ("Mennonite Quarterly Review"), Roth, Springer, and Shoemaker (2000), http://www.goshen.edu/mqr/

Mennonites

ANABAPTISTS emerged in several areas of Europe in the 1520s, including SWITZERLAND, Moravia, southern GERMANY, and AUSTRIA, as well as in northern Germany and the NETHERLANDS. MENNO SIMONS (1496–1561), a Dutch Catholic priest, converted to Anabaptism in 1536. A gifted leader and writer, he became an influential voice in the Netherlands and beyond. As early as 1545, some of Menno's followers were called Mennists. Eventually Anabaptists outside the Netherlands became known as Mennists, Mennonists, and eventually Mennonites. These groups carried the Mennonite name as they migrated to POLAND/Prussia, RUSSIA, and North America. Worldwide members of Mennonite-related churches are found in about 80 countries and number over 1.6 million.

Historical, religious, and cultural factors have produced more than 150 different Mennonite groups in North America. Some Mennonites have a Swiss–south German lineage, while others come from Dutch–north German stock. Many of the latter group came to America via Prussia and Russia. In recent years sizable numbers of members with Asian, Hispanic, Native American, African-American, and indigenous roots have expanded the Mennonite cultural mosaic. Mennonite groups fall roughly into two cultural clusters—TRADITIONAL GROUPS and ASSIMILATED GROUPS—based on their degree

of traditionalism and separation from the larger society.

OLD ORDER MENNONITES follow long-established traditions. They reject HIGHER EDUCATION, use TECHNOLOGY selectively, and practice a rural, separatist lifestyle. They typically do not have SUNDAY SCHOOLS, evening worship services, revival meetings, or evangelistic programs. Many speak both English and a German DIALECT, but others speak only English. Old Order Mennonites in Canada and the United States can be sorted into two types: those who drive automobiles and those who travel by horse and buggy. Members of these groups wear distinctive plain CLOTHING prescribed by their local churches.

Other traditional Mennonites who wear plain clothing are often labeled conservative Mennonites, not only because of their dress but because they tend to be more conservative theologically than assimilated Mennonites. Some of the conservative groups separated from more assimilated groups in the 20th century to maintain traditional practices. The conservative groups hold the middle ground between Old Order and assimilated Mennonites. The conservative groups are largely rural, but many members no longer farm. They wear church-prescribed clothing, ordain lay ministers, and emphasize cultural (but not economic) separation from the world. Although they seek to conserve traditional beliefs and practices, they have few restrictions on technology for AGRICULTURE or BUSINESS purposes. Their homes have TELEPHONES and ELECTRICITY. Many of these conservative groups do, however, forbid TELEVISION and may restrict use of the Internet to business purposes.

Like Old Orders, conservative Mennonites typically avoid higher education, professional occupations, and participation in politics. If necessary, they will excommunicate wayward members. Conservative Mennonites, unlike Old Orders, have Sunday schools, revival meetings, and topical PREACHING instead of expository preaching. Some use their own statements of faith rather than the DORDRECHT CONFES-

Table 10   Resources on Mennonite Groups

Books

Beliefs: Mennonite Faith and Practice, Roth, 2005a

Mennonite Handbook, Kehrberg, 2007

Practices: Mennonite Worship and Witness, Roth, 2009

Road Signs for the Journey, Kanagy, 2007

Stories: How Mennonites Came to Be, Roth, 2006

Through Fire and Water: An Overview of Mennonite History, Loewen and Nolt, 2010

The Upside-Down Kingdom, Kraybill, 2003b

Periodicals

Brethren in Christ History and Life (http://www.bicweb.org/ministries/histsoc/pub_act.htm)

The Canadian Mennonite (http://www.canadianmennonite.org)

Center for Mennonite Writing Journal (http://www.mennonitewriting.org/journal)

Christian Leader (http://www.usmb.org/christian-leader)

Conrad Grebel Review (http://www.grebel.uwaterloo.ca/academic/cgreview/index.shtml)

Direction (http://www.directionjournal.org)

Journal of Mennonite Studies (http://mennonitestudies.uwinnipeg.ca/jms)

The Mennonite (http://www.themennonite.org)

Mennonite Brethren Herald (http://www.mbherald.com)

Mennonite Life (http://www.bethelks.edu/mennonitelife)

Mennonite Quarterly Review (http://www.goshen.edu/mqr)

Information Centers

Amish and Mennonite Heritage Center, Berlin, OH (http://www.behalt.com; 330-893-3192)

Center for Mennonite Brethren Studies, Fresno, CA (http://www.fresno.edu/library/cmbs; 559-453-2225)

Crossroads Valley Brethren-Mennonite Heritage Center, Harrisonburg, VA (http://www.vbmhc.org; 540-438-1275)

Lancaster Mennonite Information Center, Lancaster, PA (http://www.mennoniteinfoctr.com; 717-299-0954)

Mennonite and Brethren in Christ Resource Centre, Kitchener, ON (http://www.mbicresources.org/resourcecentre; 519-745-8458)

Mennonite Heritage Center, Harleysville, PA (http://www.mhep.org; 215-256-3020)

Mennonite Heritage Centre, Winnipeg, MB (http://www.mennonitechurch.ca/heritage/mhc.html; 204-888-6781)

Menno-Hof, Shipshewana, IN (http://www.mennohof.org; 260-768-4117)

Libraries and Archives

Archives of the Mennonite Church, Goshen, IN, and North Newton, KS (http://www.mcusa-archives.org)

Brethren in Christ Historical Library and Archives, Grantham, PA (http://www.messiah.edu/archives)

Lancaster Mennonite Historical Society, Lancaster, PA (http://www.lmhs.org)

Mennonite Brethren Archives and Library, Fresno, CA (http://www.fresno.edu/library/cmbs)

Mennonite Heritage Centre Archives, Winnipeg, MB (http://www.mennonitechurch.ca/programs/archives)

Mennonite Historical Library, Goshen, IN (http://www.goshen.edu/mhl/home)

Muddy Creek Farm Library, Ephrata, PA (717-354-7635)

Web Sites

Brethren in Christ Church (http://www.bic-church.org)

Global Anabaptist Mennonite Encyclopedia Online (http://www.gameo.org)

Global Anabaptist Wiki (http://www.anabaptistwiki.org)

Mennonite Brethren, Canadian Conference (http://www.mbconf.ca)

Mennonite Brethren, United States Conference (http://www.usmb.org)

Mennonite Central Committee (http://mcc.org)

Mennonite Church USA (http://www.mennoniteusa.org)

Mennonite Church Canada (http://www.mennonitechurch.ca)

Third Way Café (http://www.thirdway.com)

SION of 1632. Conservative Mennonites oppose DIVORCE as well as the ORDINATION OF WOMEN—practices that have become more typical among assimilated Mennonites.

Over half of the Mennonites in North America are members of ASSIMILATED GROUPS. They are more likely to accept new technology, higher education, and contemporary values. Assimilated Mennonites typically embrace mainstream cultural practices related to DIVERSITY, dress, GENDER ROLES, THEOLOGICAL EDUCATION, and POLITICAL INVOLVEMENT. Members of assimilated groups more actively engage in the civic culture of North America than members of the more separatist traditional groups. Assimilated Mennonites, for example, operate numerous colleges and seminaries as well as other church-related INSTITUTIONS. The five largest assimilated bodies are MENNONITE CHURCH USA (106,000 members), MENNONITE CHURCH CANADA (33,000 members), MENNONITE BRETHREN CHURCHES (Canada: 37,000 members; United States: 35,870 members), and BRETHREN IN CHRIST (23,000 members). There are smaller bodies of assimilated Mennonites as well.

The Brethren in Christ formed in eastern Pennsylvania in the late 1770s when some former Mennonites were influenced by REVIVALISM and the PIETISM of the German Baptist Brethren. They were first known as the River Brethren and informally as River Mennonites because many lived near the Susquehanna River. The newly formed church merged Pietist themes from the BRETHREN with Anabaptist understandings from the Mennonites. Although the Brethren in Christ blend influences from Anabaptist, Pietist and Wesleyan piety, they are included in the Mennonite family of groups because of their theological affinity, their support of MENNONITE CENTRAL COMMITTEE activities, and their participation in MENNONITE WORLD CONFERENCE.

Mennonite Church USA and Mennonite Church Canada formed in 2002 through a realignment of several Mennonite groups. The Mennonite Brethren emigrated from Russia in the 1870s and established congregations in the United States and later in Canada, where over half of their members reside. Each of the major denominations has national program boards for EDUCATION, MISSIONS, publications, congregational ministries, and MUTUAL AID to serve their members as well as the larger society. Compared with stateside Mennonites, a higher percentage of Canadian Mennonites live in urban areas and participate more actively in politics at all levels of government.

Mennonites living in CENTRAL AMERICA, MEXICO, and the CARIBBEAN nations are of two broad types: those who emigrated from Canada in the early 20th century and those who joined Mennonite-related churches as the result of missions established in the last half of the 20th century. Some of the churches in the Caribbean, Central America, and Mexico are loosely affiliated with Mennonite denominations in the United States and Canada, and many of them participate in Mennonite World Conference.

Diversity flourishes in Mennonite communities. Some congregations in rural areas embody traditional beliefs and lifestyles. Congregations in urban and suburban areas are often quite cosmopolitan. Some travel in horse-drawn buggies on back country roads, while others drive expensive sports cars on metropolitan freeways. Some wear plain dress, and others sport designer clothing. Some are indigenous farmers working with hand tools in remote villages, while others operate large corporations headquartered in metropolitan areas. Mennonites in North America worship in Chinese, English, French, Pennsylvania German, Spanish, Vietnamese, and other languages.

Some congregations have informal services of WORSHIP, while others are more liturgical. Still others have a more CHARISMATIC style. The ethnic mix is growing as well. People of European ancestry dominate many church organizations, but growing numbers of HISPANIC-AMERICAN ANABAPTISTS, AFRICAN-AMERICAN ANABAPTISTS, and ASIAN-AMERICAN ANABAPTISTS participate in the life of the church.

Driedger and Kauffman (1982), Kanagy (2007),

Kraybill and Hostetter (2001), Loewen and Nolt (2010), C. Redekop (1989), M. Reimer (2008), Roth (2005a, 2006, 2009)

Mennonite Voluntary Service   *See* Voluntary
Service

Mennonite World Conference (MWC)

This international network of MENNONITE-related churches began in 1925 as a sequence of inspirational meetings that occurred about every five years. German pastor Christian Neff (1863–1946) is considered to be the father of those meetings, even though he was never elected chairman. Since the 1970s the assemblies, which occur every six to seven years, have developed an ongoing institutional identity whose purpose is to foster fellowship among MENNONITE and BRETHREN IN CHRIST members and churches in all countries and cultures. The organization also represents these groups in global ecumenical organizations.

For about the first 50 years, the assemblies were held in EUROPE and North America. The first meeting site outside of these two continents was Curitiba, Brazil, in 1972. Recognizing that Mennonite populations were growing disproportionately in the southern hemisphere, several later assemblies were held in ASIA and AFRICA. By 2010, over 60% of the 1.6 million worldwide Mennonites lived in the global South (Africa, SOUTH AMERICA, and most of Asia).

In the beginning of the 21st century, MWC sponsored the GLOBAL MENNONITE HISTORY PROJECT, which publishes Mennonite and Brethren in Christ histories of churches on the various continents. The series was inaugurated in 2003 with a history of Mennonites and Brethren in Christ in Africa (3rd ed. 2006).

In 2006, MWC adopted "Shared Convictions of Global Anabaptists," seven brief statements to help shape common theological commitments among the growing and diverse groups that affiliate with this worldwide conference. Various other theological and historical publications of MWC, including a series of explorations of core ANABAPTIST beliefs and practices called the Global Anabaptist-Mennonite Shelf of Literature, have helped to provide a common understanding of the meaning of Anabaptism around the globe.

See also Anabaptist Groups, International
GAMEO ("Mennonite World Conference"), N. Heisey (2006), Lapp and Snyder (2006a), Lapp and van Straten (2003), Lichdi and Krieder (1990), ME III ("Mennonite World Conference"), ME V ("Mennonite World Conference"), A. Neufeld (2008), C. Snyder (1997b, 1999), http://www.mwc-cmm.org

Menno Simons (1496–1561)

Although not a founder of the Anabaptist Movement, Menno Simons was its most influential leader in the NETHERLANDS and northern GERMANY in the 1500s. He was a prolific writer, and his publications spread his influence. His *Foundation of Christian Doctrine*, written in Dutch in 1539, was translated into German by 1575. His influence was so great that some ANABAPTISTS eventually became known as MENNONITES.

After receiving training in Latin and possibly Greek, Menno Simons became a Roman Catholic priest at age 28. At his first assignment in Pingjum, he began to doubt that the bread and wine of COMMUNION were changed into the literal

Table 11   Membership of Churches Affiliated with Mennonite World Conference by Region

Region	Membership	Percentage
Africa	593,500	37.0
Asia	262,000	16.3
Latin America	167,600	10.4
Europe	64,500	4.0
Canada and United States	519,600	32.3
Total	1,507,200	100.0

Source: http://www.mwc-cmm.org.

Note: Estimated number of baptized members. If children, unbaptized youth, and nonmember participants are counted, the total population in some groups may be two to three times larger than the baptized membership. Membership includes churches affiliated with the Brethren in Christ. The Latin America region includes the Caribbean, Central America, Mexico, and South America.

body and blood of Jesus Christ. After a period of intense Bible study, Menno concluded that the biblical writers presented a symbolic, rather than literal, interpretation of communion. His reading of the Bible also convinced him that the ritual of infant BAPTISM, practiced by both the Reformers and the Roman Catholics, was not scriptural.

In 1535 a group of radical Anabaptists took over the German city of Münster and attempted to establish the kingdom of God there. Eventually they became militant. Menno Simons was impressed by their commitment and zeal but repulsed by their use of violence. The leaders of the Münster rebellion were brutally executed, and Menno Simons was pained by their recourse to violence. In January 1536 he renounced his priestly vows and joined the underground Anabaptist Movement.

After 1536, Menno Simons married and had children. Between 1536 and 1554, he moved frequently to avoid being captured by civil authorities. From 1554 until his death in 1561, he found refuge in Oldesloe in the north German province of Holstein, where he was protected by a local nobleman. His Christ-centered biblicism is apparent in his favorite Bible verse: "For no one can lay any foundation other than the one that has been laid; that foundation is Jesus Christ" (I Cor. 3:11).

C. Dyck (1962), A. Friesen (1998), GAMEO ("Menno Simons"), Klaassen (1988), ME III ("Menno Simons"), Menno (1956)

Mental Health

Rather than serving in the military during WORLD WAR II, some ANABAPTISTS worked in ALTERNATIVE SERVICE programs in mental hospitals. These experiences led MENNONITE groups to form their own mental health facilities in the 1950s and 1960s. Mennonites and BRETHREN in ASSIMILATED GROUPS also entered counseling, psychiatry, and social work professions in order to bring the skills and sensitivities they learned in alternative service to bear on mental illnesses. Church leaders sought ways to incorporate these skills and these profession-

als into the healing ministries of Anabaptist churches.

Like other people, some Anabaptists struggle with mental health issues. Because the Anabaptist ethic of NONRESISTANCE emphasizes Jesus' commandment to love one's enemies, expressions of anger and aggression are often discouraged in some Anabaptist groups. This cultural inhibition may encourage people to repress their hostile feelings, and in some cases it may support clinical depression.

Another problem surfaced in the 1980s when church members and leaders began to acknowledge publicly the existence of sexual and DOMESTIC ABUSE in homes and CONGREGATIONS. Many Anabaptist groups began to offer counseling resources and develop organizational policies to address this problem, attending to the mental health of both victim and perpetrator.

Some members of TRADITIONAL GROUPS suffer from mental illnesses, although generally at lower rates than the general population. Psychiatrists and geneticists have used subjects in the AMISH community for GENETIC STUDIES to explore the genetic basis of manic depression. Since 1990, some traditional churches have established private residential care facilities for members with mental health problems. Several psychiatric care facilities have also opened special units to care for members of AMISH and OLD ORDER MENNONITE groups. In some traditional groups, networks of informally trained lay counselors/helpers aid members struggling with mental health issues.

See also Hospitals, Mental; Mennonite Health Services Alliance

J. Hostetler (1993), Schmitt and Schmitt (1984), Toews and Loewen (1995)

Mexico

About 20 different ANABAPTIST-related groups, ranging from OLD COLONY MENNONITES in rural areas to Hispanic cultural groups in urban areas, are present in Mexico. These churches, with approximately 29,775 baptized members, hail from two different cultural backgrounds. The majority (over 24,000 members) are German-DIALECT-speaking MENNONITES whose families emigrated from CANADA in the 1920s and 1940s. The second cultural heritage group includes Spanish-speaking churches that emerged as a result of missionary efforts by churches in Canada and the United States in the last half of the 20th century.

Three traditional Mennonite groups—Old Colony, Kleine Gemeinde, and Sommerfelder—comprise about 80% of the adult Anabaptist-related membership in Mexico. These people, sometimes called KANADIER, are descendants of Mennonites who settled in Russia in 1789 and 1804 and then immigrated to western Canada between 1874 and 1879. Members speak the Low German dialect, worship in High German, and maintain their German culture by living in colonies—large block settlements on thousands of acres of adjacent land. Although most earn their livelihood from farming, in some areas an increasing number work in local industries.

Conservative Mennonites in Canada in the 1920s felt threatened after new education laws in Manitoba and Saskatchewan required all children to attend publicly registered, English-language schools. In 1921 a delegation of Canadian Old Colony leaders met with Mexican President Alvaro Obregón (1880–1928) in Mexico City and negotiated an agreement for private education, military exemption, separate inheritance practices, and other economic incentives. Beginning in 1922 some 7,000 Mennonites—mostly Old Colony and some Sommerfelder—migrated to the Mexican states of Chihuahua and Durango, where they established four colonies. In 1948 about 800 more Canadian emigrants affiliated with the Kleine Gemeinde settled in the Mexican state of Chihuahua.

Many members of these traditional groups eventually left Mexico. MENNONITE CENTRAL COMMITTEE programs in the 1950s and the encroachment of Mexican government social services annoyed some of them so much that they emigrated in 1958. That year, Old Colony and Kleine Gemeinde Mennonites from Mexico settled in British Honduras (now BELIZE). The

most conservative factions moved to Bolivia in the 1960s. In another emigration during the 1990s some conservative Mexican and Belizean Mennonites moved to Bolivia, East Paraguay, and Argentina and to new regions in Mexico, especially the northern district of Chihuahua around Casas Grandes and the southern state of Campeche near the Yucatan peninsula.

Although many members of these traditional groups stayed in Mexico, some returned to Canada in the last quarter of the 20th century for various reasons. During the 1970s and 1980s, unstable economies in Mexico and endemic violence in Belize increased the migration of traditional Mennonites northward, especially to southern parts of Ontario, Alberta, and Manitoba, but also to British Columbia and Nova Scotia, and in the United States to Texas, Oklahoma, and Kansas. By the late 1990s, persistent drought had brought even more impoverished migrants to Canada and the United States. Some of these traditional Mennonites adopted a migrant lifestyle of working on vegetable fields in southern Ontario and Alberta during the summer and living in Mexico during the winter.

Although the traditional Mennonites initially settled in the states of Chihuahua and Durango, they later moved into Zacatecas in the interior and Campeche in the southeast as well as other states. There are three clusters of traditional Mennonites, all of whom live in colonies on large blocks of adjacent land. (1) The Kleine Gemeinde (about 2,800 adults) retain many German cultural traits including language but have more evangelical religious views than the Old Colony. They use electricity in their homes, drive cars, and have tractors with rubber tires. (2) The Old Colony car-driving groups (about 16,500 adults) have accepted electricity, cars, and rubber wheels on tractors, but they retain most of the older German cultural customs and do not have an evangelical outlook. (3) The Old Colony horse-and-buggy groups (about 3,200 adults) are the most conservative. About two-thirds of them live in Campeche. They have not adapted modern technology as the other two groups have done but continue living without electric-

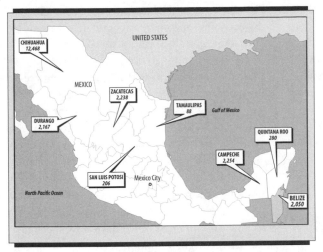

FIGURE 12 Distribution of Old Colony Mennonite Baptized Membership in Belize and Mexico

ity and using horse-and-buggy transportation and tractors with steel wheels. Although they have many economic ties, these three groups have retained a cultural separation from Mexican society by building networks of their own economic, educational, and civic organizations. In the 21st century, AMISH and OLD ORDER MENNONITES in the United States have provided teachers and assistance to improve the schools in some the Old Colony communities.

The second cultural cluster of Mexican Mennonites has a Spanish cultural background. Two Anabaptist-related groups formed about 1960 through the mission efforts of Mennonites from the United States: the Conference of Evangelical Anabaptist Mennonites, which is located near Mexico City, and the Evangelical Mennonite Church of Northeastern Mexico, which is located in the states of Sinaloa and Sonora. Another group, the Conference of Christian Mennonite Anabaptists of Tamaulipas, across the border from Brownsville, Texas, has a close relationship with the South Central Conference of MENNONITE CHURCH USA.

The MENNONITE BRETHREN began working in Mexico in the 1940s. They aided Old Colony Mennonites and conducted mission work in Guadalajara and Tamaulipas. BRETHREN IN CHRIST missionaries started churches in the

state of Tamaulipas in the mid-1990s, which have grown to eight congregations with about 250 members.

The CHURCH OF GOD IN CHRIST, MENNONITE established a mission outreach in 1927. This group has about 350 members in 31 congregations and other outreach centers in 11 states, mainly in Chihuahua and Nuevo Leon. Three other plain-dressing Mennonite groups in the United States have founded four congregations in Mexico. The NATIONWIDE FELLOWSHIP CHURCHES have two congregations and about 75 members, the Midwest Mennonite Fellowship has 50 members in one congregation, and Hope Mennonite Mission of Oregon has about two dozen members in its congregation.

Six different Mennonite groups are loosely organized under the legal umbrella of United Anabaptist Mennonite Church of Mexico, which has its offices in Mexico City. The groups, which formed the association in 1992, maintain their separate church identities but collaborate in leadership training and other projects. They held their first national assembly in 2008 for leaders and laity and plan to convene others periodically. The church bodies that participate in the association include Conference of Evangelical Anabaptist Mennonites, Conference of Christian Mennonite Anabaptists of Tamaulipas, Conference of Evangelical Missions of Mexico, Evangelical Missionary Conference, and Mennonite Conference of Mexico.

Mennonite Central Committee (MCC) has assisted the Old Colony Mennonites since the 1950s. Around 1987 MCC began community development work outside the Old Colony areas and in 1990, focused its efforts on impoverished areas of southern Mexico in Guerrero and Chiapas. About 16 MCC expatriate staff members are involved in numerous projects such as developing clean water sources and promoting sustainable agriculture. The agency also engages in public health education and environmental preservation projects including the construction of latrines and wood stoves. Several MCC staff members continue to assist Low German–speaking Mennonites in Chihuahua. Others, in collaboration with national staff, promote PEACEMAKING and social SERVICE among Spanish-speaking Mennonites and Brethren in Christ in the Mexico City area.

GAMEO ("Mexico"), R. Loewen (2004, 2008), ME V ("Mexico," Old Colony Mennonites"), Mennonite World Conference (2005), http://www.bic-church.org/wm/who-we-are/mexico.asp, http://www.mwc-cmm.org

Migration

Because of their experience of PERSECUTION and legal harassment, some ANABAPTIST groups have migrated many times. Some sought RELIGIOUS LIBERTY and searched for better economic opportunities in new lands while fleeing the oppression of their old land. From 1550 to 1850, Anabaptist groups spread from the NETHERLANDS, SWITZERLAND, AUSTRIA, and GERMANY to FRANCE, POLAND/Prussia, RUSSIA, Moravia, and the North American British colonies. Between 1719 and 1729 almost all of the BRETHREN left EUROPE for Pennsylvania. AMISH, Brethren, and HUTTERITES no longer exist in Europe, the continent of their origins.

Some Pennsylvania MENNONITES, Brethren, and BRETHREN IN CHRIST moved to Upper CANADA (now Ontario) in the 1780s and 1790s to acquire inexpensive land and to live in a British colony rather than in the recently formed UNITED STATES.

The Hutterites relocated several times in Europe before immigrating to North America in the 1870s. About the same time, Mennonites moved from Russia to the United States and Canada. These 7,000 Mennonites who immigrated to Canada became known as KANADIER MENNONITES. In the 1920s, about one-third of all Kanadier Mennonites moved from Canada to MEXICO and Paraguay. In later decades many of these Mennonites moved from Mexico to British Honduras and Bolivia. Beginning in the mid-20th century and continuing into the 21st century, many Kanadier Mennonites (especially OLD COLONY MENNONITES) have migrated

from Latin America back to Canada. Impelled by economic and environmental deprivations and some church conflicts, these Low German–speaking Mennonites sought a better life in Canada. Immigrants and their descendants returning to Canada number about 60,000.

Approximately 20,000 Russian Mennonites, known as RUSSLÄNDER, immigrated to North America (mostly to Canada) in the 1920s. Other Mennonites fleeing from war and Communism in Russia moved to Paraguay and Uruguay.

Various waves of immigration have brought Mennonites and Amish from Europe to what is now the United States. These waves include the Swiss-origin Mennonites and Amish from the German Palatinate moving to Pennsylvania in the 1700s, and the Swiss-origin Mennonites and Amish from Bavaria and France settling in the midwestern states and Ontario in the 1800s. One group of Swiss-origin Amish has a complex immigration history. From the 1600s to 1874, they immigrated to France, then to Poland, then to Russian Volhynia, and finally to Kansas. Throughout these journeys, they had contact with many different political jurisdictions and with many groups of Mennonites and Hutterites.

Since 1970 over 110,000 Mennonites and evangelicals with Mennonite ancestry have immigrated to Germany from Russia. During the decade and a half after 1993, some 15,000 of these immigrants moved once again, this time to rural properties in the southern Manitoba communities of Steinbach and Winkler.

Mennonite and Brethren groups have provided assistance for immigrants to the United States and Canada. Some of this assistance was given to fellow Anabaptists, such as the approximately 20,000 Russländer Mennonites who immigrated to North America in the 1920s. Some Anabaptist churches have also assisted non-Anabaptist refugees who moved to North America, fleeing war and persecution in AFRICA, CENTRAL AMERICA, SOUTH AMERICA, and ASIA.

In addition to immigrating to new countries, Anabaptist groups have also migrated within national boundaries. In the 1700s and 1800s many Anabaptists moved to the western frontiers of North America to take advantage of cheaper land prices. Later, the railroads and their incentives also attracted them to the West. Russian Mennonite and Hutterite immigrants of the 1870s spread across the prairies of North America, where large tracts of land, resembling the steppes of southern Russia, were available for large-scale grain farming.

In the 1900s, jobs in cities and towns pulled some assimilated Anabaptists away from their rural settings. Other reasons for migration included education, urban missions, and the desire to establish new churches in those areas. Members of ASSIMILATED GROUPS live in many cities, including Toronto, Winnipeg, Vancouver, New York, Philadelphia, Chicago, and Los Angeles, where they have founded congregations.

Members of TRADITIONAL GROUPS frequently migrate, seeking rural locations for new settlements or, in some cases, to resolve community or congregational conflict.

See also Anabaptist Groups, International; Volhynian Mennonites

BE I ("Germany"), BE II ("Migration of Brethren"), C. Dyck (1993), F. Epp (1962), GAMEO ("Migrations," "Volhynia [Ukraine]"), Juhnke (1989), R. Loewen (2004, 2008), MacMaster (1985), ME III ("Migrations of Mennonites"), ME IV ("Volhynia"), ME V ("Migrations"), J. Oyer (1968, 1974), Ruth (2001), T. Schlabach (1988), Stumpp (1973)

Military Conscription   *See* Alternative Service

Minister

This leadership role is a key ordained office in all ANABAPTIST groups. The minister's primary responsibility is PREACHING and providing spiritual leadership for the life of the congregation in TRADITIONAL GROUPS. The role is often expanded in ASSIMILATED GROUPS to include planning worship services, guiding Christian education activities, initiating service and witness projects, providing counseling services, and offering spiritual direction for individual members. Many congregations have several ministers who serve together on a team.

In traditional groups, the minister is always a male who is typically chosen from the lay members in the CONGREGATION. Ministers are subject to guidance from the congregation and, in some churches, to a BISHOP or overseer. A minister does not receive formal THEOLOGICAL EDUCATION or a salary.

As assimilated groups established colleges and Bible schools in the late 1800s and seminaries in the mid-1900s, the role of minister in these groups became more professionalized. In the last half of the 20th century many congregations expected their ministers to have some formal theological education, and many began to pay them a salary.

Some assimilated groups have three levels of ministry. A person might be licensed for ministry for a trial period, commissioned for a limited time or a specific task, or fully ordained. Many assimilated groups accept women at all three levels of ministry.

See also Deacon; Elder; Ordination; Schools, Bible

BE II ("Ministry"), C. Bowman (1995), J. Esau (1995), GAMEO ("Ordination"), May (1990), ME III ("Ministry"), ME V ("Ordination")

Mission

Sixteenth-century ANABAPTISTS believed that the church's mission is based on the Great Commission that Jesus gave to his disciples at the end of his earthly ministry: go and make disciples of all people (Matt. 28:19). EVANGELISM, the effort to spread the gospel of JESUS CHRIST, springs from this fundamental mission.

When the early Anabaptist Movement was forced underground because of PERSECUTION, it continued to grow through vigorous personal evangelism. However, by about 1600, governmental suppression, along with the Swiss Anabaptist emphasis on NONCONFORMITY and separation from the world, had dampened the earlier missionary zeal.

Biological growth and geographical diffusion became the primary mode of church growth for most Anabaptist groups from 1600 to the late 1800s. One exception was the German Baptist Brethren, who, from their beginnings in the early 1700s in GERMANY, showed a vigorous missionary impulse, even during persecution.

Throughout the 1800s various Anabaptist churches in Europe and North America became convinced of the need for mission work both at home (evangelism within the home country), and overseas (foreign missions). This missionary interest was reawakened by theological currents from outside Anabaptism, such as PIETISM, RE-VIVALISM, and EVANGELICALISM.

MENNONITES created their first mission society in the Netherlands in 1847 in order to send church workers to Indonesia. In 1872, GEN-ERAL CONFERENCE MENNONITES organized the first mission board in North America. The BRETHREN created a mission board in 1880 and later founded foreign missions in Denmark, China, Nigeria, India, and Ecuador.

By 1900, institutional support for foreign missions began to grow among some North American Anabaptists. In some instances differ-ent church groups cooperated more readily in foreign mission efforts than they did with those in their home countries. This cooperation was especially apparent in Congo Inland Mission, later known as African Inter-Mennonite Mission, a foreign missions group created in 1912 by a partnership of two small Mennonite groups. At the beginning of the 20th century, Mennonite missionaries went to AFRICA (Rhodesia, Congo), SOUTH AMERICA (Argentina), and ASIA (India, China).

During the 1920s and 1930s, FUNDAMENTAL-ISM began to influence many North American Mennonite churches. Fundamentalist theology emphasized doctrinal beliefs instead of the tra-ditional Anabaptist themes of DISCIPLESHIP, NONRESISTANCE, SERVICE, and the creation of Christian COMMUNITY. Some leaders tried to apply this more conservative theology in their mission endeavors, and during this time some missionaries were required to affirm key doc-trinal beliefs and sign a pledge to signify their orthodoxy.

After World War II, Mennonite foreign mis-sion activity increased, and these new mission efforts often combined evangelism and service

ministries. Mission work by Brethren groups such as the BRETHREN CHURCH and GRACE BRETHREN also increased in the postwar era.

After 1960 the Mennonite-related churches of Africa, Asia, and South America began to mature and expand. Indeed, over 50% of the 1.6 million Mennonites in the world live in the global South. Such growth has transformed the face of international Mennonite identity and cul-ture. MENNONITE WORLD CONFERENCE was developed to foster fellowship and communion between Mennonites of different cultures in different countries.

Among Brethren-related groups, over 500,000 members in 25 nations and some 3,500 congregations identify with the Brethren move-ment in the 21st century. The Grace Brethren report some 2,600 related congregations in 25 countries outside North America.

The most conservative TRADITIONAL GROUPS do not advocate or practice organized mission outreach. They think that the character and lifestyle of their community is a witness—a light set on a hill—to the outside world. More-over, they distrust large institutions, higher education, salaried ministry, and the relaxed behavioral standards that often accompany mission efforts. Some New Order Amish and conservative Brethren and Mennonite groups have mission organizations and programs, both foreign and domestic. CHRISTIAN AID MINIS-TRIES, a large relief and service organization that distributes Bibles and Christian literature in numerous countries in North America and beyond, is supported by many individual mem-bers of traditional groups.

See also Anabaptist Groups, International

BE II ("Missions"), D. Durnbaugh (1997a), GAMEO ("Mission [Missiology]"), Juhnke (1979), Kraybill (2003c), R. Kreider (1980), ME V ("Missiology"), G. W. Peters (1984), T. Schlabach (1980), W. Shenk (1984, 2000), http://www.aimmintl.org

Mission Organizations   *See* Anabaptist
   Groups, International; Evangelism; Mission

MMA   *See* Everence

Modernity   *See* Assimilated Groups; Traditional
Groups

Movies   *See* Cinema

Music

Congregational SINGING has been very important to most ANABAPTIST groups throughout
their history. The musical style of singing hymns
was usually a cappella, without musical instruments. TRADITIONAL GROUPS still forbid the
use of musical instruments, solo singing, and
special ensembles and choirs in WORSHIP,
although members in some of these groups
sing and play folk and gospel songs outside of
worship. The Ephrata Community (EPHRATA
CLOISTER), which branched off from the
BRETHREN in the 1720s, developed a unique
style of musical composition and larger works
for choir.

Musical styles became more complex with
the acceptance of the singing school movement
among some groups in the mid-19th century.
By the early 1900s, levels of musical education
and performance skills were rising in MENNO-
NITE- and Brethren-founded colleges. By the
mid-20th century many ASSIMILATED GROUPS
had established choirs, which sang a broader
range of music than hymns, and also had introduced organs, pianos, and other instruments in
worship to accompany congregational singing
and to provide another type of music in church
services. Members of these groups participated
in mass choirs, community choirs, and children's
choirs. Members of assimilated groups also took
active roles in musical composition, performance, teaching, and research. Mennonite organ
builders, such as the Hallmans in Ontario and
the Beckeraths in Germany, contributed to the
expanding role of instrumental music in assimilated Anabaptist worship services.

At the beginning of the 21st century, assimilated Mennonites and Brethren bring many
styles of music into worship, including African-
American, folk, contemporary Christian, Southern gospel, and praise songs.

See also *Hymnal: A Worship Book*; Hymnody

Epp and Weaver (2006), Faus (1988, 1993), GAMEO
("Music, North America," "Musical Instruments"),
Kropf and Nafziger (2001), H. Martens (2002), ME V
("Music, North America," "Music, Instrumental"),
M. Oyer (2002)

Mustache   *See* Beard

Mutual Aid

Among the early ANABAPTISTS, the HUTTER-
ITES were the only group to practice full-fledged
COMMUNAL LIVING that included economic
sharing. Although other Anabaptist communities in the 16th century held private property,
they viewed themselves as Christian stewards
of economic goods who had a responsibility to
share them with needy fellow church members
as well as with other people. Mutual aid refers
to the voluntary sharing of material goods when
fellow church members face hardships or emergencies. The practice of mutual aid, underscored
in many biblical texts, rests on a deep Anabaptist conviction that Christians have a duty to
bear one another's burdens by expressing compassion in both word and economic deed.

The real and somewhat mythic symbol of mutual aid in rural areas is the barn raising. Dozens
of neighbors drop their other duties in order to
clean up debris after a fire and construct a new
barn. In the course of the 19th and 20th centuries, new forms of mutual aid emerged with the
rise of mutual aid organizations and more formal, organized aid practices. Numerous companies related to Anabaptist churches have developed INSURANCE-like plans with premiums and
deductibles for car, fire, homeowners, health,
long-term care, life, and liability. These larger,
formal church-related insurance options supplement the informal and spontaneous sharing in
local congregations. Traditional forms of mutual
aid have diminished somewhat because many
members of assimilated churches subscribe
to commercial insurance policies provided by
employers or purchased through independent
agents.

More TRADITIONAL GROUPS discourage
commercial insurance because they think it

undercuts reliance on God and the church for help in time of disaster and emergency. Some of the Old Order groups refuse to accept government pension payments. As a general rule, mutual aid in traditional communities is more informal and spontaneous than it is in the ASSIMILATED GROUPS, whose practices more closely parallel those of the larger society.

See also Brethren Mutual Aid Agency; Credit Unions; Everence

BE II ("Mutual Aid"), GAMEO ("Mutual Aid"), Hernley (1970), ME V ("Mutual Aid"), Swartley and Kraybill (1998), http://www.brethrenbenefittrust.org

Mutual Aid Association   *See* Brethren Mutual Aid Agency

Mysticism

The term "mysticism" refers to an individual spiritual experience that culminates in union—usually ecstatic and ineffable—with the divine. According to this definition, ANABAPTISTS are not mystics. Rather than seeking such a mysterious union, Anabaptists emphasize obedience to God in mind (right belief) and in will (right action).

However, if the definition of mysticism is broadened to describe the consciousness of and reaction to the immediate presence of God, then some early 6th-century Anabaptists in Switzerland and southern Germany may be viewed as mystics. These Anabaptists emphasized the HOLY SPIRIT's role in developing a profound consciousness of sin, the need for repentance, and a complete surrender to God's will in a thoroughgoing spiritual CONVERSION. The abandonment of self and yieldedness to God's will, known as GELASSENHEIT, became integral to the spirituality of some Anabaptist groups. Similar experiences during conversion, spiritual revival, and CHARISMATIC renewal in various Anabaptist and PIETIST groups in different historical periods also border on mysticism. Among the BRETHREN, the EPHRATA CLOISTER followed the teaching of Conrad Beissel (1691–1768), which was a type of mysticism.

Bach (2003), GAMEO ("Mysticism"), ME V ("Mysticism"), Packull (1977), C. Snyder (2002)

National Committee for Amish Religious Freedom

This informal committee is comprised of people who are not AMISH but who provide advice and arrange legal counsel to support RELIGIOUS LIBERTY and the right of the Amish to freely practice their religion in the United States. It was formed in 1967 to address educational issues facing the Amish by new attendance laws and the consolidation of public schools.

The committee is especially known for its work on the 1972 landmark U.S. Supreme Court case *Wisconsin v. Yoder*. The case involved state laws that forced Amish children to attend high school, an action that threatened Amish religious values. The court ruled that Amish youth could end their formal education at 14 years of age, thus protecting free exercise of religion for Amish in the area of public education.

Because the Amish discourage involvement in LITIGATION, members of this committee provide counsel to the Amish on legal matters such as milk standards, slow-moving vehicle regulations, land use, zoning, midwife licensing, photo identification requirements, and hospitalization fees.

See also Old Order Amish Steering Committee
Keim (1975), Kraybill (2003c), Lindholm (2003), S. Peters (2003)

National Council of Churches   *See* Ecumenism

National Evangelical Guatemalan Mennonite Church

This church (Iglesia Nacional Evangélica Menonita Guatemalteca) formed in 1972 among the K'ekchi'-speaking people in the department of Alta Verapaz. It grew out of the work of MENNONITE missionaries from Eastern Mennonite Missions and Franklin-Washington Mennonite Conference who arrived in GUATEMALA in 1968. Comprised mostly of members from K'ekchi' backgrounds, the church is organized into five districts with about 115 congregations and approximately 5,000 baptized members. The K'EKCHI' MENNONITE FOUNDATION and

BEZALEEL EDUCATION CENTER are major projects related to this church.
GAMEO ("Guatemala"), ME V ("Guatemala")

Nationalism

When they originated in Europe in the 1500s, ANABAPTIST groups suffered persecution at the hands of religious and GOVERNMENT officials. They responded by subsequent emigration and sometimes were subject to deportation. This experience encouraged some churches to emphasize the judgment of God on nations—especially those nations that restricted religious freedom and demanded unquestioned allegiance. Persecution in the 16th and 17th centuries also encouraged a separatist outlook in some groups. In the 19th and 20th centuries, as Anabaptists became comfortable with and assimilated into the countries in which they lived, especially in democracies urging civic participation, some members began to identify with nationalistic ideas and practices.

Anabaptist theology affirms God's creation and love for the entire world and all its peoples regardless of tribe, nation, or ethnicity. It does not view God's blessings as unique or favoring any particular nation. Anabaptists support a healthy patriotism as long as it does not lead to uncritical national allegiance. Anabaptist churches have frequently spoken against blind loyalty to the nation-state, which in their view constitutes a subtle form of idolatry that raises obedience to the nation above obedience to the kingdom of God.

Their commitment to Christian PACIFISM makes many members uncomfortable with national military ceremonies that view sacrifice to the country as a noble virtue. Forms of patriotism that blend Christian symbols with national ones in civil religion—flag salutes, patriotic songs, military parades, public worship services, national HOLIDAYS, political proclamations—trouble some, but not all, church members. They believe that the god of civil religion is a provincial deity, a tribal god used by politicians to bless and legitimize whatever the nation does. Worshiping such a deity fosters a national idolatry, which diverts worship away from genuine devotion to God as portrayed in the New Testament.

Despite historic Anabaptist rejections of nationalism and church statements in the 20th century calling for obedience to God above nation, many members succumb to strong patriotic pressures. Others contend that the highest form of patriotism is to care for all peoples of all nations and to hold the state to high levels of integrity and accountability, even though such positions may be unpopular in the larger society.

A study of assimilated groups in the United States (CMP 2006) found that 48% of MENNONITE CHURCH USA, 73% of CHURCH OF THE BRETHREN, and 62% of BRETHREN IN CHRIST members think that God has especially blessed America. In the same study, 67% of MENNONITES, 87% of BRETHREN, and 95% of Brethren in Christ said that they pledge allegiance to the flag. When asked about the propriety of displaying a U.S. flag inside their church building, 35% of Mennonites, 72% of Brethren, and 79% of Brethren in Christ found it acceptable.

See also Anabaptism, Theology of; Church and State; Religious Liberty

CMP 2006, A. J. Dueck (1994), GAMEO ("Civil Religion, United States," "Nationalism"), Kraybill (1976), ME V ("Civil Religion," "Nationalism")

Nationwide Fellowship Churches

A number of congregations that withdrew from several different conferences of the MENNONITE CHURCH in the mid-20th century began affiliating together in the late 1950s and early 1960s. The growing acceptance of television, jewelry, and fashionable clothing in the Mennonite Church (now part of MENNONITE CHURCH USA and MENNONITE CHURCH CANADA) prompted the formation of the Nationwide Fellowship Churches. Members of the Fellowship maintain a conservative lifestyle and hold traditional doctrinal beliefs. These churches maintain a close affiliation with Rod and Staff Publishers.

In the United States the Fellowship has about 62 congregations spread over 19 states,

with some 2,850 members. In Canada, the group has 23 congregations in six provinces, with about 1,000 members. Some members of Low German–speaking, Dutch-Russian backgrounds (Old Colony, Sommerfelder, Kleine Gemeinde) have joined the Nationwide Fellowship Churches, whose initial members were primarily of Swiss MENNONITE origin. The group's mission outreach is in six other countries, including five congregations in the Dominican Republic, five in Guatemala, and two in Mexico.

Scott (1996)

Native American Anabaptists

In 1880, GENERAL CONFERENCE MENNONITES sent German-speaking missionaries to the Arapaho and Cheyenne tribes in Indian Territory (now Oklahoma). These missionaries started schools, but a congregation was not established until 1897. There were few converts, and the schools closed in the late 1890s.

In 1892, MENNONITE missionaries began a mission effort among the Cheyenne in northern Montana. They learned the Cheyenne language, produced the first English–Cheyenne dictionary, and made the first translation of the New Testament and major portions of the Old Testament into Cheyenne. Several present-day Mennonite congregations stem from these ANABAPTIST missionary efforts. Some contemporary Native American Mennonite leaders have tried to establish a theological link between the pacifist heritage of the Cheyenne peace chiefs and Anabaptist PACIFISM. The most important Native American Anabaptist is the Cheyenne peace chief Lawrence H. Hart (1933–).

Mennonites have operated MISSIONS in Canada and the United States among the Blackfeet, Cheyenne, Choctaw, Comanche, Cree, Creek, Hopi, Huoma, Lakota Sioux, Navajo, and Ojibwa people. An estimated 700 people attend some 20 Native American Mennonite congregations, which are located in Alabama, Arizona, Mississippi, Montana, New Mexico, Oklahoma, South Dakota, Manitoba, and Ontario.

Very few Native Americans joined BRETHREN groups in the 1800s. Although some

Brethren ministers had previously preached to
Native groups, the first Brethren mission to the
Native Americans began in the early 1950s in
New Mexico. There they established a school
and medical clinic for the Navajo. Volunteers
with Brethren Volunteer Service programs have
worked in Native American communities since
the late 1950s.

GAMEO ("Indians, North America"), Habegger
(1959), Juhnke (1980), Lowe (1993), ME V ("Indians,
North America")

Native Peoples   *See* Native American Anabaptists

Netherlands, The

This small country in northwestern Europe was
one of the major points of origin for ANABAP-
TISM in the 1500s. MENNO SIMONS (1496–
1561), for whom the MENNONITES are named,
was an influential Anabaptist leader in the
Netherlands. The Anabaptist Movement splintered into several factions in the Netherlands in
the late 16th and early 17th centuries because of
doctrinal differences and cultural variations. The
DORDRECHT CONFESSION OF FAITH (1632)
was written in an attempt to reconcile some of
the differences.

Mennonites experienced about 50 years
(1525–1575) of intense PERSECUTION in the
Netherlands and Flanders, a part of Belgium.
Later Mennonites wrote about this persecution
and other instances of Christian MARTYRDOM
in MARTYRS MIRROR, first published in Dutch
in 1660 in the Netherlands. In the mid-1600s,
Dutch Mennonites created the Committee for
Foreign Needs, which lobbied on behalf of persecuted Anabaptist groups and others throughout Europe. For over a century the committee
gathered material aid and financial funds, for
Anabaptists and others in need.

During the 1600s, Mennonites in Dutch cities managed to maintain some distinctive beliefs
and practices while also successfully participating in the rich cultural life of the Netherlands as
merchants, painters, poets, doctors, and writers.
In rural regions such as Friesland, they were primarily involved in AGRICULTURE.

By the 18th century, Mennonite church
membership had declined dramatically as its
members were attracted to material success and
the philosophy of the Enlightenment. From a
high of about 160,000 members in 1700, church
membership dropped sharply to about 27,000
in 1808. Some congregations started a small
seminary in 1735, and in 1811 it was enlarged with
support from all Dutch Mennonite groups. This
endeavor helped to provide some stability and
identity during the 1800s. From 1956 to 2010,
church membership declined again, from 38,500
to 9,000. Various efforts for renewal are under
way, such as the Dutch Mennonite Historical
Society, retreat centers, and an expanded ministry to youth.

Although the German Baptist Brethren originated in Germany, a significant number of them
lived in Friesland, a province of the Netherlands,
from 1720 to 1729, before they immigrated to
Pennsylvania.

BE II ("Netherlands, The"), C. Dyck (1993), GAMEO
("Netherlands"), Krahn (1963, 1981), Lowry (2007), ME
III ("Netherlands"), ME V ("Netherlands, The"), http://
www.mwc-cmm.org

New Order Amish   *See* Amish

New Testament   *See* Bible

Nicaragua

Five ANABAPTIST denominations are present
in Nicaragua. The oldest is the BRETHREN IN
CHRIST, which was initiated by Brethren in
Christ missionaries who arrived in Nicaragua
in 1964 after being forced to flee Cuba. This
church combines evangelical and social service
ministries and emphasizes the importance of
the HOLY SPIRIT in the lives of believers. It
has a membership of about 3,900 in 114 congregations and worship centers. In 1989 the
denomination sent missionaries to Honduras to
establish new Brethren in Christ congregations
in that nearby country.

The Fraternity of Evangelical Mennonite
Churches of Nicaragua was formed in 1970 by
missionaries from the Evangelical Mennonite

Conference, Canada. Legally incorporated in 1973, the church has about 2,300 members in 32 congregations. It focuses on ministries that combine SERVICE and EVANGELISM, such as educational and community development programs.

The Convention of Evangelical Mennonite Churches of Nicaragua formed in 1977 as a result of mission efforts begun in 1973 by the Rosedale (Ohio) Mennonite Missions. This large church has about 4,600 members in 117 congregations and worship centers.

These three largest Anabaptist groups formed the Anabaptist Emergency Commission for collaboration during emergencies and disasters. The social services committees of the three groups also join efforts on some projects, and in addition the groups support the LATIN AMERICAN ANABAPTIST SEMINARY in Guatemala.

The first congregation of the Christian Brotherhood Churches (six congregations and 100 members) formed in 1995 near Managua. The Brotherhood churches are supported by and affiliated with the BEACHY AMISH MENNONITE CHURCH in the United States.

The CHURCH OF GOD IN CHRIST, MENNONITE group has five mission outposts in Nicaragua, including a gospel tract distribution center, but has very few members.

CHRISTIAN AID MINISTRIES operates a material aid office in Nicaragua for the distribution of food, clothing, medicine, and seeds. This organization opened a clinic at Waslala in 1997 and encouraged some congregations of the Christian Brotherhood Churches that have emerged in northern Nicaragua since then. Additionally, a congregation initiated by Mennonite Christian Fellowship was founded in 1995 near Managua.

MENNONITE CENTRAL COMMITTEE (MCC), with an expatriate staff of about a dozen people, supports the social service commissions of the three largest Nicaraguan Anabaptist denominations: the Brethren in Christ, the Fraternity of Evangelical Mennonite Churches, and the Convention of Evangelical Mennonite Churches. These commissions work with church and community members to drill wells, build latrines,

repair schools, and improve roads. MCC also promotes sustainable agricultural practices in the Teustepe region, home to about 40 congregations of the Convention of Evangelical Mennonite Churches. MCC supports the Nicaraguan Anabaptist Peace and Justice Commission, which mediates conflicts and teaches peace in schools, churches, communities, and a prison, and the Nicaraguan Anabaptist Emergency Commission, which responds to natural and human-caused disasters.

GAMEO ("Nicaragua"), ME V ("Nicaragua"), Mennonite World Conference (2005), http://www .bic-church.org/wm/who-we-are/nicaragua.asp, http://www.mwc-cmm.org

Nonconformity

At the beginning of the Anabaptist Movement in the 1500s, many ANABAPTISTS rejected some of the practices (attending state-controlled churches, drunkenness, swearing oaths) of their surrounding societies. They focused on being disciples of Jesus, practicing love and mercy, and forming disciplined church communities that emphasized godly behavior. The concept of nonconformity is rooted in the Apostle Paul's teaching that Christians should not conform to the practices of the world (Rom. 12:2), as well as in other Scripture verses such as "Love not the world, neither the things that are in the world" (I John 2:15). Nonconformity to the world was a key aspect of Anabaptist devotional practices, literature, and worship. It also was the foundation on which MUTUAL AID and church DISCIPLINE operated. PERSECUTION heightened the desire (and sometimes the need) for nonconformity, but did not create it.

Nonconformity involves COUNTERCULTURAL values and practices. Expressions of Anabaptist nonconformity have varied by group, cultural context, and time period. Some groups have allowed individual members to decide how they translate nonconformity into daily practice. Others, especially TRADITIONAL GROUPS in the 20th century, have specified particular forms of nonconformity, such as dress, for their members.

As MENNONITES and BRETHREN became more assimilated into North American culture, their outward signs of nonconformity faded. In terms of geography, DIALECT, OCCUPATION, and CLOTHING, most members of ASSIMILATED GROUPS are indistinguishable from the wider culture. However, 80% of CHURCH OF THE BRETHREN, MENNONITE CHURCH USA, and BRETHREN IN CHRIST members in the United States reported in a survey (CMP 2006) that nonconformity to the world is important in their personal faith commitment. Their theology and actions continue to bear the marks of nonconformity, including NONRESISTANCE, PEACEMAKING, a simple lifestyle, rejection of consumerism, and participation in VOLUNTARY SERVICE.

Traditional groups continue to practice nonconformity related to clothing, LITIGATION, Sabbath observance, use of TECHNOLOGY, and LEISURE activities, which distinguish their individual and corporate life from the wider society.

BE II ("Nonconformity"), Burkholder (1989), CMP 2006, GAMEO ("Nonconformity"), Kauffman and Driedger (1991), ME III ("Nonconformity"), ME V ("Nonconformity"), J. Wenger (1974)

Noncreedalism   *See* Confessions of Faith

Nonresistance

"Nonresistance" means not resisting evil with force or retaliation. Most ANABAPTISTS believe that the use of violent, coercive force toward others is not compatible with Christian ethics based on Jesus' SERMON ON THE MOUNT (especially Matt. 5:38–48). Anabaptist groups have long emphasized loving one's enemies, turning the other cheek, and not resisting evil with force. For the Swiss BRETHREN, this belief was stated in the SCHLEITHEIM ARTICLES, which prohibited Christians from participating in politics because it involved exerting coercive force over others.

With respect to military service, most Anabaptist groups officially advocate CONSCIENTIOUS OBJECTION, although some individuals have joined the armed forces. Most groups recognize the necessity of the GOVERNMENT to use coercive police force to maintain order in society, but there is disagreement over whether Christians may enter the police force and carry lethal weapons. Whether force may be used, even for self-defense, is also debated among Anabaptists.

Some assimilated MENNONITES use the term PACIFISM or "biblical pacifism" rather than "nonresistance." A survey (CMP 2006) of assimilated groups in the United States found that 27% of BRETHREN IN CHRIST, 37% of CHURCH OF THE BRETHREN, and 70% of MENNONITE CHURCH USA members would choose to serve in ALTERNATIVE SERVICE as conscientious objectors if drafted for the armed forces.

See also Peacemaking

Bush (1998b), CMP 2006, Driedger and Kraybill (1994), D. Durnbaugh (1968), GAMEO ("Nonresistance"), M. Heisey (2003), Keim (1990), Sampson and Lederach (2000), T. Schlabach (2009), C. Snyder (1989), Swartley (2006)

Nonviolence   *See* Nonresistance; Peacemaking

Oath, Swearing of

An oath calls on God as a witness of the truth and as an avenger of untruth. ANABAPTISTS have refused to take oaths, based on Jesus' command to speak a simple yes or no (Matt. 5:33–37). Because most European GOVERNMENTS and state churches required oaths in various situations, but especially to give allegiance for defending the state through force, Anabaptists struggled to win recognition of their convictions to prohibit oaths.

Members of most Anabaptist groups believe that Christians should always tell the truth and therefore should not be required to make any special promises to God or to the government about truth-telling. Most courts in North America allow persons to affirm (rather than swear an oath to God) that they are telling the truth.

BE II ("Oaths, Taking of"), GAMEO ("Oath"), ME IV ("Oath"), Schijn (1987)

Obedience   *See Gelassenheit*

Occupations

In the early 1500s, Swiss ANABAPTISTS lived primarily in urban areas, but in order to escape PERSECUTION they soon moved to rural areas and took up agricultural vocations. Until 1920 a high percentage of Anabaptists in SWITZERLAND, southern GERMANY, FRANCE, and North America were farmers. Anabaptists in North America became widely known for their expertise in AGRICULTURE. Alongside farming, members of Anabaptist groups were also involved in trades such as carpentry and crafts in the 18th and 19th centuries.

After outright persecution of Anabaptists ceased in the Netherlands around 1580, MENNONITES in Dutch urban areas joined the professions of medicine, ship building, import-export trade, and the arts. Those who lived in rural areas remained in farming, as did many of those who immigrated to northern Germany, POLAND, and RUSSIA from the late 1500s to the late 1700s. Although the Russian Mennonite colonies were based on agricultural production, Mennonite industries such as flour mills and

farm implement factories arose in the later 1800s.

In CANADA and the UNITED STATES, the proliferation of schools and other church-supported INSTITUTIONS expanded the occupational possibilities for some young people in the 20th century. Since around 1950, ASSIMILATED GROUPS in North America have entered a wide variety of occupations, in part because of higher levels of urbanization and EDUCATION. A survey (CMP 2006) in the United States revealed that a majority of assimilated BRETHREN and Mennonites work in managerial and professional jobs or in technical professions, sales, or administrative support. In fact, fewer than 8% work in agriculture, although about a third live in rural areas.

Even among TRADITIONAL GROUPS that do not encourage or allow HIGHER EDUCATION, the percentage of full-time farmers has rapidly declined because of the high cost of farmland, the large initial investment, and the expensive machinery required for farming. Many traditional Anabaptists now work in small BUSINESSES related to agriculture and construction.

See also Anabaptism, History of

CMP 2006, GAMEO ("Occupations"), Kraybill and Nolt (2004), ME V ("Occupations"), P. Toews (1996), Urry (1985)

Old Colony Mennonite Church, Canada

Beginning in 1874 and continuing for about 10 years, about 7,000 Russian MENNONITES moved to CANADA from Imperial RUSSIA. Canada promised the immigrants exemptions from military service and public education and allowed them to settle in compact agricultural reserves in the prairie provinces. The immigrant groups of the 1870s became known as KANADIER MENNONITES.

The largest group of immigrants, about 3,200 people, were called the Old Colony (or Reinländer) Mennonites because they originated from the oldest Mennonite colony (Chortitza) in Russia and its offspring. The Old Colony Church (Altkolonier Mennonitengemeinde), the most conservative of the Kanadier groups, was noted for its strong support of village farms and use of simple buggies without tops. During the 1920s about two-thirds of the Old Colony community relocated to MEXICO after governments in Manitoba and Saskatchewan passed laws requiring English-language instruction for children. Many of those remaining in Canada moved to more isolated communities in the northern parkland regions of Alberta, Saskatchewan, and British Columbia.

During the second half of the 20th century many Old Colony Mennonites living in Mexico returned to Canada and established new congregations in Leamington and Aylmer (Ontario) and Tabor (southern Alberta). Old Colony members are distinguished by their CLOTHING—the women's simple print dresses and black kerchiefs and the men's shirts worn without neckties. Distinctive plain dress has been part of their traditional lifestyle, but that is changing in the 21st century. The group has large families and uses the Low German DIALECT in their everyday life. Old Colony Mennonites also speak Low German in their worship services, although the singing and Bible reading are done in High German. Ministers without formal theological training provide congregational leadership.

Although farming is encouraged, most male members work in the trades, in local factories, in trucking firms, or as entrepreneurs, typically in building or farm-related enterprises. Married women generally do not work outside their homes, but they are active in volunteer work. Members now drive cars and use electricity. Old Colony churches in Canada continue to resist acculturation and remain somewhat isolated from other Mennonite groups.

The Old Colony Mennonite churches in Manitoba divided in 2003. A small progressive-minded group of about 500 members, known as the Old Colony Mennonite Church of Manitoba, emerged from the division. This group adopted practices, such as using English in church services, that remain taboo among the traditional churches.

The larger, more conservative group in Manitoba uses the name German Old Colony Mennonite Church and remains a part of the Old Colony Mennonite Church in Canada. There are about 9,000 Old Colony members in some 20 congregations in five provinces. The largest concentrations are in Ontario and Alberta, with smaller communities in Manitoba, Saskatchewan, and British Columbia. A few congregations have been established in Texas and Kansas in the United States. Old Colony–related churches also exist in Mexico and BELIZE as well as Paraguay.

See also Old Colony Mennonite Church, Mexico

F. Epp (1974, 1982), J. Friesen (2007), GAMEO ("Old Colony Mennonites"), Loewen and Nolt (2010), R. Loewen (2004, 2008), ME V ("Old Colony Mennonites"), Plett (2001)

Old Colony Mennonite Church, Mexico

Beginning in 1922, some 7,000 mostly Old Colony Mennonites (Altkolonier Mennonitengemeinde) of Dutch-Russian background who had settled in CANADA in the 1870s immigrated to MEXICO. These tradition-minded MENNONITES left Canada because they were threatened by new education laws in Manitoba and Saskatchewan that required all children to attend English-language schools. They established three colonies in the Mexican states of Chihuahua (Manitoba and Swift) and Durango (Patos). Many Old Colony members eventually left Mexico in 1958 for British Honduras (now BELIZE) and Bolivia. Some impoverished members returned to Canada in the last quarter of the 20th century. At the beginning of the 21st century, the Old Colony churches have about 19,700 members in some 30 colonies in eight Mexican states. There are also Old Colony groups in Belize, Canada, and Paraguay.

See also Central America; Kanadier Mennonites; Old Colony Mennonite Church, Canada

F. Epp (1974, 1982), GAMEO ("Old Colony Mennonites"), Loewen and Nolt (2010), R. Loewen (2004, 2008), ME V ("Old Colony Mennonites")

Old German Baptist Brethren

With roots in the Schwarzenau Brethren movement of 1708, this group formed in 1881 during the three-way division of the German Baptist Brethren Church. An Old Order group, it seeks to preserve many of the traditional practices of the German Baptist Brethren but permits the ownership of motor vehicles and the use of ELECTRICITY and COMPUTERS for business, but not TELEVISION or RADIO. Members of the group are sometimes confused with the AMISH because of similar plain dress and beards worn by men. The Old German Baptist Brethren participate in the projects of BRETHREN ENCYCLOPEDIA, INC. This group of traditional BRETHREN in the United States has about 6,300 members and some 50 congregations in 16 states, with the largest number in Ohio and Indiana. A division within this group began forming in 2009. The more change-minded branch, calling itself the Old German Baptist Brethren New Conference, initially claimed about one-third (2,000) of the members.

BE II ("Old German Baptist Brethren"), Kraybill and Bowman (2001)

Old Order Amish   *See* Amish; Traditional Groups

Old Order Amish Steering Committee

During the VIETNAM WAR, many young AMISH men were granted CONSCIENTIOUS OBJECTOR status and worked in various ALTERNATIVE SERVICE programs, most often in hospitals. This program was unsatisfactory to many in the Amish community because when the men were exposed to mainstream American culture in the hospitals, only about half of them returned home, joined the church, and assumed adult roles in the Amish community.

The Old Order Amish Steering Committee was founded in 1966 to represent the Amish to federal officials. The committee worked to obtain farm deferments for drafted Amish men, which allowed them to work on Amish farms instead of serving in alternative service programs.

Since the 1960s and 1970s the committee has expanded its form and its function. It now consists of an informal network of several dozen Amish representatives from various states who

try as much as possible to speak with a unified voice to government officials regarding issues of special concern. A small executive committee coordinates the work of state committees. The full countrywide committee meets annually to discuss a wide variety of legal issues, such as occupational safety and health laws, Social Security TAXES, workers' compensation, Medicare, photo identification, Selective Service guidelines, and private Amish schools. The representatives, generally laymen rather than ordained officials, also negotiate with public officials at local, state, and federal levels to avoid conflict and LITIGATION. Despite the unified position that the steering committee seeks to present, different Amish subgroups have diverse opinions on how they prefer to respond to government regulations.

See also National Committee for Amish Religious Freedom

J. Hostetler (1993), Kraybill (2001, 2003c), Olshan (2003)

Old Order Anabaptist Groups   *See* Traditional Groups

Old Order Brethren   *See* Brethren; Traditional Groups

Old Order Mennonites

The Old Order Mennonite movement arose in the United States and Canada between 1872 and 1901 in MENNONITE communities of largely Swiss–south German origin. New developments in the broader society and the larger Protestant world—SUNDAY SCHOOLS, revival services, MISSION activities, use of the ENGLISH LANGUAGE in church services, HIGHER EDUCATION, and the growing acceptance of new TECHNOLOGY—that threatened to transform the traditional churches catalyzed the OLD ORDER MOVEMENT. Old Order groups emerged in Indiana and Ohio (1872), Ontario (1889), Pennsylvania (1893), and Virginia (1901).

More than a half-dozen different Old Order Mennonite groups have thriving congregations in the U.S. and Canada in the 21st century. (The

Hoover Church also has congregations in Belize.) The two largest groups are the Groffdale Conference (10,000) and the Weaverland Conference (7,100). A listing of all the groups appears in the Table of Groups.

Members of Old Order congregations wear distinctive plain clothing that varies somewhat by group. The most traditional ones use horse-and-buggy transportation. Some groups conduct their church services in Pennsylvania German, while others have accepted English. Unlike the AMISH, Old Order Mennonites worship in meetinghouses. Most of the groups do not have Sunday school or revival meetings. Members in some of the groups actively support and participate in service programs such as MENNONITE DISASTER SERVICE and CHRISTIAN AID MINISTRIES, but they do not operate mission agencies. The technological practices of each group related to the use of public grid electricity, telephones, and modern farm machinery varies, but all of them forbid the use of radio, television, and the Internet.

The OLD COLONY MENNONITES of CANADA and MEXICO have a completely different historical and cultural tradition unrelated to the Old Order Mennonites of Swiss background in Canada and the United States. The Old Colony Mennonites emigrated from Imperial Russia to Manitoba in the KANADIER MENNONITE migration of the 1870s.

See also Old Order Mennonites, Groffdale Conference; Old Order Mennonites, Weaverland Conference

GAMEO ("Old Order Mennonites, Pennsylvania"), A. Hoover (1982, 2006), B. Hostetler (1992), Kraybill and Hurd (2006), D. Martin (2003), ME V ("Old Order Mennonites, PA"), Joseph Miller (2004), Weiler (1993)

Old Order Mennonites, Groffdale Conference

This group of horse-and-buggy-driving MENNONITES traces its roots to the 1893 Old Order division in Lancaster, Pennsylvania. Some years later, in 1927, the OLD ORDER MOVEMENT in Lancaster divided over AUTOMOBILE use. The Groffdale Conference was the more conserva-

tive branch and became known as the team Mennonites because they continued using horse-and-buggy teams. They also are known as Wenger Mennonites because their first bishop was Joseph Wenger (1830–1907). The car-driving branch of the 1927 division became the OLD ORDER MENNONITES, WEAVERLAND CONFERENCE. Members of the Groffdale Conference speak both English and the Pennsylvania German DIALECT. The Groffdale Conference has expanded into eight other states including New York, Missouri, Ohio, Kentucky, Iowa, and Wisconsin. However, 21 of its 50 congregations remain in Pennsylvania. The OLD ORDER MENNONITES of Indiana merged with the Groffdale Conference in 1973. The total baptized membership is about 10,000. A similar horse-and-buggy group, the Old Order Mennonite Church in Ontario, with about 3,200 members, maintains a close relationship with the Groffdale Conference.

GAMEO ("Old Order Mennonites, Pennsylvania"), Kraybill and Hurd (2006), ME V ("Old Order Mennonites, PA")

Old Order Mennonites, Weaverland Conference

This group traces its roots to the Old Order division of 1893 in Pennsylvania when Bishop Jonas Martin (1839–1925) withdrew from the Lancaster Mennonite Conference. The OLD ORDER MOVEMENT in Lancaster separated into two branches in 1927 when the Weaverland Conference accepted automobiles and the OLD ORDER MENNONITES, GROFFDALE CONFERENCE continued using horse-drawn buggies. For many years MENNONITES in the Weaverland Conference were known as "black bumpers" because members were required to paint the chrome bumpers on their cars black. This practice still continues for ministers, but not for other members.

The Weaverland Conference no longer uses the Pennsylvania German DIALECT in their services, but some older members continue to speak it in daily life. The group does not have SUNDAY SCHOOL or revival meetings. Its members support some mission and service programs. They use ELECTRICITY, TELEPHONES, and modern farm machinery, but not RADIO, TELEVISION, or the Internet. Of their 40 congregations, 26 are located in Pennsylvania. Their membership is about 9,000. A similar group in Canada, the Markham-Waterloo Mennonite Conference, has about 1,400 members. *Home Messenger* is the semiofficial monthly paper of the Weaverland Conference.

GAMEO ("Old Order Mennonites, Pennsylvania"), A. Hoover (1982, 2006), Kraybill and Hurd (2006), ME V ("Old Order Mennonites, PA")

Old Order Movement

In the last half of the 19th century, industrialization began to transform the United States and Canada from small farm economies to factory-based production and to encourage migration from rural areas to cities. Protestant church agencies for evangelism, religious education, and publishing increased during this time as well. The ripple effects of industrialization and the growth of Protestant church INSTITUTIONS touched the religious ethos of ANABAPTIST churches. Between 1855 and 1901, the AMISH, MENNONITES, and BRETHREN all experienced Old Order divisions within their churches related to new developments in the broader society and the larger Protestant world: SUNDAY SCHOOLS, revival services, MISSION activities, use of the ENGLISH LANGUAGE in church services, HIGHER EDUCATION, and the growing acceptance of new TECHNOLOGY. The exact issues entangled in the church divisions varied from group to group, but they frequently reflected tensions produced by the massive process of industrialization and the growing prominence of Protestant forms of religion that threatened to transform the traditional patterns of Anabaptist churches.

Some churches welcomed the changes, which they deemed progressive and helpful to the growth and witness of the church. Others feared the changes and warned that the distinctive Anabaptist beliefs and practices would be absorbed into the mainstream of Protestant religion. TRADITIONAL GROUPS that wanted to conserve older values and customs were often called Old Order, meaning that they continued to embrace the old rules and cultural practices in the church. Those more comfortable with cultural change embarked on the path of assimilation with the larger society. Contentious debates and divisions resulted in the formation of numerous Old Order groups in the last three decades of the 19th century in Canada and the United States.

Among the Amish, a series of national ministers' meetings between 1862 and 1878 produced a division between Old Order Amish and more progressive Amish-Mennonites, who moved toward affiliation with Mennonite churches. A three-way division among the Brethren between 1881 and 1883 produced the OLD GERMAN BAPTIST BRETHREN, the BRETHREN CHURCH, and the CHURCH OF THE BRETHREN. The Old Order River Brethren in eastern Pennsylvania emerged in 1855 as an Old Order branch of the BRETHREN IN CHRIST church. In Mennonite circles, the Old Order Movement arose between 1872 and 1901, with different Old Order groups originating in Indiana and Ohio (1872), Ontario (1889), Pennsylvania (1893), and Virginia (1901).

The OLD COLONY MENNONITES of CANADA and MEXICO are not directly connected to the OLD ORDER MENNONITES of Swiss background in Canada and the United States. The Old Colony Mennonites emigrated from Imperial Russia to Manitoba in the KANADIER MENNONITE migration of the 1870s. They established Mennonite villages, or "colonies," in Manitoba similar to the ones they left in Russia. In the 1920s about two-thirds of the Old Colony Mennonites moved to Mexico when some Canadian provinces began requiring English-language instruction for children, which leaders did not want to teach in church-run schools. During the second half of the 20th century some of the Old Colony Mennonites in Mexico returned to Canada.

Although all the Old Order groups have experienced numerous changes since their origin, they continue to exhibit and practice many traditional Anabaptist values and beliefs.

See also Central America; Revivalism

A. Hoover (1982, 2006), B. Hostetler (1992), Kraybill and Bowman (2001), R. Loewen (2004), D. Martin (2003), Joseph Miller (2004), Weiler (1993), Paton Yoder (1991)

Old Order River Brethren   *See* Brethren in Christ

On Earth Peace Assembly

Begun in 1974 under the impetus of M. R. Zigler (1891–1985) of the CHURCH OF THE BRETHREN, this educational organization promotes peace-related themes and distributes resources for peace education. On Earth Peace Assembly holds conferences and provides training in areas such as CONFLICT resolution, peace witness, and peace education. Initially created within the Church of the Brethren structure, it was incorporated as an independent body in 1981. It is located at the BRETHREN SERVICE CENTER in New Windsor, Maryland.

See also Brethren; Peacemaking

BE II ("On Earth Peace"), D. Durnbaugh (1989), http://www.brethren.org/oepa

Ordinance

ANABAPTIST groups have often used the term "ordinance" rather than "sacrament" for important RITUALS or rites within the church. The term refers to the practices that Jesus ordered or instituted for his followers. Early Anabaptists rejected the medieval theology of sacraments in which visible acts/ceremonies of the church, administered by officially ordained priests, were believed to convey God's grace. Instead, Anabaptists believe that visible ceremonies symbolize God's grace given to the believer by the HOLY SPIRIT, but that such acts themselves do not convey God's grace.

Adult BAPTISM and COMMUNION (or the Lord's Supper) are the central ordinances for Anabaptists. Some Anabaptist groups also con-

sider ORDINATION, FOOTWASHING, ANOINTING WITH OIL, laying on hands, and marriage as ordinances. The BRETHREN practice the ordinance of the LOVE FEAST, which includes footwashing, the meal of fellowship, and the bread and cup of communion. The Brethren historically have considered the HOLY KISS an ordinance. Around 1900, some MENNONITES of Swiss origin considered the HEAD COVERING for women (widely used prior to then) and the holy kiss / kiss of peace as ordinances of the church.

BE II ("Ordinances"), Bender and Sell (1991), Eller (1972), GAMEO ("Ordinances"), ME IV ("Ordinances," "Sacrament"), ME V ("Ordinances"), M. Miller (1990), Rempel (1993), C. Snyder (1995)

Ordination

Church bodies call and appoint persons to exercise leadership AUTHORITY through the process of ordination, which involves a special service that usually includes the laying on of hands. The locus of authority to ordain varies among groups. In some groups the CONGREGATION has the sole prerogative; in other groups a conference or regional body ordains; and in still other groups these two levels of authority are combined in calling and ordaining leaders.

The traditional practice involved three separate lifetime ordinations for different leadership roles: BISHOP or ELDER, MINISTER or preacher, and DEACON. These roles continue in many TRADITIONAL GROUPS, but a variety of ministerial roles and titles are found in ASSIMILATED GROUPS. BRETHREN in the 18th century had two levels: elder and exhorter. Later, Brethren adopted three "degrees" or levels of ministry for elders and ministers. Brethren do not consider deacons to be ordained, even though deacons are consecrated by the laying on of hands.

Some assimilated MENNONITE and Brethren churches recognize three stages of ministry: licensing for a trial period, commissioning for a limited time or task, and full ordination. Some assimilated groups ordain women as ministers, but traditional groups prohibit this practice.

Assimilated congregations use a variety of procedures to select ordained leaders, typically in collaboration with a larger ecclesiastical body—a regional district or conference. Some congregations find leaders within their congregation and ordain them, but many select leaders from outside who have already been ordained. The process of selecting an outside pastor often involves a search committee, a trial sermon, and a vote by members of a congregation or its leadership body.

Some traditional groups select leaders for ordination by casting lots among eligible men who are first nominated by the congregation or a group of leaders. This process was used in biblical times to select leaders (I Sam. 36–42, Proverbs 16:33, Acts 1:24–26). The exact process varies by group but typically involves placing a piece of paper inside the cover of a hymnbook and randomly arranging the book with other identical hymnbooks. The total number of hymnbooks is equivalent to the number of men in the pool of nominees. Each man in the "lot" selects a book, and the one who chooses the book with the hidden paper is ordained. Typically, the congregation views the one to whom the lot fell as selected and called by God.

See also Church Authority; Ordination of Women

BE II ("Ordination"), GAMEO ("Ordination"), ME IV ("Ordination"), ME V ("Ordination"), Mosemann (1983), Shetler (1987), E. Thomas (1996), J. E. Toews (2004)

Ordination of Women

The ORDINATION of women is a key mark in the assimilation process of ANABAPTIST groups. TRADITIONAL GROUPS object to the ordination of women because they believe only men should hold major leadership roles in the church. Even among the more ASSIMILATED GROUPS, ordaining women, as well as which ministerial tasks are acceptable for women to perform, varies considerably. The majority of assimilated BRETHREN and MENNONITES in the United States favor ordaining women for pastoral ministry, but over half of those in one study (CMP 2006) said that they would prefer a man as lead pastor. Although hundreds of women have been ordained and many have served successfully as pastors in the CHURCH OF THE BRETHREN, MENNONITE BRETHREN CHURCH, MENNONITE CHURCH CANADA, and MENNONITE CHURCH USA, the issue remains contentious in many congregations.

Controversy ensued among the Brethren in the 1800s when a few women began to preach in worship services and other settings. The 1922 Annual Conference of the Church of the Brethren ruled that women could be licensed as ministers for PREACHING only, but few districts actually licensed women. In 1958 the Church of the Brethren opened full ordination to women, but some Brethren groups (Dunkard Brethren, OLD GERMAN BAPTIST BRETHREN) do not ordain women. The BRETHREN CHURCH began to ordain women in the early 21st century, after briefly having ordained women at the end of the 19th century.

Anna Beahm Mow (1893–1985) was a prominent leader in the Church of the Brethren. She served as a missionary and educator, as well as a professor of missions, Christian education, and biblical studies at Bethany Biblical Seminary in Chicago from 1940 to 1958. In 1960 she became one of the first women to be ordained in the Church of the Brethren.

Although Ann Jemima Allebach (1874–1918) was the first Mennonite woman on record to be ordained (in 1911) a minister by Mennonites in North America, she never served in a Mennonite Church. Very few, if any, Mennonite women were ordained for the next 60 years. Emma Sommers Richards (1927–) was ordained to serve in the Lombard, Illinois, congregation of the MENNONITE CHURCH in 1973 before the ordination of women had churchwide approval. Later in the 1970s both the Mennonite Church and the GENERAL CONFERENCE MENNONITE CHURCH authorized the ordination of women. Although Mennonite Church USA as a denomination embraces the ordination of women, the governance of ordination belongs to area conferences, which have varied practices. In 2010 about 350 ordained women in the denomination were active in various ministerial roles. The United States

Conference of Mennonite Brethren Churches licenses women for ministerial roles, but they generally do not serve as senior pastors.

In Canada the first ordination of a Mennonite woman took place in 1979 (Doris Weber, 1930–); in 2007, 26% of pastors listed in the Mennonite Church Canada directory were women. The Canadian Conference of Mennonite Brethren permits congregations to call women for pastoral roles, but the proportion of women who serve as pastors is lower than in Mennonite Church Canada.

A maverick bishop in the BRETHREN IN CHRIST church in Oklahoma ordained a woman in 1921, but she was never recognized by the denomination. The first official ordination of a woman by the Brethren in Christ was performed in 1987.

See also Gender Roles

BE II ("Mow, Anna Beahm"), CMP 2006, Eriksson (2007), GAMEO ("Allebach, Ann Jemima [1874–1918]," "Women"), ME V ("Women"), Schiedel (2003), Shetler (1987)

Ordnung

The ANABAPTIST theological focus on following the ways and teachings of Jesus has led to an understanding of Christian faith that typically emphasizes practice in daily life more than creeds and formal religious doctrine. Historically, German-speaking groups referred to the rules and regulations (behavioral expectations) of the local church body as *Ordnung,* a German word meaning "regulations," often translated as "discipline" in English. This collective understanding about the church's expectation for behavior encompasses issues related to moral behavior, dress, participation in the larger society, and selective ownership of TECHNOLOGY. The *Ordnung* of church bodies evolves slowly to address the changing social issues facing the church, especially those for which there is no clear-cut biblical teaching. Expectations that are addressed in the Scripture, such as honesty and marital fidelity, do not require *Ordnung,* but issues that are not directly addressed by Scripture, such as fashionable CLOTHING, gambling, and taking of PHOTOGRAPHS, might require *Ordnung* guidance.

Some TRADITIONAL GROUPS keep written *Ordnung,* but many do not. The regulations of the church typically are developed and enforced by ordained leaders, but in most groups they require ratification by the members of the congregation. For children and many adults, the *Ordnung* is simply the taken-for-granted way of life taught by the church and expected of faithful and virtuous members.

Most ASSIMILATED GROUPS no longer have the equivalent of an *Ordnung,* although they may have a mission statement, a covenant of beliefs and expectations, or a CONFESSION OF FAITH. The use of *Ordnung* continues among many conservative groups—especially AMISH, OLD ORDER MENNONITES, and OLD COLONY MENNONITES.

Kraybill and Bowman (2001)

Overseer *See* Bishop

Pacifism

One of the key earmarks of ANABAPTIST identity in the larger world is pacifism. Although Anabaptists have long emphasized the pacifist teachings of Jesus and often taught that his followers should shun violence, they have not always been comfortable with the pacifist label. On the one hand, to members of more TRADITIONAL GROUPS the word "pacifism" sounds like a philosophical or political term quite different from their rejection of force based on religious convictions. In the 16th and 17th centuries, Anabaptists often described themselves as "defenseless" Christians. Tradition-minded Anabaptists prefer to speak of NONRESISTANCE to evil, which reflects the admonition of Jesus to love enemies and not retaliate (Matt. 5:39, 44). For traditional members, pacifism is not a political strategy but a fervent commitment to follow the example of Jesus and reject the use of force even in the face of violence. This nonresistant faith is associated with a strong view that the church should not be involved in politics.

Anabaptists in many ASSIMILATED GROUPS also are uncomfortable with the pacifist label, but for a different reason. To them, pacifism is too passive. These Anabaptists believe that following the way of Jesus means being an active peacebuilder. For the more assimilated, pacifism suggests passive acceptance and noninvolvement in civic and political affairs and a reluctance to take responsibility to improve the moral condition of the larger world. This brand of Anabaptist faith believes that Christian convictions should empower people to enact the nonviolent principles of Jesus in civic and political activities. These activities include RESTORATIVE JUSTICE, protest against war, conflict mediation, PEACEMAKING, peacebuilding, and other conciliation efforts.

Organizations such as ON EARTH PEACE ASSEMBLY, the Center for Justice and Peacebuilding at Eastern Mennonite University, and MENNONITE CENTRAL COMMITTEE as well as dozens of local and regional peace-related organizations reflect these Anabaptist commitments to active peacemaking.

After the publication of *The Original Revolution: Essays on Christian Pacifism* (1971) and *The Politics of Jesus: Vicit Agnus Noster* (1972), the pacifist thought of Anabaptist theologian John Howard Yoder (1927–1997) stirred a worldwide ecumenical conversation among scholars. Yoder's knowledge of biblical scholarship, historical theology, and ethical thought contributed to his creative interpretation of the fundamental nonviolent claims of traditional Christianity.

See also Christian Peacemaker Teams; Historic Peace Churches

Driedger and Kraybill (1994), Enns, Holland and Riggs (2004), Nation (1997), Roth, (2002a), Swartley (2006), Swartley and Dyck (1987), J. H. Yoder (1971, 1972/1994, 1984b, 1992).

Panama

ANABAPTISTS first began work in Panama in 1957, when missionaries with Mennonite Brethren Mission and Services moved across the border from Colombia to start adult education and literacy programs. The missionaries worked in the Choco region in southern Panama and in 1964 established the United Evangelical Mennonite Brethren Church, which became a legal entity in 1970. The church began growing after 1999 and has several churches related to the Wounan and Emberá ethnic groups. It remains largely centered in the border region and has 13 congregations with about 550 members. Members are mainly indigenous, and the church is autonomous, with missionaries serving only as resource persons.

GAMEO ("Panama"), ME V ("Panama"), Mennonite World Conference (2005), http://www.mwc-cmm.org

Parenting   *See* Children; Family

Pathway Publishers

This PUBLISHING company was founded by two AMISH farmers, David L. Wagler (1921–) and Joseph Stoll (1935–), in 1964 in Ontario. It publishes school curricula, DEVOTIONAL LITERATURE, and general Christian literature written by and for the Amish. Although the company is not owned by the church, its activities and publications reflect the values of many TRADI-TIONAL GROUPS.

Pathway Publishers prints three monthly PE-RIODICALS. *Young Companion* is aimed at Amish youth, while *Blackboard Bulletin* addresses the needs of teachers, parents, and school board members. The third periodical, *Family Life*, began in 1968 to promote Christian living and values. It contains articles, poems, short stories, book reviews, historical research, and letters by and about Old Order Amish and OLD ORDER MENNONITES. A popular textbook series is the Pathway Readers, collections of stories for use in first through eighth grades in Amish schools.

Many of Pathway's publications articulate Amish assumptions about spiritual life and ethical behavior that have typically not been written down in the past. Historical beliefs are examined and applied to practical issues facing Amish communities. Some Amish object to having too much of their way of life in print and thus disapprove of Pathway Publishers, but the company continues to thrive with increasing sales and publications. Pathway Publishers also promotes and subsidizes the publication of books by other PUBLISHING ORGANIZATIONS that support Old Order lifestyles and beliefs. The company has also developed Heritage Historical Library, a major repository for Amish and Old Order Mennonite documents and artifacts.

GAMEO ("Pathway Publishers"), J. Hostetler (1993), ME V ("Pathway Publishers"), W[agler] (1968)

Patriarchy   *See* Gender Roles

Patriotism   *See* Nationalism

Pax   *See* Alternative Service

Peacemaking

ANABAPTIST efforts at peacemaking are rooted in their commitment to biblical NONRESIS-TANCE. In an attempt to follow Jesus' prohibition against violence in his SERMON ON THE MOUNT, many Anabaptists have created organizations that work at peacebuilding in a variety of ways. During the 1970s, ASSIMILATED GROUPS began to emphasize peacemaking more than nonresistance, which they considered too passive. They saw the possibilities for conciliation and mediation in a wide variety of conflicts, from interpersonal to organizational to international.

During the world wars and the VIETNAM WAR, the HISTORIC PEACE CHURCHES (BRETHREN, QUAKERS, and MENNONITES) established Civilian Public Service, Pax, and other options for ALTERNATIVE SERVICE for their members who were CONSCIENTIOUS OBJECTORS to war.

CHRISTIAN PEACEMAKER TEAMS (CPT) was organized by Brethren, Quakers, and Mennonites in 1986. Members of CPT intervene in situations of conflict in order to stop violence and foster reconciliation through direct nonviolent action. Often this means intervening in militarized situations and violent intergroup confrontations, such as standing between an Israeli bulldozer and a Palestinian home that is marked for destruction.

Other groups work at peace by trying to eliminate injustice. MENNONITE CENTRAL COMMITTEE and Brethren Volunteer Service were created to provide relief and advocacy in underdeveloped areas around the world. Eirene is a similar organization that provides international voluntary service opportunities for European Mennonites. In CENTRAL AMERICA, REGIONAL NETWORK OF JUSTICE AND PEACE is an Anabaptist organization that promotes reconciliation in the aftermath of civil wars.

Mediation is another important aspect of peacemaking. Mennonite Conciliation Service and Victim Offender Reconciliation Programs both offer nonviolent and creative ways to resolve conflict.

Peace education is also important to many Anabaptist groups. In 1948, Manchester College, a Brethren school in Indiana, became the first undergraduate school to offer a degree in peace studies. Since that time many colleges (Anabaptist and non-Anabaptist) have added similar degree programs in peace studies.

Table 12   Peacemaking Resources

Books

Biblical Pacifism, D. Brown, 2003

Choosing against War: A Christian View, Roth, 2002a

Covenant of Peace: The Missing Peace in New Testament Theology and Ethics, Swartley, 2006

From the Ground Up: Mennonite Contributions to International Peacebuilding, Sampson and Lederach, 2000

In Harm's Way: A History of Christian Peacemaker Teams, Kern, 2009

The Journey toward Reconciliation, J. Lederach, 1999

Mennonite Peacemaking: From Quietism to Activism, Driedger and Kraybill, 1994

The Politics of Jesus: Vicit Agnus Noster, J. H. Yoder, 1972/1994

Seeking Cultures of Peace: A Peace Church Conversation, Enns, Holland, and Riggs, 2004

Web Sites

Canadian Mennonite University (http://www.cmu.ca)

Center for Justice and Peacebuilding at Eastern Mennonite University (http://www.emu.edu/cjp)

Christian Peacemaker Teams (http://www.cpt.org)

Juniata College, Baker Institute (http://www.departments.juniata.edu/pacs)

Plowshares Peace Studies Collaborative (http://www.plowsharesproject.org)

Project Ploughshares (http://www.ploughshares.ca)

Mennonite Central Committee (http://mcc.org/whatwedo/peace)

See also Pacifism; Restorative Justice

BE IV ("Christian Peacemaker Teams"), D. Brown (2003), T. Brown (2005, 2008), Driedger and Kraybill (1994), D. Durnbaugh (1997a), Enns, Holland, and Riggs (2004), GAMEO ("Peace"), Kern (2009), ME V ("Peace"), Roth (2002a), Sampson and Lederach (2000), Swartley (2006)

Pennsylvania Dutch / Pennsylvania German   *See* Dialects

Periodicals

The publication of ANABAPTIST periodicals exploded in the second half of the 19th century. BRETHREN minister Henry Kurtz (1796–1874) began publishing *The Gospel Visitor* in 1851 as a private venture. Kurtz realized that as Brethren migrated across the UNITED STATES, they needed some way to maintain contact, and his publication provided the link. In 1882 the Brethren Annual Meeting approved it, under the title *Gospel Messenger*, as the official newspaper of the church.

When printing became easier and more available in the late 1800s in North America, the number of church-related periodicals increased dramatically. During this time hundreds of peri-

odicals were published by church conferences, districts, and church-related organizations in Anabaptist groups.

During the 20th century, after ASSIMILATED GROUPS had established colleges, academic periodicals such as BRETHREN IN CHRIST HISTORY AND LIFE, DIRECTION, MENNONITE LIFE, MENNONITE QUARTERLY REVIEW, BRETHREN LIFE AND THOUGHT, JOURNAL OF MENNONITE STUDIES, and CONRAD GREBEL REVIEW emerged. In the 21st century, Anabaptists are a diverse group—in interest, age, EDUCATION, and geographical location—and new periodicals are continuously created to serve these different groups.

Many TRADITIONAL GROUPS also publish periodicals. Christian Light Publications in Virginia is a major distributor of books and curricular materials for conservative MENNONITE groups. *The Vindicator*, begun in 1870, serves the interests of the OLD GERMAN BAPTIST BRETHREN. Amish-related publications including *Family Life, The Diary, Die Botschaft*, and *The Budget* provide information written by AMISH and OLD ORDER MENNONITE authors.

In the 21st century, dozens of Anabaptist groups have biweekly, monthly, or quarterly periodicals published for their members. These range in format from well-designed four-color magazines to simple newsletters. Increasingly, assimilated groups are shifting to electronic newsletters, online publications, and web sites.

See also Publishing; Publishing Organizations

BE II ("Publishing"), GAMEO ("Periodicals"), ME V ("Periodicals")

Persecution

As religious and political dissidents, ANABAP-TISTS in the 1500s and 1600s suffered severe persecution. They were harassed by the three major European religious groups (Roman Catholics, Lutherans, and Calvinists) for their religious beliefs, and by political authorities who were threatened by Anabaptists' refusal to baptize infants, swear OATHS, and participate in military service. Civil authorities resorted to legal restrictions, banishment, physical torture, and execution in their attempts to modify Anabaptists' beliefs and behavior.

Intense persecution and MARTYRDOM had ceased in the NETHERLANDS by 1579, but it continued throughout the rest of EUROPE. (The HUTTERITES, for example, experienced severe persecution in Moravia in the 1600s.) These early Anabaptists believed that Jesus had predicted harsh treatment for his followers (Matt. 5:10–12, 10:17–23), so they were not surprised by the persecution they suffered or by their marginal cultural status. In some groups the persecution confirmed the reality of a TWO-KINGDOM THEOLOGY and strengthened their religious belief in separation from the world. MARTYRS MIRROR, a collection of testimonies of Christian martyrs including many 16th-century Anabaptists, was published in 1660 in the Netherlands and remains in print in Dutch, German, and English.

Many Anabaptists were attracted to the prospect of RELIGIOUS LIBERTY (separation of CHURCH AND STATE) and the abundant fertile land available in Pennsylvania in the late 1600s and 1700s. MENNONITES, AMISH, and BRETHREN immigrated to this British colony, which was founded by William Penn (1644–1718),

a QUAKER pacifist. In the UNITED STATES and CANADA, Anabaptists have experienced only intermittent periods of harassment and minor persecution, primarily during wartime because of their unwillingness to participate in military service.

Even in tolerant and pluralistic democracies, Anabaptists have faced persecution in times of war because of their belief in biblical PACIFISM and their unwillingness to serve in the military. Two Hutterite brothers were drafted by the United States for military service in WORLD WAR I. When they refused to sign admission papers or don army uniforms, they were held as military prisoners. While imprisoned at Alcatraz (California) and Fort Leavenworth (Kansas), they were tortured. They died in 1918 at Fort Leavenworth from an illness that likely resulted from their torture. This experience, as well as the intense anti-German sentiment directed at the Hutterites during World War I, compelled most of them (nearly 1,000) to leave the United States and migrate to Canada. Many Hutterites returned to the United States and started new colonies after World War I.

See also Baptism

BE II ("Persecution"), Bright (1998), Hege (1998), Homan (1994), J. Hostetler (1997), MacMaster (1985), J. Oyer (2000), Oyer and Kreider (1990)

Philips, Dirk   *See* Dirk Philips

Photographs

Some TRADITIONAL GROUPS object to having their members' photographs taken. The guidelines vary by group and family, but in general, members of Old Order communities are forbidden to consent to or pose for a face-on photograph. Photographs of animals, landscapes, homes, businesses, and even children who are not church members are less objectionable. Photographs of members taken by outsiders from a distance and side- or back-view photographs of members are regarded as the moral responsibility of the photographer rather than of the subject.

The taboo on posing for photographs is

meant to discourage pride and vanity; personal photos call attention to the individual and set the individual above other members in the group. The most conservative churches view photographs of individuals as graven images and cite the second of the Ten Commandments, which rejects graven images, as their reason for the prohibition. The taboo on face-on photos of members is strongest among traditional groups, such as the AMISH, that emphasize a high level of communalism over individualism. Taboos on television, video, and film by most traditional groups are designed to limit the influence of the outside world as well as reflect the restriction on graven images.

Kraybill (2001)

Pietism

The Pietist Movement began within the state-supported churches in Europe during the 17th century and reached its peak by the middle of the 18th century. Adherents of this historical movement worked within the church, seeking a religious and moral renewal of both church and society.

Pietism was marked initially by the use of small groups *(collegia pietatis)* within the church, meeting for the purpose of strengthening their spiritual lives and, eventually, BIBLE study. Another sign of Pietism was a renewed, moderate eschatology, a hope for better times to come. Other characteristics of the Pietist Movement included biblicism and a strong emphasis on love and ethical behavior. Many Pietists also emphasized the need for CONVERSION, repentance, transformation, and spiritual rebirth.

Pietists stressed the need for religious renewal and transformation of the individual. They believed that a renewal of an individual's SPIRITUAL LIFE would manifest itself in a changed lifestyle, which in turn would influence the church and society. Pietists tried to examine the problems and issues of human life from a biblical perspective and used the Bible as the standard of truth. Religious fellowship was essential for members of the Pietist Movement. Participation in these small groups contributed a sense of distinctiveness. Pietists viewed themselves as distinct from other Christians whose lives had not been transformed, and they often saw their own lives as a critique of established Christianity. In general, Pietism emphasized practice over doctrine, spirit over form.

Pietist leader August Hermann Francke (1663–1727) established at Halle (Germany) the Francke Institutes, which included an orphanage, schools for girls and boys, a publishing house, and a pharmaceutical enterprise. Pietism was concerned with social improvement as well as spiritual uplift.

Some scholars have argued that Pietism's emphasis on the emotional aspects of faith and the commonalities that cross denominational lines has compromised distinctive ANABAPTIST convictions related to the collective nature of the church—discipline, authority, accountability, community, NONCONFORMITY, and biblical PACIFISM. Other scholars have emphasized the common elements of Pietism and Anabaptism, claiming that Pietism helped MENNONITE and BRETHREN groups to reclaim their original missionary zeal to spread the gospel and to develop church-related institutions linked to church renewal.

Although the HUTTERITES have not been strongly influenced by Pietism, it has greatly influenced some other Anabaptist groups, especially Brethren groups that combined the streams of Anabaptism and Pietism to create a tradition that attends to both the inner life (spiritual renewal) and the outer life (ethics and social action). Pietism has also greatly influenced the hymn traditions, prayers, and devotional literature of both TRADITIONAL GROUPS and ASSIMILATED GROUPS.

Although Pietism and REVIVALISM share some commonalities, traditional groups resist revivalism more than they do Pietism. Revivalism's emphasis on individualism clashes with the communal authority of traditional churches. Strong emotional expressions are inconsistent with quiet humility, and the emphasis on personal religious feelings undercuts community standards.

BE II ("Pietism"), D. Brown (1996b), Friedmann (1940), GAMEO ("Mennonite Brethren in Christ," "Pietism"), ME IV ("Pietism"), ME V ("Pietism"), Roth (1997)

Plain Dress   *See* Clothing

Plain People   *See* Traditional Groups

Plattdeutsch / Plautdietsch / Low German   *See* Dialects

Poetry

Hymn texts are the most widespread form of poetry that ANABAPTISTS have written, but other forms exist as well. The earliest MENNONITE poets wrote in the NETHERLANDS in the 1500s and 1600s, but the modern tradition began among Mennonites in the late 1800s. Higher levels of EDUCATION and more widespread availability of publications helped to inspire poetry that rose above the simple inspirational or occasional verse.

Poetry in BRETHREN circles has been primarily in the form of hymns and short informal verse in church publications. Jacob Stoll (1731–1822), a Brethren minister, wrote a book of devotional poetry in 1806. Several books by Brethren poets were published by Brethren Press in the mid-20th century.

In the last half of the 20th century, some poets from ASSIMILATED GROUPS have been published by the secular press. Canadian Mennonite poets are especially noteworthy in this regard, and several have become nationally prominent. Much of their poetry, both in German and in English, addresses Mennonite identity in contemporary society and themes of personal religious struggle and affirmation. Periodic conferences of Mennonite writers since 1990 have supported and encouraged Anabaptist-related poets. The Center for Mennonite Writing at Goshen College supports poets as well as other writers of LITERATURE.

BE II ("Poetry"), GAMEO ("Poetry"), Gundy (1997, 2005), A. Hostetler (2003), ME V ("Poetry"), Tiessen (1990), Ziegler (1980), http://www.mennonitewriting.org

Poland

ANABAPTISTS began immigrating to Poland as early as the 1530s. They came from the NETHERLANDS and Flanders (now Belgium) and settled in the delta of the Vistula River near Gdansk. These MENNONITES came to Poland at the invitation of the king and other noble families, who had heard of their reputation as good farmers. The nobles wanted the Mennonites to drain some of their swampy land and use it for AGRICULTURE.

Though Mennonites faced legal and social restrictions, they were allowed to practice their faith, and they thrived in this region. They lived primarily on farms, but some also settled in the city of Gdansk. They adopted *Plautdietsch* or Low German, the DIALECT of the German settlers in the region, and added some of their own Dutch elements. The traditions of HYMNODY, FOLK ART, and MATERIAL CULTURE that Mennonites became famous for in RUSSIA, North America, and SOUTH AMERICA originated in this region.

In the latter part of the 1700s, Poland was conquered and divided. German-speaking Prussia took over the area where the pacifist Mennonites lived and began to pressure them to serve in the military and to restrict their landholdings. From 1790 to 1820 many Mennonites emigrated from Prussia to southern Russia, just north of the Black Sea in what is now Ukraine. A small number of Swiss AMISH moved from GERMANY to Volhynia, an area of Poland, in the late 18th century; the region became part of Russia in 1795.

The Mennonites who remained in Prussia were influenced by German culture and politics. At the end of WORLD WAR II all the German-speaking Mennonites in Prussia (about 10,000) fled to western GERMANY to escape the advancing Russian army. These refugees never returned to Prussia; some stayed in western Germany, while others immigrated to CANADA, Paraguay, Uruguay, and Brazil.

See also Volhynian Mennonites

Friesen and Klassen (1992), GAMEO ("Poland"), Janzen and Janzen (1991), P. J. Klassen (1989, 2009)

Political Participation

North American ANABAPTISTS hold a diverse
array of beliefs about political participation.
Many members of the most ASSIMILATED
GROUPS actively participate in local, state, and
national politics, but the more TRADITIONAL
GROUPS strongly discourage any form of political participation apart from voting.

Henry Peter Krehbiel (1862–1940), a fervent
MENNONITE pacifist, was elected to a term in
the Kansas state legislature in 1909, and Mennonite Brethren member Harvey L. Wollman
(1935–) was governor of South Dakota from 1978
to 1979. In general, assimilated Mennonites in
CANADA participate more actively in politics
than their counterparts in the UNITED STATES.
Since 1950 numerous Canadians with Mennonite affiliations ran for and/or were elected
to provincial parliaments. Others have been
elected members of parliament at the national
level. Jake Epp (1939–), a member of the MEN-
NONITE BRETHREN, served in the Canadian
parliament from 1972 to 1993 and was the first
Mennonite to be appointed to the federal
government cabinet. Brad Wall (1965–), also a
Mennonite Brethren, was elected premier of
Saskatchewan in 2007. In 2009, seven members
of the House of Commons identified themselves
as Mennonite. Over 400 Canadian Mennonites
ran for elective office provincially or nationally
between 1867 and 1999.

Members of assimilated BRETHREN groups
have participated in the political order since the
early part of the 20th century. Martin G. Brumbaugh (1862–1930), the first Ph.D. holder in the
CHURCH OF THE BRETHREN, served as Republican governor of Pennsylvania from 1915 to
1919. Some Brethren leaders criticized his prominence as a political officeholder and his leadership of the state militia during WORLD WAR I.

Groups with a more traditional bent espouse
a TWO-KINGDOM THEOLOGY that emphasizes
a sharp separation between the kingdom of God
(the church) and the kingdoms of the world (the
state). These groups forbid GOVERNMENT office holding and political campaigning, and they
discourage voting. Apart from wanting a clean

separation from the state, they worry that office
holding might require the use of force and LITI-
GATION, which would violate the nonresistant
ethic of Jesus. Some OLD ORDER MENNONITE
and AMISH groups consider voting to be an individual choice but reject office holding unless
it is on the local municipal level, but even that
is rare. These groups may more willingly vote
in local elections than in presidential ones in
the United States because they view voting for
president—the commander in chief of military
forces—as inconsistent with PACIFISM and
CONSCIENTIOUS OBJECTION to serving in the
armed forces.

Groups that are more assimilated accept
various degrees of participation in the political
order. Some members of assimilated groups oppose political participation because they think
it should be secondary to public service through
church agencies. Others actively participate by
voting, writing to elected representatives, supporting political campaigns, and running for office at local and state or provincial levels. Sometimes political party affiliations and the fervor of
campaigns become divisive inside church communities. Political affiliation and participation
by members in assimilated churches correlates
with social factors—EDUCATION, social class,
ETHNICITY, OCCUPATION, and urbanization.
Some politicians from Anabaptist backgrounds
have drifted away from or become marginalized
in the church because of their political involvement.

In the United States, assimilated Brethren,
BRETHREN IN CHRIST, and Mennonites belong
to all of the major American political parties, but
the majority identify themselves as Republican
and describe their political views as conservative. The majority of assimilated Anabaptists
believe that Christians should actively participate in politics in order to improve society. They
support running for elected public office and
overwhelmingly think that Anabaptists should
vote in national elections, according to one survey (CMP 2006).

In Canada, assimilated Anabaptists support all of the major parties, though generally

there has been greater support for the Liberal Party because its historical support of immigration benefited Mennonite immigration. More recently, a majority of Mennonites support the Conservative party.

BE I ("Brumbaugh, Martin Grove"), C. Bowman (1995), CMP 2006, Graber Miller (1996), Kaylor (1996), Kraybill and Kopko (2007), J. Redekop (2007), Regehr (2000, 2003), Urry (2006)

Politics   *See* Political Participation

Polity   *See* Church, Polity of

Population   *See* Demography

Power   *See* Authority

Prayer

As it is for many Christians, prayer is central for ANABAPTISTS in their individual and group experiences and expressions of faith. Prayer styles tend to vary among groups and CONGREGATIONS, depending on historical and cultural influences.

In the 1800s, AMISH and MENNONITES usually prayed silently. BRETHREN groups, because of their strong roots in PIETISM, tended to use more spoken, extemporaneous, and emotive prayers. Until the late 1800s many Anabaptist groups knelt for prayer. Gradually, in the 20th century, members of most ASSIMILATED GROUPS began sitting or standing for prayer. The shift from kneeling to sitting or standing is a typical transformation away from the posture of humility (kneeling) as churches became more assimilated. In 1926 the Dunkard Brethren split from the CHURCH OF THE BRETHREN (because of conflict over how the church should relate to the world), and the new conservative-minded group forbade standing or sitting for corporate prayer.

In the 21st century, HUTTERITE prayers during worship are memorized and recited, as are their sermons. The Old Order Amish typically kneel and either pray silently (at home and at worship) or read prayers aloud from *Die Ern-*

sthafte Christenpflict (*Prayer Book for Earnest Christians*, 1708) as well as other prayer books. The use of the Lord's Prayer (Matthew 6) in worship is prominent in all the TRADITIONAL GROUPS. Assimilated Mennonites and Brethren incorporate a wide variety of prayer styles, including CHARISMATIC, liturgical, and meditative, into their WORSHIP services and individual spiritual lives. Groups with styles of worship that are more Pentecostal engage in expressive verbal prayers that may involve several people praying aloud simultaneously.

See also Devotional Literature; Ritual

BE II ("Prayer"), Boers et al. (2005), GAMEO ("Prayer"), Groff (1984), L. Gross (1997), J. Hostetler (1993, 1997), ME IV ("Prayer," "Prayer Books, Mennonite"), ME V ("Prayer")

Prayer Veiling   *See* Head Covering

Preaching

The sermon, the oral presentation and interpretation of the word of God, is the central element in the WORSHIP services of most ANABAPTIST groups. The sermon has several functions: to interpret the BIBLE, to foster DISCIPLESHIP, to provide advice and instruction, and to enrich spiritual life.

The style of preaching, as well as who is allowed to preach, has varied among historical periods and among Anabaptist groups. During the 1500s, Anabaptist worship services usually included sermons preached by multiple leaders who gave informal ethical admonition and explanations of Bible texts.

Many TRADITIONAL GROUPS continue in this style in 21st-century North America. In these groups only ordained men preach. In HUTTERITE worship services, MINISTERS read sermons written centuries earlier by Hutterite ministers. Old Order AMISH and OLD ORDER MENNONITE worship includes multiple sermons, often delivered in a stylized, semi-chanting fashion. After the primary sermon is preached, opportunity is given to other ordained men to respond to the sermon with affirmations or corrections, a practice that underscores a preacher's accountability to the community (Matt. 18:16).

BRETHREN and MENNONITES in ASSIMI-LATED GROUPS incorporate many different styles of preaching into their services. The style of preaching in assimilated congregations tends toward conversational rather than highly oratorical, except in some African-American Mennonite and Brethren congregations, where the preacher may use a chantlike style. In Hispanic cultural settings, the preaching style is often more Pentecostal. In addition to ordained pastors (both men and women), laymen and laywomen are allowed to preach in some congregations. Preachers may focus on a broad range of topics, including MISSION, CONVERSION, SOCIAL JUSTICE, and PACIFISM, or they may follow the Protestant lectionary. Some emphasize expository preaching—interpreting the themes from a particular passage of the Bible. Dramas, dialogues, and liturgical dance are also used as alternative forms of or supplements to sermons.

See also Ordination; Ordination of Women

BE II ("Sermon"), GAMEO ("Preaching," "Sermons," "Sermons, Hutterite"), Greiser and King (2003), J. Hostetler (1993), ME IV ("Sermons," "Sermons, Hutterite"), ME V ("Preaching"), Yoder, Kropf, and Slough (2005), Ziegler (1965)

Priesthood of Believers   *See* Believers Church

Professions

TRADITIONAL GROUPS are largely located in rural areas, and the OCCUPATIONS of their members are chiefly related to AGRICULTURE, trades, and small BUSINESS. Moreover, the taboo on HIGHER EDUCATION in these groups blocks their members from entering professions that require college or advanced degrees.

As some ANABAPTIST groups became assimilated into the larger society in the 20th century, their members earned college degrees and began entering professions. Members of the CHURCH OF THE BRETHREN began assuming professional occupational roles in the first half of the 20th century. Typically, EDUCATION and MEDICINE were the primary fields of entry be-

cause they explicitly embodied the key Anabaptist value of SERVICE to others. Martin G. Brumbaugh (1862–1930) was the most prominent early BRETHREN in a professional leadership role. The first to hold a Ph.D. among the Brethren, he served as superintendent of schools in Philadelphia, president of Juniata College, and governor of Pennsylvania from 1915 to 1919. Many other Brethren entered professions related to education and medicine in the first half of the 20th century.

Among MENNONITES, the entry into professions occurred largely after WORLD WAR II. Many young adults who had served in ALTERNATIVE SERVICE in lieu of military service were exposed to professional jobs in hospitals and elsewhere. The decline of farming in the mid-20th century also encouraged Mennonites to enter the professions. Like their Brethren counterparts, many first entered professions related to medicine and education. By the end of the 20th century, however, Brethren and Mennonites were serving in a wide variety of professions.

A 1972 survey of five Mennonite groups in Canada and the United States found that 21% of men and women were employed in professional and managerial jobs. A subsequent survey (CMP 2006) of members of MENNONITE CHURCH USA reported that 41% of men and women held professional or managerial jobs.

Anabaptists in some professions have created loose networks, associations, and occasional gatherings to discuss issues and challenges facing Anabaptist Christians that arise in their particular professions. These networks and gatherings also build solidarity and strengthen ethnic/Anabaptist identity among the members of these professions.

See also Mennonite Economic Development Associates

BE I ("Brumbaugh, Martin Grove"), CMP 2006, GAMEO ("Professions"), Kauffman and Harder (1975), Kraybill and Good (1982), ME V ("Professions")

Progress   *See* Assimilated Groups; Traditional Groups

Protestant Reformation   *See* Radical
Reformation

Prussia   *See* Poland

Publishing

ANABAPTIST groups have widely supported literacy. One of the earliest publishers associated with Anabaptist groups in North America was Sauer Publishers, which published many books in Philadelphia beginning around 1739. Christopher Sauer I (1695–1758) never joined the BRETHREN but was sympathetic to their beliefs. His son, CHRISTOPHER SAUER II (1721–1784), joined the Brethren in 1737 and was ordained a minister.

Until the 1800s, hymnals, devotional books, and CONFESSIONS OF FAITH were the most widely published books among Anabaptist groups. In the mid-1800s, individual Brethren and MENNONITES founded private publishing companies that produced religious and church materials. Joseph Funk (1778–1862) of Virginia was the first Mennonite printer in the United States, establishing a printing press in 1847. In 1864 John F. Funk (1835–1930), a future Mennonite bishop and leader of church renewal, began publishing the periodical *Herald of Truth* and its German edition, *Herold der Wahrheit*. This publication helped to unify far-flung Mennonite settlements. By the late 1800s, some of the publishing ventures started by individuals were taken over by church-related INSTITUTIONS. However, TRADITIONAL GROUPS initially resisted creating publishing institutions.

Throughout the 20th century, publishing by both traditional and assimilated Anabaptists increased dramatically and included church-related newspapers, PERIODICALS, and books on many subjects. By the late 1900s, assimilated Mennonites and Brethren also were creating, publishing, and distributing information through audio recordings, videos, TELEVISION, and the Internet.

See also Devotional Literature; Hymnody; Publishing Organizations

BE II ("Publishing"), GAMEO ("Publishing"), Gates et al. (1964), ME IV ("Publishers, Mennonite"), ME V ("Publishing")

Publishing Organizations

In the late 19th and early 20th centuries, many groups created church-related publishing INSTITUTIONS that printed a wide variety of materials, including church news periodicals, hymnals, missionary tracts, and books with doctrinal, devotional, evangelistic, and apologetic content. By the early 1900s these growing publishing organizations helped to shape the identities of their denominations through the distribution of printed literature.

A list of the principal publishers of materials related to ANABAPTIST interests in North America in the 21st century appears in table 13. Some of these are affiliated with denominations, while others (Good Books, Cascadia, and Pandora Press) are privately owned companies. CHRISTIAN AID MINISTRIES, Christian Light Publications, and Rod and Staff Publishers publish and distribute a wide variety of materials to serve the needs of many conservative MENNONITES and traditional churches. Friesens Corporation of Altona, Manitoba, is owned by Mennonites, and although not primarily a publishing company, it is one of Canada's largest book-printing companies.

One of the earliest AMISH publishers was Andrew Kinsinger (1921–1995), who operated the Gordonville Print Shop in Pennsylvania. PATHWAY PUBLISHERS, founded by two AMISH farmers in Ontario, publishes school curricular materials, DEVOTIONAL LITERATURE, and general Christian literature for TRADITIONAL GROUPS, especially the Amish. Although not owned by the church, its activities and publications conform to the values of traditional Anabaptists. A few other publishing companies also supply curricular materials for traditional and conservative Anabaptist schools.

Choice Books, a Mennonite-related book distribution organization, sells materials related to Christian faith and other family-oriented topics in secular retail settings throughout North America. This company was founded in the early

Table 13	Anabaptist-Related Publishers in North America	
BMH Books	Winona Lake, IN	http://www.bmhbooks.com
Brethren Encyclopedia	Philadelphia, PA	http://www.brethrenencyclopedia.org
Brethren Press	Elgin, IL	http://www.brethrenpress.com
Carlisle Press	Sugarcreek, OH	800-852-4482
Cascadia Publishing House	Telford, PA	http://www.cascadiapublishinghouse.com
Christian Aid Ministries	Berlin, OH	http://www.anabaptists.org/places/cam
Christian Light Publications	Harrisonburg, VA	http://www.clp.org
CMU Press	Winnipeg, MB	http://www.cmu.ca/cmupress.html
Evangel Press	Nappanee, IN	http://www.evangelpress.com
Faith & Life Resources	Newton, KS	http://www.faithandliferesources.org
Good Books	Intercourse, PA	http://www.goodbks.com
Herald Press	Scottdale, PA	http://www.heraldpress.com
Kindred Productions	Winnipeg, MB	http://www.kindredproductions.com
Masthof Press	Morgantown, PA	http://masthofpress.com/site
Third Way Media	Harrisonburg, VA	http://www.thirdwaymedia.org
Pandora Press	Kitchener, ON	http://www.pandorapress.com
Pathway Publishers	Aylmer, ON	R.R. 4, Aylmer, ON N5H 2R3
Rod and Staff Publishers	Crockett, KY	http://www.rodandstaffbooks.com

1960s, and by 2010 it was selling about 5.5 million books annually at over 9,400 retail locations (airports, drugstores, gift shops) throughout North America.

BE II ("Publishing"), GAMEO ("Publishing"), ME V ("Publishing")

Puerto Rico

The Brethren Service Commission (a CHURCH OF THE BRETHREN organization) operated agricultural and medical projects in Puerto Rico, beginning with a Civilian Public Service unit in 1942. The first congregation was organized in 1948 and, by 2010 there were seven BRETHREN-related congregations and 375 members in the territory.

Two MENNONITE groups, the Conference of the Mennonite Churches of Puerto Rico and the Evangelical Mennonite Mission of the Caribbean, have about 525 members in 16 congregations on the island. Started by missionaries

from the Mennonite Board of Missions in the late 1940s, the Conference of the Mennonite Churches of Puerto Rico became registered as an independent church in 1988. In the 1990s several churches left the conference to form the Evangelical Mennonite Mission of the Caribbean.

The Mennonite churches of Puerto Rico operate two schools (kindergarten through grade 12) and a Bible institute. They founded the Mennonite General Hospital in Aibonito. The churches on the island also participate in the Caribbean Anabaptist Seminary with churches from the Dominican Republic.

The Southeastern Mennonite Conference has had a small presence (two mission churches) in Puerto Rico since the 1980s, but they have fewer than 25 members.

GAMEO ("Puerto Rico"), ME V ("Puerto Rico"), Mennonite World Conference (2005)

Quakers

Formally called the Religious Society of Friends, the Quakers were founded by George Fox (1624–1691) in England in the 17th century. Quakerism was a dissenting and persecuted Protestant movement with both Puritan and ANABAPTIST affinities. Unlike Anabaptists, the Quakers do not practice water baptism or the Lord's Supper. Quakers also differ from Anabaptist groups in other beliefs and practices related to WORSHIP, ORDINANCES, and their theology of church. Both traditions emphasize the non-swearing of OATHS, COMMUNITY, SOCIAL JUSTICE, and PACIFISM. Along with MENNONITES and the CHURCH OF THE BRETHREN, the Quakers are one of the HISTORIC PEACE CHURCHES.

William Penn (1644–1718), the Quaker founder of the British colony of Pennsylvania, offered religious freedom in his colony and invited persecuted religious groups from EUROPE to settle there. Mennonites, BRETHREN, and AMISH responded to this opportunity of RELIGIOUS LIBERTY, inexpensive land, and excellent agricultural possibilities by immigrating to Pennsylvania in droves in the 18th century.

Because of their common pacifist beliefs, German-speaking Anabaptist groups and English-speaking Quaker groups often found common ground in times of war. In 1793, after the Revolutionary War in the United States, the Mennonites, Quakers, and Tunkers (Brethren in Christ) in Canada were granted exemption from military service. They worked together to convince the GOVERNMENT to recognize CONSCIENTIOUS OBJECTORS to war, to grant exemption from serving in armed forces, and to allow men to render ALTERNATIVE SERVICE in nonmilitary efforts. This cooperation peaked during WORLD WAR II, when the historic peace churches and the government created the programs of alternative service in place of military service.

Anabaptists in ASSIMILATED GROUPS and Quakers work together and support a variety of organizations related to PEACEMAKING, including CHRISTIAN PEACEMAKER TEAMS, the Fellowship of Reconciliation, and the Peace Tax Fund. Since 1994, Bethany Theological Seminary (the Church of the Brethren seminary) has been located adjacent to the Earlham School of Religion on the campus of Earlham College (Quaker) in Richmond, Indiana. The two graduate schools of religion share many intellectual, technological, and physical resources and also cooperate in a variety of programs.

BE II ("Society of Friends"), D. Durnbaugh (1994), F. Epp (1974), GAMEO ("Society of Friends"), Hamm (2003), ME IV ("Society of Friends"), Rushby (1986), http://www.peacetaxfund.org, http://www.quaker.org

Quilts

These pieced and appliquéd decorative bedcovers are a flourishing example of FOLK ART in North America. By the middle 1800s, Pennsylvania German women, including the ANABAPTISTS, had learned this tradition from their English neighbors and infused it with their own aesthetic sensibility. Even though quilt making has faded from many groups as a result of the mass production of textiles, some Anabaptist women continue the tradition.

A 1971 exhibition, "Abstract Design in American Quilts," at the Whitney Museum of American Art in New York City was instrumental in recognizing quilting as an art form, and soon after, quilts began to receive the attention of folk art enthusiasts as well as art collectors. Quilts made by Anabaptist women, especially those made by the AMISH, became popular and avidly sought by collectors and museums. Amish quilts are very distinctive, with only solid-colored fabrics and geometric designs. The abstract and minimalist qualities of these quilts have elevated them to the category of fine art in the eyes of urban art critics.

Some contemporary MENNONITES infuse their quilts with symbolic significance. They use religious symbols in designs, hang quilts as works of art on the walls of their sanctuaries, and reproduce quilt images for church-related publications.

Lancaster County, Pennsylvania, a center of Amish- and Mennonite-related TOURISM, hosts the annual Quilters' Heritage Celebration, a quilt conference that draws several thousand visitors, vendors, and participants each year. A similar gathering, Quilt and Fibre Art Festival, is held in the Waterloo region of Ontario.

Born (2005), GAMEO ("Quilts"), P. Good (1999), Herr (2000, 2004), Kraybill, Herr, and Holstein (1996), ME V ("Quilts"), J. Smucker (2006)

Race Relations   *See* Racism; Social Justice

Racism

ANABAPTIST churches are not immune from racism, both within their communities and in their views toward some groups in the larger society. For example, interracial marriage was a strong taboo in many Anabaptist churches in the first half of the 20th century, and it continues to be discouraged by more conservative congregations and families. Some white BRETHREN in the 19th and early 20th centuries substituted a handshake for the HOLY KISS when greeting African-American members.

Many Anabaptist leaders have emphasized God's love for all people regardless of skin color and ethnic background. Some Anabaptists were active in the Civil Rights Movement of the 1950s and 1960s in North America. Others have established churches in communities racially and ethnically different from their own and welcomed new members to their churches from various racial, ethnic, and minority groups. In the mid-20th century many Anabaptist efforts to promote racial integration and SOCIAL JUSTICE were conducted under the rubric of the New Testament theme of Christian reconciliation.

A more explicit focus on racism emerged in the 1990s with the organization of a training program for antiracism under the auspices of MENNONITE CENTRAL COMMITTEE. The Damascus Road Project, named for the process of transformation that Saul experienced on the road to Damascus (Acts 9:1–31), is a training effort designed to produce individual transformation and long-term institutional change in churches and faith-based organizations. Damascus Road provides workshops, training programs, networking events, consultation, and media resources aimed at education and the dismantling of racism, as well as the articulation of a theology and spirituality of antiracism. More than 1,800 individuals and 60 teams from Anabaptist-related groups have participated in Damascus Road workshops for congregations, colleges, and other church-related organizations.

A survey (CMP 2006) of MENNONITE CHURCH USA members found that 79% thought it was important for church leaders to discuss and address issues of race and racism. Fifty-three percent thought that the larger society should make intentional efforts to hire and promote racial/ethnic minorities in order to overcome historic patterns of racism in society. Forty-one percent of CHURCH OF THE BRETHREN and 36% of BRETHREN IN CHRIST members agreed with the same statement.

CMP 2006, GAMEO ("Reconciliation"), ME V ("Reconciliation"), Shearer (2008, 2010), http://antiracism.mcc.org/damascusroad

Radical Reformation

This term was coined by historian George H. Williams (1914–2000) to refer to the historical movement in the 16th century that included a wide variety of groups with alternative agendas—including ANABAPTISTS—whose adherents were rejected and persecuted by the dominant Roman Catholic, Lutheran, Calvinist, and Anglican traditions. The Anabaptists were the spiritual ancestors of the AMISH, BRETHREN, HUTTERITE, and MENNONITE groups that emerged from this radical reform movement. In 1962 Williams wrote *The Radical Reformation* (3rd ed. 1992), which became the definitive scholarly treatment of the movement.

Although scholars usually group them together for study purposes, the radical reformers held a wide variety of theological beliefs and practices—sometimes in conflict with each other. Despite their differences, most rejected the practice of GOVERNMENTS enforcing religious belief and practice, and most demanded a more purified church, one whose members would be free from the AUTHORITY of the state to live according to biblical principles. Because many of these reformers saw a drastic separation between the ways of the world and the ways of God, the lifestyles they advocated were COUNTERCULTURAL. The most notable countercultural practice among Anabaptists was believers (adult-only) BAPTISM.

In addition to adult baptism, the Anabaptists

also emphasized the life and teachings of Jesus as the pattern for Christian life, nonresistant love for enemies, strict church DISCIPLINE, the priesthood of all believers, MUTUAL AID within the church, and non-swearing of OATHS.

Until the late 1800s, most scholarly writing was biased against members of the Radical Reformation and their theological views. Since the mid-1900s there has been an explosion of more objective research and writing about this movement, by scholars both within and outside Anabaptist churches in EUROPE and North America. Mennonites in GERMANY, the NETH-ERLANDS, the UNITED STATES, and CANADA have been especially prolific in this area. Beginning in 1947, MENNONITE LIFE has published an extensive Radical Reformation and Mennonite bibliography each year.

See also Anabaptism, History of; Anabaptism, Theology of; Believers Church; Church and State; Religious Liberty

D. Durnbaugh (1968), C. Dyck (1993), GAMEO ("Anabaptism," "Reformation, Protestant"), ME V ("Anabaptism," "Reformation, Protestant"), Roth and Stayer (2007), C. Snyder (1995), Williams (1992), http://www.bethelks.edu/mennonitelife/bibliogra phies

Radio

ANABAPTIST groups reacted in various ways as radio use became widespread in North America after its introduction in the 1920s. Some TRA-DITIONAL GROUPS thought radio represented a dangerous TECHNOLOGY that would allow mainstream culture to infiltrate their separatist communities. These groups used persuasion and church DISCIPLINE to prohibit their members from owning and using radios.

ASSIMILATED GROUPS saw radio as a potential tool for MISSION outreach, and they created numerous local gospel radio programs. In 1951 the Mennonite Hour, based in Harrisonburg, Virginia, became the official voice for the mission of the MENNONITE CHURCH. Its programs offered both MUSIC (initially a cappella) and SERMONS. Later the Mennonite Hour included

a wider range of programs, including ones for women and broadcasts in Spanish, Russian, German, Navaho, Italian, and Japanese.

At the beginning of the 21st century most assimilated Anabaptists listen to a variety of religious and nonreligious radio broadcasting, while many traditional groups, including the AMISH, continue to prohibit the use of radios.

GAMEO ("Radio"), ME IV ("Radio Broadcasting, Mennonite"), ME V ("Radio"), Pellman (1979)

Recreation   *See* Leisure

Redpaz   *See* Regional Network of Justice and Peace

Reformation   *See* Radical Reformation

Regional Network of Justice and Peace (Red Regional de Justicia y Paz)

The Regional Network of Justice and Peace, also known as Redpaz, was begun in CENTRAL AMERICA in 1997 as a joint initiative of the ANA-BAPTIST churches of Central America and MEN-NONITE CENTRAL COMMITTEE. Its purpose is to contribute, from a Christian perspective, to the construction of an integral and sustainable peace in a region often characterized by social and political violence, social injustice, and prolonged wars. Redpaz works to strengthen relationships between Anabaptist churches, other Christian churches, and Latin American social organizations engaged in PEACEMAKING, with the hope of collaborating to strengthen efforts toward justice and peace in the region. From its office in Guatemala City, Redpaz carries out research, conducts training, offers degrees in peace studies, promotes conflict mediation in the schools, and works with vulnerable families and programs, among other projects. More than 100 students have graduated from the degree program and work in local social and religious-affiliated programs, promoting justice and peace in the region.

http://www.bethelks.edu/mennonitelife/2005Mar/hart.php

Relief Sales   *See* Brethren Disaster Ministries;
Mennonite Central Committee

Religious Liberty

Sixteenth-century ANABAPTISTS sought the
right to practice religious faith without external
constraints, especially those imposed by GOV-
ERNMENTS. They believed that the choice to
follow Jesus Christ should be a personal, adult
decision, free from coercion. They also believed
that the government should not have AUTHOR-
ITY over the church. Because religious liberty
did not exist in EUROPE during this time, political rulers often persecuted their subjects for
their religious beliefs. Partly to escape this PER-
SECUTION, all of the HUTTERITES and BRETH-
REN, and most of the AMISH, had immigrated to
North America by the late 1800s.

The 16th-century Anabaptist zeal for religious freedom, commitment to a BELIEVERS
CHURCH, and call for a church free from government control paved the way for modern no-
tions of the separation of CHURCH AND STATE,
which are widely taken for granted in North
America.

In colonial America the British colonies of
Rhode Island and Pennsylvania were the leading
havens of religious toleration. Initially the Caro-
linas also offered generous religious tolerance.
English Baptists, QUAKERS, and support from
Dutch MENNONITES contributed to toleration
in colonial America. Free exercise of religion was
one of the founding tenets of the U.S. Constitution (1787), even though some states continued
to have legally established denominations for a
limited time.

By the 19th century most western European
rulers, exhausted by religious wars, finally became more tolerant and ceased harsh levels of
persecution. However, even in the 20th century
some countries, especially RUSSIA, continued
to deny religious liberty to Mennonites. At the
beginning of the 21st century some Anabaptist
groups face significant restrictions on religious
liberty in countries with one dominant religious
tradition or a repressive government. This is
especially the case in some developing countries
where missionaries actively seek new members.

BE II ("Religious Liberty"), Bender (1955), Estep
(1988), GAMEO ("Religious Liberty"), ME IV ("Religious Liberty")

Religious Society of Friends   *See* Quakers

Restorative Justice

This theory of justice focuses on repairing
the harm caused by criminal behavior and attempts to transform the way COMMUNITIES
and GOVERNMENTS respond to crime. The
approach is characterized by four key values:
(1) encounter—the offender and the victim
meet to discuss the crime and its repercussions;
(2) amends—the offender is expected to try
to repair the damage caused by the crime;
(3) reintegration—an attempt is made to restore
both victim and offender as accepted members
of the community; (4) inclusion—anyone affected by the crime is welcome to participate
in the process.

Many ANABAPTISTS were drawn to the theory of restorative justice because it meshes well
with their theological understanding of God's
reconciling work in Jesus Christ, as well as biblical directions for dealing with CONFLICT (Matt.
18 and Acts 15). In 1975, MENNONITES and
like-minded colleagues began the first Victim
Offender Reconciliation Program in Kitchener,
Ontario. The program offers court-sponsored
mediation sessions between the victim and the
perpetrator of a crime. Rather than seeking
retribution, these sessions attempt to repair
the ruptured relationships caused by the crime
and attend to the harm done to the victim. The
program offers possibilities for accountability,
forgiveness, healing, closure, and restoration.

Anabaptists have created various other programs that work at SOCIAL JUSTICE through
nonviolent means. Two mediation groups were
formed out of MENNONITE CENTRAL COMMIT-
TEE: Mennonite Conciliation Services in 1977
and International Conciliation Service in 1989.
These agencies provide mediation skills that

Mennonites have attempted to use in conflict situations in Colombia, Northern Ireland, Somalia, NICARAGUA, GUATEMALA, and South Africa. CHRISTIAN PEACEMAKER TEAMS, another organization focused on peace and justice, was created in 1987 by a number of BRETHREN and Mennonite church bodies in order to train mediators to take direct nonviolent action in situations of political conflict by living with and identifying with oppressed people in their quest for justice. Brethren groups have been active in restorative justice efforts through organizations such as ON EARTH PEACE ASSEMBLY. TRADITIONAL GROUPS, in general, have not participated in social justice and restorative justice programs.

See also Peacemaking

J. Lederach (1999), Sampson and Lederach (2000), Schrock-Shenk and Ressler (1999), Zehr (1990), http://www.restorativejustice.org, http://www.vorp.com

Retirement   *See* Elderly

Retirement Communities
During the period from about 1890 to 1920, assimilated BRETHREN and MENNONITES founded many homes for the ELDERLY that offered care for the poor and homeless and for church leaders with limited resources. Since the 1940s these ASSIMILATED GROUPS have established full-service retirement and nursing centers. In 2010 there were more than 50 Mennonite- and Brethren-related retirement and/or nursing facilities in the United States, and more than 30 in Canada. These centers offer services ranging from independent living to total nursing care. Most have an open admission policy that permits the elderly from non-Anabaptist churches to live in these communities.

TRADITIONAL GROUPS have established some retirement communities, but most of the aged in these churches are cared for by their families in their homes. Members of some conservative groups also use the rehabilitation services provided by retirement homes for short-term care.

BE II ("Retirement Homes"), GAMEO ("Aged, Care for," "Homes, Retirement and Nursing"), ME V ("Aged, Care for," "Homes, Retirement and Nursing")

Revivalism
Revivalism is a concentrated effort to spread the gospel to nonbelievers and to intensify the commitment of believers by means of PREACHING and other forms of WORSHIP. Emotional appeals by the preacher are expected to elicit a personal response, which includes a change of attitude and behavior known as CONVERSION. The desired response involves an individual's deep consciousness of sin, awareness of the need for repentance, and joyful appreciation for the forgiving grace of God through the death of Jesus Christ on the cross.

TRADITIONAL GROUPS (with some exceptions) resist revivalism for several reasons: revivalism's focus on the individual and on subjective emotional responses to God undermines the AUTHORITY of the church, and the emotional response sought by revivalism tends to clash with the traditional emphasis on quiet humility and ethical behavior.

During the 1700s and early 1800s, MENNONITES who embraced revivalism usually left the denomination by choice or by expulsion. The River Brethren (later called BRETHREN IN CHRIST), who formed in the late 1770s, were more open to the spirit of revivalism and attracted Mennonites and others whose churches were less tolerant of the movement.

From 1850 and into the early 1900s, some churches began to hold revival meetings, which often encountered opposition from traditionalists. In numerous instances conflict over revivalism and related issues sparked major denominational schisms, which resulted in the formation of groups such as the MENNONITE BRETHREN in RUSSIA (many of whom later immigrated to North America), the Mennonite Brethren in Christ (now the Missionary Church in the United States, and the Evangelical Missionary Church in Canada), the Evangelical Mennonite Brethren (now the Fellowship of Evangelical Bible Churches), the Missionary Church Association (now part of the Missionary Church), and the Egly Amish (now Fellowship of Evangelical Churches). The long-term effect of revivalism, mingled with influences of FUNDAMENTALISM and EVANGELICALISM, has prompted some churches to drift away from ANABAPTIST principles over several generations.

See also Old Order Movement; Pietism

BE II ("Revival Meetings and Revivalism"), GAMEO ("Revivalism," "Revival Meetings"), B. Hostetler (1992), ME IV ("Revival and Revival Meetings"), ME V ("Revivalism"), C. Redekop (1998), T. Schlabach (1980)

Riedemann, Peter (1506–1556)

This HUTTERITE leader was born in Silesia and served as a traveling missionary throughout AUSTRIA and GERMANY. He wrote the Hutterite *Confession of Faith* around 1543 while in prison. The book begins with an extended commentary on the Apostles' Creed and, after treating other classic theological themes from the perspective of communal Anabaptism, turns to specific ethical guidelines for the Christian way of life. It has served as a major theological guide for Hutterites for four centuries. Several editions of *Confession of Faith* have been published in both German and English.

Friedmann (1970), J. Friesen (1999), GAMEO ("Riedemann, Peter [1506–1556]"), ME IV ("Riedemann, Peter"), Packull (2007)

Ritual

The term "ritual" refers to a repetitive ceremony performed in a social setting that enacts and/or reflects an important value or belief of a particular community. Distinctive rituals bolster a group's unique IDENTITY and distinguish it from other groups. ANABAPTIST communities have many distinctive rituals and ORDINANCES. Ordinances are rituals that Jesus taught his followers to practice. Some of these, such as COMMUNION, are similar to the ceremonies of other Christian churches but are performed in a different manner.

Two general statements cover all rituals in Anabaptist communities. (1) TRADITIONAL GROUPS are most likely to have distinctive ceremonies that set them off from other Christian churches. The rituals of traditional groups are collectively owned by the church and prescribed by the church, giving little space for individual adaptation of any ritual. (2) ASSIMILATED GROUPS have much greater ritual diversity because of individualistic interpretation in ritual performance. For example, in the most traditional churches the wedding ceremony is identical for all marriages, thus eliminating the need for a rehearsal. In assimilated churches, the wedding ceremony is typically crafted by the couple, thus requiring a rehearsal to prepare the participants in the ritual.

Rituals vary widely within and across the various Anabaptist communities. A partial list includes a cappella SINGING, BAPTISM, church-prescribed CLOTHING, ANOINTING WITH OIL, FOOTWASHING, LOVE FEAST, HOLY KISS, HEAD COVERING, ORDINATION by lot, and rituals related to ethnic food.

Cronk (1977), Kraybill and Bowman (2001), Roth (2005b, 2009)

River Brethren   *See* Brethren in Christ

Rumspringa

This term, which means "running around" in the Pennsylvania German DIALECT, has become widely publicized in popular portrayals of AMISH youth. *Rumspringa* begins at age 16 and continues until a young person is BAPTIZED and joins the church. It is an ambiguous time when Amish youth are suspended between the authority of their parents and the church's regulations, which do not apply until they become members. During this time they begin going out on weekends with their peers. Contrary to popular myth, parents do not encourage their offspring to experiment with the outside world; indeed, most parents want their youth to engage in activities condoned by the church. Very few Amish youth leave their homes and go to a city, for example. Most of them continue living at home and working during the week but socialize with their peers on weekends. This is typically the time when courtship begins.

The *Rumspringa* experience varies widely

from community to community. The length of
time can stretch from merely one or two years
in more conservative groups to as long as six or
eight years in some communities. The activities
that youth engage in, as well as the amount of
exposure to the outside culture, vary by locale.
In more isolated, conservative communities,
most *Rumspringa* activities occur inside the
Amish community, whereas in larger settlements, adjacent to urban areas, some youth
become involved in activities (bars, movies, and
other entertainment) outside the Amish fold.

During the *Rumspringa* years Amish youth
embark on a social life where the peer group
plays a new and dominant role in their lives.
They enjoy a newfound freedom before settling down, being baptized, joining the church,
getting married, and becoming adults. During these ambiguous years they face the most
important decisions of their lives: to be or not
to be Amish, to marry, and if so, to whom. *Rumspringa* is therefore both an exciting venture
and potentially a time of inner turmoil. Although
they have been immersed in Amish culture and
worn the distinctive garb of their community
since birth, youth are not considered members
of the church until they are baptized, typically
between the ages of 18 and 22. Although the
actual rate varies by region and community, on
average 85% or more of the youth do in fact
become baptized and join the Amish church.

Kraybill (2001), Stevick (2007)

Rural Life   *See* Agriculture

Russia

MENNONITES first immigrated to Russia from
POLAND/Prussia in 1789, after the government
of Tsarina Catherine the Great invited western European farmers to settle the steppes of
present-day Ukraine. They left Poland because
it was invaded by Prussia, and the Prussian government had imposed legal restrictions on the
Mennonites and threatened to eliminate their
exemption from military service.

These German-speaking Mennonites settled
in southern Russia just north of the Black Sea

in what is now Ukraine. They were granted extensive privileges of self-government and were
expected to share their agricultural knowledge
with other colonists and indigenous people.
Johann Cornies (1789–1848) became a leader in
advancing AGRICULTURE by introducing cattle,
sheep, silkworms, fruit trees, and potatoes into
the Russian settlement. He also vigorously
advocated educational reforms among the Mennonites.

Beginning in the late 1840s a spirit of religious PIETISM spread throughout the Mennonite settlements. Those most affected by
this renewal began to meet in their own groups
for prayer and BIBLE study and became known
as "brethren." The brethren raised objections
to the behavior of some church members and
requested their own COMMUNION service.
Relations deteriorated to the point that in 1860
the MENNONITE BRETHREN split from the
larger Mennonite group. The new denomination
stressed repentance from sin and CONVERSION
as a personal, subjective experience prior to
BAPTISM and church membership.

In 1871 the Russian government began to
withdraw some of the privileges that Mennonites and HUTTERITES had enjoyed. Officials
instituted universal military conscription and
government control of education. Faced with
forced assimilation, about one-third (nearly
18,000) of the Mennonites (including the VOL-
HYNIAN MENNONITES) and all of the Hutterites in Russia immigrated to the UNITED
STATES (Kansas, Nebraska, Minnesota, and
the Dakota Territory) and CANADA (Manitoba)
between 1874 and 1880. In Canada this wave of
immigrants from Russia were eventually called
KANADIER MENNONITES.

The Mennonites who remained in Russia
adjusted to the changes. They participated in
ALTERNATIVE SERVICE in forestry and learned
to speak the Russian language in schools while
maintaining the Low German (*Plautdietsch*) DIA-
LECT they spoke among themselves. By the late
1800s some Mennonites had found prosperity
in industrial manufacturing and in agriculture,
especially in growing grain. They developed

institutions of BENEVOLENCE, such as mental and medical hospitals, orphanages, and MISSION organizations. Some received HIGHER EDUCATION in Russia and GERMANY. As they developed a strong Mennonite community, Russian officials became suspicious of their German language and culture.

WORLD WAR I and the Communist Revolution undermined the economic basis of the Mennonite community. Postwar Russia suffered a massive famine, and Russian Mennonites appealed to Mennonites in North America for help. North American Mennonites responded by creating MENNONITE CENTRAL COMMITTEE in 1920, which provided food for those who were starving in Russia.

By 1920 some 120,000 Mennonites lived in numerous settlements throughout Russia. From 1923 to 1930 about 20,000 Mennonites left Russia for Canada, led in part by Benjamin B. Janz (1877–1964) and David Toews (1870–1947) and assisted by the enormous efforts of the Canadian Mennonite Board of Colonization. Called RUSSLÄNDER MENNONITES, this second wave of immigrants helped to reinvigorate the German language and educational institutions of Canadian Mennonites. Many other Mennonites of Russian origin migrated to Brazil and Paraguay in the 1930s and 1940s.

The Great Purge of Stalin and WORLD WAR II destroyed Mennonite institutions in Russia, but some Mennonites survived after 1945 in restricted and remote areas. Mennonites have continued to immigrate to Germany (about 112,000 people since 1970), which has drastically reduced the Mennonite population in Russia.

The Hutterites lived in Russia for about a century (ca. 1780–1880). During that period their population increased from about 380 to 1,260 members. In 1842 they relocated from the province of Tchernigov (120 miles northwest of Kiev) to Mennonite settlements in southern Russia. Between 1874 and 1879, all Hutterites left Russia and immigrated to the Dakota Territory in the United States.

See also Hospitals, Medical; Hospitals, Mental

F. Epp (1962, 1974, 1982), GAMEO ("Russia," "Union of Soviet Socialist Republics"), Hiebert and Miller (1929), J. Hostetler (1997), Kroeker (2005), Heinrich Loewen (2003), ME IV ("Russia"), ME V ("Union of Soviet Socialist Republics"), Urry (1989)

Russländer Mennonites

During the 1870s, about 7,000 MENNONITES (later known as KANADIER) left RUSSIA and immigrated to CANADA. Those who remained in Russia became more assimilated into Russian culture in some ways, but they also maintained some cultural and social distance. Although they learned some Russian in schools, most of their educational instruction was in High German, and they spoke a Low German (*Plautdietsch*) DIALECT in everyday life. Some Russian Mennonites prospered in manufacturing and agriculture; others developed hospitals, orphanages, and mission organizations.

By 1920 about 120,000 Mennonites were living in settlements throughout Russia and the Soviet Union. These Mennonites suffered from the impact of WORLD WAR I and the Communist Revolution, as well as the massive postwar famine. From 1923 to 1930 about 20,000 of these Russian Mennonites fled to Canada.

In order to distinguish between the two waves of MIGRATION to Canada, the 1870s group became known as Kanadier and the 1920s immigrants as Russländer. The Kanadier and Russländer had very different experiences in the 50 years (1875–1925) after the Kanadier left Russia. The Russländer, living in Russia, became more industrialized. They worked with the Russian GOVERNMENT to set up opportunities for ALTERNATIVE SERVICE, but they also lived through the trauma of war. When the Russländer arrived in Canada in the 1920s, they held on to the High German language, but they joined the vanguard of Mennonite urbanization.

Although the two waves of immigrants to Canada had important differences, some unrealistic intergroup stereotypes developed. The Russländer believed that the Kanadier were too conservative, too opposed to EDUCATION, too resistant to High German, and too satisfied with tradition. The Kanadier believed that the Russländer were too liberal, too educated, too embarrassed by the Low German dialect, and too ready to compromise with the government. The Russländer assimilated into Canadian society more rapidly than the Kanadier, who were more rural and traditional.

F. Epp (1974, 1982), GAMEO ("Rußländer"), Juhnke (1988), Kroeker (2005), Loewen and Nolt (2010), R. Loewen (2004, 2008), ME V ("Rußländer")

Sabbath   *See* Holidays; Religious

Sacrament   *See* Ordinance

Salvation

The doctrine of salvation—that God acted in JESUS CHRIST to redeem humanity from sin and reconcile them to God—is fundamental to Christian doctrine (Rom. 5:8–11) and to ANABAPTIST theology. Anabaptists believe that prior to the age of accountability, CHILDREN are innocent (without original sin) and are saved by the death and resurrection of Jesus Christ. After BAPTISM, members are expected to exhibit obedient DISCIPLESHIP in their lives. Anabaptists emphasize the importance of the human response to God's initiative of grace in the process of salvation and believe that genuine faith is expressed in daily social interaction. They expect that an individual's response to God's saving activity will include the fruits of the HOLY SPIRIT (Gal. 5:22–26), such as love, joy, peace, self-sacrifice, humility, and service in obedience to Christ.

The traditional Christian doctrine of atonement usually emphasizes the impact of Jesus' sacrificial death. Anabaptists have advocated different aspects of atonement theology, but most groups emphasize Jesus' life and teachings along with his death and resurrection. Some MENNONITE theologians in the late 20th century offered a nonviolent view of the atonement. According to these theologians, in saving humanity God seeks to end the sinful relationships of oppression and exploitation that are created by unjust social structures. Members of some assimilated groups seek to follow Jesus' example by striving to tear down these unjust structures and by working for peace and justice.

Many evangelical-minded Anabaptist groups emphasize a believer's assurance of eternal salvation, while leaders of some traditional groups speak about a "living hope" that God will be a merciful judge when determining one's eternal destiny at the end of life.

See also Anabaptism, Theology of
BE II ("Salvation, Doctrine of"), GAMEO ("Atonement, Anabaptist Theology of," "Salvation"), Martens (2008), ME V ("Atonement, Anabaptist Theology of," "Salvation"), J. Weaver (1997, 2001), J. H. Yoder (2002), P. B. Yoder (1987)

Sattler, Michael (d. 1527)

This theological leader of Swiss–south German ANABAPTISM was a former prior of a Benedictine monastery in Baden, Germany. He joined the Anabaptist Movement in 1526 and is believed to have been the primary author of the SCHLEITHEIM ARTICLES (1527), which emphasized the separation of the church from the world. Sattler used themes from monasticism, such as a pure and separated community of saints, self-denial, cross-bearing, and the centrality of following or imitating JESUS CHRIST, and revised them to reflect an Anabaptist perspective.

Soon after writing the Articles, Sattler, his wife, Margaretha, and others were arrested and accused of marrying (after having made monastic promises of celibacy) and advocating NONRESISTANCE toward the Turks. He and his wife were tried and executed in May 1527. A novel and film based on Sattler's life *(The Radicals)* interpreted his views and significance for present-day Anabaptists.

See also Discipleship; Martyrdom; Persecution
M. Augsburger (1967a), GAMEO ("Sattler, Michael"), ME V ("Sattler, Michael"), *Radicals* (1989), C. Snyder (1984), J. H. Yoder (1973)

Sauer, Christopher, II (1721–1784)

This printer and publisher of German-language materials in colonial Philadelphia also served as a minister among the BRETHREN in Pennsylvania. He printed German BIBLES, books, newspapers, almanacs, and a religious periodical. He and his father printed many materials for MENNONITE and Brethren readers, including the AUSBUND, the foundational Swiss–south German ANABAPTIST hymnal, and *DAS KLEINE DAVIDISCHE PSALTERSPIEL DER KINDER ZIONS*, the first Brethren hymnal in North America.

Sauer and his staff made important advances in printing technology, including the first casting of type in North America. Sauer also built a paper mill to supply his printing enterprise and became wealthy by purchasing property in Philadelphia.

Sauer was arrested in 1778 for his pacifism and refusal to support the Patriots' cause during the AMERICAN REVOLUTION. Disregarding the freedom of the press and due legal process, the revolutionary patriots seized almost all his possessions and sold them. Following the war Sauer was released and aided by Brethren friends. He spent his final years living with his daughter and ministering in Brethren congregations.

See also Publishing

BE II ("Sauer, Christopher II," "Sauer, Johann Christoph I"), Longenecker (1981)

Schism *See* Conflict

Schleitheim Articles

On February 24, 1527, a group of ANABAPTIST leaders met in Schleitheim in the Swiss canton of Schaffhausen to approve seven affirmations that gave theological shape to Anabaptism in Switzerland and southern Germany. MICHAEL SATTLER (d. 1527) was probably the primary author. The seven articles discussed BAPTISM, the ban (SHUNNING), COMMUNION, separation from the world and from evil, election of ministers by the congregation, NONRESISTANCE, and the OATH. The teachings on nonresistance, the oath, and separation of the church from the world became normative for most HUTTERITES and MENNONITES with origins in Switzerland and southern Germany.

See also Anabaptism, Theology of; Confessions of Faith; Nonconformity

GAMEO ("Schleitheim Confession"), Koop (2006), ME I ("Bruederliche Vereinigung"), ME V ("Schleitheim Confession"), C. Snyder (1989), J. H. Yoder (1973)

Schmiedeleut Hutterites, Gibb Group

The earliest HUTTERITE churches emerged around 1528 in the context of the Anabaptist Movement during the Protestant Reformation in Europe. Their distinctive trademark was (and

still is) their rejection of private property and insistence on COMMUNAL LIVING and sharing. Facing severe PERSECUTION, the Hutterites migrated to several countries in Europe. The Schmiedeleut Hutterites formed in 1859 in Russia. The leader, Michael Waldner (1823–1889), was a blacksmith *(Schmied)*; thus the groups became known as the Schmiedeleut (the blacksmith's people).

After immigrating to the Dakota Territory in North America in the 1870s, the Schmiedeleut remained a single group for over a century until they divided in an internal dispute in 1992. Jacob Kleinsasser (1922–), the senior elder of the Schmiedeleut colonies, lost his leadership role in 1992 when he was rejected by a majority of the council of ministers. The colonies that rejected Kleinsasser's leadership became known as the Gibb group, because a non-Hutterite banker with that surname supported their separation from Kleinsasser's supporters. They are also sometimes called the Committee Hutterites, because they have a committee of elders who provide leadership. Although the Gibb group is more conservative in cultural practice than the Kleinsasser group, the two Schmiedeleut branches are the most progressive of the four Hutterite groups. Twice as large as the Kleinsasser group, the Gibb group has about 4,800 members (12,000 children and adults) in some 120 colonies in North America. Nearly half are in Manitoba, with the remainder in North and South Dakota and Minnesota.

See also Anabaptism; Dariusleut Hutterites; Lehrerleut Hutterites; Schmiedeleut Hutterites, Kleinsasser Group

J. Hostetler (1997), Rod Janzen (2005), Janzen and Stanton (2010), Kraybill and Bowman (2001), Packull (1995)

Schmiedeleut Hutterites, Kleinsasser Group

The earliest HUTTERITE churches emerged around 1528 in the context of the Anabaptist Movement during the Protestant Reformation in Europe. Their distinctive trademark was (and still is) their rejection of private property and insistence on COMMUNAL LIVING and sharing. Facing severe PERSECUTION, the Hutterites migrated to several countries in Europe. The Schmiedeleut Hutterites formed in 1859 in Russia. The leader, Michael Waldner (1823–1889), was a blacksmith (*Schmied*); thus the groups became known as the Schmiedeleut (the blacksmith's people).

After immigrating to the Dakota Territory in North America in the 1870s, the Schmiedeleut remained a single group for over a century until they divided in an internal dispute in 1992. Jacob Kleinsasser (1922–), the senior elder of the Schmiedeleut colonies, lost his leadership role in 1992 when he was rejected by a majority of the council of ministers. Those colonies loyal to him became known as the Kleinsasser group. Many factors complicated the division, including the group's relationship to the BRUDERHOF (a similar communitarian group) and Kleinsasser's progress-minded views on the use of English, musical instruments, missions, and more advanced technology. This group is the least traditional of the four Hutterite groups. It permits some members to pursue college education and engages in some mission activities. The Kleinsasser Hutterites have about 2,400 members (6,000 children and adults) in 60 colonies in the United States and Canada. All but 10 of the colonies are located in Manitoba.

See also Anabaptism; Dariusleut Hutterites; Lehrerleut Hutterites; Schmiedeleut Hutterites; Gibb Group

J. Hostetler (1997), Rod Janzen (2005), Janzen and Stanton (2010), Kraybill and Bowman (2001), Packull (1995)

Schools, Bible

Bible schools and institutes typically provide secondary or postsecondary EDUCATION on the BIBLE and practical theological themes. These schools primarily serve young people, both prospective ordained leaders and laypersons. Some Bible schools offer certificates for completion of a series of classes, but most do not employ professionally accredited teachers or offer degrees. MENNONITE Bible schools are much more

prevalent in Canada than in the United States. In the United States, BRETHREN and Mennonite groups either created four-year liberal arts colleges or transformed their Bible schools into degree-granting colleges with strong denominational identities.

Mennonites established about 60 Bible schools in Canada between 1900 and 1970, primarily in the 1920s and 1930s. In some cases leaders created these schools because young Mennonites attending non-Mennonite Bible schools were learning theological beliefs that challenged ANABAPTIST views. However, by 1970 most of these schools had closed or consolidated.

Bible schools closed because of several factors. The transition from German to English among young people and the improved transportation networks in rural areas exposed young Mennonites to more opportunities. In the last half of the 20th century, many Mennonite students began attending public high schools and, in some regions, Mennonite high schools. Also, as congregations sought professional leadership, they expected their ministers to possess a higher level of education. Future pastors, missionaries, evangelists, Christian education leaders, and choir conductors needed more specialized training than that available at Bible schools.

Some Bible schools became colleges, such as Steinbach Bible College and Columbia Bible College. In 2000 the two Bible colleges established by the MENNONITE BRETHREN and the CONFERENCE OF MENNONITES IN CANADA (Concord College and Canadian Mennonite Bible College) merged with Menno Simons College to create Canadian Mennonite University in Winnipeg, Manitoba.

Brethren groups founded only a few independent Bible schools. One of these schools was established in Chicago in 1905 and eventually developed into the full-fledged seminary of the CHURCH OF THE BRETHREN: Bethany Theological Seminary.

In the mid-20th century some members of the BRETHREN CHURCH and the GRACE

BRETHREN Fellowship attended nondenomina-
tional schools, such as the Bible Institute of Los
Angeles (now Biola University), Moody Bible
Institute, and Philadelphia College of the Bible
(now Philadelphia Biblical University). Some
Brethren leaders have taught in these three
schools. Other Bible school efforts were incorporated into the Brethren colleges founded in
the late 1800s.

TRADITIONAL GROUPS, such as the HUT-
TERITES, AMISH, OLD ORDER MENNONITES,
and OLD GERMAN BAPTISTS, have not developed Bible schools, because they oppose
HIGHER EDUCATION for their members and
formal education for their pastors. Several
conservative Mennonite groups in the United
States have established Bible schools or short-
term Bible institutes since 1950, including Nu-
midia Mennonite Bible School (1966) and Faith
Builders (1992) in Pennsylvania and Rosedale
Bible College (1952) in Ohio.

See also Theological Education

BE I ("Bible Institutes"), F. Epp (1982), GAMEO
("Bible Colleges and Institutes"), ME V ("Bible
Colleges and Institutes"), Regehr (1996)

Schools, Elementary

ANABAPTIST groups show a considerable diversity of practice related to elementary school
EDUCATION. In general, the more traditional
the group, the more likely its members are to
educate their children in private, church-related
elementary schools. Although a few assimilated
groups sponsor private elementary schools,
most do not.

With a few exceptions, prior to 1950 most
Anabaptist children in the United States attended small rural public schools under the
supervision of neighborhood school boards.
Regardless of church affiliation, the bulk of
Anabaptist elementary schools were founded in
the mid-20th century for various reasons. The
massive consolidation of public schools removed
rural one-room schools from local and parental
control. Excessive nationalism and patriotism in
public schools in the context of WORLD WAR II
deeply troubled some parents and church lead-

ers. Curricular developments in some large consolidated public schools included TELEVISION,
the teaching of EVOLUTION in science courses,
and physical education classes. The National
Christian Day School Movement among many
evangelical churches in the 1950s also provided
an impetus for the beginning of some Anabaptist elementary schools.

The AMISH and OLD ORDER MENNONITES
operate 1,900 private one- or two-room schools
for over 50,000 pupils in grades 1 through 8. In
some rural areas a few Amish and Old Order
Mennonite pupils attend public elementary
schools. Many conservative MENNONITE
groups also operate elementary schools for their
children.

Although most children of assimilated Mennonites attend public schools, some of the
larger Mennonite communities have established
elementary schools. Many of these schools end
at 8th grade, but others are part of a larger
school system that extends through 12th or 13th
grade. About 30 elementary schools are related
to church groups affiliated with MENNONITE
CHURCH USA. In a survey (CMP 2006) of Mennonite Church USA members, 7% reported attending a Mennonite-related elementary school
for at least one year.

In the BRETHREN world, some elementary
schools were founded in the 1970s and 1980s
by churches affiliated with the Fellowship of
GRACE BRETHREN CHURCHES and the OLD
GERMAN BAPTIST BRETHREN. Virtually all children in the CHURCH OF THE BRETHREN and
the BRETHREN CHURCH attend public elementary schools.

Most HUTTERITE colonies have a school
building that houses both a German school
and a public school. Each colony has a German
teacher who provides about an hour of instruction related to German and church beliefs for
elementary pupils each day. A public school
teacher, supervised by a local public school
board, teaches a standard curriculum in English
to Hutterite pupils for the bulk of the school
day.

A few Anabaptist families home-school their

children in the elementary grades. Many Amish and Old Order Mennonites object to home-schooling because they want their children to learn the value of community and collaboration with peers, which is more likely to develop in a small private school setting than within an individual family.

See also Higher Education; Schools, Bible; Schools, Secondary

BE I ("Christian Day School Movement," "Elementary Education"), CMP 2006, GAMEO ("Elementary Education," "Private Christian Schools"), Johnson-Weiner (2007), ME V ("Private Christian Schools," "Education"), http://www.mennoniteschools.org, http://www.wmes.ca

Schools, Secondary

The most TRADITIONAL GROUPS do not consider formal EDUCATION beyond the eighth grade necessary for occupational preparation in Old Order communities. The AMISH and some OLD ORDER MENNONITE groups in fact discourage high school education. This view created conflict in the United States with the consolidation of public schools after World War II. Some parents were jailed for refusing to school their children beyond eighth grade. A compromise in 1955 resolved the issue in Pennsylvania. The U.S. Supreme Court, in *Wisconsin v. Yoder*, determined in 1972 that youth in Old Order communities could end formal education at age 14.

The schools in HUTTERITE colonies, operated by local public school districts, sometimes include grades 9 and 10, and a few continue through 12th grade.

All of the traditional groups place a high value on a practical education to provide youth with skills related to farming, the trades, construction, woodworking, or homemaking. Many of these groups encourage informal apprenticeships for vocational training in OCCUPATIONS within their community.

Among the ASSIMILATED GROUPS, BRETHREN and MENNONITES established numerous academies between 1870 and 1920 to provide the equivalent of a secondary education for young people at a time before public high schools were readily accessible. Many of these academies later evolved into colleges or were disbanded when public high schools became more widespread. The Mennonite Collegiate Institute, begun in 1889 in Gretna, Manitoba, is probably the oldest continuously Mennonite-owned and -operated secondary school in North America. Heinrich H. Ewert (1855–1934) was the principal for most of its first 50 years.

A second wave of interest in establishing church-related high schools emerged after World War II. The academies of the 19th century were often founded to fill a void in public education. The high schools established by ANABAPTISTS in the mid-20th century were created primarily as a reaction against the large consolidated public high schools that emerged after World War II. The main objections included loss of local control, secular values in the curriculum, lack of religious education, and excessive patriotism and NATIONALISM. Schools founded in this era were designed to protect Anabaptist youth from harmful values in the public school culture and to provide a curriculum based on Anabaptist beliefs, as well as peers from similar backgrounds.

A few high schools were established between 1950 and 1980 by the Fellowship of GRACE BRETHREN CHURCHES and the BRETHREN CHURCH. None were established by the CHURCH OF THE BRETHREN in this era. Nearly 30 Anabaptist-related high schools were built in the United States and Canada by MENNONITE BRETHREN and MENNONITE CHURCH groups between 1940 and 1960. The Mennonite Secondary Education Council was formed in 1961 to coordinate the efforts of some of the schools. In the early 21st century, assimilated churches in some of the larger Mennonite communities operate about two dozen high schools, attended by pupils from both Mennonite and non-Mennonite backgrounds. In a survey (CMP 2006) of MENNONITE CHURCH USA members, 17% reported attending a Mennonite high school for at least one year.

Numerous conservative (but not Old Order)

Mennonite churches established small high schools for their constituents in the last quarter of the 20th century and continue to operate them. Mennonite-related secondary schools are important feeder schools for Anabaptist-affiliated colleges and universities.

See also Higher Education; Theological Education

BE II ("Secondary Education"), CMP 2006, GAMEO ("Secondary Schools"), ME V ("Secondary Schools"), S. Peters (2003), www.mennoniteschools.org

Secret Societies

ANABAPTIST groups have traditionally forbidden membership in secret organizations for several reasons. They objected to the swearing of OATHS, the use of special titles, RITUALS not centered on the Christian faith, flamboyant CLOTHING, and any secrecy that might compromise loyalty to the church. In North America, Anabaptist groups traditionally prohibited membership in fraternal orders such as the Masons and the Odd Fellows. However, in the 21st century some ASSIMILATED GROUPS no longer object to membership in certain secret societies, such as the Masons.

BE II ("Secret Societies"), GAMEO ("Secret Societies"), ME IV ("Secret Societies"), Schroeder and Loewen (1958)

Sect

Cults, sects, and DENOMINATIONS are three forms of religious organization identified by social analysts. Most of the TRADITIONAL GROUPS fit the threefold description of a sect. First, they have rigorous membership requirements that make it challenging for outsiders to join. Some of these groups do have members who came from the outside the group, but newcomers face significant hurdles related to DIALECT, dress, lifestyle, and TECHNOLOGY. Second, virtually all of the traditional ANABAPTIST groups emphasize NONCONFORMITY to the world, which they express through distinctive CLOTHING and noninvolvement in politics, worldly amusements, and entertainment. Third, as sectarian groups they have few formal institutions. These churches are structured

more like a large extended family, with informal practices, face-to-face gatherings, and little bureaucratic protocol. In many ways HUTTERITE, AMISH, OLD COLONY MENNONITE, OLD ORDER MENNONITE, and traditional BRETHREN groups are what sociologists call "established sects" because they continue to exhibit these traits over several generations rather than evolve into a denomination, as often happens.

Some observers mistakenly call these groups "cults." A key attribute of a cult is a CHARISMATIC leader who exercises power over the members. Often a one-generation phenomenon, cults typically flounder and recede after the death of the first leader. The Amish and similar traditional groups do not have self-appointed charismatic leaders. Their leaders, selected by the community, typically have various congregational and affiliation ties that balance power and restrain the scope of their influence.

Yinger (1970)

SEMILLA   See Latin American Anabaptist Seminary

Seminaries   See Theological Education

Separation from the World   See Nonconformity

Separation of Church and State   See Church and State

Sermon   See Preaching

Sermon on the Mount

Many ANABAPTIST groups think this New Testament passage, which contains a sermon given by Jesus (Matt. 5–7), expresses the essence of the Christian gospel and its primary ethical values. The sermon's themes of radical DISCIPLESHIP, loving one's enemies, patient suffering under PERSECUTION, moral purity of thought and deed, non-swearing of OATHS, and PEACEMAKING have been important to Anabaptists throughout the centuries.

Written Anabaptist CONFESSIONS OF

FAITH routinely cite more verses from the Book of Matthew than any other book in the BIBLE, and within Matthew, the Sermon on the Mount is most frequently cited. This pattern offers evidence about the significance of this passage for Anabaptists. The explicit admonitions of Jesus in the Sermon on the Mount provide the ethical foundation for the Anabaptist emphasis on discipleship rather than on creeds and systematic doctrine.

Some other theological traditions have minimized the hard ethical imperatives of this sermon by relegating them to some future era or by saying that Jesus, expecting the imminent end of the world, intended them as short-term guidelines for the interim. By contrast, the Anabaptist discipleship tradition understands these teachings of Jesus as pertinent and normative for all time.

In the 1940s the writings of Harold S. Bender (1897–1962) on the Anabaptist vision helped to reawaken Anabaptist interest in and appreciation of the Sermon on the Mount. Since that time Anabaptist scholars have continued to emphasize the centrality of the Sermon on the Mount and its themes to Anabaptist theology.

See also Anabaptism, Theology of

BE II ("Sermon on the Mount"), Bender (1944), GAMEO ("Sermon on the Mount"), Kissinger (1975), Koop (2004), Kraybill (2003b), Howard Loewen (1985), ME V ("Sermon on the Mount"), John Miller (1969)

Service

ANABAPTIST groups advocate doing good works of self-sacrifice for others. Anabaptists read in the BIBLE that Jesus came "not to be served but to serve" (Matt. 20:28), and they attempt to follow his example.

Service is a prominent value in Anabaptist theology and practice. Anabaptist service in the 16th century began with the practice of MUTUAL AID, whereby members assisted one another in the event of financial loss, property damage, and the like. This type of service maintained an inward focus on the needs of members in their own communities.

However, by the 1800s and 1900s some Eu-ropean and North American Anabaptists developed a more outward focus on serving people outside their ranks and on MISSION activity. In the mid-1900s in North America, members of ASSIMILATED GROUPS became more engaged with the world as they moved into cities and towns, and they began to serve more people outside their own groups.

During WORLD WAR II the HISTORIC PEACE CHURCHES helped to create government-sanctioned programs of ALTERNATIVE SERVICE in lieu of military service. Through these programs CONSCIENTIOUS OBJECTORS to war performed service in medical and mental hospitals, as firefighters, and as farm laborers. These service programs increased rapidly in the mid-20th century among assimilated BRETHREN and MENNONITE groups. Many Anabaptist-related churches have developed various types of VOLUNTARY SERVICE programs to encourage members to serve people beyond their church. Brethren Volunteer Service and MENNONITE CENTRAL COMMITTEE were both created to provide opportunities for church members to serve others. Numerous Anabaptist-related agencies operate service programs all over the world that provide material aid, agricultural training, and social, medical, and educational services for people in underdeveloped areas.

See also Brethren Disaster Ministries; Brethren Service Commission; Hospitals, Medical; Hospitals, Mental; Mennonite Disaster Service

P. Dyck (1970), GAMEO ("Service"), Kraybill (1996), J. Kreider (2001), ME V ("Service")

Sewing Circle   *See* Gender Roles

Sexual Abuse   *See* Abuse, Domestic

Sexuality

Few written records describe ANABAPTISTS' attitudes toward sexuality before the 20th century. Their conservative views and their rural settings reinforced traditional attitudes toward sexual expression, the roles of males and females in the family, singleness, DIVORCE and remarriage, ABORTION, and BIRTH CONTROL.

Beginning in the 1960s, leaders of some AS-SIMILATED GROUPS sought to discuss these topics more openly. The official statements of several groups presented sexuality as a part of personal identity and expression as well as a means for procreation. Such statements, citing biblical texts, affirmed the sanctity of monogamous marriage and reserved sexual intercourse for heterosexual marriage.

In the last quarter of the 20th century various assimilated church bodies debated their views on HOMOSEXUALITY and on accepting practicing homosexuals into their membership. In the 21st century widely divergent views are held on these subjects.

Most assimilated Anabaptists tacitly condone artificial methods of birth control, leaving decisions to individual members. Members of these assimilated groups display a wide range of opinions regarding abortion.

Beginning in the 1980s, Anabaptist church members and leaders began to acknowledge publicly that sexual ABUSE occurs within their families and congregations. They developed programs to teach counseling skills and instituted organizational policies to try to protect both victims and church-related institutions.

TRADITIONAL GROUPS affirm conservative sexual norms but do not write extensively about them. They rarely discuss sexuality and sexual expression publicly.

See also Gender Roles

BE II ("Sexuality, Human"), GAMEO ("Sex Education," "Sexuality"), Grimsrud and Nation (2008), Heggen (1993), A. Hershberger (1999), Johansen (1977), King (2007), ME V ("Sex Education," "Sexuality"), Swartley (2003)

Shunning

Shunning, also called avoidance or the ban (*Meidung* in German), follows the EXCOMMU-NICATION of members. It is practiced by some traditional groups, especially the Old Order Amish and HUTTERITES as well as some conservative MENNONITE groups. The practice of shunning is based on I Corinthians 5:11 and four other biblical passages: Matthew 18:15–18,

II Thessalonians 3:6, Titus 3:10, and Romans 16:17. Shunning is spelled out in article 17 of the 1632 DORDRECHT CONFESSION OF FAITH. It is intended to shame wayward members who break the BAPTISMAL vows they made in the presence of church witnesses and to encourage them to confess their sins and return to the church. Shunning assumes that the violation of a baptismal vow to God is a very serious moral offense that could jeopardize one's eternal destiny. The church, acting in the role of a spiritual parent, uses shunning as a form of moral DISCIPLINE to reprimand the wayward.

Strong disagreements over the practice of shunning divided Dutch Mennonite groups in the 16th century. A distinction eventually emerged between two types of shunning: partial and full. Partial shunning meant that an ex-member was excluded from COMMUNION and church membership but could still attend WORSHIP services and participate in the community if he or she so desired. Full shunning meant greater separation in certain aspects of daily life, such as eating and business. A debate over types of shunning became a key point of contention in the 1690s Amish-Mennonite division in SWITZERLAND and Alsace, led by JAKOB AMMANN (1644–ca. 1730), that resulted in the formation of the AMISH. The Amish favored the stronger type of shunning, while the Swiss Brethren (MENNONITES) favored the partial type.

In the 21st century the practice of shunning does not necessarily end all social interaction with ex-members, but it may prohibit things such as eating at the same table, riding in vehicles driven by ex-members, accepting gifts, money, goods, or services from them, and participating with them in business enterprises. The shunned person may live with his or her family with certain restrictions. Conversation is allowed, for example, but eating meals together at the same table is not. Church members are expected to assist ex-members in times of emergency or special need.

A shunned person is welcomed back into the church with all prior privileges restored if she or he expresses repentance and offers a formal public apology in front of the congregation. Some groups practice a milder form of shunning that ends if the ex-member joins another Anabaptist group, but other groups will lift the ban only if the offender returns to his or her former church. Ex-members occasionally return, but more typically those expelled for a long period of time stridently oppose shunning and never return to their previous church.

In the 21st century the manner and severity of shunning varies greatly in the most traditional groups and by family and congregation within a particular group. Most churches require a vote of the congregation to initiate excommunication and shunning when it involves a violation of church regulations. If the offense is a serious one—adultery or murder—that is forbidden in the Bible, church leaders may act without a congregational vote.

GAMEO ("Avoidance"), J. Hostetler (1993), Kraybill (2001), Kraybill, Nolt, and Weaver-Zercher (2007)

Simons, Menno   *See* Menno Simons

Simplicity   *See Gelassenheit*

Singing
Many ANABAPTIST groups are noted for vibrant congregational hymn singing in their WORSHIP services. Some groups sing in a cappella style, without instrumental accompaniment. TRADITIONAL GROUPS prohibit musical instruments in worship because they believe that instruments distract the believer from the religious meaning of the words and focus attention on individual performance. They also prohibit vocal and instrumental solos because they think that solos foster individual pride rather than humility. Some traditional churches do not sing harmony parts during worship, but others accept four-part harmony. The Old Order Amish and MENNONITES do not sing parts in the worship service, but many of them do in youth, social, and family gatherings. Some traditional groups worship and sing in German, while others use English.

Some groups lost much of their German-language hymn tradition in Canada and the United States when they embraced four-part singing and began using English in worship in the late 1800s. Many German-speaking Mennonites who emigrated from RUSSIA in the 1870s and in the 1920s have maintained their German-origin hymns longer, despite their transition to English.

ASSIMILATED GROUPS in the 21st century include vocal solos and a wide variety of musical instruments, including pipe organs, pianos, guitars, and drums, in their worship services. Some congregations continue to sing a cappella. Others always use musical accompaniment, and still others use a combination of the two styles. Choral and instrumental music plays an important role in Anabaptist schools, colleges, and universities. Music written and sung by Anabaptist groups and choirs has been recorded and sold in many forms. "Sound in the Lands" festivals featuring Mennonite music across borders and boundaries were sponsored by Conrad Grebel University College in 2004 and 2009. Many Anabaptist groups have produced hymnbooks, some of which include songs written by members.

See also Ausbund; Folklore; *Hymnal: A Worship Book*; Hymnody

H. Durnbaugh (1999), GAMEO ("Singing"), Kropf and Nafziger (2001), ME V ("Singing"), D. Thomas (1985)

Social Avoidance   *See* Shunning

Social Class   *See* Diversity, Social

Social Justice
After World War II, many members of ASSIMILATED GROUPS began working in SERVICE and MISSION projects in urban and unfamiliar rural areas, where they learned about RACISM, racial discrimination, and social injustice. By the 1950s, assimilated MENNONITES and BRETHREN began to rethink the church's relationship to the outside world. ANABAPTISTS traditionally believed that the church should remain separate from the world and preach an ethic of love in contrast to the GOVERNMENT's ethic of justice.

However, during this time of transition some assimilated leaders contended that the church has a responsibility to respond to unjust situations in the world.

The Civil Rights Movement of the 1960s and 1970s in the UNITED STATES, led by Martin Luther King Jr. (1929–1968), advocated nonviolent direct action in the service of racial justice. Many Anabaptists admired King's nonviolent approach, and some became active in the movement. This participation sometimes led to bitter CONFLICTS within Mennonite and Brethren congregations, which mirrored the tensions between conservative and liberal perspectives in the wider society.

In 1968 MENNONITE CENTRAL COMMITTEE U.S. opened a permanent office in Washington, D.C., and in 1975 Mennonite Central Committee Canada did the same in Ottawa. These offices monitor legislation and advocate for social justice and peace-related issues to elected officials.

By the 1970s, Anabaptist theologians were highlighting justice as one aspect of Jesus' prophetic work in announcing the kingdom of God. According to Mennonite theologian John Howard Yoder (1927–1997) in *The Politics of Jesus,* a genuine Christian ethic should not precisely define social and legal policy, but it should certainly call on the government to uphold the highest expression of its own values—equitable justice, order, moral responsibility, and benefits for all citizens.

Also during this time, assimilated Anabaptists began to advocate and institutionalize programs for PEACEMAKING, including those in RESTORATIVE JUSTICE, such as victim-offender reconciliation programs. Many Anabaptist-related agencies and organizations that engage in peacebuilding include social justice in their vision and strategy.

BE II ("Social Action"), Bush (1998a), Driedger and Kraybill (1994), GAMEO ("Justice," "Sociopolitical Activism"), G. Hershberger (1958), ME V ("Justice," "Sociopolitical Activism"), Schlabach (2009), J. H. Yoder (1972/1994), Zehr (1990), http://mcc.org/us/washington, http://mcc.org/canada/ottawa

Society of Brothers   *See* Bruderhof

Society of Friends   *See* Quakers

Sommerfeld Mennonite Church

Ancestors of this church were part of the Bergthaler Colony of KANADIER MENNONITES that migrated from RUSSIA to Manitoba in the 1870s. In 1894 the Sommerfelders separated from the more progressive-minded Bergthalers and retained a traditional lifestyle. The group remained rather conservative until the last half of the 20th century, when Sunday school, youth meetings, musical instruments, and English hymnals were adopted. Restrictions on dress have also declined. Unsalaried lay ministers serve each congregation under the supervision of a bishop.

The group's 13 congregations with some 2,300 members are in southern Manitoba. Some conservative Sommerfelders moved from Canada to Mexico in the 1920s because of new Canadian education laws that required MENNONITE children to attend English-language schools. They established a colony, Santa Clara, in the state of Chihuahua. Some of their members eventually left Mexico for Bolivia in the 1960s, and others returned to Canada in the last quarter of the 20th century. About 2,000 members continue to live in Mexico.

Bergen (2001), J. Friesen (2007), M. Reimer (2008)

South America

German-speaking MENNONITES of Dutch-Russian origins began to immigrate to South America in 1926, and by 1927 they had set up colonies there. They migrated first from CANADA to Paraguay (the KANADIER), then from RUSSIA to Brazil and Paraguay (1930, 1948), and from POLAND to Uruguay (1948). In the early 21st century some 75,000 Mennonites, including European immigrants and indigenous people, live in South America.

The Evangelical Mennonite Center of Theology was created in Montevideo, Uruguay, in 1956 and later moved to Asunción, Paraguay. The seminary offers courses in both German and Spanish. Mennonite-owned farms, schools, hospitals, economic cooperatives, churches, and businesses in Paraguay have an important economic impact on the country, and some Mennonites there are entering government service.

Beginning in 1917, American Mennonite missionaries went to Argentina and Brazil, and their work there eventually led to the establishment of a significant number of indigenous congregations. These indigenous Mennonite churches have sizable communities in Argentina, Brazil, Colombia, and Bolivia. In 1972, MENNONITE WORLD CONFERENCE held its first assembly in South America, in Curitiba, Brazil, where a Bible school had earlier been founded. The 2009 Mennonite World Conference was held in Paraguay. Mennonite church PERIODICALS appear in German, Portuguese, and Spanish.

The South American congregations exhibit many ANABAPTIST emphases, such as PEACE-MAKING, CONSCIENTIOUS OBJECTION to military participation, and community SERVICE. Colombian Mennonites are active participants in an ecumenical organization, JustaPaz, that seeks to bring reconciliation to violent situations. MENNONITE CENTRAL COMMITTEE, the North American relief and development organization of Mennonite and BRETHREN IN CHRIST churches, has supported many of these efforts for peace and SOCIAL JUSTICE in South American countries.

Some Latin American Anabaptist theologians stress a connection between the Anabaptist vision and their own experiences of poverty, structural violence, and alienation from the political elite. In their radical obedience to Christ, some leaders seek to witness against social injustice and work for a peace that rejects violence and apathy.

In 1909 the BRETHREN CHURCH began a mission in Argentina, which helped to start new congregations with a Brethren identity. After World War II the Brethren sent missionaries to Ecuador. The Ecuadoran churches joined a broader body of evangelical churches. After an initial effort in the 1980s, the CHURCH OF THE BRETHREN restarted mission work in Brazil in the 1990s. There are five congregations (250 members) affiliated with the Church of the Brethren.

BE I ("Brazil"), C. Dyck (1993), Fretz (1953), GAMEO ("South America"), P. P. Klassen (1999), Martínez (2000), ME IV ("South America, Mennonites in"), ME V ("South America"), Stoesz and Stackley (1999), Warkentin (1987), http://www.anabaptistwiki.org, http://www.mwc-cmm.org

Spanish   *See* Central America; Hispanic-American Anabaptists; Language; Mexico

Spiritual Life

This term refers to those aspects of the Christian life that include PRAYER, personal devotional life, WORSHIP, and individual and communal RITUALS, but not formal doctrine or theological studies. ANABAPTIST spirituality is Christ-centered and emphasizes the use of Scripture for personal reflection and inspiration. Historical Anabaptist spirituality has been shaped by experiences of PERSECUTION and NONCONFORMITY to the wider culture.

The spiritual lives of members of TRADITIONAL GROUPS are often shaped by distinctive practices and symbols more than by words. Beliefs and ethics of the community are often transmitted through the actions of everyday life instead of through words or dogma prescribed for certain occasions. Words and expressive feelings are more typical ways of articulating spiritual experience in ASSIMILATED GROUPS.

COMMUNION services in congregations are collective spiritual moments filled with deep meaning. The LOVE FEAST ritual has traditionally embodied the spiritual essence of church life for many Brethren groups. Congregational SINGING is an important means of worship and spiritual rejuvenation for many Anabaptists in the 21st century.

Members of Anabaptist groups have also been nourished by various streams of spirituality outside historical Anabaptism.

See also Devotional Literature; *Gelassenheit*; Pietism

D. Augsburger (2006), BE II ("Spiritual Life"), Boers

et al. (2005), Cronk (1977), Faus (1994), GAMEO ("Spiritual Life"), Koontz (1996), Kraybill, Nolt, and Weaver-Zercher (2007), D. Liechty (1994), J. Liechty (1980), ME V ("Spiritual Life"), C. Snyder (2002, 2004)

Sports   *See* Leisure

Stewardship   *See* Economics; Environment

Sunday   *See* Holidays, Religious

Sunday School

During the second half of the 19th century, many BRETHREN and MENNONITES organized Sunday schools in the wake of the wider Sunday school movement that promoted special religious education classes for children. This trend sometimes fostered church schisms among ANABAPTIST groups. Opposition to Sunday schools was a major issue in fueling the OLD ORDER MOVEMENT in many churches in the 1880s and 1890s.

Some TRADITIONAL GROUPS have resisted Sunday school classes because they believe that educating children in faith matters is the parents' responsibility. They also suspect that other innovations that they deem unscriptural and too institutionalized—REVIVALISM, the salaried ministry, HIGHER EDUCATION, and the use of English for WORSHIP services—will be introduced through Sunday schools.

In many Anabaptist denominations the growing Sunday school movement in the late 19th and early 20th centuries was supported by specialized publications and curricula printed by church-owned or church-related firms. In 1977 several assimilated Mennonite and Brethren groups created the Foundation Series—age-appropriate Sunday school lessons that interpreted biblical stories from an Anabaptist perspective. The Foundation Series was replaced by another cooperative curriculum, Jubilee, in the 1990s.

In March 2006, Mennonite Publishing Network and Brethren Press launched a new Sunday school curriculum for children and youth. The curriculum, Gather 'Round, is a Bible-based se-

ries that presents issues from an Anabaptist perspective. It shares stories of Anabaptist heritage and invites questions from the learners.

BE II ("Sunday School Movement"), Boyers (1971), Brumbaugh-Cayford (2006), GAMEO ("Sunday School," "Sunday School Literature"), ME IV ("Sunday School"), ME V ("Sunday School Literature," "Sunday Schools"), T. Schlabach (1988), J. Umble (1934), http://www.gatherround.org

Swiss Volhynian Mennonites   *See* Volhynian Mennonites

Switzerland

One of the three primary locations where ANABAPTISM emerged in the early 1500s was the German-speaking part of Switzerland, primarily the three cantons of Zurich, Basel, and Bern.

Swiss Anabaptism began within the circle of Protestant reformer Ulrich Zwingli (1484–1531), a pastor in Zurich in the 1520s. Radical leaders such as CONRAD GREBEL (ca. 1498–1526), MICHAEL SATTLER (d. 1527), and Felix Manz (1498–1527) would not accept Zwingli's position that GOVERNMENTS should have some control over church reforms. They believed that the BIBLE and the spirit of Christ were the only authorities for matters of faith. By 1525 the Anabaptists in Zurich had broken with Zwingli and formed a new movement. These Anabaptists called themselves *Brüder* or "brothers," so scholars generally refer to them as Swiss BRETHREN Anabaptists.

The Anabaptists lived under intense opposition in Switzerland. Until 1614 many of their members suffered MARTYRDOM. Despite the cessation of executions, regional governments maintained policies of PERSECUTION and harassment well into the 1800s.

The Swiss Brethren suffered a church SCHISM in the 1690s, and two groups emerged: the AMISH, named after the Swiss leader JAKOB AMMANN (1644–ca. 1730), and the (Swiss) MENNONITES, named for the Dutch Anabaptist leader MENNO SIMONS (1496–1561). The Amish-Mennonite division stretched to the French Alsace and the German Palatinate. Many

Swiss-origin Mennonites, Amish, and HUTTER-
ITES emigrated or were banished to countries
outside Switzerland. Many of the Amish and
Mennonites in the eastern part of North America, especially those in traditional groups, trace
their origins to the three Swiss cantons of Basel,
Bern, and Zurich.

A renewal movement in the 1820s in Switzerland led to the formation of the APOSTOLIC
CHRISTIAN CHURCH, a group that attracted
some traditional Mennonites. The VOLHYNIAN
MENNONITES also originated in Switzerland
and migrated to areas of Germany and France
in the mid-1600s to escape persecution in Switzerland.

A modest number of Mennonites (about
2,500 baptized members) remain in Switzerland.
The oldest continuous Mennonite congregation
in the world is in Langnau, Bern. In 1950 the European Mennonite Bible School was established
near Basel, a cooperative effort of Swiss, French,
and German Mennonites.

In an effort to recognize the historical importance of Anabaptism and to attract visitors,
the Swiss government and its tourist office des-
ignated 2007 as "Täuferjahr 2007" (The Year of
the Anabaptists) and sponsored several events
related to Anabaptist history.

C. Dyck (1993), GAMEO ("Swiss Brethren,"
"Switzerland"), Gratz (1953), J. Hostetler (1993),
Keim (1998), ME IV ("Swiss Brethren," "Switzerland"),
http://www.mwc-cmm.org

Taxes

Throughout their history in EUROPE, ANABAPTIST groups were subject to special taxes or fines to finance state-supported churches, as a form of religious PERSECUTION. In North America, special fees were sometimes assessed as compensation to the GOVERNMENT for exemption from military service prior to the 20th century. Except for a few assimilated BRETHREN and MENNONITES, most Anabaptists willingly pay all taxes (even those levied specifically for military purposes). They cite both Jesus' and Paul's admonitions to pay taxes (Matt. 22:21 and Rom. 13:6) as justification for this practice. HUTTERITE colonies, which own collective property, are taxed as corporations and pay an estimated per capita income tax. The AMISH and OLD ORDER MENNONITES pay taxes like other citizens, but they have been exempt from Social Security in the United States since 1965 and from Social Insurance in Canada since 1974.

However, since the mid-20th century, especially during the VIETNAM WAR, a few assimilated Brethren and Mennonites refused to pay the portion of federal taxes used for military purposes. In 1987 the Peace Tax Foundation was created in the UNITED STATES with significant Mennonite and Brethren involvement. It advocates changing the tax code to allow CONSCIENTIOUS OBJECTORS and others to direct their federal income tax payments to a special fund to be used only for nonmilitary purposes. Some assimilated Mennonites in Canada support Conscience Canada, an organization with similar objectives that was founded by Mennonites and Quakers in 1979.

See also Church and State

BE II ("Taxes, Taxation, Tax Refusal"), GAMEO ("Taxes"), D. Kaufman (1978), ME IV ("Taxation"), ME V ("Taxes"), http://www.consciencecanada.ca/, http://www.peacetaxfund.org

Technology

The use, control, and rejection of technology vary greatly across ANABAPTIST communities. Most of the ASSIMILATED GROUPS accept new

technological developments and devices in their homes, businesses, leisure activities, and worship services. As new devices became available in the first half of the 20th century in North America, some churches were slow to adopt them—especially the AUTOMOBILE and, later, the TELEVISION. However, as those groups become more assimilated later in the century, the car and the television were more readily accepted. In the 21st century only a few families in assimilated churches choose to not have televisions or Internet access in their homes in order to limit the cultural influence of mainstream society.

TRADITIONAL GROUPS have greater reservations about technology than assimilated Anabaptists for two primary reasons. They fear that some forms of technology—ELECTRICITY, Internet, RADIO, television, COMPUTERS, DVD players—will expose their families to harmful influences from the secular values in the larger society. A second fear is that technology such as motor vehicles and farm machinery will pull their communities apart by encouraging mobility and outside employment, thereby weakening the family unit and the church community.

None of the traditional churches categorically reject technology. Rather, they *selectively* use it—making choices about what to accept, what to reject, and what to adapt in ways that will support the values of their way of life. Some groups, when screening a new piece of technology, ask, "What will it do to our families and church? How might it change our way of life over time?" The use of some devices like television or the Internet are relatively easy to discern, but others—telephones, automobiles, fax machines, and computers—may require years of informal discussion before the community can reach an agreement.

Some AMISH and OLD ORDER MENNONITE communities have also devised interesting methods of adapting technology to fit their values and way of life—for example, by placing steel wheels on tractors, using electricity from batteries rather than the public grid, and removing Internet capability from computers.

Although biblical teachings do not directly address issues of modern technology, traditional communities base many of their objections to it on the biblical principles of NONCONFORMITY to the world (Rom. 12:2) and the importance of the church being apart from the world, especially from the values that might harm the spiritual health of their communities.

Heidebrecht (2006), Kraybill (2001), Kraybill and Bowman (2001), Scott and Pellman (1990)

Telephone

Some TRADITIONAL GROUPS resisted the installation of telephones as they were adopted by the larger society in the first two decades of the 20th century. The resister groups worried that the telephone would provide a direct connection to the outside society and thus violated their religious belief in separation from the world. Many of the first telephones were installed in public places, and churches did not object to their use, but bringing phones into homes was considered connecting too close to the world. Typically, the first in-home telephone systems had party lines that enabled neighbors to eavesdrop on conversations, making it difficult to have private conversations between church members. A deeper sociological reason for telephone resistance was the loss of the face-to-face conversations that were the social glue of rural societies.

Some groups eventually adopted the telephone, but others still place restrictions on it in the 21st century. In Old Order groups members may use public telephones but not install phones on their own properties. Other groups permit installation of a community phone used by several families. Still others permit phones in businesses but not in homes. Cell phones are acceptable in some Old Order groups but not in others.

An Amish Mennonite Conference Line was established in 2004 to enable members of AMISH and conservative MENNONITE groups to hear news from their communities, discuss historical topics, and hear special speakers. Both English and Pennsylvania German phone

lines are available, with several hundred callers participating on a typical day.

Kraybill (2001), Scott and Pellman (1990), D. Umble (1996)

Television

Many Anabaptist churches resisted the adoption of television when it became available in mid-20th-century North America. Some members of ASSIMILATED GROUPS gradually purchased televisions, and they slowly became commonplace in the homes of most assimilated church members. A survey (CMP 2006) found that 97% of MENNONITE CHURCH USA and 99% of CHURCH OF THE BRETHREN and BRETHREN IN CHRIST members in the United States owned at least one television.

TRADITIONAL GROUPS, however, strongly resisted both RADIO and television, and many continue to forbid them in the 21st century. These churches view television as a medium that brings into their homes values and images that conflict with church teachings about modesty, simplicity, honesty, marital fidelity, and nonviolence. Why, they ask, should we connect our homes directly to a technological gadget that pumps objectionable values into our living rooms and bedrooms and pollutes the minds of our children? Despite ample religious and educational programming on television, most traditional churches view the bulk of television programs as propagating secularism, individualism, commercialism, alcohol, sex, and violence, all of which violate their religious convictions. Thus, many traditional churches forbid members to own televisions; in some groups a violation of that taboo could bring excommunication.

See also Counterculture; Nonconformity

BE II ("Television Viewing"), CMP 2006, Kraybill and Bowman (2001), ME V ("Television"), Scott (1996)

Temperance   *See Alcohol*

Theological Education

Informal theological education occurs continuously as believers participate in the life of the church. Some ANABAPTISTS have expressed caution or opposition to formal theological EDU-CATION, because of their understanding of the church as a priesthood of all believers. Anabaptist MINISTERS were traditionally chosen from among the CONGREGATION. In their early history Anabaptists suffered accusations of heresy by the educated clergy of the state-supported churches, which increased their distrust of formal theological education.

TRADITIONAL GROUPS do not create or support seminaries for the training of pastors, although some conservative groups do operate Bible schools for leaders and laity. The HUTTERITES, AMISH, and OLD ORDER MENNONITES do not provide any formal theological education for pastors.

ASSIMILATED GROUPS do support INSTITUTIONS for theological education. The first MENNONITE seminary was founded in Europe by the Dutch Mennonites in 1735. Assimilated Mennonite and BRETHREN groups in North America founded Bible schools, colleges, and seminaries for training pastors in the early and mid-1900s. In a 2006 survey (CMP 2006), the majority of MENNONITE CHURCH USA and CHURCH OF THE BRETHREN members in the United States wanted their pastors to have a seminary degree.

A list of Mennonite and Brethren seminaries appears in table 14. A variety of undergraduate and graduate-level theological studies are offered at Mennonite postsecondary schools in Canada, but Canadian Anabaptists do not have self-standing seminaries. Most Mennonite graduate theological programs in Canada have formal partnerships with U.S.-based Mennonite and Canadian-based non-Mennonite seminaries. The LATIN AMERICAN ANABAPTIST SEMINARY (SEMILLA) in Guatemala City is the primary center for Anabaptist theological training in the Caribbean, Central America, and Mexico.

See also Schools, Bible

Ainlay (1990), BE II ("Theological Education"), CMP 2006, GAMEO ("Seminaries"), ME IV ("Seminaries, Mennonite Theological"), ME V ("Seminaries"), Pannabecker (1975), M. Reimer (2008)

Theology

Those engaged in the discipline of theology reflect on the nature of God, explore God's relationship to creation (physical and human), and interpret doctrines of the church. Until the early and mid-1900s, ANABAPTIST theological writing tended to be occasional, implicit, and practical rather than systematic, formal, and speculative, although the 16th century saw some theological writing by Anabaptists such as MENNO SIMONS (1496–1561), DIRK PHILIPS (1504–1558), and PILGRAM MARPECK (ca. 1490s–1556). Over the centuries Anabaptist groups have published many CONFESSIONS OF FAITH.

The central pillar of Anabaptist theology is the life, teachings, death, and resurrection of JESUS CHRIST as described in the New Testament. This Christ-centered approach shapes biblical interpretation, individual spirituality, behavior, and the theology of the church. Ana-

Table 14   Anabaptist-Related Seminaries and Graduate Schools of Theology

Brethren-related		
Ashland Theological Seminary	Ashland, OH	http://seminary.ashland.edu
Bethany Theological Seminary	Richmond, IN	http://www.bethanyseminary.edu
Grace Theological Seminary	Winona, IN	http://gts.grace.edu
Mennonite-related		
Associated Mennonite Biblical Seminary	Elkhart, IN	http://www.ambs.edu
Eastern Mennonite Seminary	Harrisonburg, VA	http://www.emu.edu/seminary
Latin American Anabaptist Seminary	Guatemala City, Guatemala	http://semilla.org.gt/english%20home.html
Mennonite Brethren Biblical Seminary	Fresno, CA	http://www.mbseminary.edu
Toronto Mennonite Theological Centre	Toronto, ON	http://www.grebel.uwaterloo.ca/tmtc

baptists have traditionally valued ETHICS and DISCIPLESHIP more than theological sophistication and systematic doctrine. The authority to interpret the BIBLE, define doctrine, and regulate church life was held by the congregation, not by theologically educated MINISTERS or scholars.

This pattern changed somewhat in ASSIMILATED GROUPS as their churches switched to a salaried, theologically educated ministry in the 20th century. In the 21st century most pastors of assimilated congregations are seminary-trained, and their churches support denominational colleges and seminaries. Pastors, professors, and students encounter and are influenced by many outside theological currents, such as ECUMENISM, EVANGELICALISM, FUNDAMENTALISM, liberation theology, CHARISMATIC theology, feminist theology, PACIFISM, and MISSION theology.

A number of Anabaptist theologians have made significant contributions to formal and systematic theological thought from an Anabaptist perspective since the mid-20th century. Two North American MENNONITE theologians of the 20th century exerted influence far beyond Anabaptist circles. Mennonite Gordon D. Kaufman (1925–) received his Ph.D. from Yale University and taught theology at Harvard Divinity School for decades. Perhaps the first formally educated Mennonite to write a systematic theology, he also served as president of the American Theological Association and the American Academy of Religion.

In the last quarter of the 20th century, John Howard Yoder (1927–1997), a prominent Anabaptist scholar, made significant contributions to ecumenical discussions. After the publication of *The Original Revolution: Essays on Christian Pacifism* (1971) and *The Politics of Jesus: Vicit Agnus Noster* (1972), Yoder's thought had worldwide influence. His knowledge of biblical scholarship, historical theology, biblical ethics, pacifism, and ecumenical dynamics provided resources for his creative interpretation of a wide range of fundamental claims of traditional Christianity.

See also Anabaptism, Theology of; God, Doctrine of; Theological Education

BE II ("Theology"), Finger (1985, 1989, 2004), GAMEO ("Theologies from the Two-Thirds World," "Theology, Mennonite"), G. Kaufman (1968, 1993), Klaassen (1973), ME IV ("Theology, Anabaptist-Mennonite"), ME V ("Theologies from the Two-Thirds World," "Theology"), Nation (1997), A. Reimer (2001), Rutschman (1981), Stoffer (1989), A. Weaver (1996), J. H. Yoder (1971, 1972/1994, 1984b, 2002)

Tobacco

ANABAPTIST groups in North America have had various responses to growing and using tobacco. In the late 1800s tobacco became a key cash crop that was central to the farm economy in eastern Pennsylvania. Many farm families who were members of various Anabaptist groups raised and sold tobacco. Smoking and chewing tobacco were typical in the late 19th and early 20th centuries in some Anabaptist communities in Europe and North America. Conflict concerning tobacco has at times been intense. In the mid-20th century some church leaders in ASSIMILATED GROUPS in tobacco raising regions preached against raising it. Growing health concerns about tobacco use in the last half of the 20th century greatly diminished its use among assimilated groups. In the 21st century most assimilated groups forbid or discourage growing and using tobacco.

A few TRADITIONAL GROUPS permit their members to grow and use tobacco; however, even in those groups the practices are often contentious. Some change-resistant members in those groups argue that growing tobacco provides nearly year-round work that helps to keep large families together on the farm.

BE II ("Tobacco"), C. Bowman (1995), GAMEO ("Tobacco"), J. Hostetler (1993), ME IV ("Tobacco"), Reist (1974), Ruth (2001)

Tourism

Tourism in the ANABAPTIST world has two primary facets: non-Anabaptists who visit Anabaptist communities, and Anabaptists who visit areas related to Anabaptist history. Outsider tourism focuses heavily on the AMISH and the large tourist sites located in or near major Amish settlements. The four largest Amish-themed tourist regions in the United States, which host millions of visitors a year, are Lancaster County (Pennsylvania), Holmes County (Ohio), LaGrange County (Indiana), and Douglas County (Illinois). Most of the tourist attractions are operated by non-Anabaptists who commodify Amish images and use them to promote their tourist businesses. Several Anabaptist-owned and -operated interpretive centers provide guides and exhibits that give accurate views of Anabaptist beliefs and practices. Some of these interpretive centers are operated by local consortia of Anabaptist groups. In some tourist areas Amish people operate small roadside produce, baked goods, and craft stands, as well as retail furniture and quilt stores, that cater to tourists.

The early seeds of Amish tourism emerged in the first half of the 20th century, primarily in Lancaster County, which is only a few hours away from major cities (New York, Philadelphia, Baltimore, and Washington) in the eastern United States. Tourism in Lancaster and other sizable Amish communities expanded in the last half of the 20th century with the growth of highways, advertising (both print and online), and family vacations, and the persistence of a distinctive horse-and-buggy culture. Amish-themed tourist enterprises pump millions of dollars into the regional economies near the largest Amish settlements.

"St. Jacobs Country" in southwestern Ontario highlights the OLD ORDER MENNONITE culture of that area of Canada. This venture was initiated by MENNONITE businessmen who wanted to avoid the extremes found in some of the Amish-themed areas in the United States.

A number of Anabaptist-related information centers and museums have emerged throughout North America, often connected to regional immigration history. (See tables 15 and 16.)

The second type of tourism in the Anabaptist world developed in the last half of the 20th cen-

Table 15 Information Centers for Anabaptist-Related Groups		
Amish and Mennonite Heritage Center	Berlin, OH	http://www.behalt.com 330-893-3192
Brethren Heritage Center	Brookville, OH	http://www.brethrenheritagecenter.org 937-833-5222
Center for Mennonite Brethren Studies	Fresno, CA	http://www.fresno.edu/library/cmbs 559-453-2225
Crossroads Valley Brethren-Mennonite Heritage Center	Harrisonburg, VA	http://www.vbmhc.org 540-438-1275
Illinois Amish Interpretive Center	Arcola, IL	http://www.amishcenter.com 888-45AMISH
Lancaster Mennonite Information Center	Lancaster, PA	http://www.mennoniteinfoctr.com 717-299-0954
Mennonite Heritage Center	Harleysville, PA	http://www.mhep.org 215-256-3020
Mennonite Heritage Centre	Winnipeg, MB	http://www.mennonitechurch.ca/heritage/mhc.html 204-888-6781
Menno-Hof	Shipshewana, IN	http://www.mennohof.org 260-768-4117

Table 16	Museums of Anabaptist-Related Groups	
Hans Herr House Museum	Willow Street, PA	http://www.hansherr.org 717-464-4438
Heritage Hall Museum and Archives	Freeman, SD	http://www.freemanmuseum.org 605-925-4237
Kauffman Museum	North Newton, KS	http://www.bethelks.edu/kauffman 316-283-1612
Menno-Hof	Shipshewana, IN	http://www.mennohof.org 260-768-4117
Mennonite Heritage Museum	Goessel, KS	http://www.skyways.org/museums/goessel 620-367-8200
Mennonite Heritage Village	Steinbach, MB	http://www.mennoniteheritagevillage.com 204-326-9661
Mennonite Settlement Museum	Hillsboro, KS	http://www.hillsboro-museums.com/ Mennonite-Settlement-Museum.html 620-947-3775
The People's Place Quilt Museum	Intercourse, PA	http://www.ppquiltmuseum.com 800-828-8218

tury as access to transatlantic flights became more available. Thousands of American and Canadian BRETHREN and Mennonites whose ancestors lived in Western Europe visit historic Anabaptist sites in the Netherlands, Poland, Russia, Germany, and Switzerland. Many take organized tours guided by historians and knowledgeable interpreters. The rise of Anabaptist-themed tourism reflects a renewed interest in the European roots of the Anabaptist story. Many members of Anabaptist groups also visit North American museums and sites related to their heritage.

Biesecker-Mast (2006), GAMEO ("Museums"), Gleysteen (2007), Luthy (1994), Myers (2003), Walbert (2002), http://www.stjacobs.com/, http://www.tour magination.com/

Traditional Groups

ANABAPTIST groups can be viewed along a continuum stretching from tradition to assimilation. Two fundamental factors mark this spectrum: (1) the locus of *moral authority* and (2) how sharply the community *separates* itself from the larger society. Tradition-centered groups accent the authority of the church community over the individual and typically reject many of the prevailing practices of the larger society. AS-SIMILATED GROUPS grant greater freedom to individual choice and responsibility in religious affairs. The continuum reflects the degree to which a group rejects or accepts the values, features, and structures of modern culture as it has emerged in North America in the late 19th and 20th centuries.

One of the most prominent traits of traditional churches is that they typically stipulate some CLOTHING requirements for their members. These distinctive dress practices are symbolic of their NONCONFORMITY to the larger world and the submission of members to the authority of the church. Traditional churches have more explicit rules for membership than assimilated churches do. They reject individualism, instead emphasizing the subordination of the individual to community standards. Their distinctive practices mark sharp boundaries of separation from the outside world.

Other typical characteristics of the more traditional groups include placing a high value on traditional religious RITUAL, living in rural areas, discouraging HIGHER EDUCATION, advocating traditional GENDER ROLES, and using lay ministers who serve without seminary training or salary. Many of these churches prohibit TELEVISION, DIVORCE and remarriage, the ORDINATION OF WOMEN, and the use of musical instruments in worship.

A few traditional groups, often known as Old Orders, travel by horse and buggy. Some speak Pennsylvania German, Low German, or another DIALECT in daily discourse as well as in their WORSHIP services. The Old Orders in particular emphasize the preservation of traditional forms of religious ritual. Many traditional groups permit their members to own motor vehicles and use most forms of technology, except television and the Internet, in their homes.

Unlike assimilated groups, which tend to be more active in PEACEMAKING, international SERVICE, and MISSION activities, traditional churches emphasize a more separatist TWO-KINGDOM THEOLOGY, NONRESISTANCE, and nonconformity.

Most of the AMISH and HUTTERITE groups espouse traditional practices. The bulk of BRETHREN churches reflect the traits of assimilated groups, whereas the MENNONITES are widely dispersed across the assimilation-tradition spectrum.

See also *Gelassenheit*; *Ordnung*; Old Order Mennonites; Old Order Movement

D. Gross (1992), Kraybill and Bowman (2001), Kraybill and Hostetter (2001), Pelikan (1984)

Transportation   *See* Automobile

Trinidad and Tobago
The Mennonite Church of Trinidad and Tobago was formed in 1974 after missionaries from Virginia Mennonite Conference began radio broadcasts and worked with leprosy victims in 1969. The church, composed of people from various national and cultural backgrounds, has six congregations and about 275 members. The church operates an early childhood education project

and is involved in developing new churches in the CARIBBEAN area.

GAMEO ("Trinidad and Tobago"), ME V ("Trinidad and Tobago"), Mennonite World Conference (2005), http://www.mwc-cmm.org

Trinity   *See* God, Doctrine of

Two-Kingdom Theology
Many 16th-century ANABAPTISTS held a so-called two-kingdom view of the boundaries between the church and the political order. This view was especially strong among the Swiss–south German Anabaptists and continues to be affirmed in the 21st century by many TRADITIONAL GROUPS, such as the AMISH and conservative BRETHREN and MENNONITE groups that come from that cultural heritage. The two-kingdom perspective, shaped by Scripture and galvanized by PERSECUTION, underscored a sharp line of separation between church and government. The SCHLEITHEIM ARTICLES (1527) contains a prominent early version of this view.

The Anabaptist two-kingdom theology sees the voluntary, BELIEVERS CHURCH as a social order under the peaceful rule of Christ—one that does not use force but operates with an ethic of love and persuasion. The state, outside the perfection of Christ, is grounded in the use and threat of force. Although members of the church, according to this view, should not join the military, participate in politics, or hold GOVERNMENT office, they should respect government, pray for its leaders, and pay TAXES because it is ordained by God (Rom. 13:6). This view is based on Jesus' teachings in the SERMON ON THE MOUNT (Matt. 5–7) to not resist evil with force, to love one's enemies, and to turn the other cheek.

Those who subscribe to a two-kingdom theology consider it wrong for disciples of Jesus to engage in political lobbying, to try to influence government policies, or to protest government actions. In a sharp departure from what are typically considered the responsibilities of modern citizens in a democratic society, Anabaptist proponents of the two-kingdom model believe that they should not tell the government what to do. The Anabaptist understanding of two kingdoms differs significantly from the two-kingdom views of Saint Augustine (354–430) and Martin Luther (1483–1546).

In the last half of the 20th century, numerous critics and scholars in ASSIMILATED GROUPS rejected the sharp dualism of the two-kingdom approach for several reasons. They contended that it produced a passive NONRESISTANCE that did not challenge evil and violence in the world. It also hampered the church's public witness for truth and justice. Those who understood Jesus to call people to active PEACEMAKING and to confront oppression argued that the two-kingdom view was too simple and dualistic for citizens in democratic societies who had the opportunity, if not the responsibility, to not only witness to government but to shape its policies in ways that supported peace and alleviated injustice.

See also Nonconformity

Driedger and Kraybill (1994), Koop (2006), G. Schlabach (1993), J. H. Yoder (1973), http://peace .mennolink.org/articles/leobeyond.html, http:// personal2.stthomas.edu/gwschlabach/docs/2v1k.htm

Unions   *See* Labor Unions

United States

The first continuous ANABAPTIST presence in North America may be traced to Germantown (near Philadelphia) in 1683, when a few MENNONITES immigrated to the British colony founded by QUAKER leader William Penn (1644–1718). Many other Mennonites, AMISH, and BRETHREN immigrated to Pennsylvania from EUROPE in the first half of the 18th century, and eventually moved south and west to other states.

Anabaptist groups enjoyed freedom of religion and thrived in colonial America. Mennonite and Brethren groups were somewhat diversified in type, identity, and practices. The American Revolution caused difficulties for some Anabaptists and in part impelled a few Mennonites to migrate to CANADA in the two decades after the war.

From about 1700 to 1900, German-speaking Anabaptists (Amish, Brethren, HUTTERITES, and Mennonites) came to the United States from Switzerland, France, southern Germany, Prussia, and Russia. In the 1870s and 1880s, Kansas and other Great Plains states acquired a wide variety of Anabaptists with these origins, except for the Hutterites, who settled in the Dakota Territory. The Hutterites emigrated from Russia to the United States in the 1870s, but in the 1920s many of them moved to Canada. Most of these Anabaptist immigrants and their descendants held a vigorous belief in biblical PACIFISM. They often left Europe when governments or war threatened their pacifism or economic disruptions hurt their communities. They were attracted to a new country that offered RELIGIOUS LIBERTY and economic stability.

Until the 1900s Anabaptist groups in North America were primarily agricultural, conservative, and generally prosperous. Beginning in the mid-19th century, Brethren and Mennonites began to assimilate aspects of theology and culture from the wider society, such as EVANGELISM, EDUCATION, PUBLICATIONS, and other aspects of Protestant church life. ASSIMILATED GROUPS founded educational academies and colleges in the late 1800s and early 1900s to train leaders and members for a wider range of nonagricultural OCCUPATIONS.

TRADITIONAL GROUPS retained their rural lifestyle and conservative customs while making some adjustments to economic and technological necessities. The OLD ORDER MOVEMENT (1855–1901) consolidated the resistance to many changes under way in American society. The Amish made fewer concessions to technology than the Hutterites. Internal growth of the traditional groups increased dramatically in the mid-20th century.

Mission activity in North America in the 1900s spread Anabaptist congregations across a wide spectrum of ethnic groups. Drawn by educational and occupational opportunities, as well as SERVICE and MISSION, some rural Anabaptists, converts, and 20th-century immigrants settled in urban areas. By the dawn of the 21st century, Anabaptists worshiped in numerous languages and included people of Asian, European, South American, and African descent, as well as Native Americans.

Anabaptist groups encountered patriotic NATIONALISM in the United States, especially in times of war. Although their CONSCIENTIOUS OBJECTION to military service was usually respected, they encountered a growing tradition of civil religion—identifying God's will directly and uncritically with the behavior and ideals of the government. This sometimes blunted the Anabaptists' prophetic criticism of government policy and actions. In the 20th century, when the United States became the wealthiest and most powerful country in the world, some Anabaptists found it easy to shift their primary allegiance, obedience, and reverence toward nation rather than God and to blend the two together uncritically.

In the early 21st century the number of baptized members of Anabaptist churches in the U.S. is approximately 578,000. Pennsylvania, with over 150,000, has the largest number of any state.

C. Bowman (1995), GAMEO ("United States of America"), Haury (1981), Juhnke (1989), Juhnke and

Table 17	Anabaptist-Related Churches in the United States with 10,000 or More Baptized Members	
Group	Membership	Web site
Church of the Brethren	124,000	http://www.brethren.org
Mennonite Church USA	106,000	http://www.mennoniteusa.org
Amish	101,600	http://www.etown.edu/amishstudies
Mennonite Brethren Churches	35,875	http://www.usmb.org
Grace Brethren Churches, Fellowship of	30,400	http://www.fgbc.org
Brethren in Christ	23,000	http://www.bic-church.org
Church of God in Christ, Mennonite	14,500	http://churchofgodinchristmennonite.net
Apostolic Christian Church	12,700	http://www.apostolicchristian.org
Conservative Mennonite Conference	11,100	http://www.cmcrosedale.org
Brethren Church	10,400	http://www.brethrenchurch.org
Old Order Mennonites, Groffdale Conference	10,000	—

Note: Estimated number of adult baptized members. If children, youth, and nonmember participants are counted, the total population of some groups may be two to three times larger than the baptized membership.

Hunter (2004), Kraybill (1976), Kraybill and Hostetler (2001), MacMaster (1985), ME IV ("United States of America"), T. Schlabach (1988), Scott (1996), P. Toews (1996)

Unpartheyisches Gesangbuch

The longest enduring North American MENNO-NITE hymnal, *Unpartheyisches Gesangbuch* (Nonpartisan Hymnal) is used by the OLD ORDER MENNONITES in the United States for their worship services and by some Old Order Amish for their SINGINGS outside Sunday morning worship. Published by Mennonites in 1804 in Lancaster County, Pennsylvania, it remains in print in the 21st century. The songbook contains some hymns from the AUSBUND, which was published by Anabaptists in the 1500s, and is used by the AMISH in their worship services. Hymns by American authors as well as many Pietist hymns that are sung in German-speaking Lutheran and Reformed congregations also appear in the book.

See also Hymnody

Ruth (2001), P. Stoltzfus (1994), Weiler et al. (2004)

Urban Life

ANABAPTISM began in and around several preindustrial cities of central EUROPE in the early 16th century. However, religious PERSECUTION (especially in SWITZERLAND, GERMANY, and AUSTRIA) exterminated some members and drove others to isolated rural areas. Despite this push into the countryside, some Anabaptists continued to live and thrive in the city. Intense persecution in the NETHERLANDS ended by the 1560s, and MENNONITES survived in Dutch cities and rural areas. Mennonites have lived in Amsterdam from the beginnings of the Anabaptist Movement into the 21st century. Dutch Mennonites tended to live in towns, while Anabaptists of Swiss origin, except for the earliest years, lived in the countryside.

Although the AMISH and HUTTERITES have lived almost entirely in rural areas in Europe and North America from their origins until the present, ASSIMILATED GROUPS have lived in a variety of urban communities. Most of the assimilated groups initially settled in rural areas, but by the end of the 19th century they had begun MISSION efforts and founded congregations in small towns and cities.

Mennonites and BRETHREN developed different forms of COMMUNITY in urban settings as their congregations became more socially and occupationally diverse. Some groups renewed their interest in COMMUNAL LIVING; Reba Place Fellowship in Evanston, Illinois, was founded in 1957 when a close-knit church that met in homes began to practice economic sharing.

A survey (CMP 2006) found that at the beginning of the 21st century, about one-third of the members of MENNONITE CHURCH USA (40%), CHURCH OF THE BRETHREN (31%), and BRETHREN IN CHRIST (35%) live in a city of 10,000 people or more or in its adjacent suburbs. Mennonites in CANADA are more likely to reside in large cities (Winnipeg, Saskatoon, Vancouver, Kitchener-Waterloo) than Mennonites in the UNITED STATES, but Philadelphia, Chicago, and Los Angeles have sizable Mennonite communities. Mennonite congregations are also found in large Latin America urban areas, such as Guatemala City, Mexico City, and Tegucigalpa, Honduras.

BE II ("Urban Ministry"), CMP 2006, Driedger and Kauffman (1982), D. Friesen (2000), GAMEO ("Urban Church," "Urbanization"), Kraybill (2003c), ME V ("Urban Church," "Urbanization")

Victim Offender Reconciliation
Programs   *See* Restorative Justice

Vietnam War

This war in Southeast Asia (1963–1975) elicited diverse responses from ANABAPTIST groups. It caused intense debates among MENNONITES and BRETHREN in CANADA and the UNITED STATES. Some young American men performed ALTERNATIVE SERVICE, while others destroyed their draft cards and fled in protest to Canada. Some Mennonite and Brethren members served in the military, although the official statements of most of their churches discouraged military participation. Some adults protested the war by refusing to pay a portion of their TAXES or by paying them under protest. Other adults agreed with and supported the war effort. If drafted, AMISH and HUTTERITES generally performed alternative service as CONSCIENTIOUS OBJECTORS.

Ted Studebaker (1945–1971) and Chandler Edwards (1945–1969), conscientious objectors serving through Brethren Volunteer Service in Vietnam and Laos respectively, were killed while serving in peacemaking and development activities.

MENNONITE CENTRAL COMMITTEE (MCC) began to work in Vietnam in 1954 by helping with refugee resettlement and distributing material aid. MCC volunteer Daniel Amstutz Gerber (1940–1962) was captured in 1962 and never heard of again. Some MCC staff members stayed in the country during the war and were also active in postwar reconstruction.

BE II ("Vietnamese War"), Bush (1998b), GAMEO ("Gerber, Daniel Amstutz," "Vietnam," "Vietnam War [1954–75]"), Kreider and Goossen (1988), E. Martin (1978), ME V ("Vietnam," "Vietnam War"), Metzler (1985), Miller and Shenk (1982), P. Toews (1996)

Volhynian Mennonites

Also called the Swiss Volhynians, this ANABAPTIST group originated in SWITZERLAND. Along with many other Anabaptists in the mid-1600s, they moved to the German Palatinate and to areas in what is now northeastern FRANCE in order to escape PERSECUTION. After the Amish-Mennonite church SCHISM in 1693, the group joined the AMISH. In the late 1700s some of the families immigrated (via Galicia in Austria) to Volhynia in POLAND, which became a part of RUSSIA in 1795.

In Russia they came into contact with MENNONITES of Dutch, north German, and Prussian origins. Under the influence of these Mennonites and of PIETISM, they shed some of their distinctive Amish practices. However, they retained their folk and religious identity, including their German DIALECT (known as *Schweizer*), which originated in the Palatinate. When the Russia GOVERNMENT withdrew their exemption from military service and required that schools conduct lessons in Russian instead of German, the Swiss Volhynians began to consider emigration, as did other Mennonite groups.

Beginning in 1874 almost all of the Volhynians immigrated to Kansas, Nebraska, and the Dakota Territory. Although they adopted some of the folk culture of the other Russian Mennonites and joined their church conference organizations, their Swiss-origin dialect and distinctive surnames made them easily identifiable. Their complicated MIGRATION patterns and their contact with various political jurisdictions and with various groups of Mennonites and HUTTERITES make their history one of the most complex among North American Mennonite groups of European origin.

T. Schlabach (1988), M. Schrag (1974), Stahly (1989)

Voluntary Service

During WORLD WAR II many CONSCIENTIOUS OBJECTORS in the HISTORIC PEACE CHURCHES worked in government-approved ALTERNATIVE SERVICE programs in the UNITED STATES and CANADA as a substitute for military service. After the war various ANABAPTIST churches expanded SERVICE opportunities by creating programs whereby people could serve (for little or no salary) in various agricultural, social, medical, educational, and mission projects. The military draft continued in the United States until the 1970s, and many young men entered Voluntary Service between 1951 and 1973 as an alternative to military service.

Assimilated BRETHREN groups created the Brethren Service Committee (later called the BRETHREN SERVICE COMMISSION) in 1939 to administer alternative service programs during the war. In 1948 Brethren Volunteer Service was established with the goals of advocating justice, working for peace, serving basic human needs, and maintaining the integrity of creation.

Since 1948 thousands of volunteers have participated in CHURCH OF THE BRETHREN programs in and outside of North America. They have worked at projects in material relief, community development, EDUCATION, refugee resettlement, MENTAL HEALTH, and counseling. Beginning in the 1960s some service programs focused specifically on poverty-related needs in cities and on Native American reservations.

Assimilated MENNONITES founded MENNONITE CENTRAL COMMITTEE, an international relief, development, and service agency, in 1920. This agency sends workers, food, and material aid to people all over the world who suffer from poverty, oppression, and natural disasters. Numerous Anabaptist churches in the 21st century organize and promote voluntary service programs for various lengths of time for youth, adults, and the elderly in their ranks.

TRADITIONAL GROUPS of Mennonites and AMISH support CHRISTIAN AID MINISTRIES (founded in 1981), which has a larger component of material aid than either Brethren Volunteer Service or Mennonite Central Committee. Some conservative Anabaptist groups have also created voluntary service programs related to their MISSION outreach projects.

See also Brethren Disaster Ministries; Mennonite Disaster Service

BE II ("Brethren Volunteer Service"), GAMEO ("Voluntary Service"), J. Kreider (2001), ME V ("Voluntary Service"), J. Oyer (1970, 1996), http://www.mcc .org

Voting   *See* Political Participation

W

Walpot, Peter (1521–1578)

This HUTTERITE leader lived in Moravia during a period of relative tolerance, prosperity, and expansion. In 1565 the Moravian Hutterites choose Walpot as their primary bishop and the town of his residence, Neumühl, became the administrative center of Hutterite life.

Walpot wrote extensively to encourage Hutterite missionaries all over German-speaking lands, to counter claims by Lutherans and Calvinists, and to define Hutterite belief and practice. He wrote an instructional manual for the schools, which advocated principles of gentle discipline, meaningful rewards, evenhanded punishment, regular Bible instruction, and cleanliness. The theological themes of GELASSENHEIT and the biblical reasons for COMMUNAL LIVING were also greatly emphasized in his writings. In 1577 he wrote the *Article Book,* a lengthy justification of Hutterite theology and communal practices. Walpot was probably the author of the earliest known Hutterite sermons, some of which are still preached in Hutterite communities.

GAMEO ("Walpot, Peter L. [1521–1578]"), L. Gross (1980), ME IV ("Walpot, Peter")

War   *See* American Revolution; Civil War, U.S.; Conscientious Objectors; Historic Peace Churches; Iraq War; Pacifism; Vietnam War; World War I; World War II

War Tax Resistance   *See* Taxes

Wealth

The ANABAPTIST theology of community stresses spiritual unity and the sharing of material goods or MUTUAL AID among believers. Anabaptist groups often admonish members not to accumulate wealth, and especially not to flaunt it with displays of conspicuous consumption. Members are taught to be good stewards of wealth and to share it with others who are less fortunate. HUTTERITES stress this teaching by allowing virtually no personal property and requiring COMMUNAL LIVING.

As a consequence of religious tolerance and economic freedom in the NETHERLANDS, some Dutch MENNONITES accumulated considerable wealth in the 1600s. Some of this money was contributed to various groups in need, including their fellow believers who were persecuted in Switzerland, Germany, and France.

Anabaptists with Swiss origins experienced PERSECUTION for a longer period of time than did Mennonites in the Netherlands. They often had their property confiscated and were banished. Consequently they experienced some poverty and redistribution of wealth within the church. Mennonites in the late 1800s in Russia became quite prosperous in AGRICULTURE and industries, only to see their wealth disappear under communism in the 20th century.

For much of their history some Anabaptists accumulated wealth through successful agriculture and farm-related BUSINESSES. In the 20th century these groups witnessed a major diversification of OCCUPATIONS. North American Anabaptists today have a wide range of incomes, although most fall into the midrange with only a few at high levels. In a survey (CMP 2006) of ASSIMILATED GROUPS in the United States, 13% of CHURCH OF THE BRETHREN members, 11% of BRETHREN IN CHRIST members, and 15% of MENNONITE CHURCH USA members reported household incomes above $100,000. Many members place funds with Anabaptist-related foundations and investment companies offering options for socially responsible investing that excludes alcohol, arms manufacture, and environmentally destructive products, and favors activities that support ecological sustainability and social justice.

In addition to sharing their wealth through outright gifts to church mission and service organizations, some members provide low-interest loans to small entrepreneurs in developing countries. MENNONITE ECONOMIC DEVELOPMENT ASSOCIATES is a nonprofit organization that seeks to bring Christian values into the marketplace and businesses. One of their major emphases is providing capital and expertise to projects in less-developed countries and assistance in creating and sustaining small businesses in North America.

See also Anabaptist Foundation; Brethren in Christ Foundation; Church of the Brethren Benefit Trust; Mennonite Foundation; Mutual Aid

CMP 2006, GAMEO ("Mennonite Economic Development Associates [MEDA]," "Property," "Wealth"), Kauffman and Driedger (1991), Kauffman and Harder (1975), R. Loewen (2009), Lowry (2007), ME V ("Mennonite Economic Development Associates," "Property," "Wealth"), Urry (1985)

Weddings

Prior to the early 1900s, the weddings of many North American ANABAPTISTS took place in the bride's home, not in a church building. This practice gradually changed during the 20th century, and weddings increasingly took place in churches, especially among ASSIMILATED GROUPS. Among many TRADITIONAL GROUPS, weddings are still held at the home of the bride or a relative.

Weddings among traditional groups include few elements unique to the individuals. Instead, the ceremony is shaped by tradition and folk culture. For example, the AMISH and OLD ORDER MENNONITES follow certain specific patterns, such as the season of the year when weddings are held, where the bride and groom sit and stand during the service, which biblical passages are read, and which hymns are sung during the service. Conservative groups may have restrictions related to flowers and other accoutrements typical of the larger culture. Nevertheless, weddings are festive FAMILY occasions that typically involve meals and attendance by large extended families.

Wedding ceremonies among assimilated groups exhibit much variety. Some are conducted in churches, others at historic sites or other outdoor locations. Some ceremonies are very simple, while others conform to the expensive and elaborate styles found in the wider culture. Among assimilated groups, pastors often perform several premarital counseling sessions prior to performing wedding rites.

GAMEO ("Weddings"), J. Hoover (1990), D. Martin (2003), ME IV ("Weddings"), ME V ("Weddings"), Scott (1988)

Witness *See* Cinema

Women *See* Gender Roles

Women's Head Covering *See* Head Covering

World Council of Churches *See* Ecumenism

World War I

MENNONITES living in EUROPE suffered when the war began in August 1914. Some Mennonite farms in GERMANY and FRANCE became battlegrounds, and some of their young men abandoned their PACIFIST heritage and served in the armies.

ANABAPTISTS in the UNITED STATES, CANADA, and RUSSIA immediately drew the suspicion and hostility of their neighbors because they spoke the enemy's language (German) and because they held pacifist convictions, which prevented them from fighting. Russia allowed Mennonite men to serve in church-supported, noncombatant ALTERNATIVE SERVICE programs such as forestry and the medical corps, but no regular program of alternative service had been developed in the United States or Canada.

Canada generally granted full exemption from military service to CONSCIENTIOUS OBJECTORS from Anabaptist groups, based on laws going back to 1793 and to an exemption status negotiated with the 1870s immigrants from Russia. Some civil authorities, however, claimed that this exemption was valid only for baptized members of the church. Since many young men of draft age had not yet joined the church, some officials considered them to be eligible for the draft. Because their eligibility for exemption had to be established, some men initially spent time in jail. Negotiations eventually resolved this problem so that unbaptized young men were not drafted.

The experiences of Anabaptist men who were drafted in the United States varied. Some received farm furloughs to work in agriculture. Others reported to military camps for some type of noncombatant service. At the camps, some were harassed intensely. Those who refused to wear military uniforms or to engage in the noncombatant duty they were ordered to do were often court-martialed.

The CHURCH OF THE BRETHREN called a special conference in January 1918 in Goshen, Indiana. Delegates approved a strong directive for BRETHREN men not to join the military and not to wear the uniform. However, when conference leaders were threatened with prosecution by the War Department, they retracted the statement.

HUTTERITE brothers Joseph (d. 1918) and Michael Hofer (d. 1918) were drafted by the U.S. military. When they refused to sign admission papers or don army uniforms, they were held as military prisoners and tortured. They died in 1918 in a military hospital in Leavenworth, Kansas, from an illness that was likely a consequence of their torture. Their deaths illustrate the intense anti-German sentiment that was directed toward the Hutterites living in the United States, which impelled most of them (about 1,000) to migrate to Canada in the 1920s.

The military defeat of Russia led directly to the Communist Revolution, an event that had cataclysmic consequences for the over 100,000 Mennonites living there. The ensuing economic changes, famine, social chaos, and brutal repression of religious life placed Mennonites in a desperate situation. North American Mennonites, whose income soared during the war from the sale of their agricultural products, responded by creating MENNONITE CENTRAL COMMITTEE in 1920 in order to collect and distribute food to starving Mennonites and others in Russia. North American Mennonites also helped to organize and finance the migration of about 20,000 Mennonites from Russia to North American, primarily to Canada, after the revolution. Some Mennonite and Brethren young men participated in European reconstruction projects directed by the American Friends Service Committee after the war.

BE II ("World War I"), Clouse (1990), F. Epp (1974), GAMEO ("World War [1914–1918]"), M. Heisey (2003), Homan (1994), Juhnke (1986), ME V ("World War I"), Mock (2003)

World War II

This war had an especially devastating impact on MENNONITES in GERMANY and RUSSIA. Mennonites in Germany did not resist conscription. Some joined the armed forces, and many of these men died in Germany's defeat. Some German Mennonite civilians suffered under intense Allied bombing. The entire German Mennonite community of West Prussia—about 12,000 people—was displaced or killed by the Soviet invasion at the end of the war.

Mennonites in the Soviet Union had already suffered from Stalin's repression. By 1934–1935 all churches had been closed, and within a few years about half of all Mennonite families had lost their fathers through banishment, imprisonment, or execution. After the German army was driven out of the Ukraine, about 35,000 Mennonites fled to Germany. When Russia invaded Germany, about 23,000 of those Mennonites were forcibly returned to Russia, where many were imprisoned, were executed, or died from ill health. Some of the remaining 12,000 Russian Mennonites migrated to SOUTH AMERICA.

In North America the HISTORIC PEACE CHURCHES (BRETHREN, Mennonites, QUAKERS) were better prepared to negotiate with GOVERNMENTS for recognition of their pacifist convictions than they had been during WORLD WAR I. In the UNITED STATES, the Selective Service Act was passed in September 1940. It contained provisions for conscientious objectors that eventually resulted in the ALTERNATIVE SERVICE program called Civilian Public Service (CPS). More than 12,000 men participated in CPS programs in the areas of agriculture, forestry, and hospital work. Some Mennonite and Brethren women participated as volunteers, matrons, dieticians, and mental health workers. CPS programs in public mental hospitals spawned a series of Mennonite-operated mental hospitals soon after World War II.

About 7,500 Canadian Mennonites participated in alternative service (in road building, firefighting, or hospital work under government supervision) during World War II, and about 4,500 enlisted in the military. Some conscientious objectors remained on their farms, while others worked for limited pay in industries such as logging, sawmills, and food-processing plants, with their income having to be donated to the Red Cross. Those who joined the military were sometimes expelled from membership in their congregations, unless they confessed their transgression.

The percentages of men from the various ANABAPTIST groups who performed alternative service varied widely. Members of ASSIMILATED GROUPS more readily accepted military service. For example, less than 20% of drafted Brethren men chose CPS or noncombatant military service. In TRADITIONAL GROUPS, such as the AMISH, almost all drafted men chose alternative service.

After the war, MENNONITE CENTRAL COMMITTEE and BRETHREN SERVICE COMMISSION created programs that sent funds, material aid, and volunteers to help rebuild Europe.

See also Hospitals, Mental

BE II ("World War II"), Bush (1998b), D. Durnbaugh (1997a), M. Epp (2000), GAMEO ("Mental Health Facilities and Services, North America," "World War [1939–1945]—Germany," "World War [1939–1945]—Soviet Union"), Goossen (1997), M. Heisey (2003), J. Kreider (2001), Harry Loewen (2000), ME V ("Mental Health Facilities and Services," "World War II [Germany]," "World War II [Soviet Union]"), V. Neufeld (1983), C. Redekop (2001), Regehr (1996), E. Thiessen (2000), P. Toews (1996), http://www.alternativeser vice.ca

World Wide Web *See* Computer

Worship

The patterns of ANABAPTIST worship services are extremely varied in the 21st century. Hymn SINGING, PRAYER, BIBLE reading, and a sermon are typical and central features. Many congregations include a time for informal sharing that may include personal testimony, news, prayer requests, and responses to the sermon. The sermon, which usually includes practical admonitions, is the central event of most Anabaptist worship services.

Some TRADITIONAL GROUPS use a simple sequence of events in their worship services, which reflects the historical distrust of highly liturgical forms of worship. They sing hymns in a cappella style and listen to sermons preached by ordained men. RITUALS such as kneeling for prayer and segregated seating by sex are typical.

Among ASSIMILATED GROUPS, worship has been influenced by a variety of factors, including SUNDAY SCHOOLS, foreign MISSIONS, REVIVALISM, mainline Protestant liturgical patterns, and musical instruments. The switch to a salaried ministry, along with the increasing number of church-related publications and the creation of MENNONITE and BRETHREN colleges in the late 19th century, raised the educational level of both leaders and members in many assimilated congregations. THEOLOGICAL EDUCATION at seminaries and an appreciation of the fine arts (including dance) have also shaped worship patterns. Moreover, Pentecostalism and CHARISMATIC-style worship with clapping, raising hands to God, and praying aloud simultaneously are also typical in some groups and cultural regions.

In some congregations, traditional hymns have been replaced by simple Scripture songs. The use of contemporary Christian praise music in the worship services of many assimilated groups in the 21st century has had significant impact on the content and style of worship. Conflict occurs among some assimilated Mennonite and Brethren groups over gendered references to God, such as the use of strictly masculine or gender-neutral language.

Some assimilated groups incorporate aspects of the liturgical church calendar, such as the seasons of Lent, Pentecost, and Epiphany, into worship. These groups may also use or adapt the lectionary cycle of Bible texts that many

Protestant and Catholic groups use. HUT-
TERITE and AMISH groups follow their own
lectionary of Scripture texts, and some Brethren
and Mennonite churches follow no lectionary
pattern.

BE II ("Worship, Public"), D. Brown (1986), GAMEO
("Worship, Public"), *Hymnal* (1992), ME IV ("Worship,
Public"), ME V ("Worship"), Yoder, Kropf, and Slough
(2005)

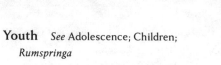

Youth *See* Adolescence; Children; *Rumspringa*

Directory of Groups

Entries in the main section of this encyclopedia provide information on each of the four major Anabaptist families and information on church groups with 5,000 or more baptized members. Entries in this section, the Directory of Groups, provide information on organized church groups with three or more congregations and/or 300 or more baptized members in North America. Some networks of independent congregations that are not formally organized are also included. In some cases similar churches with fewer than three congregations or 300 members are combined into a single entry. (The Table of Groups includes independent congregations that have at least 25 members.) The Directory of Groups includes long-established churches as well as those that formed through migration, mission, or service work or by an indigenous group affiliating with an Anabaptist church. Most churches that appear in the directory are identified with one of the four major Anabaptist families. A few have only a modest historical or present-day linkage and are loosely connected to an organized Anabaptist body.

Estimates of the number of congregations and members were gathered from various sources—primarily 2008 or 2009 official church directories and reports by knowledgeable informants who are members of the churches or work closely with them. Membership estimates refer to baptized members. If children, unbaptized youth, and nonmember participants are counted, the total population of a church group may in some cases be two or three times greater than the number of baptized members. This is especially true for traditional groups, whose members typically have large families. Among declining churches with an elderly membership, the actual number of participants may be fewer than the estimated membership.

Table 18   Presence of Churches by Anabaptist Family and Country/Region in North America

	Amish	Brethren	Hutterites	Mennonites
Canada	Yes	No	Yes	Yes
Caribbean	No	Yes	No	Yes
Central America	No	No	No	Yes
Mexico	No	No	No	Yes
United States	Yes	Yes	Yes	Yes

The directory is organized into five geographical sections: Canada, Caribbean, Central America, Mexico, and the United States. The Caribbean and Central America sections are organized by country. Within each country, the church groups are listed by their association with one of the four major families: Amish, Brethren, Hutterites, and Mennonites. If a church body has members in more than one country, separate membership estimates appear in the respective geographical sections of the directory. Web sites are listed at the end of each group's description, when available.

SECTION ONE: CANADA

AMISH-RELATED GROUPS

Old Order Amish
The Amish in Canada have about 2,450 baptized members and 34 congregations in 14 settlements, all of which are in Ontario. They use horse-and-buggy transportation, wear plain clothing, hold worship services in their homes, and speak the Pennsylvania German dialect in home and church. Some of the Canadian Amish keep in close contact with Amish communities in the United States.

Amish settlers from the Alsace region of France and southern Germany as well as a few from Pennsylvania began arriving in Ontario in 1824. In the late 1800s and early 1900s, some of the Amish joined Mennonite churches. Those who remained Amish became known as the Old Order. The 19th-century immigrants have four settlements and 11 congregations. In the 1950s and 1960s some Amish moved to Ontario from the United States. These immigrants have 10 settlements and 23 congregations. The Aylmer, Ontario, settlement is the home of Pathway Publishers, a major Amish publishing house. There are also many Amish congregations in the United States.

HUTTERITE-RELATED GROUPS

Dariusleut Hutterites
The Dariusleut, one of four Hutterite groups, formed in Russia in 1860 under the leadership of Darius Walter. Hutterites do not have private property. They live in rural self-contained colonies, which typically own several thousand acres of land. More moderate than the Lehrerleut, the Dariusleut are the most culturally diverse of the four Hutterite groups. They have about 160 colonies in North America. Of the nearly 140 colonies in Canada, over 100 are in Alberta. This group also has colonies in the United States.

Lehrerleut Hutterites
This is the most conservative and homogeneous of the Hutterite groups. The Lehrerleut formed about 1877 after they migrated from Russia to the United States under the leadership of Jacob Wipf. Hutterites do not have private property. They live in rural self-contained colonies, which typically own several thousand acres of land. The Lehrerleut have 140 colonies in North America. Over 100 of them are located in Canada, in the provinces of Alberta and Saskatchewan. This group also has colonies in the United States.

Schmiedeleut Hutterites, Gibb Group
The Schmiedeleut formed in 1859 in Russia when Michael Waldner (1823–1889) reinstituted the practice of communal property. They were a single group from their origin until they divided after an internal dispute in 1992. The Gibb Group, so-named because a non-Hutterite

banker whose surname was Gibb supported their separation from the Kleinsasser Group, is occasionally called the Committee Hutterites. Although the Gibb Group is more conservative in cultural practice than the Kleinsasser Group, the two Schmiedeleut branches are the most progressive of the four Hutterite communities. Twice as large as the Kleinsasser Group, the Gibb Group has 120 colonies in North America, nearly half of which are in Canada (Manitoba). The group also has colonies in the United States.

Schmiedeleut Hutterites, Kleinsasser Group

The Schmiedeleut formed in 1859 in Russia when Michael Waldner (1823–1889) reinstituted the practice of communal property. They were a single group from 1859 until 1992, when they divided following an internal dispute. Jacob Kleinsasser (1922–) was the senior elder of all of the Schmiedeleut colonies until that time, when his leadership was rejected by a majority of the colonies' council of ministers. He then formed his own affiliation, which became known as the Kleinsasser Group. Although there were many complicated factors in the division, Kleinsasser's progressive views on the use of English, musical instruments, missions, and more advanced technology contributed to the separation. The Kleinsasser Group has 51 colonies in Canada, all of which are in Manitoba. This group also has colonies in the United States.

MENNONITE-RELATED GROUPS

Beachy Amish Mennonite Church

With its roots in the Old Order Amish Church, the Beachy Amish Mennonite Church formed in the United States in the 1920s. Several Canadian Amish congregations affiliated with the Beachy Amish. Unlike the Old Order Amish, the Beachy Amish use automobiles and public electricity, worship in meetinghouses, use English in their church services, and engage in mission efforts in other countries. The eight Beachy Amish congregations in Canada have a total of about 225 members; four of these congregations are mission endeavors to Ojibwa people in northwestern Ontario. Four other similar congregations include two that belong to the Maranatha Amish Mennonites, and two that identify themselves as independent Amish Mennonite churches. The total membership of the 12 churches is about 500. This group has related congregations in Belize, Costa Rica, El Salvador, Nicaragua, and the United States.

Bergthal Mennonite Church of La Crete

This group, located near La Crete, in Alberta's far north, was part of the Kanadier immigration of tradition-minded Mennonites who moved from Russia to Manitoba in the 1870s. It was established in 1957 by Bergthalers from Saskatchewan. This group is similar to, but separate from, the Saskatchewan Bergthalers. It has largely made the transition from German to English and has a mainstream evangelical emphasis. Traditional Mennonite practices have mostly disappeared, except that in some congregations the ministers are elected from within the congregation and are unsalaried. Its four congregations with some 1,000 members are located in northern Alberta. The Bergthalers of La Crete associate with the Sommerfeld Mennonite Church in Manitoba and the Chortitzer Mennonite Conference.

Bergthal Mennonite Church of Saskatchewan

This group was part of the Kanadier migration of tradition-minded Mennonites from the Bergthal Colony in Russia who came to Manitoba in the 1870s. The Bergthal Mennonite community near Saskatoon, Saskatchewan, was established in the 1890s and has five congregations and about 800 members. These churches have largely made the transition from German to English and have a mainstream evangelical emphasis. Traditional Mennonite practices have faded, except that in some congregations the ministers are elected from within the congregation and are unsalaried. The Bergthalers of Saskatchewan associate with the Sommerfeld Mennonite Church in Manitoba and the Chortitzer Mennonite Conference.

Brethren in Christ

The Brethren in Christ emerged in the late 1770s in eastern Pennsylvania. They blend Mennonite-Anabaptist influences with the Pietist strains of the German Baptist Brethren and United Brethren. As early as 1788 some Brethren in Christ moved to Ontario, where they became known as Tunkers (from the German *tunken*, "to dip") because they baptized by immersion. They have about 3,600 members in 48 congregations, mostly in Ontario. The Brethren in Christ support Mennonite Central Committee, participate in Mennonite World Conference, and have active mission projects around the world. This group has related congregations in Cuba, the Dominican Republic, Honduras, Mexico, Nicaragua, and the United States. Web site: http://www.bic-church.org

Charity Christian Fellowship

This network of churches formed in 1982 in eastern Pennsylvania. Their leader, Moses Stoltzfus (1946–), came from Amish background. Members come from various plain Anabaptist groups, and they and the congregations resemble conservative Mennonites in many ways. Rather fundamentalist in doctrine and charismatic in expression, they practice footwashing and the holy kiss. Members wear modest dress, and women wear prayer coverings. They aggressively seek to convert people from traditional Anabaptist groups as well as from outside these circles. The Fellowship has 11 congregations (about 250 members) in three provinces: Alberta, Manitoba, and Ontario. The group also has congregations in the United States and some mission projects outside North America. Web site: http://www.charity ministries.org

Chortitzer Mennonite Conference

Members of this group descended from immigrants from the Bergthal Colony in Russia who came to Canada in the 1870s. This church, with some 1,700 members in 15 congregations, is located primarily in the Steinbach area of Manitoba, although there are two congregations in British Columbia, one in Saskatchewan, and one in Alberta. Some of the members come from Old Colony Mennonite Church background.

A few of the Chortitzer congregations still use German in their worship services, and the group has a radio broadcast in Low German directed to traditional Mennonites living in or returning from Latin America. Most of the congregations have shifted to English. The group has a predominant mainstream evangelical theological orientation. Some of the congregations hire trained pastors, while others continue to ordain lay ministers. The Chortitzer Mennonite Conference supports Steinbach Bible College in collaboration with Evangelical Mennonite Conference and Evangelical Mennonite Mission Conference. Web site: http:// www.chortitzer.com

Christian Anishinabec Fellowship

This group originated with an independent mission outreach in Red Lake, Ontario, that began in 1938. It was formerly known as the Northern Light Gospel Mission Conference, which was formed in 1965 by U.S. Mennonites as an outreach and church-planting program to reach Native people on northern reserves in Ontario and Minnesota. The Christian Anishinabec Fellowship was known as the Native Mennonite Conference from 1990 to 1996. By 1997 all of the former Northern Light Gospel Mission Conference churches had either become member congregations of the Christian Anishinabec Fellowship or continued as unaffiliated Mennonite churches. The group has eight congregations with 100 members.

Church of God in Christ, Mennonite

This church began in 1859 in the United States under the leadership of John Holdeman (1832–1900), who left the Mennonite Church to begin a church of his own that was stricter and held more firmly to older Mennonite practices. Holdeman's church spread to Canada in 1881, when many members of the Kleine Gemeinde in Manitoba joined it. The Holdeman Mennonites maintain a sharp separation from the outside world by their distinctive dress, rejection of worldly entertainment, and shunning of ex-members. The Church of God in Christ, Mennonite teaches the doctrine of the one true church of Christ, which emphasizes the succession of true doctrine over the centuries. The group has about 5,000 members and 50 congregations in eight Canadian provinces, with the largest concentrations in Alberta and Manitoba. It has related congregations in Belize, the Dominican Republic, El Salvador, Guatemala, Haiti, Jamaica, Mexico, and the United States.

Conservative Mennonite Church of Ontario

This group formally organized in 1960 when it withdrew from the main body of assimilated Mennonites in Ontario to form a more conservative church that upheld traditional Mennonite practices on nonconformity to the larger world—plain dress, and the rejection of radio, television, and secular entertainment. Initially the church was part of the Nationwide Mennonite Fellowship, but it separated from the Fellowship in the early 1990s. It blends plain dress, a traditional lifestyle, and an evangelical emphasis in its teaching. The Conservative Mennonite Church has 10 congregations in Ontario with some 625 members. It has mission projects in other countries and has established three congregations in India.

Conservative Sommerfeld Mennonite Churches

The congregations in this group of Sommerfeld Mennonite churches are more conservative than the Reinländ Mennonites, who withdrew from the Sommerfeld Mennonite Church in Manitoba in 1958. The Conservative Sommerfelders are similar to some of the Old Colony Mennonite churches. They have retained the German language in their worship and sing a cappella. Women wear head coverings and modest, simple dress. The eight congregations, with 2,000 members, are located in Saskatchewan, Alberta, and Ontario. The largest concentration is in the La Crete (Alberta) area, where there are four congregations with over 1,000 members.

Eastern Pennsylvania Mennonite Church

This church began in eastern Pennsylvania in 1968, when about 40 conservative leaders withdrew from the Lancaster Mennonite Conference over issues related to dress, television, and other cultural changes. The Eastern Pennsylvania Mennonite Church developed a more conservative discipline and continues to uphold traditional Mennonite standards of doctrine, dress, and practice. Some Old Order Mennonites eventually joined this group because it held Sunday schools. In 1971 the Eastern Pennsylvania Mennonite Church assumed responsibility for a mission church established by the Nationwide Mennonite Fellowship in northern British Columbia. Four congregations with over 200 members developed from this mission church. In addition to the congregations in Pennsylvania, this group also has congregations in the Bahamas and Guatemala.

Evangelical Mennonite Conference

This group stems from the Kleine Gemeinde founded in Russia in 1812 and transplanted to Manitoba in 1874. The group adopted the name Evangelical Mennonite Church in 1952 and Evangelical Mennonite Conference in 1959. It has 7,000 members in 60 congregations, the majority of which are in Manitoba. Evangelical Mennonite Conference views Scripture as its final authority for faith and practice and promotes discipleship based on the life of Christ and the teaching of Scripture. The group baptizes upon confession of faith and seeks to live out its faith together as a church family. It has both an evangelical and an Anabaptist identity, supports several educational programs, and cooperates with numerous inter-Mennonite agencies. Web site: http://www.emconf.ca

Evangelical Mennonite Mission Conference

Ancestors of this group were part of a migration from Russia to Manitoba in the 1870s. The group began in 1937 as a revivalist, evangelical division from the more traditional Sommerfeld Mennonite Church. It adopted the name Evangelical Mennonite Mission Conference in 1959. The majority (16) of its 27 congregations (4,300 members) are located in Manitoba. Some congregations still use German in their worship services. Evangelical Mennonite Mission Conference is very active in mission work among Old Colony Mennonites in Mexico and those returning to Canada from Mexico. This group has related congregations in Belize, Mexico, and the United States. Web site: http://www.emmc.ca

Kleine Gemeinde

The roots of the Kleine Gemeinde ("small church") reach back to a reform movement in Russia in 1812. Members migrated to Manitoba and Nebraska in the 1870s. In 1948 many of the more traditional members in Canada moved to Mexico, and eventually some immigrated to Belize. The progressive-minded majority who stayed in Canada formed what became Evangelical Mennonite Conference in 1959. In the 1980s some of the Kleine Gemeinde families returned to Canada and eventually established congregations in four provinces: Alberta, Manitoba, Nova Scotia, and Ontario. The group has about 700 members in eight congregations. Some of the congregations worship in German and others in English. Members practice a traditional lifestyle, and most parents send their children to church-operated schools. This group has related congregations in Belize, Mexico, and the United States.

Markham-Waterloo Mennonite Conference

This group of Swiss–south German origin traces its roots to the beginning of the Old Order Movement in Ontario in 1889 that opposed Sunday schools and the use of English in church services. The conference was part of the Old Order Mennonite Church until the two groups separated in 1939 over the use of automobiles, electricity, and the English language in church services—practices that the Markham-Waterloo Conference eventually adopted. The Markham-Waterloo Mennonites still wear plain dress and live simply, practices that are similar to those of other Old Order Mennonite communities in the United States with whom they maintain fellowship. This body of Mennonites has about a dozen congregations and 1,400 members in Ontario.

Mennonite Brethren Churches, Canadian Conference of

With some 37,000 members, this group has become the largest body of Mennonites in Canada. The Mennonite Brethren trace their roots to a renewal movement in Russian Mennonite communities in the 1860s. The first Mennonite Brethren congregation in Canada was established in the 1880s, but later emigrants from Russia in the 1920s gave the Mennonite

Brethren a lasting presence in Canada. With about 250 congregations in eight provinces, members worship in more than a dozen different languages. This denomination operates numerous mission and education programs and also cooperates in many areas with the United States Conference of Mennonite Brethren. The denomination emphasizes a strong evangelical outreach and personal piety that is similar in many ways to mainstream evangelicalism. This group also has congregations in the United States. Web site: http://www.mbconf.ca

Mennonite Church Canada

This is the second largest body of Mennonites in Canada, with about 33,000 members in 220 congregations. The denomination formed in 2002 when the Mennonite Church and the General Conference Mennonite Church united. Thus members of Mennonite Church Canada trace their roots to Russian, Swiss, and German immigrations in different time periods. This denomination has congregations in seven provinces. It is affiliated with several colleges and universities as well as Associated Mennonite Biblical Seminary in Elkhart, Indiana. Members actively support the relief and service projects of Mennonite Central Committee. Mission activities have resulted in some two dozen congregations whose members have Asian or Hispanic backgrounds. The denomination partners with Mennonite Church USA on a number of educational and publishing endeavors. Web site: http://www.mennonitechurch.ca

Mennonite Churches, Independent (Assimilated)

In addition to the larger Mennonite bodies, there are about 13 independent Mennonite congregations (with an estimated 2,000 members) that are no longer affiliated with a larger Mennonite body. Some of these congregations were at one time affiliated with Mennonite Church Canada but for a variety of reasons left the main body.

Mennonite Churches, Independent (Traditional)

There are nine plain-dressing, car-driving conservative Mennonite congregations in Canada that are independent of each other and unaffiliated with a larger group. Many of the 425 members in these churches come from Swiss–south German backgrounds.

Midwest Mennonite Fellowship

This group is part of a network of some 30 congregations in Canada and the United States that formed in the mid-1970s to maintain conservative Mennonite principles of faith and life with some flexibility regarding changing social conditions. It is similar to the Nationwide Fellowship Churches, from which it broke in 1976, but unlike that group the Midwest Mennonites permit radios. Many members come from the more traditional Markham-Waterloo Mennonite Conference. Members wear plain clothing but use English in their church services, drive cars, and engage in evangelism. The group has about 950 members in 10 congregations, all but one of which are in Ontario. This group has related congregations in Mexico and the United States.

Nationwide Fellowship Churches

In a reaction to the acculturation—especially related to dress and the use of television—that was occurring in many mainstream Mennonite churches in the late 1950s and 1960s, a number of congregations from different Mennonite backgrounds began affiliating together. This network of congregations, whose members maintain a conservative lifestyle and hold traditional doctrinal beliefs, eventually became known as the Nationwide Fellowship

Churches. In time other congregations with Dutch-Russian background (Old Colony, Sommerfeld, Kleine Gemeinde) joined this group of Swiss–south German origin. Nationwide Fellowship Churches have nearly 100 congregations in North America. A total of 23 congregations with 1,000 members are located in six Canadian provinces, with concentrations in Alberta and Ontario. This group has related congregations in the Dominican Republic, Guatemala, Mexico, and the United States.

Northwest Mennonite Conference

Swiss Mennonites and Amish Mennonites from the United States who settled in Alberta in the late 1800s and early 1900s helped to form this group. Formerly affiliated with the Northwest Conference of the Mennonite Church and later with Mennonite Church Canada, Northwest Mennonite Conference became independent in 2003. All 14 of its congregations (1,100 members) are located in Alberta.

Old Colony Mennonite Church

The name of this group traces back to 19th-century Russia. Its people descended from Chortitza, the oldest Mennonite colony founded in Russia (now Ukraine) in 1789. The group immigrated to Canada in the 1870s. Many members moved from Canada to Mexico in the 1920s because of English educational requirements in western Canadian schools. In the last decades of the 20th century many members returned to Canada. Old Colony churches in Canada continue to resist acculturation and remain somewhat isolated from other Mennonite groups. Distinctive plain dress has been part of their traditional lifestyle, but that has been changing in the 21st century. Members drive cars and use electricity. A Low German dialect is spoken in worship services, with singing and Bible reading in High German. Lay ministers provide congregational leadership.

In Manitoba the Old Colony Mennonite congregations divided in 2003. The progressive-minded group, which kept the Old Colony name, accepted a number of changes, including the use of more English in church services. It is now independent. (See Old Colony Mennonite Church, Manitoba.) In order to distinguish itself from that group, the more conservative group calls itself the German Old Colony Mennonite Church, although it remains a part of the larger Old Colony Mennonite Church in Canada.

There are about 9,000 Old Colony members in 20 congregations in five Canadian provinces. The largest concentrations are in Ontario and Alberta, with smaller communities in Manitoba, Saskatchewan, and British Columbia. This group has related congregations in Belize, Mexico, and the United States.

Old Colony Mennonite Church, Manitoba

In 2003 the Old Colony Mennonites in Manitoba divided, and this progressive-minded group became independent. It adopted some practices, such as the use of English in church services, that remain taboo for the more traditional Old Colony congregations. The Old Colony Mennonite Church of Manitoba has approximately 500 members in three congregations.

Old Order Mennonite Church

The Old Order Mennonites formed in Ontario in 1889. The emergence of Old Order groups in Ontario was part of the larger Old Order Movement among Mennonites of Swiss background in North America in the 1880s and 1890s. Old Order groups objected to the growing use of English and Sunday schools in Mennonite churches. Old Order Mennonites are similar to the Amish in that they use horse-and-buggy transportation, wear distinctive plain clothing, and speak Pennsylvania German. Unlike the Amish, they worship in meeting-houses, and the men do not wear beards. The Old Order Mennonite Church in Canada has about 3,200 baptized members in six different communities in Ontario. The total population, including children, exceeds 6,500. The group has 36 congregations and 21 meeting-houses, some of which are shared by two congregations.

Old Order Mennonite Church (David Martin)

This group branched off from the Old Order Mennonite Church in 1917 under the leadership of David Martin (1873–1959). It practices a stricter shunning of excommunicated members than the other Old Order Mennonites and retains the use of horse-and-buggy transportation and horse-drawn farm equipment. No electric lights are used in homes, but propane gas is used for kitchen appliances. For the many large businesses owned by members, computers and advanced manufacturing technology are permitted, but diesel engines are used to generate electricity. Members of the group send their children to public schools but generally do not accept government payments for insurance, health care, or pensions. The David Martin Mennonites have six congregations and about 500 members, all in Ontario.

Orthodox Mennonite Church

Members of this group broke off from the David Martin Old Order Mennonite Church in 1957 under the leadership of Elam Martin (1907–1987). After subsequent internal divisions, some members returned to the original church. In the 1980s, when more technology came to be accepted in the Old Order Mennonite Church, some of its members joined the Orthodox Mennonites. The group has about 400 members and four congregations, all in Ontario. Like other Old Order Mennonites, members drive horse and buggy, wear plain clothing, speak Pennsylvania German, and worship in meetinghouses. One distinction is that men wear beards. In 2007 a splinter group known as the Westbourne Orthodox Mennonites, consisting of about a dozen families, moved to Manitoba. The Orthodox Mennonite Church has related congregations in the United States.

Reinländ Mennonite Church (Manitoba)

This group separated from the Sommerfeld Mennonite Church in Manitoba in 1958. Of Russian background but not Old Colony, the members speak Low German, wear plain dress, and maintain a traditional lifestyle of separation from the dominant culture. However, they have adopted Sunday schools and youth meetings. Unsalaried lay ministers lead the congregations under the direction of a bishop. The church has about 3,000 members in seven congregations, five in Manitoba and two in Alberta. In 1979 a large Old Colony Mennonite settlement in Mexico affiliated with the Reinländ Mennonites, and many of the members of the group in Canada are recent immigrants from the Mexico settlement. The Old Bergthal Mennonites (two congregations and about 200 members), which divided from the Bergthal Mennonite Church of Saskatchewan in 1983, relate to the Reinländ Mennonite Church. This group has affiliated congregations in Mexico and the United States.

Reinländ Mennonite Fellowship Church (Ontario)

This group formed in 1994 when it broke away from the New Reinländ Mennonite Church in Ontario to conserve traditional Old Colony practices. (The New Reinländ Mennonite Church—one congregation, 250 members—branched off from the Old Colony Mennonites in Ontario in 1984.) The Reinländ Mennonite Fellowship Church, with three congregations and 1,000 members, is based in Ontario. In many ways the lifestyle of its members is similar to that of Old Colony Mennonites, but the dress of the women is not as distinctive. The group uses some English in its church services. It cooperates with the Reinländ Mennonite Church in Manitoba.

Sommerfeld Mennonite Church

Ancestors of this church were part of the Bergthal Colony that migrated from Russia to Manitoba in the 1870s. In 1894 the Sommerfelders separated from the more progressive-minded Bergthalers in Manitoba and retained a traditional lifestyle. The group remained rather conservative until the last half of the 20th century, when Sunday school, youth meetings, musical instruments, and English hymnals were adopted. Restrictions on dress have also declined. Unsalaried lay ministers serve each congregation under the supervision of a bishop. The 13 congregations with some 2,300 members are located in southern Manitoba. This group has related congregations in Mexico and the United States.

SECTION TWO: CARIBBEAN

Bahamas

See Bahamas *in the Entries section*

Cuba

MENNONITE-RELATED GROUPS

Brethren in Christ Cuban Missionary Society (Sociedad Misionera Cubano Hermanos en Cristo)

Several missionary efforts from the United States initiated churches in Cuba in the 1950s, including the Brethren in Christ in 1954. Most missionaries left the country after Fidel Castro assumed power in 1959, but the Brethren in Christ Cuban Missionary Society had been legally registered by 1959 and remained in the country. It has about 3,275 members and an additional 5,000 participants that meet in 75 congregations and worship centers. There are related Brethren in Christ congregations in Canada, the Dominican Republic, Honduras, Mexico, Nicaragua, and the United States.

Mennonite Church in Cuba (Iglesia Menonita en Cuba)

This church formed in 2008 as a result of contact with Canadian Mennonites over the previous two decades. The Cuban leaders have a strong commitment to an Anabaptist vision and the model of the early church described in Acts. The group has numerous cell groups and three congregations with 50 members and other participants. It is affiliated with Mennonite Church Canada.

Dominican Republic

BRETHREN-RELATED GROUPS

Church of the Brethren (Iglesia de los Hermanos Dominicana)

The Church of the Brethren began mission efforts in the Dominican Republic following Hurricane David in 1979. It has some 1,700 members in 20 congregations and numerous mission outposts. A micro-loan community development project involves about 500 people related to the congregations. In addition, the group supports health education and a medical clinic. The Church of the Brethren also has congregations in Haiti, Puerto Rico, and the United States.

MENNONITE-RELATED GROUPS

Bethel Brethren in Christ Church (Iglesia Bethel Hermanos en Cristo)
This group, established by the Brethren in Christ in 1997, has about 300 members and several hundred participants in 15 congregations and worship centers. The Brethren in Christ Church has related congregations in Canada, Cuba, Honduras, Mexico, Nicaragua, and the United States.

Church Of God in Christ, Mennonite
The Church of God in Christ, Mennonite has established three congregations and five mission outreach sites with a total membership of 50. The group has related congregations in Belize, Canada, El Salvador, Guatemala, Haiti, Jamaica, Mexico, and the United States.

Conference of the Dominican Evangelical Mennonites (Conferencia Evangélica Menonita Dominicana)
This group was started by the Fellowship of Evangelical Churches (formerly Evangelical Mennonite Conference) in the mid-1940s. It has about 2,450 members in 60 congregations.

Divine Light National Assembly of Mennonites (Concilio Nacional Menonita Faro Divino)
The Divine Light National Assembly was established by missionaries from Eastern Mennonite Missions in Pennsylvania; however, the group is no longer affiliated with that mission agency. The group has about 2,500 members in 23 congregations.

Dominican Evangelical Mennonite Council (Consejo Evangélico Menonita Dominicana)
This group was started by missionaries from Eastern Mennonite Missions in Pennsylvania. It has about 275 members in six congregations.

Koinonia Fellowship of Churches
This cluster of six congregations (400 members) is the result of mission efforts by Koinonia Fellowship of Churches based in eastern Pennsylvania and New Jersey. The group had been affiliated with Lancaster Mennonite Conference before it formed as an independent group in 2002.

Nationwide Fellowship Churches
Nationwide Fellowship Churches, based in the United States, began mission work in the Dominican Republic in 1981. The Fellowship has five congregations with about 100 members. Other congregations related to this group are in Canada, Guatemala, Mexico, and the United States.

Grenada

MENNONITE-RELATED GROUPS

Olive Branch Mennonite Missions
This group, affiliated with Keystone Mennonite Fellowship based in eastern Pennsylvania, has three congregations in Grenada with a membership of about 50.

Haiti

BRETHREN-RELATED GROUPS

Church of the Brethren
A Church of the Brethren mission project was initiated around 2000 by some Haitian Brethren congregations in Miami. The first members were baptized in 2003. There are five Brethren-related congregations and additional outreach sites with some 50 members. The Church of the Brethren also has congregations in the Dominican Republic, Puerto Rico, and the United States.

MENNONITE-RELATED GROUPS

Assembly of Grace (Assemblée da la Grace)
This group began in 1990 through the efforts of Haitian pastors to establish indigenous churches. The leaders were influenced by Mennonites in the Sonlight Mission, Mennonite Central Committee, and Florida Mennonite churches. The group, which has 25 congregations and 2,375 members, maintains an affiliation with Mennonite World Conference.

Church of God in Christ, Mennonite (Église de Dieu en Christ Mennonite, Haiti)
The Church of God in Christ, Mennonite conducted disaster relief work in Haiti after Hurricane Flora in 1963, and missionaries followed in 1968. There are 17 congregations and about 600 members in Haiti. The group has related congregations in Belize, Canada, the Dominican Republic, El Salvador, Guatemala, Jamaica, Mexico, and the United States.

Gospel Light Chapel
The Gospel Light Chapel, which grew from a mission effort in 1978, has 14 congregations and about 700 members. It is supported by the Palm Grove Mennonite Church of Sarasota, Florida, and is affiliated with the Conservative Mennonite Conference.

Mennonite Sonlight Mission
This group began as an indigenous Haitian church in 1980. Several Conservative Mennonite churches, primarily from Ohio and Pennsylvania, support Mennonite Sonlight Mission, which has five congregations and 200 members.

Jamaica

MENNONITE-RELATED GROUPS

Jamaica Mennonite Church
The Jamaica Mennonite Church began when missionaries from Virginia Mennonite Board of Missions began mission outreach there in 1955. The group has 675 members in 13 congregations scattered across the country.

Puerto Rico

BRETHREN-RELATED GROUPS

Church of the Brethren (Iglesia de los Hermanos, Puerto Rico)
Puerto Rico has seven congregations (375 members) affiliated with the Church of the Brethren. The oldest was founded in 1948. Three began in the 1980s, two in the 1990s, and one in

2004. The Church of the Brethren also has congregations in the Dominican Republic, Haiti, and the United States.

MENNONITE-RELATED GROUPS

Conference of the Mennonite Churches of Puerto Rico (Convención de las Iglesias Menonitas de Puerto Rico)
Founded in 1947 as an outgrowth of work by Mennonite Board of Missions based in Elkhart, Indiana, this group was officially registered in Puerto Rico as an independent Latin American church in 1988. In the 1990s several congregations separated from the conference to form the Evangelical Mennonite Mission of the Caribbean. The Conference of the Mennonite Churches of Puerto Rico has 11 congregations and about 400 members. It is also engaged in mission and community service work in the Dominican Republic.

Evangelical Mennonite Mission of the Caribbean (Misión Evangélica Menonita del Caribe)
This group began in the 1990s when some congregations associated with the Conference of the Mennonite Churches of Puerto Rico left to form their own group. It has five congregations and about 125 members.

Trinidad and Tobago

MENNONITE-RELATED GROUPS

Mennonite Church of Trinidad and Tobago
The Mennonite Church of Trinidad and Tobago was formed in 1974 after missionaries from Virginia Mennonite Conference began radio broadcasts and worked with leprosy victims in 1969. The church, composed of people from various national and cultural backgrounds, has six congregations and 275 members.

SECTION THREE: CENTRAL AMERICA

Belize

MENNONITE-RELATED GROUPS

Beachy Amish Mennonite Church
Immediately following the destruction caused by Hurricane Hattie in 1961, Amish Mennonite Aid, a Beachy Amish relief agency, began reconstruction work in Belize and organized the first Beachy Amish Mennonite congregation in 1962. This group has six congregations with some 175 members. This group has related congregations in Canada, Costa Rica, El Salvador, Nicaragua, and the United States.

Belize Evangelical Mennonite Church (Iglesia Evangélica Menonita de Belice)
The Belize Evangelical Mennonite Church began in 1973 as a result of service and mission activities of Mennonite Central Committee and Eastern Mennonite Missions. These agencies worked with the Low German–speaking Mennonite colonists in the early 1960s. Incorporated in 1981, the Belize Evangelical Mennonite Church has 10 congregations and 425 members. Although the official language of Belize is English, the church holds worship services in English, Spanish, and Garifuna, or a combination of these languages.

Caribbean Light and Truth

Twelve congregations (150 members) belong to this group, which began in the 1970s through mission efforts of Salem Mennonite Church in Keota, Iowa.

Evangelical Mennonite Mission Conference

Based in Manitoba, Canada, this group established a congregation near the Blue Creek colony (Old Colony Mennonite Church) in 1966 and near the Spanish Lookout colony (Kleine Gemeinde) in 1995 in order to evangelize colony members. In 2002 the group established a congregation, Gospel Fellowship Chapel, near Shipyard. Evangelical Mennonite Mission Conference has 475 members in three congregations. This group has related congregations in Canada, Mexico, and the United States. Web site: http://www.emmc.ca

Kleine Gemeinde

Similar in background to the Old Colony Mennonites, the Kleine Gemeinde ("small church") also left Mexico and settled in Belize in 1958. There they founded a colony (a block of hundreds of adjacent acres of land) known as Spanish Lookout. (Of Dutch-Russian background, the Kleine Gemeinde had settled in Canada in the 1870s and then immigrated to Mexico in 1948.) Members speak Low German and wear traditional clothing but use modern technology and have an evangelical religious view that has attracted some Old Colony Mennonite converts. The group has five congregations (about 800 members) in two colonies: Blue Creek (formerly a colony of the Old Colony Mennonites) and Spanish Lookout. This group has related congregations in Canada, Mexico, and the United States.

Old Colony Mennonite Church (Horse)

These traditional Mennonites of Russian origin settled in Canada and later moved to Mexico in 1922 to avoid assimilation in Canada. They entered Belize (then British Honduras) in 1958 and established two agricultural colonies (large blocks of hundreds of adjacent acres) known as Shipyard and Blue Creek (no longer Old Colony). In the 21st century the group has about 2,050 members in three colonies: Shipyard, Indian Creek, and Little Belize. Members speak Low German, wear distinctive dress, reject electricity, use steel-wheeled tractors for farming, and use horse-and-buggy transportation. Other Old Colony congregations are in Canada, Mexico, and the United States.

Old Order Mennonites, Hoover Church

The Hoover Mennonite Church, based in Scottsville, Kentucky, is one of several groups stemming from a 1944 division in the Stauffer Mennonite Church in Snyder County, Pennsylvania. This horse and buggy church is one of the most restrictive Old Order groups with respect to the use of technology—forbidding any use of internal combustion engines. The Hoover Church in Belize has three communities: Springfield, Upper Barton, and Lower Barton, which is loosely related to the other two. Members of the Lower Barton community have mostly Old Colony roots, whereas members of Springfield and Upper Barton have a mixture of Swiss-German, Dutch-Russian, and Belizean backgrounds. There are many participants in addition to about 175 members in the three communities. The group also has five congregations in the United States.

Costa Rica

MENNONITE-RELATED GROUPS

Beachy Amish Mennonite Church

The Beachy Amish Mennonite Church emerged in Costa Rica in 1968. The church began by establishing colonies where members lived close together, similar to the colony pattern of the Old Colony Mennonites in South America and Mexico. The Beachy Amish have 11 congregations in Costa Rica with about 275 members. This group has related congregations in Belize, Canada, El Salvador, Nicaragua, and the United States.

Convention of Mennonite Churches of Costa Rica (Asociación Convención de Iglesias Menonitas de Costa Rica)

The Convention was formed in 1974 as a result of efforts of missionaries from Rosedale (Ohio) Mennonite Missions (Conservative Mennonite Conference) that began more than a decade earlier. The mission staff initially carried out community development projects and translated the Bible into an indigenous language. Under local Costa Rican leadership, the church grew and expanded to 26 congregations with about 1,475 members. Nine of the congregations are in metropolitan areas such as Puerto Viejo, Heredia, and Canalete de Upala; the others are in rural settings.

El Salvador

MENNONITE-RELATED GROUPS

Church of God in Christ, Mennonite

This group, based in the United States, has three congregations with a total of 25 members, several mission outreach sites, and a gospel tract distribution center in El Salvador. It has related congregations in Belize, Canada, the Dominican Republic, Guatemala, Haiti, Jamaica, Mexico, and the United States.

Evangelical Mennonite Church (Iglesia Evangélica Menonita)

Several Beachy Amish workers began an agricultural aid project in El Salvador in 1962 under Amish Mennonite Aid sponsorship. Evangelization produced a local congregation by 1968. The church has 10 congregations and about 200 members. Other congregations related to this group are in Belize, Canada, Costa Rica, Nicaragua, and the United States.

Evangelical Mennonite Church of El Salvador (Iglesia Evangélica Menonita de El Salvador)

Some Salvadorans who fled into Honduras in 1969 during the so called Soccer War joined Mennonite churches in Honduras. They eventually returned to El Salvador and formed the Evangelical Mennonite Church of El Salvador, which has about 425 members in 11 congregations.

Guatemala

MENNONITE-RELATED GROUPS

Eastern Pennsylvania Mennonite Church

In 1970 the Eastern Pennsylvania Mennonite Church began mission efforts in Guatemala. It has five congregations with about 200 members. The group has related congregations in the Bahamas, Canada, and the United States.

Evangelical Mennonite Church of Guatemala (Iglesia Evangélica Menonita de Guatemala)
In 1968, Mennonite missionaries from Eastern Mennonite Missions and Washington-Franklin Mennonite Conference arrived in Guatemala and began work that produced the Evangelical Mennonite Church of Guatemala, which is located in Guatemala City. The church has about 1,700 members in 11 congregations throughout the capital city area.

Mennonite Air Missions
This group began in 1972 as an outgrowth of Conservative Mennonite Fellowship mission work. Using airplanes to reach isolated areas in the roadless interior of the country, the Air Missions group has established 17 congregations with nearly 275 members.

National Evangelical Guatemalan Mennonite Church (Iglesia Nacional Evangélica Menonita Guatemalteca)
This church formed in 1972 among the K'ekchi'-speaking people in the department of Alta Verapaz. The church grew out of the work of Mennonite missionaries from Eastern Mennonite Missions and Washington-Franklin Mennonite Conference who arrived in Guatemala in 1968. Composed mostly of members from K'ekchi ethnic backgrounds, the church is organized into five districts with 115 congregations and approximately 5,000 members.

Nationwide Fellowship Churches
The Conservative Mennonite Fellowship began mission work in 1964. Their efforts eventually produced congregations that affiliated with other church groups in the United States after the Conservative Mennonite Fellowship disbanded in the 1990s. Five congregations with a total of about 175 members relate to the Nationwide Fellowship Churches in the United States. Other congregations related to this group are in Canada, the Dominican Republic, Mexico, and the United States.

Honduras

MENNONITE-RELATED GROUPS

Evangelical Brethren in Christ Church (Iglesia Evangélica Hermanos en Cristo)
This group began in the arid areas of southern Honduras when Brethren in Christ missionaries from Nicaragua arrived there in 1989. About 1,450 members and many other participants attend 37 congregations and worship centers. Although there is a large congregation in the capital city of Tegucigalpa, most are located in rural areas of southern Honduras. The Brethren in Christ Church also has congregations in Canada, Cuba, the Dominican Republic, Mexico, Nicaragua, and the United States.

Honduran Evangelical Mennonite Church (Iglesia Evangélica Menonita Hondureña)
The Honduran Evangelical Mennonite Church was begun by missionaries from Eastern Mennonite Missions, who arrived on the north Honduran coast in 1950. This missionary effort began near the large banana-growing area in and around the cities of La Ceiba, Trujillo, and San Pedro Sula. Many, but not all, of the 136 congregations (about 4,750 members) are located in these areas.

Living Love (Amor Viviente)
Living Love formed in 1973 as the result of a Mennonite missionary couple's work with youth and alcoholics. Establishing small groups of new members, the church grew rapidly. The charismatic-style movement began in the capital city of Tegucigalpa, and by the early

21st century it was the largest Anabaptist denomination in Honduras, with about 8,650 members in 32 congregations.

Mennonite Christian Fellowship

Mennonite Christian Fellowship has five congregations and about 150 members. Some of its members came from an Old Order Amish group that settled in Honduras in 1968 but later disbanded. This group has related congregations in Cuba, Nicaragua, and the United States.

Nicaragua

MENNONITE-RELATED GROUPS

Christian Brotherhood Churches

Christian Aid Ministries opened a clinic in Waslala in 1997, an endeavor that produced six congregations with about 100 members. The churches are supported by and affiliated with the Beachy Amish Mennonite Church. Related Beachy Amish congregations are found in Belize, Canada, Costa Rica, El Salvador, and the United States.

Convention of Evangelical Mennonite Churches of Nicaragua (Convención de Iglesias Evangélicas Menonitas de Nicaragua)

The Convention was founded in 1977 as a result of mission efforts by Rosedale (Ohio) Mennonite Missions that began in 1973. It has about 4,600 members in 117 congregations and worship centers.

Evangelical Mission of the Brethren in Christ (Misión Evangélica de los Hermanos en Cristo)

This is the oldest Anabaptist-related church in Nicaragua. It was initiated by Brethren in Christ missionaries who arrived in Nicaragua in 1964 after being forced to flee Cuba. It has a membership of about 3,900 and an additional 7,000 participants who worship in 114 congregations and worship centers. In 1989 this denomination sent missionaries to Honduras to establish congregations there. Brethren in Christ–related congregations are also in Canada, Cuba, the Dominican Republic, Honduras, Mexico, and the United States.

Fraternity of Evangelical Mennonite Churches of Nicaragua (Fraternidad de Iglesias Evangélicas Menonitas de Nicaragua)

The Fraternity was started in 1970 by missionaries from Evangelical Mennonite Conference in Canada. It was legally incorporated three years later. It has about 2,300 members in 32 congregations. In addition to mission outreach, the group operates educational and community development programs.

Panama

MENNONITE-RELATED GROUPS

United Evangelical Mennonite Brethren Church (Iglesia Evangélica Unida Hermanos Menontas de Panamá)

Missionaries from the Mennonite Brethren Board of Missions and Service began work in Panama in the 1940s, coming across the Colombian border to start adult education and literacy programs. The missionaries worked with the Choco people in southern Panama and established the church in 1961. The church remains largely centered in the border region. It has 13 congregations with about 550 members. Members are mainly indigenous, and the group is autonomous, relying on missionaries only as resource persons.

SECTION FOUR: MEXICO

MENNONITE-RELATED GROUPS

Brethren in Christ Religious Association of Evangelical Churches of Mexico (Asociación Religiosa Iglesia Evangélica Hermanos en Cristo de México)
The Brethren in Christ churches in the state of Tamaulipas were organized in 1994. The Spanish-speaking group has about 250 members and several hundred additional participants who worship in eight congregations and worship centers. Other congregations related to the Brethren in Christ are in Canada, Cuba, the Dominican Republic, Honduras, Nicaragua, and the United States.

Christian Peace Church in Mexico (Iglesia Cristiana de Paz en México)
This group, based in the state of Jalisco, is associated with the Mennonite Brethren churches in the United States. It has 200 members in seven congregations.

Church of God in Christ, Mennonite (Iglesia de Dios en Cristo Menonita)
Associated with the Church of God in Christ, Mennonite denomination based in the United States, this group has about 350 members in 31 congregations. It also has numerous mission outreach sites. Other congregations related to this group are in Belize, Canada, the Dominican Republic, El Salvador, Guatemala, Haiti, Jamaica, and the United States.

Conference of Christian Mennonite Anabaptists of Tamaulipas (Conferencia Cristiana Menonita Anabautista de Tamaulipas)
This group of five Spanish-speaking congregations (50 members) is based in Tamaulipas, across the border from Brownsville, Texas. The congregations were started through mission efforts of South Texas Mennonite churches and are affiliated with the South Central Conference of Mennonite Church USA.

Conference of Evangelical Anabaptist Mennonites (Conferencia de Iglesias Evangélicas Anabautistas Menonitas de México)
Mennonite mission workers arrived in Mexico City in 1958 and started five congregations, which were under Mexican leadership by 1985. These Spanish-speaking churches developed their own mission program and goals for growth. The conference continues to affiliate with Franconia Conference (Pennsylvania), the Mennonite group in the United States that established the mission in 1958. It has some 550 members in 14 congregations in the Mexico City area. It commissioned two members to start a mission outreach in the United States in 2008.

Conference of Evangelical Missions of Mexico (Conferencia Evangélica Misionera de México)
This conference in Chihuahua consists of 16 congregations (about 450 members). These Spanish-speaking churches began through the mission work of Evangelical Mennonite Conference of Canada and the Commission on Overseas Mission of the General Conference, as well as the work of representatives of the Mexican German-speaking Mennonites.

Evangelical Mennonite Church in Mexico (Iglesia Evangélica Menonita en México)
The Hispanic Council of Lancaster (Pennsylvania) began a cluster of churches in the Huatabampo area of Sonora in the early 21st century. The group has about 250 members in 11 congregations. Other congregations related to this group are in Belize, El Salvador, Guatemala, and Honduras.

Evangelical Missionary Conference (Conferencia Misionera Evangélica)
This conference in Chihuahua was formed in 2007 by a merger of German congregations started by Evangelical Mennonite Conference of Canada and Evangelical Mennonite Mission Conference of Canada. The group has five congregations (about 350 members). Related congregations are in Belize, Canada, and the United States. Web site: http://www.emmc.ca

Kleine Gemeinde of Mexico (Kleingemeinde in Mexiko)
In 1948 about 800 Kleine Gemeinde ("small church") emigrants from Canada settled in Mexico. Ten years later some Kleine Gemeinde members moved to British Honduras (now Belize). Others returned to Canada in the last quarter of the 20th century. The group has about 2,775 members in 16 colonies. Ten of the colonies are in the state of Chihuahua, and the others are scattered in five other states. This group uses Low German but has an evangelical mindset and accepts more technology than the Old Colony Mennonites. Some Kleine Gemeinde members are converts from Old Colony groups. Other congregations related to this group are in Canada, Belize, and the United States.

Mennonite Conference of Mexico (Conferencia Menonita de México)
Founded in 1990, this conference in Chihuahua grew from the work of missionaries in 1963 to 1970. The missionaries were invited by German-speaking colonists to establish German and Spanish schools and develop mission programs for Mexican people living near the traditional Mennonite colonies. Four German-heritage congregations are in the conference, which had related to the General Conference Mennonite Church prior to 2002 but now affiliates with Mennonite Church Canada. The group operates a workshop for people with disabilities, a home for the aged, a credit union, and other social ministries. It has about 850 members in seven congregations.

Old Colony Mennonite Church (Car) (Altkolonier Mennonitengemeinde)
This group was part of the 1922 migration of Old Colony Mennonites of Dutch-Russian background from Canada to Mexico. These tradition-minded Mennonites left Canada because they were threatened by new education laws in Manitoba and Saskatchewan that required all children to attend English-language schools. Many Old Colony members eventually left Mexico for British Honduras (now Belize) and Bolivia. Some impoverished members returned to Canada in the last quarter of the 20th century.

This is the largest and most progressive branch of Old Colony people in Mexico. They accept rubber tires on tractors, travel by car and truck, and use electricity. They speak Low German and continue many traditional religious practices of their Old Colony heritage. The group has about 16,525 members in 18 colonies. Twelve of the colonies are in Chihuahua, and the rest are in Coahuila, Durango, Tamaulipas, and Zacatecas. Other congregations related to this group are in Belize, Canada, and the United States.

Old Colony Mennonite Church (Horse) (Altkolonier Mennonitengemeinde)
Beginning in 1922, some 7,000 Old Colony Mennonites of Dutch-Russian background, who had settled in Canada in the 1870s, migrated to Mexico. They established three colonies: Manitoba and Swift in Chihuahua, and Patos in Durango.

These tradition-minded Mennonites left Canada because they were threatened by new education laws in Manitoba and Saskatchewan that required all children to attend English-language schools. Many Old Colony members eventually left Mexico for British Honduras (now Belize) and Bolivia. Some impoverished members returned to Canada in the last quarter of the 20th century.

This is the most traditional subgroup. Members speak Low German, use steel-wheeled tractors, reject electricity, and travel by horse and buggy. The group has 3,200 members living in 12 colonies, seven of which are in the state of Campeche. Other congregations related to this group are in Belize, Canada, and the United States.

Reinländ Mennonite Church (Reinländer Gemeinde)

After the most conservative faction of Old Colony Mennonites in Mexico's Swift Current Colony migrated to Boliva in 1979, the remaining members affiliated with the Reinländ Mennonite Church in Manitoba, which had divided from the Sommerfeld Mennonite Church in Manitoba in 1958. The Reinländ Church in Mexico has about 1,675 members in three colonies, two in Chihuahua and one in Campeche. Other congregations related to this group are in Canada and the United States.

Sommerfeld Mennonite Church (Sommerfelder Mennonitengemeinde)

The Sommerfeld Mennonite Church was part of the migration of conservative Mennonites of Dutch-Russian background from Canada to Mexico in the 1920s. They emigrated from Canada because of new education laws in Manitoba and Saskatchewan that required all children to attend English-language schools. They established a colony, Santa Clara, in the state of Chihuahua. Some members eventually left Mexico for Bolivia in the 1960s, and others returned to Canada in the last quarter of the 20th century. The group has about 2,075 members in nine colonies, five in Chihuahua and two each in Campeche and Tamaulipas. Other congregations related to this group are in Canada and the United States.

SECTION FIVE: UNITED STATES

AMISH-RELATED GROUPS

New Order Amish

The New Order Amish emerged in 1966 in Holmes County, Ohio. They use horse-and-buggy transportation and speak Pennsylvania German. There are two primary circles of affiliation based on whether or not congregations use electricity from the public grid. Some church districts permit the use of tractors in the field, but others do not. Most New Order congregations have Sunday school, hold youth Bible study meetings, and emphasize greater individual expression of religious experience than the Old Order Amish. The group has an estimated 3,500 members in 58 congregations scattered in 13 states, with the majority in Ohio.

New Order Amish Fellowship

This group separated from the New Order Amish of Holmes County, Ohio, in 1986. Sometimes they are referred to as the New New Order Amish. The New Order Amish Fellowship places more emphasis on heartfelt experience than on rules and regulations. The group uses horse-and-buggy transportation but permits tractors in the field, electricity in the home, and ownership of computers for business operations. The Fellowship churches have a more spontaneous style of worship than the other New Order groups. Five of their seven congregations are in Ohio. A congregation in Oakland, Maryland, and one in Pencham, Kentucky, affiliate with the New Order Amish Fellowship, making a total of 400 members.

Old Order Amish

The label "Old Order" emerged in the 1860s–1880s when progressive Amish congregations became Amish-Mennonite and eventually joined various Mennonite conferences. Those keeping the traditional practices eventually became known as the Old Order Amish. Some 40 subgroups of Old Order Amish emerged in the 20th century. Subgroups emerge for various reasons: religious practices, use of technology, ethnicity, and migration history. Many refer to themselves simply as "Amish" or "Old Order Amish." Others have names such as Byler Amish, Swartzentruber Amish, and Troyer Amish. Although each subgroup has its own regulations and distinctive practices, all use horse-and-buggy transportation, wear plain clothing, and speak the Pennsylvania German dialect or a Swiss German dialect. Some of the subgroups based in large settlements in Indiana, Iowa, Michigan, Ohio, and Pennsylvania have daughter congregations in other states.

Combining all of the Old Order subgroups and excluding the New Order Amish yields a total of 1,628 congregations and about 97,700 members in the United States. If children are included, the total population exceeds 200,000. The Old Order Amish live in 27 states, mostly east of the Mississippi. About 67% of the congregations are in Ohio, Pennsylvania, and Indiana. The Old Order Amish also have congregations in Ontario, Canada.

BRETHREN-RELATED GROUPS

Brethren Church

The Brethren Church formed in 1883 when it branched off from the German Baptist Brethren, which began in 1708 in Schwarzenau, Germany. It was known as the "progressive" wing at the time of the division. Headquartered in Ashland, Ohio, the Brethren Church is sometimes called the Ashland Brethren. Its 119 congregations (about 10,400 members) are located in 18 states. About 78% of the members live in Ohio, Indiana, and Pennsylvania. Web site: http://www.brethrenchurch.org

Brethren Community Fellowship

This group branched off from the Old German Baptist Brethren in 1989. In 2007 additional members left the Old German Baptist Brethren and formed two other congregations (Greenville Fellowship and Victory in Christ Fellowship), which affiliate with the Brethren Community Fellowship. These churches have dropped many of the older requirements including plain dress. They are evangelical in their outlook and support various mission projects. Located in California, Indiana, and Ohio, they have three congregations with 270 members.

Church of the Brethren

The Church of the Brethren, the largest of the Brethren groups, traces its roots to the German Baptist Brethren who formed in 1708 in Schwarzenau, Germany. The German Baptist Brethren were influenced by both Radical Pietism and Anabaptism. At its bicentennial in 1908 the body changed its name to the Church of the Brethren. The Brethren are considered one of the three historic peace churches, along with the Quakers and the Mennonites. In addition to active peacemaking, the Brethren participate in ecumenical conversations with the National Council of Churches USA and the World Council of Churches. Six colleges and Bethany Theological Seminary are affiliated with the Church of the Brethren, whose headquarters are in Elgin, Illinois. The 1,000 congregations are found in 39 states, mostly east of the Mississippi River. About 70% of its 124,000 members live in Pennsylvania, Virginia, Maryland, Ohio, and Indiana. Other congregations related to this group are in the Dominican Republic, Haiti, and Puerto Rico. Web sites: http://www.brethren.org; http://www.cob-net.org

Conservative Grace Brethren Churches International
The Conservative Grace Brethren trace their roots to the German Baptist Brethren in Schwarzenau, Germany, and the Fellowship of Grace Brethren Churches from whom they separated. This conservative branch formed in 1989–1991 over issues related to congregational autonomy, trine immersion baptism, women in ministry, and other matters of biblical interpretation. With 38 congregations and 1,600 members, the Conservative Grace Brethren are found in 15 states; the highest concentration is in Ohio, where they have 11 congregations. In 2007, six congregations left the denomination and function as independent Conservative Grace Brethren congregations. Web site: http://www.thecgbci.org

Conservative Grace Brethren, Independent
These six congregations with about 500 members left the Conservative Grace Brethren in 2007. They each function independently but retain Grace Brethren identity.

Dunkard Brethren
The Dunkard Brethren emerged in 1926 in a conservative response to liberalizing changes in the Church of the Brethren, especially plain dress. The Dunkard Brethren continue to wear plain dress and uphold other traditional practices of the Church of the Brethren. The group has an estimated 1,000 members in 30 congregations. Its primary concentration is in Pennsylvania, but members are found in 13 other states as well. The group has a mission outreach in Kenya. Web site: http://www.dunkardbrethrenchurch.com

Grace Brethren Churches, Fellowship of
This group emerged in 1939 from a division within the Ashland-based Brethren Church. Both groups trace their origins to the German Baptist Brethren who formed in 1708 in Schwarzenau, Germany. The Fellowship of Grace Brethren Churches has about 30,400 members and 260 congregations in 29 states, with the largest clusters in Pennsylvania, Ohio, and California. The group supports aggressive evangelistic efforts by local congregations. Web site: http://www.fgbc.org

Independent Traditional Brethren (Car)
Four independent groups (two Old Brethren and two German Baptist Brethren) endorse many traditional 19th-century Brethren worship practices and reject Sunday school, revival meetings, and evangelistic outreach. The members of these churches wear plain dress and drive cars. The 10 congregations, in eight states, have a total of 375 members.

Independent Traditional Brethren (Horse)
This cluster of three independent churches (Old Order German Baptist Brethren, Old Brethren German Baptist, Christian Community) are the most traditional of all Brethren groups. They use horse-and-buggy transportation, reject public grid electricity, and wear traditional Brethren dress. They do not have Sunday school or revival meetings, nor do they support mission activities. The eight congregations affiliated with these groups have about 200 members located in six states.

Independent Traditional Evangelical Brethren
This cluster of 10 independent congregations share many characteristics. The churches formed between 1931 and 1998 as offshoots of either the Dunkard Brethren or the Church of the Brethren. The members of these churches wear plain dress and drive cars. Although espousing many traditional practices, they have an evangelical outlook, support mission activities, and have accepted Sunday school and revival meetings. Nine of the 10 congrega-

tions are located in Pennsylvania, and one is located in Virginia; they have a total of 350 members.

Old German Baptist Brethren

This group formed in 1881 during the three-way division of the German Baptist Brethren. An Old Order group, it seeks to preserve many of the traditional practices of the German Baptist Brethren but permits the ownership of motor vehicles and the use of electricity and other technology except television and radio. Members of the group are sometimes confused with the Amish because of their plain dress and the beards worn by the men. This group has about 6,300 members in 50 congregations in 16 states, with the largest number in Ohio and Indiana. A division within this group began forming in 2009. The more change-minded branch, calling itself the Old German Baptist Brethren New Conference, initially claimed about one-third (2,000) of the members.

HUTTERITE-RELATED GROUPS

Dariusleut Hutterites

The Dariusleut formed in Russia in 1860 under the leadership of Darius Walter (1835–1903). More moderate than the Lehrerleut, the Darisuleut are the most culturally diverse of the four Hutterite groups. The Dariusleut have 160 colonies in North America, 22 of which (875 members) are in the United States, mostly in Montana. The remaining colonies are in Canada, with the largest concentration in Alberta.

Lehrerleut Hutterites

The most conservative and homogeneous of the Hutterite groups, the Lehrerleut formed about 1877 after they migrated from Russia to the United States under the leadership of Jacob Wipf (1835–1896). The Lehrerleut have 140 colonies in North America; 35 of them (1,400 members) are in the United States (all in Montana), and the rest are in Canada.

Schmiedeleut Hutterites, Gibb Group

The Schmiedeleut formed in 1859 in Russia when Michael Waldner (1823–1889) reinstituted the practice of communal property. They were a single group from 1859 until they divided following an internal dispute in 1992. This group became known as the Committee Hutterites or the Gibb Group because a non-Hutterite banker whose surname was Gibb supported their separation from the Kleinsasser Group. Although the Gibb Group is more conservative in cultural practice than the Kleinsasser Group, the two Schmiedeleut branches are the most progressive of the Hutterite groups. Twice as large as the Kleinsasser Group, the Gibb Group has about 120 colonies. Nearly half of the group's members live in Manitoba, and the rest—about 2,450 members in 61 colonies—live in Minnesota and North and South Dakota.

Schmiedeleut Hutterites, Kleinsasser Group

The Schmiedeleut formed in 1859 in Russia when Michael Waldner (1823–1889) reinstituted the practice of communal property. They were a single group from 1859 until they divided following an internal dispute in 1992. Jacob Kleinsasser (1922–), the senior elder of all of the Schmiedeleut colonies until 1992, lost his leadership role when he was rejected by a majority of the colonies' council of ministers. Those colonies loyal to him separated from the others and became known as the Kleinsasser Group. Many factors complicated the division, including Kleinsasser's progressive views on the use of English, musical instruments, missions, education, and more advanced technology, and his association with the Bruderhof community. The Kleinsasser group has 60 colonies, the bulk of which are in Manitoba. Only nine of them (with some 350 members) are in the United States, in Minnesota and South Dakota.

MENNONITE-RELATED GROUPS

Alliance of Mennonite Evangelical Congregations

The Evangelical Anabaptist Fellowship organized in 1992 to promote conservative and evangelical views within Mennonite circles. Not a formally organized group of congregations, the Fellowship consisted of a network of individuals and pastors who circulated a newsletter and held seminars and workshops. In 2002 the group organized under its present name. The Alliance has 13 congregations with a membership of 2,200. Most of the congregations are in Pennsylvania. Alliance leaders hold a gathering every other year, but within regions, some associations of congregations meet on a monthly basis. Web site: http://www .aemc2000.org

Ambassadors Amish Mennonites

This group is a small, loose network of churches primarily originating from the Beachy Amish in 2008. Its formation was instigated by the Leitchfield and Summersville congregations of Kentucky, and it is more conservative than the Beachy Amish. Church members come from a variety of backgrounds, including New Order Amish, Mennonite Christian Fellowship, and the Beachy Amish Mennonite Church. The Ambassadors group strongly emphasizes rapid, successive church planting in areas without Anabaptist churches. It operates Still Waters Ministries and publishes and distributes *Beside the Still Waters*, a devotional magazine widely read in Amish and conservative Mennonite communities. With a total of about 250 members, the network has four congregations—two in Kentucky and one each in Indiana and Missouri—as well as several church-planting efforts.

Amish Mennonite Churches (Independent)

Two different clusters of independent churches are known as Amish Mennonites because they have Amish roots or historical affiliations. The two clusters are not denominations or official organizations, but loose networks of congregations that share a common outlook and some religious practices. Members drive cars, use more advanced technology, and emphasize a more subjective, emotional, religious experience than most Amish groups. They also participate in some of the programs and activities of the more traditional Mennonite groups.

The first cluster of 15 congregations has about 1,000 members. One of the largest congregations is the Spring Garden Church in Lancaster County, Pennsylvania. Other similar congregations are found in Daviess County, Indiana, and Perth County, Ontario. These churches have meetinghouses and conduct their services in English.

A second cluster of six Amish Mennonite congregations use German in their church services and adhere to very conservative dress standards that exceed those of many New Order Amish. Most of the congregations in this cluster separated from the Beachy Amish in the last quarter of the 20th century. Members drive cars, but their churches tightly restrict the use of tape and CD players and computers. In dress and lifestyle they are similar to the Old Order Amish. Three of these congregations are in Kentucky, and three are in Illinois. They have a total of about 400 members.

Amish Mennonite Churches (Tampico)

The Tampico Amish Mennonites, named for their origin in Tampico, Illinois, have a dozen congregations, primarily located in Arkansas, Colorado, Illinois, Missouri, and Wisconsin. They trace their roots to the "sleeping preacher," John D. Kauffman (1847–1913), who preached while in a trance. The Tampico Amish Mennonites are a traditional plain-dressing group similar to the Beachy Amish in some respects. Members are permitted to own automobiles. Most, but not all, congregations use the Pennsylvania German dialect in their church services. The group has about 1,450 members.

Amish Mennonite Churches of Tennessee and Kentucky

Based in Tennessee, this group formed in 1966 through the influence of individuals with Beachy Amish and Conservative Mennonite backgrounds. The group has about 350 members. Two of its eight congregations are in Kentucky, and six are in Tennessee. Members drive cars, use public electricity, hold services in meetinghouses, and use English in their church services. They espouse very traditional standards in religious doctrine, lifestyle, and dress.

Anabaptist Native Fellowship of Churches

Anabaptist Native Fellowship is a group of Native American congregations that ascribes to an evangelical, Anabaptist understanding of Scripture. The Fellowship is committed to First Nations and cross-cultural outreach. One of its goals is to develop effective Native leaders for church planting and leadership. The Fellowship formed in 2001 after United Native Ministries, a ministry of Mennonite Board of Missions, and Mennonite Indian Leadership Council, a ministry of General Conference Mennonite Church, were discontinued. The group of six congregations (150 members) is closely affiliated with Harvest Fellowship of Churches. Web site: http://www.harvestfellowshipofchurches.org/module17.html

Apostolic Christian Church of America

This group began in 1832 in Switzerland under the leadership of Samuel Froehlich (1803–1857), who was influenced by the Anabaptists and their teaching. Many converts to this church came from Swiss Mennonite backgrounds. The Apostolic Christian Church came to Lewis County, New York, in 1847 and attracted Amish there as well as in other states. Sometimes nicknamed the New Amish, the group shares many Anabaptist principles and practices with conservative Mennonite churches. Some members come from Amish and Mennonite backgrounds. The Apostolic Church occasionally supports projects sponsored by Mennonite Central Committee and Mennonite Disaster Service. The group has 12,700 members in the United States in 87 congregations scattered in 23 states, with concentrations in Illinois, Indiana, Iowa, and Ohio. It also has two congregations in Canada and two in Mexico. Web site: http://www.apostolicchristian.org

Association of Radical Church Networks

This network consists of at least five affiliated bodies with some 40 congregations and more than 7,000 members. These church groups emphasize some Anabaptist themes but have also been heavily influenced by the principles of apostolic church governance, which emphasizes the authority of elders in shaping and enacting the vision of their congregations. Leaders see the historical radical churches, including the early church described in Acts and 16th-century Anabaptists, as sources of inspiration for their vision. Many of the congregations in the network have a charismatic style of worship and strong outreach efforts. Web site: http://www.radicalrestoration.org/ARCnet.html

Beachy Amish Mennonite Church

The Beachy Amish emerged in the 1920s in Somerset County and Lancaster County, Pennsylvania, under the leadership of Bishop Moses Beachy (1874–1946). Most of the members have New Order or Old Order Amish backgrounds. The group has about 7,350 members in 97 congregations in 20 states, with heavy concentrations in Ohio, Pennsylvania, Indiana, Kentucky, and Virginia. Members wear plain dress, and men wear an abbreviated beard. They drive cars and use public electricity in their homes but typically do not permit television or radio. This group, like the Old Order Amish, has more congregational autonomy than conservative Mennonite churches, which have a more centralized governance. Many Beachy Amish congregations support evangelistic and outreach initiatives. Since 1990 three groups (Maranatha Amish Mennonite Church, Berea Amish Mennonite Fellowship, and Ambassadors Amish Mennonites) have broken off from the Beachy Amish and formed their own affiliations. The Ambassadors Amish Mennonites formed most recently and is the most conservative. Other congregations related to this group are in Belize, Canada, Costa Rica, El Salvador, and Nicaragua. Web site: http://beachyam.org

Berea Amish Mennonite Fellowship

This group officially separated from the Beachy Amish Mennonite Church in 2007. The Berea Fellowship churches are considerably more traditional in doctrine, dress, and lifestyle than the Beachy Amish and the Maranatha Amish Mennonite Church, which also separated from the Beachy Amish. The Berea group has 12 congregations in nine states with about 575 members.

Bethel Mennonite Fellowship

This cluster of congregations withdrew from the now defunct Conservative Mennonite Fellowship in 1983. It promotes conservative Mennonite practices and does not permit members to use radios. Bethel Fellowship has about 925 members in 19 congregations. Congregations are in eight states, with the largest concentration in Missouri. The Fellowship operates Bethel Bible School in Seymour, Missouri, and supports several mission efforts, including one in Wasilla, Alaska.

Biblical Mennonite Alliance

This group formed in the spring of 2000, largely because some people were concerned about the declining use of the women's prayer covering, women in ministry, and the interpretation of Scripture in their former churches. Alliance congregations take a conservative view on these issues. Initially many of the group's members came from the Conservative Mennonite Conference, but members later came from many other Mennonite groups as well. The Alliance's 47 congregations (2,375 members) are scattered among 18 states. It also has two congregations in Canada.

Brethren in Christ

The Brethren in Christ emerged about 1780 in eastern Pennsylvania. They blend Mennonite-Anabaptist influences with the Pietist strains of the German Baptist Brethren and United Brethren. An assimilated group, the Brethren in Christ reflect mainstream evangelical worship practices in many ways, including the use of contemporary Christian music. They support Mennonite Central Committee and participate in Mennonite World Conference. The Brethren in Christ have about 23,000 members and 270 congregations in 20 states, with major concentrations in Pennsylvania, Florida, Ohio, and California. About 51% of the members live in Pennsylvania. Other congregations related to this group are in

Canada, Cuba, the Dominican Republic, Honduras, Mexico, and Nicaragua. Web site: http://www.bic-church.org

Charity Christian Fellowship

This network of congregations, also known as the Remnant, formed in 1982 in eastern Pennsylvania. Their leader, Moses Stoltzfus (1946–), came from Amish background. Members come from various Plain Anabaptist groups, and they resemble conservative Mennonites in many ways. Rather fundamentalist in doctrine and charismatic in expression, they practice footwashing and the holy kiss. Members wear modest dress, and women wear prayer coverings. They support an aggressive program of evangelism that seeks converts from other Anabaptist groups as well as from outside Anabaptist circles. The Fellowship has 42 congregations (about 2,300 members) in 15 states, with the strongest concentrations in Ohio and Pennsylvania. The group also has related congregations in Canada and mission projects outside North America. Web site: http://www.charityministries.org

Church of God in Christ, Mennonite

Also known as the Holdeman Mennonites, this group formed in 1859 under the leadership of John Holdeman (1832–1900). Although similar in some ways to other conservative Mennonite groups, the Church of God in Christ, Mennonite teaches the doctrine of the one true church of Christ and practices shunning. Men wear abbreviated beards, and women wear black scarves or bonnets. The group has 135 congregations (about 14,500 members) in 33 states, with the largest concentration in Kansas. The Holdeman Mennonites have congregations and mission ventures in 24 countries, including 50 congregations in Canada. The group's total worldwide membership is about 22,000. Other congregations related to this group are in Belize, Canada, the Dominican Republic, El Salvador, Guatemala, Haiti, Jamaica, and Mexico. Web site: http://churchofgodinchristmennonite.net

Conservative Mennonite Churches of York and Adams Counties, Pennsylvania

This small conference of churches separated from the Lancaster Mennonite Conference in 1975 because it wanted to uphold more traditional practices. The group is similar in many ways to the Eastern Pennsylvania Mennonite Church. It has about 250 members in five congregations.

Conservative Mennonite Conference

Organized in 1910 in Pigeon, Michigan, this group was first known as the Conservative Amish Mennonite Conference but dropped "Amish" from its name in 1954. Virtually all of the early members came from Amish backgrounds. The Conservative Mennonite Conference is an autonomous body with fraternal relations with numerous Mennonite bodies and organizations. It emphasizes the authority of the Scriptures and nonconformity to the world. Plain dress is worn by many of the members who live in rural areas but not by many of those in urban congregations. The group's denominational headquarters and its Bible school, Rosedale Bible College, are located in Irwin, Ohio. It has over 11,000 members attending about 106 congregations in 20 states, with the largest concentration in Ohio. Web site: http://www.cmcrosedale.org

Cumberland Valley Mennonite Church

This independent conference of churches formed in 1971 in south-central Pennsylvania. Prior to that the member congregations were a conservative cluster in the northern section of Washington-Franklin Mennonite Conference. Emphasizing conservative doctrine, dress, and practice, this conference has about 400 members with four congregations in Pennsylvania and three in Maryland.

Eastern Pennsylvania Mennonite Church

This group of churches took root in eastern Pennsylvania in 1968, when five conservative bishops and some 40 other ordained leaders withdrew from the Lancaster Mennonite Conference over issues related to dress, television, and other cultural changes. The Eastern Pennsylvania Mennonite Church developed a more conservative discipline and continues to uphold traditional Mennonite standards of doctrine, dress, and practice. With some 4,500 members, this group has 56 congregations in 13 states, the majority of them in Pennsylvania. The group has additional congregations in the Bahamas, Canada, and Guatemala.

Evangelical Mennonite Mission Conference

Ancestors of this group were part of a migration from Russia to Manitoba in the 1870s. The group began in 1937 as a revivalist, evangelical division from the more traditional Sommerfeld Mennonite Church. It adopted the name Evangelical Mennonite Mission Conference in 1959. Most of its 34 congregations are in Canada. Some congregations still use German in their services. This group is actively engaged in mission work among Old Colony Mennonites in Mexico and those returning to Canada from Mexico. In the United States the group has seven congregations (about 400 members) in Texas and Kansas, which relate to Old Colony Mennonites who emigrated from Mexico in the late 20th century. Other congregations related to this group are in Belize, Canada, and Mexico. Web site: http://www.emmc.ca

Fellowship of Evangelical Churches

Formed in 1865 by individuals from Amish background, this group was known for many years as the Egly Amish because their leader was Henry Egly (1824–1890). In 1908 the group's name was changed to Defenseless Mennonite Church. In 1948 it was changed again, to Evangelical Mennonite Church, and in 2003 to Fellowship of Evangelical Churches. Shaped by modern evangelicalism, its congregations have a weak Mennonite identity. Headquartered in Fort Wayne, Indiana, the group has 43 congregations (about 6,950 members) in nine states, with about one-third of them in Illinois. Web site: http://fecministries.org

Good News Mennonite Fellowship

This group was formed in 2000, largely by congregations that had been formerly affiliated with the Lancaster Mennonite Conference. Geographical proximity, reservations about joining Mennonite Church USA, and more conservative views on women in ministry, as well as other issues, led to its formation. Good News Mennonite Fellowship has about 1,500 members in 20 congregations, mostly in Alabama, with the remainder in the panhandle of Florida.

Harvest Fellowship of Churches

Harvest Fellowship of Churches, an Evangelical Anabaptist organization, formed in 2002 as the result of a 10-year discussion. Many of the founding leaders had roots in various Mennonite churches, primarily in the New England region of the United States. The group has an explicit commitment to implementing Anabaptist principles and values in the development of outreach ministries and the establishment of new congregations. Over half of the 12 congregations (500 members) are located in the New England area. The national origin and identity of some congregations includes Ethiopian, Cambodian, Indonesian, and Vietnamese. Web site: http://www.harvestfellowshipofchurches.org/index.html

Haven Mennonite Fellowship

This group formed in about 2003 when several congregations separated from the Ohio
Wisler Mennonite Churches. The Haven group did not want Sunday school, which the
Wisler Churches had adopted. This plain-dressing, car-driving group has two congregations
in Ohio and one in Indiana, with a total membership of nearly 200.

Hope Mennonite Fellowship

This group formed in the early 1980s when an ordained leader withdrew from the Eastern
Pennsylvania Mennonite Church. Many of the early adherents objected to two issues in the
Eastern Pennsylvania Church: their use of unleavened bread in communion and their views
of prophecy related to the return of Christ. Hope Mennonite Fellowship has five congregations and about 500 members, all in Pennsylvania.

Keystone Mennonite Fellowship

The congregations in this group emerged in 1985 in the Lancaster, Pennsylvania, area and
formed a separate affiliation in 1999 because their ordained leaders wanted to preserve
more conservative standards than those held by the Lancaster Mennonite Conference. The
group encourages plain dress, discourages television, and takes a traditional stand on many
Mennonite doctrines and practices. All but one of the 18 congregations are located in eastern Pennsylvania. Keystone Mennonite Fellowship has about 1,275 members.

Koinonia Fellowship of Churches

This group, comprised of 16 congregations (1,000 members), is located primarily in eastern
Pennsylvania and New Jersey. The first congregations, affiliated with Lancaster Mennonite
Conference, began in the 1970s. The Koinonia Fellowship formed as an independent group
in 2002. The vision of these churches is to be an apostolic fellowship of Anabaptists in
urban areas. The Fellowship places a strong emphasis on dynamic, spirit-led worship and
teaching and engages in establishing new congregations.

Maranatha Amish Mennonite Church

This group emerged from the Beachy Amish Mennonites in the 1990s. It emphasizes stricter
standards than the majority of Beachy Amish congregations and a stronger central form of
church governance. The Maranatha Amish Mennonite Church has 13 congregations in the
United States, with a total of about 800 members. Related congregations are also in Canada.

Mennonite Brethren Churches, United States Conference

The Mennonite Brethren emerged among Russian Mennonites in the 1860s and migrated to
the United States and Canada in the late 19th century. Some 200 Mennonite Brethren congregations are located in 19 states, with more than 60 in California alone. Most are located
west of the Mississippi River. Maintaining a strong evangelical orientation, the Mennonite
Brethren support many Mennonite Central Committee projects as well as other inter-Mennonite activities. As a result of their evangelistic outreach and the entry of some 35 Slavic
congregations into their denomination, nearly half of the Mennonite Brethren congregations have strong Asian, Slavic, or Hispanic identities. These ethnic congregations account
for some 16,000 of the denomination's 35,875 members. Other congregations related to this
group are in Canada. Web site: http://www.usmb.org

Mennonite Christian Fellowship

This group emerged from the Beachy Amish Mennonite Church in the late 1950s but adopted its present name in the 1990s to assume a more Mennonite identity. Most of its mem-

bers come from Amish background. Like many other Amish Mennonite groups, the Fellowship emphasizes a born-again religious experience and evangelical message. It emphasizes uniformity and traditional dress and other lifestyle practices. Members typically dress more conservatively than the Beachy Amish. The group's 32 congregations (about 1,450 members) are scattered in nine different states; Pennsylvania is home to six of them. Other congregations related to this group are in Cuba, Honduras, and Nicaragua.

Mennonite Church USA

This is the largest Mennonite body in the United States. It formed in 2002 through the merger of the General Conference Mennonite Church and the Mennonite Church. Mennonite Church USA has 916 congregations in 44 states, with a membership of about 106,000. About 18% of the congregations and 11% of the members are non-Caucasian. Within the ethnic minority portion, about 50% of members are African-American, 35% are Latino/Hispanic, 9% are Asian, and 4% are Native American. The denomination supports numerous mission, publishing, and mutual aid programs and is affiliated with two seminaries, several colleges, and numerous primary and secondary schools. Many of its members support international service and relief programs operated by Mennonite Central Committee and gatherings of Mennonite World Conference. Denominational leaders participate in ecumenical discussions with representatives of other religious bodies. Other congregations related to this group are in Belize, the Dominican Republic, Guatemala, Haiti, Honduras, and Mexico. Web sites: http://www.mennoniteusa.org; http://www.thirdway.com

Mennonite Churches, Independent (Assimilated)

Approximately 50 congregations in 20 states are independent Mennonite congregations whose members do not wear plain clothing and are largely assimilated into mainstream culture. This is not an organized body. West of the Mississippi many of these congregations had formerly been a part of the General Conference Mennonite Church but have cut formal ties with that body, largely because they were influenced by fundamentalism. They adhere to evangelical and sometimes fundamentalist religious views, and many support non-Mennonite evangelical mission programs. In total, these congregations have about 5,000 members.

Mennonite Churches, Independent (Traditional)

Approximately 109 small congregations have dropped their formal affiliation with larger Mennonite bodies because of differences over doctrine, biblical interpretation, or practice. Members wear plain clothing and embrace a simple lifestyle. Although many of the churches fellowship with a cluster of similar congregations, they have no formal name or central organization. Many of the more conservative congregations associate with organized groups such as Midwest Mennonite Fellowship. Other congregations relate to one of three small, loose networks: Sharing Concerns Mennonite Fellowship, Southern Mennonite Fellowship, and Bible Mennonite Fellowship in Oregon. Approximately 6,425 members are in these independent, plain-dressing congregations. Eleven congregations are located in Pennsylvania, and the rest are distributed in 24 other states. A sizable number are in Holmes County, Ohio.

Mennonite Evangelical Church

This church began in Texas in 1978 as a result of mission work by the Morwenna Evangelical Mennonite Church in Manitoba. They have both English and German worship services. Musical instruments are used in worship, and the largest congregation has a full-time pastor. Some members wear plain dress, but that practice is declining. The largest congregation is at Seminole, Texas. Another small congregation is in Texas, and one is in Kansas. About 425 members attend the three congregations.

Mid-Atlantic Mennonite Fellowship

This group branched off from the Eastern Pennsylvania Mennonite Church in 1972 and officially organized in 1978. Congregations from Lancaster Mennonite Conference and from the Old Order Weaverland Conference have also joined this plain-dressing, car-driving church. On some practices, such as the use of radios and musical instruments, the Mid-Atlantic Fellowship is more tolerant than the Eastern Pennsylvania Mennonite Church. The Fellowship has approximately 1,650 members. All but three of its 21 congregations are located in Pennsylvania.

Midwest Mennonite Fellowship

Numerous traditional Mennonite congregations of various backgrounds formed the Midwest Fellowship in 1977 and opened Maranatha Mennonite Bible School in Lansing, Michigan, in 1978. Mission outreach tends to be initiated by individual congregations rather than by the Fellowship as a whole. The group has about 1,175 members and 24 congregations in the United States, with concentrations in Ohio, Michigan, and Indiana. Other congregations related to this group are in Canada.

Mountain Valley Mennonite Churches

Located in Virginia, the Mountain Valley Churches separated from the Virginia Mennonite Conference in 2002 as a more conservative offshoot. The group emphasizes the authority of Scripture, biblical church discipline, the Christian order of headship in the church and the home, permanence of Christian marriage, purity in sexual relationships, peace and non-resistance, and modesty in dress. These churches have six congregations and 400 members.

Nationwide Fellowship Churches

A sizable number of congregations that withdrew from several different conferences of the Mennonite Church in the mid-20th century began affiliating together in the late 1950s and early 1960s. Lifestyle changes in the Mennonite Church (now Mennonite Church USA), such as accepting television and wearing jewelry and fashionable clothing, prompted the formation of the Fellowship churches. The Fellowship has about 62 congregations spread over 19 states with a membership of about 2,850 members. The group also has related congregations in Canada, the Dominican Republic, Guatemala, and Mexico.

Ohio Wisler Mennonite Churches

This group formed in 1973 when several congregations that were part of the car-driving Old Order Mennonites, Wisler Conference in Ohio and Indiana began to affiliate together as the Ohio Wisler Mennonite Churches. Moving in a more evangelical and less traditional direction, they adopted Sunday schools and more aggressive forms of outreach. All five congregations, with nearly 300 members, are located in Ohio.

Old Colony Mennonite Church

The name of this group traces back to 19th-century Russia. Its people descended from Chortitza, the oldest Mennonite colony founded in Russia (now Ukraine) in 1789. The group immigrated to Canada in the 1870s. Some members moved from Canada to Mexico in the 1920s because of English educational requirements in western Canadian schools. In the last decades of the 20th century, many families returned to Canada, and some came to the United

States. Old Colony churches continue to resist acculturation and remain somewhat isolated from other Mennonite groups. Distinctive plain dress has been part of their traditional lifestyle, but that has been changing in the 21st century. They drive cars and use electricity. A Low German dialect is still spoken in worship services. The group has three congregations in Texas and one in Kansas. The largest congregation, with about 500 members, is in Seminole, Texas. Total membership in the United States is about 950. There are related congregations in Belize, Canada, and Mexico.

Old Order Mennonites, Groffdale Conference

This sizable group of horse-and-buggy-driving Mennonites traces its roots to the 1893 Old Order division in Lancaster, Pennsylvania. Some years later, in 1927, the Old Order community in Lancaster divided over automobile use. The Groffdale Conference was the more conservative branch, which became known as the "team" Mennonites because they continued using horse-and-buggy "teams." The Old Order Mennonites of Indiana merged with the Groffdale Conference in 1973. Of the group's 50 congregations, 21 are located in Pennsylvania. The Groffdale Conference has congregations in eight other states as well, including New York, Missouri, Ohio, Kentucky, Iowa, and Wisconsin. Total membership is about 10,000.

Old Order Mennonites, Hoover Church

The Hoover Mennonites, based in Scottsville, Kentucky, are one of several groups stemming from a 1944 division in the Stauffer Mennonite Church in Snyder County, Pennsylvania. The group moved to Scottsville in 1978. This horse-and-buggy church is one of the most restrictive Old Order groups with respect to the use of technology, forbidding any use of internal combustion engines. The Hoover Church has five communities with about 400 members: two in Kentucky, two in Missouri, and one in Tennessee. The group also has three communities in Belize.

Old Order Mennonites, Reidenbach Churches

In 1942 several families withdrew from the Old Order Groffdale Conference because they felt that participation in Civilian Public Service camps would compromise their stance on separation from the world. They formed the Reidenbach Mennonite Church in 1946 in Lancaster County, Pennsylvania. The group is also known as the 35-ers because about 35 people were involved in the original division. The group is composed of numerous subgroups, identified by the names of the various leaders. The Reidenbach Churches have strict restrictions on technology—no tractors, telephones, electricity, or rubber on buggy wheels. The group has an estimated 375 members in 10 congregations. Most of the congregations are located in Pennsylvania, but several have been established in Kentucky and Missouri.

Old Order Mennonites, Stauffer Church

The Stauffer Mennonites are an Old Order group that broke off from the Lancaster Mennonite Conference in Pennsylvania in 1845, before the national Old Order Movement in the last quarter of the 19th century. Sometimes called the Pike Mennonites, this is a horse-and-buggy group that does not use electricity or tractors for field work. Their dress and buggies are more austere than those of other horse-and-buggy Mennonites such as the Groffdale Conference and the Reidenbach Churches. The Stauffer Church also applies shunning more strictly than these other groups. Five of their 13 congregations are located in Pennsylvania, and the rest are scattered in seven other states. The Stauffers have about 1,300 members.

Old Order Mennonites, Virginia Conference

Part of the nationwide Old Order Movement, this group separated from the Virginia Mennonite Conference in 1901. It is similar to the Old Order Groffdale Conference of Mennonites,
although Virginia Conference members do not speak Pennsylvania German, and they have
pulpits in their meetinghouses and use rubber tires on their tractors. The community has
divided into three subgroups. Most of the 500 members who make up this conference live in
Virginia (three congregations), with one congregation in Ohio.

Old Order Mennonites, Weaverland Conference

This group traces its roots to the Old Order division of 1893 in Pennsylvania when Bishop
Jonas Martin (1839–1925) withdrew from the Lancaster Mennonite Conference. The Old
Order community in Lancaster separated into two branches in 1927, when the Weaverland
Conference accepted automobiles and the Groffdale Conference continued using horse-
drawn buggies. For many years members of the Weaverland Conference were known as
"black bumpers" because they were required to paint any chrome on their cars black. This
practice still continues for ministers but is not required for members; however, members
are expected to drive black cars, at least to church. The Weaverland Conference no longer
uses the Pennsylvania German dialect in church services, but some older members speak it
in daily life. The group does not have Sunday school or revival meetings. Although the conference does not operate its own programs, its members support some mission and service
programs of other churches. They are permitted to use electricity, telephones, and modern
farm machinery, but not radio, television, or the Internet. Twenty-six of the Weaverland
Conference's 40 congregations are in Pennsylvania. Total membership is about 7,100.

Old Order Mennonites, Wenger (Virginia)

This horse-and-buggy group branched off from the Old Order Mennonite Virginia Conference in 1952. It has one congregation (located in Virginia) and slightly over 300 members.
In many ways it is similar to the Old Order Groffdale Conference based in Pennsylvania;
however, this group does not speak Pennsylvania German and permits the use of pneumatic
tires on tractors and farm machinery.

Old Order Mennonites, Wisler Conference

Tracing its roots to a 1907 division of Old Order Mennonites in Ohio and Indiana, this auto-
mobile-driving group is similar to the Weaverland Conference of the Old Order Mennonites.
The name Wisler comes from an early Old Order Mennonite leader, Jacob Wisler (1808–
1889). The group is commonly known as the Ohio-Indiana Wisler Conference. Their seven
congregations, with 925 members, are located in Ohio, Indiana, Michigan, and Minnesota.

Old Order River Brethren

The Old Order River Brethren trace their roots to an 1856 division among the River Brethren in eastern Pennsylvania who a few years later became known as the Brethren in Christ.
The Old Order River Brethren are the traditional strand of the Brethren in Christ. Members
wear plain clothing and hold worship services in homes as well as in schools and community
centers. Although they drive cars, they are sometimes mistaken for Amish because of their
similar dress and the men's long, flowing beards. There are three subgroups of Old Order
River Brethren, including a small one of about a half-dozen members that uses horse-drawn
transportation. Four of their five congregations are in Pennsylvania. The total number of
members in all of the subgroups is about 350.

Orthodox Mennonite Church

Members of this group broke off from the David Martin Old Order Mennonite Church in Canada in 1957. After subsequent internal divisions, some members returned to the original church. In the 1980s when more technology was accepted in the Old Order Mennonite Church in Canada, some of its members joined the Orthodox Mennonites. Like other Old Order Mennonites, Orthodox Mennonites drive horse and buggy, wear plain clothing, speak Pennsylvania German, and worship in meetinghouses. One distinction is that men wear beards. The Orthodox Mennonite Church has three congregations (two in Kentucky and one in Pennsylvania), with about 200 members. Related congregations are in Canada.

Pilgrim Mennonite Conference

Twelve of this group's 22 congregations are located in Pennsylvania, the state where it began in 1991. The Pilgrim Conference was formed by members who withdrew from the Eastern Pennsylvania Mennonite Church because they differed on ideas about church leadership and wanted to place less emphasis on preserving traditional practices not specifically mentioned in the Bible. This plain-dressing group of 1,300 members is similar in many respects to the mother body. The Pilgrim Conference has an active prison ministry, holds tent meeting revivals, and operates numerous schools, including Pilgrim Mennonite Bible School. Related congregations are in Honduras.

Reformed Mennonite Church

One of the first Mennonite subgroups to form in the United States, the Reformed Mennonites separated from the Lancaster Mennonite Conference in about 1785 and officially organized in 1812. Because they wanted to restore some traditional practices of the Mennonite Church as well as to establish new ones, the group was sometimes known as the New Mennonites. Members wear plain dress and own automobiles. Although they had some 2,000 members in 1900, the Reformed Mennonites experienced a steady decline in the 20th century. The group has fewer than 175 members in 10 congregations, most of which are in Ohio and Pennsylvania.

Reinländ Mennonite Church

Members of this group have Old Colony, Russian-Mennonite roots. Some came to the United States from Mexico and others from Canada. They live a simple lifestyle but use cars and electricity. The group has six congregations in Texas and Kansas, with a total membership of about 1,200. Other congregations related to this group are in Canada and Mexico.

South Atlantic Mennonite Conference

This group formed in the 1990s, initially as a subgroup in Southeastern Mennonite Conference. It has four congregations in Georgia and South Carolina with about 250 members.

Southeastern Mennonite Conference

This body withdrew from the Virginia Conference of the Mennonite Church in 1971 in order to maintain more conservative dress requirements. Many of the staff members of Christian Light Publications are affiliated with Southeastern Conference congregations. The group has 16 congregations (about 725 members) in Virginia and West Virginia. It also has two mission projects in Puerto Rico. A regional subgroup, the South Atlantic Mennonite Conference, left Southeastern Mennonite Conference in the 1990s to form its own group.

United Zion

Originally called United Zion's Children, this group emerged from a division among the River Brethren (now Brethren in Christ) in 1855. Led by Matthias Brinser (1795–1889), the group constructed a meetinghouse before such facilities were sanctioned by the River Brethren. United Zion members dress modestly, and some of the women wear prayer coverings. The group has about 600 members in 11 congregations, all of which are located in Pennsylvania.

Washington-Franklin Mennonite Conference

This group of Mennonites was part of the (Old) Mennonite Church in the 20th century until it became an independent conference in 1965. Although not part of the Old Order Movement, it is a very traditional, plain-dressing Mennonite group whose members use cars but adhere to a simple and conservative lifestyle. The group is similar to the Eastern Pennsylvania Mennonite Church except that it does not endorse the latter's premillennial view of the return of Christ. Most of its 17 congregations (1,600 members) are located in the Hagerstown, Maryland, area with others in Kentucky and Pennsylvania and mission outposts in Haiti and Africa.

Western Conservative Mennonite Fellowship

The group was started in 1973 by several congregations in Oregon that had previously belonged to the Nationwide Mennonite Fellowship. Several churches from other states also later joined the Western Conservative Mennonite Fellowship. It is a plain-dressing group that promotes traditional Mennonite doctrines and practices. The Fellowship has about 450 members in eight congregations in the United States. There is another one in Canada, and one in Belize.

Table of Groups

The table includes identifiable groups with one or more congregations and at least 25 baptized members. Estimates are based on 2008 and 2009 group directories and reports of informants. Numbers of members are rounded to the nearest 25.

Groups are organized by region (Caribbean and Central America) and country and, within country, by affiliation with one of the four Anabaptist families.

Region	Affiliation	Group	Congregations	Members
Canada	Amish	Old Order Amish	34	2,450
		Amish Total	*34*	*2,450*
	Hutterite	Dariusleut Hutterites	136	5,450
		Lehrerleut Hutterites	105	4,200
		Schmiedeleut Hutterites, Gibb Group	59	2,350
		Schmiedeleut Hutterites, Kleinsasser Group	51	2,050
		Hutterite Total	*351*	*14,050*
	Mennonite	Amish Mennonite Churches, Independent	2	125
		Apostolic Christian Church	2	25
		Beachy Amish Mennonite Church	8	225
		Bergthal Mennonite Church of La Crete	4	1,000
		Bergthal Mennonite Church of Saskatchewan	5	800
		Bethel Fellowship	1	25
		Biblical Mennonite Alliance	2	50
		Brethren in Christ	48	3,600
		Charity Christian Fellowship	11	250
		Chortitzer Mennonite Conference	15	1,700
		Christian Anishinabec Fellowship	8	100
		Church of God in Christ, Mennonite	50	5,000
		Conservative Mennonite Church of Ontario	10	625
		Conservative Mennonite Conference	1	75
		Conservative Sommerfeld Mennonite Churches	8	2,000
		Eastern Pennsylvania Mennonite Church	4	200
		Evangelical Mennonite Conference	60	7,000
		Evangelical Mennonite Mission Conference	27	4,300
		Kleine Gemeinde	8	700
		Maranatha Amish Mennonites	2	150
		Markham-Waterloo Mennonite Conference	12	1,400
		Mennonite Brethren Churches, Canadian Conference of	250	37,000

(continued)

Region	Affiliation	Group	Congregations	Members
		Mennonite Church Canada	220	33,000
		Mennonite Churches, Independent (Assimilated)	13	2,000
		Mennonite Churches, Independent (Traditional)	9	425
		Midwest Mennonite Fellowship	10	950
		Nationwide Fellowship Churches	23	1,000
		New Hope Mennonite Church	2	2,100
		New Reinländ Mennonite Church of Ontario	1	250
		Northwest Mennonite Conference	14	1,100
		Old Bergthal Mennonites	2	200
		Old Colony Mennonite Church	20	9,000
		Old Colony Mennonite Church, Manitoba	3	500
		Old Order Mennonite Church	36	3,200
		Old Order Mennonite Church (David Martin)	6	500
		Orthodox Mennonite Church	4	400
		Reformed Mennonite Church	2	125
		Reinländ Mennonite Church (Manitoba)	7	3,000
		Reinländ Mennonite Fellowship Church (Ontario)	3	1,000
		Sommerfeld Mennonite Church	13	2,300
		Westbourne Orthodox Mennonites	1	50
		Western Conservative Mennonite Fellowship	1	50
		Mennonite Total	*928*	*127,500*
Grand Total, Canada			**1,313**	**144,000**
Caribbean				
Bahamas	Mennonite	Eastern Pennsylvania Mennonite Church	1	25
		Mennonite Total	*1*	*25*
		Bahamas Total	**1**	**25**
Cuba	Mennonite	Brethren in Christ Cuban Missionary Society (Sociedad Misionera Cubano Hermanos en Cristo)	75	3,275
		Mennonite Christian Fellowship	1	25
		Mennonite Church in Cuba (Iglesia Menonita en Cuba)	3	50
		Mennonite Total	*79*	*3,350*
		Cuba Total	**79**	**3,350**
Dominican Republic	Brethren	Church of the Brethren (Iglesia de los Hermanos Dominicana)	20	1,700
		Brethren Total	*20*	*1,700*
	Mennonite	Bethel Brethren in Christ Church (Iglesia Bethel Hermanos en Cristo)	15	300
		Church of God in Christ, Mennonite	3	50

Region	Affiliation	Group	Congregations	Members
		Conference of the Dominican Evangelical Mennonites (Conferencia Evangélica Menonita Dominicana)	60	2,450
		Divine Light National Assembly of Mennonites (Concilio Nacional Menonita Faro Divino)	23	2,500
		Dominican Evangelical Mennonite Council (Consejo Evangélico Menonita Dominicana)	6	275
		Koinonia Fellowship of Churches	6	400
		Nationwide Fellowship Churches	5	100
		Mennonite Total	*118*	*6,075*
		Dominican Republic Total	**138**	**7,775**
Grenada	Mennonite	Olive Branch Mennonite Missions	3	50
		Mennonite Total	*3*	*50*
		Grenada Total	**3**	**50**
Haiti	Brethren	Church of the Brethren	5	50
		Brethren Total	*5*	*50*
	Mennonite	Assembly of Grace (Assemblée de la Grace)	25	2,375
		Church of God in Christ, Mennonite (Église de Dieu en Christ Mennonite, Haiti)	17	600
		Gospel Light Chapel	14	700
		Mennonite Sonlight Mission	5	200
		Salem Amish Mennonite Church	1	25
		Washington-Franklin Mennonite Conference	1	25
		Mennonite Total	*63*	*3,925*
		Haiti Total	**68**	**3,975**
Jamaica	Mennonite	Christ's Ambassadors	1	25
		Church of God in Christ, Mennonite	2	25
		Jamaica Mennonite Church	13	675
		Mennonite Total	*16*	*725*
		Jamaica Total	**16**	**725**
Puerto Rico	Brethren	Church of the Brethren (Iglesia de los Hermanos, Puerto Rico)	7	375
		Brethren Total	*7*	*375*
	Mennonite	Conference of the Mennonite Churches of Puerto Rico (Convención de las Iglesias Menonitas de Puerto Rico)	11	400
		Evangelical Mennonite Mission of the Caribbean (Misión Evangélica Menonita del Caribe)	5	125
		Mennonite Total	*16*	*525*
		Puerto Rico Total	**23**	**900**

(continued)

Region	Affiliation	Group	Congregations	Members
Trinidad and Tobago	Mennonite	Mennonite Church of Trinidad and Tobago	6	275
		Mennonite Total	*6*	*275*
		Trinidad and Tobago Total	**6**	**275**
Grand Total, Caribbean			**334**	**17,075**

Central America

Region	Affiliation	Group	Congregations	Members
Belize	Mennonite	Beachy Amish Mennonite Church	6	175
		Belize Evangelical Mennonite Church (Iglesia Evangélica Menonita de Belice)	10	425
		Bethel Fellowship	2	50
		Caribbean Light and Truth	12	150
		Church of God in Christ, Mennonite	2	50
		Evangelical Mennonite Mission Conference	3	475
		Kleine Gemeinde	5	800
		Old Colony Mennonite Church (Horse)	3	2,050
		Old Order Mennonites, Hoover Church	3	175
		Western Conservative Mennonite Fellowship	1	50
		Mennonite Total	*47*	*4,400*
		Belize Total	**47**	**4,400**
Costa Rica	Mennonite	Amish Mennonites of Tennessee and Kentucky	2	50
		Beachy Amish Mennonite Church	11	275
		Convention of Mennonite Churches of Costa Rica (Asociación Convención de Iglesias Menonitas de Costa Rica)	26	1,475
		Mennonite Christian Fellowship	1	25
		Mennonite Total	*40*	*1,825*
		Costa Rica Total	**40**	**1,825**
El Salvador	Mennonite	Church of God in Christ, Mennonite	3	25
		Evangelical Mennonite Church (Iglesia Evangélica Menonita)	10	200
		Evangelical Mennonite Church of El Salvador (Iglesia Evangélica Menonita de El Salvador)	11	425
		Mennonite Total	*24*	*650*
		El Salvador Total	**24**	**650**
Guatemala	Mennonite	Bethel Mennonite Fellowship	1	25
		Church of God in Christ, Mennonite	2	25
		Eastern Pennsylvania Mennonite Church	5	200
		Evangelical Mennonite Church of Guatemala (Iglesia Evangélica Menonita de Guatemala)	11	1,700
		Mennonite Air Missions	17	275
		National Evangelical Guatemalan Mennonite Church (Iglesia Nacional Evangélica Menonita Guatemalteca)	115	5,000

Region	Affiliation	Group	Congregations	Members
		Nationwide Fellowship Churches	5	175
		Mennonite Total	*156*	*7,400*
		Guatemala Total	**156**	**7,400**
Honduras	*Mennonite*	Evangelical Brethren in Christ Church (Iglesia Evangélica Hermanos en Cristo)	37	1,450
		Honduran Evangelical Mennonite Church (Iglesia Evangélica Menonita Hondureña)	136	4,750
		Living Love (Amor Viviente)	32	8,650
		Mennonite Christian Fellowship	5	150
		Pilgrim Mennonite Conference	2	50
		Mennonite Total	*212*	*15,050*
		Honduras Total	**212**	**15,050**
Nicaragua	*Mennonite*	Christian Brotherhood Churches	6	100
		Convention of Evangelical Mennonite Churches of Nicaragua (Convención de Iglesias Evangélicas Menonitas de Nicaragua)	117	4,600
		Evangelical Mission of the Brethren in Christ (Misión Evangélica de los Hermanos en Cristo)	114	3,900
		Fraternity of Evangelical Mennonite Churches of Nicaragua (Fraternidad de Iglesias Evangélicas Menonitas de Nicaragua)	32	2,300
		Mennonite Christian Fellowship	1	25
		Mennonite Total	*270*	*10,925*
		Nicaragua Total	**270**	**10,925**
Panama	*Mennonite*	United Evangelical Mennonite Brethren Church (Iglesia Evangélica Unida Hermanos Menonitas de Panamá)	13	550
		Mennonite Total	*13*	*550*
		Panama Total	**13**	**550**
Grand Total, Central America			**762**	**40,800**
Mexico	*Mennonite*	Apostolic Christian Church	2	50
		Brethren in Christ Religious Association of Evangelical Churches of Mexico (Asociación Religiosa Iglesia Evangélica Hermanos en Cristo de México)	8	250
		Christian Peace Church in Mexico (Iglesia Cristiana de Paz en México)	7	200
		Church of God in Christ, Mennonite (Iglesia de Dios en Cristo Menonita)	31	350
		Conference of Christian Mennonite Anabaptists of Tamaulipas (Conferencia Cristiana Menonita Anabautista de Tamaulipas)	5	50

(continued)

Region	Affiliation	Group	Congregations	Members
		Conference of Evangelical Anabaptist Mennonites (Conferencia de Iglesias Evangélicas Anabautistas Menonitas de México)	14	550
		Conference of Evangelical Missions of Mexico (Conferencia Evangélica Misionera de México)	16	450
		Conservative Mennonite Conference	1	25
		Evangelical Mennonite Church in Mexico (Iglesia Evangélica Menonita en México)	11	250
		Evangelical Missionary Conference (Conferencia Misionera Evangélica)	5	350
		Hope Mennonite Mission	1	25
		Kleine Gemeinde of Mexico (Kleingemeinde in Mexiko)	16	2,775
		Mennonite Conference of Mexico (Conferencia Menonita de México)	7	850
		Midwest Mennonite Fellowship	1	50
		Nationwide Fellowship Churches	2	75
		Old Colony Mennonite Church (Car) (Altkolonier Mennonitengemeinde)	18	16,525
		Old Colony Mennonite Church (Horse) (Altkolonier Mennonitengemeinde)	12	3,200
		Reinländ Mennonite Church (Reinländer Gemeinde)	3	1,675
		Sommerfeld Mennonite Church (Sommerfelder Mennonitengemeinde)	9	2,075
		Mennonite Total	*169*	*29,775*
Grand Total, Mexico			**169**	**29,775**
United States	*Amish*	New Order Amish	58	3,500
		New Order Amish Fellowship	7	400
		Old Order Amish	1,628	97,700
		Amish Total	*1,693*	*101,600*
	Brethren	Brethren Church	119	10,400
		Brethren Community Fellowship	3	270
		Church of the Brethren	1,000	124,000
		Conservative Grace Brethren Churches International	38	1,600
		Conservative Grace Brethren, Independent	6	500
		Dunkard Brethren	30	1,000
		Grace Brethren Churches, Fellowship of	260	30,400
		Independent Traditional Brethren (Car)	10	375
		Independent Traditional Brethren (Horse)	8	200
		Independent Traditional Evangelical Brethren	10	350
		Old German Baptist Brethren	50	6,300
		Brethren Total	*1,534*	*175,395*

Region	Affiliation	Group	Congregations	Members
	Hutterite	Dariusleut Hutterites	22	875
		Lehrerleut Hutterites	35	1,400
		Schmiedeleut Hutterites, Gibb Group	61	2,450
		Schmiedeleut Hutterites, Kleinsasser Group	9	350
		Hutterite Total	***127***	***5,075***
	Mennonite	Alliance of Mennonite Evangelical Congregations	13	2,200
		Ambassadors Amish Mennonites	4	250
		Amish Mennonite Churches (Independent)	21	1,400
		Amish Mennonite Churches (Tampico)	12	1,450
		Amish Mennonite Churches of Tennessee and Kentucky	8	350
		Anabaptist Native Fellowship of Churches	6	150
		Apostolic Christian Church of America	87	12,700
		Association of Radical Church Networks	40	7,000
		Beachy Amish Mennonite Church	97	7,350
		Berea Amish Mennonite Fellowship	12	575
		Bethel Mennonite Fellowship	19	925
		Biblical Mennonite Alliance	47	2,375
		Brethren in Christ	270	23,000
		Charity Christian Fellowship	33	2,050
		Church of God in Christ, Mennonite	135	14,500
		Conservative Mennonite Churches of York and Adams Counties, Pennsylvania	5	250
		Conservative Mennonite Conference	106	11,100
		Cumberland Valley Mennonite Church	7	400
		Eastern Pennsylvania Mennonite Church	56	4,500
		Evangelical Mennonite Mission Conference	4	400
		Fellowship of Evangelical Churches	43	6,950
		Good News Mennonite Fellowship	20	1,500
		Harvest Fellowship of Churches	12	500
		Haven Mennonite Fellowship	3	200
		Hope Mennonite Fellowship	5	500
		Keystone Mennonite Fellowship	18	1,275
		Kleine Gemeinde	2	100
		Koinonia Fellowship of Churches	16	1,000
		Maranatha Amish Mennonite Church	13	800
		Mennonite Brethren Churches, United States Conference	200	35,875
		Mennonite Christian Fellowship	32	1,450
		Mennonite Church USA	916	106,000
		Mennonite Churches, Independent (Assimilated)	50	5,000
		Mennonite Churches, Independent (Traditional)	109	6,425
		Mennonite Evangelical Church	3	425
		Mid-Atlantic Mennonite Fellowship	21	1,650
		Midwest Mennonite Fellowship	24	1,175
		Mountain Valley Mennonite Churches	6	400

(continued)

Region	Affiliation	Group	Congregations	Members
		Nationwide Fellowship Churches	62	2,850
		Ohio Wisler Mennonite Churches	5	300
		Old Colony Mennonite Church	4	950
		Old Order Mennonites, Groffdale Conference	50	10,000
		Old Order Mennonites, Hoover Church	5	400
		Old Order Mennonites, Reidenbach Churches	10	375
		Old Order Mennonites, Stauffer Church	13	1,300
		Old Order Mennonites, Virginia Conference	4	500
		Old Order Mennonites, Weaverland Conference	40	7,100
		Old Order Mennonites, Wenger (Virginia)	1	300
		Old Order Mennonites, Wisler Conference	7	925
		Old Order River Brethren	5	350
		Orthodox Mennonite Church	3	200
		Pilgrim Mennonite Conference	22	1,300
		Reformed Mennonite Church	10	175
		Reinländ Mennonite Church	6	1,200
		Sommerfeld Mennonite Church	1	125
		South Atlantic Mennonite Conference	4	250
		Southeastern Mennonite Conference	16	725
		United Zion	11	600
		Washington-Franklin Mennonite Conference	17	1,600
		Western Conservative Mennonite Fellowship	8	450
		Mennonite Total	*2,779*	*296,125*
Grand Total, United States			**6,133**	**578,195**
Grand Total, North America			**8,711**	**809,845**

References

Abrahams, Ethel Ewert. 1980. *Frakturmalen und Schönschreiben: The Fraktur Art and Penmanship of the Dutch-German Mennonites While in Europe, 1700–1900*. Hillsboro, Kans.: Mennonite Press.

Ainlay, Stephen C. 1990. "The 1920 Seminary Movement: A Failed Attempt at Formal Theological Education in the Mennonite Church." *Mennonite Quarterly Review* 64 (4): 325–51.

Anabaptist (Mennonite) Directory 2009. 2009. Harrisonburg, Va.: Sword and Trumpet.

And When They Shall Ask. 1984. Directed by John Morrow. Winnipeg, Man.: Dueck Film Productions.

Armour, Rollin S. 1966. *Anabaptist Baptism: A Representative Study*. Scottdale, Pa.: Herald Press.

Arthur, Linda Boynton. 1997. "Clothing Is a Window to the Soul: The Social Control of Women in a Holdeman Mennonite Community." *Journal of Mennonite Studies* 15:11–30.

Augsburger, David. 2006. *Dissident Discipleship: A Spirituality of Self-Surrender, Love of God, and Love of Neighbor*. Grand Rapids, Mich.: Brazos Press.

Augsburger, Myron S. 1967a. *Pilgrim Aflame*. Scottdale, Pa.: Herald Press.

———. 1967b. *Principles of Biblical Interpretation*. Scottdale, Pa.: Herald Press.

———. 1983. *Evangelism as Discipling*. Scottdale, Pa.: Herald Press.

———. 1990. *The Christ-Shaped Conscience*. Wheaton, Ill.: Victor Books.

Bach, Jeff. 2003. *Voices of the Turtledoves. The Sacred World of Ephrata*. University Park, Pa.: Pennsylvania State Univ. Press.

Baecher, Robert. 2000. "Research Note: The 'Patriarche' of Sainte-Marie-aux-Mines." *Mennonite Quarterly Review* 74 (1): 145–58.

Bailey-Dick, Matthew. 2005. "The Kitchenhood of All Believers: A Journey into the Discourse of Mennonite Cookbooks." *Mennonite Quarterly Review* 79 (2): 153–78.

Baum, Markus. 1998. *Against the Wind: Eberhard Arnold and the Bruderhof*. Farmington, Pa.: Plough Publishing House.

BE. See *Brethren Encyclopedia*.

Beach, Mark, and Julie Kauffman. 2006. *Simply in Season Children's Cookbook*. Scottdale, Pa.: Herald Press.

Bechler, Le Roy. 1986. *The Black Mennonite Church in North America, 1886–1986*. Scottdale, Pa.: Herald Press.

Beck, Ervin. 1989. "Mennonite and Amish Painting on Glass." *Mennonite Quarterly Review* 63 (2): 115–49.

———. 1997. "Plain and Fancy: A Review of Research in Mennonite Folk Arts." *Mennonite Quarterly Review* 71 (1): 69–91.

———. 2004. *MennoFolk: Mennonite and Amish Folk Traditions*. Scottdale, Pa.: Herald Press.

———, ed. 2005. *MennoFolk2: A Sampler of Mennonite and Amish Folklore*. Scottdale, Pa.: Herald Press.

Bender, Harold S. 1944. *The Anabaptist Vision*. Scottdale, Pa.: Herald Press.

———. 1955. "The Anabaptists and Religious Liberty in the 16th Century." *Mennonite Quarterly Review* 29 (1): 83–100.

———. 1962. *These are My People: The Nature of the Church and Its Discipleship According to the New Testament*. Scottdale, Pa.: Herald Press.

Bender, Ross T., and Alan P. F. Sell. 1991. *Baptism, Peace, and the State in the Reformed and Mennonite Traditions*. Waterloo, Ont.: Wilfrid Laurier Univ. Press.

Bergen, Peter, comp. 2001. *History of the Sommerfeld Mennonite Church: That Is the Background and First Hundred Years of the Sommerfeld Mennonite Church*. Altona, Man.: Sommerfeld Mennonite Church.

Bertsche, Jim. 1998. *CIM/AIMM: A Story of Vision, Commitment, and Grace*. Elkhart, Ind.: Fairway Press.

Bible Doctrine and Practice: Church of God in Christ, Mennonite. 1998. Moundridge, Kans.: Gospel Publishers.

Biesecker-Mast, Susan. 2006. "Tourism in Holmes County and the Ministry of Behalt." *Mennonite Historical Bulletin* 61 (1): 1–6.

Bird, Michael S. 1977. *Ontario Fraktur: A Pennsylvania-German Folk Tradition in Early Canada*. Toronto: M. F. Feheley.

———. 2002. *O Noble Heart / O Edel Herz: Fraktur and Spirituality in Pennsylvania German Folk Art*. Lancaster, Pa.: Heritage Center Museum.

Bittinger, Emmert F. 1980. "Marking 100 Years of Brethren Higher Education." *Brethren Life and Thought* 25 (2): 71–82.

Block, Isaac I. 1990. "Mennonite Pastors' Response to Domestic Abuse." *Journal of Mennonite Studies* 8:189–97.

Boers, Arthur Paul, Eleanor Kreider, John Rempel, Mary Schertz, and Barbara Nelson Gingerich, eds. 2005. *Take Our Moments and Our Days: An Anabaptist Prayer Book; A Four-Week Cycle of Morning and Evening Prayers for Ordinary Time*. Elkhart, Ind.: Institute of Mennonite Studies.

Bontrager, Edwin. 1978. *Divorce and the Faithful Church*. Scottdale, Pa.: Herald Press.

Born, Daniel. 2005. "From Cross to Cross-Stitch: The Ascendancy of the Quilt." *Mennonite Quarterly Review* 79 (2): 179–90.

Bowman, Carl F. 1995. *Brethren Society: The Cultural Transformation of a "Peculiar People."* Baltimore: Johns Hopkins Univ. Press.

———. 2008. *Portrait of a People: The Church of the Brethren at 300*. Elgin, Ill.: Brethren Press.

Bowman, Warren D. 1942. *Anointing for Healing: An Entrusted Means of God's Grace*. Elgin, Ill.: Brethren Press.

Boyers, Auburn A. 1971. "The Brethren, Annual Conference, and Education: Sunday Schools." *Brethren Life and Thought* 16 (4): 215–26.

Braght, Thieleman J. van. 1998. *The Bloody Theater, or, Martyrs Mirror of the Defenseless Christians. . . .* Rev. ed. Scottdale, Pa.: Herald Press.

Brensinger, Terry L., ed. 2000. *Focusing Our Faith: Brethren in Christ Core Values*. Nappanee, Ind.: Evangel Publishing House.

Brethren Encyclopedia. 1983. Volumes I–II. Philadelphia: Brethren Encyclopedia, Inc.

————. 1984. Volume III. Philadelphia: Brethren Encyclopedia, Inc.

————. 2005. Volume IV. Philadelphia: Brethren Encyclopedia, Inc.

Brethren World Assembly. 1994. *Report of the Proceedings of the Brethren World Assembly: Elizabethtown College, Elizabethtown, Pennsylvania, July 15–July 18, 1992.* Ambler, Pa.: Brethren Encyclopedia, Inc.

————. 1999. *Report of the Proceedings of the 1998 Brethren World Assembly: Bridgewater College, Bridgewater, Virginia, July 15–18, 1998.* Ambler, Pa.: Brethren Encyclopedia, Inc.

————. 2004. *The Brethren Presence in the World and the World Directory of Brethren Bodies: Proceedings of the 3rd Brethren World Assembly: July 23–26, 2003, Grace College, Winona Lake, Indiana.* Philadelphia, Pa.: Brethren Encyclopedia, Inc.

Bronner, Simon J. 2006. *Encyclopedia of American Folklife.* Armonk, N.Y.: M. E. Sharpe.

Brown, Dale W. 1978. *Flamed by the Spirit: Biblical Definitions of the Holy Spirit: A Brethren Perspective.* Elgin, Ill.: Brethren Press.

————. 1983. "A Baptismal Theology with Implications for Evangelism, Conversion, and Church Growth." *Brethren Life and Thought* 28 (3): 151–60.

————. 1986. "People without a Liturgy? An Essay on Brethren Worship, Past and Present." *Brethren Life and Thought* 31 (1): 24–32.

————. 1996a. "Love Theology: Pietism, Anabaptism, and the Brethren in Christ Tradition." *Brethren in Christ History and Life* 19 (2): 306–18.

————. 1996b. *Understanding Pietism.* Rev. ed. Nappanee, Ind.: Evangel Publishing House.

————. 2003. *Biblical Pacifism.* 2nd ed. Nappanee, Ind.: Evangel Publishing House.

————. 2005. *Another Way of Believing: A Brethren Theology.* Elgin, Ill.: Brethren Press.

Brown, Tricia Gates, ed. 2005. *Getting in the Way: Stories from Christian Peacemaker Teams.* Scottdale, Pa.: Herald Press.

————, ed. 2008. *One Hundred Eighteen Days: Christian Peacemaker Teams Held Hostage in Iraq.* Telford, Pa.: Cascadia Publishing House.

Brubaker, Pamela. 1985. *She Hath Done What She Could: A History of Women's Participation in the Church of the Brethren.* Elgin, Ill.: Brethren Press.

Brumbaugh-Cayford, Cheryl. 2006. "New Sunday School Curriculum Launched by Brethren and Mennonites." Church of the Brethren Newsline.

Brunk, George R., II, ed. 1972. *Encounter with the Holy Spirit.* Scottdale, Pa.: Herald Press.

Bucher, Christina, ed. 1994. "Homosexuality." Special issue, *Brethren Life and Thought* 39 (2).

Buffington, Albert F. 1942. "The Pennsylvania German Dialect." In *The Pennsylvania Germans,* ed. Ralph Wood, 259–81. Princeton: Princeton Univ. Press.

Burkhardt, Ferne. 2006. "Sider Calls Church to Economic Sharing." *Canadian Mennonite* 10 (8): 18.

Burkholder, J. Lawrence. 1989. *The Problem of Social Responsibility from the Perspective of the Mennonite Church.* Elkhart, Ind.: Institute of Mennonite Studies.

Burridge, Kate, and Werner Enninger. 1992. *Diachronic Studies on the Languages of the Anabaptists.* Bochum, Germany: N. Brockmeyer.

Bush, Perry. 1998a. "The Flexibility of the Center: Mennonite Church Conflict in the 1960s." *Mennonite Quarterly Review* 72 (2): 189–206.

————. 1998b. *Two Kingdoms, Two Loyalties: Mennonite Pacifism in Modern America.* Baltimore: Johns Hopkins Univ. Press.

Carter, Karen S. 1985. "Anna Mow: She Said Yes to Life." *Messenger* 134 (8): 11.

Christian Aid Ministries 2008 Annual Report. 2008. Berlin, Ohio: Christian Aid Ministries.

Church Member Profile 2006. A Survey of Members of the Brethren in Christ, Church of the

Brethren, and Mennonite Church USA in the United States. Unpublished reports. Elizabethtown, Pa.: The Young Center of Elizabethtown College (www.etown .edu/youngctr). Denominational results published in Kanagy (2007) and C. Bowman (2008).

Church, Richard P. 2008. *First Be Reconciled: Challenging Christians in the Courts.* Scottdale, Pa.: Herald Press.

Clouse, Robert G. 1979. "Henry R. Holsinger." *Brethren Life and Thought* 24 (3): 134–41.

———. 1990. "The Church of the Brethren and World War I: The Goshen Statement." *Mennonite Life* 45 (4): 29–34.

CMP. *See* Church Member Profile 2006.

Confession of Faith in a Mennonite Perspective. 1995. Scottdale, Pa.: Herald Press.

Correll, Ernst H. 1991. "The Mennonite Agricultural Model in the German Palatinate." *Pennsylvania Mennonite Heritage* 14 (4): 2–14.

Cronk, Sandra L. 1977. "Gelassenheit: The Rites of the Redemptive Process in Old Order Amish and Old Order Mennonite Communities." Ph.D. diss., Univ. of Chicago. Excerpts under same title appear in *Mennonite Quarterly Review* 55 (1): 5–44.

Cross, Harold E., and Andrew H. Crosby. 2008. "Amish Contributions to Medical Genetics." *Mennonite Quarterly Review* 82 (3): 449–67.

Davis, Kenneth R. 1979. "Anabaptism as a Charismatic Movement." *Mennonite Quarterly Review* 53 (3): 219–34.

Detweiler, Lowell. 2000. *The Hammer Rings Hope: Photos and Stories from 50 Years of Mennonite Disaster Service.* Scottdale, Pa.: Herald Press.

Dirk Philips. 1992. *The Writings of Dirk Philips.* Trans. and ed. Cornelius J. Dyck, William E. Keeney, and Alvin J. Beachy. Scottdale, Pa.: Herald Press.

Driedger, Leo, and J. Howard Kauffman. 1982. "Urbanization of Mennonites: Canadian and American Comparisons." *Mennonite Quarterly Review* 56 (3): 269–90.

Driedger, Leo, and Donald B. Kraybill. 1994. *Mennonite Peacemaking: From Quietism to Activism.* Scottdale, Pa.: Herald Press.

Driedger, Leo, Roy Vogt, and Mavis Reimer. 1983. "Mennonite Intermarriage: National, Regional, and Intergenerational Trends." *Mennonite Quarterly Review* 57 (2): 132–44.

Dueck, A. J., ed. 1994. *Canadian Mennonites and the Challenge of Nationalism.* Winnipeg, Man.: Manitoba Mennonite Historical Society.

Dueck, Al. 1989. "Story, Community and Ritual: Anabaptist Themes and Mental Health." *Mennonite Quarterly Review* 63 (1): 77–91.

Durnbaugh, Donald F. 1958. *European Origins of the Brethren.* Elgin, Ill.: Brethren Press.

———. 1968. *The Believers' Church: The History and Character of Radical Protestantism.* New York: Macmillan Books.

———, ed. 1975. *To Serve the Present Age: The Brethren Service Story.* Elgin, Ill.: Brethren Press.

———. 1978. *On Earth Peace: Discussions on War/Peace Issues between Friends, Mennonites, Brethren, and European Churches.* Elgin, Ill.: Brethren Press.

———. 1989. *Pragmatic Prophet: The Life of Michael Robert Zigler.* Elgin, Ill.: Brethren Press.

———. 1991. "M. R. Ziegler and Civilian Public Service." *Brethren Life and Thought* 36 (2): 83–91.

———. 1994. "Brethren and Friends in a New Land: A Shared History." *Brethren Life and Thought* 39 (4): 227–40.

———. 1997a. *Fruit of the Vine: A History of the Brethren, 1708–1995.* Elgin, Ill.: Brethren Press.

———. 1997b. "Sustainers or Seducers: The Rise and Meaning of Church-Related Institu-
    tions." *Mennonite Quarterly Review* 71 (3): 345–64.

———. 2002. "The Fundamentalist/Modernist Struggle within the Church of the Brethren,
    1910–1950." *Brethren Life and Thought* 47 (1–2): 52–88.

Durnbaugh, Hedwig T. 1986. *The German Hymnody of the Brethren, 1720-1903.* Philadelphia:
    Brethren Encyclopedia, Inc.

———. 1999. "The Amish Singing Style: Theories of Its Origin and Description of Its Singu-
    larity." *Pennsylvania Mennonite Heritage* 22 (2): 24–31.

Dyck, Cornelius J., ed. 1962. *A Legacy of Faith: The Heritage of Menno Simons.* Newton, Kans.:
    Faith and Life Press.

———. 1985. "The Suffering Church in Anabaptism." *Mennonite Quarterly Review* 59 (1): 5–23.

———, ed. 1993. *An Introduction to Mennonite History: A Popular History of the Anabaptists
    and the Mennonites.* 3rd ed. Scottdale, Pa.: Herald Press.

Dyck, Peter J. 1970. "A Theology of Service." *Mennonite Quarterly Review* 44 (3): 262–80.

Earnest, Corinne, and Russell Earnest. 2003. *To the Latest Posterity: Pennsylvania-German
    Family Registers in the Fraktur Tradition.* University Park, Pa.: Pennsylvania State Univ.
    Press.

Eberly, William R., ed. 1991. *The Complete Writings of Alexander Mack.* Winona Lake, Ind.:
    BMH Books.

Eby, Larry, and Mary Jane Brenneman Eby. 2006. *In Harmony with Creation: Seeking God's
    Face in Mennonite Camping, 1980-2005.* Elkhart, Ind.: Mennonite Camping Association.

Ediger, Gerald C. 2001. *Crossing the Divide: Language Transition among Canadian Mennonite
    Brethren, 1940-1970.* Winnipeg, Man.: Centre for Mennonite Brethren Studies.

Eicher, Lovina, and Kevin Williams. 2008. *The Amish Cook at Home: Simple Pleasures of Food,
    Family, and Faith.* Kansas City, Mo.: Andrews McMeel Publishing.

———. 2009. *The Amish Cook's Baking Book.* Kansas City, Mo.: Andrews McMeel Publishing.

Eller, Vernard M. 1972. *In Place of Sacraments.* Grand Rapids, Mich.: Wm. B. Eerdmans.

Enns, Fernando. 2007. *The Peace Church and the Ecumenical Community: Ecclesiology and the
    Ethics of Nonviolence.* Kitchener, Ont.: Pandora Press.

Enns, Fernando, Scott Holland, and Ann K. Riggs. 2004. *Seeking Cultures of Peace: A Peace
    Church Conversation.* Telford, Pa · Cascadia Publishing House.

Ens, Adolf. 2004. *Becoming a National Church: A History of the Conference of Mennonites in
    Canada.* Winnipeg, Man.: CMU Press.

Epp, Frank H. 1962. *Mennonite Exodus: The Rescue and Resettlement of the Russian Mennonites
    Since the Communist Revolution.* Altona, Man.: D. W. Friesen and Sons.

———. 1974. *Mennonites in Canada, 1786-1920: The History of a Separate People.* Toronto:
    Macmillan of Canada.

———. 1982. *Mennonites in Canada, 1920-1940: A People's Struggle for Survival.* Scottdale,
    Pa.: Herald Press.

———, ed. 1983. *Partners in Service: The Story of Mennonite Central Committee Canada.*
    Winnipeg, Man.: MCC Canada.

Epp, Marlene. 1987. "Women in Canadian Mennonite History: Uncovering the 'Underside,'"
    Journal of Mennonite Studies 5:90–107.

———. 2000. *Women without Men: Mennonite Refugees of the Second World War.* Studies in
    Gender and History Series. Toronto: Univ. of Toronto Press.

———. 2008. *Mennonite Women in Canada: A History.* Winnipeg, Man.: Univ. of Manitoba
    Press.

Epp, Maureen, and Carol Ann Weaver, eds. 2006. *Sound in the Land: Essays on Mennonites and Music.* Kitchener, Ont.: Pandora Press.

Epp, Reuben. 1993. *The Story of Low German and Plautdietsch: Tracing a Language across the Globe.* Hillsboro, Kans.: Reader's Press.

Erb, Paul. 1939. "Nonresistance and Litigation." *Mennonite Quarterly Review* 13 (2): 75–82.

———. 1969. *Orie O. Miller: The Story of a Man and an Era.* Scottdale, Pa.: Herald Press.

Eriksson, Sven. 2007. "Women Pastors: Are We Practicing What We Preach?" Mennonite Church Canada. http://www.mennonitechurch.ca/resourcecentre/FileDownload/6308/Denominational_Minister.pdf.

Esau, Alvin J. 2004. *The Courts and the Colonies: The Litigation of Hutterite Church Disputes.* Vancouver, B.C.: Univ. of British Columbia Press.

Esau, John A., ed. 1995. *Understanding Ministerial Leadership: Essays Contributing to a Developing Theology of Ministry.* Elkhart, Ind.: Institute of Mennonite Studies.

Estep, William R. 1988. *Religious Liberty: Heritage and Responsibility.* North Newton, Kans.: Bethel College.

———. 1996. *The Anabaptist Story: An Introduction to 16th-Century Anabaptism.* 3rd ed. Grand Rapids, Mich.: Wm. B. Eerdmans.

Falcon, Rafael. 1986. *The Hispanic Mennonite Church in North America, 1932–1982.* Scottdale, Pa.: Herald Press.

Faus, Nancy R., ed. 1988. "Worship and Music." Special issue, *Brethren Life and Thought* 33 (4).

———, ed. 1993. *The Importance of Music in Worship.* Elgin, Ill.: Brethren Press.

———. 1994. "Spirituality and Worship in the Church of the Brethren." *Brethren Life and Thought* 39 (4): 241–50.

Faw, Chalmer E. 1974. "Profile of the Brethren in Mission: An Evaluation of 50 Years in Nigeria." *Brethren Life and Thought* 19 (2): 85–100.

Fike, Earle W. 1979. *A Raspberry Seed under God's Denture: The Wisdom and Wit of William McKinley Beahm, Missionary, Preacher, Educator.* Elgin, Ill.: Brethren Press.

Finger, Thomas N. 1985 and 1989. *Christian Theology: An Eschatological Approach.* 2 vols. Scottdale, Pa.: Herald Press.

———. 2004. *A Contemporary Anabaptist Theology: Biblical, Historical, Constructive.* Downers Grove, Ill.: InterVarsity Press.

Fisher, Gideon L. 1978. *Farm Life and Its Changes.* Gordonville, Pa.: Pequea Publishers.

Flores, Gilberto. 1984. "A Third Way." *Mennonite Quarterly Review* 58 (3): 399–409.

———. 2001. "Hispanic Mennonites in North America." *Mennonite Life* 56 (3).

Fretz, J. Winfield. 1953. *Pilgrims in Paraguay: The Story of Mennonite Colonization in Paraguay.* Scottdale, Pa.: Herald Press.

———. 1978. *The MEDA Experiment: Twenty-five Years of Economic Development.* Waterloo, Ont.: Conrad Press.

Friedmann, Robert. 1940. "Anabaptism and Pietism." *Mennonite Quarterly Review* 14 (2): 90–128; 14 (3): 144–69.

———. 1949. *Mennonite Piety through the Centuries: Its Genius and Its Literature.* Goshen, Ind.: Mennonite Historical Society.

———. 1958. "Hutterian Pottery or Haban Fayences." *Mennonite Life* 13 (4): 147–52.

———. 1970. "Peter Riedemann: Early Anabaptist Leader." *Mennonite Quarterly Review* 44 (1): 5–44.

Friesen, Abraham. 1998. "Present at the Inception: Menno Simons and the Beginnings of Dutch Anabaptism." *Mennonite Quarterly Review* 72 (3): 351–88.

Friesen, Duane K. 2000. *Artists, Citizens, Philosophers: Seeking the Peace of the City.* Scottdale, Pa.: Herald Press.

Friesen, John J., ed. 1989. *Mennonites in Russia, 1788–1988: Essays in Honour of Gerhard Lohrenz.* Winnipeg, Man.: CMBC Publications.

———, trans. and ed. 1999. *Peter Riedemann's Hutterite Confession of Faith.* Scottdale, Pa.: Herald Press.

———. 2007. *Building Communities: The Changing Face of Manitoba Mennonites.* Winnipeg, Man.: CMU Press.

Friesen, John J., and Peter J. Klassen, eds. 1992. "Mennonites in Poland and Prussia." Special issue, *Mennonite Quarterly Review* 66 (2).

GAMEO. *See* Global Anabaptist Mennonite Encyclopedia Online.

Gardner, Richard B. 1983. "Brethren and the Bible." *Brethren Life and Thought* 28 (1): 7–15.

Garrett, Ruth Irene. 2001. *Crossing Over: One Woman's Exodus from Amish Life.* With Rick Farrant. Allen, Tex.: Thomas More.

Gates, Gary. 1987. *How to Speak Dutchified English.* Intercourse, Pa.: Good Books.

Gates, Helen Kolb, John Funk Kolb, J. Clemens Kolb, and Constance Kolb Sykes. 1964. *Bless the Lord, O My Soul: A Biography of Bishop John Fretz Funk, 1835-1930, Creative Pioneer for Christ and Mennonite Leader.* Scottdale, Pa.: Herald Press.

Gingerich, Hugh F., and Rachel W. Kreider. 1986. *Amish and Amish Mennonite Genealogies.* Gordonville, Pa.: Pequea Publishers.

Gingerich, Melvin. 1949. *Service for Peace: A History of Mennonite Civilian Public Service.* Akron, Pa.: Mennonite Central Committee.

———. 1964. "Harold S. Bender and *The Mennonite Encyclopedia.*" *Mennonite Quarterly Review* 38 (2): 172–74.

———. 1970. *Mennonite Attire through Four Centuries.* Breinigsville, Pa.: Pennsylvania German Society.

Gingerich, Orland. 1972. *The Amish of Canada.* Waterloo, Ont.: Conrad Press.

Gleysteen, Jan. 2007. *Mennonite Tourguide to Western Europe.* Rev. ed. Morgantown, Pa.: Masthof Press.

Glick, Lester, and Doris Glick. 1988. *Adolescence: Becoming Adult.* Scottdale, Pa.: Herald Press.

Global Anabaptist Mennonite Encyclopedia Online. http://www.gameo.org.

Good, E. Reginald. 1988. *Frontier Community to Urban Congregation: First Mennonite Church, Kitchener, 1813-1988.* Kitchener, Ont.: First Mennonite Church.

Good, Merle. 1985. "Reflections on *Witness* Controversy." *Gospel Herald* (Mar. 5): 161–64.

Good, Phyllis Pellman. 1999. *Quilts from Two Valleys: Amish Quilts from the Big Valley, Mennonite Quilts from the Shenandoah Valley.* Intercourse, Pa.: Good Books.

———. 2000. *Fix-It and Forget-It Cookbook: Feasting with Your Slow Cooker.* Intercourse, Pa.: Good Books.

Goossen, Rachel Waltner. 1994. "Piety and Professionalism: The Bethel Deaconesses of the Great Plains." *Mennonite Life* 49 (1): 4–11.

———. 1997. *Women against the Good War: Conscientious Objection and Gender on the American Home Front, 1941-1947.* Chapel Hill, N.C.: Univ. of North Carolina Press.

Graber Miller, Keith. 1996. *Wise as Serpents, Innocent as Doves: American Mennonites Engage Washington.* Knoxville: Univ. of Tennessee Press.

———. 2001. "Complex Innocence, Obligatory Nurturance, and Parental Vigilance: 'The Child' in the Work of Menno Simons." In *The Child in Christian Thought,* ed. Marcia J. Bunge, 194–226. Grand Rapids, Mich.: Wm. B. Eerdmans.

Granddaughter's Inglenook Cookbook. 1942. Elgin, Ill.: Brethren Publishing House.

Gratz, Delbert L. 1953. *Bernese Anabaptists and Their American Descendants.* Scottdale, Pa.: Herald Press.

Graybill, Beth. 2002. "'To Remind Us Who We Are': Multiple Meanings of Conservative Women's Dress." In *Strangers at Home: Amish and Mennonite Women in History,* ed. Kimberly D. Schmidt, Diane Zimmerman Umble, and Stephen Reschly, 53–77. Baltimore: Johns Hopkins Univ. Press.

Gregory, Brad S. 1999. *Salvation at Stake: Christian Martyrdom in Early Modern Europe.* Cambridge, Mass.: Harvard Univ. Press.

Greiser, David B., and Michael A. King, eds. 2003. *Anabaptist Preaching: A Conversation between Pulpit, Pew, and Bible.* Telford, Pa.: Cascadia Publishing House.

Grimsrud, Ted, and Mark Thiessen Nation. 2008. *Reasoning Together: A Conversation on Homosexuality.* Scottdale, Pa.: Herald Press.

Groff, Warren, 1975. "Response to Brethren Identity and the Unity of the Church." *Brethren Life and Thought* 20 (4): 236–38.

———. 1984. *Prayer: God's Time and Ours.* Elgin, Ill.: Brethren Press.

Gross, David. 1992. *The Past in Ruins: Tradition and the Critique of Modernity.* Amherst, Mass.: Univ. of Massachusetts Press.

Gross, Leonard. 1980. *The Golden Years of the Hutterites: Witness and Thought of the Communal Moravian Anabaptists during the Walpot Era, 1565–1578.* Scottdale, Pa.: Herald Press.

———. 1986. "The Doctrinal Era of the Mennonite Church." *Mennonite Quarterly Review* 60 (1): 83–103.

———, trans. and ed. 1997. *Prayer Book for Earnest Christians.* Scottdale, Pa.: Herald Press.

Gross, Paul S. 1965. *The Hutterite Way.* Saskatoon, Sask.: Freeman Publishing Company.

Gundy, Jeff. 1997. "U.S. Mennonite Poetry and Poets: Beyond Dr. Johnson's Dog." *Mennonite Quarterly Review* 71 (1): 5–41.

———. 2005. *Walker in the Fog: On Mennonite Writing.* Telford, Pa.: Cascadia Publishing House.

Guth, Hermann. 1995. *Amish Mennonites in Germany: Their Congregations, the Estates Where They Lived, Their Families.* Morgantown, Pa.: Masthof Press.

Haas, J. Craig, and Steven M. Nolt. 1993. *The Mennonite Starter Kit.* Intercourse, Pa.: Good Books.

Habegger, Lois. 1959. *Cheyenne Trails: A History of Mennonites and Cheyennes in Montana.* Newton, Kans.: Mennonite Publication Office.

Hallock, Daniel. 1998. *Hell, Healing, and Resistance: Veterans Speak.* Farmington, Pa.: Plough Publishing House.

Hamm, Thomas D. 2003. *The Quakers in America.* New York: Columbia Univ. Press.

Hanks, Gardner C. 1997. *Against the Death Penalty: Christian and Secular Arguments against Capital Punishment.* Scottdale, Pa.: Herald Press.

Harrison, Wes. 1997. *Andreas Ehrenpreis and Hutterite Faith and Practice.* Kitchener, Ont.: Pandora Press.

Haury, David A. 1981. *Prairie People: A History of the Western District Conference.* Newton, Kans.: Faith and Life Press.

Hege, Nathan B. 1998. *Beyond Our Prayers: Anabaptist Church Growth in Ethiopia, 1948–1998.* Scottdale, Pa.: Herald Press.

Heggen, Carolyn Holderread. 1993. *Sexual Abuse in Christian Homes and Churches.* Scottdale, Pa.: Herald Press.

Heidebrecht, Paul C. 2006. "Walking with Yoder toward a Theological Approach to the Automobile from a Mennonite Perspective." *Conrad Grebel Review* 24 (2): 59–80.

Heisey, M. J. 2003. *Peace and Persistence: Tracing the Brethren in Christ Peace Witness through Three Generations.* Kent, Ohio: Kent State Univ. Press.

Heisey, Nancy. 2006. "Pilgrimage, Place, and People: A History of the Locations of Mennonite World Conference Assemblies, 1925–2003." *Church History* 75 (4): 849–79.

Heppner, Jack. 1987. *Search for Renewal: The Story of the Rudnerweider/EMMC, 1937–1987.* Winnipeg, Man.: Evangelical Mennonite Mission Conference.

Hernley, H. Ralph, comp. 1970. *The Compassionate Community.* Scottdale, Pa.: Association of Mennonite Aid Societies.

Herr, Patricia T. 2000. *Quilting Traditions: Pieces from the Past.* Atglen, Pa.: Schiffer Publishing.

———. 2004. *Amish Quilts of Lancaster County.* Atglen, Pa.: Schiffer Publishing.

Hershberger, Anne Krabill, ed. 1999. *Sexuality: God's Gift.* Scottdale, Pa.: Herald Press.

Hershberger, Guy F. 1939. "Nonresistance and Industrial Conflict." *Mennonite Quarterly Review* 13 (2): 135–54.

———. 1958. *The Way of the Cross in Human Relationships.* Scottdale, Pa.: Herald Press.

Hershey, Mary Jane Lederach. 2003. *This Teaching I Present: Fraktur from the Skippack and Salford Mennonite Meetinghouse Schools, 1747–1836.* Intercourse, Pa.: Good Books.

Hess, Clarke E. 2002. *Mennonite Arts.* Atglen, Pa.: Schiffer Publishing.

Hiebert, Clarence. 1973. *The Holdeman People: The Church of God in Christ, Mennonite, 1859–1969.* Pasadena, Calif.: William Carey Library.

Hiebert, Peter C., and Orie O. Miller, eds. 1929. *Feeding the Hungry: Russia Famine, 1919–1925.* Scottdale, Pa.: Mennonite Central Committee.

Higueros, Mario. 1995. "The Anabaptist Vision in the Church of Central America." *Mennonite Quarterly Review* 69 (3): 389–404.

Hinojosa, Felipe. 2009. "Making Noise among the 'Quiet in the Land': Mexican American and Puerto Rican Ethno-Religious Identity in the Mennonite Church, 1932–1982," Ph.D. diss., University of Houston.

Homan, Gerlof D. 1994. *American Mennonites and the Great War: 1914–1918.* Scottdale, Pa.: Herald Press.

Hoover, Amos B., trans., ed., and comp. 1982. *The Jonas Martin Era (1875–1925).* Denver, Pa.: Muddy Creek Farm Library.

———, ed. 2006. *Whether by Word or Epistle: Letters of Frank W. Hurst and Other Weaverland Conference Mennonites of Pennsylvania to Thomas Reesor of Ontario, 1920–1948.* Ephrata, Pa.: Muddy Creek Farm Library.

Hoover, John David. 1990. "An Old Order Mennonite Wedding Ceremony in Pennsylvania." *Pennsylvania Mennonite Heritage* 13 (3): 11.

Horst, Irvin B. 1956. "Rembrandt Knew Mennonites." *Mennonite Life* 11 (4): 148–54.

———. 1982. "The Dordrecht Confession of Faith: Three Hundred Fifty Years." *Pennsylvania Mennonite Heritage* 5 (3): 2–8.

———, ed. 1986. *Dutch Dissenters: A Critical Companion to their History and Ideas, with a Bibliographical Survey of Recent Research Pertaining to the Early Reformation in the Netherlands.* Boston: Brill.

———, trans. and ed. 1988. *Mennonite Confession of Faith* [Dordrecht Confession]. Lancaster, Pa.: Lancaster Mennonite Historical Society.

Hostetler, Ann, ed. 2003. *A Cappella: Mennonite Voices in Poetry.* Iowa City: Univ. of Iowa Press.

Hostetler, Beulah. 1992. "The Formation of the Old Orders." *Mennonite Quarterly Review* 66 (1): 5–25.

Hostetler, John A. 1992. "An Amish Beginning." *American Scholar* 61 (Autumn): 552–62.

———. 1993. *Amish Society.* 4th ed. Baltimore: Johns Hopkins Univ. Press.

———. 1997. *Hutterite Society.* Baltimore: Johns Hopkins Univ. Press. (Orig. pub. 1974.)

Hostetler, John A., and Donald B. Kraybill. 1988. "Hollywood Markets the Amish." In *Image Ethics: The Moral Rights of Subjects in Photographs, Film, and Television,* ed. L. Gross, J. Katz, and J. Ruby, 220–35. New York: Oxford Univ. Press.

Huffines, Marion Lois. 1988. "Pennsylvania German among the Plain Groups: Convergence as a Strategy of Language Maintenance." *Brethren Life and Thought* 33 (3): 242–49.

Hüppi, John. 2000. "Research Note: Identifying Jacob Ammann." *Mennonite Quarterly Review* 74 (2): 329–39.

Hurst, Charles E., and David L. McConnell. 2010. *An Amish Paradox: Diversity and Change in the World's Largest Amish Community.* Baltimore: Johns Hopkins Univ. Press.

Hutterian Brethren, trans. and eds. 1987. *The Chronicle of the Hutterian Brethren, Volume I.* Rifton, N.Y.: Plough Publishing House.

———, trans. and eds. 1998. *The Chronicle of the Hutterian Brethren, Volume II.* Ste. Agathe, Man.: Crystal Spring Colony.

Hymnal: A Worship Book Prepared by Churches in the Believers Church Tradition. 1992. Elgin, Ill.: Brethren Press.

Inglenook Cook Book. 1901. Repr. of 1901 ed., Elgin, Ill.: Brethren Publishing House, 1981.

Janzen, Reinhild Kauenhoven. 1992. "Sources and Styles of the Material Culture Life of Mennonites in the Vistula Delta." *Mennonite Quarterly Review* 66 (2): 167–98.

———. 1994. "Mennonite Furniture: The Dynamics of a Migrant Cultural Tradition." *Kansas Quarterly* 25 (2): 31–45.

Janzen, Reinhild Kavenhoven, and John M. Janzen. 1991. *Mennonite Furniture: A Migrant Tradition (1766–1910).* Intercourse, Pa.: Good Books.

Janzen, Rod. 1999. *The Prairie People: Forgotten Anabaptists.* Hanover, N.H.: University Press of New England.

———. 2005. "The Hutterites and the Bruderhof: The Relationship between an Old Order Religious Society and a 20th-Century Communal Group." *Mennonite Quarterly Review* 74 (4): 505–44.

Janzen, Rod, and Max Stanton. 2010. *The Hutterites in North America.* Baltimore: Johns Hopkins Univ. Press.

Janzen, William. 1990. *Limits on Liberty: The Experience of Mennonite, Hutterite, and Doukhobor Communities in Canada.* Toronto: Univ. of Toronto Press.

Jérôme, Claude. 2005. "Agriculture and Religion: The Success of Anabaptists in Alsace in the 18th and 19th Centuries." Trans. Kevin J. Ruth. *Pennsylvania Mennonite Heritage* 28 (1): 14–23.

Jeschke, Marlin. 1983. *Believers Baptism for Children of the Church.* Scottdale, Pa.: Herald Press.

———. 1988. *Discipling in the Church: Recovering a Ministry of the Gospel.* 3rd ed. Scottdale, Pa.: Herald Press.

Johansen, Ruthann Knechel. 1977. *Coming Together: Male and Female in a Renamed Garden.* Elgin, Ill.: Brethren Press.

Johnson-Weiner, Karen M. 2001. "The Role of Women in Old Order Amish, Beachy Amish, and Fellowship Churches." *Mennonite Quarterly Review* 75 (2): 231–56.

————. 2007. *Train up a Child: Old Order Amish and Mennonite Schools.* Baltimore: Johns Hopkins Univ. Press.

————. 2010. *New York Amish: Life in the Plain Communities of the Empire State.* Ithaca: Cornell Univ. Press.

Juhnke, James C. 1979. *A People of Mission: History of General Conference Mennonite Overseas Missions.* Newton, Kans.: Faith and Life Press.

————. 1980. "General Conference Mennonite Missions to the American Indians in the Late 19th Century." *Mennonite Quarterly Review* 54 (2): 117–34.

————. 1983. "Gemeindechristentum and Bible Doctrine: Two Mennonite Visions of the Early 20th Century." *Mennonite Quarterly Review* 57 (3): 206–21.

————. 1986. "Mennonite Benevolence and Revitalization in the Wake of World War I." *Mennonite Quarterly Review* 60 (1): 15–30.

————. 1988. "Mennonite History and Self Understanding: North American Mennonitism as a Bipolar Mosaic." In *Mennonite Identity: Historical and Contemporary Perspectives,* ed. Calvin Wall Redekop, 83–99. Lanham, Md.: University Press of America.

————. 1989. *Vision, Doctrine, War: Mennonite Identity and Organization in America, 1890–1930.* The Mennonite Experience in America, vol. 3. Scottdale, Pa.: Herald Press.

————, ed. 1990. "*Martyrs Mirror.*" Special issue, *Mennonite Life* 45 (3).

————. 1999. "Shaping Religious Community through Martyr Memories." *Mennonite Quarterly Review* 73 (3): 546–56.

Juhnke, James C., and Carol M. Hunter. 2004. *The Missing Peace: The Search for Nonviolent Alternatives in United States History.* 2nd ed. Kitchener, Ont.: Pandora Press.

Kanagy, Conrad L. 2007. *Road Signs for the Journey.* Scottdale, Pa.: Herald Press.

Kauffman, J. Howard. 1996. "Mennonite Charismatics: Are They Any Different?" *Mennonite Quarterly Review* 70 (4): 449–72.

Kauffman, J. Howard, and Leo Driedger. 1991. *The Mennonite Mosaic: Identity and Modernization.* Scottdale, Pa.: Herald Press.

Kauffman, J. Howard, and Leland Harder. 1975. *Anabaptists Four Centuries Later.* Scottdale, Pa.: Herald Press.

Kauffman, Jess. 1984. *A Vision and a Legacy: The Story of Mennonite Camping, 1920–80.* Newton, Kans.: Faith and Life Press.

Kaufman, Donald D. 1978. *The Tax Dilemma: Praying for Peace, Paying for War.* Scottdale, Pa.: Herald Press.

Kaufman, Edna Ramseyer. 1974. *Melting Pot of Mennonite Cookery, 1874–1974.* North Newton, Kans.: Bethel College Women's Association.

Kaufman, Gordon D. 1968. *Systematic Theology: A Historicist Perspective.* New York: Charles Scribner's Sons.

————. 1993. *In Face of Mystery: A Constructive Theology.* Cambridge, Mass.: Harvard Univ. Press.

Kaylor, Earl C., Jr. 1996. *Martin Grove Brumbaugh: A Pennsylvanian's Odyssey from Sainted Schoolman to Bedeviled World War I Governor, 1862–1930.* Cranbury, N.J.: Associated University Presses.

Keating, Christopher. 1982. "You Can't Go Home the Same." *Messenger* 131 (Sept.): 38–40.

Kehrberg, Sarah, ed. 2007. *Mennonite Handbook.* Scottdale, Pa.: Herald Press.

Keifer, Luke L., Jr. 1990. "American Motifs in Anabaptist Heritage." *Brethren in Christ History and Life* 13 (3): 293–323.

Keim, Albert N., ed. 1975. *Compulsory Education and the Amish: The Right Not to Be Modern.* Boston: Beacon Press.

———. 1990. *The CPS Story: An Illustrated History of Civilian Public Service.* Intercourse, Pa.: Good Books.

———. 1998. *Harold S. Bender, 1897–1962.* Scottdale, Pa.: Herald Press.

Keim, Albert N., and Grant M. Stoltzfus. 1988. *The Politics of Conscience: The Historic Peace Churches and America at War, 1917–1955.* Scottdale, Pa.: Herald Press.

Kern, Kathleen. 2009. *In Harm's Way: A History of Christian Peacemaker Teams.* Eugene, Ore.: Cascade Books.

King, Michael A., ed. 2007. *Stumbling toward a Genuine Conversation on Homosexuality.* Telford, Pa.: Cascadia Publishing House.

Kissinger, Warren S. 1975. *The Sermon on the Mount: A History of Interpretation and Bibliography.* Metuchen, N.J.: Scarecrow Press.

———, ed. 1983. "Brethren Biblical Interpretation." Special issue, *Brethren Life and Thought* 28 (1).

Klaassen, Walter. 1973. *Anabaptism: Neither Catholic Nor Protestant.* Waterloo, Ont.: Conrad Press.

———. 1981. "The Anabaptist Critique of Constantinian Christendom." *Mennonite Quarterly Review* 55 (3): 218–30.

———. 1988. "Menno Simons: Molder of Tradition." *Mennonite Quarterly Review* 62 (3): 368–86.

Klaassen, Walter, and William Klassen. 2008. *Marpeck: A Life of Dissent and Conformity.* Scottdale: Pa.: Herald Press.

Klassen, A. J., ed. 1997. *Alternative Service for Peace in Canada during World War II, 1941–1946.* Abbotsford, B.C.: Mennonite Central Committee of British Columbia.

Klassen, Doreen. 1989. *Singing Mennonite: Low German Songs among the Mennonites.* Winnipeg, Man.: Univ. of Manitoba Press.

Klassen, Peter J. 1964. *The Economics of Anabaptism, 1525–1560.* London: Mouton.

———. 1989. *A Homeland for Strangers: An Introduction to Mennonites in Poland and Prussia.* Fresno, Calif.: Center for Mennonite Brethren Studies.

———. 2009. *Mennonites in Early Modern Poland and Prussia.* Baltimore: Johns Hopkins Univ. Press.

Klassen, Peter P. 1999. "Worship and Churches in the Development of Mennonite Settlements in Paraguay and Brazil." *Mennonite Quarterly Review* 73 (2): 286–301.

Klassen, William, and Walter Klaassen. 1978. *The Writings of Pilgram Marpeck.* Scottdale, Pa.: Herald Press.

Klippenstein, Lawrence. 1979. *That There Be Peace: Mennonites in Canada and World War II.* Winnipeg, Man.: Manitoba CO Reunion Committee.

Klippenstein, Lawrence, and Jacob Dick. 2002. *Mennonite Alternative Service in Russia: The Story of Abram Dück and His Colleagues, 1911–1917.* Kitchener, Ont.: Pandora Press.

Klopfenstein, Perry A. 1984. *Marching to Zion: A History of the Apostolic Christian Church of America, 1847–1982.* [Eureka, Ill.?]: Apostolic Christian Church of America.

Kniss, Fred L. 1997. *Disquiet in the Land: Cultural Conflict in American Mennonite Communities.* New Brunswick, N.J.: Rutgers Univ. Press.

Koontz, Ted. 1996. *Godward: Personal Stories of Grace.* Scottdale, Pa.: Herald Press.

Koop, Karl. 2004. *Anabaptist-Mennonite Confessions of Faith: The Development of a Tradition.* Kitchener, Ont.: Pandora Press.

———, ed. 2006. *Confessions of Faith in the Anabaptist Tradition, 1527–1660*. Kitchener, Ont.: Pandora Press.

Koop, Karl, and Mary H. Schertz, eds. 2000. *Without Spot or Wrinkle: Reflecting Theologically on the Nature of the Church*. Elkhart, Ind.: Institute of Mennonite Studies.

Kotva, Joseph J., Jr. 2005. "The Question of Abortion: Christian Virtue and Government Legislation." *Mennonite Quarterly Review* 79 (4): 481–504.

Krahn, Cornelius. 1956. "The Office of Elder in Anabaptist-Mennonite History." *Mennonite Quarterly Review* 30 (2): 120–27.

———. 1957. "The Artist Govert Flinck." *Mennonite Life* 12 (2): 52–55, 95.

———, ed. 1963. "Dutch Mennonites in the 1960s." Special issue, *Mennonite Life* 18 (4).

———. 1981. *Dutch Anabaptism: Origin, Spread, Life, and Thought*. Scottdale, Pa.: Herald Press.

Kraus, C. Norman, ed. 1979. *Evangelicalism and Anabaptism*. Scottdale, Pa.: Herald Press.

———. 1987. *Jesus Christ Our Lord: Christology from a Disciple's Perspective*. Scottdale, Pa.: Herald Press.

———, ed. 2001. *To Continue the Dialogue: Biblical Interpretation and Homosexuality*. Telford, Pa.: Pandora Press.

Kraybill, Donald B. 1976. *Our Star-Spangled Faith*. Scottdale, Pa.: Herald Press.

———. 1978. "The Mennonite Woman's Veiling: The Rise and Fall of a Sacred Symbol." *Mennonite Quarterly Review* 61 (3): 298–320.

———. 1988. "Modernity and Identity: The Transformation of Mennonite Ethnicity." In *Mennonite Identity: Historical and Contemporary Perspectives*, ed. Calvin Wall Redekop, 153–72. Lanham, Md.: University Press of America.

———. 1996. "MCC and the Transformation of Mennonite Identity." *Mennonite Quarterly Review* 70 (1): 23–58.

———. 2001. *The Riddle of Amish Culture*. Rev. ed. Baltimore: Johns Hopkins Univ. Press.

———, ed. 2003a. *The Amish and the State*. 2nd ed. Baltimore: Johns Hopkins Univ. Press.

———. 2003b. *The Upside-Down Kingdom*. 3rd ed. Scottdale, Pa.: Herald Press.

———. 2003c. *Who Are the Anabaptists? Amish, Brethren, Hutterites, and Mennonites*. Scottdale, Pa.: Herald Press.

Kraybill, Donald B., and Carl Desportes Bowman. 2001. *On the Backroad to Heaven: Old Order Hutterites, Mennonites, Amish, and Brethren*. Baltimore: Johns Hopkins Univ. Press.

Kraybill, Donald B., and Phyllis P. Good, eds. 1982. *Perils of Professionalism: Essays on Christian Faith and Professionalism*. Scottdale, Pa.: Herald Press.

Kraybill, Donald B., Patricia T. Herr, and Jonathan Holstein. 1996. *A Quiet Spirit: Amish Quilts from the Collection of Cindy Tietze and Stuart Hodosh*. Los Angeles: UCLA Fowler Museum of Cultural History.

Kraybill, Donald B., and C. Nelson Hostetter. 2001. *Anabaptist World USA*. Scottdale, Pa.: Herald Press.

Kraybill, Donald B., and James P. Hurd. 2006. *Horse-and-Buggy Mennonites: Hoofbeats of Humility in a Postmodern World*. University Park, Pa.: Pennsylvania State Univ. Press.

Kraybill, Donald B., Karen M. Johnson-Weiner, and Steven M. Nolt. Forthcoming. *The Amish in America*. Baltimore: Johns Hopkins Univ. Press.

Kraybill, Donald B., and Kyle C. Kopko. 2007. "Bush Fever: Amish and Old Order Mennonites in the 2004 Presidential Campaign." *Mennonite Quarterly Review* 81 (2): 165–205.

Kraybill, Donald B., and Steven M. Nolt. 2004. *Amish Enterprise: From Plows to Profits*. 2nd ed. Baltimore: Johns Hopkins Univ. Press.

Kraybill, Donald B., Steven M. Nolt, and David L. Weaver-Zercher. 2007. *Amish Grace: How Forgiveness Transcended Tragedy.* San Francisco: Jossey-Bass.

———. 2010. *The Amish Way: Patient Faith in a Perilous World.* San Francisco: Jossey-Bass.

Kraybill, Donald B., and Marc A. Olshan, eds. 1994. *The Amish Struggle with Modernity.* Hanover, N.H.: University Press of New England.

Kreider, Carl. 1980. *The Christian Entrepreneur.* Scottdale, Pa.: Herald Press.

Kreider, Eleanor. 1987. "Let the Faithful Greet Each Other: The Kiss of Peace." *Conrad Grebel Review* 5 (1): 29–49.

———. 1997. *Communion Shapes Character.* Scottdale, Pa.: Herald Press.

Kreider, J. Kenneth. 2001. *A Cup of Cold Water: The Story of Brethren Service.* Elgin, Ill.: Brethren Press.

Kreider, Robert S., ed. 1980. "Images of Mennonite Missions in India, China, Congo, Japan, Taiwan, Colombia, Paraguay." Special issue, *Mennonite Life* 35 (2).

Kreider, Robert S., and Rachel Waltner Goossen. 1988. *Hungry, Thirsty, a Stranger: The MCC Experience.* Scottdale, Pa.: Herald Press.

Kroeker, Wally, ed. 2003. "MEDA History." Special issue, *The Marketplace* 33 (Nov.–Dec.).

———. 2005. *An Introduction to the Russian Mennonites.* Intercourse, Pa.: Good Books.

Kropf, Marlene, and Kenneth James Nafziger. 2001. *Singing: A Mennonite Voice.* Scottdale, Pa.: Herald Press.

Labi, Nadya. 2005. "The Gentle People." *Legal Affairs* 4 (1): 24–32.

Lapp, John A. 1972. *The Mennonite Church in India, 1897–1962.* Scottdale, Pa.: Herald Press.

Lapp, John A., and C. Arnold Snyder, eds. 2006a. *Anabaptist Songs in African Hearts.* Global Mennonite History Series: Africa. 3rd ed. Intercourse, Pa.: Good Books.

———. 2006b. *Testing Faith and Tradition.* Global Mennonite History Series: Europe. Intercourse, Pa.: Good Books.

Lapp, John A., and Ed van Straten. 2003. "Mennonite World Conference, 1925–2000: From Euro-American Conference to Worldwide Communion." *Mennonite Quarterly Review* 77 (1): 7–45.

Lederach, John Paul. 1999. *The Journey toward Reconciliation.* Scottdale, Pa.: Herald Press.

Lederach, Paul M. 2002. *The Road to Goodville: The Story of Goodville Mutual Casualty Company through 75 Years.* New Holland, Pa.: Goodville Mutual Casualty Company.

Lehman, James O. 2002. *Mennonite Tent Revivals: Howard Hammer and Myron Augsburger.* Kitchener, Ont.: Pandora Press.

Lehman, James O., and Steven M. Nolt. 2007. *Mennonites, Amish, and the American Civil War.* Baltimore: Johns Hopkins Univ. Press.

Leichty, Paul D. 2006. "Mennonite Advocacy for Persons with Disabilities." *Journal of Religion, Disability, and Health* 10 (1/2): 195–205. http://secure.mennonite.net/.cWtools/download.php/mnF=Jo95V10No1_13.pdf,mnOD=Papers%20-%20PDF,mnOD=Papers,mnOD=My%20Documents,dc=adnet,dc=mennonite,dc=net.

Leisy, Bruce R. 1976. "The Last of the Mennonite Brewers." *Mennonite Life* 31 (1): 4–9.

Lesher, Emerson. 1985. *The Muppie Manual: The Mennonite Urban Professional's Handbook for Humility and Success.* Intercourse, Pa.: Good Books.

Letkemann, Peter. 2001. "The German Hymnody of Prussian Mennonites: A Tale of Two Gesangbücher." *Preservings* 18 (June): 120–30.

Lichdi, Diether Götz, and Loretta Kreider, eds. 1990. *Mennonite World Handbook: Mennonites in Global Witness.* Carol Stream, Ill.: Mennonite World Conference.

Liechty, Daniel. 1994. *Early Anabaptist Spirituality: Selected Writings.* Mahwah, N.Y.: Paulist Press.

Liechty, Joseph L. 1980. "Humility: The Foundation of the Mennonite Religious Outlook in the 1860s." *Mennonite Quarterly Review* 54 (1): 5–31.

Lind, Mary Beth, and Cathleen Hockman-Wert. 2005. *Simply in Season: A World Community Cookbook.* Scottdale, Pa.: Herald Press.

Lind, Millard C. 2004. *The Sound of Sheer Silence and the Killing State: The Death Penalty and the Bible.* Telford, Pa.: Cascadia Publishing House.

Lindholm, William C. 2003. "The National Committee for Amish Religious Freedom." In *The Amish and the State,* ed. Donald B. Kraybill, 109–24. 2nd ed. Baltimore: Johns Hopkins Univ. Press.

Loewen, Harry. 1999. "Mennonite Literature in Canadian and American Mennonite Historiography: An Introduction." *Mennonite Quarterly Review* 73 (3): 557–70.

———. 2000. *Road to Freedom: Mennonites Escape the Land of Suffering.* Kitchener, Ont.: Pandora Press.

Loewen, Harry, and Steven M. Nolt. 2010. *Through Fire and Water: An Overview of Mennonite History.* Rev. ed. Scottdale, Pa.: Herald Press.

Loewen, Heinrich. 2003. "Mennonite Historical Interest in Germany." *Mennonite Historian* 29 (4): 1–2.

Loewen, Howard John. 1985. *One Lord, One Church, One Hope, and One God: Mennonite Confessions of Faith in North America, an Introduction.* Elkhart, Ind.: Institute of Mennonite Studies.

Loewen, Royden, ed. 2004. "Old Colony Mennonites." Special issue, *Journal of Mennonite Studies* 22.

———. 2005. "The Quiet on the Land." *Journal of Mennonite Studies* 23:151–64.

———. 2006. *Diaspora in the Countryside: Two Mennonite Communities and Mid-20th-Century Rural Disjuncture.* Urbana, Ill.: Univ. of Illinois Press.

———. 2008. "To the Ends of the Earth: An Introduction to the Conservative Low German Mennonites in the Americas." *Mennonite Quarterly Review* 82 (3): 427–48.

———, ed. 2009. "Mennonites and Money: Wealth and Poverty in the Past and Present." JMS Forum issue, *Journal of Mennonite Studies* 27.

Longacre, Doris Janzen. 1976. *More-with-Less Cookbook: Suggestions by Mennonites on How to Eat Better and Consume Less of the World's Limited Food Resources.* Scottdale, Pa.: Herald Press.

Longenecker, Stephen L. 1981. *The Christopher Sauers: Courageous Printers Who Defended Religious Freedom in Early America.* Elgin, Ill.: Brethren Press.

———. 2006. *The Brethren during the Age of World War: The Church of the Brethren Encounter with Modernization, 1914–1950.* Elgin, Ill.: Brethren Press.

Louden, Mark L. 2006. "Pennsylvania German in the 21st Century." In *Sprachinselwelten— The World of Language Islands,* ed. Nina Berend and Elisabeth Knipf-Komlósi, 89–107. Frankfurt: Peter Lang.

Lowe, John W., Jr. 1993. "Brethren and Native Americans: An Unfulfilled History." *Brethren Life and Thought* 38 (3): 137–50.

Lowry, James W. 2003. *Hans Landis: Swiss Anabaptist Martyr in 17th Century Documents.* Millersburg, Ohio: Ohio Amish Library.

———. 2007. *Documents of Brotherly Love: Dutch Mennonite Aid to Swiss Anabaptists, Volume 1, 1635–1709.* Millersburg, Ohio: Ohio Amish Library.

Luthy, David. 1994. "The Origin and Growth of Amish Tourism." In *The Amish Struggle with Modernity*, ed. Donald B. Kraybill and Marc A. Olshan, 113–29. Hanover, N.H.: University Press of New England.

———. 1995. *Amish Folk Artist Barbara Ebersol: Her Life, Fraktur, and Death Record Book*. Lancaster, Pa.: Lancaster Mennonite Historical Society.

MacMaster, Richard K. 1985. *Land, Piety, and Peoplehood: The Establishment of Mennonite Communities in America, 1683–1790*. The Mennonite Experience in America, vol. 1. Scottdale, Pa.: Herald Press.

———. 2006. *Mennonite and Brethren in Christ Churches of New York City*. Kitchener, Ont.: Pandora Press.

MacMaster, Richard K., Samuel L. Horst, and Robert F. Ulle. 1979. *Conscience in Crisis: Mennonites and Other Peace Churches in America, 1739–1789*. Scottdale, Pa.: Herald Press.

Marr, Lucille. 2003. *The Transforming Power of a Century: Mennonite Central Committee and Its Evolution in Ontario*. Kitchener, Ont.: Pandora Press.

Martens, Helen. 2002. *Hutterite Songs*. Kitchener, Ont.: Pandora Press.

Martens, Peter. 2008. "The Quest for an Anabaptist Atonement: Violence and Nonviolence in J. Denny Weaver's *The Nonviolent Atonement*." *Mennonite Quarterly Review* 82 (2): 281–313.

Martin, Andrew C. 2007. "Creating a Timeless Tradition: The Effects of Fundamentalism on the Conservative Mennonite Movement." M.T.S. thesis, Univ. of Waterloo.

Martin, Clarence E. 1994. "Time Line of the Development of the Bahamas Church." *The Eastern Mennonite Testimony of the Pennsylvania Mennonite Church and Related Areas*. 26 (May): 8–9.

Martin, Donald. 2003. *Old Order Mennonites of Ontario: Gelassenheit, Discipleship, Brotherhood*. Kitchener, Ont.: Pandora Press.

Martin, Earl S. 1978. *Reaching the Other Side: The Journal of an American Who Stayed to Witness Vietnam's Postwar Transition*. New York: Crown Publishers.

Martínez, Juan Francisco. 1999. "Training Leaders for the Latin American Anabaptist Churches in the 21st Century." *Courier* 14 (2): 10–12.

———. 2000. "Latin American Anabaptist-Mennonites: A Profile." *Mennonite Quarterly Review* 74 (3): 463–77.

———. 2005. "Toward a Latino/a Mennonite History." *Journal of Mennonite Studies* 23: 37–46.

———. 2006. "When Anabaptists Relate to Pentecostals." *Courier* 21 (1 and 2): 2–3.

May, Melanie A., ed. 1990. *For All the Saints: The Practice of Ministry in the Faith Community*. Elgin, Ill.: Brethren Press.

McCauley, Daniel, and Kathryn McCauley. 1988. *Decorative Arts of the Amish of Lancaster County*. Intercourse, Pa.: Good Books.

McClendon, James William, Jr. 1994. *Doctrine: Systematic Theology, Volume 2*. Nashville: Abingdon Press.

———. 2000. *Witness: Systematic Theology, Volume 3*. Nashville: Abingdon Press.

———. 2002. *Ethics: Systematic Theology, Volume 1*. 2nd ed. Nashville: Abingdon Press.

McKusick, Victor A. 1978. *Medical Genetic Studies of the Amish: Selected Papers*. Baltimore: Johns Hopkins Univ. Press.

ME. See *Mennonite Encyclopedia*.

Menno Simons. 1956. *The Complete Writings of Menno Simons, c. 1496–1561*. Ed. John Christian Wenger. Trans. Leonard Verduin. Scottdale, Pa.: Herald Press.

Mennonite Church Directory 2009. 2009. Harrisonburg, Va.: Christian Light Publications.

Mennonite Church USA 2009 Directory. 2009. Scottdale, Pa.: Faith and Life Resources.

Mennonite Encyclopedia. 1955–1959. Volumes I–IV. Hillsboro, Kans.: Mennonite Brethren Publishing House.

———. 1990. Volume V. Scottdale, Pa.: Herald Press.

Mennonite World Conference. 2005. "Global Gifts Sharing Project: Caribbean, Central and South America." Available from MWC offices.

Mennonite World Conference News Service. 2005. "Ethiopian Conference Tops in Membership." *Mennonite Weekly Review* 24 (June 13): 1.

———. 2008. "07 Jan. 2008—Anabaptism and Living the Gospel Are the Same." http://www.mwc-cmm.org/en15/index.php?option=com_content&view=article&id=162:07-jan-2008-anabaptism-and-living-the-gospel-are-the-same&catid=28:news-releases-current&Itemid=108.

Metzler, James E. 1985. *From Saigon to Shalom: The Pilgrimage of a Missionary in Search of a More Authentic Mission.* Scottdale, Pa.: Herald Press.

Miller, Donald E., Scott Holland, Lon Fendall, and Dean Johnson, eds. 2007. *Seeking Peace in Africa: Stories of African Peacemakers.* Telford, Pa.: Cascadia Publishing House.

Miller, Ivan J. 1985. *History of the Conservative Mennonite Conference, 1910-1985.* Grantsville, Md.: Ivan J. Miller.

Miller, John W. 1969. *The Christian Way: A Guide to Christian Life Based on the Sermon on the Mount.* Scottdale, Pa.: Herald Press.

Miller, Joseph, S. 2004. "The Peculiar Beauty of *Gelassenheit*: An Interview with Amos B. Hoover." In *The Measure of My Days: Engaging the Life and Thought of John L. Ruth,* ed. Reuben Z. Miller and Joseph S. Miller, 201–27. Telford, Pa.: Cascadia Publishing House.

Miller, Levi, ed. 1977. *The Meetinghouse of God's People.* Scottdale, Pa.: Mennonite Publishing House.

Miller, Marlin E. 1990. "Baptism in the Mennonite Tradition." *Mennonite Quarterly Review* 64 (3): 230–58.

Miller, Melissa, and Phil M. Shenk. 1982. *The Path of Most Resistance.* Kitchener, Ont.: Pandora Press.

Miller, Roman J., Beryl H. Brubaker, and James C. Peterson, eds. 2005. *Viewing New Creations with Anabaptist Eyes: Ethics of Biotechnology.* Telford, Pa.: Cascadia Publishing House.

Miller, Sharon Wyse. 1998. "The Anabaptist Witness in Haiti: Proclaiming the Gospel of Peace." Master's thesis, Eastern Mennonite Seminary.

Mock, Melanie Springer. 2003. *Writing Peace: The Unheard Voices of Great War Mennonite Objectors.* Telford, Pa.: Pandora Press.

Morse, Kenneth I. 1977. "Margaret and John Metzler: World Citizens." *Messenger* 126 (Feb.): 10–13.

Mosemann. John H. 1983. *Ordination, Licensing, and Installation.* Newton, Kans.: Faith and Life Press.

Moyer, J. Harold. 1994. "Review of *Hymnal: A Worship Book.*" *Mennonite Quarterly Review* 68 (1): 132–35.

Myers, Thomas J. 2003. "Amish Tourism: 'Visiting Shipshewana Is Better Than Going to the Mall,'" *Mennonite Quarterly Review* 77 (1): 109–26.

Nation, Mark Thiessen. 1997. *A Comprehensive Bibliography of the Writings of John Howard Yoder.* Goshen, Ind.: Mennonite Historical Society.

Neufeld, Alfred. 2008. *What We Believe Together: Exploring the "Shared Convictions" of Anabaptist-Related Churches.* Intercourse, Pa.: Good Books.

Neufeld, Tom Yoder. 1989. "Christian Counterculture: Ecclesia and Establishment." *Mennonite Quarterly Review* 68 (2): 193–209.

Neufeld, Vernon H. 1983. *If We Can Love: The Mennonite Mental Health Story.* Newton, Kans.: Faith and Life Press.

Nolt, Steven M. 2003. *A History of the Amish.* Rev. ed. Intercourse, Pa.: Good Books.

———. 2005. "Mennonite Identity and the Writing on the 'New Giving' since 1945." *Journal of Mennonite Studies* 23:59–76.

———. 2008. "Who Are the Real Amish? Rethinking Diversity and Identity among a Separate People." *Mennonite Quarterly Review* 82 (3): 377–94.

Nolt, Steven M., and Thomas J. Meyers. 2007. *Plain Diversity: Amish Cultures and Identities.* Baltimore: Johns Hopkins Univ. Press.

Olshan, Marc. 2003. "The National Amish Steering Committee." In *The Amish and the State,* ed. Donald B. Kraybill, 67–84. 2nd ed. Baltimore: Johns Hopkins Univ. Press.

Oyer, John S., ed. 1968. "Mennonite Migration." Special issue, *Mennonite Quarterly Review* 42 (3).

———, ed. 1970. "Mennonite Central Committee." Special issue, *Mennonite Quarterly Review* 44 (3).

———, ed. 1974. "Russian Mennonite Immigration." Special issue, *Mennonite Quarterly Review* 48 (4).

———, ed. 1982. "Mennonites and Mental Health Ministries." Special issue, *Mennonite Quarterly Review* 56 (1).

———, ed. 1992. "Mennonites and Alternative Service in World War II." Special issue, *Mennonite Quarterly Review* 66 (4).

———, ed. 1996. "Mennonite Central Committee." Special issue, *Mennonite Quarterly Review* 70 (1).

———. 2000. *They Harry the Good People out of the Land: Essays on the Persecution, Survival and Flourishing of Anabaptists and Mennonites.* Ed. John D. Roth. Goshen, Ind.: Mennonite Historical Society.

Oyer, John S., and Robert S. Kreider. 1990. *Mirror of the Martyrs: Stories of Courage, Inspiringly Retold, of 16th Century Anabaptists Who Gave Their Lives for Their Faith.* Intercourse, Pa.: Good Books.

Oyer, Mary K. 2002. "The Sound in the Land." In *Sound in the Land: Essays on Mennonites and Music,* ed. Maureen Epp and Carol Ann Weaver, 21–33. Kitchener, Ont.: Pandora Press.

Packull, Werner O. 1977. *Mysticism and the Early South German Anabaptist Movement: 1525–1531.* Scottdale, Pa.: Herald Press.

———. 1995. *Hutterite Beginnings: Communitarian Experiments during the Reformation.* Baltimore: Johns Hopkins Univ. Press.

———. 2007. *Peter Riedemann: Shaper of the Hutterite Tradition.* Kitchener, Ont.: Pandora Press.

Pannabecker, Samuel F. 1975. *Ventures of Faith: The Story of Mennonite Biblical Seminary.* Elkhart, Ind.: Mennonite Biblical Seminary.

Peachey, Paul. 1968. "Identity Crisis among American Mennonites." *Mennonite Quarterly Review* 42 (4): 24–25.

Pelikan, Jaroslav. 1984. *The Vindication of Tradition.* New Haven: Yale Univ. Press.

Pellman, Hubert. 1979. *Mennonite Broadcasts: The First 25 Years.* Harrisonburg, Va.: Mennonite Broadcasts.

Peters, G. W. 1984. *Foundations of Mennonite Brethren Missions*. Hillsboro, Kans.: Kindred Press.

Peters, Galen, and Robert A. Riall. 2003. *The Earliest Hymns of the Ausbund*. Kitchener, Ont.: Pandora Press.

Peters, Shawn Francis. 2003. *The Yoder Case: Religious Freedom, Education, and Parental Rights*. Lawrence, Kans.: Univ. Press of Kansas.

Plett, Delbert F., ed. 2001. *Old Colony Mennonites in Canada, 1875–2000*. Steinbach, Man.: Crossway Publications.

Preheim, Rich. 2005. "To Every Food, a Season." *Mennonite Weekly Review* 24 (June 20): 1–2.

Prieb, Wesley J. 1990. *Peter C. Hiebert: He Gave Them Bread*. Hillsboro, Kans.: Center for Mennonite Brethren Studies.

The Radicals. 1989. VHS. Directed by Raul V. Carrera. Worcester, Pa.: Gateway Films / Vision Video.

Ramirez, Frank. 2000. *The Love Feast*. Elgin, Ill.: Brethren Press.

———. 2004. *The Meanest Man in Patrick County and Other Unlikely Brethren Heroes*. Elgin, Ill.: Brethren Press.

———. 2008. *Brethren Brush with Greatness: Thirty-two Stories*. Elgin, Ill.: Brethren Press.

Ramseyer, Robert L., and Alice P. Ramseyer. 1988. *Mennonites in China*. Winnipeg, Man.: China Educational Exchange.

Redekop, Benjamin W., and Calvin W. Redekop. 2001. *Power, Authority, and the Anabaptist Tradition*. Baltimore: Johns Hopkins Univ. Press.

Redekop, Calvin W. 1989. *Mennonite Society*. Baltimore: Johns Hopkins Univ. Press.

———. 1998. *Leaving Anabaptism: From Evangelical Mennonite Brethren to Fellowship of Evangelical Bible Churches*. Telford, Pa.: Pandora Press.

———, ed. 2000. *Creation and the Environment: An Anabaptist Perspective on a Sustainable World*. Baltimore: Johns Hopkins Univ. Press.

———. 2001. *The Pax Story: Service in the Name of Christ, 1951–1976*. Telford, Pa.: Pandora Press.

Redekop, Calvin W., Stephen C. Ainlay, and Robert Siemens. 1995. *Mennonite Entrepreneurs*. Baltimore: Johns Hopkins Univ. Press.

Redekop, Calvin W., Victor A. Krahn, and Samuel J. Steiner. 1994. *Anabaptist/Mennonite Faith and Economics*. Lanham, Md.: University Press of America.

Redekop, Calvin W., and Benjamin W. Redekop. 1996. *Entrepreneurs in the Faith Community*. Scottdale, Pa.: Herald Press.

Redekop, Calvin W., and Samuel J. Steiner, eds. 1988. *Mennonite Identity: Historical and Contemporary Perspectives*. Lanham, Md.: University Press of America.

Redekop, John H. 2007. *Politics under God*. Scottdale, Pa.: Herald Press.

Regehr, T. D. 1996. *Mennonites in Canada, 1939–1970: A People Transformed*. Toronto: Univ. of Toronto Press.

———. 2000. *Peace, Order, and Good Government: Mennonites and Politics in Canada*. Winnipeg, Man.: CMBC Publications.

———. 2003. *Faith, Life, and Witness in the Northwest, 1903–2003: Centennial History of the Northwest Mennonite Conference*. Kitchener, Ont.: Pandora Press.

Reimer, A. James. 2001. *Mennonites and Classical Theology: Dogmatic Foundations for Christian Ethics*. Kitchener, Ont.: Pandora Press.

———. 2003. *The Dogmatic Imagination: The Dynamics of Christian Belief*. Waterloo, Ont.: Herald Press.

Reimer, Margaret Loewen. 2008. *One Quilt, Many Pieces: A Guide to Mennonite Groups in Canada.* 4th ed. Scottdale, Pa.: Herald Press.

Reist, Arthur. 1974. *Tobacco Lore of Lancaster County, Pennsylvania.* Ephrata, Pa.: Science Press.

Rempel, John D. 1993. *The Lord's Supper in Anabaptism: A Study in the Christology of Balthasar Hubmaier, Pilgram Marpeck, and Dirk Philips.* Scottdale, Pa.: Herald Press.

Rich, Elaine Sommers. 1983. *Mennonite Women: A Story of God's Faithfulness, 1683–1983.* Scottdale, Pa.: Herald Press.

Rogers, John, ed. 1988. *Medical Ethics, Human Choices: A Christian Perspective.* Scottdale, Pa.: Herald Press.

Roth, John D. 1997. "Pietism and the Anabaptist Soul." In *The Dilemma of Anabaptist Piety,* ed. Stephen L. Longenecker, 17–34. Bridgewater, Va.: Forum for Religious Studies.

———, ed. 1998. "Conflict." Special issue, *Mennonite Quarterly Review* 72 (2).

———, ed. 1999a. "Anabaptist-Mennonite Church Architecture." Special issue, *Mennonite Quarterly Review* 73 (2).

———, ed. 1999b. "Mennonite Historical Writing." Special issue, *Mennonite Quarterly Review* 73 (3).

———, ed. 2001. "Family in the Anabaptist-Mennonite Tradition." Special issue, *Mennonite Quarterly Review* 75 (2).

———. 2002a. *Choosing against War: A Christian View.* Intercourse, Pa.: Good Books.

———, trans. and ed. 2002b. *Letters of the Amish Division: A Sourcebook.* 2nd ed. Goshen, Ind.: Mennonite Historical Society.

———, ed. 2003. "Mennonite/s Writing in the U.S. and Canada." Special issue, *Mennonite Quarterly Review* 77 (4).

———. 2005a. *Beliefs: Mennonite Faith and Practice.* Scottdale, Pa.: Herald Press.

———, ed. 2005b. "Ritual." Special issue, *Mennonite Quarterly Review* 79 (1).

———. 2006. *Stories: How Mennonites Came to Be.* Scottdale, Pa.: Herald Press.

———. 2009. *Practices: Mennonite Worship and Witness.* Scottdale, Pa.: Herald Press.

Roth, John D., Nelson Springer, and Janet Shoemaker, eds. 2000. *Mennonite Quarterly Review: Cumulative Index, Volumes 1–74 (1926/1927–2000).*

Roth, John D., and James M. Stayer, eds. 2007. *A Companion to Anabaptism and Spiritualism, 1521–1700.* Boston: Brill.

Rupel, Esther Fern. 1994. *Brethren Dress: A Testimony to Faith.* Philadelphia: Brethren Encyclopedia, Inc.

Rushby, William F. 1986. "A Comparative Study of Plain Garb in the Religious Society of Friends and the Mennonite Church." *Brethren Life and Thought* 31 (3): 180–88.

Ruth, John L. 1978. *Mennonite Identity and Literary Art.* Scottdale, Pa.: Herald Press.

———. 1984. *Maintaining Right Fellowship: A Narrative Account of Life in the Oldest Mennonite Community in North America.* Scottdale, Pa.: Herald Press.

———. 2001. *The Earth Is the Lord's: A Narrative History of the Lancaster Mennonite Conference.* Scottdale, Pa.: Herald Press.

Ruth-Heffelbower, Duane. 1991. *The Christian and Jury Duty.* Scottdale, Pa.: Herald Press.

Rutschman, LaVerne A. 1981. "Anabaptism and Liberation Theology." *Mennonite Quarterly Review* 55 (3): 255–70.

Rutt, Harry W. 1997. "A Measure of the Impact of Holy Spirit Renewal among Lancaster Conference Mennonites in 1990." *Pennsylvania Mennonite Heritage* 20 (2): 25–27.

Sampson, Cynthia, and John Paul Lederach. 2000. *From the Ground Up: Mennonite Contributions to International Peacebuilding.* New York: Oxford Univ. Press.

Sappington, Roger E. 1985. *The Brethren in Industrial America*. Elgin, Ill.: Brethren Press.

Sareyan, Alex. 1994. *The Turning Point: How Men of Conscience Brought about Major Change in the Care of America's Mentally Ill*. Washington, D.C.: American Psychiatric Press.

Sawatsky, Rodney J. 1987. *Authority and Identity: The Dynamics of the General Conference Mennonite Church*. North Newton, Kans.: Bethel College.

———. 1997. "Leadership, Authority, and Power." *Mennonite Quarterly Review* 71 (3): 439–51.

Scheer, Herfried. 1980. "The Hutterian German Dialect: A Study in Sociolinguistic Assimilation and Differentiation." *Mennonite Quarterly Review* 54 (3): 229–43.

Schiedel, Mary A. 2003. *Pioneers in Ministry: Women Pastors in Ontario Mennonite Churches, 1973–2003*. Kitchener, Ont.: Pandora Press.

Schijn, Herman. 1987. "Concerning the Nonswearing of Oaths." *Mennonite Quarterly Review* 61 (2): 228–35.

Schlabach, Gerald W. 1993. "Beyond Two- vs. One-Kingdom Theology: Abrahamic Community as a Mennonite Paradigm for Christian Engagement in Society." *Conrad Grebel Review* 2 (3): 187–210.

Schlabach, Joetta Handrich, and Kristina Mast Burnett. 1991. *Extending the Table: A World Community Cookbook*. Scottdale, Pa.: Herald Press.

Schlabach, Theron F. 1980. *Gospel versus Gospel: Mission and the Mennonite Church, 1863–1944*. Scottdale, Pa.: Herald Press.

———. 1988. *Peace, Faith, Nation: Mennonites and Amish in 19th Century America*. The Mennonite Experience in America, vol. 2. Scottdale, Pa.: Herald Press.

———. 2009. *War, Peace, and Social Conscience: Guy F. Hershberger and Mennonite Ethics*. Scottdale, Pa.: Herald Press.

Schlachta, Astrid von. 2009. *From the Tyrol to North America: The Hutterite Story through the Centuries*. Kitchener, Ont.: Pandora Press.

Schmidt, Henry J., ed. 1986. *Witnesses of a Third Way: A Fresh Look at Evangelism*. Elgin, Ill.: Brethren Press.

Schmidt, Kimberly, Diane Zimmerman Umble, and Steven D. Reschly, eds. 2002. *Strangers at Home: Amish and Mennonite Women in History*. Baltimore: Johns Hopkins Univ. Press.

Schmidt, Leigh Eric. 1995. *Consumer Rites: The Buying and Selling of American Holidays*. Princeton, N.J.: Princeton Univ. Press.

Schmidt, Melvin D. 1980. *Funerals and Funeral Planning*. Newton, Kans.: Faith and Life Press.

Schmitt, Abraham, and Dorothy Schmitt. 1984. *When a Congregation Cares: A New Approach to Crisis Ministries*. Scottdale, Pa.: Herald Press.

Schrag, Martin H. 1964. "The Early Brethren Concept of Authority." *Brethren Life and Thought* 9 (4): 109–26.

———. 1974. *The European History of the Swiss Mennonites from Volhynia*. Ed. Harley J. Stucky. North Newton, Kans.: Swiss Mennonite Cultural and Historical Association.

Schrag, Paul. 2004. "North Americans Seek Their Place in a New Global Mission Context." *Mennonite Brethren Herald* 43 (3). www.mbherald.com/43/03/news-4.en.html.

Schrock-Shenk, Carolyn, and Lawrence Ressler, eds. 1999. *Making Peace with Conflict: Practical Skills for Conflict Transformation*. Scottdale, Pa.: Herald Press.

Schroeder, David, and Esko Loewen. 1958. "Loyalty and Lodges." In *Studies in Church Discipline*, Mennonite General Conference, 173–81. Newton, Kans.: Mennonite Publication Office.

Schwartz, Hillel. 1973. "Early Anabaptist Ideas about the Nature of Children." *Mennonite Quarterly Review* 47 (2): 102–14.

Scott, Stephen E. 1981. *Plain Buggies: Amish, Mennonite, and Brethren Horse-Drawn Transportation*. Intercourse, Pa.: Good Books.

———. 1986. *Why Do They Dress That Way?* Intercourse, Pa.: Good Books.

———. 1988. *The Amish Wedding and Other Special Occasions of the Old Order Communities*. Intercourse, Pa.: Good Books.

———. 1996. *An Introduction to Old Order and Conservative Mennonite Groups*. Intercourse, Pa.: Good Books.

Scott, Stephen E., and Kenneth Pellman. 1990. *Living without Electricity*. Intercourse, Pa.: Good Books.

Séguy, Jean. 1973. "Religion and Agricultural Success." *Mennonite Quarterly Review* 47 (3): 182–224.

———. 1984. "The French Anabaptists: Four and One-Half Centuries of History." *Mennonite Quarterly Review* 58 (3): 206–17.

Sharp, John E., ed. 2001. *Gathering at the Hearth: Stories Mennonites Tell*. Scottdale, Pa.: Herald Press.

Shearer, Tobin Miller. 2008. "Moving beyond Charisma in Civil Rights Scholarship: Vincent Harding's Sojourn with the Mennonites." *Mennonite Quarterly Review*. 82 (2): 213–48.

———. 2010. *Daily Demonstrators: The Civil Rights Movement in Mennonite Homes and Sanctuaries*. Baltimore: Johns Hopkins Univ. Press.

Shenk, Sara Wenger. 2005. *Thank You for Asking: Conversing with Young Adults about the Future Church*. Scottdale, Pa.: Herald Press.

Shenk, Wilbert R. 1973. "The Planting and Growth of the Muria Christian Churches." *Mennonite Quarterly Review* 47 (1): 20–30.

———, ed. 1984. *Anabaptism and Mission*. Scottdale, Pa.: Herald Press.

———. 2000. *By Faith They Went Out: Mennonite Missions, 1850–1999*. Elkhart, Ind.: Institute of Mennonite Studies.

Shetler, Sanford. 1987. *Biblical Perspectives on Women in Ministry*. Harrisonburg, Va.: Fellowship of Concerned Mennonites.

Showalter, Mary Emma. 1950. *Mennonite Community Cookbook: Favorite Family Recipes*. Philadelphia: John C. Winston.

Sider, E. Morris. 1982. *Messenger of Grace: A Biography of C. N. Hostetter, Jr.* Nappanee, Ind.: Evangel Press.

———. 1988. *The Brethren in Christ in Canada: Two Hundred Years of Tradition and Change*. Nappanee, Ind.: Evangel Press.

———. 2002. "Conversion Narratives in Anabaptist and Pietist Groups." *Brethren in Christ History and Life* 25 (2): 220–36.

Sider, Erma, ed. 1998. *Celebration of Hospitality: A Brethren in Christ World Cookbook*. Nappanee, Ind.: Evangel Publishing House.

Siegrist, Joanne Hess. 1996. *Mennonite Women of Lancaster County: A Story in Photographs from 1855 to 1935*. Intercourse, Pa.: Good Books.

Slough, Rebecca, and Shirley Sprunger King. 2007. *Nurturing Spirit through Song: The Life of Mary K. Oyer*. Telford, Pa.: Cascadia Publishing House.

Smith, C. Henry. 1962. *Mennonite Country Boy: The Early Years of C. Henry Smith*. North Newton, Kans.: Faith and Life Press.

Smith, C. Henry, and Cornelius Krahn. 1981. *Smith's Story of the Mennonites*. 5th ed. North Newton, Kans.: Faith and Life Press.

Smucker, David Rempel, ed. 1993. "Mennonite Mergers." Special issue, *Mennonite Life* 48 (1).

————, ed. 1994. "Mennonite Hymnology." Special issue, *Pennsylvania Mennonite Heritage* 17 (2).

Smucker, Janneken. 2006. "Destination Amish Quilt Country: The Consumption of Quilts in Lancaster County, Pennsylvania." *Mennonite Quarterly Review* 80 (2): 185–206.

Snyder, C. Arnold. 1984. *The Life and Thought of Michael Sattler.* Scottdale, Pa.: Herald Press.

————. 1989. "The Influence of the Schleitheim Articles on the Anabaptist Movement: An Historical Evaluation." *Mennonite Quarterly Review* 63 (4): 323–44.

————. 1995. *Anabaptist History and Theology: An Introduction.* Kitchener, Ont.: Pandora Press.

————. 1997a. *Anabaptist History and Theology: An Introduction.* Rev. student ed. Kitchener, Ont.: Pandora Press.

————, ed. 1997b. "Toward a Global Mennonite / Brethren in Christ Historiography." Special issue, *Conrad Grebel Review* 15 (1–2).

————. 1999. *From Anabaptist Seed: The Historical Core of Anabaptist-Related Identity.* Kitchener, Ont.: Pandora Press.

————, ed. 2001. *Biblical Concordance of the Swiss Brethren, 1540.* Kitchener, Ont.: Pandora Press.

————. 2002. "Mysticism and the Shape of Anabaptist Spirituality." In *Commoners and Community: Essays in Honour of Werner O. Packull,* ed. C. Arnold Snyder, 195–215. Kitchener, Ont.: Pandora Press.

————. 2004. *Following in the Footsteps of Christ: The Anabaptist Tradition.* Maryknoll, N.Y.: Orbis Books.

Snyder, C. Arnold, and Linda Huebert Hecht. 1996. *Profiles of Anabaptist Women: Sixteenth Century Reforming Pioneers.* Waterloo, Ont.: Wilfrid Laurier Univ. Press.

Snyder, C. Arnold, and Galen A. Peters, eds. 2002. *Reading the Anabaptist Bible: Reflections for Every Day of the Year.* Kitchener, Ont.: Pandora Press.

Snyder, Graydon F. 1995. *Health and Medicine in the Anabaptist Tradition.* Valley Forge, Pa.: Trinity Press.

Songs of the Ausbund, Volume I: History and Translation of Ausbund Hymns. 1998. Millersburg, Ohio: Ohio Amish Library.

Speicher, Sara, and Donald F. Durnbaugh. 2003. "Historic Peace Churches." World Council of Churches Ecumenical Dictionary, Article of the Month Series. World Council of Churches. www.wcc-coe.org/wcc/who/dictionary-article8.

Springer, Nelson P., and A. J. Klassen. 1977. *Mennonite Bibliography, 1631–1961.* Scottdale, Pa.: Herald Press.

Stahly, Jerold A. 1989. "The Montbéliard Amish Move to Poland in 1791." *Mennonite Family History* 8 (1): 13–17.

Stauffer, Ardell, Pearl Sensenig, and Howard Good, eds. 1993. *Natural Connections: Faith Stories from African and African-American Christians.* Akron, Pa.: Mennonite Central Committee.

Stauffer, Ethelbert. 1945. "The Anabaptist Theology of Martyrdom." *Mennonite Quarterly Review* 19 (3): 179–214.

Stayer, James M. 2002. "Numbers in Anabaptist Research." In *Commoners and Community: Essays in Honour of Werner O. Packull,* ed. C. Arnold Snyder, 51–73. Kitchener, Ont.: Pandora Press.

Stayer, James M., Werner O. Packull, and Klaus Depperman. 1975. "From Monogenesis to Polygenesis: The Historical Discussion of Anabaptist Origins." *Mennonite Quarterly Review* 49 (2): 83–121.

Stellet Licht (Silent Light). 2007. DVD. Directed by Carlos Reygadas. New York: Palisades Tartan.

Stevick, Richard A. 2007. *Growing up Amish: The Teenage Years.* Baltimore: Johns Hopkins Univ. Press.

Stoesz, Edgar, and Muriel T. Stackley. 1999. *Garden in the Wilderness: Mennonite Communities in the Paraguayan Chaco, 1927–1997.* Winnipeg, Man.: CMBC Publications.

Stoffer, Dale R. 1989. *Background and Development of Brethren Doctrines, 1650–1987.* Philadelphia: Brethren Encyclopedia, Inc.

Stoltzfus, Louise. 1995. *Two Amish Folk Artists: The Story of Henry Lapp and Barbara Ebersol.* Intercourse, Pa.: Good Books.

Stoltzfus, Philip E. 1994. "Tradition and Diversity in *Ein Unpartheyisches Gesangbuch.*" *Pennnsylvania Mennonite Heritage* 17 (2): 29–36.

Stone, Steven F. 1987. "Church of the Brethren Survey: Retirement Communities and Nursing Homes—Economic, Management and Personnel Trends." *Brethren Life and Thought* 32 (3): 185–91.

Stumpp, Karl. 1973. *The Emigration from Germany to Russia in the Years 1763 to 1862.* Lincoln, Neb.: American Historical Society of Germans from Russia.

Swartley, Willard M., ed. 1984. *Essays on Biblical Interpretation: Anabaptist-Mennonite Perspectives.* Elkhart, Ind.: Institute of Mennonite Studies.

———. 2003. *Homosexuality: Biblical Interpretation and Moral Discernment.* Scottdale, Pa.: Herald Press.

———. 2006. *Covenant of Peace: The Missing Peace in New Testament Theology and Ethics.* Grand Rapids, Mich.: Wm. B. Eerdmans.

Swartley, Willard M., and Cornelius J. Dyck, eds. 1987. *Annotated Bibliography of Mennonite Writings on War and Peace: 1930–1980.* Scottdale, Pa.: Herald Press.

Swartley, Willard M., and Donald B. Kraybill, eds. 1998. *Building Communities of Compassion: Mennonite Mutual Aid in Theory and Practice.* Scottdale, Pa.: Herald Press.

Taylor, Steven J. 2009. *Acts of Conscience: World War II, Mental Institutions, and Religious Objectors.* Syracuse, N.Y.: Syracuse Univ. Press.

Thiesen, John. 1984. "Film Review: And When They Shall Ask." *Mennonite Life* 39 (3): 25–26.

Thiessen, Edna. 2000. *A Life Displaced: A Mennonite Woman's Flight from War-Torn Poland.* Kitchener, Ont.: Pandora Press.

Thiessen, Jack. 1989. "Origins of the Variations in Mennonite *Plautdietsch.*" *Mennonite Quarterly Review* 63 (3): 285–96.

Thomas, Dwight. 1985. "The Singing Servants Chorus: An Expression of Mennonite Identity." *Pennsylvania Mennonite Heritage* 8 (2): 6–17.

Thomas, Everett J. 1996. *A Mennonite Polity for Ministerial Leadership.* Newton, Kans.: Faith and Life Press.

Tiessen, Hildi Froese, ed. 1990. "Mennonite Writing." Special issue, *Prairie Fire* 11 (Summer).

Toews, Aron A. 1990. *Mennonite Martyrs: People Who Suffered for Their Faith, 1920–1940.* Trans. John B. Toews. Winnipeg, Man.: Kindred Press.

Toews, John, and Eleanor Marie Loewen. 1995. *No Longer Alone: Mental Health and the Church.* Scottdale, Pa.: Herald Press.

Toews, John B. 1982. *Czars, Soviets and Mennonites.* Newton, Kans.: Faith and Life Press.

Toews, John E. 2004. "Rethinking the Meaning of Ordination: Towards a Biblical Theology of Leadership Affirmation." *Conrad Grebel Review* 22 (1): 5–25.

Toews, Paul. 1983. "Fundamentalist Conflict in Mennonite Colleges: A Response to Cultural Transition?" *Mennonite Quarterly Review* 57 (3): 241–56.

———. 1996. *Mennonites in American Society, 1930–1970: Modernity and the Persistence of Religious Community*. The Mennonite Experience in America, vol. 4. Scottdale, Pa.: Herald Press.

Toews, Paul, and Kevin Enns-Rempel, eds. 2002. *For Everything a Season: Mennonite Brethren in North America, 1874–2002*. Winnipeg: Kindred Productions.

Ulrich, Daniel, and Janice Fairchild. 2002. *Caring Like Jesus: The Matthew 18 Project*. Elgin, Ill.: Brethren Press.

Umble, Diane Zimmerman. 1996. *Holding the Line: The Telephone in Old Order Mennonite and Amish Life*. Baltimore: Johns Hopkins Univ. Press.

Umble, Diane Zimmerman, and David L. Weaver-Zercher, eds. 2008. *The Amish and the Media*. Baltimore: Johns Hopkins Univ. Press.

Umble, John S. 1934. "Seventy Years of Progress in Sunday School Work among Mennonites of the Middle West." *Mennonite Quarterly Review* 8 (4): 166–79.

Urry, James. 1985. "Through the Eye of a Needle: Wealth and the Mennonite Experience in Imperial Russia." *Journal of Mennonite Studies* 3:7–35.

———. 1989. *None but Saints: The Transformation of Mennonite Life in Russia, 1789–1889*. Winnipeg, Man.: Hyperion Press.

———. 2006. *Mennonites, Politics, and Peoplehood: Europe—Russia—Canada, 1525–1980*. Winnipeg, Man.: Univ. of Manitoba Press.

Voth, Norma Jost. 1990–1991. *Mennonite Foods and Folkways from South Russia*. 2 vols. Intercourse, Pa.: Good Books.

W[agler], D[avid]. 1968. "Editorials." *Family Life* 1 (Jan.): 3.

Walbert, David. 2002. *Garden Spot: Lancaster County, the Old Order Amish, and the Selling of Rural America*. New York: Oxford Univ. Press.

Waldrep, G. C. 2008. "The New Order Amish and Para-Amish Groups: Spiritual Renewal within a Tradition." *Mennonite Quarterly Review* 82 (3): 395–426.

Waltner, Rachel. 1982. "From Anabaptism to Mennonitism: *The Mennonite Encyclopedia* as a Historical Document." *Mennonite Life* 37 (4): 13–19.

Warkentin, Abe. 1987. *Gäste und Fremdlinge / Strangers and Pilgrims, Hebrews 11:13*. Steinbach, Man.: Derksen Printers.

Weaver, Alain Epp, ed. 1996. *Mennonite Theology in Face of Modernity: Essays in Honor of Gordon D. Kaufman*. North Newton, Kans.: Bethel College.

Weaver, J. Denny. 1983. "A Believers' Church Christology." *Mennonite Quarterly Review* 57 (2): 112–31.

———. 1997. *Keeping Salvation Ethical: Mennonite and Amish Atonement Theology in the Late 19th Century*. Scottdale, Pa.: Herald Press.

———. 2001. *The Nonviolent Atonement*. Grand Rapids, Mich.: Wm. B. Eerdmans.

———. 2005. *Becoming Anabaptist: The Origin and Significance of 16th-Century Anabaptism*. 2nd ed. Scottdale, Pa.: Herald Press.

Weaver-Zercher, David. 2001. *The Amish in the American Imagination*. Baltimore: Johns Hopkins Univ. Press.

———, ed. 2002. *Minding the Church: Scholarship in the Anabaptist Tradition*. Telford, Pa.: Pandora Press.

Weiler, Lloyd M. 1993. "An Introduction to Old Order Mennonite Origins in Lancaster County, Pennsylvania, 1893–1993." *Pennsylvania Mennonite Heritage* 16 (4): 2–13.

Weiler, Lloyd, John B. Martin, James K. Nolt, and Amos B. Hoover. 2004. "The *Unpartheyisches Gesang-Buch*: Two Hundred Years of a Mennonite Hymnal." *Pennsylvania Mennonite Heritage* 27 (4): 20–29.

Wenger, J. C. 1974. *Separated unto God: A Plea for Christian Simplicity of Life and for a Scriptural Nonconformity to the World.* Scottdale, Pa.: Mennonite Publishing House.

———. 1991. *What Mennonites Believe.* Rev. ed. Scottdale, Pa.: Herald Press.

Wenger, Mark R. 2005. "The Origins and Development of Anointing among 19th-Century Mennonites." *Mennonite Quarterly Review* 79 (1): 19–50.

Williams, George H. 1992. *The Radical Reformation.* 3rd ed. Kirksville, Mo.: Sixteenth Century Journal Publishers.

Witness. 1985. VHS. Directed by Peter Weir. Hollywood, Calif.: Paramount Pictures Corp.

Wittlinger, Carlton O. 1978. *Quest for Piety and Obedience: The Story of the Brethren in Christ.* Nappanee, Ind.: Evangel Press.

Wright, Edward N. 1931. *Conscientious Objectors in the Civil War.* Philadelphia: Univ. of Pennsylvania Press.

Yinger, J. Milton. 1970. *The Scientific Study of Religion.* New York: Macmillan Company.

Yoder, Elizabeth G., ed. 1992. *Peace Theology and Violence against Women.* Elkhart, Ind.: Institute of Mennonite Studies.

Yoder, Elmer S. 1987. *The Beachy Amish Mennonite Fellowship.* Hartville, Ohio: Diakonia Ministries.

Yoder, Glee. 1978. *Passing on the Gift: The Story of Dan West.* Elgin, Ill.: Brethren Press.

Yoder, John Howard. 1958. *The Ecumenical Movement and the Faithful Church.* Scottdale, Pa.: Mennonite Publishing House.

———. 1961. *The Christian and Capital Punishment.* Newton, Kans.: Faith and Life Press.

———. 1971. *The Original Revolution: Essays on Christian Pacifism.* Scottdale, Pa.: Herald Press.

———. 1972/1994. *The Politics of Jesus: Vicit Agnus Noster.* 2nd ed. Grand Rapids, Mich.: Wm. B. Eerdmans.

———, comp., trans., and ed. 1973. *The Legacy of Michael Sattler.* Scottdale, Pa.: Herald Press.

———. 1984a. *God's Revolution: The Witness of Eberhard Arnold.* New York: Paulist Press.

———, ed. 1984b. *The Priestly Kingdom: Social Ethics as Gospel.* Notre Dame, Ind.: Univ. of Notre Dame Press.

———. 1991. "The Believer's Church Conferences in Historical Perspective." *Mennonite Quarterly Review* 65 (1): 5–19.

———. 1992. *Nevertheless: The Varieties and Shortcomings of Religious Pacifism.* Rev. and exp. ed. Scottdale, Pa.: Herald Press.

———. 2002. *Preface to Theology: Christology and Theological Method.* Grand Rapids, Mich.: Brazos Press.

Yoder, June Alliman, Marlene Kropf, and Rebecca Slough. 2005. *Preparing Sunday Dinner: A Collaborative Approach to Worship and Preaching.* Scottdale, Pa.: Herald Press.

Yoder, Lawrence M. 2006. *The Muria Story: A History of the Chinese Mennonite Churches in Indonesia.* Kitchener, Ont.: Pandora Press.

Yoder, Nathan E. 1999. "Mennonite Fundamentalism: Shaping an Identity for an American Context." Ph.D. diss., Notre Dame University.

———. 2011. *A History of the Conservative Mennonite Conference: Evangelical Anabaptists in 20th-Century America.* Scottdale, Pa.: Herald Press.

Yoder, Paton. 1991. *Tradition and Transition: Amish Mennonites and Old Order Amish, 1800–1900*. Scottdale, Pa.: Herald Press.

Yoder, Paul M. 1964. *Four Hundred Years with the Ausbund*. Scottdale, Pa.: Herald Press.

Yoder, Perry B. 1982. *From Word to Life: A Guide to the Art of Bible Study*. Scottdale, Pa.: Herald Press.

———. 1987. *Shalom: The Bible's Word for Salvation, Justice, and Peace*. Newton, Kans.: Faith and Life Press.

Zablocki, Benjamin. 1971. *The Joyful Community: An Account of the Bruderhof*. Baltimore: Penguin Books.

Zehr, Howard. 1990. *Changing Lenses: A New Focus for Crime and Justice*. Scottdale, Pa.: Herald Press.

Ziegler, Edward K., ed. 1956. "Family Life among the Brethren." Special issue, *Brethren Life and Thought* 1 (3).

———, ed. 1959. "Healing." Special issue, *Brethren Life and Thought* 4 (3).

———, ed. 1965. "Sermons." Special issue, *Brethren Life and Thought* 10 (3).

———, ed. 1966. "Consultation on Church Union." Special issue, *Brethren Life and Thought* 11 (1).

———, ed. 1975. "Brethren Identity." Special issue, *Brethren Life and Thought* 20 (4).

———, ed. 1976. "Divorce." Special issue, *Brethren Life and Thought* 21 (3).

———, ed. 1977. "Women and the Church." Special issue, *Brethren Life and Thought* 22 (3).

———, ed. 1979. "Outdoor Ministries." Special issue, *Brethren Life and Thought* 24 (1).

———, ed. 1980. "Poems." Special issue, *Brethren Life and Thought* 25 (3).

List of Entries

Topic Finder

Index of Names

Names in **bold** refer to subjects with dedicated entries.